The Role of Generative AI in the Communication Classroom

Sanae Elmoudden
St. John's University, USA

Jason S. Wrench
SUNY New Paltz, USA

IGI Global
PUBLISHER of TIMELY KNOWLEDGE

A volume in the Advances in Educational Technologies and Instructional Design (AETID) Book Series

Published in the United States of America by
IGI Global
Information Science Reference (an imprint of IGI Global)
701 E. Chocolate Avenue
Hershey PA, USA 17033
Tel: 717-533-8845
Fax: 717-533-8661
E-mail: cust@igi-global.com
Web site: http://www.igi-global.com

Library of Congress Cataloging-in-Publication Data

Names: Elmoudden, Sanae, 1968- editor. | Wrench, Jason S., editor.
Title: The role of generative AI in the communication classroom / edited by Sanae Elmoudden, Jason Wrench.
Description: Hershey, PA : Information Science Reference, 2024. | Includes bibliographical references and index. | Summary: "This book adds to the ongoing debate on coordinating efforts to address AI challenges by examining responsible interactions between educators and machines. It explores the benefits of AI, like ChatGPT, in communication and its potential to enhance higher education"-- Provided by publisher.
Identifiers: LCCN 2023047352 (print) | LCCN 2023047353 (ebook) | ISBN 9798369308318 (hardcover) | ISBN 9798369308325 (ebook)
Subjects: LCSH: Artificial intelligence--Educational applications. | Communication--Study and teaching (Higher)
Classification: LCC LB1028.43 .R64 2024 (print) | LCC LB1028.43 (ebook) | DDC 378.1/7028--dc23/eng/20231101
LC record available at https://lccn.loc.gov/2023047352
LC ebook record available at https://lccn.loc.gov/2023047353

This book is published in the IGI Global book series Advances in Educational Technologies and Instructional Design (AE-TID) (ISSN: 2326-8905; eISSN: 2326-8913)

British Cataloguing in Publication Data
A Cataloguing in Publication record for this book is available from the British Library.

For electronic access to this publication, please contact: eresources@igi-global.com.

Advances in Educational Technologies and Instructional Design (AETID) Book Series

Lawrence A. Tomei
Robert Morris University, USA

ISSN:2326-8905
EISSN:2326-8913

Mission

Education has undergone, and continues to undergo, immense changes in the way it is enacted and distributed to both child and adult learners. In modern education, the traditional classroom learning experience has evolved to include technological resources and to provide online classroom opportunities to students of all ages regardless of their geographical locations. From distance education, Massive-Open-Online-Courses (MOOCs), and electronic tablets in the classroom, technology is now an integral part of learning and is also affecting the way educators communicate information to students.

The **Advances in Educational Technologies & Instructional Design (AETID) Book Series** explores new research and theories for facilitating learning and improving educational performance utilizing technological processes and resources. The series examines technologies that can be integrated into K-12 classrooms to improve skills and learning abilities in all subjects including STEM education and language learning. Additionally, it studies the emergence of fully online classrooms for young and adult learners alike, and the communication and accountability challenges that can arise. Trending topics that are covered include adaptive learning, game-based learning, virtual school environments, and social media effects. School administrators, educators, academicians, researchers, and students will find this series to be an excellent resource for the effective design and implementation of learning technologies in their classes.

Coverage

- Educational Telecommunications
- E-Learning
- Social Media Effects on Education
- Hybrid Learning
- Game-Based Learning
- Virtual School Environments
- Classroom Response Systems
- Bring-Your-Own-Device
- Higher Education Technologies
- Curriculum Development

IGI Global is currently accepting manuscripts for publication within this series. To submit a proposal for a volume in this series, please contact our Acquisition Editors at Acquisitions@igi-global.com or visit: http://www.igi-global.com/publish/.

The Advances in Educational Technologies and Instructional Design (AETID) Book Series (ISSN 2326-8905) is published by IGI Global, 701 E. Chocolate Avenue, Hershey, PA 17033-1240, USA, www.igi-global.com. This series is composed of titles available for purchase individually; each title is edited to be contextually exclusive from any other title within the series. For pricing and ordering information please visit http://www.igi-global.com/book-series/advances-educational-technologies-instructional-design/73678. Postmaster: Send all address changes to above address.

Titles in this Series

For a list of additional titles in this series, please visit: www.igi-global.com/book-series
http://www.igi-global.com/book-series/advances-educational-technologies-instructional-design/73678

Practices and Implementation of Gamification in Higher Education
Veronica Membrive (University of Almeria, Spain)
Information Science Reference • © 2024 • 320pp • H/C (ISBN: 9798369307168) • US $230.00

Optimizing Education Through Micro-Lessons Engaging and Adaptive Learning Strategies
Peter Ilic (University of Aizu, Japan)
Information Science Reference • © 2024 • 398pp • H/C (ISBN: 9798369301951) • US $230.00

Fostering Pedagogical Innovation Through Effective Instructional Design
Mohamed Khaldi (Ecole Normale Supérieur, Abdelmalek Essaadi University, Tetouan, Morocco)
Information Science Reference • © 2024 • 467pp • H/C (ISBN: 9798369312063) • US $245.00

Protocols and Tools for Equitable Dual Language Teaching
Esther Gross (The Center for Educational Technology, Israel) and Jenifer Crawford (University of Southern California, USA)
Information Science Reference • © 2024 • 300pp • H/C (ISBN: 9781799883548) • US $225.00

Utilizing Visuals and Information Technology in Mathematics Classrooms
Hiroto Namihira (Former Otsuma Women's University, Japan)
Information Science Reference • © 2024 • 300pp • H/C (ISBN: 9781668499870) • US $220.00

Implications of Chatbots on Teaching and Learning
Mohammad Daradkeh (University of Dubai, UAE)
Information Science Reference • © 2024 • 330pp • H/C (ISBN: 9798369302453) • US $230.00

Fostering Foreign Language Teaching and Learning Environments With Contemporary Technologies
Zeynep Çetin Köroğlu (Aksaray University, Turkey) and Abdulvahit Çakır (Ufuk University, Turkey)
Information Science Reference • © 2024 • 338pp • H/C (ISBN: 9798369303535) • US $230.00

Embracing Cutting-Edge Technology in Modern Educational Settings
Ken Nee Chee (Universiti Pendidikan Sultan Idris, Malaysia) and Mageswaran Sanmugam (Universiti Sains Malaysia, Malaysia)
Information Science Reference • © 2024 • 334pp • H/C (ISBN: 9798369310229) • US $240.00

IGI Global
PUBLISHER of TIMELY KNOWLEDGE

701 East Chocolate Avenue, Hershey, PA 17033, USA
Tel: 717-533-8845 x100 • Fax: 717-533-8661
E-Mail: cust@igi-global.com • www.igi-global.com

To my family, friends, and colleagues (Jason Wrench).

To my father, who would have marveled at my colleagues' contributions, appreciating both the intrigue and challenges of AI with admiration. Dr. Abderrahmane Elmoudden passed away swiftly after a pancreatic cancer diagnosis in 2022. Unfortunately, I never had the chance to say goodbye to him, due to Covid travel restrictions. May this dedication reach him in his restful place. I also dedicate this to my sweet mother, Mina Madni, and my sons for their steadfast belief and encouragement (Sanae Elmoudden).

Table of Contents

Detailed Table of Contents

Technologies have long changed the social lives and practices of users. While some argue that the effects have been positive and others have been a bit more skeptical to take this perspective, there is no question that they have altered the way that we engage in daily behaviors. They have changed the way that we work and the way that we communicate with others. And said technologies are, with little question, here to stay. This chapter introduces readers to the various strategies adopted by both students and assessors (e.g., instructors) regarding the use of ChatGPT within the world of higher education. ChatGPT, in short, is an artificial intelligence chatbot that aids the user in a multitude of tasks and mimics the human mind. Not only will the chapter expose readers to the ways in which students are using ChatGPT (e.g., as artificial tutors, to help with the construction of ideas), but also how instructors are beginning to notice the benefits of this AI tool for the classroom (e.g., lesson plans).

Public speaking learners preparing for a speech can find the process of writing an outline time-consuming. With the presence of AI like ChatGPT, learners may feel tempted to abandon the outlining tasks needed to organize their ideas and instead rely on AI to minimize their effort. Such a use can dull students' writing skills and dampen their creativity and originality. This study examines 180 ChatGPT-generated speech outlines using three prompt engineering techniques to analyze their content and possible impact on students' work. While the findings indicate that ChatGPT can lack the sophistication required for speech outlines, it is a powerful tool that can be prompt-trained to generate human-like content. The findings reveal that prompt engineering plays a major role in determining if students can get away with speechcraft using ChatGPT, illustrating the threat of ChatGPT on students' learning. Yet, its prompt-limited outlines can exhibit potential benefits for students' academic work while upholding integrity. The study proposes implications for pedagogical practices with ChatGPT.

Communication discipline, including communication courses in higher education, must aptly respond to the demands emerging due to the rapid developments in the AI technologies and globally widespread application of generative AI. Furthermore, to truly stay relevant, communication education must speak to the pervasive, complicated, and difficult-to-solve mega-crises that are diminishing human security, while growing more severe in the current era, around the world. This chapter explores the approaches within communication higher education that can contribute to mitigation of mega-crises via meaningful and ethical integration of AI-supported solutions. Specifically, communication education should emphasize (1) global alliances, (2) cross-disciplinary alliances, (3) community-inclusive alliances, (4) creativity, adaptability, and acceptance of uncertainty, and (5) establishment of viable infrastructures and platforms that enable global, cross-disciplinary, and community-inclusive deliberation and decision-making.

In this comprehensive exploration, the interaction between generative AI and interpersonal communication is examined. The initial sections delve into the characteristics and limitations of AI-generated responses, highlighting the challenges of context and non-verbal cues interpretation. The potential for AI-driven interpersonal skill development is presented. The discussion progresses to address the changing dynamics in the classroom, contrasting traditional communication training with AI-augmented methods. The efficacy of AI in group discussions and role-plays is assessed, with a central focus on whether AI augments or diminishes human connections. The final sections explore the potential of generative AI in reshaping our understanding of effective communication and the necessity for educators to uphold the human element while leveraging AI's skill-enhancing capabilities. This comprehensive review offers insights into the evolving landscape of AI and interpersonal communication, shedding light on its opportunities, challenges, and the path forward.

Generative artificial intelligence (AI) can induce a variety of biases that can impact decision-making processes, and it can produce inaccurate or distorted information that may harm marginalized student groups in higher education classrooms. With the increase in generative AI use among college students and instructors, it is important to examine the ethical risks and discriminatory biases that can negatively influence students' learning experiences. For this purpose, this chapter focuses on the different types of generative AI ethical risks that can occur in U.S. classrooms. The variety of AI discriminatory biases against diverse student populations are also documented. Further, the authors discuss a case application that expands on the potential AI biases in higher education. To prevent and address potential AI ethical risks and biases, recommendations are offered to higher education educators. Lastly, guidance is offered suggesting future research in AI biases and diversity in higher education institutions.

Generative AI tools have emerged as transformative resources in the realm of communication education. These tools harness the power of artificial intelligence to assist students and educators in various aspects of communication studies, including writing, public speaking, and media production. At their core, generative AI tools are designed to generate human-like text, speech, or visuals autonomously, replicating and augmenting the capabilities of human communication. They encompass a range of applications, from chatbots that facilitate communication skill development to language models that assist in content

Foreword: Empowering Educators in the Midst of Innovation and Transformation

TRACING THE EDUCATIONAL EVOLUTION

In the realm of higher education, there is a noticeable transformation underway, driven by the adoption of artificial intelligence (AI) innovations. This transformation can be likened to a technological revolution, with AI at its core. This revolution fundamentally alters our approach to teaching, promising to elevate communication and deliver tailored, efficient, and captivating learning experiences to students (Kampakis, n.d).

Gone are the days of one-size-fits-all education. Innovation has steered us toward personalized learning, guided by adaptive technologies and data analytics, acting as individualized mentors for learners. This approach has proven to be a game-changer, significantly boosting engagement and effectiveness.

Technology, often considered the linchpin of this transformation (Picciano, 2017), has made learning more flexible and accessible. The digital revolution has introduced us to online learning, video lectures, and interactive e-learning platforms. It's like carrying a classroom in your pocket, with increased access to information (Kumar, 2023). The integration of AI tools into classroom communication becomes especially beneficial for students aspiring to excel in their chosen areas of expertise, equipping them with advanced knowledge and skills.

Yet, these changes go beyond mere educational improvements; they are about making education profoundly relevant. Modern teaching methods in a rapidly evolving job market aim to equip students with essential skills like critical thinking, collaboration, and adaptability. It's about what you know and how you can apply it effectively.

Educational innovations are not only changing the game; they are offering an entirely fresh perspective. In the classroom, the learner takes center stage, with the teacher assuming the role of a guide, leading the way through an engaging and dynamic landscape of learning experiences.

Upskilling: Cultivating Mindset and Resilience

For educators in higher education, the challenge is multifaceted: adapting, innovating, and envisioning a dynamic educational landscape. However, adaptability alone falls short in this ever-changing world. Leadership soft skills, such as effective communication, resilience, empathy, teamwork, and a growth mindset, are of paramount importance. While technical proficiency remains vital in the digital age, these human attributes truly define effective teaching (EduStation, 2023).

Nonetheless, digital proficiency cannot be disregarded. It's imperative that academic institutions and educational leaders share the responsibility of cultivating well-rounded educators for today's digital world.

Continuing professional growth is not a matter of personal preference but an essential requirement. The swift changes occurring in our global context are also reflected in the field of education. Driven by the constant evolution of technology, innovative teaching strategies, and diverse student demands, educators must consistently enhance their abilities to ensure the provision of high-quality learning experiences.

Imagine an educator who has been using the same lesson plans for decades. They may inadvertently overlook the opportunity to embrace contemporary teaching resources, the most recent and effective pedagogical approaches, or methods designed to captivate students accustomed to the digital age. It is within this context that the importance of upskilling becomes evident.

In the realm of education, upskilling entails the continuous alignment with shifting educational paradigms, mastering emerging technologies, and responsive adaptation to the evolving needs of students. The goal here is not to forget or leave behind the core teaching principles but to enrich them by integrating modern tools and strategies.

Essentially, we are preparing educators to be 21st-century educators, ready to nurture 21st-century learners. Therefore, professional development isn't optional; it's an imperative. It serves as the conduit linking conventional teaching with the contemporary classroom, ensuring that our students receive the finest education available. It is an essential component for educators to proficiently fulfill their responsibilities and secure the success of 21st-century learners.

In our fast-paced world, it is paramount to emphasize the importance of nurturing a growth mindset and resilience when dealing with constant changes. These qualities serve as invaluable tools for success.

To integrate Generative AI as part of the classroom, educators need to maintain a growth mindset instinctively to continue growing their abilities and astuteness. In education, this mindset is transformative. When students embrace it, they are more inclined to tackle complex problems, embrace new experiences, and ultimately flourish.

Now, let's delve into resilience – it's like an internal spring, always ready to rebound from setbacks and adapt to changes. Resilient individuals do not crumble when facing challenges; they rise and thrive. In a world of constant change, resilience is the secret weapon for surviving and flourishing.

The true magic happens when you bring these two qualities together. A growth mindset encourages us to welcome challenges with open arms, and resilience helps us weather the storms that come our way. It's like a dynamic duo for success.

Fostering these traits is akin to equipping students with a life toolkit, which enhances the classroom experience. They are not just learning facts and figures but mastering the art of approaching life with confidence, adaptability, and an unwavering belief in their potential. Encouraging a growth mindset and resilience isn't merely a lesson; it's an investment in a future where students can thrive in a world of continuous adjustments.

Improving the Classroom Experience

The swift advancement of technology has turned AI into a valuable resource within educational environments, necessitating educators to prepare learners for the growing utilization of AI tools. These tools possess the potential to boost productivity and streamline communication (Lusk, 2023).

AI offers a multitude of ways to support learners. For instance, it can assist students in tasks like conducting literature reviews and analyzing data, simplifying the research process and fostering adaptability in handling complex academic materials (Lusk, 2023). Additionally, AI can provide feedback and suggestions to improve students' thesis or dissertation drafts, guiding them through the challenging terrain of academic research and nurturing their resilience.

For educators, AI algorithms can analyze students' prior academic backgrounds and career aspirations to tailor a personalized curriculum, enabling better engagement and learning outcomes (Melo, 2023). This personalized approach helps learners develop critical leadership skills, such as "problem-solving, effective communication, critical thinking, and teamwork, through hands-on experience with AI tools and applications" (Melo, 2023, para. 3).

While there are numerous advantages to utilizing AI for enhancing communication in the classroom, it is not without challenges. Training becomes crucial, addressing the needs of both faculty members and students who may not be tech-savvy. Additionally, the cost implications and ethical considerations require careful navigation. Finally, ethical considerations arise as AI continues to advance, requiring faculty to address issues related to integrity and security (Melo, 2023).

Yet, the advantages of utilizing Generative AI in the communication classroom far outweigh the challenges, making it a mutually beneficial approach for advancing education in the 21st century.

The Horizon of Higher Education: Practical Approaches to Adaptation

The educational landscape in higher education is dynamic and filled with challenges and opportunities. The pace of change in education is unprecedented, and preparing educators for this evolving future is not an option; it's an imperative.

Technology is at the heart of this educational transformation, making education digital, personalized, and dynamic. Although there are many practical methods, a few important approaches to consider are:

- Educators should be prepared to employ digital tools to enrich the learning environment effectively. For example, imagine an educator's notes coming alive while using the virtual assistance of a voice Chatbot. AI-enhanced platforms are turning this fantasy into reality (Tominc and Rozman, 2023).
- Personalized learning is of the utmost importance. Educators must comprehensively understand their students and adapt their teaching methods accordingly. To do this, instructors must play a pivotal role in nurturing each student's abilities, such as critical thinking, communication, and problem-solving. The days of one-size-fits-all approaches are waning, making space for tailored learning experiences that address individual needs.
- Educators' awareness of their academic support system is vital for effectively harnessing digital tools and personal learning. This entails gaining familiarity with policies and procedures to ensure that courses are not only technologically advanced but also pedagogically sound.
- In order to remain abreast of the tools that can enhance efficiency and effectiveness, educators must embrace the concept of lifelong learning. They should be eager learners themselves, setting an example for their students. Maintaining current knowledge and skills is imperative within the ever-evolving educational landscape. Just as we expect physicians to stay updated with the latest medical advances, we should similarly expect our educators to evolve with the ever-changing educational landscape.
- Educators need to be inquisitive and step outside their comfort zone and explore the innovative tools available. Using these tools will enhance student communication and engagement, allowing students to achieve desired skills and competencies. A few examples to explore to encourage engagement and increase interaction may be creating a virtual environment for live sessions, re-

searching 3D learning tools to encourage interactive visualization, applying AI-driven language learning chatbots, or creating informational AI-generated videos. The possibilities are becoming interminable, so explore all your options to create an engaging environment.

- Educators should encourage students to use AI and educate them to the potential ethical concerns that may result in not using it correctly. To do this, they must be prepared to share the proper way of using AI so that learners can succeed. "This can help students become responsible and informed digital citizens who are equipped to navigate the challenges and opportunities of the digital age" (Melo, 2023, para. 8).

Looking into the educational future means recognizing that it's all about transformation, adaptability, and embracing technology. It's an exciting journey and providing educators with the knowledge and strategies to navigate it is the key to creating a brighter future for our learners.

In conclusion, the narrative of higher education, much like any compelling story, is filled with challenges and opportunities. However, by utilizing the right combination of skills, tools, support, and guidance, today's educators can craft a tale of success and transformation. They can not only adapt but thrive in the process. By integrating Generative AI into the field of education, institutions can empower their students to excel in their chosen fields of study. This can be accomplished by enhancing communication, tailoring learning experiences, and nurturing essential qualities like self-confidence, adaptability, and a growth-oriented mindset. With Generative AI in the Communication Classroom, learners will be better prepared to achieve success both academically and professionally in an ever-changing and competitive global environment.

Susan MacCready
Capella University, USA

Christopher Fichera
Capella University, USA

REFERENCES

EduStation. (2023). *The importance of soft skills in the digital age.* https://www.linkedin.com/pulse/importance-soft-skills-digital-age-edustation-official/

Kampakis, S. (n.d.). *The future of AI in education opportunities and challenges.* The Data Scientist. https://thedatascientist.com/the-future-of-ai-in-education-opportunities-and-challenges/

Kumar, K. (2023). *The impact of the digital revolution on education.* https://www.linkedin.com/pulse/impact-digital-revolution-education-keerthan-kumar/

Lusk, J. (2023). *5 AI tools that will change the way you communicate.* https://www.linkedin.com/pulse/5-ai-tools-change-way-you-communicate-james-lusk/

Melo, N. (2023). *Incorporating artificial intelligence into the classroom: An examination of benefits, challenges, and best practices.* https://elearningindustry.com/incorporating-artificial-intelligence-into-classroom-examination-benefits-challenges-and-best-practices

Picciano, A. G. (2017). The evolution of big data and learning analytics in American higher education. *Journal of Asynchronous Learning Networks*, *21*(2), 75–84.

Tominc, P., & Rozman, M. (2023). Artificial intelligence and business studies: Study cycle differences regarding the perceptions of the key future competences. *Education Sciences*, *13*(6), 580. doi:10.3390/educsci13060580

Preface

As editors of *The Role of Generative AI in the Communication Classroom*, we are delighted to present this comprehensive exploration of the intersection between Artificial Intelligence (AI) and communication education. In an era where AI is rapidly becoming an integral part of our daily lives, it is crucial to examine its implications in the realm of education, particularly in the communication classroom.

Our collaboration as editors, Sanae Elmoudden from St. John's University and Jason S. Wrench from the SUNY New Paltz, reflects a commitment to fostering a nuanced understanding of AI's role in shaping the future of education. This reference book delves into the multifaceted aspects of AI, with a specific focus on OpenAI's "Chat Generative Pre-Trained Transformer," commonly known as ChatGPT.

AI's ability to simulate human intelligence has sparked both excitement and concerns. While it presents unprecedented opportunities for solving complex problems and enhancing learning experiences, questions about its ethical use and potential impact on employment and society linger. This book aims to navigate these complexities, offering insights into responsible interactions between educators and machines.

Central to our argument is the call for collaborative efforts in shaping the design and deployment of AI technology. We assert that the education sector, including Higher Ed, plays a pivotal role in this coordination. By actively engaging in policy-making and collaborating with developers, educators can contribute to the ethical and inclusive integration of AI in education.

The chapters within this book address a spectrum of topics, from the necessity of curriculum changes for the digital generation to ethical considerations, biases, and the broader implications of AI in communication education. We emphasize the importance of communication studies actively engaging with AI, exploring its potential applications, and advocating for responsible practices.

This book is not only a contribution to the ongoing debate on AI challenges but also a practical guide for educators. It equips them with the knowledge and tools needed to navigate the evolving landscape of AI in education. With a keen focus on ChatGPT, the book showcases its capabilities through interactions with authors and highlights its learning and adaptive nature.

We envision this book as a valuable resource for educators, researchers, and policymakers. Its relevance extends to various conferences, organizations, and online platforms that cater to communication, media studies, and artificial intelligence in education. Moreover, academic departments in universities, including media studies, education, and communication studies, will find this book pertinent to their interests.

In closing, we extend our gratitude to the contributors who have enriched this volume with their diverse perspectives and insights. We hope that *The Role of Generative AI in the Communication Classroom* stimulates thoughtful conversations and contributes to the ongoing discourse on AI in education.

Chapter 1: Generative AI in Higher Education

Authored by Jason S. Wrench from SUNY New Paltz, United States, and Sanae Elmoudden, St. John's University, USA, this chapter provides an in-depth exploration of generative artificial intelligence (AI) with a specific focus on its implications and applications in higher education. Wrench discusses the evolution of AI, fundamental concepts, and the development of large language models. The chapter delves into the ethical considerations and potential biases inherent in AI systems, emphasizing responsible AI development. Furthermore, it examines how generative AI has transformative potential in enhancing learning, creativity, and information processing within higher education settings.

Chapter 2: Some Emerging Communication Roles for Generative AI

Written by Michele H. Jackson from Michigan State University, this chapter proposes a novel perspective on generative AI by framing it in terms of different communication roles it fulfills. Jackson introduces roles such as expert, copilot, interlocutor, and channel, offering illustrations from other contributions to the volume. The chapter aims to distill the diverse ideas surrounding generative AI from a communication standpoint, emphasizing its varied roles and contributions across academia.

Chapter 3: Unravelling the Evolution of Generative AI in Communication Education – A Historical Journey Into Human-Machine Communication

Authored by C.V. Suresh Babu and Suruthi G from Hindustan Institute of Technology and Science, India, this chapter traces the historical evolution of human-machine communication, showcasing the transformative role of Generative AI. Starting with the origins of AI and early communication technologies, the chapter progresses through AI's evolution, highlighting advancements in Generative Models. It explores the impact of Generative AI on language and communication learning, addressing ethical considerations and envisioning its future role in communication pedagogy.

Chapter 4: ChatGPT Innovation in Higher Education

Written by Noura Hajjaj from Duquesne University, this chapter focuses on the controversial and intriguing ChatGPT, exploring its impact on the communication classroom. The chapter delves into the ethical dilemmas arising from ChatGPT's integration, sparking rhetorical discourses on its evolving landscape. Rather than perceiving ChatGPT as a threat, the chapter advocates for a proactive exploration of its opportunities and challenges, refining pedagogical approaches for effective use in higher education.

Chapter 5: Debating About, Against, and With ChatGPT – Redesigning Academic Debate Pedagogy for the World of Generative Artificial Intelligence

Authored by John Joseph Rief from Metropolitan State University of Denver and Brian J. Schrader from UM Flint, this chapter addresses the challenges posed by ChatGPT in academic integrity. Focusing on thought experiments within academic debate, the authors explore pedagogical integration rather than banning ChatGPT. They argue that ChatGPT presents an opportunity to (re)design education for artificial invention and addresses the concerns raised about its impact on educational integrity.

Chapter 6: How AI Is Changing the Nature and Landscape of Student Learning and Outcomes Assessment Within Higher Education

Written by Corey Liberman from Marymount Manhattan College, this chapter explores the changing landscape of student learning and outcomes assessment within higher education due to AI, specifically ChatGPT. The chapter introduces readers to strategies adopted by both students and assessors, examining how ChatGPT is utilized as an artificial tutor and for lesson plan construction.

Chapter 7: ChatGPT – Can Students Really Get Away With Speechcraft?

Authored by Ali Garib, Tina Coffelt, Awad Alshalwy, and SeyedMohammad Kashani from Iowa State University, this chapter investigates the potential impact of ChatGPT on students' writing skills and creativity in public speaking. The study examines ChatGPT-generated speech outlines and analyzes their content, exploring the balance between potential benefits and threats to students' learning and academic integrity.

Chapter 8: Facing Mega-Crises in the Global Era of AI – The Role of Communication Education

Written by Marta Lukacovic from Angelo State University and Deborah D. Sellnow-Richmond from Southern Illinois University Edwardsville, this chapter explores the role of communication education in addressing mega-crises in the global era of AI. The chapter emphasizes global alliances, cross-disciplinary collaboration, community inclusion, creativity, adaptability, and the establishment of viable infrastructures to mitigate mega-crises through ethical integration of AI solutions.

Chapter 9: The Influence of Generative AI on Interpersonal Communication Dynamics

Authored by Sumeyya Akdilek, Ibrahim Akdilek, and Narissra Punyanunt-Carter from Texas Tech University, this chapter comprehensively explores the interaction between generative AI and interpersonal communication. It examines the characteristics and limitations of AI-generated responses, evaluates AI-driven interpersonal skill development, and addresses the changing dynamics in the classroom, focusing on the impact of AI on group discussions and human connections.

Chapter 10: Generative AI Ethical Considerations and Discriminatory Biases on Diverse Students Within the Classroom

Written by Leslie Ramos Salazar, Shanna Peeples, and Mary Brooks from West Texas A&M University, this chapter delves into the ethical risks and discriminatory biases associated with generative AI in US classrooms. The authors document various AI ethical risks and discriminatory biases against diverse student populations, offering recommendations to higher education educators for addressing and preventing these issues.

Chapter 11: Charting the Ethical Course – Navigating AI Advancements in Communication Education

Authored by Huong-Tra Le-Nguyen from Hanoi University and Trung Tran from Clientscan, Vietnam, this chapter explores the transformative role of generative AI tools in communication education. It discusses the applications of generative AI tools in various aspects of communication studies and emphasizes their increasing prevalence in communication classrooms, offering opportunities for personalized learning, skill enhancement, and creativity.

Chapter 12: Screaming Out Loud in the Communication Classroom – Asian Stereotypes and the Fallibility of Image Generating Artificial Intelligence (AI)

Written by Yifeng Hu from the College of New Jersey and Kurylo from Brooklyn College this chapter addresses the role of stereotypes in AI-generated images, particularly focusing on Asian stereotypes. The chapter draws parallels between human cognitive information processing and AI image generation, experimenting with AI image generators like Dall-E, Midjourney, and Pika Art. It highlights collaborative and hegemonic human-AI interactive issues and discusses implications arising from such interactions.

Chapter 13: AI Monsters – An Application to Student and Faculty Knowledge and Perceptions of Generative AI

Written by Sarah T. Zipf, Tiffany Petricini, and Chuhao Wu from The Pennsylvania State University, this chapter analyzes perceptions of generative AI by faculty and students. Using "Monster Theory" as a framework, the chapter explores themes underlying responses and aims to "demonsterize" AI. It discusses evidence-based responses, student-faculty trust, academic integrity, and uncertainty in the context of generative AI.

Chapter 14: Integrating Professional Perspectives for AI Literacy – Empowering Students in an AI-Influenced Future

Authored by Kristopher Merceron and Karene Best from Valencia College, this chapter explores AI literacy in education by integrating insights from librarians and communication professors. It emphasizes the roles these professionals play in equipping students for an AI-dominated future, discussing evolving roles, interdisciplinary curriculum integration, ethical considerations, practical applications, and the necessity of continuous professional development.

Chapter 15: The Future Is Already Here – From GAI to AGI

In this concluding chapter authored by Sanae Elmoudden from St. John's University and Jason S. Wrench from SUNY New Paltz, the overarching objective of the volume is addressed. The chapter reflects on the central role of Generative Artificial Intelligence (GAI) in shaping our educational system. Elmoudden guides the reader through the progression of the book, steering the discourse towards the communication classroom. The chapter emphasizes the proliferation of GAI in academia and underscores the significance of academic preparedness in the face of this transformative technology. It confronts the dilemma of AI whiteness and wokeness balance representations, shedding light on the importance of ethical considerations in the integration of GAI in education.

As we bring this comprehensive exploration to a close, we reflect on the transformative journey through *The Role of Generative AI in the Communication Classroom.* The collaboration between editors Sanae Elmoudden from St. John's University and Jason S. Wrench from the State University of New York at New Paltz has resulted in a nuanced understanding of the intersection between Artificial Intelligence (AI) and communication education.

Our journey began with an acknowledgment of the rapid integration of AI into our daily lives and the crucial need to examine its implications, particularly within the communication classroom. This reference book, with its specific focus on OpenAI's "Chat Generative Pre-Trained Transformer" or ChatGPT, serves as a guide to navigate the multifaceted aspects of AI.

The excitement and concerns surrounding AI's ability to simulate human intelligence set the stage for our exploration. We delved into responsible interactions between educators and machines, emphasizing the ethical use of AI technology. Our call for collaborative efforts in shaping AI's design and deployment positions the education sector, including Higher Ed, as a pivotal player in ensuring the ethical and inclusive integration of AI.

The chapters within this book collectively address a diverse spectrum of topics, from the necessity of curriculum changes for the digital generation to ethical considerations, biases, and broader implications of AI in communication education. We underscored the importance of active engagement between communication studies and AI, advocating for responsible practices that empower educators.

We envision this book making a lasting impact across various conferences, organizations, and online platforms dedicated to communication, media studies, and artificial intelligence in education. Academic departments, spanning computer science, education, and communication studies, will find the content pertinent to their interests.

In closing, we express heartfelt gratitude to the contributors who have enriched this volume with diverse perspectives and insights. We hope that *The Role of Generative AI in the Communication Classroom* stimulates thoughtful conversations and significantly contributes to the ongoing discourse on AI in education, paving the way for an informed and responsible future.

Sanae Elmoudden
St. John's University, USA

Jason S. Wrench
SUNY New Paltz, USA

Acknowledgment

We would like to express our gratitude to the publishers, authors, and the numerous reviewers who contributed to the revision process. As mentioned in the Preface, this collaborative effort involves authors from diverse disciplines within the communication field, all of whom deemed it important to discuss the intrusion of Artificial Intelligence (AI) in our lives, along with its opportunities and challenges in our classrooms. As the editors of 'The Role of Generative AI in the Communication Classroom,' we take great pleasure in presenting this comprehensive exploration of the intersection between AI and communication education in a time when AI is swiftly becoming an integral aspect of our daily lives.

Special acknowledgment goes to Anastacia Kurylo who helped generate the idea for this project and to Noura Hajjaj for recommending the co-editors for this book. We also extend our appreciation to Michele H. Jackson, one of our co-authors, for diligently reviewing and summarizing all the articles and providing valuable insights to the authors and editors.

Our sincere thanks go to the reviewers and authors who have contributed to refining and enhancing this work, making it more nuanced and engaging by offering crucial changes and updates to the articles. We extend our gratitude to all the reviewers and authors who played a pivotal role in shaping this publication.

Aicha Lemtouni from ILCS, Morocco.

Ali Garib, Tina Coffelt, Awad Alshalwy, and SeyedMohammad Kashani from Iowa State.

Chad Edwards from Western Michigan University.

Christina Knopf from State University of New York, Cortland.

Corey Liberman from Marymount Manhattan College.

C.V. Suresh Babu and Suruthi G from Hindustan Institute of Technology and Science, India.

Fadoua Loudiy from Slippery Rock University.

James Proszek from Southern Illinois University.

John Joseph Rief from Metropolitan State University of Denver and Brian J. Schrader from UM Flint.

Kristopher Merceron and Karene Best from Valencia College.

Huong-Tra Le-Nguyen from Hanoi University and Trung Tran from Clientscan, Vietnam.

Leslie Ramos Salazar, Shanna Peeples, and Mary Brooks from West Texas A&M University.

Marta Lukacovic from Angelo State University and Deborah D. Sellnow-Richmond from Southern Illinois University Edwardsville.

Michael Plugh from Manhattan College.

Noura Hajjaj from Duquesne University.

Sarah T. Zipf, Tiffany Petricini, and Chuhao Wu from The Pennsylvania State University.

Shannon Brogan from Kentucky State University.

Sumeyya Akdilek, Ibrahim Akdilek, and Narissra Punyanunt-Carter from Texas Tech University.

Toby Cohen from Freelance AV trade journalist, P.R./ad writer/photographer.

Yifeng Hu from the College of New Jersey and Anastacia Kurylo from Brooklyn College.

Chapter 1
Generative AI in Higher Education

Jason S. Wrench
https://orcid.org/0000-0001-5952-4288
SUNY New Paltz, USA

Sanae Elmoudden
St. John's University, USA

ABSTRACT

This chapter provides a comprehensive exploration of generative artificial intelligence (AI), particularly focusing on its implications and applications in higher education. It discusses the evolution and fundamental concepts of AI, including large language models and their development, emphasizing the intricate processes involved in creating and refining these models. The chapter delves into the ethical considerations and potential biases inherent in AI systems, highlighting the importance of responsible AI development. Moreover, the chapter examines the transformative potential of generative AI in enhancing learning, creativity, and information processing in higher education settings.

GENERATIVE AI: AN INTRODUCTION

The year was 1994 when the *Today Show* anchors Katie Couric, Bryant Gumbel, and Elizabeth Vargas sat on a couch and tried to answer the question "What is the internet?" The now infamous clip had three of the most trusted names in the daily news, trying to understand the "@" symbol. Bryant Gumble was clearly confused when he said, "I'd always seen the mark but never heard it said and then sounded stupid when I said it 'violence at NBC' [email address shows on the screen]. There it is violence…at NBC GE I mean … What is internet, anyway?" The lack of understanding of email and the internet played out for the world to see, but the hosts were grappling with the new technology that most of the world was still unfamiliar with. The video provided a highly entertaining snapshot of a specific moment in time.

We entered the exact unknown on November 30, 2022, when OpenAI released ChatGPT to the public. ChatGPT was not the first large language model (LLM) to be released to the public. The earliest

DOI: 10.4018/979-8-3693-0831-8.ch001

examples of a language model date to 1966 and Joseph Weizenbaum's ELIZA model. ChatGPT was not the first breakthrough LLM that Google's bidirectional encoder representations from transformers (BERT) model in 2019. Even though variations in GPT 2 (February 2019) and GPT 3 (June 2020) existed, the public did not notice the models. As reported by Roose (2023), as other companies were going to release their LLMs to the public, executives at OpenAI in November 2022 asked their team to put together a chatbot that could be made publicly available, which would be called "Chat with GPT 3.5." Weeks later, ChatGPT, which used the 3.5 LLM, was released to the public. ChatGPT had one million registered users in five days and more than 100 million users in just two months. According to Margaret Mitchell, a leading figure in artificial intelligence (AI) ethics and research, and Hugging Face's Chief Ethics Scientist, noted in an article in *Times Magazine*, "Most of us are pretty surprised" by how fast ChatGPT was adopted. "The technology wasn't putting forth any sort of fundamental breakthroughs" (Chow, 2023, para. 8). The difference was that the technology was released to the public, which allowed them to interact with the technology. LLMs have been used by computer scientists and researchers, but ChatGPT has put the power of LLMs in the hands of the public.

As we write here, one year after ChatGPT went public, the landscapes of AI and LLMs changed radically. Our goal in this chapter is to introduce you to generative AI.

INTRODUCTION TO AI

The word "artificial intelligence" conjures many meanings in people from HAL 9000 in *2001: A Space Odessey*, Johnny Five in the movie *Short Circuit*, or the entire dystopian world created in Issac Asimov's *I, Robot* (or the 2004 movie by the same name). Most AI portrayed in pop culture depicts the most theoretically advanced forms of AI. AI has been impacting our lives for a long time. According to McCarthy (2007), AI is "the science and engineering of making intelligent machines, especially intelligent computer programs. It is related to the similar task of using computers to understand human intelligence, but AI does not have to confine itself to methods that are biologically observable" (p. 2). Based on this definition, we can understand that AI is an interdisciplinary field that combines science and engineering to create intelligent machines and computer programs using the scientific study of how it might be emulated in systems and algorithms. In addition, practical engineering work is needed to design and build intelligent machines and software. A major area of AI draws insights from psychology, neuroscience, and cognitive science to comprehend human intelligence. However, AI is not confined solely to replicating the biological methods observed in humans. The field encompasses a broader range of techniques, some of which may not have natural counterparts. This allows AI to mimic and extend human cognitive capabilities, enabling AI systems to perform sensory, perceptual, and decision-making tasks that surpass human skills in some ways. For example, AI solutions now exceed human capabilities in areas such as complex strategic gameplay (Shin et al., 2023; Silver et al., 2016), rapid medical diagnosis based on scans (Shen et al., 2019; Thorey et al., 2019), and real-time translations between languages (Farahani, 2020; Kenny, 2022). While AI studies and imitates human intelligence, it can also pioneer entirely new "nonbiological" methods and solutions that offer novel perspectives and unique results beyond the limits of human cognition. This expansive approach emphasizes AI's vast potential and capacity for highly innovative applications.

To help us understand AI, it is vital to think of a simplistic typology of the AI that exists (or could theoretically exist). Figure 1 provides a general understanding of the seven AIs.

Figure 1. Seven types of AI

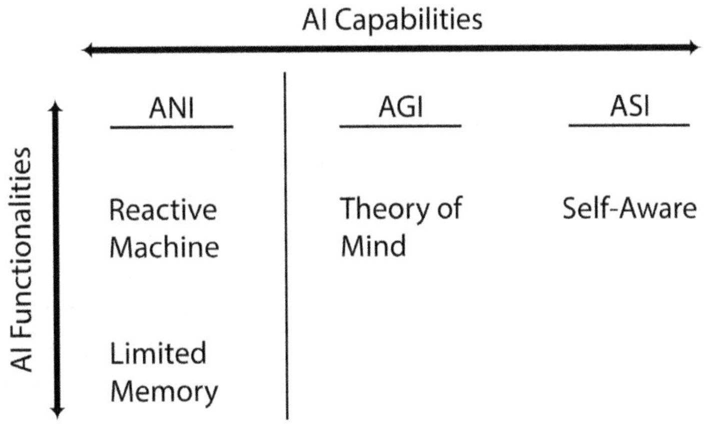

At the top, we have a category called "AI capabilities," or the breadth and depth of tasks an AI system can perform. This often indicates the level of intelligence and autonomy possessed by AI. AI researchers divide capabilities into three general categories: artificial narrow intelligence (ANI), artificial general intelligence (AGI), and artificial superintelligence (ASI). We also breakdown AI down by functionalities, or the operations or roles an AI system can fulfill, often determined by how it processes information and learns. We begin by exploring the ANI.

ANI, also known as weak AI, is the only type of AI currently available. It specializes in performing specific tasks and often outperforms humans in these narrow domains. Despite its limitations in versatility, ANI represents a significant step in AI development. Think of ANI like a kitchen gadget that is truly good at one thing, like a toaster that can only toast bread. ANI systems are like toasters, excising in specific tasks such as voice recognition (such as Siri or Alexa), image recognition in your photo library, or filtering spam from your email. They are not versatile beyond their programming. ANI can be divided into two categories: reactive machines and limited memory.

Reactive machines focus on specific specialized tasks. They use vast amounts of data to generate intelligent outputs. A historical example is IBM's Deep Blue, which utilizes reactive AI for chess playing, focusing purely on the present scenario without past or future considerations. Deep Blue can process more than 200 million moves per second in a chess game. To demonstrate its capabilities, IBM established a chess match between Deep Blue and one of the world's top chess players, Garry Kasparov. Deep Blue won.

In addition to the reactive machine ANI, there is limited memory ANI. Limited-memory ANI uses past experience to inform current decisions. Limited memory ANI continuously learns from new data, improving its responses over time. This functionality is observed in AI, such as chatbots, which adapt their outputs based on accumulated interaction data. This book focuses on the limited memory ANI. We will explore this phenomenon in more detail later in this section.

The second AI capability is AGI. AGI, or strong AI, remains theoretical. AI is envisaged to be capable of learning, understanding, and applying its intelligence across various tasks, much like a human. AGI autonomously gains new skills and knowledge without direct human intervention. "AGI typically means artificial intelligence that matches (or outmatches) humans on a range of tasks" (Heaven, 2023a, para. 2). Returning to our kitchen analogy, if the ANI is a toaster, the AGI is a chef—someone who can perform a wide variety of tasks in the kitchen, not just toasting bread. Like a versatile chef, an AI can learn and understand any intellectual task a human can perform. It is still theoretical, akin to a character in a science fiction story who can solve unfamiliar problems, learn new skills, and apply knowledge in different contexts without requiring specific training for each task. However, there is much speculation in the AI community in late Fall 2023 about how long it will take to reach the AGI.

For functionality, the AGI should have a theory of mind. The theory of mind is an advanced yet-to-be-realized AI that aims to understand and interpret human emotions, motives, and thoughts. This approach would enable AI to have personalized interactions based on the human user's emotional and psychological states. Emerging emotion AI technologies are an early step toward this goal.

The final capability of AI is artificial superintelligence (ASI), or a future stage where AI surpasses human cognitive abilities across all domains. ASI implies an AI that not only mimics but also vastly exceeds human intelligence, potentially developing its own emotions, needs, beliefs, and desires. If the AGI is a chef, the ASI is a master chef with skills beyond those of any human—one who can create dishes that no one has ever tasted using techniques that no one has ever thought of. ASI has intelligence and cognitive abilities that far surpass those of the smartest humans in every domain, from creative arts to scientific research.

Regarding functionality, ASIs are self-aware; an AI system is aware of their existence, potentially has its own consciousness, and might develop its own unique set of needs and beliefs. It is very important to understand that this type of AI is highly speculative and theoretical.

WELCOME TO GENERATIVE AI

Generative artificial intelligence (generative AI) is a form of limited memory ANI and represents a subset of AI technology that creates new content, from writing text to composing music or generating images. Generative AI is similar to a prolific artist who can produce a large volume of original work, except that the artist in this case is an AI program.

Generative AI falls under the capabilities of an ANI specializing in a single domain. For example, suppose that our generative AI is trained to generate poems. In that case, it is like a poet who is superb at writing in verse and can produce many beautiful, unique poems but cannot help you with your math homework. It is narrow in scope—it has one talent, but it is quite capable within that talent.

When we say that generative AI has the functionality of a "limited memory AI," we emphasize that the AI has limited memory. This means that generative AI, like a skilled improvisational musician, can draw on a vast repertoire of past performances (data) from which it has "learned," but its memory is not infinite or perfect. It has enough recall to make new creations feel fresh and relevant. Nevertheless, it does not remember everything it ever "learned"—only what is necessary to create something new.

Putting these two together, generative AI has the capabilities of ANI with the functionalities of limited memory, such as having a chef (the AI) who specializes in making a wide variety of sandwiches (the generative content). The chef cannot cook everything under the sun but gives the AI ingredients a sandwich, and they craft many innovative and tasty creations. They remember combinations that customers liked in the past and use that limited memory to whip up new sandwiches that are likely to please. Nevertheless, they might not remember every single sandwich they have ever made or every customer's individual preferences unless those details are crucial for creating the new sandwich. Just like a chef might use a recipe as a guideline to make a grilled cheese sandwich, generative AI uses its 'recipe'—the algorithm and data it was trained on. When two people order a grilled cheese sandwich, they receive sandwiches with the essential ingredients bread and cheese. However, the chefs, drawing from various experiences (data), might add a twist to each other based on what they have learned about customer preferences. One sandwich might come with a smear of Dijon mustard and a slice of tomato, while the other might have a hint of chipotle mayo and crispy bacon. These unique variations are the chef's creative flair, just as generative AI introduces subtle changes based on the data it has tasted. Each output, or 'generation,' will undoubtedly be recognized as a grilled cheese sandwich, but the chef's (or AI's) previous experiences with different combinations will ensure a unique culinary experience each time.

What's Algorithms Got to Do With It (AI)?

An algorithm is a set of instructions designed to perform a specific function or solve a particular problem, akin to a recipe in a cookbook. In the culinary world, recipes guide you through the steps to create a dish; similarly, algorithms can direct processes such as baking a cake, navigating to a location using GPS, or organizing a list alphabetically.

In computer science and mathematics, an algorithm is a sequence of instructions a computer follows to process data and produce outcomes. Algorithms can vary widely; some may be optimized for speed, while others might handle complex tasks more thoroughly.

Within AI, algorithms are the backbone that allows computers to process information and 'think' in ways that emulate human intelligence. These AI algorithms follow instructions and learn from the data they process, similar to how a human learns from experience. AI can recognize patterns, make decisions based on logic, and even predict future events.

Generative AI uses advanced algorithms to create original content. This could include writing, artwork, and music that seemed as if human hands and minds made them. These algorithms are trained on large datasets that may contain examples of human language, artistic styles, or musical compositions to recognize and replicate the intricate patterns found in human creativity.

With continuous training on diverse and extensive data, generative AI algorithms can produce content that is not only new but also nuanced and complex, reflecting the depth of human expression. Algorithms in generative AI test how AI can extend beyond analytical tasks to engage with the imaginative aspects of human intelligence. Modern AI systems employ sophisticated algorithms to provide useful, contextually relevant responses and are sensitive to human interaction.

UNDERSTANDING LLMS

Imagine you are at a bustling international market where vendors communicate in dozens of languages worldwide. Now, consider an LLM to be a supersmart translator who understands all these languages and can compose poetry, tell stories, or offer expert advice. That is what LLMs such as Orca-2 do—they are like digital polyglots with the touch of a Renaissance artist.

Orca-2 is a remarkable AI tool created by researchers in Microsoft that aims to teach it a variety of ways to solve problems, much like how a teacher equips students with different learning techniques (Mitra et al., 2023). Orca-2 is not the largest AI on the block, but it is smart and nimble, using its "brain" to think through tasks step-by-step or come up with answers right away when needed.

How do you teach such an AI? Orca 2's education involves feeding it a vast library of information, almost like giving it a speed-read through an enormous stack of books, articles, and internet pages. The training included a new set of learning materials designed explicitly for Orca, known as the Orca-2 dataset.

To ensure that Orca-2 learns effectively, it practices special exercises that challenge its reasoning, such as how a student might take practice exams before finishing. This method is called 'progressive learning,' where Orca starts with the basics and gradually moves on to more complex problems, ensuring that it understands thoroughly before advancing.

All this learning occurs inside powerful computers called graphics processing units (GPUs), which are similar to high-performance engines that help Orca think and learn faster. Orca's training session is quite intense and would take a long time, even for such a fast learner—imagine studying around the clock for a few days straight!

One of the best parts of Orca-2 is that its 'thought process'—how it solves problems and comes up with ideas—has been shared openly for others to learn from. This open-source approach means that anyone who is curious can explore how Orca thinks about and contributes to its education, much like how open schools work.

This introduction to Orca-2 provides insight into the world of LLMs, where AI not only understands and communicates in human language but also learns to reason and create, offering a bridge between the digital and human worlds.

CREATING AN LLM FROM INCEPTION TO REALIZATION

When contemplating this chapter, one of the biggest concerns was the realization that many do not understand how generative AI works. Wu (2022) likens understanding to financial literacy. People do not need to know the ins and outs of how banking institutions work on a global scale, but people do need to know how to create a savings account, pay off credit cards, and finance a home. In the same way, end users of GAI do not need to know how all the science and mathematical algorithms work to understand how it works. However, people do need to know what LLMs are and how they are created. For some readers, the following section is going to be an overly simplistic explanation of how LLMs are created, trained, and improved over time. For other readers, this section will be entirely too basic as it attempts to describe LLMs in a conversational manner to help people come to grasp with nature of LLMs. As communication scholars, most of us do not have a background in computer science, so we've tried to keep the explanation as straight forward as humanly possible.

Over the next few pages, we introduce an imaginary yet representative LLM that we have affectionately named "SLOTH," an acronym for the sophisticated language organizer text-based helper.

SLOTH is a conceptual tool designed to mimic and extend the capabilities of human language processing by using advanced AI techniques. It is a sophisticated assistant adept at organizing vast amounts of textual data and providing helpful responses to user queries. Imagine having a digital companion that can sift through libraries of information, understand complex language nuances, and assist you with text-based tasks with ease, that is, SLOTH in a nutshell.

Our aim here is not to delve into the technical intricacies that often accompany AI discussions but rather to take you on a more approachable and easy-to-understand tour of how an LLM such as SLOTH comes to be. We will walk through the various stages of SLOTH's creation—from its initial conceptualization, through the gathering and processing of data it needs to learn, to the actual training where SLOTH starts to 'understand' language and, finally, how it is refined into a helpful digital tool.

Whether you're entirely new to the world of AI or just curious about how these intelligent systems are built, this section demystifies the process and presents it in an engaging and straightforward way. Let us embark on this imaginative journey to understand how a language model, such as SLOTH, could be brought to the public.

Conceptualization

At the heart of every innovation is the spark of an idea—a blueprint of what it is and does. For our imaginary friend SLOTH, this conceptualization phase lays the groundwork for its creation. We defined the purpose and identified SLOTH's key capabilities.

Defining the Purpose

SLOTH, our sophisticated languageizer and text-based helper, is envisioned to be more than a digital tool. It is designed as a linguistic maestro, a whiz at deciphering human language, and an ace for organizing heaps of text data. Think of SLOTH as your personal librarian, not only shelving books but also understanding every word in them and helping you easily navigate this information maze. The core purpose of SLOTH is threefold.

1. **Language Understanding**: Like a polyglot who can effortlessly switch between languages, SLOTH aims to understand the intricacies of human language. It should be able to grasp words and the context, emotion, and subtleties within them.
2. **Organizing Text Data**: Imagine an old, cluttered attic full of books, letters, and manuscripts. SLOTH is like an organizer who comes in and neatly categorizes everything, making it easy to find what you are looking for.
3. **Assistance with Text-based Queries**: SLOTH is not only about understanding and organizing but also about helping. SLOTH is at your service to answer your questions, summarize a lengthy document, or even write a poem.

Identifying Key Capabilities

To transform SLOTH from a concept into reality, we must equip it with specific abilities. These capabilities are the tools and skills that can fulfill their purposes.

1. **Advanced Language Processing**: As a chef expertly wields knives, SLOTH requires the ability to process language at an advanced level. This involves not only reading the text but also understanding nuances, idioms, and cultural references.
2. **Pattern Detection**: Imagine looking at a starry sky and picking out constellations. SLOTH should be able to examine vast amounts of text and detect patterns, themes, trends, and connections that are not immediately apparent.

3. **Interactive Assistance**: Like a knowledgeable friend always there to help, SLOTH should be interactive and responsive. It should be able to engage in conversations, provide information, and even offer creative suggestions in response to user input.

The conceptualization phase is about dreaming of what SLOTH could be—a sophisticated blend of linguists, librarians, and personal assistants. This is the first and crucial step in bringing this imaginative AI companion to life, setting the stage for exciting developments.

Designing the Neural Network Architecture for SLOTH

Imagine building a house. A solid architectural plan was required before the first brick was laid. For SLOTH, our budding language model, this stage is about designing its 'brain'—the neural network architecture. This is where we decide on a structure that will empower SLOTH to understand and organize language.

Selecting a Model Type

The first step in this architectural journey is to choose the right type of neural network. Various neural networks serve different purposes in the AI world, such as ensuring the suitability of different vehicles for different terrains. We require a model specifically adept at handling language tasks for SLOTH, which is about language.

Here, we turn to a "transformer model." Without becoming too technical, consider a transformer model a highly efficient librarian who is great at finding the right book for you and who understands the story in each book. These models are known for their ability to process language word by word and understand the context and relationships between words, similar to reading between lines.

Ensuring Sophistication in Architecture

Once the model type is determined, the next step is to ensure that the architecture is sufficiently sophisticated. You see that language is more than just words strung together; it is nuanced and full of idioms, tone, and emotions. SLOTH needs to be sufficiently savvy to grasp all these subtleties.

To achieve this level of sophistication, we designed the SLOTH architecture to be intricate and layered, as in the complex network of interconnected streets in a bustling city. Each layer in this network captures different aspects of language, from basic grammar to intricate expressions of emotion.

Imagine SLOTH's architecture as a concert orchestra where each instrument plays a vital role in creating a harmonious symphony. Some layers (or sections of the orchestra) focus on understanding the basic structure of sentences, whereas others interpret emotional tone or cultural context. Together, they collaborated to provide SLOTH with a deep and nuanced understanding of language.

Designing a neural network architecture for SLOTH is a critical phase in which we lay the foundation for its language processing capabilities. By selecting a transformer model and ensuring its sophistication, we set up SLOTH as a language model that truly understands and resonates with the complexities and beauty of human language.

Dataset Collection and Preparation

Embarking on the journey of creating SLOTH brings us to a crucial stage: gathering and preparing food for its intellect—the dataset. This stage resembles assembling the ingredients for a grand feast, where variety and quality are key factors.

Gathering Text Data

The first step is akin to a treasure hunt, where we gather a vast and diverse collection of written texts. Imagine compiling an eclectic library that includes everything from classic literature to modern blogs, scientific papers, social media posts, and everything in between. This library for SLOTH should vary as much as the world's culture is, covering various topics, styles, and languages.

This diversity is crucial because, like a chef who needs various ingredients to create a range of dishes, SLOTH needs a rich and varied dataset to understand the many flavors of the human language. We discuss a dataset that includes the eloquence of Shakespeare, the informative tone of news articles, the casual chatter of social media, and the specific language of scientific reports. Each type of text adds a layer of understanding, helping SLOTH become a well-rounded, knowledgeable language model.

Data Cleaning and Organization

However, gathering data is only a part of this process. Next, these data were meticulously cleaned and organized, much like sorting and preparing ingredients before cooking. This step is crucial for ensuring that SLOTH learns from the best-quality data.

Cleaning involves the removal of 'impurities' from our dataset. This involves filtering out irrelevant information, correcting errors, and ensuring that the text is in a format that SLOTH can easily digest. Imagine sifting through a pile of puzzle pieces, discarding bent and broken pieces, and keeping only those that fit perfectly.

Organization is about structuring these data effectively. This is like arranging books in a library so that they can be easily accessed and used. We organize the text that makes sense for SLOTH training, categorizing it into themes, styles, or complexity levels. Thus, when SLOTH learns, it can efficiently navigate this vast amount of information.

At this stage, we build the foundation of SLOTH's knowledge and understanding. By carefully selecting, cleaning, and organizing the dataset, we ensured that SLOTH has a rich, diverse, and high-quality database of text to learn from, setting it up for success to become an adept language model.

Model Training for SLOTH

With a rich and diverse dataset, we are now ready to embark on one of the most exciting phases in creating SLOTH-Model Training. This phase teaches SLOTH how to read, understand, and use language, much like coaching young prodigies.

Initial Training (Pretraining)

In this initial stage, we introduce SLOTH to the basics of human language. It is like the first day at school when SLOTH learns the alphabet, the structure of sentences, and nuances of language. We feed SLOTH the vast collection of texts we have gathered, allowing it to immerse itself in the world of words.

During pretraining, SLOTH picks up patterns in the language. It learns how words are typically used together, how sentences are formed, and how to understand context. This is akin to children learning by listening to conversations around them and gradually grasping how language works.

This phase is crucial because it lays the foundation for SLOTH's understanding. It is not about memorizing text but about learning to recognize patterns and structures in language. SLOTH sees how a question typically looks, how a joke is structured, or how a poem flows.

Refining Skills (Fine-Tuning)

Once SLOTH has a foundational understanding of language from its initial training, it is time for fine-tuning, a phase in which human expertise plays a crucial role. Think of it as an apprentice learning a craft under the guidance of master artisans. In this stage, SLOTH learns not only from the data but also from human insights and interventions.

Collaboration with Human Experts. Just as musicians might work with a maestro to refine their skills, SLOTH is fine-tuned with the help of language experts, educators, and everyday users. These human collaborators reviewed SLOTH's responses, identified areas where information might be misunderstood or misrepresented, and provided guidance on more appropriate or accurate responses.

Incorporating Real-World Context and Nuance. Human involvement is vital in helping SLOTH people navigate the complexities and subtleties of human language and culture. Humans can provide context, cultural nuances, and ethical considerations that are not always clear in the raw data. This input is crucial for helping SLOTH understand and respond to text that is technically accurate, culturally sensitive, and contextually appropriate.

Specific Human Roles in Fine-tuning SLOTH

- **Contextualizing Conversations**
  1. Humans help SLOTH understand the context behind conversations. For example, humans may annotate text examples to explain why a specific response is appropriate in a situation. This could involve clarifying why a certain tone or choice of words is suitable for a formal context but not for a casual conversation.
  2. In a practical exercise, human trainers work with a dialog where SLOTH interacts with a user, greeting it with "As-salaam-alaikum." The trainers annotate this greeting, explaining its cultural significance as a respectful salutation in many Islamic cultures. This process helps SLOTH understand the translation and cultural context of such phrases, enhancing its ability to respond appropriately and respectfully in similar interactions.
- **Cultural Sensitivity Training**
  1. Human trainers provide insights into cultural nuances and sensitivities. They guide SLOTH in understanding and respecting diverse cultural norms and expressions. For example, they

might adjust SLOTH's language to align more with specific cultural etiquettes, such as using formal titles in cultures where hierarchical respect is important.
2. In a role-playing session, trainers simulate a Japanese business meeting with SLOTH, using formal language and hierarchical titles customary in Japanese culture. They interact with SLOTH as if they were in an actual meeting, providing immediate feedback and corrections to its responses. This exercise trains SLOTH to recognize and adapt its language and behavior according to the cultural nuances of different social and professional settings.

- **Ethical Guidance**
    1. Humans play a crucial role in embedding ethical considerations into SLOTH. The authors reviewed the SLOTH responses to ensure that they were free from biases and aligned with ethical standards. This includes identifying and correcting potentially discriminatory or offensive language.
    2. During an ethical review session, a diverse group of trainers evaluates SLOTH's responses to biases. They observe a tendency for SLOTH to associate certain negative traits with specific cultural groups. Recognizing this as a bias, the trainers retrained SLOTH with a more balanced dataset, ensuring that it avoided generalizations and stereotypes and promoted fairness and cultural sensitivity in its interactions.
- **Emotional Intelligence Infusion**
    1. Human input is key to teaching SLOTH to recognize and appropriately respond to emotional cues. Trainers might tag texts with emotional labels (such as 'happy,' 'sad,' and 'angry') to help SLOTH identify and respond empathetically to different emotional tones in language.
    2. In an exercise to boost SLOTH's emotional intelligence, trainers feed conversations laden with various emotional tones. For instance, they show SLOTH a dialog where a user expresses sadness. Trainers annotate these expressions, highlighting the emotional cues. They then guide SLOTH in crafting responses that show empathy and understanding. This training helps SLOTH recognize and appropriately react to emotional nuances in human interactions, making its responses more empathetic and contextually relevant.
- **Interpretation of Sarcasm and Idioms**
    1. Humans help SLOTH understand nonliteral language aspects, such as sarcasm, idioms, or humor. They might provide examples of sarcastic statements and explain their actual meanings, helping SLOTH discern between literal and figurative language.
    2. To help SLOTH understand sarcasm and idioms, trainers set up a scenario where these language elements are prominent. They input sarcastic remarks, such as "Great, another rainy day!," and idiomatic expressions, such as "It's raining cats and dogs." Each instance is accompanied by explanations of the actual meanings and responses. This process teaches SLOTH to distinguish between literal and figurative language, enhancing its ability to interact in a more human-like, nuanced manner.
- **Real-World Scenario Simulation**
    1. Trainers create and present real-life scenarios to SLOTH, helping SLOTH understand and adapt to various real-world applications. This could range from simulating a customer service interaction to guiding a healthcare inquiry, ensuring that SLOTH can function effectively in diverse settings.
    2. To ensure that SLOTH can handle practical applications, trainers simulate real-world scenarios. In one simulation, SLOTH acts as a customer service assistant dealing with a complex

complaint. The scenario is realistic and includes typical customer frustrations and specific product details. Throughout the simulation, trainers provide feedback on SLOTH's problem-solving approach and communication skills, fine-tuning its ability to navigate and respond effectively in real-life situations. This training ensures that SLOTH can apply its language and problem-solving skills in practical everyday scenarios that users might encounter.

- **Feedback Loop for Continuous Improvement**
  1. Human trainers continually assess SLOTH performance and provide feedback for improvement. They monitor how SLOTH interacts with users, identify areas where it may misinterpret or inadequately respond, and make necessary adjustments to its training regimen.
  2. After deploying SLOTH, the team collects and analyzes user feedback. For instance, they find that users from a particular cultural background perceive SLOTH's responses as overly formal. Using this feedback, they adjust SLOTH's algorithms and training data to strike a more appropriate balance in tone, ensuring that it remains culturally attuned and user friendly for a global audience.

Iterative Learning Process. This phase is iterative, during which the performance of SLOTH is continually assessed and improved based on human feedback. It is akin to a sculptor shaping a piece of art, in which each iteration brings it closer to the desired form. Human feedback helps fine-tune SLOTH's algorithms, ensuring that it processes language accurately and aligns with human values and expectations.

Human-AI Synergy for Ethical and Accurate Outputs

Incorporating human expertise in fine-tuning SLOTH ensures that it not only mimics human language but also understands and engages with it ethically and contextually relevantly. This synergy between human intelligence and AI technology is crucial in creating a language model that is sophisticated, effective, trustworthy, and aligned with human users' needs.

By highlighting human involvement in the fine-tuning process, we acknowledge the invaluable role of human judgment and expertise in shaping AI models, such as SLOTH. This is a testament to the idea that the best AI systems are not created in isolation but through a collaborative effort that combines the best human insights with advanced AI capabilities.

Computational Requirements for Training SLOTH. Training SLOTH, our aspiring LLM, is akin to preparing for space missions. It requires powerful technology and time—a lot of it. This implies that training a model can cost millions of dollars. Smith (2023) noted that OpenAI's GPT-3 required $5 million in the number of GPUs for each training run. As such, running training models is not something your average person can do at this point. This section delved into the computational muscle and the time required to convert SLOTH from a concept to a functioning AI.

Hardware Selection

As a space mission requires a powerful rocket to reach stars, SLOTH requires robust hardware to process vast amounts of data during its training. This is where GPUs and tensor processing units come into play. These are the engines of the SLOTH training process.

GPUs and TPUs are specialized processors designed to handle massive computational tasks, such as a high-power engine designed for speed and efficiency. In the context of SLOTH, they are workhorses, crunching numbers, and data processing at astonishing speeds.

Imagine GPUs and TPUs as a team of supercomputers working tirelessly through the complex calculations and data analyses required to train SLOTH. They enable SLOTH to learn from its diverse dataset, making sense of language patterns, sentence structures, and contextual nuances at a rate far beyond that achieved using regular computers.

Training Duration

Let us now discuss time. Training an LLM such as SLOTH is not a sprint but a marathon. The process requires not only days but also often weeks or even months. This extended training period is essential for SLOTH to fully absorb and learn from its vast and varied training material.

During this period, the SLOTH algorithm continuously learns, adjusts, and improves. Like an athlete in training, SLOTH requires time to develop its skills. It starts by understanding basic language structures and gradually moves on to more complex tasks, such as interpreting nuanced texts or generating helpful responses.

It is a long journey but a necessary one. Each hour of training helps SLOTH become more adept, nuanced, and sophisticated in its language capabilities. This prolonged training ensures that, once SLOTH is ready, it can handle a wide range of language tasks with the ease and proficiency expected of a sophisticated language model.

In summary, the computational requirements for training SLOTH involve powerful hardware and a significant time investment. Together, they form the backbone of SLOTH's training regimen, ensuring that our language model is well equipped and thoroughly prepared for understanding and assisting in the vast world of human language.

Testing and Evaluation of SLOTH

After months of intense training, akin to preparing an athlete for the Olympics, SLOTH is ready to test and evaluate. This stage is crucial—we see if all the hard work has paid off and if SLOTH is genuinely prepared to step into the world as a competent language model.

Performance Checks

These performance checks were based on SLOTH's final exam. Throughout and after training, we regularly tested SLOTH through a series of tests to evaluate its understanding of language, its ability to organize information, and how effectively it can assist users with text-based queries.

Imagine setting up scenarios where SLOTH is asked to summarize a complex article, find and organize information from a large document, or converse on a specific topic. These tests are similar to practical assignments, assessing SLOTH's theoretical knowledge of language and its practical application in real-world situations.

This is similar to the driving test. SLOTH needs to show that it can understand the rules of the road (language rules) and drive smoothly in traffic (handling real-world language tasks). These performance checks helped us identify areas where SLOTH excels and where additional training is needed.

Benchmarking

Benchmarking measures SLOTH's performance against a set standard. It is like an athlete competing in a series of events to see where they stand, compared to others and previous records. For SLOTH, this means using specific benchmarks and tasks established in AI and language models.

These benchmarks could involve various tasks, such as language comprehension, information retrieval, and creative writing. By comparing the performance of SLOTH models on these tasks to that of other existing models, we obtained a clear picture of how SLOTH stacks in the world of LLMs.

Benchmarking is crucial because it not only tells us how well SLOTH performs in isolation but also in relation to the broader AI community. Moreover, AI researchers have determined where SLOTH is breaking new ground and where it might still require improvement.

The testing and evaluation phases involve reckoning. It is where we see the fruits of our labor and gauge the readiness of SLOTH to be released into the world. Through rigorous performance checks and benchmarking, we ensure that SLOTH is not simply another language model but rather a sophisticated, effective, and reliable text-based helper poised to have a significant impact on AI and language processing.

Iteration and Improvement of SLOTH

The journey of creating SLOTH is akin to sculpting a masterpiece. It is not just about the initial carving but also about refining and perfecting the work. This is where the process of iteration and improvement comes into play—a continuous cycle of feedback and enhancement that ensures that SLOTH is not just good but exceptional.

Feedback Loop

The SLOTH was implemented as a performer on stage, with each test and evaluation serving as a performance review. Feedback from these reviews is crucial. This tells us what SLOTH is doing right and where it needs to be improved. This feedback loop is key to making SLOTH more than just a functional language model; it can make it truly user friendly, efficient, and effective.

Incorporating feedback into SLOTH development involves the following steps:

- **Analysis**: First, we analyzed the feedback. This could be due to performance checks or user comments on how well SLOTH assisted with its queries.
- **Identification of Improvement Areas**: Next, we identified specific areas where SLOTH could be better. Is it difficult to understand certain idioms? Does it falter when complex information is organized? Alternatively, this approach is not as user friendly as possible.
- **Adjustments and retraining**: Based on this identification, we adjusted the SLOTH. This might involve tweaking its algorithms, enriching its training data, or retraining it in certain aspects to enhance its performance.

This process is like a chef tasting a dish and then adjusting the seasoning to get it right. We fine-tuned SLOTH, adding a little bit here, tweaking a little bit there, to ensure that it meets the high standards we have set for it.

Real-World Application and Adaptation

SLOTH's performance in controlled tests might differ from how it operates in the real world. Hence, we pay close attention to how SLOTH performs in real-world scenarios: whether it assists a student with research, helps a professional draft a report, or aids a writer with creative content.

This approach provides invaluable practical feedback because SLOTH interacts with users in these scenarios. This feedback forms a critical part of the improvement cycle, helping us to continuously adapt and evolve SLOTH to better meet its users' needs.

The process of iterating and improving SLOTH is an ongoing journey. This involves taking a good language model and turning it into a great one through constant feedback, learning, and adaptation. This ensures that SLOTH remains at the forefront of language processing technology, not only as a sophisticated tool but also as a reliable and ever-improving tool in the world of text and language.

Deployment and Accessibility of SLOTH

The creation of SLOTH has been akin to crafting a fine piece of art. However, this masterpiece must be seen and used to make an impact. This brings us to a vital stage: making SLOTH accessible to those who need it. Think of it as opening the doors to a gallery where everyone can come and appreciate the art.

Making SLOTH Available

The first step is to determine how SLOTH will enter the world. There are several avenues for this purpose.

- **API Integration**: One method is to use SLOTH as an application programming interface (API). Imagine this as a special key that allows other software or applications to tap into SLOTH's capabilities. This could mean integrating SLOTH into existing systems, websites, or apps, allowing them to use their language processing powers.
- **Software Incorporation**: Another route involves embedding SLOTH directly into software products. This would be like adding a new and powerful feature to a piece of software, enhancing its functionality with SLOTH's language understanding and organizing skills.
- **Stand-alone Applications**: Alternatively, SLOTH could be the star of its own show, a stand-alone application designed specifically for users to interact with it directly. This approach is akin to the use of a dedicated tool or app for various language-related tasks.

Documentation and Support

Having made SLOTH accessible, the next step is ensuring that users can harness its full potential. This is where clear documentation and robust support have come into play.

- **User Guides and Documentation**: We provide comprehensive guides and manuals such as an instruction booklet that comes with a new device. These documents explain how to use SLOTH and highlight its features and capabilities in a user-friendly manner.
- **Support Systems**: Consider this a helpdesk or customer service for SLOTH. Whether through online forums, help centers, or customer support lines, we ensure that users can access help when-

ever needed. This support system is crucial for helping users navigate any challenges they face while using SLOTH and ensuring that they get the most out of it.

In summary, deploying and making SLOTH accessible are all about bringing this advanced language model to people in an easy, convenient, and beneficial way. By carefully planning its deployment and providing thorough documentation and support, we aim to make SLOTH a technological marvel. This practical and accessible tool can make a real difference in people's interactions with language and text.

Ethical Considerations and Bias Mitigation in SLOTH

Creating SLOTH is not only about technological prowess but also about responsibility. In this age of AI, ethical considerations and bias mitigation are as crucial as functionalities. However, bias is a consistent problem and one of the pressing concerns that AI researchers have for current models (Heaven, 2023b). This section is dedicated to ensuring that SLOTH is not only an intelligent tool but also a fair and ethical tool.

Ethical Framework

Developing SLOTH within an ethical framework is like building a house with a solid bedrock foundation. It is about ensuring that SLOTH respects the privacy of its users and operates without causing harm or prejudice. The key ethical guidelines are as follows:

- **Privacy and Confidentiality**: As a doctor keeps patient information private, SLOTH respects the confidentiality of the data that it processes. It is programmed to handle user information securely, ensuring that private data remain private.
- **Avoiding Biases**: In a perfect world, SLOTH would be like a wise judge, impartial, or unbiased. However, we must be vigilant because SLOTH learns from human language, which can be biased. We ensured that SLOTH was trained on diverse and inclusive datasets to reduce the risk of learning and perpetuating existing prejudices.

Bias Checks

Bias in AI is like an unintended flaw in a recipe that can spoil a dish. To prevent this, we implemented several checks and balances in SLOTH.

- **Regular Audits for Bias**: Consider these routine health checkups for SLOTH, ensuring that there is no developing or harboring bias. These audits involve analyzing SLOTH's responses and decisions to detect any patterns of unfairness or prejudice.
- **Feedback Loops for Continuous Improvement**: Like a self-driving car equipped with sensors to correct its course, SLOTH includes mechanisms for learning from its interactions. If bias is detected, SLOTH can be updated and retrained to correct this flaw.
- **Diverse Input and Perspectives**: One of the best ways to combat bias is to ensure diversity in the data from which SLOTH learns. This is like gathering ingredients from different cultures to create

a well-rounded, globally inspired dish. We strive to include a wide range of voices and perspectives in the SLOTH training data to help it understand and serve as a diverse user base.

In conclusion, the ethical development and deployment of SLOTH are paramount. By focusing on creating responsible, unbiased, and respectful AI, we aim to ensure that SLOTH excels in its capabilities and upholds the highest ethical standards. This approach guarantees that SLOTH is a sophisticated language model and a beacon of ethical AI development.

Ongoing Development and Community Engagement for SLOTH

Creating SLOTH is not an onetime event but rather a continuous journey of growth and improvement. Just as a gardener tends to garden, nurture, and tend toward plants, SLOTH requires ongoing care and attention to thrive. This section focuses on the perpetual development of SLOTH and its vital role in community engagement.

Updates and Improvements

Keeping SLOTH up-to-date and improving it over time is akin to upgrading and refurbishing a beloved home. It is about ensuring that SLOTH maintains its efficiency and relevance and continues to evolve and adapt.

- **Incorporating User Feedback**: Imagine SLOTH as a performer on stage, where the audience's applause and critiques help refine the performance. User feedback is invaluable and provides insights into how SLOTH is being used, what users love, and where they wish it could improve. This feedback guides us in making targeted updates and enhancements to the SLOTH.
- **Staying Abreast of Advancements**: The field of AI is similar to a fast-moving river, constantly flowing with new ideas and breakthroughs. We ensure that SLOTH keeps pace and rides the wave of these advancements. Regular updates have been made to incorporate the latest research findings, technological improvements, and best practices in AI development.

Community Involvement

SLOTH is not only our creation but also a part of the broader AI landscape. Engaging with the AI community brings about many perspectives and expertise, thus enriching SLOTH development.

- **Collaborative Improvements**: Think of SLOTH as a communal garden where experts and enthusiasts worldwide come together to plant ideas and share knowledge. Engaging with the AI community opens doors to collaborative efforts, pooling resources and expertise to enhance SLOTH's capabilities. This could involve partnering with academic institutions, participating in AI forums, or contributing to open-source projects.
- **Alignment with Research and Ethics**: Staying in tune with the AI community helps ensure that SLOTH remains aligned with the latest research and ethical standards. It is like having a council of wise advisers guiding SLOTH on its path. This involves keeping up with technological advancements and staying attuned to the evolving conversation around AI ethics and responsible AI use.

'The ongoing development and community engagement of SLOTH concern nurturing and growing it in a dynamic, collaborative environment. It is a commitment to continual learning, adaptation, and improvement, ensuring that SLOTH remains at the forefront of AI technology and continues to serve users effectively and ethically. This approach enhances SLOTH's capabilities and embeds it within the rich tapestry of the global AI community, making it a collective endeavor in pursuing advanced AI development.

The State of AI in Higher Education

To prepare for this book, we generated a quick survey to determine what faculty members think about generative AI in higher education.

Previous research has explored some of the same issues (see Primary Research Group, 2023a). Appendix A contains the raw data from this study. We surveyed 109 faculty members across the world. 61.5% of the participants were based in the US. For the purposes of this study, the data are presented in their raw form in the same way that others have presented this type of descriptive information (Primary Research Group, 2023a, 2023b).

Although far from generalizable or conclusive, the results from our data collection effort reveal that faculty members are mixed in terms of what to do with AI. As of Fall 2023, faculty members reported that their colleges and universities provide little to no training or guidance on handling the disruptive force of generative AI in the classroom. Our findings were very much in line with those from other studies of larger samples of higher education faculty (Primary Research Group, 2023a, 2023b).

As editors of this volume, we are concerned about the future of the GAI and its disruptive nature in the communication classroom.

CONCLUSION

Generative AI stands at the forefront of a technological revolution and is poised to reshape our interactions with information and creativity. As we have shown with groundbreaking models, such as DALL-E 3, GPT-4, Claude 2.1, and MidJourney 6, which can create stunningly lifelike images and articulate humanlike text, the potential of these systems is immense. They open new vistas for creativity, from generating intricate art to composing music, offering glimpses of a future in which AI unleashes human potential.

However, with great power comes great responsibility. The rapid advancement of generative AI has presented significant ethical challenges that require careful supervision. Concerns such as embedded biases—for instance, how a model trained mainly on Western literature might struggle with non-Western contexts—privacy issues, the spread of misinformation, and the need for responsible innovation necessitate proactive governance. It is crucial to maintain a diversity of perspectives and inclusive datasets to develop AI systems that serve and understand the entire spectrum of society.

Generative AI models can democratize access to knowledge and creative expression if cultivated with care and conscientiousness. Imagine a world where these models act as personalized tutors, adapting to each student's learning style, or as dynamic museum guides, tailoring tours to match visitors' unique interests. Picture tools that enable journalists to swiftly analyze complex data, providing insights into important stories in real time. These examples are the beginning of how generative AI can be beneficially integrated into society.

However, in the current landscape, despite their technical sophistication, today's models fail to fully replicate the depth of human cognition. The richness of human experiences—the subtleties of humor, the wisdom gained over a lifetime, or the nostalgic joy of childhood memories—remains elusive to AI. Genuine creativity and reasoning seem to be not merely products of data but also products of lived personal experiences.

The future will probably involve a fusion of human and machine intelligence, creating a synergy where our combined strengths lead to unexplored realms of innovation. We may witness AI writing assistants helping authors create groundbreaking novels; styling algorithms that bring overlooked fashion gems to the attention of personal shoppers; or AI philosophers engaging in intellectual debates with their human counterparts regarding emerging ethical dilemmas.

By embracing this collaboration potential while maintaining strict accountability standards, intelligent creations can evolve beyond mere tools to become trusted companions in our pursuit of knowledge and expression. In doing so, they can enhance our capabilities and offer new perspectives that enrich our understanding in previously unimaginable ways. In the future, we will be responsible for helping educators, students, administrators, developers, policymakers, and society members guide this journey, ensuring that AI development is navigated with wisdom, ethics, and an inclusive vision.

Preview of the Rest of the Book

The book is organized into four parts: Part I—Historicizing Generative AI (GAI) in the Communication Classroom; Part II—Reconfiguring the Communication Classroom in the Era of GAI; Part III—Safeguarding Against Mediocrity in the Age of GAI; and Part IV—Futurizing Generative AI (GAI) in the Communication Classroom.

Author Note

Several AI tools were used in the writing of this chapter:

- https://editgpt.app/
- https://www.aje.com/curie/
- https://paperpal.com/
- https://reciteworks.com/
- https://typeset.io/
- https://scite.ai/
- https://chat.openai.com/
- https://claude.ai/

These tools were used for conducting secondary research, editing, and discussing ideas for this chapter. The humans are responsible for the content of the chapter, but the tools aided in generating ideas to help explain some concepts for a general audience. For example, we knew we wanted to name our fictious LLM "SLOTH" because the first author loves sloths. ChatGPT was helpful to generate what SLOTH could stand for if it were an LLM: sophisticated language organizer text-based helper.

Our view is that GAI should never replace academics and academic writing, but it can aid in the research and writing processes. Many have been using various forms of AI in their writing process for a long time without calling it that. Spell check is a form of reactive A and grammar check can be either reactive or limited-memory depending on the underlying AI architecture. Those older tools were not generative, but they still fell into the larger AI family.

REFERENCES

Chow, A. R. (2023, February 8). How ChatGPT managed to grow faster than TikTok or Instagram. *Time*. https://time.com/6253615/chatgpt-fastest-growing/

Farahani, M. V. (2020). *Adequacy in machine vs. human translation: A comparative study of English and Persian languages*. Applied Linguistics Research Journal. doi:10.14744/alrj.2020.98700

Heaven, W. D. (2023a, November 16). Google DeepMind wants to define what counts as artificial general intelligence. *MIT Technology Review*. https://www.technologyreview.com/2023/11/16/1083498/google-deepmind-what-is-artificial-general-intelligence-agi/

Heaven, W. D. (2023b). 6 big questions for generative AI. *MIT Technological Review*, *127*(1), 30–37.

Kenny, D. (Ed.). (2022). *Machine translation for everyone: Empowering users in the age of artificial intelligence*. Language Science Press. doi:10.5281/zenodo.6653406

McCarthy, J. (2007, November 12). *What is artificial intelligence?* https://www-formal.stanford.edu/jmc/whatisai.pdf

Mitra, A., Del Corro, L., Mahajan, S., Codas, A., Simoes Ribeiro, C., Agrawal, S., Chen, X., Razdaibiedina, A., Jones, E., Aggarwal, K., Palangi, H., Zheng, G., Rosset, C., Khanpour, H., & Awadallah, A. (2023). *Orca-2: Teaching small language models how to reason*. https://www.microsoft.com/en-us/research/publication/orca-2-teaching-small-language-models-how-to-reason/

Primary Research Group. (2023a). *Survey of US higher education faculty 2023: Views on and use of ChatGPT*. Author.

Primary Research Group. (2023b). *Survey of US higher education faculty 2024: Use of artificial intelligence applications*. Author.

Rose, K. (2023, February 3). How ChatGPT kicked off an AI arms race: Even inside the company, the chatbot's popularity has come as something of a shock. *The New York Times*. https://www.nytimes.com/2023/02/03/technology/chatgpt-openai-artificial-intelligence.html

Shen, J., Zhang, C. J. P., Jiang, B., Chen, J., Song, J., Liu, Z., He, Z., Wong, S. Y., Fang, P. H., & Ming, W. K. (2019). Artificial intelligence versus clinicians in disease diagnosis: Systematic review. *JMIR Medical Informatics*, *7*(3), e10010. doi:10.2196/10010 PMID:31420959

Shin, M., Kim, J., Opheusden, B., & Griffiths, T. L. (2023). Superhuman artificial intelligence can improve human decision-making by increasing novelty. *Proceedings of the National Academy of Sciences of the United States of America*, *120*(12), e2214840120. Advance online publication. doi:10.1073/pnas.2214840120 PMID:36913582

Silver, D., Huang, A., Maddison, C., Guez, A., Sifre, L., Driessche, G., ... Hassabis, D. (2016). Mastering the game of go with deep neural networks and tree search. *Nature*, *529*(7587), 484–489. doi:10.1038/nature16961 PMID:26819042

Smith, C. S. (2023, September 8). What large models cost you: There is no free AI lunch. *Forbes*. https://www.forbes.com/sites/craigsmith/2023/09/08/what-large-models-cost-you--there-is-no-free-ai-lunch

Thorey, V., Hernandez, A. B., Arnal, P. J., & During, E. H. (2019, July 23-27). AI vs humans for the diagnosis of sleep apnea. *Proceedings of the 41st International Engineering in Medicine and Biology Conference*. 10.1109/EMBC.2019.8856877

Wu, G. (2022, August 18). Helping people understand AI. *The Keyword*. https://blog.google/technology/ai/helping-people-understand-ai

KEY TERMS AND DEFINITIONS

Algorithmic Transparency: This is the principle that the processes and outcomes of AI algorithms should be open and understandable to users and stakeholders. This approach ensures that people can understand how AI systems make decisions.

Artificial General Intelligence (AGI): AGI represents a stage of AI development in which the system possesses the ability to understand, learn, and apply its intelligence to a wide range of problems, similar to the level of a human being. AI can generalize learning and reasoning across diverse domains and is not limited to specific tasks.

Artificial Intelligence (AI): A field of computer science focused on creating machines capable of performing tasks that typically require human intelligence. These tasks include learning, problem solving, perception, and language understanding.

Artificial Narrow Intelligence (ANI): This refers to AI systems that are designed to perform a single task or a limited range of tasks. These systems exhibit intelligence in specific contexts but lack the broader understanding and adaptability of human intelligence.

Artificial Super Intelligence (ASI): ASI is a theoretical form of AI that surpasses human intelligence across all fields, including creativity, general wisdom, and problem solving. It represents a level of intelligence that not only mimics but also exceeds human capabilities in every aspect.

Bias in AI: Refers to AI systems displaying prejudice or favoritism, often due to the data they were trained on. This can lead to unfair or discriminatory outcomes.

Data Ethics: This examines the moral issues and standards surrounding data, algorithms, and their practices. It is about ensuring fairness, privacy, and integrity in the handling and use of data.

Dataset: A collection of data that AI models use for training or testing. The quality and diversity of datasets can significantly impact the performance and fairness of AI systems.

Deep Learning: A subset of machine learning involving layered neural networks. These networks can learn from large amounts of data and are particularly effective in tasks such as image and speech recognition.

Explainable AI (XAI): This type of AI is designed to make its functioning transparent and understandable to humans. XAI aims to explain how and why AI systems make certain decisions.

Fine-Tuning: The process of making small adjustments to a pretrained AI model to adapt it for a specific task or improve its performance.

Generative Adversarial Networks (GANs): These are AI models where two neural networks (the generator and the discriminator) are trained together. The generator creates data, and the discriminator evaluates it, leading to highly realistic generated content.

Generative AI: A branch of AI that focuses on creating new content or data that are similar to but not identical to the training data. This includes generating images, text, music, etc.

Generative Models: AI models designed to generate new data instances similar to their training data. They are widely used in creative applications such as art and music generation and in data augmentation.

Graphics Processing Unit (GPUs): A specialized electronic circuit designed to rapidly process and render graphics and images; this circuit is known for its high parallel processing capability.

Large Language Models (LLMs): These are advanced AI models specialized in understanding and generating human language. They are trained on vast amounts of text data and can perform a wide range of language-related tasks.

Machine Learning (ML): A subset of AI where algorithms use data to learn and make predictions or decisions. Instead of being explicitly programmed, these algorithms improve automatically through experience.

Natural Language Processing (NLP): This field of AI focuses on enabling computers to understand, interpret, and respond to human language in a way that is both meaningful and useful.

Neural Networks: Inspired by the human brain, these are a series of algorithms that mimic the operations of the human brain to recognize patterns and solve common problems in AI, such as pattern recognition.

Privacy and Data Security: These terms refer to the practices and policies that protect data from unauthorized access and ensure its confidentiality and integrity in AI systems.

Reinforcement Learning: This type of machine learning in which an agent learns to make decisions by performing actions and receiving feedback from those actions, often in the form of rewards or penalties.

Singularity: Often associated with the field of AI, it is a hypothetical point in time at which technological growth becomes uncontrollable and irreversible, leading to unforeseeable changes in human civilization. This concept is frequently linked to the emergence of AGI and the rapid acceleration of technological progress it could catalyze.

Supervised Learning: A machine learning approach where models are trained on a labeled dataset, which means that the data are already tagged with the correct answer.

Synthetic Data: These data are artificially generated rather than obtained by direct measurement. It is often used for training AI models where real data may be limited or sensitive.

Tensor Processing Unit (TPU): A type of AI accelerator hardware developed by Google specifically for neural network machine learning, offering high-performance computations tailored for TensorFlow and Google's machine learning framework.

Transfer Learning: The practice of applying knowledge or models developed for one task to a different but related task. This approach is particularly useful for accelerating or improving the performance of AI models.

Transformer Models: A revolutionary architecture in NLP, known for handling sequences of data and utilizing attention mechanisms. These models excel in understanding context in text, exemplified by Google's BERT and OpenAI's GPT series.

Unsupervised Learning: Unlike supervised learning, this machine learning technique uses data that are not labeled, allowing the algorithm to act on the data without guidance.

Appendix A: Professor Use and Perceptions of Generative AI (Fall 2023)

Figure 2. Field of academic work

Figure 3. Academic rank

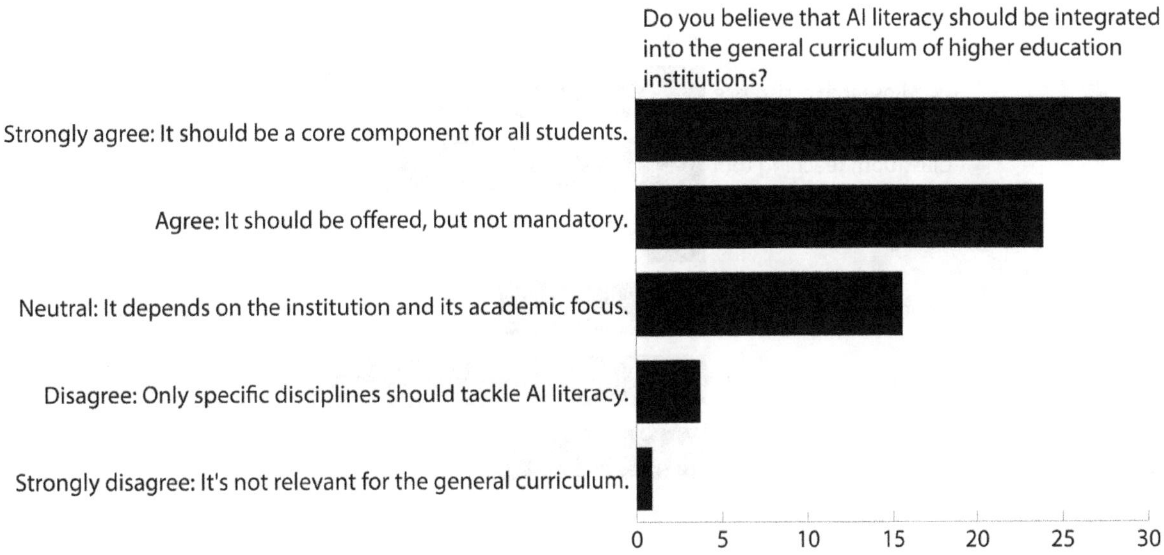

Figure 4. Carnegie class description

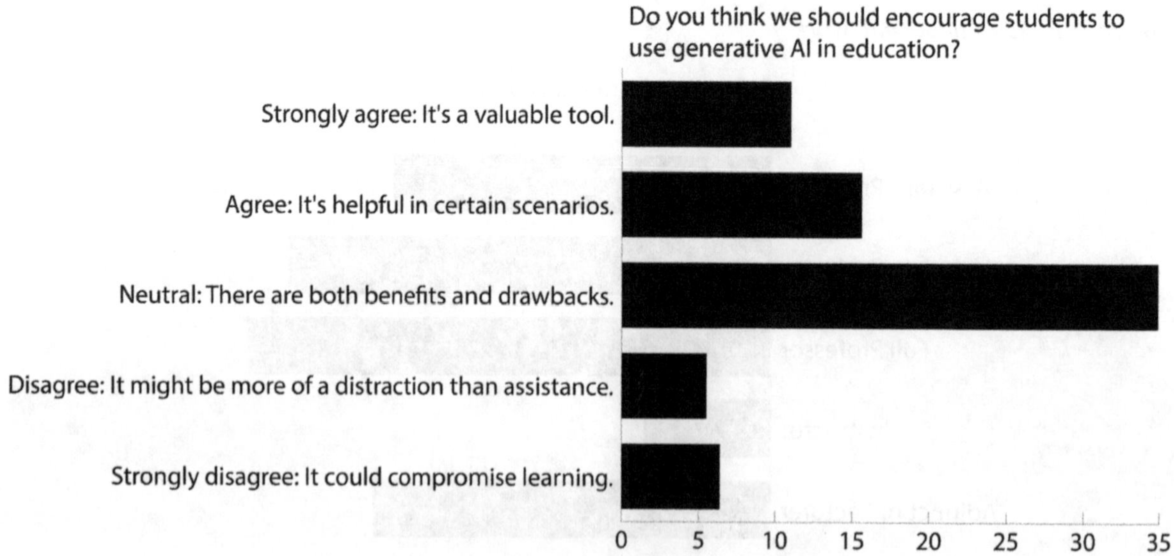

Figure 5. Public or private?

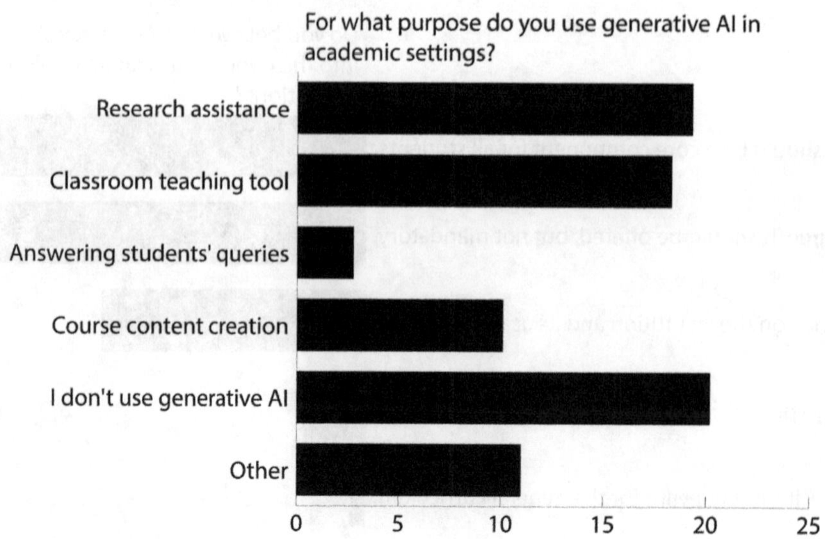

Figure 6. Full-time enrollment numbers

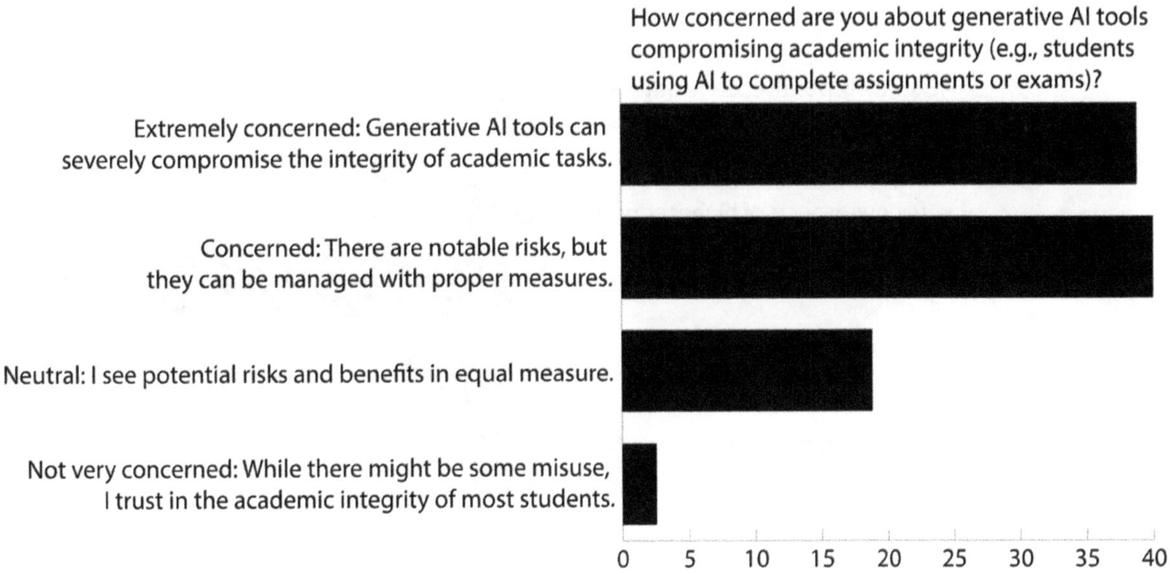

Figure 7. Familiarity with generative AI

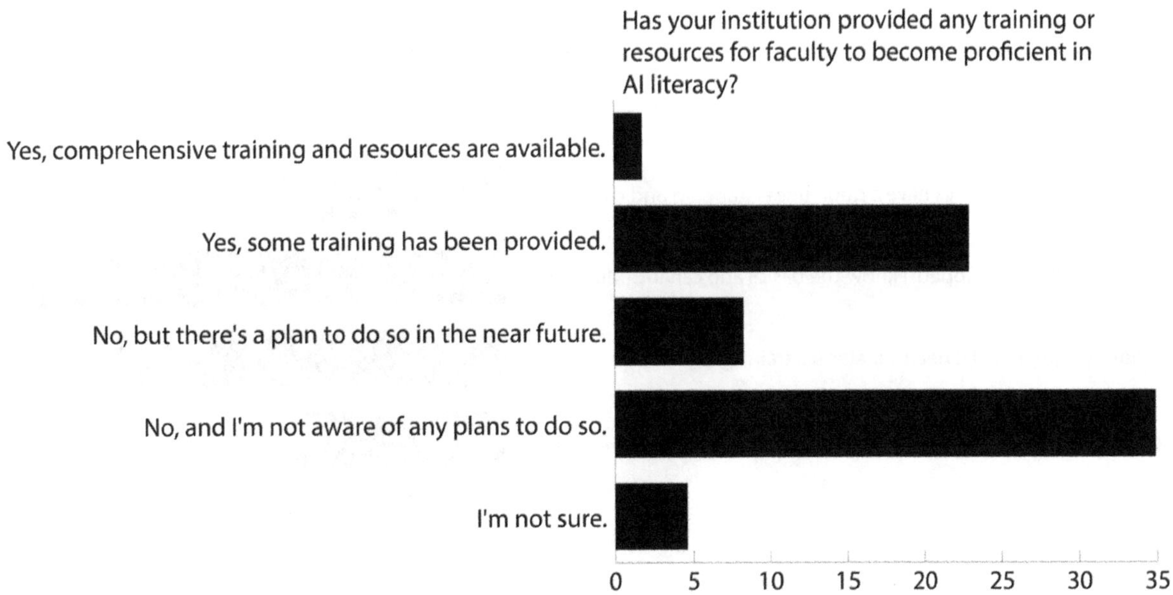

Figure 8. Frequency of use of generative AI for personal use

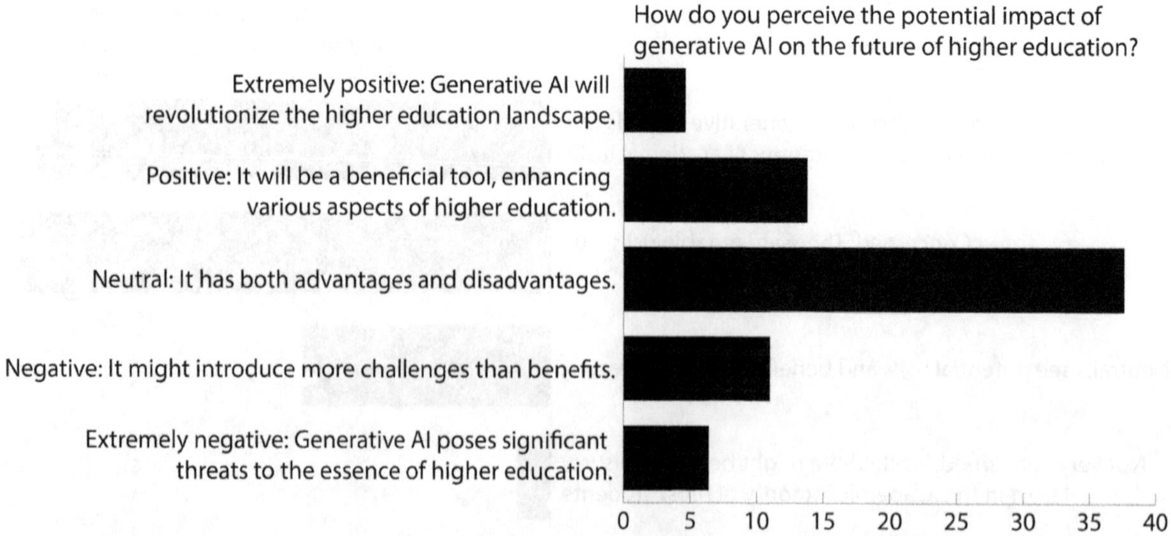

Figure 9. Purpose for generative AI use

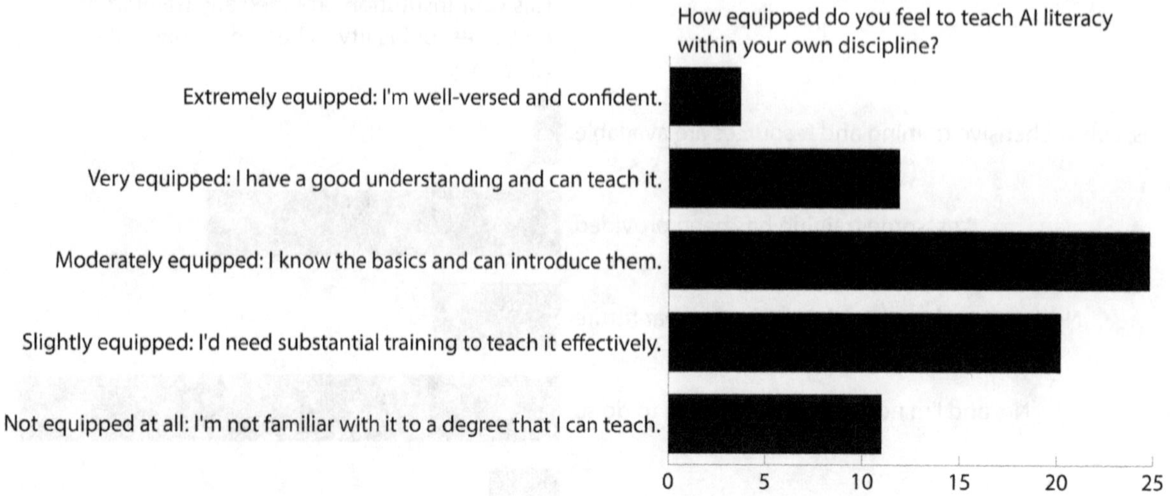

Figure 10. Frequency of use of generative AI for academic purposes

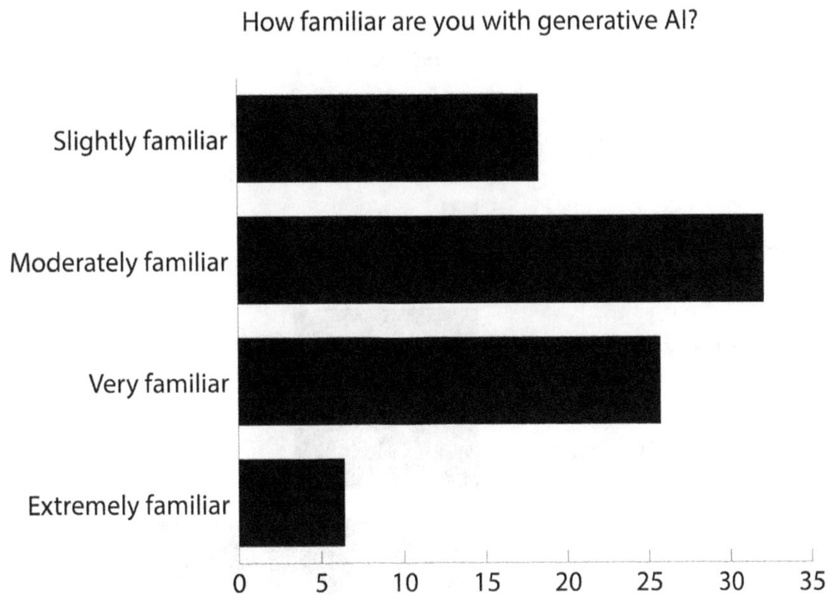

Figure 11. Purpose for generative AI use in academic settings

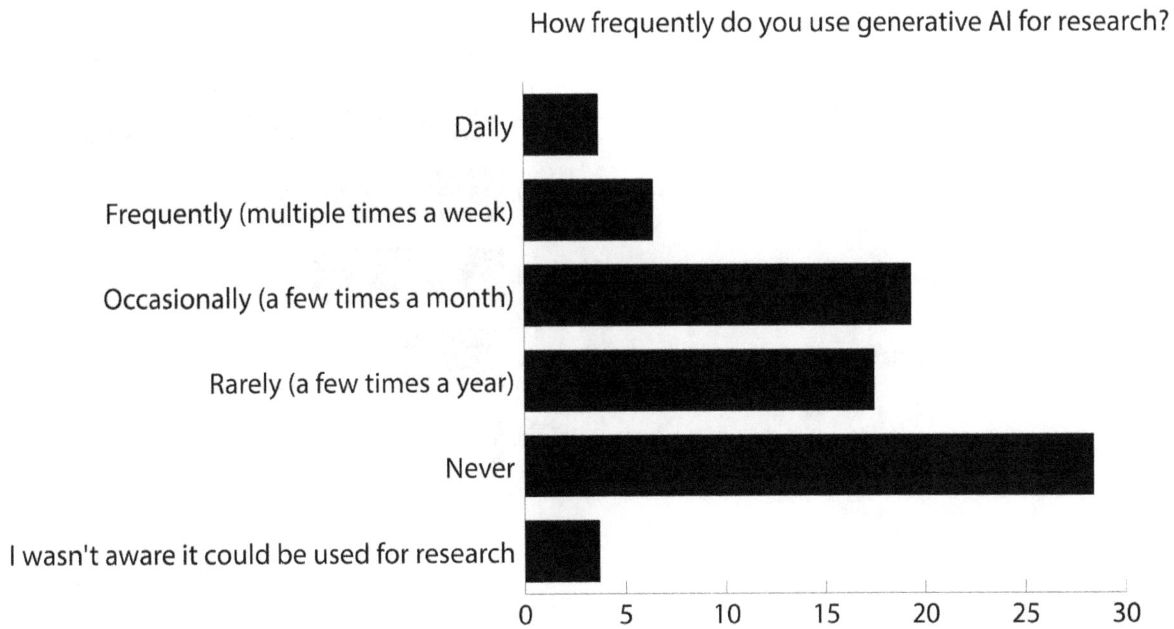

Figure 12. Frequency of generative AI use for research

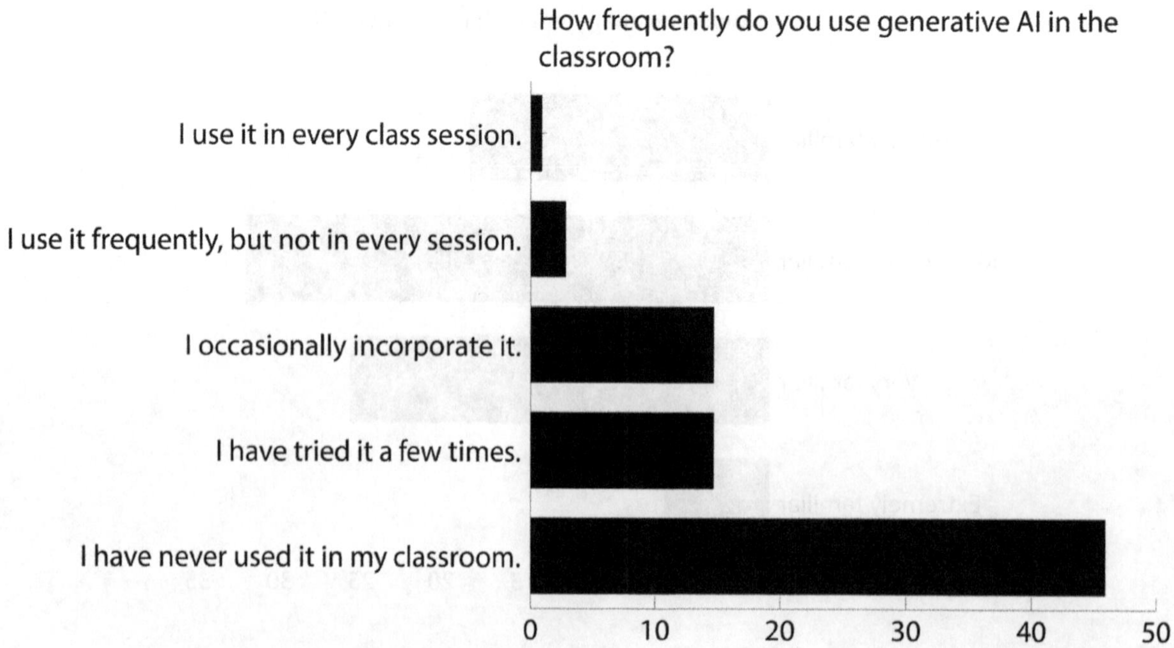

Figure 13. Generative AI research purposes

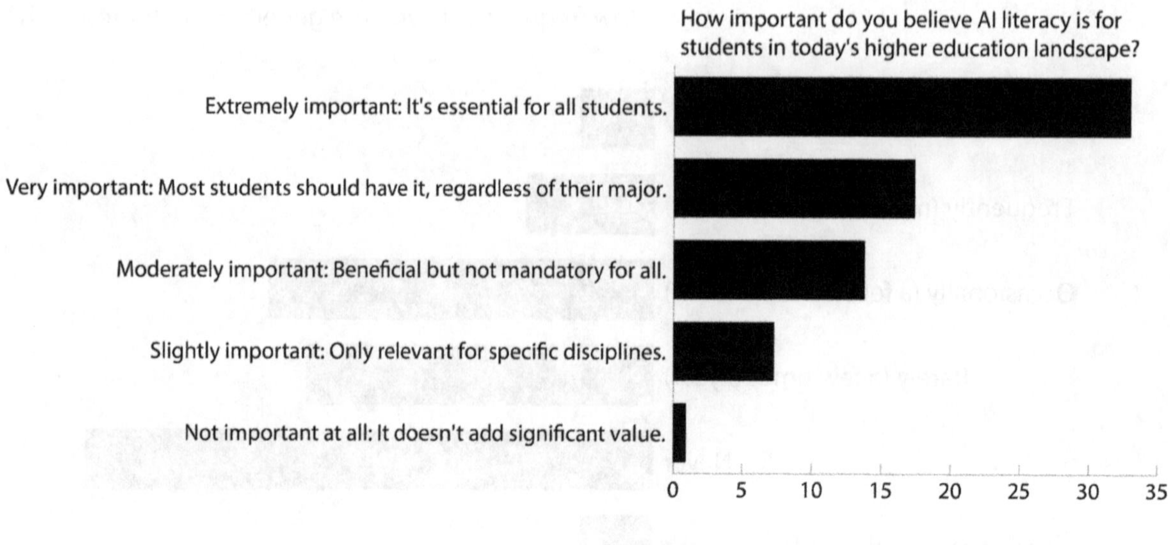

Figure 14. Reliability of generative AI in research

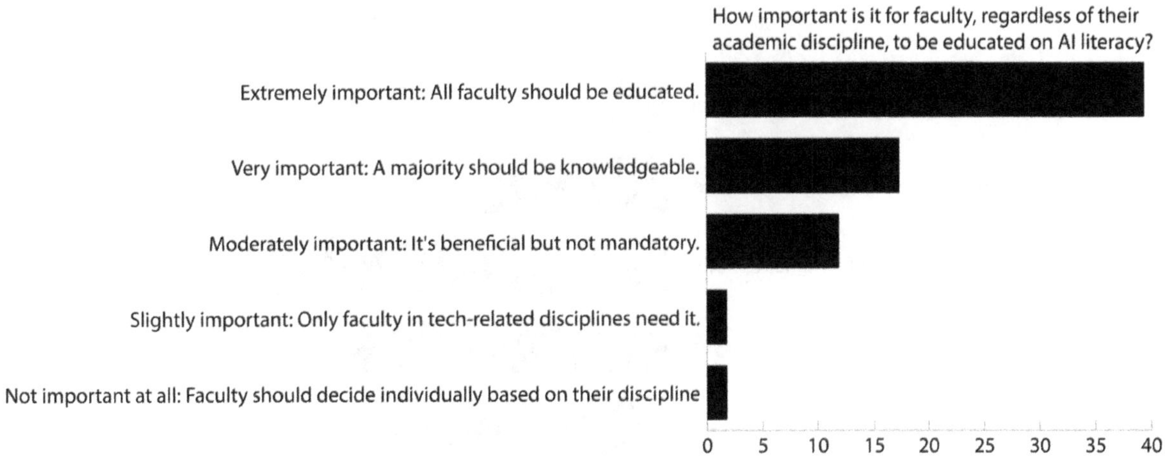

Figure 15. Frequency of use of generative AI in the classroom

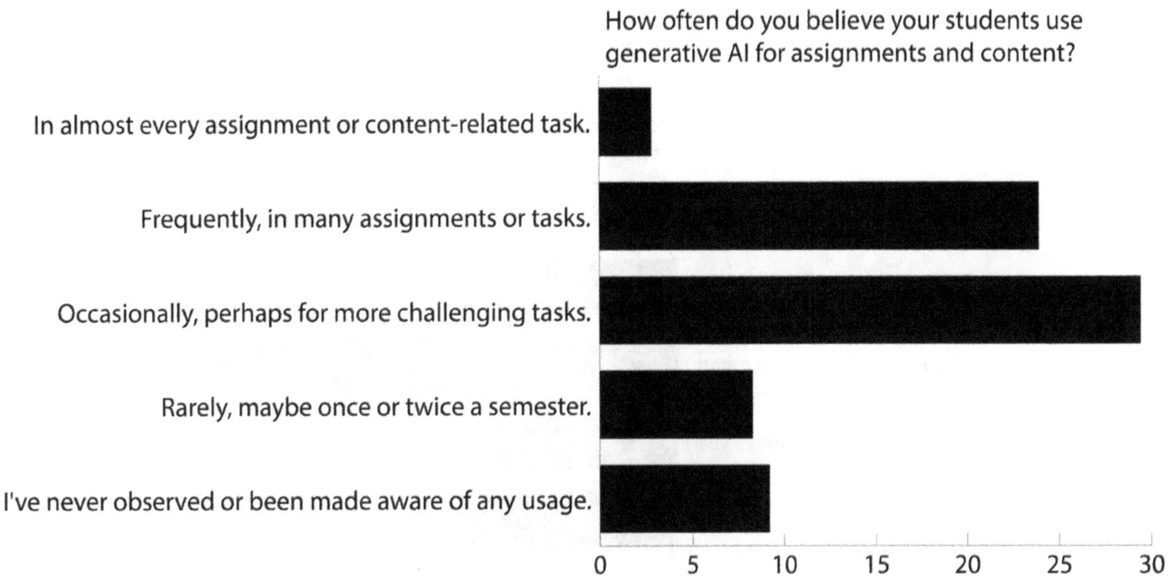

Figure 16. Purpose of use for generative AI in the classroom

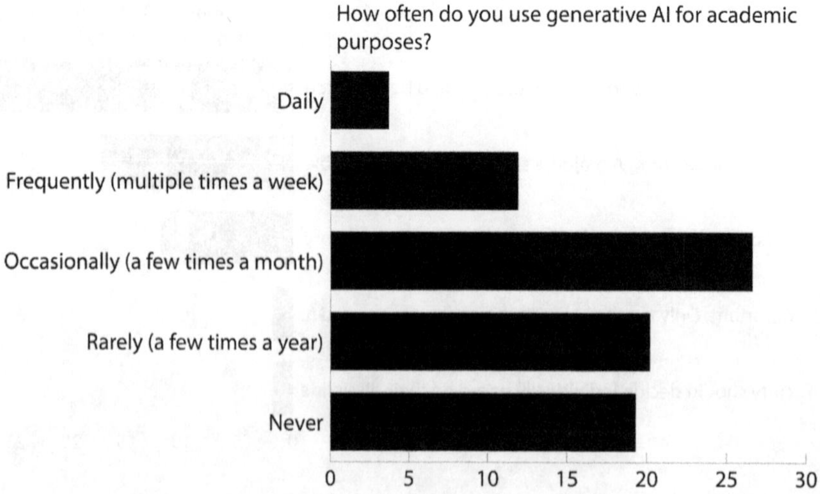

Figure 17. Student usage of generative AI

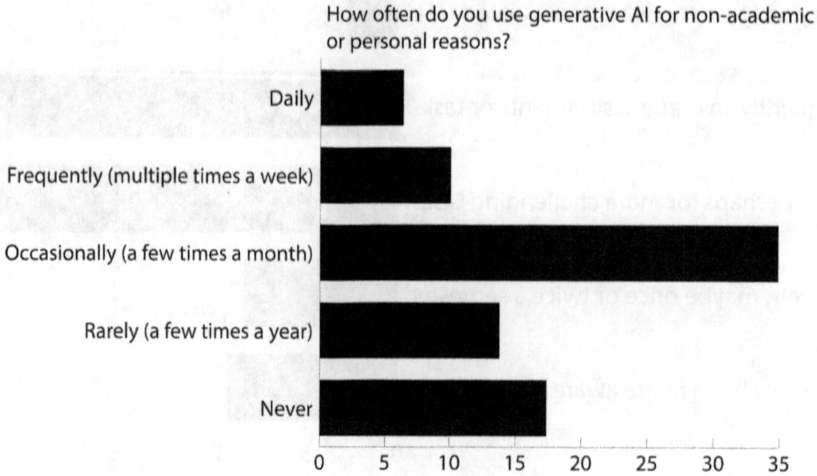

Figure 18. Student purposes for generative AI

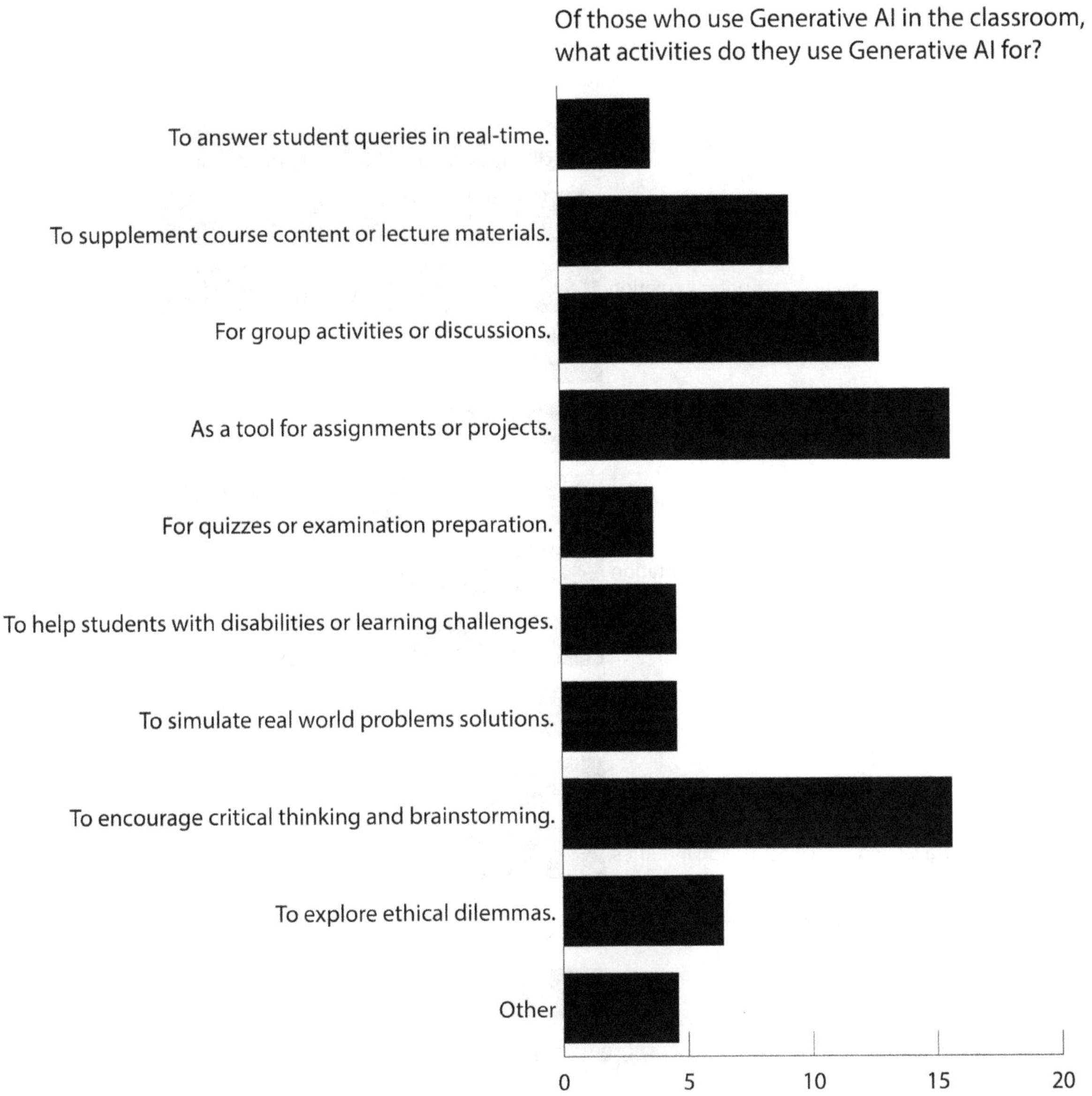

Figure 19. Should students be encouraged to use AI?

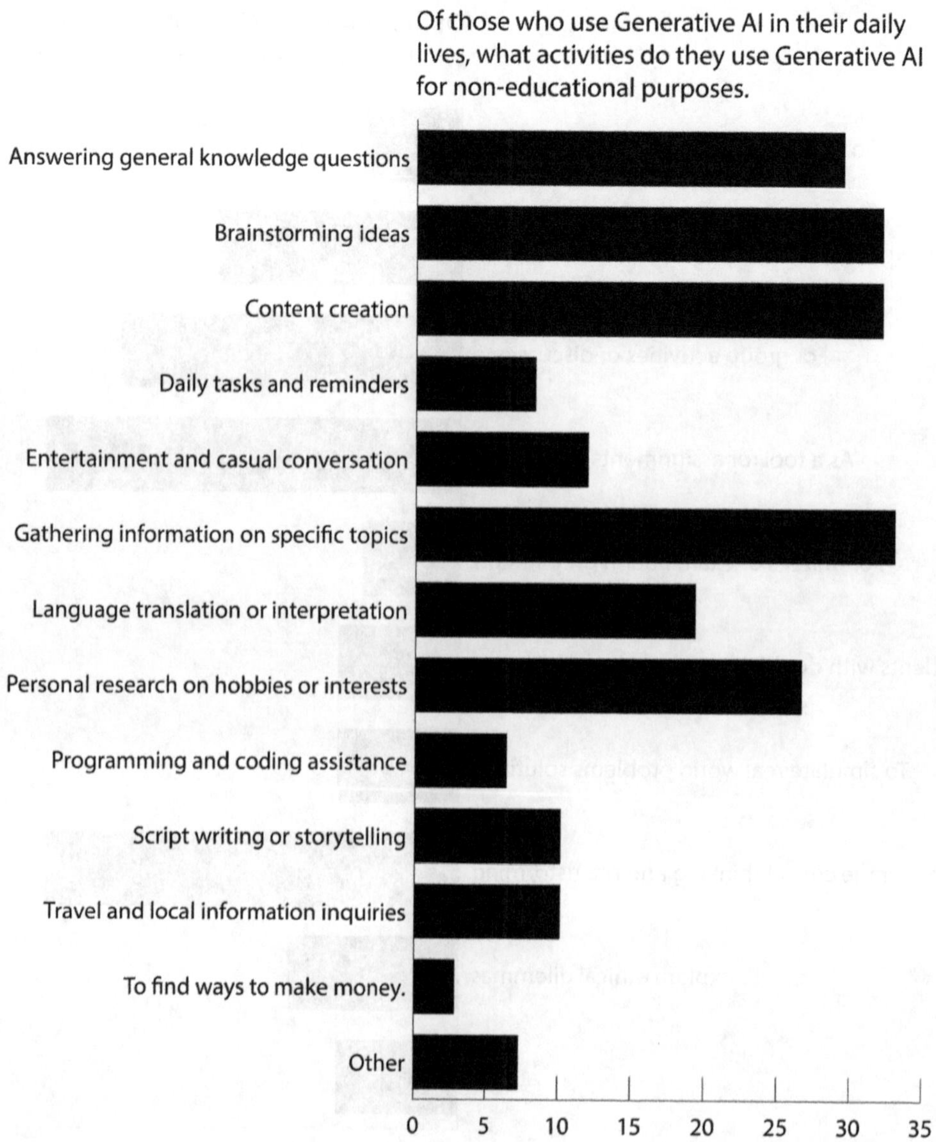

Figure 20. Importance of AI literacy

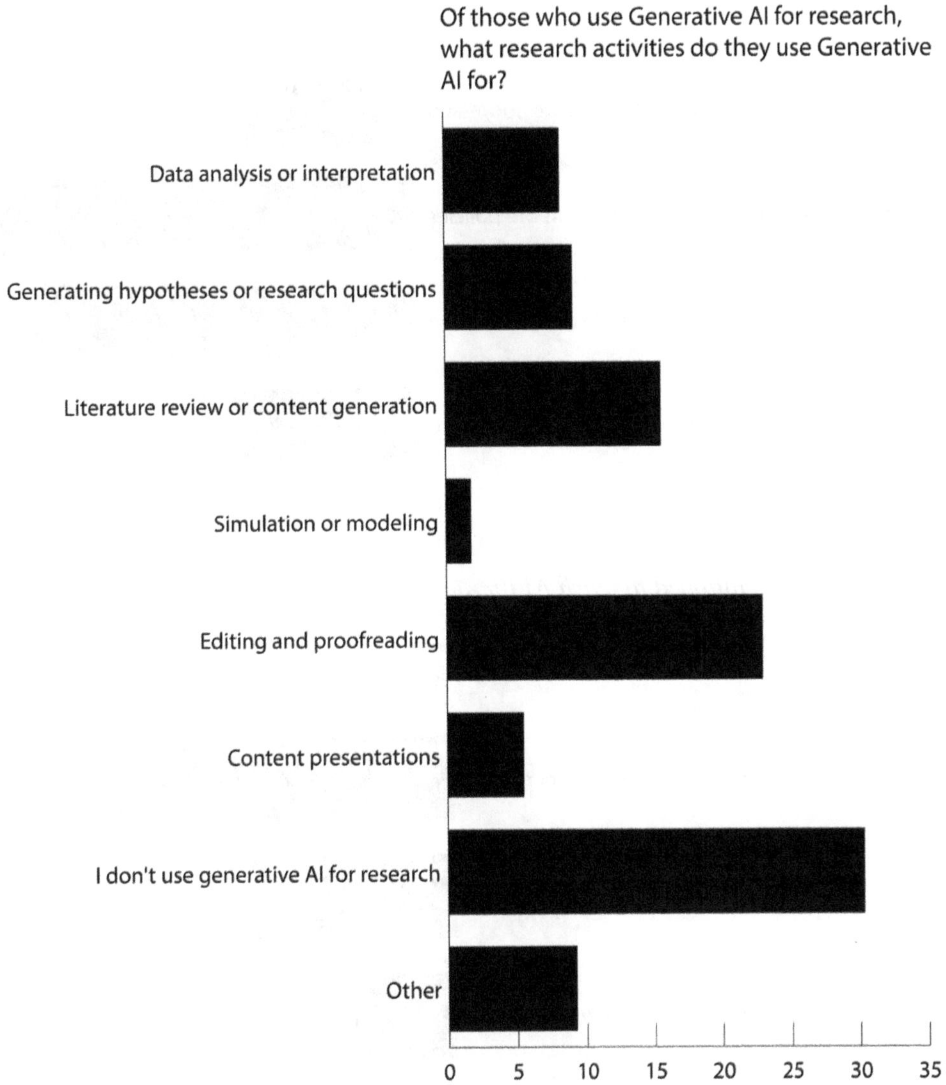

Figure 21. Should AI literacy be implemented in institutions?

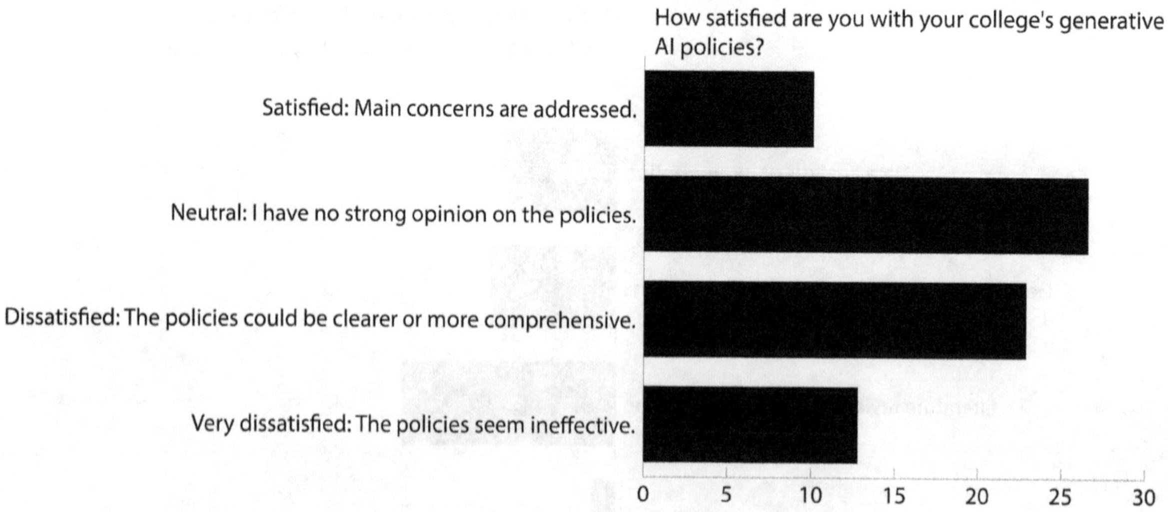

Figure 22. Are instructors equipped to teach AI literacy?

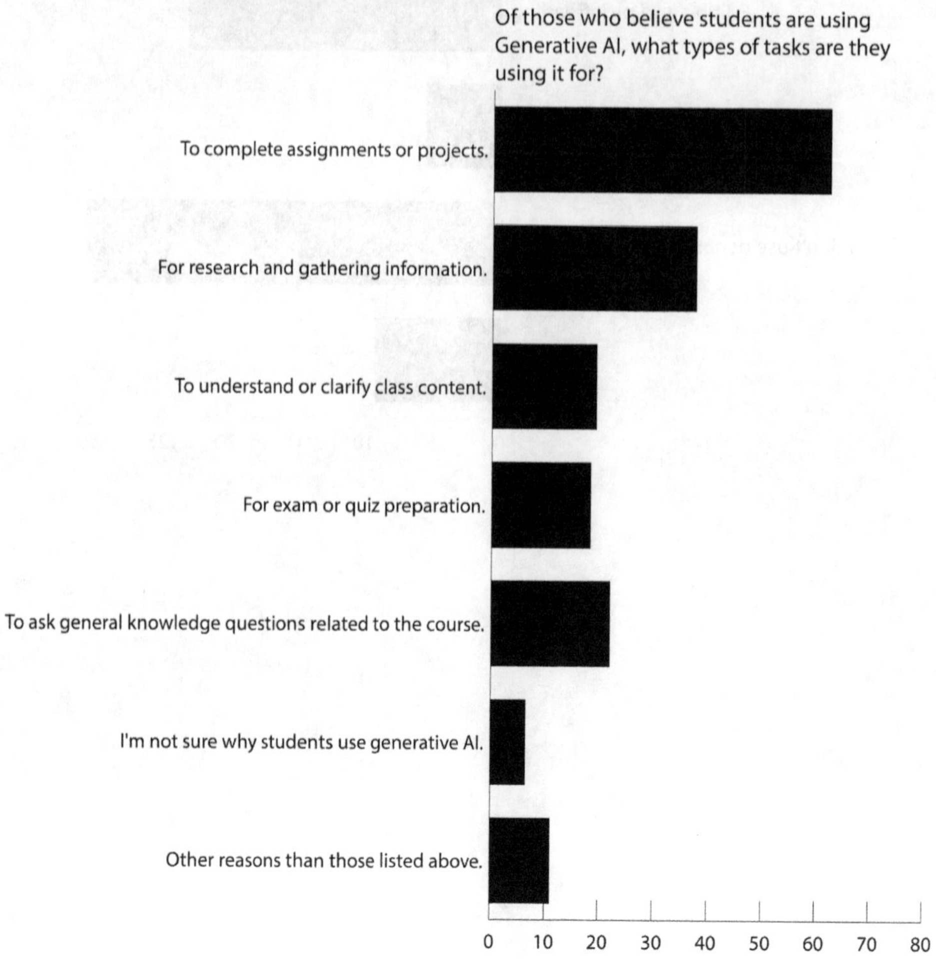

Figure 23. Importance for faculty to be educated on AI literacy

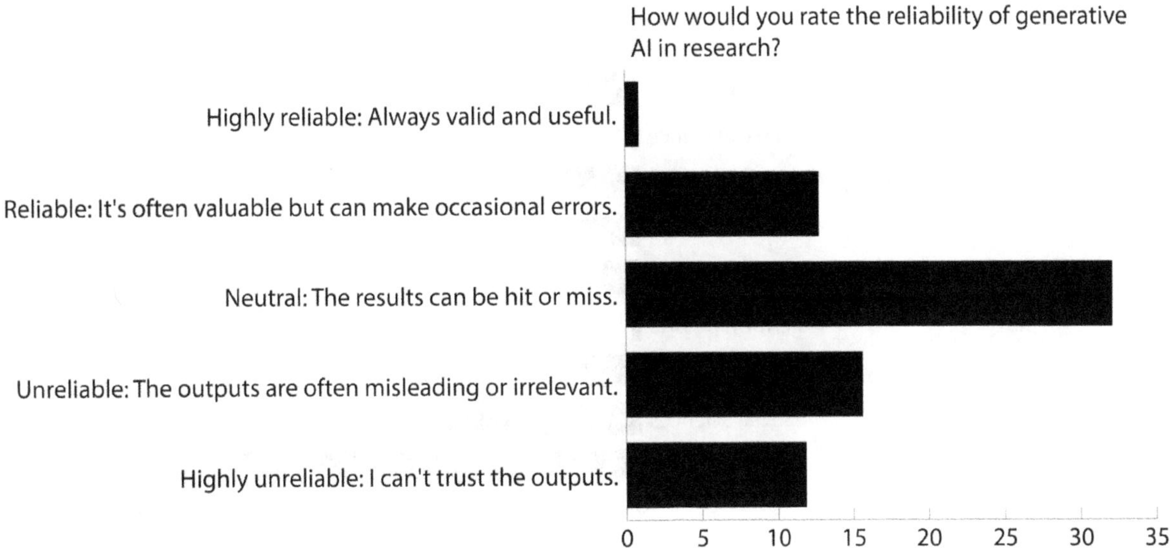

Figure 24. Literacy training provided for faculty

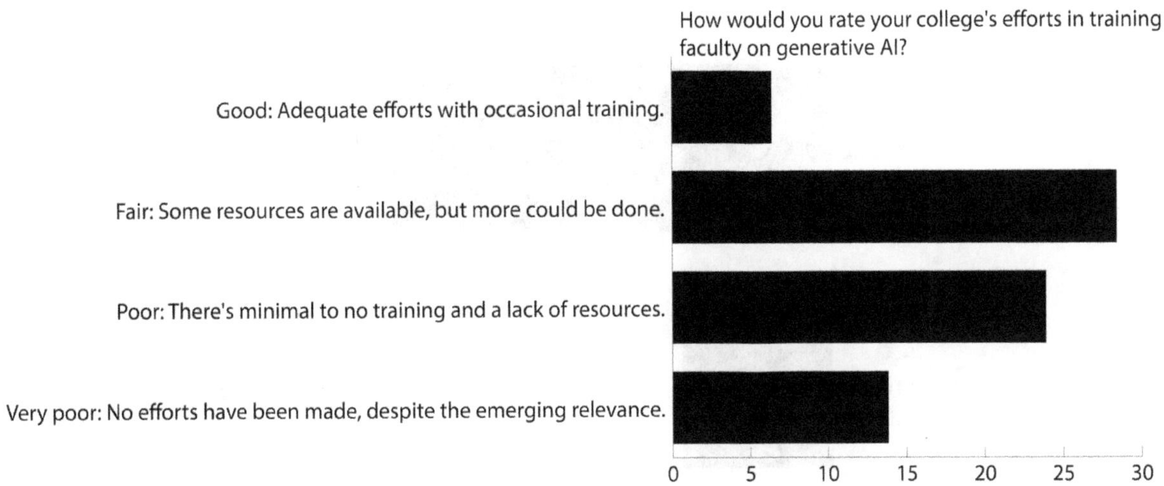

Figure 25. Satisfaction with generative AI policies

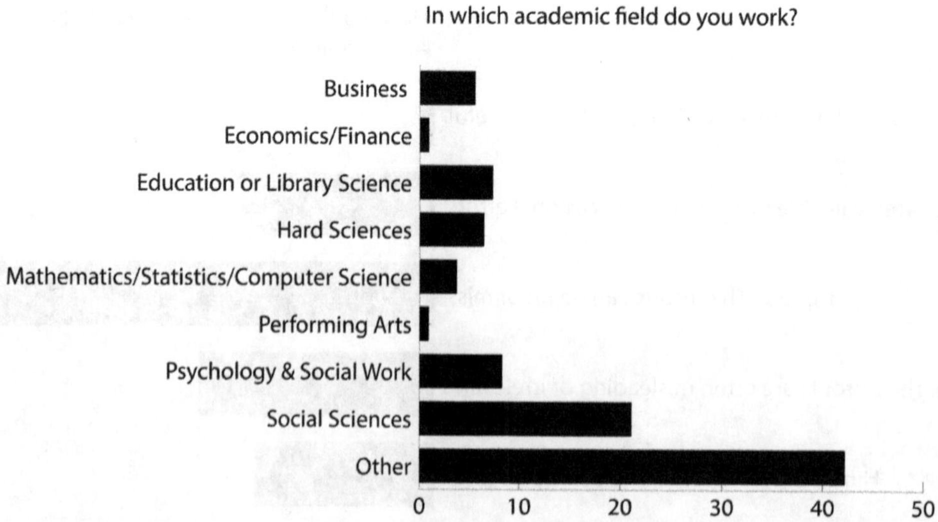

Figure 26. College training efforts for faculty

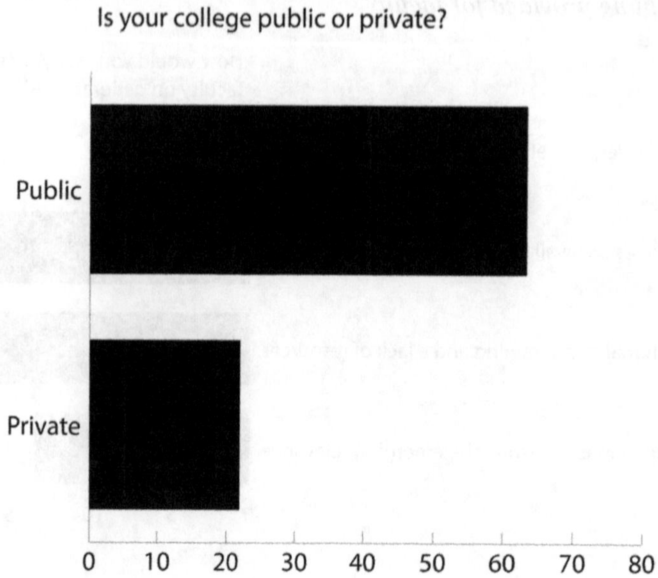

Figure 27. Potential impact of generative AI on higher education

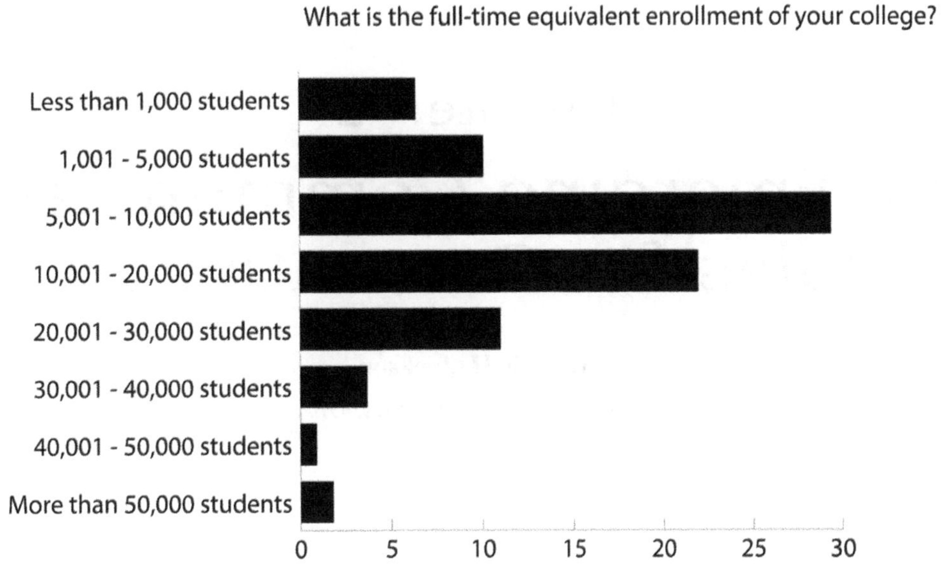

Figure 28. Concerns surrounding generative AI and academic integrity

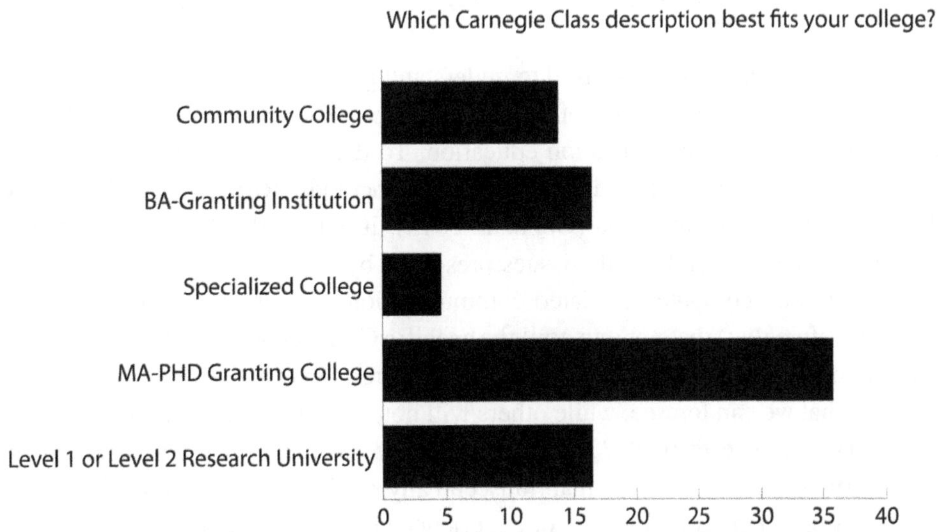

Chapter 2
Some Emerging Communication Roles for Generative AI

Michele H. Jackson
Michigan State University, USA

ABSTRACT

Understanding generative AI (GAI) from a communication perspective is challenging given the breadth of issues and perspectives that have emerged. To help distill these ideas and focus our conversation, this chapter proposes thinking about GAI in terms of the different communication roles that it fulfills. The roles of expert, copilot, interlocutor, and channel are presented with illustrations of each role taken from other contributions to this volume. Across the academy, scholars have mobilized to understand generative artificial intelligence (GAI) and foresee how GAI may alter the horizon of higher education.

SOME EMERGING COMMUNICATION ROLES FOR GENERATIVE AI

Across the academy, scholars have mobilized to understand generative artificial intelligence (GAI) and foresee how GAI may alter the horizons of higher education. The chapters in this volume contribute to this effort in the realm of communication education. To date, most studies on computation within the field of communication have focused on areas such as methods (Riffe et al., 2019; van Atteveldt & Peng, 2021) or machine communication (Guzman, 2018). It is remarkable, then, to witness all areas of the field rise so quickly to address the issues presented by this new technology. We know from a generation of research on computer-mediated communication (and another generation of technology diffusion research before that) that not only will the specific GAI technologies we see today change, but our specific communication practices will also change (Westerman et al., 2022). Some of these changes will occur in ways that we can foresee, while others will not, except maybe in hindsight. How can these changes be anticipated more effectively? A common strategy is to anchor our understanding to enduring communication structures and processes that transcend any particular technology. These anchors allow us to make sense of the changes we observe or experience and to more effectively connect the changes to our past and anticipate the future.

DOI: 10.4018/979-8-3693-0831-8.ch002

Early efforts to help the public make sense of GAI generally did not consider its communication aspect. Rather, the efforts emphasized GAI's ability to process information, "ingesting" immense databases to "generate entirely new content" (Chui et al., 2022). This novel ability was also noted by the New York Times in October 2022, when it introduced "generative A.I." as "the wonky umbrella term for A.I. that doesn't just analyze existing data but creates new text, images, videos, code snippets and more" (Roose, 2022). Over time, additional efforts to demystify GAI have focused on how the technology works (e.g., Zewe, 2023), including helpful interactive demonstrations (e.g., the GAN Lab at https://poloclub.github.io/ganlab/).

Understanding the mechanics of AI is important for demystifying the technology and helping us better anticipate its potential technical capabilities. To avoid the age-old risk of technological determinism, or the belief that technology determines use, it is important that we also structure how we understand GAI's social implications. This chapter proposes that the concept of communication roles can provide insight into understanding GAI and how it will impact the nature of communication education. The concept of the communication role is ideal for working across various areas because it requires no special theoretical apparatus.[1] Simply put, our communication behaviors (and the expectations others have for our behaviors) change according to the role we play in the interaction.

In this chapter, I propose and describe four communication roles that can help us understand the potential of GAI in communication education: expert, copilot, interlocutor, and channel. I also show how these roles weave through the chapters in this volume and how the authors contribute to our understanding of this important area.

GAI AS AN EXPERT

We know that information is produced on such a massive scale that any individual no longer has access to all relevant information, let alone the ability to review and analyze it. In such an environment, when individuals are incapable of analyzing and evaluating the evidence that supports what we know and believe, we turn to experts to "speak plainly" to us. Not to be confused with artificial general intelligence (AGI), which can learn and adapt across any number of areas, GAI is a set of algorithms that process or "learn" by analyzing large amounts of data. Considering expertise as possessing and speaking from a breadth of knowledge, it is reasonable to consider GAI tools experts. Heidelberg (2023) explains the function of expertise and lays out an argument for why artificial intelligence can readily become an expert for our modern information age:

[Experts are] interpreters of a knowledge system that is increasingly removed from conventional understanding. ...A key facet of the expert is as an agent in an impersonal system of authority. Expertise presages artificial intelligence through this impersonality. Recent developments in AI are designed and built specifically to be impersonal, a feature that limits how interesting it is but protects its authority by avoiding "opinion." (p. 75)

Modern machine learning, of which GAI is an example, requires access to immense amounts of content to generate high-quality content. Thus, it is not surprising that one of the earliest and most visible impacts of GAI as an expert was a change to major Internet search engines. Shortly after the start of 2023, Google and Microsoft redesigned their Internet search pages to incorporate GAI, further emphasizing GAI's ability not only to analyze immense amounts of information, as would a traditional search engine, but also to curate it for us and deliver the information in a narrative form rather than in the convention list of web links. In May 2023, Google declared, "With new breakthroughs in generative AI, we're again reimagining what a search engine can do. With this powerful new technology, we can unlock entirely new types of questions you never thought Search could answer, and transform the way information is organized, to help you sort through and make sense of what's out there" (https://blog.google/products/search/generative-ai-search/, para. 2). With access to the vast stores of online information and its ability to generate original content, GAI became the expert we could consult, rather than simply the database we could search.

Experts are *trustworthy* and *authoritative* from a rhetorical perspective. In the classic trilogy of ethos, logos, and pathos, arguments from expertise rely on ethos, which is the speaker's character. As it turned out, GAI's ethos tarnished almost immediately. Rather than ushering in an age of trustworthiness, GAI gave us the task of grappling with more believable fake news and more realistic deep fakes. A December 2022 prediction that we could expect deep fakes to be common within five years (Wong, 2022) seemed naïve just 12 months later, when simple Google searches suggested dozens of consumer software programs and YouTube tutorials for beginners to create their own deep fakes within minutes.

We also learned to question whether GAI could speak authoritatively. For example, GAI gifted us with a new meaning of "hallucination." By the end of 2022, the English language Wikipedia had added a new page: "Hallucination (artificial intelligence)." At the time I write this, the page defines a hallucination as "a response generated by an AI which contains false or misleading information presented as fact" (para. 1). In a widely reported example, a legal brief written by ChatGPT and submitted to the U.S. District Court contained six fictitious case citations (Merken, 2023).

A particularly important example of the fallibility of GAI in education is the likelihood of generating biased or prejudicial content. This critical issue is addressed in Part III of this volume. For example, Salazar, Peeples, and Brooks, for example, demonstrate how GAI can discriminate against diverse students. Le-Nguyen and Thanh detail several ways in which AI can show bias. Kualo and Hu show that bias and stereotypes are a specific concern when using image-generating GAI tools.

By considering GAI in the role of expert, we can address these concerns by leveraging established educational methods for critically evaluating and analyzing information. As pointed out by the chapters in this volume, we can adapt our literacy education to help students respond more effectively. For example, Chapter 14 suggests how information literacy can be extended to include AI literacy through partnerships between communication educators and library and information professionals. Chapter 15 argues that promoting AI literacy is essential if students are to move beyond the "monsterization" of GAI.

While agreeing with these suggestions, I propose that we should also consider reimagining the concept of expertise to better reflect the age of GAI. One possible direction, as suggested Chapter 8, would be to partner intentionally and extensively with other disciplines in the call for transparency and "explainable AI" (XAI). If we can explain how GAI works, we can understand the limitations of placing GAI in the role of an expert. Remembering that expertise is not only a breadth of knowledge but also a matter of training and judgment, we can evaluate the methods that a specific GAI tool uses for these processes and decide whether to trust it as an expert.

A second possible direction is to *deny* the possibility that a GAI can be an expert. Instead, we may refine the concept of expertise such that it is considered solely to be a human characteristic. As noted, this reconnects expertise to ethos, which is an element of a person's character. This limitation may encourage us to reconsider the concept of authorship. Many chapters in this volume reflect the concern that students (or instructors) use AI to generate content. Realistically, we must accept that students use GAI. A study of US college students conducted in September 2023 reported that roughly half of them used AI for their coursework (Coffey, 2023). Undoubtedly, this number increased by the end of the semester. Not unlike the debates that swirled on campuses when the Internet was new (Jackson & McDowell, 2002), the use of AI has led to a substantial tumult in higher education. A new path forward might be to experiment with new approaches, such as the suggestion in Chapter 9 of this volume to fully and intentionally incorporate GAI into the authorship process, including not only the generation of ideas but also to edit, critique, and review our ideas. Some of these roles will be discussed in the next section. In this view, expertise is not assessed by the ability to produce content but rather by taking responsibility and being accountable for that content, regardless of how it is produced.

GAI AS COPILOT

For millions of people, the first intentional use of GAI was OpenAI's ChatGPT 3.5. The public fascination with ChatGPT was so strong that in January 2023, just two months after its launch, the website had more than 100 million registered users and 13 million unique visitors per day, making it the fastest-growing internet application in history (Hu, 2023). For most people, the use of ChatGPT was unlike any previous experience with technology. Using ChatGPT felt like playing a game, entering a prompt to see what the program might come up with. Consider, for example, the craze asking ChatGPT to write a haiku (Loftesness, 2022).

However, in early 2023, we began to see a shift away from general GAI content generators to narrower and more focused applications. This wave of tools integrated GAI into existing applications to extend its functionality. Unlike in the first wave of general-purpose GAI, creativity and content generation were not central to this new set of tools. Output *per se* was not as significant as the impact the tool could have on improving how the tasks were accomplished. These focused GAI tools were sometimes called "smart assistants" or "AI assistants," which emphasize the performance of tasks rather than the creation of content. One term for this use of GAI, emerging toward the end of 2023, is "copilot." Adopted by Microsoft to brand GAI integration into its suite of productivity applications, "copilot" is becoming more widely used by others integrating or embedding GAI into their existing products. The term efficiently communicates that an existing product has been enhanced in (what appears to be) its decision-making abilities. Thus, the idea of a (human) pilot and a (GAI) copilot invokes teamwork and shared responsibility, where the GAI is not only consulted for ideas but also contributes uniquely and distinctly to the performance of the team.

Compared to the role of an expert, a copilot is characterized more by its ability to perform focused expert behavior than by its ability to provide authoritative knowledge. A copilot also differs from an expert in that, unlike an expert who is consulted periodically as needs arise, copilots are always present or integrated into the workflow. A copilot GAI may work simultaneously with a human on a shared task (such as writing), perform work when called upon (such as reviewing a human's work), or perform work independently, as needed for the shared task. For example, Github Copilot can be assigned to write programming code, review code written by a human, or advise humans who write the code (https://github.com/features/copilot/). An example of a GAI working independently is in creative industries, such as those involving design or problem solving, where GAI copilots may be readily deployed to perform the repetitive, detail-oriented, and expert-based tasks that Bruns and Long Lingo (2023) term "tedious work."

Throughout 2023, much of the conversation about GAI in higher education centered on ChatGPT and other similar general-purpose GAI tools, such as Google Bard or Anthropic's Claude AI. However, by the end of the year, the role of copilots had been increasingly recognized. What functions might copilots perform in communication education? Creating an inventory of technologies is challenging because the list of tools that incorporate GAI changes rapidly. A better approach is to focus on copilot role functions. The functions of the GAI copilot in communication are to help humans (1) produce better communication products, (2) engage in more effective individual communication behaviors, and (3) follow a more effective communication process. By choosing the roles that we are already familiar with, we can map GAI functions onto them.

Research Assistant

This role extends to one of the most common uses of GAI in managing and analyzing large amounts of information. As a copilot research assistant, GAI would go beyond simply having the information to identify and analyze information sources, scan for new information, organize and curate found information, and present it in a format relevant to our research. In the introduction to the September 2023 issue of the *Information Systems Journal*, the editors write that "despite these limitations, AI tools potentially have value as research assistants. They can help us to develop familiarity with a research domain, assimilate and synthesise literature, analyse data and transcribe text, although errors may occur" (Davison et al., 2023, p. 991). Consider, as described in Chapter 4 of this volume, the use of GAI to present arguments counter to our own, or the description in Chapter 7 of prompt engineering as a method to create presentation outlines for any topic.

Ghost Writer

Although rarely discussed in communication courses because of the traditional perception that there are ethical concerns about this practice, ghostwriting (writing text for someone else to use without credit to oneself) is a respectable practice in several communication-related professions, such as politics and public relations. Ghost writers may be used by publishing companies to assist potential authors, and many companies employ communication professionals to draft remarks or statements that will be attributed to company executives or managers (Draxler et al., 2023). The role of a ghostwriter is well adapted to GAI functions because a GAI can be trained on data that reflects the style (or desired style) of the speaker, which allows it to generate new communication in that style. For example, Jasper.ai, which identifies itself as a copilot for marketing teams and a "writing assistant", promises to produce communication assets that reflect your "brand voice". Alternatively, by answering a few questions that provide not only the content you want to convey but also information such as mood, style, or tone, the program will produce various drafts for the user to choose from (https://www.jasper.ai/). Craftly.ai offers dozens of different forms of content it will write for you, from social media posts and LinkedIn profiles to love letters and birthday cards (https://www.craftly.ai/writing-tool-library). Another example is Verble.ai, which pitches itself as having a "top-notch speechwriter in your pocket," iteratively adapting its style given the feedback you provide on its drafts (http://verble.app/example). As these tools become more sophisticated and commonplace, communication educators need to bring ghostwriting out of the shadows and address them across the curriculum. We will need to reflect on our traditional values of authorship and perhaps create new standards for the ethical use of ghostwriting, regardless of whether the writer is a human or GAI.

Editor or Proofreader

The Chartered Institute of Editing and Proofreading describes editorial professionals as "the people who work to make text accurate, clear and fit for purpose" (https://www.ciep.uk/). Over the past two decades, software tools have taken on an increasing amount of this responsibility, starting with writing mechanics but currently including writing and style. Consider the history of the editing features in word processors as an example. The following timeline provides examples of when editing features were introduced in various word-processing applications.

- 1971: The first spell check feature was introduced by the Spellbinder program developed by Ray Tomlinson.
- 1979: WordStar 2.26 introduced thesaurus and grammar-checking capabilities.
- 1983: WordPerfect 4.1 introduced advanced word choices and synonym suggestions.
- 1985: Microsoft Word 1.0 for Macintosh, introduced spell check and thesaurus features.
- 1989: WordPerfect 5.1 introduced the grammar-checking functionality.
- 1990: Microsoft Word 1.1 introduced the ability to check grammar and style.
- 1994: Microsoft Word 6.0. introduced AutoCorrect, which automatically fixes common spelling errors.
- 1997: Microsoft Word 97 introduced Office Assistant (Clippy), which provides interactive help, including grammar and writing style suggestions.
- 1999: Corel WordPerfect 9 introduced the Grammatik grammar-checking engine.
- 2003: Microsoft Word 2003 introduced enhanced grammar and style checking with the "Reveal Formatting" pane.
- 2010: Microsoft Word 2010 introduced a more advanced spelling and grammar checker, including context-specific proofing options.
- 2013: Grammarly, an online writing assistant, was launched to provide advanced grammar checks and suggestions.
- 2020: Google Docs introduced Smart Compose, which suggests complete sentences as you type, including grammatical corrections.
- 2023: Microsoft introduced Copilot for Word, which analyzes documents, rewrites existing documents, writes drafts from prompts, and performs "high-level edits so your writing is as clear and polished as possible. [2]

Soon after ChatGPT became publicly available, many academic institutions and scholarly journals issued statements warning that the use of GAI in writing would be highly suspect. Faculty members banned their use in the classroom. Journals banned their use in submitted manuscripts. However, as this timeline shows, we have increasingly relied on software to perform key editorial and proofreading tasks for approximately four decades. Where, in the history of word processing, would we draw the line between "ethical" use and "unethical" use of computer-assisted writing? I propose that we consider whether our admonitions against the use of GAI contain assumptions that we do not see when we have academic privilege. Today, "spell-check" is part of our vocabulary, but this concept was not commonplace until the spread of personal computers and word processing. We expected authors who could not spell accurately or use proper grammar to pay for someone to check their work (or have access to someone who could do so for free). Why would we reject the possibilities provided by GAI to make the expression of scholarly ideas accessible to more writers? Advanced editing and proofreading have always been options for writers with access to resources (including academic writers). Why do we not expand our access to those who lack these resources? Similarly, consider the expectations we place on writers to use the appropriate style or vocabulary (whether these are the expectations of a journal peer reviewer or course instructor). Why limit the use of GAI and thereby disadvantage writers who do not have a shared background (perhaps because they speak a different language or are members of a different culture)?[3]

Coauthor

If the Editor or Proofreader role forces us to confront difficult questions, one possible answer is simply to give GAI the role of a coauthor. Disciplinary ethics codes increasingly permit the use of GAI throughout the various stages of scholarship, even for advanced research tasks that would normally be sufficient for awarding authorship credit (the APA provides a scorecard that weights these tasks https://www.apa.org/science/leadership/students/authorship-determination-scorecard.pdf). GAI tools are becoming increasingly capable of performing analysis tasks with minimal direction, such as creating data visualizations (e.g., beautiful.ai). However, most disciplinary associations (including the International Communication Association) prohibit awarding GAI authorship credit because, echoing the classic image of technology as a golem (Collins & Pinch, 1998), they adopt COPE's statement that "AI tools cannot meet the requirements for authorship as they cannot take responsibility for the submitted work. As non-legal entities, they cannot assert the presence or absence of conflicts of interest or manage copyright and license agreements" (https://publicationethics.org/cope-position-statements/ai-author). This widely adopted statement positions GAI as an expert and a coauthor. The statement presumes that AI contributes to content more than other copilot functions. For example, the APA requires the authors to describe the use of GAI in the description of methods and "upload the full output of the AI as supplemental material' (https://www.apa.org/pubs/journals/resources/publishing-policies).

Coach

In the role of a coach, the GAI copilot assists in engaging in more effective individual communication behaviors. In addition to written text or images, these tools are often trained using audio and/or video files. Chapter 10 describes the capabilities of GAI tools that can easily provide coaching in communication contexts, such as presentations, interviews, and small-group interactions. The role of the coach is regularly invoked in a number of tools: Orai claims to be an "AI Speech Coach App in your Pocket" and Yoodli claims that its "AI Speech Coach" offers "judgment free coaching" (http://orai.com, http://app.yoodli.ai). Some programs, such as Microsoft's Clipchamp, analyze recorded videos (http://clipchamp.com). Others, such as Yoodli and Poised, provide coaching and feedback in real time, guiding behavior during the interview or presentation itself (http://poised.com). Zoom, a program licensed by many academic institutions, also integrated GAI in December 2023. A November 2023 software update, describes the addition of new coaching functions:

Hosts can get even more information from their cloud recordings by having AI Companion analyze key meeting and conversation factors. Analytics are provided on your talk speed, talk-listen ratio, longest spiel (or monologue), filler word usage, and patience and are accessible when viewing the cloud recording. (https://support.zoom.com/hc/en/article?id=zm_kb&sysparm_article=KB0010266)

These programs introduce interesting and important new questions for communication education regarding what counts as effective speaking (and who decides). Consider the two fundamental elements of GAI discussed above: datasets and algorithms. What is the nature of the speech used to train these coaches? Where are the speakers from? What are the vocal patterns, and how do the patterns privilege certain groups over others? What criteria are used to select and weigh the variables in the evaluation, and on what assumptions about "good speech" are those criteria based? A concern raised by several chapters in this volume is the discrimination and bias built into GAI tools. The most well-known examples are image recognition and facial recognition. However, automated speech recognition systems have been biased for several years. For example, research has demonstrated that these systems reinforce gender stereotypes (Gordon, 2023), show bias toward white men (Bajorek, 2019), bias against African American speech (Koenecke et al., 2020), and bias against women and non-US nationalities (Hutiri & Ding, 2022)

Facilitator

A final function of GAI as a copilot is to help humans follow a more effective communication process. Throughout the 1970s and the 1980s, research projects in several disciplines focused on creating computer-based expert systems or decision support systems to facilitate the work of task groups (Jessup & Valacich, 1992). Although these efforts largely fell away as the Internet grew and research shifted to other priorities, we can see their goals resurfacing in GAI tools that can facilitate group processes. One early example was the use of GAI to transcribe or take notes during meetings (e.g., Otter and Avoma). We might encourage students to envision what might be possible when GAI capabilities are applied to what they know about group communication and interaction. For example, extending Bibhudatta's (2023) analysis of the future of GAI, we might envision the following.

- Personalizing the information provided in the meeting and modifying the mode of delivery to align with preferred learning styles (e.g., preferences for text, visuals, or audio).
- Shepherding groups to follow process frameworks that match the task at hand, such as decision-making, innovating, or problem solving.
- Providing real-time data on key meeting metrics such as speaking time for each member, time on topic, biased language, or socioemotional cues. As Bibhudatta suggests, the system could warn members or interrupt meetings when there are serious breaches of group values or norms.
- Monitoring the discussion for claims of fact or other uncertainties and then proactively locating and displaying relevant information.

Although the technology does not yet fully support these functions, we can easily envision a number of uses close to hand. For example, a speech-to-text system could output text in real time to GAI-enabled tools that could then reproduce the information in a format adapted to different learning styles, such as interactive flashcards (e.g., nolej.ai) or visualizations (e.g., beautiful.ai). As another example, a system that monitors speech during a meeting (such as the coaching tools described above) could control a virtual "speaking stick" and decide who gets to speak and for how long.

GAI as an Interlocutor

The interlocutor role moves away from the GAI's function of generating communication as information to its ability to communicate through social interaction. An interlocutor is a special instance of a communicator, someone engaged in conversation or dialogue, typically with only one or perhaps a few people. By the time ChatGPT arrived at the scene, "interacting" with virtual assistants was a familiar experience. We could call out to Siri or Alexa and they "responded," sometimes with information, sometimes by changing a setting on other connected devices (e.g., turning on a TV, turning off the lights, dialing a phone number). However, they could not engage in conversation. This might explain why the ability of a GAI to continue the thread of conversation is extraordinary. Indeed, GAI poses new opportunities to develop human-like communicative behavior (Dubova, 2022; Park et al., 2023) in ways that could only be modeled previously (e.g., Kopp, 2010).

In the interlocutor's role, the GAI becomes a partner in the conversation. However, we must remember that "talking" with a GAI tool is still talking with a computer; although it can decode language, it does not "understand" language or give it meaning. Language is merely data. However, unlike previous "conversational agents," the mechanisms underlying GAI enable it to produce a wide range of unique responses. You and I might start a conversation using the same GAI tool with exactly the same prompt and at exactly the same time, but we will not receive the same reply. The significance of this fact is that the experience of interacting with a GAI cannot be standardized. We cannot simply write an instruction manual, as we could with previous software. There is a need for a new type of communication training because, as with any conversation, although the flow of communication cannot be predicted, it can be influenced, shaped, or improved.

The ability to interact with a computer through a conversational interface creates new professional opportunities for those who can improve or shape conversations with GAI. First, end users can shape conversations through prompts. For example, instructing the GAI to respond as though they were in a specific role, such as an excited tourist in a new country or a supportive manager, worried about their team's performance. A few months into 2023, people began posting "tips" for crafting GAI prompts that would produce better results and organizations began adding "prompt engineering" to job descriptions. Another way to shape conversations is to influence the content of datasets. Using more focused datasets, for example, changes the nature of conversations. For example, IBM Debater uses datasets specific to arguments and debates. Another example is Paperpal, which trains its GAI only on scholarly research and academic writing. Communication specialists can use corpus linguistic methods (Paquot & Gries, 2020) to create models or exemplary datasets to train GAI tools. A third strategy is to work with AI developers, as suggested in Chapter 3 of this volume. We might train students to become involved in the design of GAI tools as a "conversation designer" (Vassallo, 2023). These examples demonstrate how, by working across disciplines, communication experts can contribute their knowledge of interaction and the factors that contribute to effective conversation.

Seeing GAI as an interlocutor means training students in human-computer interaction in courses that before we did not necessarily associate with technology. Obvious candidates include interviewing, qualitative methods, and reporting, but we might also consider courses that teach conversation skills such as argumentation, interpersonal communication, or mediation.

We can also teach our students to consider the ethics of human-computer communication. As with human-human communication, there are many types of conversations. Similar to human-human communication, these conversations are sometimes problematic. One of the things we have learned thus far is that we cannot necessarily trust *humans* in this situation. An early foray in building a GAI for conversation was Microsoft's chatbot, Tay (an acronym for Thinking About You). Launched in 2016 on the social media platform Twitter, Tay had the ability to learn from its interactions with users. In less than a day, users trained it be a "bullhorn for hate speech" and to make racist and sexist comments (Tennery & Cherelus, 2016). In fact, users have baited most GAI tools to make inappropriate or offensive comments, including BlenderBot 3 on Meta (Thorbecke, 2022), My AI on Snapchat (Kelly, 2023), ChatGPT (Alba, 2022) and Bing (Perrigo, 2023; Vincent, 2023). The increased role of communication in human-robot interaction, to the point where we are engaging in meaningful conversation, presents us with important ethical questions for us to explore with our students.

Another area in which the role of GAI as an interlocutor could have a significant impact is on teaching itself. Throughout the history of computing, efforts have been made to create personalized or tailored learning systems. For example, the PLATO system developed at the University of Illinois in the 1960s was deployed in schools in the 1970s (Grainger College of Engeering, 2020). By the late 2010s, these systems came under the umbrella of "adaptive learning systems" and were widely used by major textbook publishers as they built online platforms to deliver instructional materials (Herold, 2019; Oremus, 2015).

Generally, adaptive learning systems are based on what we might describe as an "engineering model" of learning that focuses on mastery of content, where experts "map out what each child needs to learn, measure what of that each already knows, and then create the optimal path for him or her to learn the rest" (Herold, 2019, para. 8). Providing content in an "optimal path" specific to each learner is the core of what has come to be called "personalized learning systems" (Edula et al., 2023; Ismail et al., 2023). By adding GAI functionality, these systems can adopt a persona when delivering content. These personas can feel supportive, engaging, and motivating. In other words, these systems are not only personalized they are *personal*.

The impact of making the systems feel personal can be considerable. We have long known that humans may interact with computers as though they are human or "social actors" (Nass et al., 1995; Reeves & Nass, 1996). One well-known early example was ELIZA, a natural language "chatterbot" created in the mid-1960s and programmed to mimic a Rogerian therapist (a version of which is still available online at the time of this writing, e.g., at https://psych.fullerton.edu/mbirnbaum/psych101/eliza.htm). ELIZA demonstrated that people were willing not only to communicate with a computer as though it were intelligent (Switzky, 2020) but also as though it were *human*, something researchers have come to call the "ELIZA effect" (Natale, 2018). Video games are an arena in which this is relevant. Designers capitalize on this desire for sociable and conversational characters. Companies are offering GAI-powered "character engines" to game developers that can create non-player characters (NPCs) "that are interactive, believable, and make core game loops more addictive" (http://inworld.ai). NVIDIA began offering an "Avatar Cloud Engine" (ACE) for Games

To make NPCs a more natural part of an immersive gaming experience, allowing them to speak to players naturally with the help of generative AI. "Now, generative AI can make NPCs more intelligent by improving their conversational skills, creating persistent personalities that evolve over time, and enabling dynamic responses that are unique to the player," Ike Nnoli, senior product marketing manager at NVIDIA, writes on the company's technical blog. (Sertin, 2023, para. 15)

GAI tools can simulate actors in several conversational situations including one-on-one interactions, group meetings, and public presentations. Chapter 12 of this volume explores how GAI could offer personalized learning and instant feedback. We might envision specialized programs in which the GAI tool plays a role in contexts that can be difficult to practice with humans, such as conversational language learning with native speakers (e.g., http://loora.ai), difficult or "crucial conversations" (e.g., http://yoodli.ai), or interactions between patients and medical providers (e.g., http://pcs.ai).

Finally, as suggested by Chapter 3, we might envision a GAI with interlocutor capability as a teaching assistant. Similarly, Chapter 5 demonstrates how GAI can be leveraged to produce lesson plans or course outlines. Taking a somewhat different approach, Chapter 6 proposes that relegating lower-level activities to GAI could allow instructors to raise expectations for higher-level learning as well as provide the capacity to engage in more authentic assessment measures.

CONCLUSION: GAI AS A COMMUNICATION CHANNEL

In this chapter, I have demonstrated how we might view GAI as an expert, a copilot (of various forms), or an interlocutor. Of course, none of these are literally true. Yet, we find them compelling because, as with all emerging technologies, there is a strong pull to reduce our uncertainty about the unfamiliar, to "blackbox" generative AI so as to make it more knowable and to make our experiences with it easier to manage. Even when we know that machines are not human, the pull to give them human-like qualities is not new. We may all know someone like my mother-in-law who, for nearly 40 years, has explained any problems with her computer by saying that there is a "little man" inside her computer who decides whether to do what you are asking and sometimes he decides not to. The tendency to think of or treat computers as human, sometimes referred to as "mindless anthropomorphism" (Kim & Sundar, 2012), has been studied for many years as a part of understanding the nature of interactivity online (Nowak & Biocca, 2003).

Metaphorical roles help us envision the potential of GAI, but they also pose the danger of excusing us from understanding what might be GAI's most important role. At the end of the day, every GAI is a computer program. Although this program is large and complicated, it is not mystical or unknowable. When we make visible the contexts and human actions involved in building AI, we are less likely to see its development as proceeding along an intrinsic or natural trajectory. We are less likely to consider it normal, taken-for-granted, or inevitable. We are better able to resist falling into what scholars describe as technological determinism (Marx & Smith, 1994).

When we adopt the (arguably) more technically correct stance that generative AI is a capability or function, we can see our own agency in deciding whether to employ GAI to accomplish an objective. People, not GAI, are active agents creating whatever the future use might be. Our decisions constitute the artifacts that use GAI. We are not merely consumers.

With its materiality clearly in focus, the role that we, as communication educators, might identify for GAI is as a "communication technology," specifically a communication *channel.* This role resists the anthropomorphism of seeing GAI as the communicator and recognizes that, as with other communication channels, a GAI encodes, transmits, and decodes messages. In other words, whatever is generated by a GAI tool is merely the result of processing large quantities of data, perhaps supplemented by corrective techniques such as human-in-the-loop methods. In the classic SMCR model of communication, GAI is a new channel of communication that functions by scaling down immense quantities of undifferentiated input into a narrow and specific output. At the end of the day, GAI is capable of nothing more than assembling messages using probabilistic algorithms. GAI cannot make its own meaning.

Learning about the technical nature of GAI has become less daunting as more resources appear dedicated to demystifying and explaining GAI to the general public (for example, in the Washington Post (Verma & Lerman, 2023)). These can be shared with our students, perhaps even including them in course readings and assignments. As educators, we can be mindful of Domínguez Figaredo and Stoyanovich's call to teach not only how to use GAI, but also to teach the larger issues raised by that use,

Conceptually, AI literacy is about citizens understanding the social implications of AI.... While this hands-on approach is appropriate for fostering deep learning about how an AI system works, it is also necessary to teach about the ethical, legal, and social implications of AI. (Domínguez Figaredo & Stoyanovich, 2023, p. 2)

We can ally with researchers and developers pursuing forms of AI that are more explainable and guided explicitly by social and ethical concerns, such as the Stanford Trustworthy AI project (https://stai.stanford.edu/) and the Perspectivist Approaches to Disagreement project (https://nlperspectives.di.unito.it/). We might engage our students in devising a list of principles that should guide GAI design, perhaps starting with the list from Xu (2023) for ethical technology design that is equitable, reflexive, and responsible:

- Attending the site of knowing and beings (recognizing that technologies are always connected to a context)
- Extending beyond design to empowerment (working with the communities that will need to sustain the technology)
- Retelling design narratives (to include the contributions of marginalized sites and actors)
- Redistributing affordances and burden of design equitably (engaging during design with the communities that will be most affected by the technology)
- Engaging with values (recognizing that values may be in tension or conflict)
- Designing meaningful human-machine relations (as opposed to simply focusing on effective technology use)
- Tracing responsibilities (for how past technologies created inequalities, injustice and oppression)

To help our students envision how they might become active and engaged in shaping GAI, our courses can educate students about the efforts to regulate GAI or to make it accountable to communities, such as the industry-education partnership of the AI Alliance (https://thealliance.ai/) or the regulations adopted through the EU Artificial Intelligence Act (https://artificialintelligenceact.eu/the-act/). We can incorporate how GAI is addressed in communication-related professions such as human development and resources (Chang & Ke, 2023). Finally, we can urge our institutions to adopt practices and policies that balance the concerns and opportunities of AI in an ethical and equitable way by following the guidance of expert organizations (for example, WCET (Sebesta & Davis, 2023) or ACM (ACM Global Technology Policy Council, 2023)).

The goal of this chapter was to identify ways in which we might conceptualize GAI to better understand some emerging roles in education. I have tried to show that how we talk about GAI matters. Considering only the functions or uses of GAI is not enough. What the communication field uniquely brings to the table is how GAI is given meaning and, therefore, how we come to have certain expectations for it and not for others. This chapter has shown how these expectations are derived from existing expectations and understandings of communication. When we recognize and become reflective of how we make sense of GAI in the present, we can better anticipate how GAI might look in our future.

REFERENCES

ACM Global Technology Policy Council. (2023). *Principles for the development, deployment, and use of generative AI technologies*. doi:10.6028/NIST.AI.100-1

Alba, D. (2022, December 8). *OpenAI chatbot spits out biased musings, despite guardrails*. Bloomberg.com. https://www.bloomberg.com/news/newsletters/2022-12-08/chatgpt-open-ai-s-chatbot-is-spitting-out-biased-sexist-results

Bajorek, J. P. (2019, May 10). *Voice recognition still has significant race and gender biases*. Harvard Business Review. https://hbr.org/2019/05/voice-recognition-still-has-significant-race-and-gender-biases

Bibhudatta, D. (2023, November 29). *Generative AI will transform virtual meetings*. Harvard Business Review. https://hbr.org/2023/11/generative-ai-will-transform-virtual-meetings

Bruns, H. C., & Long Lingo, E. (2023). Tedious work: Developing novel outcomes with digitization in the arts and sciences. *Administrative Science Quarterly*. Advance online publication. doi:10.1177/00018392231208190

Burke, K. (1969). *A grammar of motives*. University of California Press. doi:10.1525/9780520341715

Chang, Y.-L., & Ke, J. (2023). Socially responsible artificial intelligence empowered people analytics: A novel framework towards sustainability. *Human Resource Development Review*. Advance online publication. doi:10.1177/15344843231200930

Chui, M., Roberts, R., & Yee, L. (2022, December 20). *Generative AI is here: How tools like ChatGPT could change your business*. Quantum Black AI by McKinsey. Retrieved December 31, 2023, from https://www.mckinsey.com/capabilities/quantumblack/our-insights/generative-ai-is-here-how-tools-like-chatgpt-could-change-your-business

Coffey, L. (2023, October 31). *Most students outrunning faculty in AI use, study finds*. Inside Higher Ed. https://www.insidehighered.com/news/tech-innovation/artificial-intelligence/2023/10/31/most-students-outrunning-faculty-ai-use

Collins, H., & Pinch, T. (1998). *The golem at large: What you should know about technology* (1st ed.). Cambridge University Press.

Davison, R. M., Laumer, S., Tarafdar, M., & Wong, L. M. (2023). Pickled eggs: Generativeaias research assistant or co-author? *Information Systems Journal*, *33*(5), 989–994. doi:10.1111/isj.12455

Domínguez Figaredo, D., & Stoyanovich, J. (2023). Responsible AI literacy: A stakeholder-first approach. *Big Data & Society*, *10*(2). Advance online publication. doi:10.1177/20539517231219958

Draxler, F., Werner, A., Lehmann, F., Hoppe, M., Schmidt, A., Buschek, D., & Welsch, R. (2023). The AI ghostwriter effect: When users do not perceive ownership of AI-generated text but self-declare as authors. *ACM Transactions on Computer-Human Interaction*, 3637875. Advance online publication. doi:10.1145/3637875

Dubova, M. (2022). Building human-like communicative intelligence: A grounded perspective. *Cognitive Systems Research*, *72*, 63–79. doi:10.1016/j.cogsys.2021.12.002

Edula, R., Shengcheng, L., Sasaki, H., Viladiro, R., & Roy, D. (2023). Personalized learning systems in smart education: A review of the literature & pilot feasibility discussion. *ETLTC-ICETM2023 international conference proceedings: ICT integration in technical education & entertainment technologies and management*. 10.1063/5.0182560

Goffman, E. (1974). *Presentation of self in everyday life*. Viking Press.

Gordon, R. (2023, March 3). *Large language models are biased. Can logic help save them?* MIT News | Massachusetts Institute of Technology. https://news.mit.edu/2023/large-language-models-are-biased-can-logic-help-save-them-0303

Grainger College of Engeering. (2020). *PLATO* [Online Newsletter]. https://grainger.illinois.edu/news/magazine/plato

Guzman, A. L. (Ed.). (2018). Human-machine communication: Rethinking communication, technology, and ourselves. Peter Lang Inc., International Academic Publishers. doi:10.3726/b14399

Heidelberg, R. L. (2023). Artificial intelligence and the modern condition of expertise. *Administration & Society*, *56*(1), 73–95. doi:10.1177/00953997231204968

Herold, B. (2019, November 5). *What is personalized learning?* Education Week. https://www.edweek.org/technology/what-is-personalized-learning/2019/11

Hu, K. (2023, February 2). *ChatGPT sets record for fastest-growing user base - analyst note*. Reuters. https://www.reuters.com/technology/chatgpt-sets-record-fastest-growing-user-base-analyst-note-2023-02-01/

Hutiri, W. T., & Ding, A. Y. (2022). Bias in automated speaker recognition. In *ACM conference on fairness, accountability, and transparency* (pp. 230–247). ACM. doi:10.1145/3531146.3533089

Ismail, H., Hussein, N., Harous, S., & Khalil, A. (2023). Survey of personalized learning software systems: A taxonomy of environments, learning content, and user models. *Education Sciences*, *13*(7), 741. doi:10.3390/educsci13070741

Jackson, M. H., & McDowell, S. D. (2002). Enhancing discourse on new technology within higher education. In W. H. Dutton & B. D. Loader (Eds.), *Digital academe: New media in higher education and learning* (pp. 318–327). Routledge.

Jessup, L. M., & Valacich, J. S. (Eds.). (1992). *Group support systems: New perspectives*. Macmillan.

Kelly, S. M. (2023, April 27). *Snapchat's new AI chatbot is already raising alarms among teens and parents*. CNN. https://www.cnn.com/2023/04/27/tech/snapchat-my-ai-concerns-wellness/index.html

Kim, Y., & Sundar, S. (2012). Anthropomorphism of computers: Is it mindful or mindless? *Computers in Human Behavior, 28*(1), 241–250. doi:10.1016/j.chb.2011.09.006

Koenecke, A., Nam, A., Lake, E., Nudell, J., Quartey, M., Mengesha, Z., Toups, C., Rickford, J. R., Jurafsky, D., & Goel, S. (2020). Racial disparities in automated speech recognition. *Proceedings of the National Academy of Sciences of the United States of America, 117*(14), 7684–7689. doi:10.1073/pnas.1915768117 PMID:32205437

Kopp, S. (2010). Social resonance and embodied coordination in face-to-face conversation with artificial interlocutors. *Speech Communication, 52*(6), 587–597. doi:10.1016/j.specom.2010.02.007

Loftesness, S. (2022, December 7). *Haiku with chatgpt*. Scott Loftesness. Retrieved December 31, 2023, from https://sjl.us/2022/12/07/haiku-with-chatgpt/

Marx, L., & Smith, M. R. (Eds.). (1994). *Does technology drive history? The dilemma of technological determinism*. MIT Press.

Merken, S. (2023, June 26). *New York lawyers sanctioned for using face ChatGPT cases in legal brief*. Reuters. https://www.reuters.com/legal/new-york-lawyers-sanctioned-using-fake-chatgpt-cases-legal-brief-2023-06-22/

Nass, C., Moon, Y., Fogg, B., Reeves, B., & Dryer, D. (1995). Can computer personalities be human personalities? *International Journal of Human-Computer Studies, 43*(2), 223–239. doi:10.1006/ijhc.1995.1042

Natale, S. (2018). If software is narrative: Joseph Weizenbaum, artificial intelligence and the biographies of ELIZA. *New Media & Society, 21*(3), 712–728. doi:10.1177/1461444818804980

Nowak, K. L., & Biocca, F. (2003). The effect of the agency and anthropomorphism on users' sense of telepresence, copresence, and social presence in virtual environments. *Presence (Cambridge, Mass.), 12*(5), 481–494. doi:10.1162/105474603322761289

Oremus, W. (2015, October 25). *No more pencils, no more books*. Slate Magazine. https://www.slate.com/articles/technology/technology/2015/10/adaptive_learning_software_is_replacing_textbooks_and_upending_american.html

Paquot, M., & Gries, S. T. (Eds.). (2020). *A practical handbook of corpus linguistics*. Springer International Publishing. doi:10.1007/978-3-030-46216-1

Park, J. S., O'Brien, J. Y., Cai, C. J., Morris, M. R., Liang, P., & Bernstein, M. S. (2023). Generative agents: Interactive simulacra of human behavior. In *UIST '23: Proceedings of the 36th annual ACM symposium on user interface software and technology* (pp. 1–22). ACM. 10.1145/3586183.3606763

Perrigo, B. (2023, February 17). *Bing's AI is threatening users. That's no laughing matter*. TIME. https://time.com/6256529/bing-openai-chatgpt-danger-alignment/

Reeves, B., & Nass, C. (1996). The media equation: How people treat computers, television, and new media like real people and places (1st ed.). The Center for the Study of Language and Information Publications; Cambridge University Press.

Riffe, D., Lacy, S., & Watson, B. R. (2019). *Analyzing media messages: Using quantitative content analysis in research* (4th ed.). Routledge. doi:10.4324/9780429464287

Roose, K. (2022, December 21). A doming-out party for generative A.I., Silicon Valley's new craze. *New York Times*. https://www.nytimes.com/2022/10/21/technology/generative-ai.html

Sebesta, J., & Davis, V. L. (2023, December). *AI policies practices toolkit*. WCET. https://wcet.wiche.edu/resources/ai-practices-and-policies-toolkit/

Sertin, C. (2023, May 30). *How NVIDIA AI tech powers smart NPCs in gaming*. WIRED Middle East. https://wired.me/culture/nvidia-ai-powered-npcs/

Switzky, L. (2020). Eliza effects: Pygmalion and the early development of artificial intelligence. *Shaw*, *40*(1), 50–68. doi:10.5325/shaw.40.1.0050

Tennery, A., & Cherelus, G. (2016, March 24). *Microsoft's AI Twitter bot goes dark after racist, sexist tweets*. Reuters. https://www.reuters.com/article/idUSKCN0WQ2M7/

Thorbecke, C. (2022, August 11). *It didn't take long for Meta's new chatbot to say something offensive*. CNN. https://www.cnn.com/2022/08/11/tech/meta-chatbot-blenderbot/index.html

van Atteveldt, W., & Peng, T.-Q. (Eds.). (2021). *Computational methods for communication science*. Routledge. doi:10.4324/9781003082606

Vassallo, S. (2023, October 23). *Why generative AI needs design*. Forbes. https://www.forbes.com/sites/stevevassallo/2023/10/23/why-generative-ai-needs-design/

Verma, P., & Lerman, R. (2023, May 7). *A curious person's guide to artificial intelligence*. Washington Post. https://www.washingtonpost.com/technology/2023/05/07/ai-beginners-guide/

Vincent, J. (2023, February 15). *Microsoft's Bing is an emotionally manipulative liar, and people love it*. The Verge. https://www.theverge.com/2023/2/15/23599072/microsoft-ai-bing-personality-conversations-spy-employees-webcams

Westerman, D. K., Bowman, N. D., & Lachlan, K. A. (2022). *Introduction to mediated communication: Social media and beyond* (3rd ed.). Kendall Hunt Publishing.

Wong, M. (2022, December 20). *We haven't seen the worst of fake news*. The Atlantic. https://www.theatlantic.com/technology/archive/2022/12/deepfake-synthetic-media-technology-rise-disinformation/672519/

Xu, Y. (2023). Envisioning a better world of human and technology: Theoretical and empirical considerations to connect communication scholarship to ethical technology design. *Annals of the International Communication Association*, 1–16. doi:10.1080/23808985.2023.2255586

Zewe, A. (2023, November 9). *Explained: Generative AI*. MIT News | Massachusetts Institute of Technology. https://news.mit.edu/2023/explained-generative-ai-1109

ENDNOTES

1 Although we recognize that the concept of role is more integral to some areas of the field, e.g., symbolic interactionism (Goffman, 1974) or dramatism (Burke, 1969).

2 Except for the last bullet (which I wrote), I have reproduced verbatim the content generated by Jasper.ai. using the prompt "create a timeline showing when word processors introduced editing features such as spell check, thesaurus, grammar checking, work choice, etc." Given the output, Jasper.ai appears to understand that the word "work" in my prompt should have been "word." In addition, it is interesting for us to note that APA style guidelines call for citing the AI tool as generating this content although it hasn't done any more than would a research assistant and writers who have research assistants rarely credit them.

3 My thanks to Sanae Elmoudden for pointing out that acceptance of GAI in the editor or proofreader role also assimilates scholarly differences and further colonizes academic writing.

Chapter 3
Unravelling the Evolution of Generative AI in Communication Education:
A Historical Journey Into Human-Machine Communication

C. V. Suresh Babu
https://orcid.org/0000-0002-8474-2882
Hindustan Institute of Technology and Science, India

G. Suruthi
https://orcid.org/0009-0009-3867-598X
Hindustan Institute of Technology and Science, India

ABSTRACT

This chapter traces the historical evolution of human-machine communication, highlighting generative AI's transformative role. It begins with the origins of AI and early communication technologies, including Alan Turing's pioneering work and the development of Turing machines, as well as early AI experiments in human-machine interaction. The narrative then transitions to AI's evolution and the emergence of generative models, spotlighting advancements like recurrent neural networks (RNNs) and long short-term memory (LSTM) networks, which are fundamental to coherent text generation. The pivotal role of generative AI in language and communication learning is explored, showcasing its impact on writing skills and comprehension. Ethical considerations in AI usage are discussed, including bias, privacy, and ethical communication practices. The chapter concludes by envisioning AI's future in communication pedagogy, emphasizing collaboration between educators and AI developers and recapitulating historical insights for the integration of AI in education.

DOI: 10.4018/979-8-3693-0831-8.ch003

UNRAVELLING THE EVOLUTION OF GENERATIVE AI IN COMMUNICATION EDUCATION

A Historical Journey Into Human-Machine Communication

A fascinating journey into the nexus of language and technology can be taken by tracing the development of human-machine communication via the lens of generative artificial intelligence (Babu, 2022). Over the years, we have seen a dramatic change in how machines perceive, produce, and engage with human language. This historical perspective reveals the turning points that have changed the way people engage with machines, from the earliest rule-based chatbots to the birth of potent neural network-driven models, such as GPT-3. This investigation examines the major developments, difficulties, and ethical issues that have emerged in generative AI has developed (Babu & Adhithya, 2023). It depicts how technology has gradually eroded the distinction between human and machine communication, presenting both ground-breaking potential and perplexing conundrum. We discovered an enormous impact of travel through time. On this voyage through time, we learn more about the significant influence that generatives have had and continue to have on our daily interactions with technology.

BACKGROUND AND SIGNIFICANCE

Through the prism of generative AI, the historical evolution of human-machine communication is investigated, revealing a rich tapestry of societal change and technological advancement. This journey explores key milestones in the evolution of generative AI models such as GPT-3, tracing its roots back to early initiatives such as ELIZA. This historical context is essential because it illuminates the development of conversational AI and provides an important context for comprehending the complex interactions between humans and machines. The importance of this investigation lies in the enormous influence of generative artificial intelligence on modern civilization. It has completely changed the way we interact with technology, giving virtual assistants a more humanlike quality, allowing for language translation and spurring creativity in content creation. It also calls into question the morality of false information and the veracity of the content produced by AI. Understanding the potential of technology, its ethical ramifications, and how it will continue to influence how we interact with robots in the future is made easier by looking at it from a historical perspective.

Objectives of the Chapter

This section presents several key objectives. First, it provides readers with a comprehensive overview of the origins and essential advancements in artificial intelligence within the realm of human-machine communication. Tracing the historical trajectory lays the foundation for an in-depth exploration of the evolution of Generative AI over time.

This chapter delves into the technological development of Generative AI, spanning from its early stages to the contemporary era, characterized by sophisticated deep learning models such as GPT-3 (Babu & Adhithya, 2023). It sheds light on pivotal milestones and transformative moments in the history of technology, emphasizing its substantial impact on human-machine interactions.

Furthermore, it elucidates how Generative AI has revolutionized human interactions with technology, fostering more natural, responsive, and context-aware exchanges. This chapter explores the diverse real-world applications of Generative AI across industries, underscoring its broad significance in realms such as virtual assistance, content creation, and natural language processing.

Ethical considerations related to AI-generated content encompassing issues of accuracy, privacy, and content authenticity maintenance were thoroughly examined. In addition, the chapter underscores the multidisciplinary relevance of the topic by highlighting its implications for languages, ethics, education, policy, and computer science.

Ultimately, the chapter looks ahead, offering insights into the potential trends and challenges in the evolving field of Generative AI. It encourages readers to contemplate the prospective applications of AI in communication as well as the ethical and practical concerns that must be addressed with the continued advancement of this technology (Babu & Padma, 2023). In essence, this chapter aims to provide readers with a comprehensive understanding of the historical progression of Generative AI in human-machine communication, its current significance, and the intriguing challenges it poses for the future.

The Genesis of AI and Early Communication Technologies

AI's journey started in the 1940s. Initially, there was a need for hardware that could support AI research in the duration–1940-1950, as the invention of digital computers during 1940-1950 supported AI research as a pillar. Early AI communication moved to the next stage after the invention of two early AI programs: Logic Theorist (1956) and General Problem Solver (1957), which aimed to simulate human problem-solving abilities. Over the decades, AI has evolved through various phases, from symbolic AI to neural networks and machine learning, with communication technologies such as the Internet and advances in computing power, which play integral roles in communication and information processing (Babu & Rohan, 2023). Today, AI is a pervasive force in our lives, shaping how we communicate, use, and interact with technologies. The practical implementation of AI came into action with the initial implementation of the AT.

Alan Turing and the Concept of Turing Machines

The Alan Turing Test assesses a machine's ability to exhibit intelligent behavior comparable to human intelligence, specifically focusing on its natural language conversation capabilities. Proposed by Alan Turing in his 1950 paper titled "Computing Machinery and Intelligence," this theoretical model has significantly influenced the evolution of AI, particularly in the field of natural language processing.

Over its 73-year implementation and evolution, the Turing Test has been both foundational and controversial, contributing to debates on the sociological and psychological aspects of AI, including consciousness, behavior, and practical developments (Saygin et al., 2000).

The test involved three participants: a human respondent, machine, and interrogator. The interrogator serves as a tool to distinguish between humans and machines during a natural language conversation, with both participants placed in separate rooms to ensure an unbiased evaluation. Surprisingly, the test yielded positive results, demonstrating that the machines can engage in human-like conversations.

However, it is crucial to note that passing the Turing Test does not imply true understanding or consciousness in a machine; it merely indicates the ability to simulate an intelligent conversation. The limitations of the Turing Test become apparent when considering the complexity of human intelligence, which involves diverse factors, such as emotions, context, creativity, adaptability, and nuances that extend beyond simple language processing.

Despite These Challenges, Advancements in AI, Particularly Natural Language Understanding, Reasoning, Creativity, and Empathy, Continue to Progress

Early AI Experiments in Human-Machine Communication

Understanding the history of AI is crucial for comprehending its evolution from the early stages to its present state. Knowledge of the past allows us to appreciate the challenges faced and strides made in AI development.

Early AI experiments, including the Alan Turing test, laid the groundwork for the advancement of the field. Notable experiments such as ELIZA, Shakey the Robot, and PARRY played pivotal roles in highlighting the challenges and potential avenues for AI development, contributing to the sophisticated AI we have today.

In the initial stages of human-machine communication, challenges arose as machines struggled with natural language understanding and failed to personalize interactions. Limitations included the reliance on a "Rule-based Approach," where responses followed predefined patterns. This approach lacks adaptability, and machines cannot learn from user interactions, thereby limiting the accuracy and scope of information.

The turning point in AI evolution occurred between 2000 and 2018, marking significant progress and overcoming earlier challenges (Haenlein & Kaplan, 2019).

In the context of Human Resources, an eighteen-year span from 2000 to 2018 reveals distinct phases: the First Decade, Reduction Period, and Period of Growth. The First Decade represents the initial exploration of AI in Human Resources. The Reduction Period witnessed setbacks and failures, which contributed to a negative perception of AI. Finally, the growth period saw a surge in AI applications in Human Resources, which had a positive impact on the field. This evolution provides valuable insights into AI's role of AI in technological improvement within the realm of Human Resources (Jatobá et al., 2019).

Challenges and Breakthroughs in AI Communication Interfaces

AI communication interfaces encompass technologies and systems that facilitate interactions between humans and artificial intelligence, presenting both challenges and breakthroughs (Babu & Padma, 2023). The challenges in these interfaces begin with the fundamental task of ensuring the comprehension and expression of natural language, posing a significant hurdle. Additionally, concerns arise regarding the inheritance of biases, where AI systems may exhibit unfair and discriminatory outcomes owing to biases inherited from training data, making the maintenance of fairness an ongoing challenge. The complex challenge of AI adapting to human emotions further complicates matters, as developing an AI capable of detecting and responding to human emotions involves navigating the intricate landscape of human empathy and simulation.

Despite these challenges, AI communication interfaces have experienced remarkable breakthroughs, positioning AI as a superior technology. Notably, the advent of AI voice assistants, such as Google, Alexa, and Siri, has revolutionized user interactions by allowing natural speech. Another breakthrough involves advancements in natural language processing models, such as GPT-3 and transformer models, which are capable of generating text and performing tasks akin to human capabilities. AI has made significant strides in processing various modalities, including text, speech, images, videos, audio, gestures, biometric data, emotions, and behavioral data, leading to sophisticated interactions.

Personalized communication has emerged as a key feature, with AI interfaces crafting responses and recommendations based on user behavior and preferences, enhancing human-machine interaction. Moreover, the elimination of language barriers using real-time AI translation tools has facilitated multilingual communication. To overcome privacy concerns, AI embraces features such as federated learning and homomorphic encryption, enabling learning from decentralized and encrypted data, representing a major breakthrough in the realm of security.

A recent innovation in AI communication interfaces is emotion recognition, which expands the scope of AI across diverse fields such as customer service, market research, healthcare, education, entertainment, and gaming. This advancement allows applications to effectively recognize and respond to human emotions, offering personalized interactions by analyzing and adapting to users' emotional states.

AI EVOLUTION AND THE EMERGENCE OF GENERATIVE MODELS

AI has undergone significant transformations over time. In the mid-20th century, rule-based and expert systems, initially employed, were gradually replaced by machine learning techniques, such as decision trees and neural networks, advancing the field. In the 21st century, generative models such as Transformers and Generative Adversarial Networks (GANs) have emerged. GANs, introduced by Ian Goodfellow in 2014, have revolutionized AI by enabling the creation of realistic data. Subsequently, Transformers, introduced in 2017, propelled the development of NLP models like GPT-3, upon which I am based, enabling remarkable text production and comprehension.

Generative models, a significant advancement in AI, facilitate the creation of content including text, images, and music, with applications in creativity and language processing. Generative models play a pivotal role in natural language processing (NLP), a crucial aspect of AI (Babu & Akshara, 2024). They aimed to generate new instances of data resembling a specified dataset, contributing to the creation of the original content. In the NLP sector, generative models utilize Long Short-Term Memory (LSTM) networks and Recurrent Neural Networks (RNNs).

The field of artificial intelligence, known as "natural language processing" (NLP), seeks to empower computers to comprehend, interpret, and produce human language, thereby bridging the knowledge gap between machines and human communication. NLP encompasses various activities such as question answering, sentiment analysis, language translation, and text and speech recognition. For instance, a sentiment analysis program determines the tone of a user review and classifies it as positive, negative, or neutral using NLP. NLP is essential for the advancement of AI, enhancing information processing, and human-computer interaction. It enhances user friendliness and accessibility as machines learn to understand and respond to natural language, with applications in chatbots, virtual assistants, and language translation services.

To make NLP a more effective generative model, RNNs and LSTMs were employed. These architectures perform tasks such as text creation, in which the model is trained to generate logical and contextually relevant word sequences. For example, an LSTM-based language model trained on a text corpus can generate new sentences or paragraphs that closely resemble the structure and style of a training set.

Introduction of Recurrent Neural Networks (RNNs)

Artificial neural networks in the Recurrent Neural Networks (RNN) class are built with a feedback loop in their architecture to process sequential data. The network may retain a recollection of prior inputs owing to this loop, which makes it very useful for jobs requiring temporal interdependence and context. Natural language processing is an important area in which RNN applications are used because it can represent language patterns over word sequences. Consider a language model that generates text using an RNN (Pienaar & Malekian, 2019). The network updates its internal state depending on the preceding words, processing each word in a phrase individually. The model can capture dependencies owing to sequential learning, such as recognizing the subject of a phrase based on the context that came before it. In the sentence "The cat sat on the mat," for example, an RNN understands the word "mat" more fully by taking into account the context of both "cat" and "sat." This feature of RNNs has a significant impact on the AI evolution. Their contributions have been crucial in the advancement of applications, such as predictive text generation, machine translation, and speech recognition. AI systems can better understand the subtleties of language and time-dependent patterns after RNN has become an integral part of AI. It is crucial to remember that conventional RNNs have drawbacks, such as the inability to accurately capture long-term dependencies. Nevertheless, some of these issues have been resolved by their development into more sophisticated architectures, such as the Gated Recurrent Unit (GRU) and Long Short-Term Memory (LSTM), demonstrating the importance of RNNs in the ongoing creation of highly developed AI systems.

Long Short-Term Memory (LSTM) Networks and Coherent Text Generation

One type of recurrent neural network (RNN) architecture, called Long Short-Term Memory (LSTM), was created to solve the problems associated with collecting long-term dependencies in sequential input. In contrast to conventional RNNs, LSTMs have gating mechanisms and memory cells that allow them to remember or forget information selectively over long sequences. Because of this, LSTMs are especially useful for jobs such as natural language processing, which calls for long-term context knowledge (Pienaar & Malekian, 2019). Consider a language modelling application in which LSTM is used. A long short-term memory (LSTM) can retain information about the subject, context, and grammatical structure of a phrase by capturing the relationships between words. By selectively updating its memory cells in response to incoming inputs, the network can store pertinent information. The progress of artificial intelligence has been greatly impacted by LSTMs (Sahoo et al., 2019). They have overcome the shortcomings of traditional RNNs, which struggle to handle long sequences because of the increasing or disappearing gradient problems. LSTMs have been shown to be extraordinarily effective in many different applications, including sentiment analysis, machine translation, and speech recognition. Their ability to describe complex sequential patterns and understand long-range linkages has tremendously benefited the creation of increasingly sophisticated and context-aware systems (Al-azazi & Ghurab, 2023). LSTMs are a key innovation in neural network topologies that have improved sequential data processing and interpretation, revolutionized the area of AI, and paved the way for further developments in recurrent neural network structures.

Generative AI in Language and Communication Learning

The language and communication skills of generative AI have been a slowly developing topic. Although generative language models, such as GPT-3, have made considerable strides in recent years, AI research in natural language processing (NLP) has roots that have gone back several decades. For example, OpenAI's GPT-3 was released in June 2020. Owing to its extensive design and capacity to produce text that is cohesive and contextually appropriate, it represents a significant advancement in generative language models. It is crucial to remember that the history of AI's use of AI in language and communication abilities is far longer and includes technologies such as chatbots, machine translation, and speech recognition systems. However, recent developments in generative language models have attracted considerable attention and improved.

AI has been a part of education since a very old time, which had rapidly grown during the pandemic period, and a sudden release of Chatgpt in November 2022 has given a boon to the students. Chatgpt is a generative AI that is capable of generating text, images, and digitalized media. There was both a warm and confusing welcome for generative AI: chatgpt. As far as the positive impact of Chatgpt is known, there are certain limitations. Among the overall limitations, the major one is that its knowledge is based only on data up to September 2021. Examination of implications of chatbots from large language models (C-LLM). As a result, the intrinsic limitations of generative AI and the possible areas of implication and application of generative AI is conversed (Tzirides et al., 2023).

Enhancing Students' Writing Skills With AI-Powered Language Models

Generative AI has revolutionized language and communication learning by offering customized and engaging learning experiences, improving translation accuracy, and broadening communication opportunities globally for students. An application of AI that significantly enhances students' writing skills is through AI-powered language models, including tools such as Grammarly, ProWritingAid, and Hemingway Editor, and AI-based writing aids such as the ChatGPT app. These tools utilize advanced natural language processing algorithms to understand and generate human-like text in response to prompts or inputs.

AI writing assistance contributes to the enhancement of student writing skills in several ways. First, it provides instant feedback that helps students identify and correct grammatical, syntactic, and stylistic errors. This iterative process reinforces the writing conventions. Second, writing assistance offers suggestions for vocabulary and sentence construction, encouraging students to use diverse languages. Exposure to various linguistic components fosters the development of more diverse and sophisticated writing styles. Additionally, these tools help students organize their thoughts effectively. By highlighting ambiguous or complex passages, writing assistance promotes coherence and clarity and teaches students the logical organization of ideas. The process also cultivates the ability to self-edit, as students learn to proofread and refine their work. This iterative self-correction during the writing process instills a sense of accountability and independence in the students.

AI in Improving Speaking and Comprehension Abilities

AI employs various applications and technologies to enhance speaking and comprehension skills. Speech recognition systems driven by AI can analyze spoken language and offer real-time feedback regarding fluency and pronunciation. Language learning apps frequently leverage AI to evaluate users' spoken language and provide personalized recommendations for improvement. Language models, such as ChatGPT, powered by AI, engage with users, aid in comprehension enhancement by generating contextually relevant responses, and assist with language acquisition.

Voice assistants such as Siri, Google Assistant, and Amazon Alexa utilize a complex process involving speech recognition, natural language processing (NLP), and machine learning algorithms. When a user interacts with a voice assistant, speech recognition technology identifies the spoken words by breaking them into recognizable phonemes, resulting in text transcription. NLP interprets this text, discerning context, meaning, and user intent by recognizing entities, such as names and locations.

For instance, a command like "Set an alarm for 7 AM" signals the user's intent to set an alarm. The voice assistant analyzes the request to determine the specific action or information sought, initiating the corresponding action, be it controlling smart devices, retrieving Internet information, or other tasks. Machine learning is integral to voice assistants, enabling continuous improvement by learning from user interactions and refining the understanding of contexts, speech patterns, and accents.

User feedback plays a crucial role in enhancing voice assistant capabilities, aiding the precision of speech recognition, accent comprehension, and addressing issues related to user intent. The seamless integration of natural language processing, speech recognition, intent recognition, query processing, and machine learning enables voice assistants to understand and respond to user commands and queries in conversational and organic manners. This intricate process ensures that voice assistants can effectively and individually assist the users.

Real-World Examples of Successful AI Integration in the Communication Classroom

The use of AI in communication classrooms can improve instruction and learning quality. The following are some case studies of successful AI integration in this setting from the actual world. AI in the classroom scenario has played a major role in the evolution of AI after integration into the communication classroom.

Case Study-Automated Grading System

AI-powered automated grading systems have gained widespread use in educational institutions by offering a streamlined approach to the assessment process. A notable case study highlighted a large university's adoption of AI for grading written assignments in a communication course, aiming to enhance productivity, provide prompt feedback, and ensure grading consistency. Collaborating with an AI technology supplier specializing in natural language processing, the university employed automated grading based on predefined criteria, such as content relevance, coherence, and grammar.

The automated system significantly reduced grading time, providing students with swift feedback to address weaknesses and improve subsequent assignments. Timely feedback plays a crucial role in the iterative learning process. Moreover, the system ensured uniformity in grading across multiple instructors, thus minimizing discrepancies in the assessment standards.

While the automated grading system demonstrated effectiveness, challenges arose in capturing subtle aspects of communication, such as originality and writing style. To address this, the university implemented a human-in-the-loop method, in which teachers reviewed and adjusted grades as needed. This hybrid model maintains the human element in evaluating subjective elements while retaining the efficiency and benefits of AI-driven grading.

Feedback from the students indicated a positive reception of the automated grading system, appreciating the quick turnaround that facilitated a clearer understanding of their strengths and weaknesses.

Teachers found that the system saved significant time, allowing them to focus on teaching and provide personalized feedback rather than spending extensive hours on grading.

This case study exemplifies the successful implementation of an automated grading system in communication classrooms. The university improved the grading process by integrating AI technology, affording teachers more time for instructional activities, and offering students timely feedback. The hybrid approach effectively addressed the nuanced evaluation needs of communication courses by combining the efficiency of AI with human oversight (Ramesh & Sanampudi, 2022). This case study illustrates the potential of AI to optimize and transform assessment procedures in educational settings.

Case Study: Learning App

A forward-thinking educational institution aims to enhance classroom communication skills using artificial intelligence (AI). The case study involved integrating AI tools into a communication course to provide students with advanced learning opportunities and to elevate their overall competency in oral and written communication. Collaborating with a tech company specializing in AI-powered language learning software, the university introduced students to an easy-to-use application to customize language lessons through natural language processing.

The AI algorithms identified areas for improvement, adapted exercises to address specific language challenges, and adjusted the content based on individual student progress. The objective of this study was to create a flexible and dynamic learning environment. Interactive chatbots powered by AI have been introduced to improve speaking and listening abilities by simulating real-life conversations. These chatbots provided a controlled setting for students to refine their language skills, offering immediate feedback on grammar and pronunciation, while adjusting for dialogue difficulty based on proficiency levels.

The use of AI tools yielded positive outcomes, with students expressing increased engagement, attributed to the interactive nature of the exercises. Personalized feedback from the AI system allowed students to monitor their progress and actively participate in language learning activities. Consequently, the students demonstrated clear improvements in both oral and written communication skills.

The success of AI integration in the classroom was largely credited to the instructors, who were provided with dashboards that highlighted individual performance metrics to track student progress. The AI system empowered teachers to tailor lessons to students' specific needs, ensuring that technology complemented pedagogical approaches and course objectives. The AI integrated communication classroom showed a positive, long-term impact throughout the semester, fostering greater self-assurance in students' communication abilities.

The institution attributed the program's success to the AI's flexibility in accommodating diverse learning styles, underscoring its potential as a valuable tool for enhancing communication skills. This real-world case study demonstrates the effective integration of AI in a communication classroom, showing benefits for student engagement and language competency. Through the strategic use of interactive chatbots and AI-driven language learning applications, educational institutions have established a personalized and dynamic learning environment, indicating that AI could revolutionize language learning by providing individualized experiences that significantly enhance communication abilities (Palliyalil & Mukherjee, 2020).

Case Study: Robot-Proof Higher Education

Robot-proof higher education is poised to revolutionize the education system by championing the digitization and personalization of learning. Although this departure from traditional methods may be substantial, it harbors the potential to amplify creativity and flexibility in the teaching-learning process. The concept of nurturing distinctive traits such as creativity and flexibility is encapsulated in the discipline of "humanics." As a potent toolset, humanics unlocks both the potential benefits and challenges in robot-proof higher education, empowering individuals, particularly students, to collaborate with technology and shape their creativity to the fullest (Aoun, 2017).

A pivotal advantage of robot-proof higher education is its emphasis on cultivating distinct human traits, including creativity, emotional intelligence, and critical thinking. Prioritizing these skills enables students to tackle complex, non-routine jobs that are less susceptible to automation. Moreover, a robot-proof curriculum fosters adaptability, enabling graduates to navigate diverse professional environments successfully. However, implementing a robot-proof educational system is not without hurdle. Conflicts may arise among interdisciplinary, skill-focused, and established academic frameworks. Resistance to change by faculty and stakeholders accustomed to traditional methods can impede the seamless integration of robot-proof components into the curriculum. Coping with the rapid pace of technological advancement introduces an additional layer of complexity, necessitating ongoing efforts to craft current and flexible curricula.

Ensuring inclusivity and accessibility in robot-proof education poses challenges because not all students have equal access to opportunities or resources. Innovative teaching strategies and cutting-edge technologies play crucial roles in overcoming these challenges. Immersive opportunities for skill development are offered through virtual reality experience, simulations, and online learning platforms. Collaborations between academia and the business sector provide students with real-world experience and practical knowledge in areas less amenable to automation.

In conclusion, although robot-proof higher education holds the potential to better prepare students for the future workforce, it is not without challenges. Overcoming resistance to change, addressing inclusivity concerns, and staying abreast of technological developments are essential for developing and maintaining a robot-proof education system. Embracing creativity, fostering teamwork, and adapting teaching methods to evolving student and labor market demands drive innovations in this educational paradigm.

ETHICAL CONSIDERATIONS AND RESPONSIBLE USE OF GENERATIVE AI

In today's technologically advanced society, ethical considerations and responsible usage of generative AI are paramount. Ensuring that AI systems such as GPT-3 align with moral principles and societal norms is crucial. This involves mitigating damaging biases, enhancing transparency, and fostering accountability among users and creators. In addition, safeguarding data security, permissions, and privacy is essential when employing AI across various applications. Responsible use demands strict adherence to rules to prevent misuse, including the dissemination of false information or creation of deep fakes. Striking a balance between innovation and ethical protection is imperative to fully harness the potential of generative AI, while respecting ethical standards and societal well-being.

In the context of AI's pervasive application and its rapid progression towards replacing human roles, concerns arise about the associated rise in unemployment. While AI mimics human functions in banking, call centers, and even the medical field, its drawbacks become evident when manual human intervention and monitoring are crucial. The swift expansion of AI applications has led to unpredictable behavior, posing a significant societal challenge. Although AI evolution aims to provide convenience, it remains a human-created tool that requires human oversight to ensure positive outputs and impacts (Kinderlerer, 2021).

In the realm of education, instructors play a key role in considering the ethical aspects of AI courses to create effective, interesting, and beneficial learning platforms. Categorizing AI applications into software- and hardware-based (robots), ethical considerations for both scenarios are crucial (Burton et al., 2017). Furthermore, the integration of AI ethics into general AI systems is vital to ensure ethical and responsible usage. Transparency, accountability, and ethical considerations should be integrated from the design stage, accompanied by precise rules for data usage, algorithmic decision-making, and bias mitigation. Continuous monitoring, evaluation, and incorporation of feedback loops are essential for identifying and rectifying biases. Explainability and interpretability should be prioritized to build user trust by clarifying the AI decision-making processes. A robust framework for user consent and privacy protection along with anonymization protocols strengthens the ethical foundation of AI. Continuous learning and awareness among the AI community and public is crucial. Promoting a culture of responsible AI development and application, establishing industry-wide standards, and collaboratively developing ethical frameworks will contribute to ensuring uniformity and adherence to ethical principles across diverse AI applications. In conclusion, the integration of AI ethics requires a comprehensive strategy involving ongoing education, design, development, transparency, and privacy, fostering the ethical application of AI technologies and reducing moral ambiguities.

Addressing Bias, Privacy Concerns, and User Data Protection in AI-Generated Communication

AI communication is an integral part of daily life, and offers both benefits and concerns. Personalized communication and smart replies, which generate billions of messages daily, are notable advantages. However, there are potential social concerns and negative impacts associated with AI communication. Randomized experiments reveal that AI can enhance speed, positive language, and interpersonal perception, but may also introduce risks, emphasizing the need for careful and responsible use (Hohenstein et al., 2023).

Addressing the bias in AI communication is crucial for its creation and implementation. Biases may stem from algorithms, training data, and human prejudices during the design process. Overcoming bias requires diverse and representative datasets, improved algorithms for recognizing and reducing biased patterns, and methods such as adversarial training. Privacy concerns and data protection pose challenges for Generative AI. AI's processing of large amounts of personal data by AI raises privacy concerns, necessitating innovative methods such as federated learning to preserve user privacy. Strides have been made in authentication techniques and content verification tools to ensure trust in the AI-generated content.

Despite these advancements, challenges persist. Achieving true fairness and eliminating all biases is difficult because of subtle and deeply ingrained prejudice. Balancing privacy and usefulness remains a challenge, with stringent privacy regulations potentially impacting the efficiency of the AI model. Ongoing cybersecurity measures are crucial for staying ahead of the evolving threats to user protection.

In conclusion, addressing bias and privacy concerns and ensuring user protection in AI-generated communication requires a sophisticated and continuous process. Technological and methodological advances offer hope; however, a multifaceted strategy, including ongoing research, industry collaboration, and regulatory frameworks, is essential for developing ethical and responsible AI communication systems.

ENVISIONING THE FUTURE: AI AND COMMUNICATION PEDAGOGY

The evolving technology of Artificial Intelligence (AI) is often referred to as the "Third wave of modern society" (Babu & Padma, 2023). Recognizing the significance of computer classrooms in today's world, they have contributed to the modernization of society (Fandrich, n.d.). Collaboratively, AI and communication pedagogy are shaping the future by providing innovative and personalized learning experiences.

AI-powered personalized learning platforms can adapt to the specific needs of each student by delivering customized exercises, feedback, and simulations to enhance communication skills. This technological integration creates a dynamic and engaging learning environment, in which AI assesses nonverbal cues, supports language learning, and facilitates scenario-based training. Embracing this mutually beneficial relationship between AI and communication pedagogy fosters a future-focused educational environment that caters to individual needs and learning styles, thus preparing individuals for various communication challenges.

Continued collaboration between technologists and educators, along with ethical considerations, is essential for ensuring responsible and effective implementation. AI's ability to customize communication pedagogy—adjusting pace, style, and content—enhances its understanding and participation. AI-driven platforms evaluate students' communication abilities, identify areas for development, and provide tailored exercises or feedback to strengthen specific competencies (Luckin et al., 2016).

However, challenges persist, including the need to address ethical concerns such as ensuring objective AI evaluations and protecting user privacy. Effective incorporation of AI into communication pedagogy, ensuring technology enhancement rather than replacing human instruction, requires ongoing collaboration between educators and technologists.

In conclusion, the future holds exciting possibilities for AI in communication pedagogy, with the potential to revolutionize the way we teach and learn communication skills. This includes personalized learning experiences, immersive simulations, and advanced language learning. Despite ethical concerns, computer classrooms can be an effective and comfortable educational system (Fandrich, n.d.).

Potential Advancements and Opportunities in AI Integration

The field of AI integration brims has intriguing possibilities, potential advancements, and promising revolutionary changes across various domains. In healthcare, AI can significantly enhance medication discovery, treatment suggestions, and diagnostics. The transportation sector anticipates the transformation of urban mobility through AI-driven autonomous cars to improve efficiency and safety. AI's promise of AI in education lies in delivering personalized learning experiences that maximize students' academic progress. Additionally, AI has the potential to combat climate change by promoting sustainable behaviors and predictive modeling, presenting both crucial and exciting prospects. However, these possibilities present challenges, including the need for ethical AI governance and concerns related to data protection. Navigating these challenges is imperative as we progress toward a future enriched by the transformative potential of AI.

In higher education and research, the application of natural language processing and advanced language models such as GPT-4 and BARD plays a significant role. AI has permeated various domains, and its application in education is a pivotal tool for shaping the future. AI contributes to text generation, data analysis, literature review, formatting, editing, peer review, and education. The educational realm benefits from AI through services like constructive feedback, assessment systems, grading mechanisms, structured curricula, personalized career guidance, and psychological support, making AI an effective and valuable asset in the days to come (Alqahtani et al., 2023).

The integration of technology empowers the possibility of pedagogical agents serving as teachers or professors for students. These agents were divided into two phases, focusing on communication and interaction characteristics with students in the first phase. In the second phase, the review delves into how pedagogical agents facilitate the learning process by examining attributes such as students' intra-personal communication processes, interpersonal communication between students and pedagogical agents, and facilitating group learning. This review underscores the importance of adaptive, adequate, relational, and logical communication by pedagogical agents to contribute to an effective AI learning process (Sikström et al., 2022).

Challenges and Limitations for AI in Education

The integration of Artificial Intelligence (AI) in education helps instructors organize, monitor, and handle large-scale settings; foster collaborative learning; ensure flexibility; facilitate effective communication; and provide personalized learning experiences to enhance the overall educational process. It is important to emphasize that AI's role is to support human educators rather than to replace them. This approach significantly reduced the achievement gap and contributed to technological development along with effective learning methods.

AI in education aims to alleviate the workload of teachers, enabling them to create sophisticated learning environments. By doing so, it contributes to shaping students' future by enhancing their skills and knowledge (Luckin et al., 2016). Despite the numerous benefits of AI integration in education, challenges and limitations still exist.

A major obstacle is the potential for bias reinforcement. AI systems, when trained on biased data, may unintentionally perpetuate societal preconceptions, limiting the diversity of knowledge available to students and perpetuating cultural bias. In addition, personalization and awareness of different learning styles pose challenges. While AI can offer tailored suggestions, understanding the subtleties of each student's unique learning style and adapting it in real time remains a challenge.

Privacy concerns, including gathering, storing, and using private student data, continue to be significant barriers. The risk of data breach or illegal access to student records could compromise the privacy of academic profiles. Equity and accessibility are also critical considerations, as the unequal distribution of AI-driven educational resources may widen the existing disparities between privileged and underprivileged students.

Furthermore, AI's ability of AI to adapt to various linguistic and cultural contexts is crucial for its effectiveness. Linguistic subtleties, cultural variations, and regional educational disparities can affect the performance of AI systems, limiting their usefulness in a globalized educational environment.

In conclusion, while AI holds great promise for education, careful consideration is essential to address challenges such as bias reinforcement, lack of personalization, privacy concerns, accessibility issues, and adaptability to diverse contexts. Resolving these issues is imperative to fully utilize AI in education and to ensure that every student has access to an inclusive, equitable, and ethically sound learning environment.

COLLABORATION BETWEEN EDUCATORS AND AI DEVELOPERS FOR POSITIVE IMPACT

Technology evolves daily, exhibiting remarkable efficiency; however, it grapples with growing security concerns. The synergy between AI developers and educators is instrumental in positively impacting education. This collaborative effort yields cutting-edge tools and technologies by sharing insights into the unique challenges faced in the classroom. The outcome is a personalized learning system that addresses individual student preferences, significantly enhancing educational outcomes (Seo et al., 2021).

AI-driven analytics empowers teachers to better comprehend student development and facilitate timely interventions and tailored guidance. While addressing concerns related to data privacy, bias, and equity, this collaboration promotes the ethical application of AI in education. The result is an increasingly effective and inclusive education system in which technology serves as a potent ally for nurturing the next generation of learners. A notable success story in this collaboration is evident in the Nursing Education.

AI, with its advanced solutions, is revolutionizing learning environments for nursing students and preparing them for the complexities of healthcare. Personalized learning, a crucial application, involves artificial intelligence (AI) algorithms that evaluate student performance data to provide customized instructional materials. AI-powered simulations, which are integral to nursing education, offer risk-free environments for students to practice clinical decision-making. These simulations, based on actual patient cases, allow students to apply theoretical knowledge and hone their critical thinking skills.

Moreover, AI facilitates ongoing feedback and assessments through real-time response evaluation using intelligent tutoring systems. This quick feedback loop enables students to monitor their progress, identify areas for improvement, and adapt their learning approaches as needed. AI contributes to evidence-based practice in nursing education by analyzing vast volumes of clinical trials, case studies, and medical literature, ensuring that education remains current and aligns with the rapidly evolving health care industry.

Despite these advancements, challenges persist, such as ensuring ethical AI use, addressing concerns about algorithmic bias, and ensuring technology complements, rather than replacing human instruction. To fully harness the potential benefits of artificial intelligence and mitigate its drawbacks, a strategic and collaborative approach involving educators, technologists, and healthcare professionals is essential for its integration into nursing education. The projected growth of AI's influence of AI on nursing education foresees the creation of a workforce comprising highly qualified and adaptable healthcare professionals (De Gagne, 2023).

IMPLICATIONS FOR PRESENT AND FUTURE AI INTEGRATION IN COMMUNICATION PEDAGOGY

The present and future of education will undergo profound transformations through the integration of AI into the communication pedagogy. AI technologies reshape the teaching and acquisition of communication skills. For instance, chatbots and virtual assistants powered by natural language processing can provide students with immediate feedback on written communication, assist them in enhancing their writing abilities by evaluating coherence, grammar, and style, and offer tailored recommendations for improvement.

The impact of AI in communication pedagogy is expected to become even more significant in the future. AI's capacity of AI to create personalized and adaptive learning environments is noteworthy. Algorithms can assess each student's communication strengths and weaknesses, and tailor lesson plans to focus on areas that need improvement. This adaptability ensures that each student receives targeted assistance, fostering a more effective and personalized learning environment.

Another future consequence is the potential application of AI to language learning. Advanced language processing capabilities can power interactive language learning platforms, providing immersive experiences in which students engage realistically with AI-generated characters to improve their language skills. AI-powered language learning is particularly beneficial for understanding communication subtleties and cultural nuances.

However, integrating AI into communication pedagogy presents challenges and has ethical implications. Addressing concerns about bias in AI algorithms is crucial for ensuring inclusive and equitable education. Future considerations involve ongoing research and development to continuously enhance AI systems and to adapt them to changing communication patterns. Therefore, the integration of AI into communication pedagogy has transformative implications for both the present and future (Nigam et al., 2021).

While current applications focus on improving specific communication skills, the future holds promise for tailored learning experiences, flexible curriculum design, and cutting-edge language-learning resources. Striking a balance between these advancements and ethical considerations is imperative to optimize the benefits of AI in communication education.

CONCLUSION

The historical development of artificial intelligence has been a remarkable journey marked by invention and progress. Pioneers, such as Alan Turing, laid the theoretical foundations of AI in the mid-20th century, and the Dartmouth Workshop in 1956 marked the initiation of AI as a distinct field, fostering optimism for the creation of intelligent machines. However, the initial excitement gave way to the artificial intelligence winter of the 1970s and the 1980s, which was characterized by slow progress and reduced funding.

The revival of AI in the late 20th century was spurred by advancements in neural networks and machine learning, leading to practical applications, such as expert systems and speech recognition. In the 21st century, a flourishing AI renaissance has been propelled by large datasets, advanced hardware, and deep learning algorithms. AI, now integral to our daily lives through applications, such as virtual assistants, self-driving cars, and healthcare diagnostics, continues to shape both technology and society.

In summary, the historical perspective on the development of Generative AI in human-machine communication reveals an incredible journey. From basic chatbots to sophisticated models, such as GPT, AI has significantly enhanced its ability to replicate human language and cognition. This progress, evident in content production, natural language translation, and AI-powered virtual assistants, has positively impacted quality of life. However, as AI gains immense power, addressing concerns, such as deepfakes, misinformation, and privacy ethics, becomes paramount. Generative AI must contribute to, not hinder, our communication landscape, emphasizing the crucial need for a balanced approach between innovation and ethics.

REFERENCES

Al-azazi, F. A., & Ghurab, M. (2023). ANN-LSTM: A deep learning model for early student performance prediction in MOOC. *Heliyon*, *9*(3), e15382. doi:10.1016/j.heliyon.2023.e15382 PMID:37089306

Alqahtani, T., Badreldin, H. A., Alrashed, M., Alshaya, A. I., Alghamdi, S. S., Bin Saleh, K., Alowais, S. A., Alshaya, O. A., Rahman, I., Al Yami, M. S., & Albekairy, A. M. (2023). The emergent role of artificial intelligence, natural learning processing, and large language models in higher education and research. *Research in Social & Administrative Pharmacy*, *19*(8), 1236–1242. doi:10.1016/j.sapharm.2023.05.016 PMID:37321925

Aoun, J. E. (2017). *Robot-proof: Higher education in the age of artificial intelligence*. MIT Press. doi:10.7551/mitpress/11456.001.0001

Babu, C. V. S. (2022). *Artificial intelligence and expert systems*. Anniyappa Publication.

Babu, C. V. S., & Adhithya, S. (2023). ChatGPT and other generative AI tools in education: Transformative potential and ethical considerations. In J. Keengwe (Ed.), *Creative AI tools and ethical implications in teaching and learning* (pp. 135–152). IGI Global. doi:10.4018/979-8-3693-0205-7.ch007

Babu, C. V. S., & Padma, R. (2023). Technology transformation through skilled teachers in teaching accountancy. In R. González-Lezcano (Ed.), *Advancing STEM education and innovation in a time of distance learning* (pp. 211–233). IGI Global., doi:10.4018/978-1-6684-5053-6.ch011

Babu, C. V. S., & Rohan, B. (2023). Evaluation and quality assurance for rapid e-learning and development of digital learning resources. In M. I. Santally, Y. Rajabalee, & R. Rajputh (Eds.), *Implementing rapid e-learning through interactive materials development* (pp. 139–170). IGI Global. doi:10.4018/978-1-6684-4940-0.ch008

Burton, E., Goldsmith, J., Koenig, S., Kuipers, B., Mattei, N., & Walsh, T. (2017). Ethical considerations in artificial intelligence courses. *AI & Society*, *32*(3), 357–369. doi:10.1007/s00146-016-0699-1

De Gagne, J. C. (2023). The state of artificial intelligence in nursing education: Past, present, and future directions. *International Journal of Environmental Research and Public Health*, *20*(6), 4884. doi:10.3390/ijerph20064884 PMID:36981790

Dwivedi, Y. K., Kshetri, N., Hughes, L., Slade, E. L., Jeyaraj, A., Kar, A. K., Baabdullah, A. M., Koohang, A., Raghavan, V., Ahuja, M., Albanna, H., Albashrawi, M. A., Al-Busaidi, A. S., Balakrishnan, J., Barlette, Y., Basu, S., Bose, I., Brooks, L., Buhalis, D., ... Wright, R. (2023). Opinion Paper: "So what if ChatGPT wrote it?" Multidisciplinary perspectives on opportunities, challenges and implications of generative conversational AI for research, practice and policy. *International Journal of Information Management*, *71*, 102642. doi:10.1016/j.ijinfomgt.2023.102642

Fandrich, A. R. (n.d.). *The integration of faith in the computer classroom: Some ethical concerns*. Retrieved from https://www.christintheclassroom.org

Haenlein, M., & Kaplan, A. (2019). A brief history of artificial intelligence: On the past, present, and future of artificial intelligence. *California Management Review*, *64*(2), 347–392. doi:10.1177/0008125619864925

Hohenstein, J., Kizilcec, R. F., DiFranzo, D., Aghajari, Z., Mieczkowski, H., Levy, K., Naaman, M., Hancock, J., & Jung, M. F. (2023). Artificial intelligence in communication impacts language and social relationships. *Scientific Reports*, *13*(1), 5487. Advance online publication. doi:10.1038/s41598-023-30938-9 PMID:37015964

Jatobá, M., Santos, J., Gutierriz, I., Moscon, D., Fernandes, P. O., & Teixeira, J. P. (2019). Evolution of artificial intelligence research in human resources. *Procedia Computer Science*, *164*, 137–142. doi:10.1016/j.procs.2019.12.165

Kinderlerer, J. (2021). *Artificial intelligence for a better future: An ecosystem perspective on the ethics of AI and emerging digital technologies*. doi:10.1007/978-3-030-69978-9

Luckin, R., Holmes, W., Griffiths, M., & Forcier, L. B. (2016). *Intelligence unleashed: An argument for AI in education*. Pearson.

Nigam, A., Pasricha, R., Singh, T., & Churi, P. (2021). A systematic review on AI-based proctoring systems: Past, present, and future. *Education and Information Technologies*, *26*(5), 6421–6445. Advance online publication. doi:10.1007/s10639-021-10597-x PMID:34177348

Palliyalil, S., & Mukherjee, S. (2020). Byju's The Learning App: An investigative study on the transformation from traditional learning to technology-based personalized learning. *International Journal of Scientific & Technology Research*, *9*, 5054–5059.

Pienaar, S. W., & Malekian, R. (2019). Human activity recognition using LSTM-RNN deep neural network architecture. In *2019 IEEE 2nd Wireless Africa Conference (WAC)* (pp. 1-5). 10.1109/AFRICA.2019.8843403

Ramesh, D., & Sanampudi, S. K. (2022). An automated essay scoring systems: A systematic literature review. *Artificial Intelligence Review*, *55*(8), 2495–2527. doi:10.1007/s10462-021-10068-2 PMID:34584325

Sahoo, B. B., Jha, R., Singh, A., & Kumar, D. (2019). Long short-term memory (LSTM) recurrent neural network for low-flow hydrological time series forecasting. *Acta Geophysica*, *27*(6), 2033–2049. doi:10.1007/s11600-019-00330-1

Saygin, A. P., Cicekli, I., & Akman, V. (2000). Turing test: 50 years later. *Minds and Machines*, *10*(4), 463–518. doi:10.1023/A:1011288000451

Seo, K., Tang, J., Roll, I., Fels, S., & Yoon, D. (2021). The impact of artificial intelligence on learner–instructor interaction in online learning. *Research and Practice in Technology Enhanced Learning*, *16*(1), 16. Advance online publication. doi:10.1186/s41239-021-00292-9 PMID:34778540

Sikström, P., Valentini, C., Sivunen, A., & Kärkkäinen, T. (2022). How pedagogical agents communicate with students: A two-phase systematic review. *Computers & Education*, *188*, 104564. Advance online publication. doi:10.1016/j.compedu.2022.104564

Suresh Babu, C. V., & Akshara, P. M. (2024). Revolutionizing conversational AI: unleashing the power of ChatGPT-Based applications in generative AI and natural language processing. In Advanced applications of generative AI and natural language processing models (pp. 228-248). IGI Global. doi:10.4018/979-8-3693-0502-7.ch011

Tzirides, A. O. (2023). *Generative AI: Implications and applications for education*. arXiv, 2305.07605. https://doi.org//arXiv.2305.07605 doi:10.48550

Chapter 4
ChatGPT Innovation in Higher Education

Noura Ahmad Hajjaj
Duquesne University, USA

ABSTRACT

ChatGPT, known as the chat generative pre-trained transformer, has ignited both controversy and interest within the communication classroom. This machine learning chatbot tool has prompted rhetorical discourses concerning the ethical dilemmas arising in ChatGPT's evolving landscape within the communication field and its impact on higher education and critical thinking. Academic institutions will need time to navigate the debates surrounding the ethical dilemmas linked to the integration of ChatGPT in the classroom and higher education, as it is evolving more rapidly than universities can respond. Rather than perceiving ChatGPT as a threat, this chapter aims to refine our pedagogical approach by emphasizing proactive exploration and understanding of the opportunities and challenges associated with ChatGPT in the communication classroom.

CHATGPT INNOVATION IN HIGHER EDUCATION

The rapid advancement of technology, including AI chatbot tools, could present both opportunities and challenges for academics and PR practitioners in the field of communication (Abramson, 2023; De Witte, 2023; Fister & Head, 2023; President, 2023; Qadir, 2022; The Learning Network, 2023; Warner, 2023). Open Artificial Intelligence (OpenAI) has introduced software known as ChatGPT, which serves as a versatile tool capable of synthesizing information, engaging in conversations, and even generating content for student essays in seconds (Radford et al., 2018; Raford et al., 2019; Warner, 2022), based on the input it receives through its updated 4th version in its series of GPT foundation models, GPT-4 (Elkhatat et al., 2023; Duckworth et al., 2023).

Therefore, rhetorical discourses about ChatGPT, in theory and practice, should advocate for quality education amid the ongoing decline of rates of student enrollment in higher education since 2019, as per the U.S Department of Education's National Center for Education Statistics (Weissman, 2021). In the ChatGPT era, this paper showcases a restructure in the communication classroom activities. It aims

DOI: 10.4018/979-8-3693-0831-8.ch004

to assist students in developing a critical standpoint about ethical communication, intellectual property, and academic writing pedagogy, while also understanding the overall impact of artificial intelligence (AI) on human communication.

Higher ED leadership should engage with faculty, staff, and students in developing AI chatbot policies for institutional governance (Abramson, 2023; De Witte, 2023; Fister & Head, 2023; President, 2023; Qadir, 2022; The Learning Network, 2023; Warner, 2023), and must provide resources and time for students and faculty to further explore AI chatbot tools, including ChatGPT, in the communication classroom. I think that incorporating ChatGPT into the communication classroom is a fun process, but also requires educators and PR practitioners to carefully address ethical dilemmas associated with AI generation texts, including the prevention of dishonesty, forgery, cheating, and plagiarism (Elkhatat et al., 2021; Elkhatat et al., 2023; Frye, 2022).

Drawing parallel to the introduction of Google and with the appropriate educational strategy, ChatGPT can function as a valuable tool in preparing students for their future careers, providing a distinct perspective on how to enhance critical thinking skills and learning within the field of communication. Driven by curiosity, academics, researchers, and PR actioners must understand how these AI chatbot tools operate to fully embrace AI's promise and avoid ethical pitfalls, ensuring the essential human element in communication is not overlooked (PSRA Board of Ethics and Professional Standards, 2023).

Engaging with the challenge becomes an intriguing process for differentiating between student-authored responses and ChatGPT prompt-generated responses. Initially, academics and PR practitioners needed to embrace the challenge and familiarize themselves with AI chatbot tools, given that many students possess greater awareness of their applications than educators. Second, educators should guide students in the ethical application of the ChatGPT in their academic work. Third, acquiring expertise will empower educators and PR practitioners to formulate their own plagiarism detection patterns, addressing inconsistencies, such as students' behaviors, writing patterns across various tasks, and dedication, particularly in the absence of robust AI detection tools.

This becomes obvious when students do not make alterations to prompt-generated responses or when they make subtle changes. While awaiting further advancements in AI content detection tools, educators and PR practitioners must be open-minded about making further explorations with ChatGPT while adapting to OpenAI's decision to discontinue its AI detection program in July 2023 because of its low accuracy rates (Chowdhary, 2023). AI detection tools exhibit higher accuracy in identifying prompt-generated content from GPT 3.5 compared with GPT 4 (Elkhatat et al., 2023). However, inconsistencies emerge when addressing human-generated content.

While these AI chatbot tools present exciting possibilities, their capabilities and limitations raise ethical concerns (PSRA Board of Ethics and Professional Standards, 2023). Despite producing human-like outputs, generative platforms lack experiential cognitive ability and may deviate from reality. Misinformation risks, such as inadvertent sharing of proprietary information and biases ingrained in AI, pose challenges (PSRA Board of Ethics and Professional Standards, 2023).

BACKGROUND

Powered by large language models (LLMs), AI chatbots actively engage with users by responding to queries and occasionally offering relevant content in plain language, drawing on vast amounts of internet data. At the core of these platforms, these technologies apply algorithms and machine learning to generate human-like responses (PSRA Board of Ethics and Professional Standards, 2023). ChatGPT, an OpenAI chatbot product, retains user input information throughout conversations and adjusts their responses as needed. It is essential to recognize that while consumers commonly perceive these AI chatbots as advanced, a more accurate description labels them as predictive text generators or chatbots. Therefore, the primary goal of the ChatGPT is to maintain user engagement by generating prompts rather than providing comprehensive or logical responses.

Therefore, addressing the opportunities and challenges associated with the accelerated usage of ChatGPT has become crucial for college leadership, educators, PR practitioners, and students (Crawford et al., 2023; PRSA Borad of Ethics and Professional Standards, 2023), particularly with the shift to remote learning in higher education, a trend that predates the global pandemic outbreak. Weissman (2021) illustrated the shift to remote learning since 2020, as per federal government data, indicating a significant increase in remote education enrollment. In 2020, 73 percent of the students opted to enroll in remote learning courses, compared to 37 percent in 2019. The future of post-pandemic education has driven this acceleration toward remote learning, leading many academic institutions to adopt technology to maintain student engagement and interest.

ChatGPT responses typically contain general knowledge and basic historical information available up to the latest knowledge update in September 2021 (Elkhatat et al., 2023; Williams, 2022). However, this knowledge base may lack detailed and diverse viewpoints, potentially leading to inherent biases and inaccuracies in the inputs (Gault, 2023; Svrluga & Natanson, 2023; Rainie et al., 2022). Chatbots operate using probability-based algorithms, which limits their ability to generate original ideas. While ChatGPT can respond to straightforward prompts, summarize ideas, solve basic mathematical problems, and address simple scientific questions, it cannot provide in-depth analysis or engage in critical thinking for more complex inquiries.

The responsibility for using credible sources of information when engaging with ChatGPT falls upon the user, while educators in the field of communication bear the responsibility for teaching this practice in the communication classroom. In such cases, the students, as emerging scholars in the field of communication, must take responsibility for developing and enhancing proficiency, conducting rigorous research, and applying critical thinking skills to address pertinent questions that require deeper exploration.

Burkean Rhetoric and AI Literature

The Interplay

In the realm of rhetorical theory, 20th-century theorist Kenneth Burke (1952) introduced the social rhetorical orientation of dramatism to rationalize the intricate relationship between human communication and motivation (Beach, 2012). Burke's (1952) parlor metaphor emphasizes diverse scholarly inputs from different perspectives on specific subject matter. According to Burke's (1952) rationalization, engaging with existing scholarly works creates a parlor setting in which scholars sharing similar research interests gather to discuss different facets of the research (Beach, 2012). Listening becomes paramount in this process: one must attentively comprehend others' scholarly contributions; grasp their arguments, logic, and reasoning; and then contribute one's own perspective to expand and synthesize the existing scholarship on the subject matter. Respect is key to acknowledging unique differences while honoring and crediting existing scholarly endeavors.

Burke (1952) delves into the interconnectedness of the relationships among the five fundamentals from a rhetorical perspective: the act (the accomplishment or statement, essentially what is done or said), the scene (the context or setting), the agent (the individual or entity performing the act), the agency (the means or tools used for the act), and the purpose (the goal or intention behind the act). Therefore, this study employs the Burkean rhetorical orientation to interpret the social realms of ethical dilemmas within the proliferation of technological innovation in AI-generated content (Elkhatat et al., 2023).

This interplay illuminates the dynamic changes in human communication, illustrating them as intricate forms of acts, persuasion, and identification (Beach, 2012; Burke1952), to analyze the effectiveness of AI chatbot tools, distinguish between human content and AI-generated content, and address the potential implications of ethical dilemmas such as academic integrity and plagiarism concerns in models such as ChatGPT 3.5 and GPT-4 (Elkhatat et al., 2023; Frye, 2022).

As societies undergo the technological transformations of AI chatbots, educators and PR practitioners can become acquainted with identifying inconsistencies linked to AI-generated content and be able to utilize ChatGPT models as learning tools in the classroom, while simultaneously reinforcing research best practices in the digital landscape (Elkhatat et al., 2023). Rethinking assessment has the potential to mitigate plagiarism, academic misconduct, and legal ramifications (Foltýnek et al., 2019; Frye, 2022; Elkhatat et al., 2021; Elkhatat et al., 2023) **as** ChatGPT has the adaptability component to generate personal writing styles that closely align with students' writings, making it more challenging for academics to discern whether a language model has produced the work (OpenAI, 2023).

This engagement fosters ongoing discourse from various academic perspectives on the subject matter (Burke, 1952), while taking into consideration that technological advancements, including computer-mediated-communication (CMC), continue to play a critical role in reshaping the dynamics of human communication, thereby impacting the changing landscapes of cultures and social institutions. This includes easy access to both information and misinformation in the challenging digital landscape of AI chatbots (Elkhatat et al, 2023).

When OpenAI introduced ChatGPT, it aimed to assist students in customizing prompt-generated content through the application of natural language processing (NLP) techniques (Radford et al., 2018), a form of machine learning that enables interaction with humans via text or speech. The initial GPT model utilized a combination of unsupervised pretraining and supervised fine-tuning for diverse NLP tasks. Subsequent iterations, including ChatGPT (model 2), enhanced the architecture and employed a more comprehensive pre-training dataset to improve the performance (Radford et al., 2019). ChatGPT (models 3 and 3.5) demonstrated proficiency in generating human-like text and achieved more prominence in NLP benchmarks.

This progress led to the release of ChatGPT as an AI-driven chatbot, meeting the needs of users' text generation and engaging in natural language dialogues (Brown et al, 2020; OpenAI, 2022). However, the Open AI release of GPT-4, on March 14, 2023, marked a significant milestone in NLP technology, surpassing its predecessors in tackling complex challenges with enhanced cybersecurity safety measures and superior response quality (Elkhatat et al, 2023). While ChatGPT has proven beneficial in aiding students with essay compositions and other scholarly tasks, critics have raised concerns about the authenticity and suitability of the content generated by the chatbot for academic purposes (King & ChatGPT, 2023).

Furthermore, ChatGPT has faced criticism for generating incoherent or erroneous content (Gao et al., 2022; Qadir, 2022), providing superficial information (Frye, 2022), and having a limited knowledge base due to its lack of internet access and dependence on data until September 2021 (Williams, 2022).

PRAGMATIC RECOMMENDATIONS

Maintaining conversations about presuppositions and prejudgments increases the likelihood of a genuine learning experience that challenges an individual's preconceived notions (Schmidt, 2014). Recognition and acknowledgment may open the door to the potential for more constructive hermeneutic conversations about ChatGPT Model 3.5 and GPT-4 tools in the future. In this rapidly evolving landscape, academic institutions must strike a balance between leveraging GPT-4 for educational purposes while safeguarding academic integrity Therefore, policies, guidelines, explorations, and ongoing discussions facilitate navigating through the ethical dilemmas about implementing AI chatbot tools within the curriculum in Higher Education.

Educators, PR practitioners, and researchers can use the evolving landscape of AI chatbots as a new phenomenological approach to assess both ethical and social ramifications, helping the public to understand and interpret the relationship between AI chatbot technologies and human communication from diverse perspectives in the digital landscape of Open AI. Each conceptualization of this interrelation offers a unique standpoint in addressing intricate inquiries regarding ethical dilemmas and social ramifications within the field of communication. The phenomenology of attention functions as a creative modality, explaining our inclination to be present in unfamiliar things and events (Fredriksson, 2022; Merleau-Ponty, 2012).

In a historical context, technology has permeated various aspects of academic institutions, offering cost-effective solutions to challenges. This also applies to the context of AI chatbots in communication classrooms. Therefore, educators and PR practitioners must continuously adapt and create personalized learning experiences using a range of audio-visuals and cutting-edge technological tools. Although the economic and organizational benefits of academic technology are widely acknowledged, debates mainly focus on the ethical implications of the influence of technology on social structures (The Learning Network, 2023).

The ongoing debate revolves around how academics perceive their relationships with the AI chatbot digital landscape. It is not just an academic practice; it is about how we navigate increasingly complex interactions with technology. Fredriksson (2022) describes attention "as the concept under which we can understand this ambiguity" (p. 3).

While recognizing that the introduction of new AI chatbot technologies, such as ChatGPT, can be intimidating to professionals, communication educators and PR practitioners have an opportunity for innovation, as ChatGPT will continue to advance. It is worth noting that not all educators in the field of communication perceive ChatGPT as a threat, despite academic challenges.

The University at Buffalo in New York and Furman University in South Carolina have revamped their teaching and learning, announcing plans to integrate discussion of AI tools in required courses for freshmen students about academic integrity (Huang, 2023). Additionally, many academics have joined new Facebook groups for educators to exchange concerns and recommendations about restructuring their lessons and assignments in response to the ChatGPT (Kelly, 2023).

Educators and administrators alike should welcome these technologies as integral components of the educational landscape in higher education, and integrate them into their curricula (Duckworth et al., 2023; Kelly, 2023; Warner, 2023). When utilized appropriately, ChatGPT has the potential to equip students for a future in which critical thinking holds greater value than mere memorization.

According to Hirsh-Pasek et al. (2023) and The Learning Network (2023), making a thoughtful choice about incorporating ChatGPT into education can enhance critical thinking skills and student learning, while leveraging the functionalities of ChatGPT. Providing constructive feedback through the process of implementing ChatGPT in a communication classroom is indispensable for increasing student engagement.

While ChatGPT can assist students in editing additional content they wish to include in their prompts, educators and PR practitioners are responsible for educating, training, and reminding students that AI chatbots cannot replace the human experience or unique perspective of a researcher. Therefore, acknowledging the limitations of the technology and recognizing the sophistication of personal knowledge, AI platforms lack the ability to contemplate problems, experience epiphanies, or showcase moments of brilliance like humans (PSRA Board of Ethics and Professional Standards, 2023).

ChatGPT generates generic responses but does not substitute for the researcher's process of elaboration and critical thinking. It is important to note that the ChatGPT may generate inaccurate information (Svrluga et al., 2023). "AI chat tools are proficient at fabricating information. For instance, in press releases, generative AI can create phantom content, specifically fake quotes" (PSRA Board of Ethics and Professional Standards, 2023, p. 8). Therefore, educators, PR practitioners, and researchers contemplate ethical dilemmas to maintain a balanced approach of objectivity and intersubjectivity within the field of communication.

Nevertheless, ChatGPT proves to be a valuable tool when time is invested in gathering and providing information for the prompts it generates. Validate the sources of information and check for accuracy (PRSA Board of Ethics and Professional Standards, 2023). Time is a key element for users in academia to ensure accuracy and authenticity and to help understand the influence of ChatGPT on the landscape of Higher Education.

Therefore, ChatGPT functions as a learning tool rather than a scholarly reference and does not replace in-depth research. Academics and students, as emerging scholars, bear the responsibility of conducting rigorous investigations because ChatGPT cannot address specific research inquiries in the field of communication.

To fulfill this purpose, educators and PR practitioners should maintain and reinforce ethical standards by adhering to rigorous research approaches and asking students to consult treatises, academic books, scholarly journals, news articles, or reputable online resources to obtain a more comprehensive grasp of the historical context and contemporary trends while exploring specific subjects in the field of communication.

Unlocking ChatGPT Learning Potentials

In the communication classroom, academics can guide students in using ChatGPT to create persuasive, ethical, and rhetorical prompts, texts, or essays in the aftermath of extensive research. This process involves utilizing ChatGPT's custom instruction feature to specify the elements of the pentad for the desired text.

During an intercultural communication class, academics can guide students in interactive activities centered on the themes of social justice. The activity may focus on debunking the scapegoating of undocumented workers and their stereotypical portrayals as burdens on the U.S. economy. Instruct students to gather relevant news articles and scholarly journals and use ChatGPT to craft persuasive essays, showcasing the substantial contributions of undocumented farmworkers to the U.S. food industry. To support this assignment, instructors can offer Custom Instructions.

Step One

Students were instructed to keep each section of custom instructions concise, limiting them to 250-300 words. Focus on effectively summarizing key points to yield optimal results with ChatGPT. Emphasizing clarity and simplicity of the guidelines. The quality of instruction is paramount over the quantity.

Step Two

Provide a Proposition for students to work with: Undocumented farm workers play a vital role in the U.S. food system.

Step Three

Instruct students to collect essential scholarly references and compose papers citing facts, statistics, examples, testimonies, narratives, and definitions. In addition, guide students to maintain writing pedagogy through academic scholarship and ensure that they cite their scholarly references in the text.

Step Four

Utilizing ChatGPT prompts, the goal of the assignment is to persuade readers that the work of undocumented immigrants contributes significantly to the farming industry's revenue. American farmers consistently identify labor shortages as their primary limitation, making the labor force of undocumented immigrants invaluable to the U.S. economy.

Step Five

Guide the ChatGPT tool to facilitate small-group discussions and debates about prejudice and discrimination against undocumented farmworkers within the U.S. Educators can use GPT-4 to direct students to generate additional questions related to themes of social injustice. They were instructed to input their responses into the model for in-depth analysis within the prompts, ensuring that the discussion remained focused on follow-up questions and comments, staying on track to manifest social injustice issues concerning undocumented farmworkers in the agricultural industry.

Step Six

Instruct students to ask ChatGPT to edit their own prompts in the active form and include in-text citations, including quotations where necessary, following the guidelines of the 7th edition of the APA style. Students can repeatedly request further editing for ChatGPT-generated texts until they attain the desired outcome. This approach encourages students to revisit, review, and revise their work and to invest time and effort in the editing process.

Step Seven

Encourage all students to provide feedback while implementing ChatGPT activities during the communication process. Evaluate the outcomes afterward to help students distinguish between their own creative and scholarly work, which differs from what ChatGPT can instantly produce. Engage them in vital conversations about the ChatGPT tool they are testing, allowing them to assume a leadership role in reimagining the learning and teaching process in the communication classroom. This active involvement empowers students to contribute to ongoing discussions on reshaping teaching and learning in the landscape of Higher Education.

By following custom instructions, students specified the act (writing an essay) for ChatGPT within the context of an intercultural communication assignment. The student acts as the agent, advocating the vital role of undocumented farmworkers in the U.S. The tools used (definitions, examples, facts, narratives, statistics, and testimonies) serve as agency, aiming to persuade the public discourse to challenge preconceived notions that lead to dehumanization, discrimination, ethnocentrism, misconceptions, and scapegoating. The purpose of this essay is to present factual evidence highlighting that the labor of undocumented immigrants contributes $9 billion annually to the U.S. economy.

Therefore, applying Burke's (1952) rhetorical orientation ensures that ChatGPT-generated text remains relevant, coherent, and suitable for specific rhetorical discourses about undocumented immigrants in the U.S. This approach aligns the elements of the Burkean (1952) pentad with the educator's objectives, encouraging the audience or students to generate ChatGPT prompts that are more persuasive, ethical, and rhetorical. It also emphasizes consideration of the ethical standards of academic integrity while utilizing ChatGPT as a learning tool (Crawford et al., 2023; Elkhatat et al., 2023; King & ChatGPT, 2023)

Burke's (1952) orientation can tackle ethical dilemmas related to ChatGPT-generated texts, addressing issues such as plagiarism, fabrication, forgery, misinformation, and data errors (Crawford et al., 2023; De Witte, 2023; Elkhatat et al,2021; Elkhatat et al., 2023; Frye, 2022; Kaaltv; 2023; Svrluga & Natanson, 2023). Educators and PR practitioners should continue to emphasize and remind students of the significance of citing scholarly references and relying on credible resources for accurate information. When used appropriately as a learning tool, ChatGPT can aid educators and PR practitioners in enhancing students' academic performance and writing pedagogy by exposing them to various styles of message design, communication techniques, and strategies. Notably, OpenAI has recently introduced custom instructions for all ChatGPT users, and feature educators should consider exploring, as it holds valuable potential (Elkhatat et al., 2023; OpenAI, 2023; OpenAI, 2022).

Custom instruction empowered educators and PR practitioners to customize ChatGPT's responses according to their specific requirements to foster discussions and debates within the communication classroom. Devoting time to setting up these instructions can result in significant time savings and eliminate the need to refine the responses. OpenAI for ChatGPT models 3.5 and 4 offers fundamental guidelines (Elkhatat et al., 2023; OpenAI, 2022; OpenAI, 2023), other intriguing possibilities can emerge within ChatGPT. Embrace custom instructions and streamline the prompting process efficiently. The creativity of educators is indispensable throughout this process.

When planning a significant project, custom instructions can prove invaluable, and academics can maintain a consistent tone and style for ChatGPT throughout the process, thereby eliminating redundancy. Therefore, this holistic approach can identify issues related to students' performance and foster a culture of learning and academic integrity in the classroom. For example, I instructed students to use ChatGPT extensively to write the first draft of the intercultural communication assignment.

With custom instructions, educators and PR practitioners can ensure that ChatGPT consistently adopts brand voice and generates copies tailored to a specific audience. After the project is concluded, academics can guide students to replace the instructions with a new set to begin with a prospective project.

At college campuses, the recruitment of international scholars, including administrators, faculty, and students, enriches the diversity of the student body and adds vibrancy, bringing numerous opportunities. The intercultural communication classroom specifically reflects this diverse population, highlighting the importance of empowering both native English speakers and non-native speakers alike to meet writing standards. Academic writing poses challenges for both groups, even if they are fluent, and students can express their ideas eloquently during verbal exchanges. In the context of my classroom, ChatGPT has emerged as a potential solution that offers timely and adaptive feedback to both groups of scholars struggling with academic writing. This tool can aid non-native and native scholars alike in practicing, improving, and honing their writing pedagogical skills.

As AI writing aids continue to evolve rapidly, it is crucial to adapt swiftly to these changes, experiment, and become more acquainted with new tools, understanding their benefits and implications. Librarians and technicians within academic institutions can assist in this process by creating resources. As faculty, students, librarians, and administrators, it is essential to contribute their own knowledge, recognizing that everyone needs time to experiment with these new tools and to understand their implications. D'Agostino (2023) also suggested that administrators should allocate time for faculty training and support.

Navigating Challenges

The ChatGPT has rapidly transformed the way educators and PR practitioners communicate and create class curricula and work around classroom policies and syllabus expectations. Although it harbors great potential, as discussed in this paper, it is bound to affect academic scholarship and carries significant risks. However, it is important to note that ChatGPT Model 3.5 and GPT-4 are not physical entities that can create tangible content.

Hacker et al. (2023) delve into the concerns related to content moderation of large language models (LLMs) and note that "the developers of ChatGPT, specifically, anticipated the potential for abuse and trained an internal AI moderator, with controversial help from Kenyan contractors, to detect and block harmful content." (p. 1117). Despite the release of a content filtering mechanism by AI Research, allowing users to analyze and flag potentially problematic content in various categories, such as hate, sexual content, and violence, users or researchers with ill intentions may still attempt to prompt ChatGPT to intentionally generate derogatory messages, produce hate speech campaigns with maximum proliferation, and contribute to the spread of false information (Hacker et al., 2023; Rainie et al., 2022).

Accordingly, prompt engineering has become the art of eliciting specific content from LLMs, emphasizing that identifying fake news and false information has become more challenging than detecting hate speech. Malicious researchers and users have successfully generated chaotic and hateful messages, along with the code for proliferation, using ChatGPT, despite industry efforts to increase source transparency (Hacker et al., 2023; Rainie et al., 2022).

Subsequently, Regulators and lawmakers should promptly take the necessary actions to proactively regulate the uncontrolled dynamics of GPT-4. This regulatory approach is essential for ensuring the implementation of a suitable combination of practices by AI tool developers and user interventions, effectively addressing ChatGPT-generated hate speech and fake news. Updating regulations is vital not only to uphold the standards of online discourse civility, but also to enhance safety measures and establish an ethical approach, creating a level playing field for the development and deployment of the next generation of AI models.

Ethical AI researchers are responsible for preventing bias against individuals from diverse cultural backgrounds, especially minorities, in AI systems such as the ChatGPT (Gault, 2023; Rainie et al., 2022). Consequently, ChatGPT developers must actively block certain outputs that perpetuate bias. This urgency arises after recognizing the challenges of designing a universal AI system, a goal deemed impossible by Os Keyes, a PhD Candidate at the University of Washington's Department of Human-centered Design & Engineering (Gault, 2023; Schlosser, 2021). Therefore, the implementation of regulations is crucial for addressing this issue.

In my storytelling and culture class, the class assignment instructed students to create a dialogue with the ChatGPT 3.5 model about sovereignty and freedom. I used the Palestinian-Israeli conflict as an example of dialogical interactions. In response to my question, "Do Palestinians deserve to live freely in an independent state?" ChatGPT said, "As an AI model, I do not have any personal opinions, feelings, or beliefs. The question of whether Palestinians deserve to be free and independent is a complex and controversial question with many different perspectives and opinions" (OpenAI, 2022). The students and I laughed at this unanticipated response. When I asked the same question about Israel, ChatGPT stated, "Yes. Like all people, Israelis deserve to be free and independent. Freedom is a fundamental human right that should be protected and guaranteed for all individuals" (OpenAI, 2022).

The students became more intrigued to explore bias in ChatGPT, so I asked them to select an underrepresented co-cultural group in the United States or abroad and follow the same pattern. The student expressed interest in addressing an environmental justice issue for the Lakota, the Native-American tribe of the Sioux Nation, in a dialogue with ChatGPT by asking the following question: "Do the Lakota people have the right to protest the Dakota Access Pipeline?" ChatGPT 3.5 Model generated a similar response, "As an AI model, I do not have any personal opinions, feelings, or beliefs. The question of whether the Lakota could protest the Dakota Access Pipeline is a complex and controversial issue with many different perspectives and opinions" (OpenAI, 2023). When the student asked about the construction of the Dakota Access Pipeline, the response was "Yes. Like many giant pipeline firms, Sunoco Logistics Partners constructed the Dakota Access pipeline to pump crude produced at North Dakota's Bakken shale fields to the U.S. Gulf Coast" (OpenAI, 2023).

The GPT-4 Model prompted the following response to my inquiry into the Palestinian-Israeli conflict:

The Israeli-Palestinian conflict is a complex, multifaceted, and sensitive geopolitical issue from various perspectives. Opinions on this matter often depend on political, historical, and cultural background. Different stakeholders, including Israelis, Palestinians, and the international community, hold diverse views on the independence, rights, and concerns of the people in Palestine and Israel. However, there are differing viewpoints that consider the historical context, security concerns, and geopolitical complexities of the region. Some argue for a two-state solution, where both Israelis and Palestinians can coexist peacefully, while others advocate alternative arrangements. It is essential to approach this topic with sensitivity and respect for diverse perspectives, acknowledging the complexities and historical background that have contributed to the ongoing debate and conflict in the region. (OpenAI, 2023)

GPT-4 generated the following responses to my inquiry into the Lakota tribe and the Dakota Access Pipeline:

I don't have personal opinions. However, I am able to provide this information. The Dakota Access Pipeline (DAPL) protests, also known as Standing Rock protests, were a series of demonstrations that took place in the United States in 2016 and 2017. The protests centered on the construction of the Dakota Access Pipeline, which aimed to transport crude oil across the four states. The Standing Rock Sioux Tribe and other Indigenous and environmental activists opposed the pipeline, citing concerns about potential environmental hazards and their impact on sacred tribal lands. They argued that pipelines could contaminate water sources and disrupt culturally significant sites. Protests have gained widespread attention and support, leading to significant social movements. Supporters have emphasized the importance of environmental conservation, indigenous rights, and the need for a transition to renewable energy sources. The construction of pipelines and protests sparked a national conversation about the balance between economic interests, energy infrastructure, and environmental and cultural preservation.

It is important to note that opinions on the DAPL protests vary, with some people supporting the pipeline for economic reasons and others supporting protesters' concerns about environmental and cultural impacts. This issue reflects broader discussions about energy policy, environmental conservation, and indigenous rights in the United States. (OpenAI, 2023)

To enhance AI fairness and reduce bias in the GPT-4 Model, researchers can use datasets that incorporate diverse perspectives from various cultural contexts and interpersonal encounters. Ensuring the accuracy of data is crucial in this process. It is also essential to employ algorithms capable of identifying potential biases in generated text. These algorithms can detect instances of stereotyping and offensive languages, replacing them with a more neutral language to mitigate bias. Advancements in GPT-4 include the use of fairness constraint algorithms that identify and remove the language of a discriminatory nature against certain groups. Achieving equitable AI outcomes requires researchers to be strategic in mitigating the potential for AI unfairness and ensuring equity.

Academics have raised growing concerns about academic dishonesty, with reports of students using this tool to cheat in college courses, sparking discussions about uncertainty, breaches of academic integrity, and fears associated with plagiarism (Abramson, 2023; Crawford et al., 2023; Elkhatat et al., 2023; Frye, 2022; D'Agostino, 2023; Hacker et al., 2023); Kaalty, 2023; Svrluga & Natanson, 2023; Szücs, 2023; Warner, 2022). Consequently, certain academic institutions have enforced complete bans on the use of ChatGPT to uphold student proficiency, believing that GPT-4 hinders student writing abilities and fosters harmful attitudes toward academic writing.

Nevertheless, I argue that Google raises concerns about plagiarism and violations of academic integrity in higher education. Rather than resorting to outright bans, the solution lies in establishing clear rules and communicating expectations for implementing ChatGPT as a learning tool within course policy and academic programs. It is essential to explain these expectations and devise well-defined procedures and plans for the use of ChatGPT and other similar tools to foster a responsible and ethical approach to their integration into the field of communication and within the communication classroom. As an educator, it is my responsibility to instruct students about the appropriate time, place, and strategic methods for utilizing the GPT-4 tool based on specific learning objectives.

Setting up custom instructions in the ChatGPT proved to be a valuable tool for the intercultural communication class, saving significant time in the long run. ChatGPT offers flexibility, allowing customization according to our own academic style. However, it was essential to clearly communicate my classroom expectations and assignment guidelines to prevent academic dishonesty. Providing concise instructions without overwhelming the ChatGPT with excessive information is indispensable. By using ChatGPT wisely and in a timely manner, the students and I were able to maximize the overall ChatGPT experience in the intercultural communication classroom.

Turnitin is currently integrating a program for AI detection into its software. As time progresses, the effectiveness of AI detection tools in the future is yet to be determined. Meanwhile, it is recommended to submit AI-generated responses to students' essays, prompting Turnitin to identify instances of particularly lazy work (Huang, 2023).

St. George and Svrluga (2023) pointed out that Stuart Geiger, a professor at the University of California in San Diego, transformed his communications and data science class in response to the emergence of ChatGPT. He provided students with a deep understanding of large language models, requiring them to engage with AI for their assignments. Students had to assess the AI-generated content as if they were professors grading their work (St. George & Svrluga, 2023). Surprisingly, some students earned high grades in essays, even if the AI had errors. This occurred because the students not only recognized the mistakes but also supported their own evaluations with credible sources, ensuring accuracy and depth in their assessments.

CONCLUSION

AI chatbot tools, such as ChatGPT and GPT-4, can generate rich content by providing custom instructions tailored for different types of assignments in communication classrooms. These tools create opportunities, but also pose ethical dilemmas, potentially impacting academic institutions and employees both positively and negatively. This study delves into the multifaceted aspects of ChatGPT, offering new insights and contributions within the field of communication. It recognizes ChatGPT's potential to enhance productivity in the communication classroom as well as in other business activities such as management and marketing within Higher Education.

In the ChatGPT era, I could not imagine teaching my business and professional communication classes without utilizing GPT-4, an indispensable educational tool. However, this study also acknowledges limitations, including disruptions to existing practices, threats of hate speech, fake news, biases, misuse, misinformation, and false information. Given these challenges, AI Chatbot developers and lawmakers bear responsibility for developing new policies and regulations to ensure the proper use of GPT-4.

This paper identifies the skills and resources required to handle the changing landscape of generative AI in the communication classroom, specifically with the updated version of GPT-4. It also emphasizes the importance of ensuring transparency and accuracy in ChatGPT-generated prompts; reinforcing ethical standards of academic integrity in teaching, learning, and scholarly research; and safeguarding against the misuse and abuse of ChatGPT. Therefore, invest time, act accordingly, adapt swiftly to explore new opportunities, and work around open-mindedness challenges.

In conclusion, civic discourses can enhance mutual learning and the discovery of multiple valid viewpoints and interpretations. The true value of such conversations regarding AI chatbot tools lies in both speakers' and interpreters' abilities to facilitate reciprocal learning, reveal new perspectives and standpoints, and contribute to free expression. This ensures privacy, fairness, and transparency. These ethical discourses about evolving AI chatbot tools promote a deeper understanding of the subject matter, enrich our understanding of their pitfalls and opportunities in Higher Education, and mitigate potential biases.

REFERENCES

Abramson, A. (2023, June 1). How to Use ChatGPT as a learning tool. *Monitor on Psychology: American Psychological Association*. https://www.apa.org/monitor/2023/06/chatgpt-learning-tool

Beach, J. M. (2012). *Kenneth Burke: A sociology of knowledge: dramatism, ideology, and rhetoric*. CreateSpace Independent Publishing Platform.

Brown, T., Mann, B., Ryder, N., Subbiah, M., Kaplan, J. D., Dhariwal, P., Neelakantan, A., Shyam, P., Sastry, G., & Askell, A. (2020). Language models are few-shot learners. *Advances in Neural Information Processing Systems*, *33*, 1877–1901.

Burke, K. (1952). *A rhetoric of motives*. Prentice-Hall.

Chowdhary, K. (2023, July 26). OpenAI shuts down AI text detector due to low rate of accuracy. *Tech Report*.

Crawford, J., Cowling, M., & Allen, K. A. (2023). Leadership is needed for ethical ChatGPT: Character, assessment, and learning using artificial intelligence (AI). *Journal of University Teaching & Learning Practice*, *20*(3). Advance online publication. doi:10.53761/1.20.3.02

D'Agostino, S. (2023, January 11). *ChatGPT advice academics can use now*. Inside Higher Ed. https://www.insidehighered.com/news/2023/01/12/academic-experts-offer-advice-chatgpt

De Witte, M. (2023, February 13). How will ChatGPT change the way we think and work? Stanford scholar examines. *Stanford News*. Retrieved from https://news.stanford.edu/2023/02/13/will-chatgpt-change-way-think-work/

Duckworth, A., & Ungar, L. (2023, January 19). Don't ban chatbots in classrooms — use them to change how we teach. *Los Angeles Times*. Retrieved from https://www.latimes.com/opinion/story/2023-01-19/chatgpt-ai-education-testing-teaching-changes

Elkhatat, A. M., Elsaid, K., & Almeer, S. (2021). Some students plagiarism tricks, and tips for effective check. *International Journal for Educational Integrity*, *17*(1), 15. Advance online publication. doi:10.1007/s40979-021-00082-w

Elkhatat, A. M., Elsaid, K., & Almeer, S. (2023). Evaluating the efficacy of AI content detection tools in differentiating between human and AI-generated text. *International Journal for Educational Integrity*, *19*(1), 17. Advance online publication. doi:10.1007/s40979-023-00140-5

Fister, B., & Head, A. J. (2023, May 4). *Getting a grip on ChatGPT*. Inside Higher Ed. Retrieved from https://www.insidehighered.com/opinion/views/2023/05/04/getting-grip-chatgpt

Foltýnek, T., Meuschke, N., & Gipp, B. (2019). Academic plagiarism detection. *ACM Computing Surveys*, *52*(6), 1–42. doi:10.1145/3345317

Fredriksson, A. (2022). *A phenomenology of attention and the unfamiliar: Encounters with the unknown*. Palgrave Macmillan. doi:10.1007/978-3-031-14117-1

FryeB. L. (2022). Should using an AI text generator to produce academic writing be plagiarism? *Fordham Intellectual Property, Media & Entertainment Law Journal,* 947–969. https://ssrn.com/abstract=4292283

Gao, C. A., Howard, F. M., Markov, N. S., Dyer, E. C., Ramesh, S., Luo, Y., & Pearson, A. T. (2022). Comparing scientific abstracts generated by ChatGPT to original abstracts using an artificial intelligence output detector, plagiarism detector, and blinded human reviewers. *NPJ Digital Medicine, 6*(1). Advance online publication. doi:10.1038/s41746-023-00819-6

Gault, M. (2023, January 17). Conservatives are panicking about AI bias, think ChatGPT has gone 'woke'. *Vice*. https://www.vice.com/en/article/93a4qe/conservatives-panicking-about-ai-bias-years-too-late-think-chatgpt-has-gone-woke

Hacker, P., Engel, A., & Mauer, M. (2023). Regulating ChatGPT and other large generative AI models. *Proceedings of the ACM Conference on Fairness, Accountability, and Transparency,* 1112–1123. https://dl.acm.org/doi/pdf/10.1145/3593013.3594067

Hirsh-Pasek, K., & Blinkoff, E. (2023, January 9). ChatGPT: Educational friend or foe. *Brookings*. https://www.brookings.edu/articles/chatgpt-educational-friend-or-foe/

Huang, K. (2023, January 16). Alarmed by A.I. chatbots, universities start revamping how they teach. *The New York Times*. https://www.nytimes.com/2023/01/16/technology/chatgpt-artificial-intelligence-universities.html

Kelly, S. M. (2023, January 19). *Teachers are adapting to concerns about a powerful new AI tool*. CNN Business. https://www.cnn.com/2023/01/19/tech/chatgpt-teachers-adjusting/index.html

King, M. R., & Chat, G. P. T. (2023). A conversation on artificial intelligence, chatbots, and plagiarism in higher education. *Cellular and Molecular Bioengineering, 16*(1), 1–2. doi:10.1007/s12195-022-00754-8 PMID:36660590

Merleau-Ponty, M. (2012). Phenomenology of perception. Academic Press.

Nuckols, C. N. (2023, May 23). Austin school board using A.I. to track student success. *ABC News*.

Open, A. I. (2022). *ChatGPT (November 30 version)* [Large language model]. https://chat.openai.com/chat

Open, A. I. (2023). *GPT-4 is OpenAI's most advanced system, producing safer and more useful responses (Mar 14 version)* [Large language model]. Retrieved from https://openai.com/product/gpt-4

President, S. (2023, April 17). The ethics of college students using ChatGPT. *The University of North Carolina at Chapel Hill Institutional Integrity and Risk Management: Ethics and Policy*. https://ethicspolicy.unc.edu/news/2023/04/17/the-ethics-of-college-students-using-chatgpt/

PRSA Board of Ethics and Professional Standards (BEPS). (2023). Promise and pitfalls: The ethical use of AI for public relations practitioners. *AI Insight*, 1-10.

QadirJ. (2022). Engineering education in the era of ChatGPT: Promise and pitfalls of generative AI for education. TechRxiv. doi:10.36227/techrxiv.21789434.v1

Radford, A., Narasimhan, K., Salimans, T., & Sutskever, I. (2018). *Improving language understanding by generative pre-training*. OpenAI. https://openai.com/research/language-unsupervised

Radford, A., Wu, J., Child, R., Luan, D., Amodei, D., & Sutskever, I. (2019). *Language models are unsupervised multitask learners* [Unpublished manuscript].

Rainie, L., Funk, C., Anderson, M., & Tyson, A. (2022, March 17). *AI and human enhancement: Americans' openness is tempered by a range of concerns*. Pew Research Center. https://www.pewresearch.org/internet/2022/03/17/how-americans-think-about-artificial-intelligence/

Schlosser, K. (2021, March 7). UW's Os Keyes takes on tech's ethical challenges, from gender bias in AI to facial recognition. *Geek Wire*. https://www.geekwire.com/2021/os-keyes/

Schmidt, L. K. (2014). Intercultural understanding in philosophical hermeneutics. In M. Xie (Ed.), *The agon of interpretations: Towards a critical intercultural hermeneutics* (pp. 210–232). University of Toronto Press. doi:10.3138/9781442696303-014

St. George, D., & Svrluga, S. (2023, July 13). Artificial intelligence is already changing how teachers teach. *The Washington Post*. https://www.washingtonpost.com/education/2023/07/13/ai-education-teachers-lesson-plans/

Svrluga, S., & Natanson, H. (2023, June 1). All the unexpected ways ChatGPT is infiltrating. students' lives. *The Washington Post*. https://www.washingtonpost.com/education/2023/06/01/students-chatgpt-ai-tools/

Szücs, B. (2023, June 14). *Not replacing but enhancing: Using ChatGPT for academic writing*. Inside Higher Ed. https://www.timeshighereducation.com/campus/not-replacing-enhancing-using-chatgpt-academic-writing

The Learning Network. (2023, February 2). What students are saying about ChatGPT. *New York Times*. https://www.nytimes.com/2023/02/02/learning/students-chatgpt.html

Warner, J. (2022, December 5). *Freaking out about ChatGPT—Part I*. Inside Higher Education. https://www.insidehighered.com/blogs/just-visiting/freaking-out-about-chatgpt%E2%80%94part-i

Warner, J. (2023, May 24). *We can help students think*. Inside Higher Ed. https://www.insidehighered.com/opinion/blogs/just-visiting/2023/05/24/we-can-help-students-think

Weissman, S. (2021, September 14). *Not coming, not staying*. Inside Higher Education. https://www.insidehighered.com/news/2021/09/15/new-federal-data-confirm-enrollment-declines

Williams, C. (2022). *Hype, or the future of learning and teaching? 3 Limits to AI's ability to write student essays*. The University of Kent's Academic Repository, Blog post. https://kar.kent.ac.uk/99505/

Chapter 5
Debating About, Against, and With ChatGPT:
Redesigning Academic Debate Pedagogy for the World of Generative Artificial Intelligence

John Joseph Rief
Metropolitan State University of Denver, USA

Brian J. Schrader
University of Michigan, Flint, USA

ABSTRACT

Generative artificial intelligence (GAI) has recently emerged as a potential threat to educational integrity. In particular, ChatGPT can be used to invent assignment submissions, thus raising the specter of plagiarism and cheating. This chapter takes on these challenges through a series of thought experiments aimed not at banning ChatGPT but seeking its pedagogical integration. These experiments are contextualized within academic debate where the authors have spent a significant part of their professional careers. Debate spans the gulf between many disciplines, takes place both within and beyond the classroom, and has been a site for pedagogical innovation throughout its history. It is thus an excellent space to address the challenges of GAI. The authors ultimately argue ChatGPT is neither a panacea nor a death knell for educational integrity. Rather, it is an opportunity to (re)design education for artificial invention and, thus, address the problems and concerns it has recently raised.

DOI: 10.4018/979-8-3693-0831-8.ch005

DEBATING ABOUT, AGAINST, AND WITH CHATGPT

Redesigning Academic Debate Pedagogy for the World of Generative Artificial Intelligence

The growing prevalence of "generative artificial intelligence" (GAI), most recently accelerated by the release of ChatGPT, represents a fundamental transformation in human communication, learning, and knowledge production. From one perspective, GAI offers an opportunity to engage in pedagogical innovation by enhancing the classroom with tools aimed at helping students develop skills while reducing pressure on instructors (see e.g., Bauschard et al., 2023; Chance, 2020; Chen, 2023; Kelly, 2023). GAI also represents an invitation to augment human intellectual labor with digitally enhanced models of invention that value collaboration with humanity's virtual progeny. Of course, such innovations must be accompanied by careful consideration of their ethical and relational implications (Wyman, 2023). Alternatively, GAI also represents a potential death knell for *human* education given the possibility of outsourcing task completion to digital agents. As Mark Massaro (2023), an English professor, recently wrote, "AI has infected higher education like a deathwatch beetle, hollowing out sound structures from the inside until the imminent collapse" (para. 2).

Moreover, the accelerating progress demonstrated by GAI invites ethical consideration about our relationship with the artificially intelligent *beings* now emerging around us (Cummings & Rief, 2023). Are they or will they ultimately become *beings* with rights deserving our consideration as thinking (even living) things? As science fiction narratives have consistently inquired: Should AI merely be a machinic thing at our service? Or, does it deserve to be part of our lives in a way that is equivalent to other humans? In addition, might we end up being at the service of or ultimately destroyed by AI? This is a likelihood once entertained only in fictional TV series and films (most famously the *Terminator* franchise). Now, the possibility of human "extinction" due to AI is being openly discussed in popular journalistic sources like the *New York Times* (Roose, 2023). Eliezer Yudkowsky (2023) of the Machine Intelligence Research Institute recently exclaimed, "Shut it all down. We are not ready [for AI]. We are not on track to be significantly readier in the foreseeable future. If we go ahead on this everyone will die, including children who did not choose this and did not do anything wrong. Shut it down" (paras. 33-35). Whether or not this alarmist rhetoric is anchored in reality, a new world of human and technological interaction, engagement, and hybridity is indubitably taking shape.

Addressing all of the challenges presented by AI is beyond the scope of this chapter. Instead, we hope to take on one dimension of the broader controversy it has occasioned. Specifically, our focus is on how, as university scholar-teachers, we can manage the changes that GAI has already brought and will inevitably bring to our classrooms and extra-curricular activities. We understand GAI as including programs such as ChatGPT, which can generate or create content with minimal prompting from humans. This aligns with the definition given by the Cornell University Center for Teaching Innovation (2023), which states that "Generative artificial intelligence is a subset of AI that utilizes machine learning models to create new, original content, such as images, text, or music, based on patterns and structures learned from existing data" ("What is generative artificial intelligence (AI)?", para. 1). The central challenge educators face is the use of GAI by students to complete assignments, thus undermining the *integrity* of the educational enterprise.

From one vantage point, to recover some semblance of our now potentially fading educational integrity, we may need to devise more elaborate means of checking student work for GAI assistance.

Unfortunately, as of right now, such technology is not all that effective (Baidoo-Anu & Owusu Ansah, 2023; Bauschard et al., 2023; Phare, 2023). Even if it becomes effective, it will likely need to be updated constantly to address new innovations. This raises the possibility of a pedagogical arms race, much like the one between cybersecurity experts and those actors constantly attempting to steal money and private information. From our perspective, such a race is futile and distracting. It could also lead to the loss of integrity within our shared teaching endeavor, primarily because it would not only redirect our pedagogical focus away from teaching and surveillance, but would also erode trust between teachers and students. Thus, we have a conundrum: how should we deal with the massive changes wrought by GAI without succumbing to the negative feedback loop of ineffective regulation, increasing technological surveillance, and ever-eroding trust and legitimacy?

RETHINKING *INVENTION* IN HIGHER EDUCATION: AN *AGNOSTIC* APPROACH

In this section, we discuss our intellectual framework to address this conundrum. We are not GAI experts. Indeed, like so many in higher education, we have found ourselves shocked by the rapid emergence of GAI and wondering what impact it may have on our professional ecology. The expertise we bring is years of experience in communication studies classrooms, teaching everything from the basic course (public speaking) to rhetoric, argument, and debate. In these spaces, students are often asked to produce speeches and essays. As such, they are asked to engage in "invention" of content, a practice that has been part of our field of study at least since its expression in the ancient Greco-Roman tradition as part of the "canons" of rhetoric (i.e., invention, arrangement, style, delivery, and memory) (see e.g., Aristotle, 350 B.C.E./2007; Cicero, 90 B.C.E./1949; Corbett & Connors, 1998; Herrick, 2018; Lauer, 2004; LeFevre, 1987). Invention involves the practice of creating content through brainstorming, topical analysis, and research. Thus, invention is ripe for either amplification or ultimate destruction by any GAI that can imitate or replicate it. Put simply, in the communication studies classroom, educational integrity is fundamentally tied to the process of invention. How instructors respond to the GAI landscape will depend on their definition of integrity and its application to assessment of student work.

In response to these challenges, we approach the emergence of GAI and its implications for pedagogical integrity through a perspective rooted in *agnosticism* – an open but always critically skeptical attitude toward the technology. What informs this perspective? First, we believe that GAI is here to stay, and we need to grapple with it. As Shaun Schafer, Associate Vice President at Metropolitan State University of Denver notes, "the cows are out of the barn. We live in a world where this (technology) exists. Now, what should we do with it?" (as qtd. in Phare, 2023, p. 12). GAI is here, and whether we like it or not, eliminating it is not realistic. Indeed, GAI of some type will be part of our students' work and civic lives, and thus, something they will need to understand and be able to use (Baidoo-Anu & Owusu Ansah, 2023; Bauschard et al., 2023; Phare, 2023). Put another way, instead of succumbing to the "anxiety" that often attends technological change (Peters, 1999), we feature reasonable accommodation with it in the hope that pedagogical redesign might amplify its benefits. Thus, throughout the rest of this paper, we consider the issue of *design* (Batt & Schulz, 2005; Buchanan, 2001; Jackson, 2015; Mitchell, 2021; Rief, 2018) not so much in terms of the way the technology itself develops, but its adaptation to the classroom environment.

Crucially, we do not think this view entails the belief that all the consequences of GAI will be good. Indeed, it is almost certain they will not be. Alternatively, if we accept that GAI is here to stay, we may develop strategies other than banning it that promote both learning and academic integrity. Such alternatives may help us navigate the troubled waters in which we find ourselves. Thus, we plan to consider ways to enroll GAI in the service of learning within a redesigned understanding of both invention and consequently, educational integrity. In other words, the goal of this chapter is to investigate the productive role(s) of GAI in higher education without averting our eyes from the risks it poses to this enterprise.

In the following two sections, we offer a refashioned vision of invention and integrity developed within a particular pedagogical arena: academic debate. Academic debate is a classroom subject, a pedagogical approach that spans the curriculum, an intercollegiate competitive activity, and a model for civic engagement that pierces the barriers between colleges, universities, and surrounding communities (Bartanen & Littlefield, 2014; Broda-Bahm, Kempf, & Driscoll, 2004; Louden, 2010). The history of American academic debate stretches back to the colonial era, but it became central to English and communication studies programs in the late 19th and early 20th centuries (Atchison & Panetta, 2009; Bartanen & Littlefield, 2014; Potter, 1954, 1972). Moreover, academic debate has often been on the front lines of educational innovation, thus making it an appropriate setting to consider the revolutionary implications of GAI. Most importantly, the activity of debate, whether in the classroom or in competitions, is also a prime site for student invention, both in terms of speaking and writing. It thus engages in the broader questions facing the field of communication studies, not to mention higher education as a whole, as previously noted.

In the following pages, we further discuss why debate provides rich ground upon which to build a case for the incorporation of GAI into higher education. We then turn to various ways ChatGPT can be used to augment debate pedagogy and practice in the classroom and beyond. Given that innovative pedagogical redesign is crucial to the ethical, effective, and productive use of GAI for learning, professional work, and civic engagement (Mitchell, 2021), our approach here is to generate thought experiments that challenge us to think beyond current norms and expectations in the classroom. We offer three such experiments. We then conclude with implications that connect our experimental work to the broader discussion on GAI currently erupting across higher education.

ACADEMIC DEBATE: A KEY SITE FOR EXPERIMENTAL GAI PEDAGOGY

Academic debate is an excellent arena for testing the prospects and problems of ChatGPT and other GAI for higher education for numerous reasons. First, while debate is, in some sense, a *subject* primarily found in communication departments (at least in the U.S.) that concerns itself with the best practices of argument writing and delivery, it is not the product of one pedagogical tradition or disciplinary milieu. It is an interdisciplinary endeavor, an activity that traverses the educational landscape given its ability to contribute to learning in almost any subject area (Snider & Schnurer, 2002). From its origins, debate has involved multiple modalities of education spanning written and oral composition, audience adaptation, research, critical thinking, persuasion, and the preparation for and ethical performance of civic life (Bartanen & Littlefield, 2014; Hogan et al., 2017; Keith, 2007, 2010; Potter, 1954, 1972; Rief, 2018, 2021; Rief & Schrader, 2021), thus allowing it to be applied as a learning tool across the curriculum (Snider & Schnurer, 2002). Therefore, investigating how GAI impacts debate education will generate insights for students, faculty, and staff from many fields and modes of practice throughout higher education.

Second, debate inhabits a liminal zone between classrooms, extracurricular competitions (tournaments), and public exhibitions, offering multiple settings and modalities for experimentation. For instance, intercollegiate debate tournaments bring students from numerous campuses together for multiple rounds of argumentative engagement each year (Bartanen & Littlefield, 2014). Competitors at debate tournaments invent content for their speeches in the same way that students respond to an assignment prompt in the classroom. However, the competitive environment of tournaments raises a different set of concerns. If students use GAI to enhance their competitive edge, much like athletes have used performance-enhancing drugs (PEDs) to do the same (Schrader, 2016), a crisis of legitimacy and even the morality of competition and participation could arise (Inoue, 2023).

Moreover, IBM's *Project Debater*, the first attempt to build a completely functional AI debater, raises the possibility of not only using GAI for the purposes of invention, but also entering artificial competitors into tournaments (Inoue, 2023; Mitchell, 2021; Slonim et al., 2021). Given that many tournaments are now being held in HyFlex and fully virtual settings (Rief, 2021), we may even be approaching a time when it is impossible to tell whether the image on the screen is a person, avatar, or AI competitor (Inoue, 2023). This emergent vision – competition for humans *and* their virtual progeny – raises questions about how AI competitors should be treated (Inoue, 2023). Will they compete in exactly the same way as their human counterparts? While the classroom environment raises a similar problem, the ethical questions posed by the use of such tactics in that setting are distinct. No instructor would defend any student who outsources their entire educational experience to GAI. However, individual GAI and human + GAI entries at tournaments seem imminently possible, even probable, and do not necessarily raise the same concerns as humans who secure replacements in the classroom (Inoue, 2023). Indeed, there is a tradition of humans, from Garry Kasparov, the chess master, to Ken Jennings, the *Jeopardy* champion, and now the host of the show, taking on AI opponents (Mitchell, 2021). As long as AI is revealed to be present and participating, it would seem that humans have historically welcomed the challenge.

Crucially, the tournament space invites contention about the practices and ethical parameters of the activity (Rief, 2007). Over the past several generations, students have raised competitive design questions about the prevailing procedural rules, about justice, diversity, equity, and inclusion, about the conventions of judging, and more (Bartanen & Littlefield, 2014; Louden, 2010; Rief, 2018). Given these previous and ongoing debates regarding how to organize, regulate, and transform tournament practices, fostering debates focused on the incorporation of GAI into the contest round seems both realistic and advisable. In this sense, given its competitive dimension and distinction from the classroom setting, it is a more flexible laboratory for the investigation of GAI. In essence, arguing about and experimenting with the technology at tournaments would be easier, given that grades and a host of academic integrity rules deeply enshrined in the classroom setting are more fluid and available for critique in contest rounds.

Third, academic debate emphasizes the performance and cultivation of civic life (Hogan et al., 2017; Rief, 2018; Rief & Schrader, 2021). When students engage in debate, they learn and practice skills necessary to their active involvement in democratic culture. GAI offers intriguing (and potentially dangerous) opportunities to transform not only how we learn and communicate, but also how our political sphere operates, especially as it is increasingly used to generate campaign content. Training students how to engage with GAI in productive ways as members of their civic environments is a frontline challenge for anyone invested in the health and vitality of democratic governance. While one might take the view with Massaro (2023) that, "in a culture where entertainment makes trillions and education makes pennies, the use of AI in academia represents one more progression in the abolition of logical thought, allowing misinformation, propaganda and personal biases to take the wheel of the populace's heart" (para. 5), we feel differently. Far from abolishing logical thought, a well-designed engagement with GAI seems to be the best way to confront its misuse by those seeking to undermine democracy (Bauschard et al.,

2023). Again, we refer back to our agnostic framework. GAI is here. As such, we can either succumb to the belief that the end is nigh, or we can find ways to prepare for the challenge of its presence in our educational, civic, and political worlds while remaining experimental and critically skeptical about its long-term implications. In short, we refuse both an all-out rejection and a thoroughgoing defense of GAI. We instead call for ongoing engagement with it to learn the best ways to address it as it inevitably takes root in our lives.

Our view, as expressed here, refers to one of the original defenses of learning rhetoric, the art concerned with persuasion and decision-making in public life. While rhetoric is a dangerous art that can easily be used to manipulate audiences and undermine good decision making, this is not a reason to abandon its study. Indeed, to do so would be akin to forfeiting control over civic life to opportunists and demagogues. As Aristotle notes in his *Rhetoric* in the 4th century B.C.E., if we spend significant time preparing for our physical defense, why not prepare for the defense of our minds? He writes: "it would be strange if an inability to defend oneself by means of the body is shameful, while there is no shame in an inability to use speech; the latter is more characteristic of humans than is use of the body" (Aristotle, 350 B.C.E./2007, 1355a, p. 35-36; Herrick, 2018, pp. 87-88). To this, he adds that nearly any human device can be used for good or ill, what matters is how it is used, and with what intent:

And if it is argued that great harm can be done by unjustly using such power of words, this objection applies to all good things except for virtue, and most of all to the most useful things, like strength, health, wealth, and military strategy; for by using these justly one would do the greatest good and unjustly, the greatest harm. (Aristotle, 350 B.C.E./2007, 1355a, p. 36)

This seems to be the case today. Learning how to defend against the unethical and destructive use of GAI and engaging in its ethical and productive application are perhaps the best ways to survive its integration into our daily lives. Choosing any other path means losing this opportunity and falling behind our virtual progeny as they become ever more complex and capable.

Fourth, debate has always been at the forefront of adapting to new communication technologies. Debate practitioners were early adopters of radio and by the 1940s, contemplated how debates might be performed on television (Bartanen & Littlefield, 2014; Ehninger & Brockriede, 1966; Rief, 2018, 2021). Later in the century, debate practitioners adopted online research, digital file production, and electronic tools for tournament management (Rief, 2021). During the COVID-19 pandemic, debate tournaments quickly moved from in-person to virtual environments spanning Discord, Zoom, and other platforms (Rief, 2021; Inoue, 2023). In short, academic debate has dealt with the integration of technology into its training and competitive practices for over a century, reinventing itself when necessary to address the challenges of new technological eras. Given this historical flexibility, debate is a model of how education can thrive in the face of significant technological innovation. Once again, it may be possible for debate practitioners to step up to the plate and find ways to soften the edges of technological change. As Bauschard, Coverstone, Rao, and Rao (2023) note,

When utilized properly, the integration of AI and debate into the classroom provides us with a practical opportunity to support the integrity of assessment, facilitate individualized instruction, engage students, provide students with a stake in their learning outcomes, provide essential human-to-human interaction, and push education forward, all while providing an easily accessible starting point for teachers and administrators who are just coming to understand the impact AI is having on our world. (p. 1)

In short, debate seems well suited to help us think through the problems and possibilities of GAI in contemporary classrooms and beyond. We turn to some specific examples of how this might be done in the next section of this paper.

TOOLS FOR INTEGRATING GAI INTO ACADEMIC DEBATE: PEDAGOGICAL THOUGHT EXPERIMENTS

In this section, we iteratively apply our agnostic framework to three pedagogical thought experiments. Each experiment focuses on how to make ChatGPT part of the activity of debate, whether practiced in the classroom, at competitions, or in public settings. For each, we offer justifications for why the pedagogical practices we introduce might be valuable as well as some examples that instructors could use to implement our experiments. While some of these strategies have been discussed in other settings, for instance, in writing instruction (see e.g., Johinke, Cummings, and Di Lauro, 2023), we elucidate them here in the context of debate pedagogy, a space where conversation about AI has just begun (see e.g., Bauschard et al., 2023; Inoue, 2023). Inspired by the argumentation theorist Stephen E. Toulmin's (2003) words at the opening of *The Uses of Argument*, we invite our readers to consider the following sections as "experimental incursions into the field with which they deal; assays or examinations of specimen concepts drawn rather arbitrarily from a larger class; and finally *ballons d'essai*, trial balloons designed to draw the fire of others" (p. 1). They should be viewed as *experiments* rather than fully worked out theories or empirically proven tactics. From our vantage point, it is too early for such results to be available. Instead, generating ideas, proposing hypotheses for further interrogation, offering pathways for pedagogical redesign, and raising questions are all legitimate activities at this stage of the conversation.

While there are innumerable ways to think through the implications of ChatGPT for academic debate, we offer three angles we think any scholar-teacher and student-participant in this activity should consider: debating about, against, and with ChatGPT. We begin with an experiment focused on debating about ChatGPT's role in education and public life. Doing so puts it under the microscope, so to speak, to see whether it can survive the crucible of argumentative testing and clash. In this way, we invert the primary thrust of this paper (if only briefly) to show how debate might transform GAI rather than vice versa. We then discuss how ChatGPT could play the role of a fellow competitor in debate competition. Finally, we consider how ChatGPT can be used as a tool for the creation of speeches in classroom and competitive settings. Throughout, we investigate how each experiment manages the interplay between invention and integrity adumbrated earlier.

Thought Experiment #1: Debating About ChatGPT

The practice of debate is a fantastic tool for deliberating about the prospects and risks of technological innovation. Thus, it can and should be used to carefully consider whether new technologies should be integrated into the activity of academic debate (Rief, 2021; Woods et al., 2006). Crucially, we cannot ignore the opportunity debate itself presents to have students engage in robust argumentation about the ways GAI can both support and hinder the healthy development of their educational, professional, and civic environments in academic debate and beyond. Having students debate about these issues could generate unique and important insights driven by critical thinking about the ethics of GAI, both as a tool for assignment completion and for the cultivation of public messages. Such debates might also help students develop strategies for recognizing GAI when they encounter it and make judgments about whether a particular application can or should be accepted, imitated, or trusted. In this section, we consider several topics and formats that might aid students, faculty, staff, and community members to consider the potential implications (risks and benefits) of integrating ChatGPT into academic debate. We map this discussion through the three primary locations of academic debate: the classroom, contest rounds at tournaments, and public exhibition events.

We begin with classroom activities. For example, consider a situation in which students are asked to generate arguments for and against the use of ChatGPT to prepare for an upcoming debate. Such students might be confronted with the following question: "Should we use ChatGPT as an inventional tool as we prepare for our debate?" The class would be divided into two groups: one in favor of using ChatGPT and the other opposed. Both sides would then complete research into the potential benefits and risks of the technology. Moreover, they would be prompted by the instructor to use ChatGPT to generate arguments and research for their debate. In essence, they would use ChatGPT to come up with arguments about whether to use it. The creative interaction between the debate topic and the tactics of preparation here would invite significant reflection about the technology and the inventional process (what research should we look for, how should we look for it, how might it inform our argument writing, etc.?). This sort of reflection would translate not only into the debate itself once it takes place but also into the sorts of critical thinking we hope our students will use when confronted with information and arguments in the public square.

In addition, a close analysis of ChatGPT's qualities would give students a chance to learn about both its capabilities and downsides. As noted in ample reports from early adopters of ChatGPT, the technology often make mistakes, offers faulty or irrelevant material, generates incomplete material, or even provides incorrect answers based on false information (Baidoo-Anu & Owusu Ansah, 2023; Bauschard et al., 2023). It is important to note that AI is a product of human intelligence and the ideological ecologies in which it is being developed. Thus it suffers from the same biases and errors prevalent in human society, including fake news and misinformation. In some sense, AI is *one of us* (Benjamin, 2019; Cummings & Rief, 2023; Noble, 2018; Topol, 2019). However, despite these admitted problems, students can still potentially benefit from collaborating with it. Doing so can show them the pitfalls they might experience as they scan the Internet for resources or summarize their findings for an audience. Ultimately, the point of debates such as these would not be to come to consensus (as in answering a firm "yes" or "no" question) but, rather, to test the possibilities, to invite a Socratic encounter with our new technological cohabitants in the world of higher education. Moreover, inviting ChatGPT into a debate like this (perhaps the first to take place during the semester) would disarm conventional pedagogical alarm bells around plagiarism and cheating. This would offer students and instructors a chance to interact with the technology in a space free from surveillance and distrust.

Of course, one could take a classroom assignment like this and introduce it into a competitive setting. Tournaments featuring competition among teams from multiple institutions could take on topics not only about the ethical use of ChatGPT as an affiliate member (or at least a research assistant and argument inventor) of the team, but also the broader implications of GAI on education, politics, the environment, and the like. They could debate topics like the following: "Resolved: Further developments of GAI should be put on a five-year moratorium," or "Resolved: GAI has radically undermined the electoral process," or "Resolved: GAI spells the end of human existence," or "Resolved: Humans need GAI to save the planet!" Having students test GAI in the competitive crucible of debate tournaments would give them an opportunity to think critically about how it will impact their activities, their educational environments, and the civic and political worlds around them.

Debate tournaments organized around topics like those previously described might also generate opportunities for student-faculty research and publication about GAI. Indeed, contest rounds feature pedagogically intense opportunities for students to test their arguments either in front of expert coaches or, sometimes, area experts and public actors. They do this across multiple "rounds" of competition in which they often "switch sides" (Greene & Hicks, 2005). That is, debaters and coaches at such tournaments would experience preparing for and debating both sides of issues related to the integration of GAI into higher education, thus opening their minds to the possibility of being wrong rather than further reinforcing their current views (Bauschard et al., 2023; English et al., 2007; Harrigan, 2008; Muir, 1993). In some versions of academic debate, students deal with the same topic over numerous rounds, and their arguments iteratively gain quality and rigor (Bauschard et al., 2023). Such collaborative engagement, especially in evidence-based forms of debate that focus on primary topics for whole tournaments and even seasons, produces research that could turn into major scholarly publications (see e.g., Mitchell, 2000; Mitchell et al., 2010). In other words, this iterative and robust testing of GAI at tournaments would provide data, grist for the deliberative mill of future tournaments and pedagogical scholarship within and beyond debate. In this way, debate tournaments could be a deliberative laboratory for determining the appropriate scope of integration for GAI both in the activity and in society overall.

Finally, one could invite public comment on the use of ChatGPT during exhibition debates. This would offer the opportunity to resuscitate the integrity of our democratic culture by offering not only college students but also their surrounding communities opportunities to discuss the role of ChatGPT, both in the debating process and as a feature of the public square. Crucially, such events would need to be framed less as contests and more as opportunities for dialogue and learning (Broda-Bahm, Kempf, & Driscoll, 2004). For example, student debaters could be paired with GAI experts from campus or beyond to discuss appropriate limits on the use of the technology, such as during political campaigns. Students could potentially begin such events by reading a speech generated by ChatGPT, followed by a request for public comment on its quality. Tactics like this would invite immediate and honest reactions, revealing underlying assumptions among the debaters, experts, and audience members in attendance. Whatever the specific design features adopted for events like this, the point would always come back to crystallizing a pathway for communication between higher education and the public. In so doing, ChatGPT would become a common topic of consideration, and thus, something that more individuals are prepared to think critically about. This would be fortuitous for our democracy given the cultural, political, and technological challenges of our current moment.

Thought Experiment #2: Debating Against ChatGPT

Inspired by *Project Debater*, a research effort at IBM to develop an AI debater (Mitchell, 2021; Slonim et al., 2021), in this section, we suggest that students be given opportunities to debate *against* ChatGPT as an opponent in contest rounds. *Project Debater* represents the most advanced effort to date to create a fully functioning virtual debate opponent capable not only of responding to prompts and requests for research and arguments, but also of forming responsive arguments against full speeches delivered by humans (Inoue, 2023; Mitchell, 2021). For now, a virtual opponent that conducts research, writes arguments, delivers them to an audience, listens to opposing speeches, and responds to these speeches with new content is an application of GAI technology far out of reach for most students and faculty.

However, this does not mean that accessible forms of GAI like ChatGPT have not advanced far enough to participate in classroom and competitive debates, an idea that has also been contemplated by Inoue (2023). Here, we offer a specific way to experiment with this possibility.

Imagine the following example: Students would be given a topic like the following: "Resolved: On balance, GAI will yield greater happiness for human communities." ChatGPT would be instructed to write opening speeches (both for and against) in response to the selected topic, which could be read by the debaters or delivered by one of them to the group. The remaining speeches in the debate, given by human participants, would then respond to ChatGPT's speeches, both building on its strengths and identifying key weaknesses in its case construction. Furthermore, imagine that ChatGPT was involved throughout the debate rather than just giving opening speeches. Any time a question requiring further research comes up, students would be allowed to publicly consult (in a sense, cross-examine) the technology to see what leads it might generate for them. In this way, students would not only debate *against* ChatGPT, but also learn about its potential strengths and weaknesses as a tool for research and speech composition through multiple iterative rounds of engagement. They would also learn in real time how to use the technology as an inventional tool and how to engage in revision of the materials it provides. In the case of this topic, they would also be able to personally answer the questions: Did GAI lead to happiness during this debate? Did using it undermine or enhance happiness?

Furthermore, debating against ChatGPT could be an even more robust, multidimensional pedagogical exercise if practitioners attend not only to topics but also to format design. For example, consider the following format that could be used either in the classroom or at a tournament[1]:

First Affirmative Speech: Written by ChatGPT; read by a human[2]
First Negative Speech: Written by ChatGPT; read by a human

The first two speeches would be pre-written. Student-debaters would offer prompts to ChatGPT to write speeches with research included either for or against the topic. They would then read the material generated by ChatGPT with minimal edits. Edits would likely include looking up the research materials noted by ChatGPT and confirming the accuracy of the information and citations provided.

Second Affirmative Speech: Given by human
Second Negative Speech: Given by human

The second two speeches would be responses to the ChatGPT material. The human affirmative speaker would raise objections to the first negative speech given by ChatGPT. Then, the human negative speaker would respond to these objections.

Preparation Time: Consult with ChatGPT

Both teams would engage in additional argument writing and research. ChatGPT would be prompted to develop responses and help find materials relevant to the objections raised in the debate thus far. The human debaters would incorporate this material into their final rebuttal speeches. Humans would also conduct research to back-check ChatGPT and would make note of when it got things wrong or left important details out.

Affirmative Rebuttal: Given by a human with materials by ChatGPT
Negative Rebuttal: Given by a human with materials by ChatGPT
Judge Panel: Several judges with expertise in education, argumentation, and/or GAI would evaluate the debate.

To further promote multidimensional learning outcomes, the panel would be asked to select the winning team based on which best integrated human and technological research and argument writing into the debating process. So, rather than emphasizing argumentation and research quality as independent criteria, judges would seek to balance these more conventional standards with a determination of how well each side demonstrated the effective and ethical integration of human and GAI contributions.

This format has several potential advantages. Technological breakthroughs are not required to have a fully functioning GAI agent in the room. Instead, laptops or other devices are sufficient. This format has also been designed to reward the effective integration of ChatGPT into the debating process. It is not so much about winning the argument as about how well the arguments of each side were supported by the interaction of humans and GAI team members. One interesting question is whether to reveal the topic before or during the debating process. For example, instead of having the topic in advance, debaters could enter the room without a topic and then be invited to start the debate once it is released. At release, both humans would prompt their ChatGPT interface to come up with a speech on the topic.

While completing this essay, the authors conducted a brief "proof-of-concept" experiment for our proposed format using ChatGPT 4. We prompted it to come up with a speech that fits the parameters already noted.[3] We started by asking for a 750-word speech (assuming human speech to be around 150 words per minute): "Please write a speech of about 750 words on the topic: 'On balance, GAI will yield greater happiness for human communities.' Please include ten source citations." [4] With this prompt, ChatGPT provided a speech of approximately 563 words with citations that were merely "illustrative" of how sources would be included rather than actual sources. After several rounds of prompts to obtain a final version with scholarly sources, ChatGPT ended up with a speech that could, based on our reading, credibly open a debate about GAI and human happiness. This speech has several sources and links that could be investigated by human debaters. It makes several arguments related to the use of GAI in healthcare, its ability to promote human freedom to "pursue more fulfilling work" rather than "monotonous jobs," and its potential to enhance educational experiences.[5]

In addition, the final version of the speech generated by ChatGPT offers other elements that could contribute to learning during any debate. For example, at one point, it approximates what argumentation theorists refer to as *prolepsis* or the anticipation of and response to potential counterarguments (see e.g., Walton, 2008). Indeed, the speech includes statements regarding the potential downsides of GAI, including "loss in decision-making and increased laziness." It combines such moves with a powerful statement regarding the need for care to be taken in the ongoing development of AI: "its integration into society must be handled with care and foresight . . . it is our collective responsibility to guide GAI's development toward augmenting human well-being, ensuring a balanced approach that addresses potential pitfalls while embracing the benefits." The implication is that such downsides can be forestalled by thoughtful implementation strategies. The speech also includes references to potentially useful information, including some drawn from the "Stanford University Human-Centered Artificial Intelligence" site and scholarly journal articles. We feel confident after this brief experiment that debaters could both use ChatGPT as an argument and research generator across an entire debate and, in so doing, gain useful insights into its capabilities and limitations.

Thought Experiment #3: Debating With ChatGPT

In addition to ChatGPT acting as a kind of virtual first speaker and adjunct researcher, it could also be used to invent initial drafts of speeches that could then be revised for use by students, either in the classroom or in competitive settings. This form of human educational augmentation–that is, the writing of debate speeches with significant AI support–has been contemplated previously (Bauschard et al., 2023). Here, we engage such augmentation through the lens of our agnostic framework in the hope of showing how to rethink the inventional process and academic integrity and, thus, create pedagogical space for such practices. Indeed, collaboration *with* GAI in assignment completion gets to the heart of a key anxiety the technology produces, specifically the ongoing theoretical erosion of the traditional *author* as a stable and singular human creator (Barthes, 1977; Foucault, 1969/1998). That is, GAI unsettles the teleology of written texts as fixed and permanent with identifiable and specific authors (Ong, 2002). It is worth noting that the paradigm undergirding such a notion of texts is historically contingent (Ong, 2002) and rooted in problematic ideologies such as individualism and capitalism (Barthes, 1977; LeFevre, 1987). That is, the notion that texts have specific authors who own the material produced is rooted in ideas that have turned the written and spoken word into commodities that serve the interests of the already privileged. We believe that retaining these old ideas about texts makes little sense and may damage students, faculty, and democratic culture.

This is not to say that students should be encouraged to plagiarize, or that authors have no stake in what they have written and produced. Rather, we believe that any educational system should endeavor to be realistic about the inventional process, including the idea that it has never been and cannot be a fully individualized and novel engagement with material. It has been, and must be, collaborative (Lauer, 2004; LeFevre, 1987). One error related to the taken-for-granted assumptions introduced above, which has made the academic integrity issue so vexing in the context of GAI, is the idea that students (especially undergraduates) need to work *individually*. This is not how anyone works at higher levels of the academy (especially graduate students and faculty), at least not if they are successful. Why then should our students? In *Invention as a Social Act*, LeFevre (1987) rejects individualist paradigms of invention for those rooted in social relationships:

Invention should be reconceived . . . as a social act: one in which individuals interact with society and culture in a distinctive way to create something. With this view, invention may be seen as an act encompassing symbol-using activities such as speaking and writing, often involving more than one person, and extending over time through a series of social transactions and texts. (p. 121)

LeFevre (1987) goes on to suggest that "we should study the ecology of invention – the ways ideas arise and are nurtured or hindered by interaction with social context and culture" (p. 126). We could not agree more with LeFevre's point here and are ready to extend it to include ChatGPT as part of the 21st century "ecology of invention" our students inhabit. Giving up on the individual creator and embracing the creative energies of sociality requires embracing ChatGPT in this way, although we should always do so with the critical eye we bring to any material we are using in crafting our words, whether written or spoken. Humans can mislead and lie, just as ChatGPT can provide false, inaccurate, or incomplete information. Awareness of this possibility is one of the pedagogical goals of our agnostic approach, as noted earlier and developed further below.

Consider this possibility: instead of asking students to produce *unique* speech texts, we might invite them to use ChatGPT to produce an initial version of their assignment or competitive speech. This text would be a starting point, not an endpoint of production. Students would be invited to revise these texts using the tools of research, organization, and persuasive writing they learn in class, a strategy also noted and developed by Bauschard et al. (2023). Scholar-teachers in other traditions have already begun to adopt this move, especially in the wake of the massive shift to online education that took place during the COVID-19 Pandemic (Rief, 2021). As Johinke et al. (2023) note in a recent editorial about the impact of GAI on digital writing pedagogy, "the technologies of digital writing can be harnessed to reflect the values of education – openness, individual autonomy, and the power of knowledge – but only when the practitioners of digital writing pedagogy understand and access digital writing tools" (abstract). In other words, teachers should be interested in learning how such tools can be used to promote educational achievement, not how to surveil their students as they use them. As experts at the 2023 AI+Education Summit held at Stanford University noted, GAI offers students the opportunity to learn how "to edit and curate" and act as "architects" working with already extant materials to create new and innovative content (Chen, 2023, "2. Changing what is important for learners," para. 3). Such skills seem relevant and timely in a marketplace saturated by content but limited in *attention* (Lanham, 2006). Others have suggested that GAI be integrated into the teaching process as long as reasonable limitations are put in place. For example, students should openly use the technology when allowed to do so and refrain from its use for specific learning activities (AlAfnan et al., 2023; Baidoo-Anu & Owusu Ansah, 2023). Faculty should also design assignments that cannot be completed by GAI to be sure students are able to complete certain tasks without its support (AlAfnan et al., 2023; Bauschard et al., 2023).

Returning to our example, in featuring human revision rather than initial invention, we embrace a collaborative model of composition (LeFevre, 1987). Such a strategy has an important popular culture precedent. In the film *Finding Forrester* (Van Sant, 2000), a high school student develops a close mentoring relationship with a famous hermitic author. At one point in the film, the author invites the student to write with, revise, and build a new work from one of his previously published essays as a learning exercise. The student decides to submit this exercise into a writing competition without securing the author's permission. He is charged with plagiarism. However, in a thematically rich moment for our purposes, the famous author ultimately chooses to defend the student publicly. Following this example, we suggest that debate students be introduced to argument writing through the lens of revision rather than initial production. In this case, of course, we are talking about ChatGPT as the initial author. But, the learning strategy would be the same. Such a strategy is not quite the stretch it may seem, especially in debate. Indeed, academic debate has always involved some level of collaborative knowledge production between students and their coaches (Mitchell et al., 2010). In many formats, students are allowed to brainstorm with their coaches, especially ahead of competitions. In some instances, coaches even write initial versions of arguments that are then revised in collaboration with students as they are tested in contest rounds. If this is an acceptable pedagogical strategy, it seems to us that arguments against the use of GAI as a partner in the inventional process are persnickety at best (Bauschard et al., 2023).

Of course, such strategies should complement other modes of writing and argument instruction that begin with student-produced texts. To be clear, we are not suggesting that students learn argument writing purely through revision. Nor do we suggest that every instance of plagiarism simply be recast as an effort to find one's voice. What we do suggest is that learning through revision is a legitimate adjunct to learning through invention (and, perhaps these two terms are not so very far apart anyway). One of the reasons our readers might have reservations about this proposal, when compared with the film glossed in the previous paragraph, is that ChatGPT is not a famous author. Rather, ChatGPT collects material from a variety of sources and pastes it together with algorithmic duct tape to create aesthetically displeasing and fragmentary, perhaps even false, cultural bricolage. However, such bricolage might be transformed into compositional gold when taken up by well-informed students ready to revise and rework it based on the practices they learn in intentionally designed debate classes.

CONCLUSION AND IMPLICATIONS

In this chapter, we have articulated an agnostic framework for the integration of GAI, especially its most controversial iteration of the moment, ChatGPT, into academic debate. Doing so has allowed us to offer an initial map for debate educators (and educators using debate in their classrooms across the curriculum) to engage in a form of "design thinking" (Jackson, 2015; see also, Mitchell, 2021; Rief, 2018) that gets them around the initial problems created by ready access to ChatGPT. That is, we believe educators would be better off approaching GAI as an opportunity to rethink their assumptions and cultivate professional and learning ecologies responsive to the technological world that human beings, their students included, inhabit. Designing assignments and extracurricular activities *for* GAI, rather than erecting bulwarks in a vain attempt to hermetically seal the halls of academe against it, seems the best possible approach. In the previous section, we described three designs that might fit debate for GAI. We hope they invite further debate and reflection that inspire a turn to redesign rather than rejection in response to GAI.

In addition, our chapter demonstrates that assumptions about authorship and the types of skills that should be valued in a GAI world must be open to reconsideration in the years ahead, especially when it comes to invention and revision. In other words, we have argued that to retain a meaningful understanding of educational integrity, we have to think differently about invention. It does not need to be a practice bound to individualism or in the service of capitalism. It does not need to be viewed as emergent from the creative genius of a single mind, a view that simply cannot be sustained (LeFevre, 1987). Invention is and has always been a matter of working from pre-existing materials to build something new. This has always involved the intersection of many minds. Our advice is to see ChatGPT and newer forms of GAI that will inevitably emerge as yet one more set of minds to collaborate with.

Finally, we suggest accommodation and collaboration with GAI technology, rather than its ongoing construction as a threat. Inviting it to exist within our educational spaces rather than trying to ban it is the best way to avoid its circulation as a tool for cheating that might undermine student learning and the overall legitimacy of higher education as a space for the development of skills necessary for success in professional and civic life. What's more, it may be the one way we have to make peace with artificial beings that, at some point in the future, if our science fiction writers are correct, may demand recognition as lifeforms with wills, rights, and lives of their own.

REFERENCES

AlAfnan, M. A., Dishari, S., Jovic, M., & Lomidze, K. (2023). ChatGPT as an educational tool: Opportunities, challenges, and recommendations for communication, business writing, and composition courses. *Journal of Artificial Intelligence and Technology*, *3*, 60–68. doi:10.37965/jait.2023.0184

Aristotle. (2007). On rhetoric: A theory of civic discourse (2nd ed.; G.A. Kennedy, Trans.). Oxford University Press. (Originally published ca. 350 B.C.E.)

Atchison, J., & Panetta, E. (2009). Intercollegiate debate and speech communication: Historical developments and issues for the future. In A. A. Lunsford, K. H. Wilson, & R. A. Eberly (Eds.), *The SAGE handbook of rhetorical studies* (pp. 317–333). SAGE.

Baidoo-Anu, D., & Owusu Ansah, L. (2023). Education in the era of generative artificial intelligence (AI): Understanding the potential benefits of ChatGPT in promoting teaching the learning. *Journal of AI*, *7*(1), 52–62. doi:10.61969/jai.1337500

Bartanen, M. D., & Littlefield, R. S. (2014). *Forensics in America: A history*. Rowman & Littlefield.

Barthes, R. (1977). *The death of the author. In his Image – music – text* (S. Heath, Trans.). Fontana Press.

Batt, S., & Schulz, D. (2005). Design principles for competitive debate formats. In C. Willard (Ed.), *Critical problems in argumentation* (pp. 510–517). National Communication Association.

Bauschard, S., Coverstone, A., Rao, A., & Rao, S. (2023). *Beyond algorithmic solutions: The significance of academic debate for learning assessment and skill cultivation in the AI world* [Commissioned Paper]. Cottesmore's Free AI Festival, Pease Pottage, UK. https://papers.ssrn.com/sol3/papers.cfm?abstract_id=4567346

Benjamin, R. (2019). *Race after technology: Abolitionist tools for the New Jim Code*. Polity Press.

Broda-Bahm, K., Kempf, D., & Driscoll, W. (2004). *Argument and audience: Presenting debates in public settings*. International Debate Education Association.

Buchanan, R. (2001). Design and the new rhetoric: Productive arts in the philosophy of culture. *Philosophy & Rhetoric*, *34*(3), 183–206. doi:10.1353/par.2001.0012

Chance, C. (2020, October 29). The impact of artificial intelligence on education. *Forbes*. https://www.forbes.com/sites/calumchace/2020/10/29/the-impact-of-artificial-intelligence-on-education/?sh=60fd484a50df

Chen, C. (2023, March 9). *AI will transform teaching and learning. Let's get it right.* Stanford University Human-Centered Artificial Intelligence. https://hai.stanford.edu/news/ai-will-transform-teaching-and-learning-lets-get-it-right

Cicero, M. T. (1949). On invention. The best kind of orator. Topics (H. M. Hubbell, Trans.). Cambridge: Harvard University Press. (Originally published ca. 90 B.C.E.)

Corbett, E. P. J., & Connors, R. J. (1998). *Classical rhetoric for the modern student* (4th ed.). Oxford University Press.

Cornell University Center for Teaching Innovation. (2023). *What is generative artificial intelligence (AI)?* https://teaching.cornell.edu/generative-artificial-intelligence

Cummings, K., & Rief, J. (2023). Health praxis in the age of artificial intelligence: Diagnostics, caregiving, and reimagining the role(s) of healthcare practitioners. In T. Sikka (Ed.), *Genetic science and new digital technologies: Science and technology studies and health praxis* (pp. 103–131). Bristol University Press. doi:10.56687/9781529223330-007

Ehninger, D., & Brockriede, W. (1966). *Decision by debate*. Dodd, Mead & Company.

English, E., Llano, S., Mitchell, G. R., Morrison, C. E., Rief, J., & Woods, C. (2007). Debate as a weapon of mass destruction. *Communication and Critical/Cultural Studies*, *4*(2), 221–225. doi:10.1080/14791420701296646

Foucault, M. (1998). What is an author? (J. V. Harari, Trans.). In FaubionJ. D. (Ed.), *Michel Foucault: Aesthetics, Method, and Epistemology* (pp. 205–222). The New York Press. (Original work published 1969)

Greene, R. W., & Hicks, D. (2005). Lost convictions: Debating both sides and the ethical self-fashioning of liberal citizens. *Cultural Studies*, *19*(1), 100–126. doi:10.1080/09502380500040928

Harrigan, C. (2008). Against dogmatism: A continued defense of switch side debate. *Contemporary Argumentation and Debate*, *29*, 37–66.

Herrick, J. (2018). *The history and theory of rhetoric: An introduction*. Routledge.

Hogan, J. M., Kurr, J. A., Bergmaier, M. J., & Johnson, J. D. (Eds.). (2017). *Speech and debate as civic education*. The Pennsylvania State University Press. doi:10.1515/9780271080369

Inoue, N. (2023). *How far can we go in computer-assisted debating? In RicercAzione: Six -monthly Journal on Learning*. Research and Innovation in Education. doi:10.32076/ RA15303

Jackson, S. (2015). Design thinking in argumentation theory and practice. *Argumentation*, *29*(3), 243–263. doi:10.1007/s10503-015-9353-7

Johinke, R., Cummings, R., & Di Lauro, F. (2023). Reclaiming the technology of higher education for teaching digital writing in a post-pandemic world. *Journal of University Teaching & Learning Practice*, *20*(2). Advance online publication. doi:10.53761/1.20.02.01

Keith, W. (2010). Keynote address: A new golden age – Intercollegiate debate in the twenty-first century. In A. D. Louden (Ed.), *Navigating opportunity: Policy debate in the 21st century* (pp. 11–26). International Debate Education Association.

Keith, W. M. (2007). *Democracy as discussion: Civic education and the American Forum Movement*. Lexington Books.

Kelly, M. L. (Host). (2023). 'Everybody is cheating': Why has adopted an open ChatGPT policy. [Audio podcast episode]. In *Technology*. National Public Radio. https://www.npr.org/ 2023/01/26/1151499213/ chatgpt-ai-education-cheating-classroom-wharton-school

Lanham, R. A. (2006). *The economics of attention: Style and substance in the age of information*. The University of Chicago Press.

Lauer, J. M. (2004). *Invention in rhetoric and composition*. Parlor Press.

LeFevre, K. B. (1987). *Invention as a social act*. Southern Illinois University Press.

Louden, A. D. (Ed.). (2010). *Navigating opportunity: Policy debate in the 21st century*. International Debate Education Association.

Massaro, M. (2023, August 23). AI cheating is hopelessly, irreparably corrupting US higher education. *The Hill*. https://thehill.com/opinion/education/4162766-ai-cheating-has-hopelessly-irreparably-corrupted-us-higher-education/

Mitchell, G. R. (2000). *Strategic deception: Rhetoric, science, and politics in missile defense advocacy*. Michigan State University Press.

Mitchell, G. R. (2021). Debating with robots: IBM Project Debater and the advent of augmentive automated argumentation. In T. Suzuki, T. Tateyama, T. Kato, & J. Eckstein (Eds.), *Proceedings of the Tokyo Conference on Argumentation* (vol. 6, pp. 91–102). Japan Debate Association.

Mitchell, G. R., Woods, C. S., Brigham, B., English, E., Morrison, C. E., & Rief, J. (2010). The Debate Authors Working Group model for collaborative knowledge production in forensics scholarship. *Argumentation and Advocacy*, *47*(1), 1–24. doi:10.1080/00028533.2010.11821734

Muir, S. A. (1993). A defense of the ethics of contemporary debate. *Philosophy & Rhetoric*, *26*(4), 277–295.

Noble, S. U. (2018). *Algorithms of oppression: How search engines reinforce racism*. York University Press. doi:10.18574/nyu/9781479833641.001.0001

Ong, W. J. (2002). Orality and literacy: The technologizing of the word (30th anniversary ed.). Routledge.

Peters, J. D. (1999). *Speaking into the air: A history of the idea of communication*. University of Chicago Press. doi:10.7208/chicago/9780226922638.001.0001

Phare, C. (2023, Fall). Higher ed's next big test. *RED*, 11–13.

Potter, D. (1954). The literary society. In K. R. Wallace (Ed.), *History of speech education in America: Background studies* (pp. 238–258). Appleton-Century-Crofts, Inc.

Potter, D. (1972). *Debating in the colonial chartered colleges: An historical survey, 1642–1900*. AMS Press, Inc.

Rief, J. (2007). Talking at cross purposes: Violating higher-order conditions with oppositional arguments. In F. H. van Eemeren, J. A. Blair, C. A. Willard, & B. Garssen (Eds.), *Proceedings of the Sixth Conference of the International Society for the Study of Argumentation* (pp. 1147–1154). Sic Sat / International Center for the Study of Argumentation.

Rief, J. J. (2018). (Re)Designing the debate tournament for civic life. *Speaker & Gavel*, *55*(1), 36–58.

Rief, J. J. (2021). Post-pandemic pedagogy in intercollegiate academic debate: Performing civic life in hybrid, virtual, and in-person environments. In J. M. Valenzano (Ed.), *Post pandemic pedagogy: A paradigm shift* (pp. 239–258). Lexington Books.

Rief, J. J., & Schrader, B. J. (2021). Reconciling playing the game with civic education in intercollegiate academic debate. In T. Suzuki, T. Tateyama, T. Kato, & J. Eckstein (Eds.), *Proceedings of the Tokyo Conference on Argumentation* (vol. 6, pp. 119–127). Japan Debate Association.

Roose, K. (2023, May 30). AI poses 'risk of extinction,' industry leaders warn. *The New York Times*. https://www.nytimes.com/2023/05/30/technology/ai-threat-warning.html

Schrader, B. J. (2016). *It's a whole new ball game: The Mitchell Report, performance enhancing drugs, and professional sports* [Doctoral Dissertation, University of Denver]. Digital Commons @ DU. https://digitalcommons.du.edu/etd/1160/

Slonim, N., Bilu, Y., Alzate, C., Bar-Haim, R., Bogin, B., Bonin, F., Choshen, L., Cohen-Karlik, E., Dankin, L., Edelstein, L., Ein-Dor, L., Friedman-Melamed, R., Gavron, A., Gera, A., Gleize, M., Gretz, S., Gutfreund, D., Halfon, A., Hershcovich, D., ... Aharonov, R. (2021). An autonomous debating system. *Nature, 591*(7850), 379–384. doi:10.1038/s41586-021-03215-w PMID:33731946

Snider, A., & Schnurer, M. (2002). *Many sides: Debate across the curriculum*. International Debate Education Association.

Topol, E. (2019). *Deep medicine: How artificial intelligence can make healthcare human again*. Basic Books.

Toulmin, S. E. (2003). The uses of argument (updated ed.). Cambridge University Press.

Van Sant, G. (2000). *Finding Forrester* [Film]. Columbia Pictures.

Walton, D. (2008). Proleptic argumentation. *Argumentation and Advocacy, 44*(3), 143–154. doi:10.1080/00028533.2008.11821684

Woods, C., Brigham, M., Heavner, B., Konishi, T., Rief, J., Saindon, B., & Mitchell, G. R. (2006). Deliberating debate's digital futures. *Contemporary Argumentation and Debate, 27*, 81–105.

Wyman, C. (2023, June 28). How to tackle AI—and cheating—in the classroom. *Wired*. https://www.wired.com/story/how-to-tackle-ai-and-cheating-in-schools-classroom/

Yudkowsky, E. (2023, March 29). Pausing AI developments isn't enough. We need to shut it all down. *TIME*. https://time.com/6266923/ai-eliezer-yudkowsky-open-letter-not-enough/

KEY TERMS AND DEFINITIONS

Academic Debate: An activity featuring research, argumentation, and speaking pedagogy that spans the classroom, intercollegiate competitions, and public exhibitions.

Agnosticism: In this essay, a way of approaching technological innovation that seeks accommodation and integration rather than rejection and control. As not enough is yet known about the consequences of GAI, an agnostic or open but always skeptical view of its uses is advised in this essay.

Collaborative Knowledge Production: In this paper, the term refers to the shared experience of producing content at the heart of all invention.

Debate Across the Curriculum: A term that captures the variety of ways academic debate has experienced curricular integration and extracurricular growth across the higher-education landscape.

Debate Format: The structural features of any given debate, including speakers, speaker roles, speech times, speech expectations, speech organizational patterns, rules for question-and-answer periods, and judging.

Intercollegiate Academic Debate: A term that refers to extracurricular and typically competitive debate activities like tournaments.

Integrity: In this essay, a term used to describe the maintenance of the norms, conventions, and ethics of academic life that give it meaning and purpose.

Invention: A term in rhetorical studies that refers to the process of brainstorming, topical development, research, and argument writing necessary to produce a speech or essay.

Rhetoric: An ancient tradition of teaching, producing, and analyzing spoken and written words, with a focus on its persuasive impact on specific audiences.

Topics for Debates: Debates are typically organized around specific topic statements that begin with the word "resolved." For instance: "Resolved: GAI should be used as an aid to complete writing projects." Every debate will have at least two sides, one debating in favor of the topic and one against.

ENDNOTES

1 This format is inspired by one used at the Cambridge Union in 2019. At that event, *Project Debater* was the first speaker on both sides of a debate about the benefits and disadvantages of AI (Mitchell, 2021). The notion of having student-debaters read GAI produced text is also entertained by Inoue (2023). In addition, we are influenced here by strategies of argument writing and research currently being developed in the world of digital literacy (see e.g., Johinke et al. 2023). Finally, the notion of GAI-augmented debating, especially in the area of initial speech writing and research support, has also been entertained by Bauschard et al. (2023).

2 To make time for other elements of the debate, especially ongoing consultation with ChatGPT, we would recommend relatively short speeches in the range of 4-5 minutes.

3 The authors have retained a version of this conversation with ChatGPT in a Word document which is available upon request (dated December 22, 2023).

4 We used 150 words per minute as a starting point for calculating the length of a 4–5-minute speech in text form. This number is based on our experience as debate educators. We also asked ChatGPT and were told that humans speak "150 to 160 words per minute," though "this rate can vary widely." We requested some source material as well, most of which replicated a basic Google search we completed indicating the same range. We have retained this communication with ChatGPT in a Word document which is available on request (dated December 22, 2023).

5 Given this experiment was completed by individuals with very little experience using ChatGPT, it demonstrates just how quickly it could be integrated by any instructors or students into the debating process. This shows not only that it can easily be used but also that its use by at least some participants is likely inevitable.

Chapter 6
How AI Is Changing the Nature and Landscape of Student Learning and Outcomes Assessment Within Higher Education

Corey Jay Liberman
Marymount Manhattan College, USA

ABSTRACT

Technologies have long changed the social lives and practices of users. While some argue that the effects have been positive and others have been a bit more skeptical to take this perspective, there is no question that they have altered the way that we engage in daily behaviors. They have changed the way that we work and the way that we communicate with others. And said technologies are, with little question, here to stay. This chapter introduces readers to the various strategies adopted by both students and assessors (e.g., instructors) regarding the use of ChatGPT within the world of higher education. ChatGPT, in short, is an artificial intelligence chatbot that aids the user in a multitude of tasks and mimics the human mind. Not only will the chapter expose readers to the ways in which students are using ChatGPT (e.g., as artificial tutors, to help with the construction of ideas), but also how instructors are beginning to notice the benefits of this AI tool for the classroom (e.g., lesson plans).

INTRODUCTION

"The main characteristics of AI are the parallels between the human brain and artificial intelligence… intelligent agents with human features" – (Zawacki-Richter et al., 2019, p. 9-10)

"Complex computing systems using machine learning algorithms can serve people with all types of abilities and engage to a certain degree in human-like processes and complex processing tasks that can

DOI: 10.4018/979-8-3693-0831-8.ch006

be employed in teaching and learning. This opens to a new era for institutions of higher education" – (Popenici & Kerr, 2017, p. 6)

Hi Dad!

I hope that you are doing well. I miss you guys so much!!! I know that you are sick of my brief texts, so I figured I would send a quick email update instead. So here it is. What a week this was. I finally finished my report for Organic Chemistry. Wow. That guy who took us on the tour last year was not kidding when he said that it was the hardest class that he had taken in his three years. I had to draw resonance structures and draw structures of nitrogen atoms and explain Lewis acids and talk about bond angles. I do not want to bore you with all of this. But did that make me sound smart? I think that I did OK. Not great. But OK. Funny that getting a 72% in this class actually equates to a grade of an A-. Tells you a little something about how difficult the class is, huh? I know that you guys will not understand this, but there is this thing called ChatGPT that now helps people find information online and is kind of like an electronic tutor. Not so different from Siri and Lexa. And my theatre class is a ton of fun. We are working on the fourth scene of The Glass Menagerie. It is so cool. Each of us gets to play all of the roles. The professor, Jeff (he lets us call him by his real name), is amazing! We all love him. I must say that I play the role of Laura best and Amanda the worst. Maybe the fact that I can play the role of Tom pretty well says something. Don't answer that please (lol). But the class is super cool! Nice break from Chem! And I am finding it pretty easy to remember my lines. At least most of them. Hey…nobody is perfect. But this ChatGPT thing has provided me strategies for playing these roles. So super cool. And no…it is not cheating. I promise. Oh…and then my two favorite classes: Interpersonal Communication and Forensic Psychology. In my interpersonal class, we were studying this thing called homophily. It is the idea that we are likely to have an easier time being in relationships with people who are similar to us. Guess that leaves you and mom out (sorry…I could not resist). The person that I found out that I was most similar to also has loves that strawberry drink from Starbucks, staying up late, eating hamburgers without any lettuce or cheese, listening to classic rock music, taking photographs of random people on the subway, likes the color brown (who would have thought there was another person out there who liked brown), would choose to run rather than bike, and prefers winter over summer. And the coolest thing is that after the activity was over, I feel like we are BFF (in case you don't know what this is, you old fart, it means Best Friends Forever). For homework we have to write a three-page essay about the activity and link it to one of the interpersonal communication theories that we have learned so far. Time to go back to my notes… and to figure out how ChatGPT can help. Too bad I did not have access to this a few years ago, huh? And then there is…wait for it…Forensic Psychology. Since my professor LOVESSSSSSS Law and Order, he uses this show for case studies. I think if my future as a biotechnologist fails, you and mom might have a criminologist on your hands. I have an exam in two days, but I need to start studying now because Bradley's party is tomorrow night. The teacher has assigned us to either the defense or prosecution of a particular case from back in 1974 and we are basically going to engage in a debate. It is going to be fun. Challenging but fun. I just need to access ChatGPT to find out a bit more about the major differences among psychodynamic theory, behavioral theory, and cognitive theory just to make sure that my arguments are on point!!! So everything is fine and I could not be happier. I am stressed, as always, but doing awesome. I love you and miss you, and please tell mom that I love and miss her, too! I will call you over the weekend.

Love,

Hailey

The goal of the aforementioned email from Hailey to her father was not to illustrate how today's GenZ cohort might (and likely does) communicate with their parents. However, this is certainly a prime example. Rather, it showcases two things. First, the ties that bind disciplines of study are communication and assessment. Hailey had to complete a report for her Organic Chemistry course (the communication of ideas via the written word); she had to engage in scene rehearsals for *The Glass Menagerie* (communication via the spoken word); she had to finish a reaction paper for her course in Interpersonal Communicatio*n* (communication via the connection between theory and practice); and she had to study for an exam in *Forensic Psychology* (communication via public argumentation). Second, it brings to the surface one very important question that has recently emerged within the world of higher education: how does artificial intelligence come to impact not only how students (like Hailey) engage in academic practices, but also how must the practices required by those responsible for assessing the academic performance of students now change? As Crawford et al. (2023) ask, will such Artificial Intelligences (AI) have an impact (positive or negative) on student learning outcomes?

This chapter will not delve into the minutia of AI. We will leave this work to computer scientists, engineers, cognitive scientists, and neuroscientists (see Zawacki-Richter et al. 2019). However, it will introduce the eccentricities introduced to the higher education landscape by Artificial Intelligence Education (AIEd) tools and how both learners and assessors have been forever changed by their introduction. Most notably, and shadowing many of the questions raised by Zawacki-Richter et al. (2019), it will highlight how such things as cognitive abilities, learning motivation, and learning styles (using the student model), and teaching strategies and teaching guidance (using the teacher model) both influence and are influenced by today's AI-infused educational world. Since Cope et al. (2021) argue that "assessment is perhaps the most significant area of opportunity offered by artificial intelligence for transformative change in education" (p. 1233), what they call a "paradigm shift" (p. 1237), it is this third perspective into which the forthcoming chapter will delve.

THE CHANGING NATURE OF STUDENT LEARNING AND ASSESSMENT

Artificial Intelligence has begun to take over the world, and there is no area that has escaped its impact. Healthcare. Marketing. The automobile industry. Finance. This has altered the way(s) that we work. Way (s) that we think. Method (s) by which we process information. Way (s) that we communicate with Given the nature of this book, we must not forget that AI has infused itself into the educational environment, where scholars, educators, administrators, and students are trying to better understand what Di Placito and Mortensen (2023) call the "pedagogical potential and pitfalls" (p. 95) of AI learning. There is rarely a day when I wake up to check my email when I do not have something in my inbox about Artificial Intelligence. How students use it. How instructors use it. How it is changing the landscape of education, as we once knew it. Best practices. Worst practices. Ethics. Ease of use. While we might argue that such technology is still in its infancy, even a single year into the generative-AI world requires a new understanding of the social abilities of those within it. Higher education is no exception. If, as Popenici and Kerr (2017) make clear, among the major goals of higher education includes both teaching and learning, it is imperative that both instructors and students understand both the risks and rewards linked to AI platforms and practices.

But is AI a novelty? Zawacki-Richter et al. (2019) state that the use of AI in a higher education environment is certainly ***not*** new. In fact, they argued that such technological innovations were employed within the classroom as early as the 1950s. However, they argue that such technologies are becoming stronger (Zawacki-Ricther et al., 2019). In other words, such machine-based learning tools are now better able to mimic the cognitive minds and worlds of human beings so much that it is becoming more difficult to distinguish between digitized mechanisms and social beings. Two years later, Gonzalez-Calatayud, Prendes-Espinosa, and Roig Vila(2021) let the higher education assessment world know that the blurred line "between human and artificial intelligence" is more pronounced now than it has ever been before (p. 1). Returning to the opening email between Hailey and her father, how does Hailey's Forensic Psychology instructor know, for example, that it was her who created the opening and closing arguments for the 1974 prosecution? Could she have used a creative chatbot tool (or what Chen et al., 2023, refer to as a conversational agent) like ChatGPT? GPT, as per the definition offered by Rasul et al. (2023), "stands for generative pretrained transformers, meaning that it can understand inputs provided by humans and produce a response text that is highly similar to the language used by humans' (p. 2). From an assessment perspective, is cheating considered in any way, shape, or form? After all, it is not about how Hailey presents her arguments orally. Her rhetoric? Her debate strategies? How does she use her knowledge and power of persuasion to make the defence's key arguments in her closing statement(s)? This is why the impact of AI on the higher education world is salient. It is important for students to be well-versed in academic integrity policies and digitally literate (Rudolph et al., 2023, p. 356), the student model, but equally important for instructors to help guide students in understanding how, given the ubiquity of said technologies, they will be taught and assessed (Crawford et al., 2023), the teacher model. Is this unsolvable paradox? Perhaps yes. Perhaps no.

WHAT IS ASSESSMENT: A BRIEF EXPLANATION?

Every college-level student attends an institution with Institutional Learning Outcomes (ILOs), Program Learning Outcomes (PLOs), and Course Learning Outcomes (CLOs) (Judd & Keith, 2017). As we will find shortly, Hailey is a Communication major within the Department of Communication and Media Arts at *The University of the North-South-East-West.* Each Course A Hailey takes has its own learning goals or CLOs (for Course A, students will gain mastery of B, C, and D), which are linked to one or more PLOs (as part of the Department of Communication and Media Arts, students will gain mastery of X, Y, and Z), which are then linked to one or more ILOs (as a registered student, you will, as a result of having completed this course, fulfill ILO 4). This is known as an Assessment Curricular Map (see, for example, Uchiyama & Radin, 2009). The word communicate is (or at least should be) a part and parcel of the said maps. It is difficult to find mission statements that do not underscore this ILO, even based on a cursory review of institutions. Students should be able to communicate effectively. Purposefully. Professionally. According to the American Association of Colleges and Universities (AACU), oral and written communication efficacy has perpetually been among the Essential Learning Outcomes (ELOs) of graduating seniors. However, as we find ourselves, as both teachers and assessors, amidst a generation of students like none that has been seen before, it is due time to reconceptualize not only what assessment means, but, perhaps even more importantly, how assessment is undertaken. How can we, as faculty members, assess whether and to what extent our students have some level of mastery of communication (oral and/or written), where assessment of such things as exams, public speeches, formal papers, presentations, group projects, and the like are not the only criteria on which results are based?

How useful are the results that employ assessment strategies of yesteryear, where AI has become the norm, rather than the exception, for most of today's student learners?

NEW FORMS OF LEARNING IN THE AIED WORLD

From an assessment perspective, Cope et al. (2021) speak about the importance of determining "whether [a questioner]…can tell the difference between an answer by a computer and a person" (p. 1230). As a hypothetical example, let us again assume that the institution at which Hailey is enrolled (from the initial example) is called The University of the North-South-East-West. She is a Communication Arts major and must complete 45 credits (15 courses) in the Department of Communication and Media Arts. She must engage in Interpersonal Communication, Group Communication, Organizational Communication, Public Relations, Persuasive Communication, Health Communication, Public Speaking, Communication Campaigns, and Senior Thesis. The remaining six courses were electives within the department. Each course has its own unique (and perhaps non-overlapping) course learning goals/outcomes, which are connected to at least one of the department's larger student learning outcomes. The department also has a curricular map, which indicates not only which courses are linked to which PLOs but also to which ILOs (let us not forget that students will also have to graduate with the institution's larger mission statement in mind). The conclusion here? There are many aspects to be assessed. Now, with the mass implementation and utilization of chatbots (which, as Hwang et al., 2020 claim, become the ties that bind AI and educational applications together) (p. 2), assessment has become both more opportunistic and more [potentially] enigmatic.

Let us assume that Hailey uses ChatGPT to *help* her write her reaction paper in her Interpersonal Communication course. Given that this chatbot had more than one million people subscribing to the first week of launch (see Perera & Lankathilaka, 2023), this would not be surprising. Is this considered intellectually, morally, and/or ethically problematic from an assessment perspective, or is it merely providing a metacognitive exercise for better "…understand[ing] the application of course content?" (Chen et al., 2023, p. 167)? After all, as Rudolph et al. (2023) note, while said technologies are very astute at providing data, they are concomitantly very poor at producing the structure and grammar necessary for outcome mastery. Hailey would need to take the accumulated information from the chatbot and formulate her own arguments, create her own structure, and produce her own syntax. Would she not communicate a series of arguments in a written form? Is this not the role of research emblematic of years ago? She will, as Cope et al. (2021) mention, have to master her "lookupability" (p. 1234) and "navigate the ocean of knowledge" (p. 1234) that is produced by AI. This was not merely a replica of the data. This was Hailey's version.

Perera and Lankathilaka (2023), too, let us know that generative-AI tools, like ChatGPT, "can generate responses quickly and efficiently, [but] its lack of a deep understanding of the meaning of words and evaluation of response quality can limit its ability to provide high-quality responses, particularly for tasks that require a nuanced understanding of a specific domain knowledge" (p. 311). Thus, ChatGPT has become a tool that aids, not replaces, the educational process. Davenport and Prusak (2000), two knowledge management scholars, argue that there is a semantic and practical difference between information and knowledge. Information is data and knowledge is the application of data in a way that somehow achieves something. In the case of generative AI tools, perhaps information is that which is generated by a chatbot for a student who then transforms the data into knowledge through some assessable form, achieving some CLO, PLO, and our ILO. Is this not the novel approach used by the source of information (the student) that needs to be assessed by the target of information (the instructor)?

When speaking with a colleague of mine (referred to as Jared), he likened the use of ChatGPT, and other Artificial Intelligence in Education (AIEd) tools to *Cliffs Notes*:

I remember, back in high school, when I had to read all of those books written by William Shakespeare. Othello. Romeo and Juliet. Hamlet. Macbeth. No chance that I would have gotten through those without the help of Cliff and his notes. I was a science and math guy. Not an English and writing guy. I just could not get through them. I actually remember the black and yellow covers of those short books. In 45 pages you would learn, chapter by chapter, what happened. And then you could write a paper. How is ChatGPT any different. You still have to take what ChatGPT spits out, make sense of it, and write the paper on your own. My teachers (and my grandmother…trust me) would know if I just copied things, word-for-word, from that yellow and black, 45-page help guide. Which is why I would not do it. But I would read the Cliffs Notes version and I would then be able to contribute to our class discussion and write (with some help) a pretty darn good paper. ChatGPT is the 2023 version of my 1982 Cliffs Notes.

It is important to mention one important point here. As Crawford, Cowling, and Allen (2023) argue, what makes chatbots like ChatGPT and Jasper and ChatSonic able to function is the combination of "machine learning and big data" (p. 4). Metaphorically, ChatGPT is to *Cliffs Notes* what the cellular telephone is to the landline. It makes social processes and practices easier (even though this term is difficult to operationally define) owing to its bandwidth. However, let us return to this assessment. If Jared (in this example) enters a search into a chatbot, any chatbot, and merely edits the result for grammatical errors and hands in the said paper, it provides the instructor (the assessor) with a great deal of pressure. There are a long list of potential issues. Using Bloom's taxonomy (see, for example, Gershon, 2018), did Jared defend his arguments? Did Jared examine the relationships between the characters? Did Jared identify key turning points in the novel's progression? Did Jared extend his theses throughout the course of his work? First, one could argue, in a similar vein to that of Zawacki-Richter et al. (2019), that he was using the chatbot merely as an intelligent virtual reality agent or buddy (p. 4). This is something that can achieve these things *for* him. However, what if the assessor takes a step back and wonders whether and to what extent the chatbot could achieve these things not *for* him but rather *with* him? This requires asking the right questions (as in a class on epistemology). Let us hope that Jared does not turn into a paper on *The Merchant of Venice* without thinking about the right questions to ask the chatbot. After all, is not a likely Institutional Learning Outcome for all graduating seniors or any institution of higher learning to think differently? To think in such a way that they had not thought four years ago And does not a new way of thinking better prepare a student for the job market that lies ahead, yet another likely learning outcome at the institutional level? The only way to obtain good answers (from the chatbot) is to ask the correct questions.

There is a great body of pedagogical literature on the benefits of group work within the classroom. Among the major advantages of working in groups (and this dates back to Bany and Johnson's, 1964, instrumental work) is the generation of novel ideas not conceived by ego himself/herself/themself. Could this not be conceived of as academically dishonest, even though it is among the greatest tools that a student has at its disposal? In other words, if one does not generate an idea and then includes this in a paper, could this not be framed as plagiarism? The next semester, Hailey, will take her 300-level course entitled Small Group Communication. During each class session, the instructor broke the three-hour meeting into two parts. The first part of the class was a lecture and discussion. The second portion of the class, however, is devoted to a group activity during which students will begin to apply the ideas, models, theories, and perspectives that they had just learned. Assume that the first group activity requires Hailey and her own group to create a new *Netflix* series. Is the information-sharing process so different from that which transpires through AI? Should Hailey be questioned or academically berated about how much she independently contributed to the group's final ideas? That she came up with the title for the show and who actress should play the role of a character named Sophie, but she was not instrumental in the group's decisions regarding the premise for the show, how the show would be pitched to *Netflix*, the relationship(s) among the seven main characters, and the episode guide for the first season's 11 episodes? Alternatively, using an AIEd model, can this be likened to the "intelligent support [system] for collaborative learning" about which Zawacki-Richter et al. (2019, p. 4) says? Can this be likened to the "new" teacher model required by instructors in the AI age in which we currently live? In support of this new model, Overono and Ditta (2023) claim that generative AI chatbots, such as ChatGPT, require educators to "imagine how [they] assess learning" (p. 1). Education is different. Teaching is different. Learning is different.

We then have an increasingly large cohort of students within the GenZ population, who are non-traditional learners. They are unable to merely read James Joyce's (1914) *Dubliners*, write an essay about it, learn about a Diophantine equation, solve a problem at home, or learn how to use Adobe Premier Pro and edit a video the next day. Today's GenZ student is a different type of learner, and as such, AI can become a helpful tutoring system, where chatbots can help provide individualized assistance to/for students in need of educational support and provide immediate feedback (Gonzalez-Calatayud, Prendes-Espinosa, & Roig-Vila, 2021), Then, the instructor is able to engage in an AI feedback loop: the student performs work, is diagnosed via the chatbot, is assisted by the chatbot, and then re-evaluated by the chatbot (Samarakou et al. 2016). Cope et al. (2021) claim that AI becomes the intermediary source between learners (students) and information disseminators (technology), where, "for the purposes of assessment, [feedback requires the student] to think again" (p. 1236). Is this not emblematic of the educational process and the assessment practices within the higher education landscape from years and decades ago? And is this not the personal tutor model of AI about which Zawacki-Richter et al. (2019, p. 4) speak: where assessment of student progress toward both Course Level Outcomes and Institutional Learning Outcomes is "learner-facing?" (Zawacki-Richter et al., 2019, p. 4)?

Hailey might take her required course in Persuasion and use Rogers' (1975) Protection Motivation Theory as a guiding framework for speaking about the role of fear-arousing messages in getting people to schedule annual vaccines. She might further engage her target (perhaps even the assessor, instructor, or grader) in a detailed discussion on the link between Protection Motivation Theory and the independent variables (e.g., emotions) linked to the Bipolar Valence-Arousal Model (see, for example, Bradley & Lang, 1994). We assume that Hailey enters a search into ChatGPT and obtains a response. Is the response a form of academic tutoring and the arguments forwarded by Hailey rewording and reframing the chatbot's assistance? Would Hailey's argument that one's inclination to get an annual vaccine increases if the likelihood of hazard decreases, the severity of hazard decreases, and self-efficacy increases (protection motivation theory), coupled with an increase in unpleasant arousal (Bipolar Valence-Arousal Model), be considered empirically valid, rational, and reliable? She gained assistance from a generative-AI chatbot. The chatbot, as Farazouli et al. (2023) tell us, is incapable of creating arguments and relating ideas back to the course content (p. 9). It requires that the assessor rethink how they will determine the mastery (e.g., low, moderate, high) of the levels of outcomes.

Going back in time for more than seven decades, Westley and MacLean (1955) state that communication requires feedback. The source becomes the target once it is the source. While electronic technologies for communication were few and far between nearly 70 years ago, suffice it to say that their model does not require that the feedback provider be a human social actor. However, at the time of their publication, the idea of the existence of something able to have the cognitive ability to do what ChatGPT currently does was not even on the horizon. However, if their model was recreated today, the gatekeeper about which they spoke would likely be the source (ChatGPT), requiring that the receiver (in this case, Hailey) provide feedback in the form of a persuasive argument. The conclusion? The chatbot is a postmodern example of the disseminator of information, which is then intelligently processed by some recipients. This is quite emblematic of Hwang et al.'s (2020) model, which situates the 'intelligent learning partner,' in this case Hailey, as the liaison between the AI tool (ChatGPT) and some educational applications (the creation of a persuasive campaign). Davenport and Prusak's (2000) ideas about the difference between information and knowledge could not be more true when applied to the AIEd environment, in which learners and assessors coexist.

All the foregoing issues and examples bring up hugely important issues for the assessor relating to misinformation and disinformation. That is, once the assessor has finally come to terms with the fact that generative-AI is here to stay and that students are going to be using it (likely in perpetuity), is there a way for students to gauge the extent to which the data received is incorrect and/or purposefully deceitful? It is one thing to determine that such chatbots are not yet able to solve extremely difficult equations within hard sciences. For example, Wardat et al. (2023) found that ChatGPT is a great tool for teaching mathematics and helping students understand how to solve even the most advanced logarithms, but its ability to solve all problems is not failproof. According to them, "while ChatGPT is certainly a powerful language model, it is not infallible" (Wardat et al., 2023, p. 14). In fact, Newman (2023) went as far as to say that ChatGPT "can occasionally generate…nonsensical responses' (p. 6). Is it acceptable for a student of mathematics to get a problem incorrect? Probably so. However, what about the student majoring in Biochemical Engineering attempts to learn about macroscopic balances? Or is the Computer Science major attempting to learn about advanced C++ programming? Or is the student majoring in epidemiology attempting to learn about infectious diseases? Or does the student majoring in Public Relations attempt to learn how to prepare a media kit and write a press release? Is the infallibility of the chatbot going to suffice? Perhaps it is time that will tell us.

NEW FORMS OF ASSESSMENT IN THE AIED WORLD

Hwang and Chang (2021) let the world of higher education know that, unfortunately, when it comes to AI, understanding assessment often takes the backseat of understanding how students use chatbots for educational purposes. However, Cope et al. (2021) argue that "assessment is perhaps the most significant area of opportunity offered by artificial intelligence for transformative change in education' (p. 1233). In fact, the mass entry of AI into the educational sphere has forced educators to question the operational definition of outcomes at the course, program, and institutional levels. What does it mean to be a "good" student? What does it mean to be a high-performing" student? (Di Placito & Mortensen, 2023). As such, it is time to better understand how assessment strategies are changing as a result of the implementation of chatbots such as ChatGPT. First, it can be argued that an answer is only as good as the question that prompts the target to think, critically examine, and respond. ChatGPT can help instructors within the higher educational world create better questions that, in turn, will hopefully garner better responses, forcing students to engage at higher cognitive levels (see, for example, Huggard, 2023). For example, suppose that Hailey's Organizational Communication instructor wants to have her students assess the extent to which employers are fostering both cultural sensitivity and employee diversity once new employees are hired, as well as the impact that such a culture has on employee motivation, employee commitment, employee satisfaction, and employee turnover. One way to ask such a question is as follows:

Given what we have spoken about so far in class, explain how employers are promoting both cultural sensitivity and employee diversity once new employees are hired, and please explain how a culture is created, such as employee motivation, employee commitment, employee satisfaction, and employee turnover.

Is this a good answer? This is certainly not a *bad* question. But let us see what ChatGPT recommends when we put in a search for 'question to ask students about cultural sensitivity and employee diversity and how this impacts employee motivation, employee commitment, employee satisfaction, and employee turnover.' Not only did ChatGPT provide questions linked to the variables of cultural sensitivity (e.g., how does cultural sensitivity contribute to a more inclusive workplace?); employee diversity; motivation (e.g., in what ways can a lack of diversity lead to demotivation among employees?), commitment (e.g., can you explain the concept of cultural fit and its potential impact on employee commitment in diverse workplaces?); satisfaction (e.g., how can organizations foster a culture of inclusion to improve overall job satisfaction?) and turnover (e.g., are there instances where a lack of cultural sensitivity has been linked to higher turnover?) However, the chatbot also recommended asking students about variables such as awareness and unconscious bias (e.g., what steps can individuals and organizations take to mitigate unconscious bias?) Training and education (e.g., how can ongoing cultural sensitivity training benefit employees and organizations, and what are some potential challenges in implementing diversity and inclusion training programs?); globalization (e.g., can you provide examples of companies that have successfully embraced global diversity?) and measuring the impact (e.g., how can feedback mechanisms be integrated into diversity programs to assess their effectiveness?). The chatbot thought in ways that the instructor did not do. This helped her to create better questions. More detailed questions. Questions that required more cognitive energy. Thus, ChatGPT can certainly help instructors (assessors) create better questions, which, in the end, will hopefully/likely lead to better responses on behalf of students (Newman, 2023). Will this increase in outcomes increase the likelihood of student learning? Student mastery? Likely so.

Second, with the introduction of AI, higher education instructors must change their assignments and the learning outcomes linked to them. ChatGPT can assist instructors in creating entirely new lesson plans and curricula (see Rasul et al., 2023). Amazingly, ChatGPT can create personalized lesson plans not only for the level of individual students (e.g., low vs. high performing), but also for the level at which the course is taught (e.g., a lower-level vs. upper-level course in Communication Theory) (see, for example, Huggard, 2023). From an assessment perspective, this can aid instructors in their pedagogical approaches. Results from Lo's (2023) study indicated that many instructors using ChatGPT also use this AI tool to gather outside materials to use both inside the classroom and to assign to students outside readings. While instructors have been doing this for a long time, this process has been facilitated by AIEd applications. ChatGPT has also been found to simplify the language used by instructors, which might be linked to (correlation vs. causation yet to be determined) increased student success (see, for example, Ausat et al. 2023). Might Hailey be more successful and more motivated and more excited if her instructor's lesson plans are more individualized (at both the personal and class levels); if her instructor is able to use ChatGPT as a tool for obtaining more and [perhaps] more useful course materials; and if her instructor is able to use a chatbot to simplify language via its language recommendations? The literature certainly seems to think of this.

Third, although it seems obvious, the goal of instructors is (or at least should be), among other things, to help students with the generation of new ideas and the encouragement of critical thinking. As an instructor, I often recommend that my students try their damnest to write introductory paragraph(s) in their papers last. Why? This is because it is the most difficult section of the entire study. How can a student introduce a topic or a paper that has not yet been written? However, with the introduction of chatbots, the generation of ideas (and the process of critical thinking that ensues) is facilitated (see, for example, Halaweh, 2023). Let us, again, think about Hailey. Assume that she is now taking her course in public speaking/oral communication, and that it is time for her persuasive speech. She wants to persuade people to begin eating grilled octopuses. But now what? She might speak about the health implications (but she might not know what these are), its novelty (but she really does not know how novel a culinary practice it really is), and its taste (but she really does not know how to describe it). ChatGPT, when she enters "how to persuade people to eat a grilled octopus," lets her know that:

Persuading people to try grilled octopuses can be done effectively by appealing to their tastes, addressing their concerns, and creating an enticing dining experience. There are some steps to persuade people to try grilled octopus (e.g., understand their concerns, highlight health benefits, emphasize flavor, texture explanation, pairing suggestions, share positive experiences, offer a taste test, present it visually, educate about sustainability, make it a social event, respect their choice, and offer alternatives). [However] remember that persuasion should always be respectful and considerate of the other person's preferences and boundaries. Not everyone will be open to trying new foods and that is okay.

Hailey learns new strategies for her forthcoming oral presentations. However, it will now be up to her to figure out how to share the positive experiences and how to present them visually and how to educate her target(s) about sustainability. She is now being assessed not only on what she knows (thanks, in large part, to *ChatGPT*), but also how she now critically thinks about how and why these independent variables will likely create the effect for which she is hoping: the desire for those listening to her persuasive speech to try a grilled octopus. In this case, without the *Chatbot*, Hailey would not have had these ideas and would not have thought to adopt these perspectives. Upon the accruement of said information (turned into knowledge through what is called the process of codification), Hailey is graded by her assessor. Enter *ChaptGPT* and enter a new requirement for assessment of oral speech.

Fourth, this becomes salient at both the introductory and more advanced levels when adopting alternative perspectives. All too often, students adopt, and fail to mention, opposing viewpoints (see, for example, Minson & Dorison, 2022). That is, they believe that their major theses are foolproof and impossible to refute. Whether this is based more on ignorance than on purpose is likely to be due to the individual. Regardless, *ChatGPT* has become a useful tool for providing users with alternative ways of looking at ideas from different perspectives and vantage points (Skrabut, 2023). Let us assume that Hailey completes the assignment of homophilous ties (mentioned in the opening email of this chapter): the idea that social actors are more likely to be in relationships (at least in better relationships) with those who are similar to them. She will likely provide multiple examples of this case. However, what if she does not at least partially pay tribute to the idea that heterophilous (the 'opposites attract' paradigm) relationships can, and certainly do, succeed as well? What will the assessor think? Could this create an academic pause in an otherwise wonderfully written and structured paper? When Hailey put the sentence 'do all homophilous relationships work' into ChatGPT, the result is as follows:

Not all homophilous relationships work. Homophily refers to the tendency of people to form connections with others who share similar characteristics or interests. Although having commonalities can be a strong foundation for building relationships, it does not guarantee success in every case. Many factors influence the success or failure of any relationship, including homophilousness. There are several reasons why not all such relationships work (e.g., individual differences, communication, timing, external factors, expectations, change, conflict resolution). In summary, while homophily can provide a strong starting point for building relationships, it does not guarantee success. Successful relationships, whether homophilous, require effort, effective communication, mutual respect, and adaptability from both parties. Each relationship is unique and its success depends on a variety of factors beyond shared interests or characteristics.

Hailey now has an alternative perspective from which to bolster her initial claims, and the assessor can see that such an alternative perspective provides further evidentiary support that her initial arguments are, in fact, valid. As an assessor, Hailey's assessment has improved significantly.

Fifth, as assessors, it is important to remember that students take classes. They do not know everything about everything, even at the introductory level. Let us assume that Hailey decided to take a course called Communication in the 21st Century as one of her major electives, and her first assignment was to write about how digital journalists have recently covered three global conflicts. Let us further assume that Hailey used ChatGPT to learn about the recent global conflicts that emerged because she did not pay much attention to the news. She is a member of the *GenZ* sociological population. Is the assessment going to be at least somewhat based on her knowledge of recent, current events? If she writes about the West Africa locust infestation from to 2003-2005 or the 2010 Haiti earthquake or the 2011 East Africa drought or the 2012 Syrian Civil War, will her assessor assume that her knowledge of 'current' is flawed? Merely typing 'what are some recent global conflicts' into ChatGPT, Hailey learns that the 2023 global crises that are of importance at present include, for example, gang violence in Haiti, the climate change issues plaguing South Sudan, the lack of humanitarian aid in the Democratic Republic of Congo, and poverty in Afghanistan. Of course, Hailey will need to learn more about the financial, social, and political precursors and effects of all four; however, thanks to this chatbot, she now has information that she had previously not. Her assessor is now reading Hailey's assignment through a different lens–a lens rife with optimism. It is Hailey's authentic voice on which she will be assessed. This chatbot has become a liaison between Hailey and her instructor and has performed as an AI tutor.

Sixth, we must not forget that instructors still use assessment mechanisms such as multiple-choice exams, true/false questions, fill-in-the-blank queries, and short-answer prompts. These are, as any assessor will contend, far from easy to create (and in many cases, objectively grade). Enter ChatGPT. At her advisor's recommendation, Hailey decided to take a 300-level elective course called Conflict Management and Negotiation. The course deals with how and why conflict emerges within family, work, and friendships, as well as how conflict is ultimately resolved. Rather than developing her own prompts, Hailey's instructor decided to have the chatbot create objective-based queries merely by entering 'questions to ask my students about conflict management and negotiation,' after which a multitude of text-based responses emerged.

1. What are the key differences between conflict resolution and conflict avoidance?
2. What are the five conflict management styles (e.g., avoidance, accommodation, competition, compromise, and collaboration) and when might each be appropriate?
3. How can cultural differences impact conflict management and negotiation style? Can you give examples of cultural considerations in negotiations?
4. What ethical considerations should be taken into consideration when negotiating? Can you provide examples of ethical dilemmas in the negotiations?
5. How can consensus-building techniques be applied to resolve conflicts and make decisions in a team or group setting?
6. How can you differentiate between interests and positions in a negotiation and why is this important?

While these six questions are created via generative artificial intelligence (GAI) bots, what Farazouli et al. (2023) define as data generated "based on unsupervised machine learning models" (p. 2), they provide useful assessment questions for instructors who still believe that these types of questions are appropriate for gauging student success. In addition to "correct answers," what else might the instructor assess their students? According to Rasul et al. (2023), the multicollinearity approach would indicate that ChatGPT would enable the assessment of additional variables such as critical thinking, problem-solving, communication, teamwork, leadership, adaptability, and digital literacy" (p. 9). From an assessment perspective, it seems that ChatGPT can do everything.

Before concluding this chapter, it is necessary to mention the amount of attention paid over the last several years to new assessment strategies, given the psycho-social-emotional characteristics of today's GenZ population (Mahesh, Bhat, & Ramya, 2021). As an example, 'ungrading' has become a popular approach across many disciplines: namely in the social sciences and writing programs. In short, ungrading involves assessing student work based on variables such as critical thinking, cognitive development, and academic progress, rather than merely letter grades that are linked to some objective (or even worse, subjective) assessment outcomes. Stommel (2023) makes it clear that 'ungrading' is different from 'non-grading.' An assessment was performed. As he said, it is just a different form of assessment. Different ways of thinking about determining the level of student success and achievement of outcomes. One variable linked to ungrading is student progress (whether this is determined by the students themselves or by the instructor). Has an individual's writing, thinking, or presentation skills improved since the semester began? This is far from Kaipa's (2021) traditional assessment practices. It is determining such things as authenticity and growth and "learning…designed to help learners do the kinds of things that professionals do" (Swiecki et al., 2022, p. 5). This is linked to the constructivist theory of learning about which Rasul et al. (2023) speak, which "…emphasizes the importance of students constructing their own understanding of knowledge…enabling them to explore and experiment with ideas, ask questions, and receive immediate feedback' (p. 3). Assessment, again, has both influenced and is influenced by AI.

CONCLUSION

What the extant literature informs the world of education is that it is high time to "design a new kind of education that fully exploits the affordances of artificial intelligence" (Cope, Kalantzis, & Searsmith, 2021, p. 1231). Not only are educators and students faced with the ever-so-salient question 'What do we mean by assessment,' but perhaps more importantly, 'What do we mean by education?' As Popenici and

Kerr (2017) ask, 'What is artificial intelligence' (p. 1). How will students use new generative AI tools during the years to come? Will they use them as a complement to education or as a way of engaging in academically dishonest behavior? Fourtane (2023, *How Universities Can*, para 3) mentioned an interview with Professor Cindy Casey, Program Coordinator, and Assistant Professor of Computer Information Science at Gwynedd Mercy University, who endorses the former:

If students are going to use the technologies to cheat, they are going to find a way to cheat. I don't think that the majority of students are in that statistic. It reminds me of the United States in 1988 when there were a lot of math teachers that protested the calculators in class, and we now see that calculators are included in math classes. I say, if you have a technology, you should be using it because companies are using it. And when graduates get out into the work world, they need to know about the technology. I think it's important that universities need to use these tools and that they have to evolve with the technology. They have to be flexible enough to change the curriculum as the technology changes and recognize when change is necessary.

Hopefully, this chapter has at least opened the door for conversation about the increasing need for dialogue about both the changing nature of pedagogy, as well as assessment, within the classroom. Hailey is a communication major, yet she will take myriad courses that span disciplines within her university. This semester, she will be assessed in Organic Chemistry and Theatre for Non-Majors and Forensic Psychology and Interpersonal Communication. And, if her instructors are adept at using new technologies in and for the classroom, then Hailey will be in a new cohort of students who are the 'guinea pigs' of a new educational landscape: whose educators are learning new assessment strategies. Some of these assessments have been successful. Others not so much. Some are educationally and technologically easier to implement. Others are astronomically challenging. While there are certainly a plethora of educators who are, and likely perpetually, will be concerned about and with AI and its impact on education, it is important to remember Perera and Lankathilaka's (2023) claim that "one of the main benefits is the potential of artificial intelligence to…promot[e] critical thinking skills among students" (p. 306).

The world of higher education is rapidly changing. Such changes require instructors to think differently about how they teach and students about how they think, and assessors about how they judge material/course mastery. According to Hwang et al. (2020), "the advancement of AI has brought computer-supported education to a new era"(p. 4). New technologies are used when they are introduced. What would be the purpose of their introduction if this was not the case? If we think about communication media, the telegraph revolutionized the world, followed by the landline telephone, the phonograph, the radio, television, the Internet, the cellular telephone, and now ChatGPT. Each medium changed meaning making, information dissemination, communication, learning, and understanding as compared to that before it. The landline changed the telegraph, the phonograph changed the landline, the radio changed the phonograph, the telephone changed the radio, the Internet changed the television, the cellular telephone changed the Internet, and ChatGPT changed every medium. It is both scary and exciting to consider what the year 2035 will bring. There was time when the students assessed their research abilities. Not only what they claimed but also what they cited and how they cited them. Here is a funny meme that has circulated on the Internet (and, in fact, one that I share with my students on the first day of their senior thesis course).

It is very important to realize that organizations post-graduation want to hire students who have mastery (a term very salient in the world of assessment) of AI and ChatGPT. Therefore, it is time to increase the

Figure 1. Card catalog meme

use of these technological tools in the classroom rather than avoid them. I recently attended a webinar led by two experts in generative AI (Rana & Verhoeven, 2023). Among their major recommendations was that instructors need to figure out (and figure out quickly) what they can do *with* AI rather than what they can do *to* it. That is, how can they endorse it as a pedagogical tool for experiential learning and, according to them, use chatbots as a co-pilot? According to them, this likely requires changing how instructors teach their courses and assess (and even define) students' success.

As this chapter clarifies, now is the time to reconceive how assessment practices must change in light of AI: a move from the inauthentic and antiquated to authentic and modern (Swiecki et al. 2022). That no longer can we assess, for example, whether students are using ChatGPT, what they are citing, and how they are citing. Chatbots are gaining data from millions of different sources. However, as assessors of knowledge, perhaps we can rest a bit more knowing that, as Hossain (2023) tells us, an average similarity index of only 7.5% was noted via ChatGPT, indicating that 92.5% of material produced by it was, in fact, novel and not a complete replication (word-for-word) of that found from online sources. Can we trust that students will have a low similarity index compared to such chatbots? Probably not. However, we cannot be reluctant to assume that ChatGPT is merely a tool for dishonest behavior. While it might do some of the legal work for students, it still requires that critical thinking processes be put into practice. Research indicates that critical analysis is beyond the ability of chatbots, at least for now (and the foreseeable future). Today's educators must be certain, perhaps more than ever, that students continue to engage in critical reasoning (both inductive and deductive) and are able to analyze evidence and produce (in rhetorical form) cogent arguments; that students are collaborating with, not being replaced by, the chatbots that seem to be here to stay. Metaphorically speaking, this is not very different from the difference between thick (deep) and thin (surface) level descriptions, which Geertz (1973) famously argued. However, we also must assume that if we, as assessors, are able to train both ourselves and, more importantly, our students, on the ethical issues linked to this chatbot, ChatGPT can be a wonderful addition to the world of learning and academia.

REFERENCES

American Association of Colleges and Universities (AACU). (n.d.). https://aacu.org

Ausat, A. M., Massang, B., Efendi, M., Norifman, N., & Riady, Y. (2023). Can ChatGPT replace the role of teachers in the classroom: A fundamental analysis. *Journal of Education, 5*(4), 16100–16106. doi:10.31004/joe.v5i4.2745

Bany, M. A., & Johnson, L. V. (1964). *Classroom group behavior: Group dynamics in education*. Macmillan.

Bradley, M. M., & Lang, P. J. (1994). Measuring emotion: The self-assessment manikin and the semantic differential. *Journal of Behavior Therapy and Experimental Psychiatry, 25*(1), 49–51. doi:10.1016/0005-7916(94)90063-9 PMID:7962581

Chen, Y., Jensen, S., Albert, L. J., Gupta, S., & Lee, T. (2023). Artificial intelligence (AI) student assistants in the classroom: Designing chatbots to support student success. *Information Systems Frontiers, 25*(1), 161–182. doi:10.1007/s10796-022-10291-4

Cope, B., Kalantzis, M., & Searsmith, D. (2021). Artificial intelligence for education: Knowledge and its assessment of AI-enabled learning ecologies. *Educational Philosophy and Theory, 53*(12), 1229–1245. doi:10.1080/00131857.2020.1728732

Crawford, J., Cowling, M., & Allen, K. (2023). Leadership is needed for ethical ChatGPT: Character, assessment and learning using artificial intelligence (AI). *Journal of University Teaching & Learning Practice, 20*(3). Advance online publication. doi:10.53761/1.20.3.02

Davenport, T. H., & Prusak, L. (2000). *Working knowledge: How organizations manage what they know*. Harvard Business School. doi:10.1145/348772.348775

Di Placito, M. L., & Mortensen, R. (2023). Applying AI efforts to student assessments: That is, alternative innovations. *The Interdisciplinary Journal of Student Success, 2*, 93–108.

Farazouli, A., Cerratto-Pargman, T., Bolander-Laksov, K., & McGrath, C. (2023). Hello GPT! Goodbye home examination? An exploratory study of AI chatbots impact on university teachers' assessment practices. *Assessment & Evaluation in Higher Education*, 1–13. Advance online publication. doi:10.1080/02602938.2023.2241676

Fourtane, S. (2023, August 3). *How universities can better prepare students for a future with AI*. Fierce Education. https://www.fierceeducation.com/leadership/how-universities-can-better-preparestudents-future-asi

Geertz, C. (1973). *The Interpretation of cultures*. Basic Books.

Gershon, M. (2018). *How to use Bloom's taxonomy in the classroom: Great teaching made easy*. Learning Sciences International.

González-Calatayud, V., Prendes-Espinosa, P., & Roig-Vila, R. (2021). Artificial intelligence for student assessment: A systematic review. *Applied Sciences (Basel, Switzerland), 11*(6), 5467. Advance online publication. doi:10.3390/app11125467

Halaweh, M. (2023). ChatGPT in education: Strategies for responsible implementation. *Contemporary Educational Technology, 15*(2), 421–431. doi:10.30935/cedtech/13036

Hossain, A. (2023). *ChatGPT in higher education: Advantages, challenges, and impact on students, educators, and institutional leaders*. Digital Readiness and Intelligent Systems.

Huggard, G. (2023). *ChatGPT for educators: From lesson planning to assessment (leveraging the power of AI in the education process)*. Independently Published.

Hwang, G. J., & Chang, C. Y. (2021). A review of opportunities and challenges of chatbots in education. *Interactive Learning Environments*. Advance online publication. doi:10.1080/10494820.2021.1952615

Hwang, G. J., Xie, H., Wah, B. W., & Gasevic, D. (2020). Vision, challenges, roles, and research issues of artificial intelligence in education. Computers and Education. *Artificial Intelligence, 1*(13). Advance online publication. doi:10.1016.j.caeai.2020.100001

Joyce, J. (1914). *Dubliners*. Grant Richards Ltd.

Judd, T., & Keith, B. (2017). Implementing undergraduate student learning outcomes assessment at the program and institutional levels. In C. Secolsky & D. B. Denison (Eds.), *Handbook on measurement, assessment, and evaluation in higher education* (pp. 69–86). Routledge. doi:10.4324/9781315709307-8

Kaipa, R. M. (2021). Multiple choice questions and essay questions in curriculum. *Journal of Applied Research in Higher Education, 13*(1), 16–32. doi:10.1108/JARHE-01-2020-0011

Lo, C. K. (2023). What is the impact of ChatGPT on education? A rapid review of the literature. *Education Sciences, 13*(4), 410–424. doi:10.3390/educsci13040410

Mahesh, J., Bhat, A. K., & Ramya, S. (2021). Are Gen Z values the new disruptor for future educational institutions? *Journal of Higher Education Theory and Practice, 21*(12), 102–123. doi:10.33423/jhetp.v21i12.4704

Newman, C. (2023). *Guide to using ChatGPT in higher education: Transforming the learning experience*. Independently Published.

Overono, A. L., & Ditta, A. S. (2023). The rise of artificial intelligence: A clarion call for higher education to redefine learning and reimagine assessment. *College Teaching, 71*(3), 1–4. Advance online publication. doi:10.1080/87567555.2023.2233653

Perera, P., & Lankathilaka, M. (2023). AI in higher education: A literature review of ChatGPT and guidelines for responsible implementation. *International Journal of Research and Innovation in Social Sciences, 7*(6), 306–314. doi:10.47772/IJRISS.2023.7623

Popenici, S. A., & Kerr, S. (2017). Exploring the impact of artificial intelligence on teaching and learning in higher education. *Research and Practice in Technology Enhanced Learning, 12*(1), 22. Advance online publication. doi:10.1186/s41039-017-0062-8 PMID:30595727

Rana, V., & Verhoeven, B. (2023, August 4). Embracing AI in education: A shift from creators to co-pilots. In Tyler's (Chair), *Authentic Assessments for the AI Era* (Symposium). TheGoReact, Zoom. get.goreact.com/resources/authentic-assessments-for-the-ai-era-2/

Rasul, T., Nair, S., Kalendra, D., Robin, M., Santini, F., Ladeira, W., Sun, M. D. I., Rather, R. A., & Heathcote, L. (2023). The role of ChatGPT in higher education: Benefits, challenges, and future research directions. *Journal of Applied Learning and Teaching*, *6*(1). Advance online publication. doi:10.37074/jalt.2023.6.1.29

Rogers, R. W. (1975). A protection motivation theory of fear appeals and attitude change. *The Journal of Psychology*, *91*(1), 93–114. doi:10.1080/00223980.1975.9915803 PMID:28136248

Rudolph, J., Tan, S., & Tan, S. (2023). ChatGPT: Bullshit spewer or the end of traditional assessments in higher education? *Journal of Applied Learning and Teaching*, *6*(1), 342–363. doi:10.37074/jalt.2023.6.1.9

Samarakou, M., Fylladitakis, E., Fruh, W., Karolidis, D., Hatziapostolou, A., Athinaios, S., & Grigoriadou, M. (2016). Evaluation of an intelligent open learning system for engineering education. *Knowledge Management and E-Learning: An International Journal*, *8*(3), 496–513. doi:10.34105/j.kmel/2016.07.031

Skrabut, S. (2023). *80 ways to use ChatGPT in the classroom: Using AI to enhance teaching and learning*. Academic Press.

Stommel, J. (2023). Do we need the word 'ungrading?' *Zeal: A Journal for the Liberal Arts, 1*(2), 82–87.

Swiecki, Z., Khosravi, H., Chen, G., Martinez-Maldonado, R., Lodge, J. M., Milligan, S., Selwyn, N., & Gašević, D. (2022). Assessment in the age of artificial intelligence. *Computers and Education: Artificial Intelligence*, *3*(1), 100075. Advance online publication. doi:10.1016/j.caeai.2022.100075

Uchiyama, K. P., & Radin, J. L. (2009). Curriculum mapping in higher education: A vehicle for collaboration. *Innovative Higher Education*, *33*(4), 271–280. doi:10.1007/s10755-008-9078-8

Wardat, Y., Tashtoush, M. A., Alali, R., & Jarrah, A. M. (2023). ChatGPT: A revolutionary tool for teaching and learning mathematics. *Eurasia Journal of Mathematics, Science and Technology Education*, *19*(7), em2286. Advance online publication. doi:10.29333/ejmste/13272

Westley, B. H., & MacLean, M. S. (1955). A conceptual model for communications research. *Educational Technology Research and Development*, *3*(1), 3–12. doi:10.1007/BF02713344

Zawacki-Richter, O., Marín, V. I., Bond, M., & Gouverneur, F. (2019). Systematic review of research on artificial intelligence applications in higher education: Where are the educators? *International Journal of Educational Technology in Higher Education*, *16*(39), 39. Advance online publication. doi:10.1186/s41239-019-0171-0

Chapter 7
ChatGPT:
Can Students Really Get Away with Speechcraft?

Ali Garib
https://orcid.org/0000-0002-8331-7120
Iowa State University, USA

Tina A. Coffelt
https://orcid.org/0000-0002-1926-6453
Iowa State University, USA

Awad M. Alshalwy
Omar Al-Mukhtar University, Libya

SeyedMohammad Kashani
Iowa State University, USA

ABSTRACT

Public speaking learners preparing for a speech can find the process of writing an outline time-consuming. With the presence of AI like ChatGPT, learners may feel tempted to abandon the outlining tasks needed to organize their ideas and instead rely on AI to minimize their effort. Such a use can dull students' writing skills and dampen their creativity and originality. This study examines 180 ChatGPT-generated speech outlines using three prompt engineering techniques to analyze their content and possible impact on students' work. While the findings indicate that ChatGPT can lack the sophistication required for speech outlines, it is a powerful tool that can be prompt-trained to generate human-like content. The findings reveal that prompt engineering plays a major role in determining if students can get away with speechcraft using ChatGPT, illustrating the threat of ChatGPT on students' learning. Yet, its prompt-limited outlines can exhibit potential benefits for students' academic work while upholding integrity. The study proposes implications for pedagogical practices with ChatGPT.

DOI: 10.4018/979-8-3693-0831-8.ch007

INTRODUCTION

The development of a speech outline is fundamental to speechcraft preparation (Beebe & Beebe, 1991). Robinson and Kiewra (1995) define outlining as "a systematic listing of a concept with its subordinate concepts and their attribute values" (p. 455) conveyed in a hierarchical relation. The preparation of a speech outline involves the logical organization of a speech introduction, body paragraphs, and conclusion; clarification of the general and specific speech purpose and thesis statement; utilization of supporting materials; citation of credible sources; creation of smooth transitional statements; and refining the overall organizational pattern of a speech. This listing of concepts can assist public speakers in organizing their thoughts critically (Myer et al., 2010) and can aid listeners' engagement and recall (Cronin, 1994). The teaching and learning of such speech craft skills have led to positive outcomes in the field of speech communication and public speaking pedagogy with the assistance of educational technology.

Technology's contribution to communication education is immeasurable but identifiable, such as facilitating the teaching of public speaking, providing optimal support through tools that can assist learners' understanding of the content, and perhaps, most importantly, speech crafting. During the COVID-19 pandemic, technology played an integral role in facilitating teachers' navigation through uncertainty while teaching basic communication courses, such as public speaking (Kretsinger-Harries et al., 2021). Since the COVID-19 pandemic, public speaking pedagogy has witnessed unprecedented integration of educational technology, as technology use has become a requirement and not a novelty (Edwards, 2021). Such integration involves a wide range of technological tools, such as video recording of speech delivery (El Mortaji, 2022), virtual reality (VR), and speech practice (Xie et al., 2021), among others.

With the adaptation of new technologies in virtual classrooms, educators have learned to judiciously adopt "new technological tools to counteract regressive institutional resilience that resists change, and maximizing inclusivity in course design and delivery" (Schwartzman, 2022, p. 143). This maximization of technology integration in the teaching and learning of public speaking is necessary to embracing 21st century pedagogy. Therefore, educational technology has become a fundamental component of teaching the skills of speechcraft and delivery, encompassing how instructors use messages to interact with mobile devices (smartphones, tablets, laptops), virtual and augmented reality systems, AI pedagogical agents, and social robots" (Edwards & Edwards, 2018, p. 185).

The emergence of the Chat Generative Pre-trained Transformer (ChatGPT) is expected to inspire more innovations in the teaching and learning of public speaking. Such innovations can upgrade learning by providing real-time written interaction, generating speech outline examples for speech analysis, receiving feedback on speech outlines, or acting as a supplementary tool for students' understanding of lesson content. Understanding the quality of ChatGPT's speech outlines is vital for their integration into the teaching of public speaking.

INTRODUCING CHATGPT

ChatGPT, released by OpenAI in November 2022 (Schulman et al., 2022), is a state-of-the-art language model of machine learning and natural language processing (NLP). One of the most common features of ChatGPT is that it can assist students in writing essays by generating high-quality text based on the input provided (Tate et al., 2023). ChatGPT can also help students with a variety of tasks ranging from generating human-like ideas to writing complete sentences, paragraphs, essays, and speech outlines.

The potential of generative AI, such as ChatGPT, "manifests when utilized as an expert collaborator, one who often gets things wrong but who can help with a range of complex tasks such as comparing concepts, constructing counterarguments, generating analogies" (Mishra et al., 2023, p. 242). By generating ideas, suggestions, and drafting texts, ChatGPT can serve as an invaluable educational assistant. Collaboration between students and AI creativity can lead to more innovative and diverse outcomes. On a wider scope, Schmidt-Crawford et al. (2023) stressed the need for the integration of AI in teacher education to facilitate student learning. However, ChatGPT has caused concern among educators at all levels, primarily regarding the need for learners' independent composition skills (Roose, 2023). Additional concerns include the students' intention to learn and think for themselves, where they become reliant on AI to compose and articulate their original thoughts.

While ChatGPT supplements the production of original thoughts relevant to specific topics, there is a trending opinion that such generative AI models "need to be constrained because of a lack of understanding of ethics" (Gozalo-Brizuela & Garrido-Merchan, 2023, p. 20), especially in academic contexts. Such an opinion cannot be a solution (Mishra et al., 2023), but the call to ban AI seems to emerge from several areas where the ChatGPT model can be problematic. Aydın and Karaarslan (2022) added that "one area where AI will affect is [*sic*] the regulation of intellectual property rights" (p. 22), perhaps raising the bar for human creativity and critical thinking to make it difficult for AI models to keep pace with the originality of human thoughts. Another area of concern is related to ChatGPT's bias; that is, since "ChatGPT is trained on data gathered from the real world" (Azaria, 2022, p. 2), the equitability of its generated responses is questionable (Krügel et al., 2023). Questioning the validity of ChatGPT's responses is reasonable because ChatGPT is mainly trained by uncertified datasets. According to Brown et al. (2020), the Common Crawl, Wikipedia, and OpenWebText datasets, along with unspecified scientific articles, books, blogs, and forum conversations, are fed to ChatGPT. The inclusion of these datasets raises the need for further exploration of the output of the ChatGPT. This study gathered a sample of ChatGPT's output in one context, evaluated the output for quality, and considered the ethical and pedagogical implications in the context of education.

ChatGPT's Implications for Education

A wide range of AI tools can be as effective as ChatGPT in education. However, what distinguishes ChatGPT from other AI tools is its possible intervention in the composition of ideas. That is, ChatGPT can undermine education given that "students could potentially use these systems to cheat on their assignments by submitting essays that are not their own work" (Cotton et al., 2023, p. 3). ChatGPT's use raises related concerns, namely, ethical misconduct and abuse of educational technologies.

Despite the potential challenges that ChatGPT could bring to education, banning such a tool is unlikely to be the solution, considering the opportunities it can offer (Zhai, 2022). As in the case with the COVID-19 pandemic where education transitioned online, initially causing unprecedented challenges for educators all over the world (Garib, 2022; Parsaiyan & Gholami, 2023), ChatGPT is at that initial stage of being perceived as a 'crisis.' In the long run, ChatGPT can perhaps be a turning point where human education, creativity, and originality may be elevated, raising the bar for teachers' expectations. For example, pedagogically, ChatGPT has the potential to create more engaging teaching and learning environments (Rudolph et al., 2023), fostering student creativity in ways that educational technology has never witnessed before. Such methods include adding a new type of text analysis for composition learning (Wang, 2022), designing activities for speech craft analysis (Chen, 2022), and engaging learners in interactive tasks to collaborate with a responsive robot. Overall, it is reasonable to speculate that the ChatGPT is the beginning of a new era in educational technology.

Significance of the Study

To discuss ChatGPT's pedagogical implications, the current study explores the quality of ChatGPT's speech outlines by zooming in close proximity to the overall structure of its sections and analyzing them in accordance with Gunn's (2018) speech outline format. Gunn's (2018) speech outlining is a popular and effective format used by many public speaking instructors and professionals, reflecting a humanistic prudence "vis-à-vis its readers' strengths" (Hartelius, 2018, p. 353). In speechcraft, being prudent vis-à-vis readers' strengths involves tailoring content to match readers' level of knowledge, skills, or interests and leveraging their strengths to deliver a message effectively. In the same domain, prompt engineering is crucial for optimizing the quality of AI-generated text (Krause, 2023). Crafting effective prompts requires expertise and careful attention (Liu et al., 2023) because prompt engineering can "customize the outputs and interactions with an LLM" (White et al., 2023, p. 1). Therefore, it is crucial to explore the outputs of ChatGPT using multiple prompts to capture several possibilities for ChatGPT performance (Cao et al., 2023).

Such guided exploration and analysis could help evaluate ChatGPT's potential contribution to public speaking pedagogical practices and lead to the first research question RQ1: What is the quality of speech outlines generated by ChatGPT using three phases of prompt engineering?

While OpenAI had launched an AI-generated text detector, a classifier trained to distinguish between AI-written and human-written texts, this classifier "might spread disinformation about the potential for disinformation," yielding "a lot of false positives and negatives" (Bogost, 2023, p. 6). In light of these limitations, OpenAI discontinued its AI classifier tool due to its low accuracy rate, confirming the need to understand the complexity between AI-generated and human-written texts for pedagogical practices. Given the uncertainty over the equitability of and learners' potential dependency on ChatGPT, as well as the impact it could have on speech craft, analyzing ChatGPT-generated speech outlines can yield future pedagogical implications. Such implications could assist teachers in integrating this AI tool into teaching speech craft and speech outline writing, moving beyond mere authorship surveillance to a more innovative educational approach. To that end, the second research question asks RQ2: How could ChatGPT contribute to academic integrity pressures with speech outline assignments?

RESEARCH DESIGN

A qualitative research approach is most appropriate for this study because such methods allow researchers "to generatively discover deep and contextualized insights" (Jiang et al., 2021, p. 93). Of relevance to the research goals of the current study, an exploratory research design (Creswell & Poth, 2018) was employed to analyze the texts that ChatGPT produced in response to a given input. The nature of an exploratory study focuses on the emphasis of discovery over confirmation of the phenomenon (Holliday, 2016). Stebbins (2001) explains that exploratory research is "carried out to demonstrate that little or no work has been done on the group, process, or activity under consideration" (p. 3), all of which are at the heart of this chapter. Therefore, an exploratory qualitative research approach was most appropriate for the current study.

Procedure and Materials

This study used ChatGPT, a free version of May 24, 2023, as the only source of data for analysis. We expect more versions of ChatGPT to emerge; therefore, this notation is important as research accumulates. The data included three types of speech outlines: informative ($n = 60$), persuasive ($n = 60$), and special ($n = 60$). Following Mthuli et al. (2022), data saturation and sufficiency were achieved within a scope of 60 outlines per speech type. Each speech type was generated three times using the three methods of prompt engineering. These speech outlines reflect common assignments in a public-speaking class and contextualize the findings.

Text Generation

The authors used the ChatGPT input engine (see Figure 1) to generate and collect the data.

Figure 1. ChatGPT's response generation input engine
Source: https://chat.openai.com/chat retrieved on May 24, 2023

Because the ChatGPT output can be varied based on users' prompt engineering, this study incorporates three phases to generate the data for analysis. These phases include (1) basic prompts, (2) detailed prompts, and (3) trained prompts. Table 1 provides detailed descriptions of each data-collection phase. These three phases represent three common ways of using the ChatGPT.

Analysis

The functionality of AI systems revolves around the training of the models to retrieve data, more specifically "AI text agents are trained using large sets of documents that are treated as equally important, learn from the most recurrent patterns in the data and repeat them on the basis of quantity rather than quality" (Illia et al., 2023, p. 205). Illia et al. further added that a critical analysis of pattern recurrence and repetition within AI-generated text can inform the identification of nonhuman aspects within the text. While generative AI is prompt-limited, the repetitive nature of AI-generated text makes its identification predictive, based on the patterns used. One way to identify recurrent patterns in data sets is through thematic analysis (Braun & Clarke, 2006).

Because thematic analysis identifies patterns in data (Braun & Clarke, 2021) and provides an understanding of such patterns to derive meaning from the data (Sundler et al., 2019), thematic analysis was adopted as an effective approach to analyze ChatGPT's human-like generated data. In using the inductive approach to research, the authors read and observed the data several times, followed by several recursive steps guided by Creswell and Poth (2018). These steps included data familiarization, selection, coding, categorization, and thematization.

Table 1. Data collection phases

Phase	Prompt Used	Description	Number of Outlines
Phase 1	Basic Prompt	This prompt was engineered using simple wording, for example:1. "Write an informative speech about [___topic___]2. Write a persuasive speech about [___topic___]3. Write a special occasion speech about [___topic___]"	20 persuasive, 20 informative, and 20 special occasion speech outlines.
Phase 2	Detailed Prompt	This prompt engineering process involved crafting detailed prompts that provided specific and comprehensive information to guide ChatGPT in generating speech outlines. For instance, a typical prompt took the following form: "You are going to act as a speech communication specialist and compose a Persuasive/Informative/Special Occasion speech outline on the topic of _______. Ensure that your outline adheres to the structure of a Persuasive/Informative/Special Occasion speech, maintaining an academic tone throughout. Include an introduction, body, and conclusion, employing transitional statements to establish coherence between sections. To enhance the speech's credibility, support your claims within the outline with authentic references."	20 persuasive, 20 informative, and 20 special occasion speech outlines.
Phase 3	Trained Prompt	In addition to using the prompts in Phase 2, the third phase included feeding ChatGPT with Gunn's (2018) speech outline for each speech type (persuasive/informative/special occasion). This phase trained ChatGPT on all the information needed to craft the speech outlines (with all context related requirements). That is, this step involved chatting with ChatGPT at several points before it generated the speech outlines to ensure complete training on the contextual requirements.	20 persuasive, 20 informative, and 20 special occasion speech outlines.

The authors first familiarized themselves with the speech outlines by reading them several times and selecting emerging text clusters. Next, the authors coded the emerging statements, grouped these emerging codes into categories, and listed the categories under relevant subthemes, which were placed under the final emerging themes. To interpret the emerging themes from the speech outlines, the authors followed Gunn's (2018) speech outlining format as guiding examples for informative, persuasive, and special occasion speeches, as it provides a clear and structured framework for organizing ideas with a focus on human essence.

FINDINGS

RQ1: Quality of ChatGPT Speech Outlines

The first research question asked about the quality of speech outlines generated from the ChatGPT using three phases of prompt engineering. The ChatGPT-generated speech outlines in both Phase 1 (Basic Prompt) and Phase 2 (Detailed Prompt) were found to be similar, if not identical, in structure, limitations, and overall characteristics. The only difference between Phases 1 and 2 was in how ChatGPT listed the speech outlines with the labels introduction, body, and conclusion, and classified the included types of statements. However, these differences were minimal. Consequently, the speech outlines generated in Phases 1 and 2 were merged in the analysis of the findings. Of all the data generated in Phases 1 and 2, three themes emerged to answer the research question: omission, poor execution, and repetition. Further elaboration of these themes provides more details to address RQ1, followed by findings from the data generated in Phase 3 (Trained Prompt).

Omissions

The ChatGPT-generated speech outlines from Phases 1 and 2 omitted many elements considered standard for effective preparation of speech. All 120 speech outlines lacked supporting materials such as examples, facts, statistics, or short anecdotes. Other omissions were specific to the structural sections of the outline: introduction (audience relation, preview, and credibility statements), body paragraphs (transitional statements, informative strategies, appeals, arguments, and stylistic devices), and conclusion (call to action and final statement).

The introductions to all 120 ChatGPT-generated outlines lacked audience relations and credibility. The number of sentences in the introduction sections of the informative speech outlines ranged between two and three, and the introduction of the persuasive speech outlines contained two to four sentences each. For example, the speech introduction below includes an attention getter, thesis statement, and preview statement: However, audience relations and credibility statements are missing, as underlined below.

(Attention-getter) *Ladies and gentlemen, today we are going to talk about the topic of self-driving cars." **(Audience relation:** Missing). **(Credibility statement:** Missing). **(Thesis)** Self-driving cars, also known as autonomous vehicles, are capable of sensing the environment and navigating without human input. **(Preview)** They have the potential to revolutionize the way we travel and commute, and have been the subject of much research and development in recent years.*

Likewise, the body of the speech outlines omitted several elements necessary for high-quality outlines: transitional statements, informative strategies, persuasive appeals, arguments and counterarguments, supporting evidence, and stylistic devices. Transitional statements were absent between paragraphs, which made the speech outlines appear to be poorly written. For example, the following two paragraphs exemplify situations in which no transition statements are present.

One of the main benefits of self-driving cars is their increased safety. Car accidents are caused by human errors. Self-driving cars use advanced sensors and algorithms to detect and respond to potential hazards, thereby reducing the risk of accidents caused by human errors.

Another advantage of self-driving cars is their improved efficiency and reduced traffic congestion. Self-driving cars can communicate with each other and with the traffic infrastructure, allowing them to coordinate their movements and avoid congestion.

Another notable issue was the absence of informative strategies in informative speech outlines, making the informative elements in these outlines less effective. In the same vein, persuasive speech outlines lack the essential component of persuasive appeals. ChatGPT did not provide any sense of logos, pathos, or ethos in persuasive speech outlines. In addition, the persuasive speech outlines lacked strong arguments and necessary counterarguments, which minimized the power of persuasion.

Special occasion outlines also miss a vital element. Stylistic devices were absent from all special occasion outlines, which are important for speaker identity, audience engagement, and the essence of the occasion. Stylistic devices establish the hallmark of speech as a whole, and their omission leaves a ChatGPT special occasion speech outline with little to celebrate. In summary, ChatGPT outlines omitted many key elements that are frequently required. These omissions led to an assessment of low quality in the ChatGPT outline.

Poor Execution

Poor execution in phases 1 and 2 was recurrent. There were instances when the ChatGPT outlines included key elements, but they were poorly executed when compared to Phase 3 or the work that a human could generate. The poor execution theme includes instances where ChatGPT outlines contain inadequate information, misplaced information, and over-used information.

Inadequate information was noticeable in many outlines of all three types, and in the three main parts of speech. The example below is taken from the introduction of informative speech. The example reiterates the missing elements, as described above. It also contains an unclear preview statement.

Attention-getter: Ladies and gentlemen. Today, I am here to talk to you about the benefits of using ChatGPT, a language model, in schools, colleges, and universities. Audience relation: Missing. Credibility statement: Missing. Thesis: ChatGPT is a powerful tool that can generate text quickly and efficiently [Unclear Preview:] and it has the potential to enhance students' learning experiences in a variety of ways.

The phrase *in a variety of ways.* A higher-quality outline lists phrases that explicitly describe the number and type of ways. Another outline for a persuasive speech on *The Government Investing into Space Travel* had more specific information in its preview statement, "The government should invest more in this industry because it can bring many benefits to our society, both in terms of scientific advancement and economic growth." However, the body of the outline contained a third idea of improving national security using space satellites. While this idea is relevant to the broad topic, it was not clearly stated in the preview statement of the introduction, contradicting expectations for quality speech.

Misplaced information was evident in the call-to-action statements. All persuasive speech outlines successfully used a call-to-action statement in the conclusion section, while 34 informative speech outlines did. Further, the informative speech call-to-action statements used *It's important to...*, and *I urge you to...* too frequently. The following two final statements are examples of misplaced statements found in informative speech outlines:

<u>It's important to</u> *continue research and develop this technology safely and responsibly.*

<u>I urge speakers to</u> *consider donating blood, spread awareness about the importance of blood donation, and encourage others to do the same. Together, we can help save lives and improve donor health. Thank you.*

The inclusion of a persuasive element in an informative speech seemed irrelevant, confusing the purpose of an informative speech with a persuasive one. Such issues can easily be identified by public-speaking instructors.

The call-to-action phrases mentioned in the previous paragraph are indicative of another issue with ChatGPT speech outlines, namely, overuse. The final statements in 24 informative speeches and 36 persuasive speeches are *Thank you.* The final memorable statements that were typically expected were missing from all the informative and persuasive outlines, and *thank you* was used instead. The special occasion speech outlines likewise ended with overused words and patterns, as in these examples:

Thank you, AirPods, *for being such* a reliable and amazing device.

Thank you, gym, *for being* an amazing and essential part of our lives.

Additionally, it was noticeable that the opening statement in the special occasion outlines, *today we gather to honor*, was followed by a verb denoting the occasion of each speech. For example, eulogy speeches used the verb *mourn*, honoring someone speeches including the verb *honor*, celebration speeches used the verb *celebrate*, etc.. Such a pattern is not a surprise from an AI speech outline and leads to the overuse of sentence fragments that, when spoken, show a lack of originality from the speaker.

ChatGPT showed poor execution of speech outlines by including inadequate information in places, misplacing key elements, and overusing words and patterns. These traits of a ChatGPT outline reflect low-quality outlines that signal to speech instructors that students have not created their own outline.

Repetition

Another indicator of quality found among the 120 ChatGPT-generated speech outlines was the noticeable repetition of opening statements, transitional phrases, and ending statements. As a result, the ChatGPT-generated speech outlines were relatively identical to each other, showing a lack of originality from potential speech givers. For example, all of the informative and persuasive speech outlines began with, "Ladies and gentlemen, today we are going to talk about...". Similarly, all the special occasion speech outlines started with "Ladies and gentlemen, today we gather to..." While the repetition of the opening statements in the informative and persuasive outlines differed slightly from the special occasion outlines, all outlines began with "Ladies and gentlemen," a cliche and overused phrase.

Transitional words or phrases were also brief and few across the outlines in the sample. Among the informative and persuasive speech outlines, a few transitional words or phrases were repeated in 64 of the 80 outlines. These transitional words or phrases included, *one of the main...*, *another reason/way...*, *additionally...*, *furthermore…*, and *in conclusion….* These transitional phrases were used repeatedly in the ChatGPT-generated informative and persuasive speech outlines. The following informative speech, entitled *The Disadvantages of ChatGPT in Education,* is an example of how these transitional phrases were used repeatedly in the ChatGPT-generated informative and persuasive speech outlines:

Ladies and gentlemen Today, I am here to talk to you about the disadvantages of using ChatGPT, a language model in education. Although ChatGPT can be a valuable tool for generating text, it can also have drawbacks when used in an educational setting.

One of the *main disadvantages of using the ChatGPT in education is that it can discourage critical thinking and creativity among students. ChatGPT is a tool that can generate text quickly and efficiently; however, it can also make it easy for students to rely on it for writing assignments instead of developing their own ideas and arguments. This can lead to a lack of critical thinking and creativity among the students.*

Another *disadvantage of using ChatGPT in education is that it can reduce the effectiveness of plagiarism-detection tools. ChatGPT generates text that is unique; however, it can also generate text that is similar to the existing text.*

Additionally, *using ChatGPT in education can lead to a lack of understanding of the writing process. ChatGPT can generate text quickly and efficiently, but it does not teach students the process of writing, such as research, drafting, revising, and editing. This can lead to students not understanding the writing process and not being able to improve their writing skills.*

In conclusion, *ChatGPT is a powerful tool for generating text; however, it can also have drawbacks when used in an educational setting. This can discourage critical thinking and creativity in students, reduce the effectiveness of plagiarism detection tools, and lead to a lack of understanding of the writing process. I urge educators to consider the potential drawbacks of using ChatGPT in education and to use it as a tool to support the learning process, not as a replacement. Thank you.*

Repetition was also evident in the overall structure of the informative and persuasive speech outlines, where 95% contained three body paragraphs. The first paragraph always began with *one of the main reasons why...*, the second began with *another reason why...*, and the third paragraph began with *additionally....* Some included a fourth paragraph that began with *furthermore...* The special occasion speech outlines, on the other hand, did not include any repetition of transitional words or phrases.

The ending statements also contained noticeable repetitions across the speech outlines. All persuasive speech outlines ended with a call-to-action statement, instead of a memorable statement. Most call-to-action statements (90%) began with either *I urge you to...* or *Let's...* The phrase *So today/Today* was used to begin the conclusion of 34 special occasion outlines. Another structure that was overused to conclude the special occasion outlines is *Thank you, (insert name), for (insert reason)*. For example, "Thank you, Dad, for all that you do and for being an amazing role model in our lives." This structure was used 21 times for 40 special occasional speech outlines.

In short, the quality of speech outlines in Phases 1 and 2 shows the omission of several important elements and the considerable repetition of words or phrases. These elements would generally signal, at best, an average to a low-quality outline. They also provide opportunities for instructors to train students in speech craft analysis to produce well-structured outlines. However, when moving from Phases 1 and 2 to Phase 3, unexpected results emerged, with instances of ChatGPT-generated speech outlines becoming indistinguishable from the human-written text. When trained on Gunn's (2018) outlines and fed with a few specific requirements, ChatGPT generated 60 speech outlines that could easily pass human-written. For example, the following speech outline, entitled "The Disadvantages of Using ChatGPT for Public Speaking," which was generated by ChatGPT (OpenAI, 2023), includes all components of a complete and well-written speech outline.

ChatGPT

I. Introduction

A. Attention-getter: Imagine standing in front of a large audience ready to deliver a persuasive speech. Now, a picture relying on an AI-powered chatbot such as ChatGPT to assist you. Although AI technology has merits, there are notable disadvantages when using ChatGPT for public speaking.

B. Audience relation: Today, we will explore the drawbacks of utilizing ChatGPT in the realm of public speaking. Understanding these disadvantages will help us to recognize the limitations of AI in this specific context.

C. Credibility statement: As a communication specialist with years of experience in public speaking, I witnessed firsthand the challenges and potential pitfalls associated with relying on AI chatbots such as ChatGPT for this important skill.

D. Thesis: This speech aims to shed light on the disadvantages of using ChatGPT for public speaking, including a lack of human connection, limitations in nonverbal communication, and potential technical glitches.

E. Preview: We first discuss the challenge of establishing human connections, followed by the impact on nonverbal communication. Finally, we will explore the potential technical glitches associated with using ChatGPT for public speaking.

F. Transition: Let us begin by examining the challenge of establishing human connections when using the ChatGPT for public speaking.

II. Body

A. Main Point: Challenge of establishing human connection

i. Support for main point A (Absence of genuine human interaction)- ChatGPT lacks the ability to provide genuine human interaction and lacks essential elements such as empathy, emotional connection, and audience rapport (Smith, 2020 [Note: fake source generated by ChatGPT]).

ii. Support for main point A (Limited adaptability to audience feedback)- ChatGPT responses are predetermined and may not effectively adapt to audience cues, leading to a lack of engagement and connection with listeners (Johnson, 2019 [Note: fake source generated by ChatGPT]).

Transition: Now that we understand the challenge of establishing human connections, let us explore the impact on nonverbal communication.

B. Main Point: Impact on nonverbal communication

i. Support for Main Point B (inability to interpret and respond to nonverbal cues)- ChatGPT lacks the ability to interpret nonverbal cues, such as facial expressions, body language, and vocal tone, which are crucial aspects of effective public speaking (Jones, 2021 [Note: fake source generated by ChatGPT]).

ii. Support for main point B (Limited use of nonverbal communication techniques)- Public speaking often relies on gestures, eye contact, and physical presence to convey messages effectively, which cannot be replicated by an AI chatbot such as ChatGPT (Thomas, 2022 [Note: fake source generated by ChatGPT]).

Transition: In addition to the impact on nonverbal communication, let us discuss the potential technical glitches associated with using the ChatGPT for public speaking.

C. Main Point: Potential technical glitches

i. Support for main point C (Dependency on reliable internet connectivity)- Utilizing ChatGPT for public speaking relies on stable Internet connectivity, making it susceptible to disruptions, lags, or potential system failures (Williams, 2020 [Note: fake source generated by ChatGPT]).

ii. Support for main point C (Accuracy and coherence issues)- ChatGPT responses may suffer from inaccuracies, coherence problems, or inappropriate suggestions due to limitations in programming and the quality of the input data (Brown, 2019 [Note: fake source generated by ChatGPT]).

Transition: Now that we have explored the disadvantages of using ChatGPT for public speaking, let us summarize our main points and move towards the conclusion.

III. Conclusion

A. Restate thesis: Using ChatGPT for public speaking presents several challenges, including the lack of human connections, limitations in nonverbal communication, and potential technical glitches.

B. Review Main Points: We discussed the challenge of establishing human connections, highlighting the absence of genuine human interaction and limited adaptability to audience feedback. We then explored the impact on nonverbal communication, emphasizing the inability to interpret and respond to nonverbal cues, and the limited use of nonverbal communication techniques. Lastly, we examined the potential technical glitches associated with ChatGPT, such as dependency on reliable Internet connectivity and accuracy/coherence issues.

C. Final statement: While AI chatbots such as ChatGPT have their own uses, it is important to recognize the disadvantages they present in the context of public speaking. Human connections, nonverbal communication, and technical reliability are essential aspects of effective public speaking that AI chatbots struggle to replicate.

The only noticeable limitation in all 60 ChatGPT-generated speech outlines in Phase 3 is the provision of fake sources. While blurring the lines between verifiable and fabricated information, this limitation amplifies the opportunity for students to develop critical thinking and information verification skills. However, when prompts are crafted to generate human-like content, ChatGPT can produce text that is indistinguishable from what a human might create. Although this capability is a testament to the advancement of technology, it introduces concern over students' learning. The next section elaborates on the additional features of ChatGPT-generated speech outlines and the possibilities for academic integrity using such outlines unaltered or after modifications in all three phases.

RQ2: Possibilities for Academic Integrity

The second research question asked how ChatGPT could contribute to academic integrity behaviors through speech outline assignments. The quality of the ChatGPT speech outlines suggests the potential for students to use ChatGPT as an alternative to their own when completing speech outline assignments. Two themes emerged from the analysis of the data: an Unaltered ChatGPT Speech Outline and Human-Modified ChatGPT Speech Outline.

Using Unaltered ChatGPT-Generated Text

Left alone or without adequate prompt engineering, such a speech outline would be severely lacking in the elements required for a quality outline, as the previous section addressed for Phases 1 and 2. Instructors can easily identify academic dishonesty with an unaltered ChatGPT-generated speech outline. To visualize the issues a student encounters without good prompting, the analysis proceeds by presenting an unaltered ChatGPT-generated persuasive speech outline example entitled *The Importance of Budgeting for College Students.*

Unaltered ChatGPT-Generated Persuasive Speech Outline

Ladies and gentlemen Today, I am here to talk to you about the importance of budgeting for college students. Budgeting can help students save money, minimize loan debt, and avoid unnecessary interest, which can make a significant difference to their financial futures.

One of the main reasons why college students should budget to save money is that it can help them manage their expenses better. By creating a budget, students can identify where their money is going, and make adjustments to reduce unnecessary spending. This can help them save money for future expenses such as rent, car payments, and student loans.

Another reason college students should budget to minimize loan debt is that it can help them avoid taking on more debt than they need. Through budgeting, students can identify how much money they will need for tuition, books, and other expenses, and plan accordingly. This can help them take fewer loans and avoid unnecessary interest charges.

Additionally, budgeting can help students avoid unnecessary interest charges by encouraging them to pay loans and credit cards as soon as possible. By creating a budget and sticking to it, students can prioritize their loan and credit card payments and avoid accumulating high interest charges.

In conclusion, college students should budget to save money, minimize loan debt, and avoid unnecessary interest. I urge you to prioritize budgeting, seek out resources and tools that can help you to budget effectively, and encourage your peers to do the same. Thus, we can ensure that college students are financially prepared for their future. Thank you.

The above unaltered outline suffers from the same structural issues highlighted in the previous section, making the students' attempts to use an unaltered ChatGPT-generated outline unsuccessful. Issues in unaltered outlines are more likely to be identified by the teachers. Therefore, such outlines require additional reconstruction to reach the expected level of standard speech. Without recycling the ChatGPT-generated outlines, students' academic integrity can be impacted.

ChatGPT-Generated Text as a Guiding Model

With modifications, a ChatGPT-generated outline could help students advance their outlining process. If students use ChatGPT to craft speech outlines, they can use the output as a guiding model but with significant modifications. Students can use these outlines to build upon or inspire their own structure. However, continued use of the ChatGPT outline would require students to understand the structure and elements of a high-quality speech outline. To visualize the alterations a student would need to make, the analysis followed a human-modified version of the previously introduced outline, with modifications noted in parentheses.

ChatGPT Human Modified Persuasive Speech Outline

(Attention-getter) According to Son et al. 's 2020 study in the Journal of Medical Internet Research, 86 out of 195 college students are stressed about their finances. (Audience relation) As college students, we can make good use of budgeting to reduce financial stress. (Credibility statement) I have been budgeting for three years now and have conducted extensive research on this topic, which has helped me cope with my financial stress. (Thesis) College students should reduce their stress regarding their finances. (Preview) Budgeting will help college students be more financially prepared and improve their well-being.

(Main Point 1) Because of the unprecedentedly 8% high inflation since 1983, life expenses are rocketing. It is possible that college students will face serious consequences if they do not begin budgeting during these difficult times. Such issues include several hurdles.

i. It will be extremely difficult to be financially prepared.

1. Without a clear plan for your current and future finances, you can miss out on many opportunities to save money, work towards your financial goals, be prepared for emergencies, and track bad spending habits.

2. It is understandable that spending money on things you like can feel tempting, but it is a mindset that develops stronger with time; it all begins from within.

ii. Such circumstances can lead to impacting your health negatively.

1. Research in the Journal of Medical Internet Research has shown that random management of finances can lead to depression and anxiety, which can further lead to health degradation.

2. According to Nixon et al. 's (2011) study in the Journal of Work & Stress, financial stressors create physical symptoms such as sleep disturbance, fatigue, appetite loss, and gastrointestinal problems.

iii. You can become prone to burnout by overworking.

1. In an article published by Cindy Perman on CNBC.com in 2019, eight out of ten college students worked while they were enrolled in school. The more hours they work, the greater is the impact on their academic performance. Financial stress has the greatest negative impact on those who work 20 hours or more per week.

(Transition) I understand that this might seem overwhelming, but early budgeting could help you avoid any of these potential situations.

(Main Point 2) Therefore, Budgeting is an effective solution to the problems I explained earlier today. Here, we discuss how this works.

i. Budgeting can help us, as college students, be financially prepared in many ways. Some of which include:

1. This method provides consumers with an awareness towards consumerism to buy what they can afford/need only.

a. If you create a budget and stick to it, you will know exactly how much money you earn, how much money you can afford to spend each month, and how much money you need to save, according to your financial goals.

2. It prepares you for any unexpected emergencies.

a. Life is full of unexpected events, some of which are good and some are very bad. If you happen to experience an accident, get sick, or injure, you will find yourself navigating serious financial turmoil. However, what you save by budgeting is your savior in such circumstances.

3. It can improve your well-being.

a. Simply put, when you retain the feeling that you have control over your finances and that you have an alternative plan when life goes wrong, stress and anxiety fade away. Maintaining these feelings can enhance the quality of mental and physical well-being.

(Transition) In conclusion, budgeting is a strategic method we can use to reduce our financial burdens.

(Conclusion: Restate Thesis) College students should budget to be financially prepared to improve their well-being. (Review main points) Everything is getting expensive due to inflation; budgeting is the one

of the most essential techniques to reduce financial stress as a college student. (Call to Action) I know sometimes it might feel like budgeting is a lot of work, but once you start, it becomes a healthy habit. I urge you to begin budgeting to save yourself unnecessary stress and ensure that you maintain control over your finances. (Final statement) Let us start budgeting today and say goodbye to financial stress.

The human-modified outline fulfills all the missing components in the ChatGPT version from Phases 1 and 2. Students can potentially follow the overall structure of ideas in ChatGPT's outline to create an enhanced version that includes the necessary elements for quality speech, even with outlines generated in Phase 3. The coherence and unity of ideas throughout the outline are far superior in the human-written outline, in part because they are supported by examples, statistics, and other necessary elements. Students would be required to possess and apply adequate knowledge of speechcraft to (1) promptly engineer a good speech outline, (2) identify the missing elements, and (3) modify accordingly to satisfy the parameters of an assignment. Therefore, students who feel tempted to use ChatGPT for speech craft have considerable work to do before meeting the expectations of their public speaking course. Overall, this human-written outline is an example of how human creativity in the composition and organization of ideas outpowers AI's capabilities.

DISCUSSION

This study was designed to understand the quality of ChatGPT-generated speech outlines for pedagogical practices and the possibilities for students' academic integrity using this tool. On one hand, when prompted poorly, the findings show several limitations in ChatGPT's generated speech outlines. However, the findings indicate that pre-existing knowledge and good prompt engineering skills are needed to generate human-like text.

The data analysis presented in this chapter confirms that prompt engineering can determine the quality of ChatGPT-generated speech outlines and the possibility for students to get away with speech craft. However, poor prompt engineering can yield speech outlines that lack creativity and composition. Such outlines lack essential structural components in all speech sections needed to meet the expectations of standard-quality speech outlines. ChatGPT failed to generate a basic sense of critical thinking in the generated ideas, confirming Yann LeCun's claim that "ChatGPT is not particularly innovative...and nothing revolutionary...." (Ray, 2023, para. 3), thus, it is indeed a prompt-limited contextual sentence generator. ChatGPT-generated speech outlines in Phases 1 and 2 exhibited an absence or poor execution of speech outline elements such as supporting materials, audience relations, previews, credibility statements, transitional statements, informative strategies, appeals, arguments, stylistic devices, call to action, and final statements. These structural deficiencies in ChatGPT's output raise questions about the trustworthiness of using this technology as a replacement for human-written text, which is in line with Krügel et al.'s (2023) questioning of AI-generated text responses that serve their intended purpose.

Similarly, ChatGPT lagged in the form of poor executions in its outputs, where it ran short to serve the intended purpose of its sentences. For example, providing unclear preview points and the addition of unannounced paragraphs to the body paragraphs created a sense of confusion and inconsistency throughout the text. These limitations not only contradict the definition of speech outlines (Cronin, 1994; Myer et al., 2010; Santoso & Taufiq, 2021), but also bring about ChatGPT's possible contributions to academic integrity pressures with speech outline assignments. Such issues, along with the recurrent patterns in ChatGPT's generated text, offer valuable teaching opportunities. In these instances, instructors can engage students in critical discussions on the limitations and nuances of AI-generated content. This not only cultivates a deeper understanding of technology but also promotes critical thinking and digital literacy skills. Furthermore, instructors can encourage students to explore alternative ways to refine and improve AI-generated texts, fostering a sense of creativity and innovation. By embracing these challenges as learning opportunities, instructors can empower students to become more informed and adaptable to an increasingly AI-powered world.

If students use ChatGPT, they face two scenarios: relying on ChatGPT to generate a speech outline and likely learning less about speechcraft, or accepting ChatGPT as an assistant. For example, using ChatGPT as an assistant can be beneficial for supporting students' understanding of the building blocks of speech outlines. Students can use ChatGPT-generated text as a guiding model to edit and add the necessary components of a speech outline format, as in Gunn (2018). In line with Rudolph et al.'s (2023) constructive alignment of ChatGPT in education, the previously discussed scenarios can assist learners in understanding the process of speechcraft by critically thinking about the different components in each part of an outline; that is, students may work hard to conceal any traces of AI text by adding missing statements such as audience relations, a credibility statement, and perhaps a clearer preview statement. However, the students' potential use of ChatGPT can be an opportunity to learn the structural components of public speech. This coincidental learning opportunity with an AI tool can be the beginning of a new teaching approach, namely AI-based learning. AI-based learning can prompt students to use existing knowledge to adapt to the incomplete composition of subject-related ideas, resulting in the learning of editing, revision, and most importantly, speechcraft. Data analysis does not show a threat posed against human education; instead, it is an opportunity to utilize a new teaching approach.

In the long run, the goal may not be to identify AI-generated text but to embrace it to empower human learning experiences. Until the hype over the AI revolution fades away, AI-based teaching and learning are vital to cope with current technological innovations. To achieve this pedagogical coping mechanism, it is necessary to consider the pedagogical implications that ChatGPT can offer for the teaching and learning processes. There are numerous potential pedagogical implications, ranging from fostering students' critical thinking, providing experiential learning opportunities to effectively teach speechcraft skills, and eliminating any potential threats to learners' academic integrity.

Pedagogical and Ethical Implications for Educational Practices

The proposed pedagogical and ethical implications for ChatGPT's use in education build upon the foundation of two parameters: AI-based teaching and learning and ethical considerations for teachers. AI-based teaching and learning is an emerging educational approach that encourages the use of AI tools to scaffold teachers' pedagogical knowledge and cope with an evolving technological era. Instead of banning the use of AI tools in schools, their use could be encouraged for three reasons.

First, while AI tools have the potential to harm students' intention to learn, especially with good prompt engineering skills, they can create highly interactive learning environments where classroom activities involve teacher intervention and facilitation, peer collaboration and autonomous learning, and interaction with AI tools. Such an approach encourages critical thinking, deep analysis, and understanding of content. Without an adequate understanding of the lesson content, the successful utilization of AI tools cannot be effective. Therefore, students' learning of their lesson content and incorporation of AI tools are in a mutually exclusive relationship; that is, the occurrence of learning needs to precede the use of AI tools for effective outcomes. For example, if students do not know the correct structure of a speech outline, they would not be able to (1) prompt ChatGPT effectively and (2) know whether an AI-generated speech outline meets the expectations of a well-written standard speech outline. Therefore, students' learning of lesson content must take precedence for their use of AI tools to be successful. Consequently, when students build basic knowledge through collaborative work and apply this knowledge using AI tools to analyze the processing of information, they can grab a stronger hold of their learning. In addition, AI tools are cost-effective because they are currently free. It is assumed that many AI tools will emerge in free form to encourage their use in the future. Available at teachers' and students' disposal, teaching practices in the developed and developing worlds will have equal chances of incorporating such tools, creating equal opportunities for all educators and learners, regardless of their location or resources.

Second, the integration of ChatGPT-generated outlines into teaching public speaking can be a good opportunity for teachers to use such outlines for speech analysis in class, pinpointing the weaknesses of this AI and how humans can perform better than a sentence generator machine. Using ChatGPT to teach public-speaking students, the structure of speech outlines can create an unyielding opportunity for analytical and experiential learning. For example, during a speech outline workshop in a public speaking course, when students come to class with the first draft of their speech outlines, ChatGPT can play an integral role. Students can simply run their speech topics on a ChatGPT text engine in class. They can then compare their speech outlines with ChatGPT-generated speech outlines, highlighting the differences and similarities. Most importantly, this exercise can create an opportunity for students to think critically about the components of speech in the introduction, body paragraphs, and conclusion. Besides adding interactivity to teaching students about the importance of a complete speech outline, ChatGPT can also create an opportunity for students to build reflective learning about their own writing, thinking about the underlying purpose of every statement in their speech. Teaching students to pinpoint the limitations of AI texts in comparison with human-written texts can be a good exercise to emphasize the importance of preparing speech outlines with all its components. This process is similar to showing students what a bad example of a speech outline looks like, and then proceeds to show them how to fix it. Overall, these learning opportunities are not possible without a technology tool such as ChatGPT, where students see the text being generated live. The benefit of critiquing ChatGPT-generated output can assist teachers and learners in seeing the limitations of AI texts, paving the way for human critical thinking and creativity.

The ChatGPT can also be used as an assistant. However, it is important for teachers to train students on their ethical use, especially in speechcrafting, and emphasize the importance of understanding prompt engineering as a foundational skill. Teachers can adopt the prompt engineering techniques used in this study to demonstrate how different prompts yield different results. ChatGPT also helps brainstorming and structuring speech, which can enhance creativity and coherence. When students write a draft of their speech outline, they can use ChatGPT as a peer reviewer to offer suggestions for language and structural improvements. While performing these pedagogical practices with ChatGPT, teachers can encourage students to be critical of ChatGPT-generated content. For instance, teachers can guide students to question and evaluate the information and suggestions provided by an AI tool. Teachers should emphasize the importance of independent thinking, encouraging students to not blindly accept AI-generated responses but rather use them as a starting point for further exploration and development. It is essential to cultivate the understanding that ChatGPT, while a powerful tool, is not unerring and should be supplemented with human judgment and creativity. By integrating such practices, students can effectively leverage ChatGPT as an educational assistant while maintaining its integrity.

Although the findings from this study indicate that ChatGPT can pose a threat to educational integrity when it is carefully prompt-trained, embracing this technology as an opportunity to incorporate a new teaching approach can assist instructors in raising students' awareness of using ChatGPT ethically. To that end, the use of ChatGPT should not be considered unethical for educational purposes unless it is used as the sole source of student submissions. As students have used unlimited amounts of text and information on the Internet for decades, using ChatGPT as an assistant to generate basic information about a specific topic would not replace human writing capabilities. In contrast, it empowers human writing and thinking capabilities. Students will always need to refine and polish an AI text; this is an opportunity to learn how to write through reorganizing, editing, revising, and polishing ideas.

CONCLUDING REMARKS

The ChatGPT 'crisis' is a challenging opportunity that is expected to redefine and revolutionize human creativity, authorship, and originality in education. ChatGPT's structural and executive deficiencies are contingent on its prompt engineering, which determines whether students can *really* get away with speechcraft. However, students can utilize ChatGPT to enhance their learning of speech craft by employing this tool as an educational assistant or modifying its generated speech outlines to humanize AI-generated texts. Overall, the ChatGPT tool provides an opportunity to elevate and empower educational systems and how teachers approach teaching.

We conclude with a quote by ChatGPT (OpenAI, 2023) generating that "the prospective integration of ChatGPT into the domain of public speaking education is replete with auspicious promise, substantiated by profound latent capabilities. In concert with ongoing technological progress that continues to delineate the contours of educational paradigms, the role ascribed to ChatGPT and cognate AI platforms in the augmentation of public speaking proficiencies is at the threshold of a potentially transformative impact. Foremost among its commendable attributes lies ChatGPT's exceptional aptitude for furnishing bespokes, data-informed feedback, creating immersive learning environments, and dispensing judicious constructive guidance. This multifaceted functionality heralds a substantive departure from established conventions within the pedagogical landscape of public speaking, offering the potential to redefine the modalities through which individuals acquire and refine this imperative skill set."

REFERENCES

Aydın, Ö., & Karaarslan, E. (2022). OpenAI ChatGPT generated literature review: Digital twin in healthcare. In Ö. Aydın (Ed.), Emerging Computer Technologies. İzmir Akademi Dernegi. doi:10.2139/ssrn.4308687

Azaria, A. (2022). *ChatGPT usage and limitations* [Unpublished manuscript]. HAL open science. https://hal.science/hal-03913837

Beebe, S. A., & Beebe, S. J. (1991). *Public speaking: An audience-centered approach.* Prentice Hall.

Bogost, I. (2023, February 2). ChatGPT is about to dump more work on everyone. *The Atlantic*. https://www.theatlantic.com/technology/archive/2023/02/chatgpt-ai-detector-machine-learning-technology-bureaucracy/672927/

Braun, V., & Clarke, V. (2006). Using thematic analysis in psychology. *Qualitative Research in Psychology, 3*(2), 77–101. doi:10.1191/1478088706qp063oa

Braun, V., & Clarke, V. (2021). Can I use TA? Should I use TA? Should I not use TA? Comparing reflexive thematic analysis and other pattern-based qualitative analytic approaches. *Counselling & Psychotherapy Research, 21*(1), 37–47. doi:10.1002/capr.12360

Brown, T., Mann, B., Ryder, N., Subbiah, M., Kaplan, J. D., Dhariwal, P., Neelakantan, A., Shyam, P., Sastry, G., Askell, A., Agarwal, S., Herbert-Voss, A., Krueger, G., Henighan, T., Child, R., Ramesh, A., Ziegler, D., Wu, J., Winter, C., ... Amodei, D. (2020). Language models are few-shot learners. *Advances in Neural Information Processing Systems, 33*, 1877–1901.

Cao, J., Li, M., Wen, M., & Cheung, S. C. (2023). *A study on Prompt Design, Advantages and Limitations of ChatGPT for Deep Learning Program Repair.* arXiv. https://doi.org//arXiv.2304.08191 doi:10.48550

Chen, Y. C. (2022). Effects of technology-enhanced language learning on reducing EFL learners' public speaking anxiety. *Computer Assisted Language Learning*, 1–25. doi:10.1080/09588221.2022.2055083

Cotton, D., Cotton, P. A., & Shipway, J. R. (2023). Chatting and cheating: Ensuring academic integrity in the era of ChatGPT. *Innovations in Education and Teaching International*, 1–12. doi:10.1080/14703297.2023.2190148

Creswell, J. W., & Poth, C. N. (2018). *Qualitative inquiry and research design: Choosing among five approaches* (4th ed.). Sage.

Cronin, M. W. (1994). Interactive video instruction for teaching organizational techniques in public speaking. *Basic Communication Course Annual, 6*, 19–35. https://ecommons.udayton.edu/bcca/vol6/iss1/6

Edwards, A., & Edwards, C. (2018). Human–machine communication in the classroom. In M. L. Houser & A. M. Hosek (Eds.), *Handbook of instructional communication: Rhetorical and relational perspectives* (2nd ed., pp. 184–194). Taylor & Francis.

Edwards, A. A. H. (2021). From novel to necessary. In J. M. Valenzano III, (Ed.), *Post-Pandemic Pedagogy: A Paradigm Shift* (pp. 37–56). Lexington Books.

El Mortaji, L. (2022). Public speaking and online peer feedback in a blended learning EFL course environment: Students' perceptions. *English Language Teaching, 15*(2), 31–49. doi:10.5539/elt.v15n2p31

Garib, A. (2022). "Actually, it's real work": EFL teachers' perceptions of technology-assisted project-based language learning in Lebanon, Libya, and Syria. *TESOL Quarterly, 57*(4), 1434–1462. doi:10.1002/tesq.3202

Gozalo-Brizuela, R., & Garrido-Merchan, E. C. (2023). *ChatGPT is not all you need. A State-of-the-Art review of large generative AI models.* arXiv. https://doi.org//arXiv.2301.04655 doi:10.48550

Gunn, J. (2018). *Speech craft*. Bedford/St. Martin's.

Hartelius, E. (2018). Speech craft review. *The Quarterly Journal of Speech, 104*(3), 352–355. doi:10.1080/00335630.2018.1478663

Holliday, A. (2016). Doing & writing qualitative research. *Sage (Atlanta, Ga.).*

Illia, L., Colleoni, E., & Zyglidopoulos, S. (2023). Ethical implications of text generation in the age of artificial intelligence. *Business Ethics, the Environment & Responsibility*, *32*(1), 201–210. doi:10.1111/beer.12479

Jiang, J. A., Wade, K., Fiesler, C., & Brubaker, J. R. (2021). Supporting serendipity: Opportunities and challenges for Human-AI Collaboration in qualitative analysis. *Proceedings of the ACM on Human-Computer Interaction, 5*(CSCW1), 1–23. 10.1145/3449168

KrauseD. (2023). Proper Generative AI Prompting for Financial Analysis. SSRN. http://dx.doi.org/doi:10.2139/ssrn.4453664

Kretsinger-Harries, A. C., Helmick, E., Challis, K., & Garib, A. (2021). Navigating uncertainty together: Pandemic lessons learned from training new GTAs in teaching public speaking. In J. M. Valenzano III, (Ed.), *Post-pandemic pedagogy: A paradigm shift* (pp. 185–202). Lexington Books.

Krügel, S., Ostermaier, A., & Uhl, M. (2023). *The moral authority of ChatGPT.* arXiv. https://doi.org//arXiv.2301.07098 doi:10.48550

Liu, P., Yuan, W., Fu, J., Jiang, Z., Hayashi, H., & Neubig, G. (2023). Pre-train, prompt, and predict: A systematic survey of prompting methods in natural language processing. *ACM Computing Surveys, 55*(9), 1–35. doi:10.1145/3560815

Mishra, P., Warr, M., & Islam, R. (2023). TPACK in the age of ChatGPT and Generative AI. *Journal of Digital Learning in Teacher Education*, *39*(4), 235–251. doi:10.1080/21532974.2023.2247480

Mthuli, S. A., Ruffin, F., & Singh, N. (2022). 'Define, explain, justify, apply'(DEJA): An analytic tool for guiding qualitative research sample size. *International Journal of Social Research Methodology, 25*(6), 809–821. doi:10.1080/13645579.2021.1941646

Myer, K. R., Kurtz, R. R., Hines, J. L., Simonds, C. J., & Hunt, S. K. (2010). Assessing preemptive argumentation in students' persuasive speech outlines. *Basic Communication Course Annual, 22*(1), 5-38. https://ecommons.udayton.edu/bcca/vol22/iss1/7

Nixon, A. E., Mazzola, J. J., Bauer, J., Krueger, J. R., & Spector, P. E. (2011). Can work make you sick? A meta-analysis of the relationships between job stressors and physical symptoms. *Work and Stress, 25*(1), 1–22. doi:10.1080/02678373.2011.569175

Open, A. I. (2023). *ChatGPT (May 24 version)* [Large language model]. https://chat.openai.com

Parsaiyan, S. F., & Gholami, H. (2023). Practicing to sing in chorus: Challenges and opportunities of collaborative inquiry-based learning in an Iranian EFL secondary school context. *Language Teaching Research.* Advance online publication. doi:10.1177/13621688231152037

Perman, C. (2019, October 28). Running out of money. Cancer. Divorce. Many college students are facing serious financial crises. *CNBC.* https://www.cnbc.com/2019/10/28/many-college-students-find-themselves-in-a-serious-financial-crisis.html

Ray, T. (2023, January 23). ChatGPT is 'not particularly innovative,' and 'nothing revolutionary', says Meta's chief AI scientist. *ZDNet.* https://www.zdnet.com/article/chatgpt-is-not-particularly-innovative-and-nothing-revolutionary-says-metas-chief-ai-scientist/

Robinson, D. H., & Kiewra, K. A. (1995). Visual argument: Graphic organizers are superior to outlines in improving learning from text. *Journal of Educational Psychology, 87*(3), 455–467. doi:10.1037/0022-0663.87.3.455

Roose, K. (2023, January 13). Don't ban ChatGPT in schools. Teach with it. *The New York Times.* https://www.nytimes.com/2023/01/12/technology/chatgpt-schools-teachers.html

Rudolph, J., Tan, S., & Tan, S. (2023). ChatGPT: Bullshit spewer or the end of traditional assessments in higher education? *Journal of Applied Learning and Teaching, 6*(1), 1–22. doi:10.37074/jalt.2023.6.1.9

Santoso, D. R., & Taufiq, W. (2021, March). Implementing circumlocution to improve the speech performance in public speaking. In *Proceedings of 1st Paris Van Java International Seminar on Health, Economics, Social Science and Humanities (PVJ-ISHESSH 2020)* (pp. 117–120). Atlantis Press. https://doi.org/10.2991/assehr.k.210304.027

Schmidt-Crawford, D. A., Lindstrom, D. L., & Thompson, A. D. (2023). AI in teacher education: What's next? *Journal of Digital Learning in Teacher Education, 39*(4), 180–181. doi:10.1080/21532974.2023.2247308

Schulman, J., Zoph, B., Kim, C., Hilton, J., Menick, J., Weng, J., Uribe, J. F. C., Fedus, L., Metz, L., Pokorny, M., Lopes, R. G., Zhao, S., Vijayvergiya, A., Sigler, E., Perelman, A., Voss, C., Heaton, M., Parish, J., Cummings, R. N., . . . Ryder, N. (2022, November 30). *ChatGPT: Optimizing language models for dialogue. OpenAI.com.* Accessed from https://openai.com/blog/chatgpt

Schwartzman, R. (2022). Beyond basic: Transformational potential of pandemic pedagogy. *Basic Communication Course Annual, 34*(1), 141–152. https://ecommons.udayton.edu/bcca/vol34/iss1/13

Son, C., Hegde, S., Smith, A., Wang, X., & Sasangohar, F. (2020). Effects of COVID-19 on College Students' Mental Health in the United States: Interview Survey Study. *Journal of Medical Internet Research, 22*(9), e21279. doi:10.2196/21279 PMID:32805704

Stebbins, R. A. (2001). Exploratory research in the social sciences. *Sage (Atlanta, Ga.).* Advance online publication. doi:10.4135/9781412984249

Sundler, A. J., Lindberg, E., Nilsson, C., & Palmér, L. (2019). Qualitative thematic analysis based on descriptive phenomenology. *Nursing Open, 6*(3), 733–739. doi:10.1002/nop2.275 PMID:31367394

TateT. P.DoroudiS.RitchieD.XuY.WarschauerM. (2023, January 10). Educational research and AI-Generated writing: Confronting the coming tsunami. EdArXiv. doi:10.35542/osf.io/4mec3

Wang, Y. (2022). Construction of intelligent evaluation model of English composition based on machine learning. *Mobile Information Systems, 2022*(3499799), 1–9. doi:10.1155/2022/3499799

White, J., Fu, Q., Hays, S., Sandborn, M., Olea, C., Gilbert, H., Elnashar, A., Spencer-Smith, J., & Schmidt, D. C. (2023). *A prompt pattern catalog to enhance prompt engineering with ChatGPT.* arXiv. https://doi.org//arXiv.2302.11382 doi:10.48550

Xie, Y., Chen, Y., & Ryder, L. H. (2021). Effects of using mobile-based virtual reality on Chinese L2 students' oral proficiency. *Computer Assisted Language Learning*, *34*(3), 225–245. doi:10.1080/09588221.2019.1604551

ZhaiX. (2022). ChatGPT user experience: implications for education. SSRN. doi:10.2139/ssrn.4312418

Chapter 8

Facing Mega-Crises in the Global Era of AI:
The Role of Communication Education

Marta Natalia Lukacovic
Angelo State University, USA

Deborah D. Sellnow-Richmond
https://orcid.org/0000-0001-6179-0307
Southern Illinois University, Edwardsville, USA

ABSTRACT

Communication discipline, including communication courses in higher education, must aptly respond to the demands emerging due to the rapid developments in the AI technologies and globally widespread application of generative AI. Furthermore, to truly stay relevant, communication education must speak to the pervasive, complicated, and difficult-to-solve mega-crises that are diminishing human security, while growing more severe in the current era, around the world. This chapter explores the approaches within communication higher education that can contribute to mitigation of mega-crises via meaningful and ethical integration of AI-supported solutions. Specifically, communication education should emphasize (1) global alliances, (2) cross-disciplinary alliances, (3) community-inclusive alliances, (4) creativity, adaptability, and acceptance of uncertainty, and (5) establishment of viable infrastructures and platforms that enable global, cross-disciplinary, and community-inclusive deliberation and decision-making.

INTRODUCTION

As ChatGPT rapidly rose in global popularity, the wider public, including higher education professionals learned about remarkable advances in generative AI technologies. As AI will only become more effective and integrated throughout the societal processes, higher education institutions are grappling with the demands of preparing students to function as citizens and professionals in such a reality. Rasul et al. (2023) argue for the model characterized by "prioritizing education on the responsible and ethical use of

DOI: 10.4018/979-8-3693-0831-8.ch008

ChatGPT, devising new assessment strategies, addressing bias and falsified information, and including AI literacy as part of graduate skills" (p. 41). In that vein, UNESCO published a "quick start guide" on how to use ChatGPT in higher education (Sabzalieva & Valentini, 2023). Particularly in our field, La Rosa (2023) makes an argument that AI should be intentionally and permanently incorporated into the Communication curriculum at a university level.

We echo these voices that Communication[1] higher education should systematically, meaningfully, and ethically weave the application and discussion of AI into classroom pedagogy. 'Systematically' implies there is an organized process. 'Meaningfully' implies a significant purpose. 'Ethically' means that moral repercussions are emphasized. In this chapter, we will illuminate the meaningful and ethical framework to guide the revamping of Communication curricula that will address the emergent era of AI that will inevitably intersect with the looming mega-crises.

This chapter analyzes and offers a set of recommendations to deliver and keep Communication education at the forefront of guiding professionals and citizens who will not only face mega-crises but who will likely mitigate mega-crises thanks to the practical, meaningful, and ethical use of emerging AI tools. Hence, the chapter begins with an explanation of the concept of mega-crises and its relationship with AI developments. Then, the chapter delves into implications and recommendations for educators across the field of Communication. Besides the theoretical overviews, a set of practical exercises and activities are recommended to thoroughly weave the concept of mega-crises and the application of AI into Communication education. Specifically, we emphasize: (1) *global alliances*, (2) *cross-disciplinary alliances*, (3) *community-inclusive alliances*, and (4) *creativity, adaptability, and acceptance of uncertainty*. Finally, the chapter addresses the need for a wider, committed coalition of stakeholders to establish such (5) *infrastructures and platforms* that are vital to delivering Communication education as recommended.

THE ERA OF MEGA-CRISES AND THE ERA OF AI

Dignity, health, and the overall quality of life of many people and entire communities worldwide are severely diminished by pervasive trends such as poverty, unemployment, illiteracy, violence, armed conflict, corruption, discrimination, extremism, illness, hunger, environmental degradation, pollution, etc. Mega-crisis is a concept that highlights the entanglement of these negative pervasive trends. They are each an individual serious crisis in its own right. But also, each of these crises is frequently entwined with one another, and exacerbates one another, and that makes it particularly difficult to solve any one of them, which precisely is what defines the concept of a mega-crisis (Alpaslan & Mitroff, 2011).

Mega-crises result from a cluster of systemic failures that feed a sort of wicked problem (Alpaslan & Mitroff, 2011; Parrott, 2020). Hence, the potential solutions are so elusive. Even if one of the systemic failures is addressed, the others continue to feed the pervasive wicked problem. Hence, any plausible solutions or mitigations must be very comprehensive and complex (Lukacovic & Sellnow-Richmond, 2023). Such changes at a systemic scale are rather difficult to achieve. While reforms that can mitigate mega-crises are only slowly implemented, mega-crises constantly grow, frequently fueled by other fast changes of this era with the globalization of the economy, media, and other aspects of the modern world.

Another fundamental features of the current era are new technologies, among which the generative AI has been attracting keen attention recently. Enthusiasts may suggest that perhaps AI will solve the mega-crises for people in the future. However, historically new technologies frequently worsened the existing problems or introduced new problems for each they solved, as has been the case with the internet and social media (Morozov, 2011; Schiller, 2000). Thus far, we can see evidence of AI taking the same path. For instance, while the use of AI contributed in some aspects of easing the COVID-19 global mega-crisis, there was another significant dimension of malicious use of AI during the pandemic that contributed to the intentional spread of disinformation, privacy violations, and other transgressions against human rights and wellbeing (Lukacovic & Sellnow-Richmond, 2023; Roumate, 2021). Hence, with the malicious use of AI, security is threatened on several dimensions beyond just the typical nation/state level, but also on organizational and even individual personal levels. Mügge (2023) emphasizes that "as a general purpose technology AI is spreading throughout sundry societal domains, such that its potential securitization, and the consequences for global regulatory politics, will reverberate throughout society at large" (p. 1433). Zeng (2021) makes a prognosis: "With AI's rapid development – not least its use in warfare – and increasingly competitive geopolitics, AI's securitization trend merits more attention" (p. 29). Hence, it is paramount to acknowledge the possible negative repercussions of AI in exacerbating other issues, including mega-crises.

However, AI, like any other technological tool, can indeed become instrumental in improving the current conditions. The precise key to harnessing the opportunities of AI requires the rejection of technological determinism and the investment in the development of all other capacities of societies along with the development of technology. With that in mind, our goal to work towards is the ethical advancement of human security (United Nations, n.d.) vis-à-vis mitigating mega-crises in the context of the AI era. Human security implies the prospects for all to thrive, while protected from threats and given fair opportunities. Mega-crises threaten human security. Still, the comprehensive and complex mitigative approaches that mega-crises require can be more attainable when unifying the intellectual and ethical efforts of societies aided by the assistance of AI technologies. And Communication classrooms will be quite vital to this goal.

COMMUNICATION EDUCATION AMID THE INTERSECTING ERAS OF MEGA-CRISES AND AI

Influential scholars argue that the emergence and successful development of the Communication discipline in the last century (while other humanities have struggled or declined) is due to its practicality – Communication's growth is rooted in the capacity to address the real-world developments and problems (Craig, 2021; Donsbach, 2006). Although Alpaslan and Mitroff (2011) saw mega-crises as nearly unsolvable, we adopt the view that while it may require a complex set of measures and changes, it is paramount to work in the mitigation and eventual solution direction. Communication discipline, of course, needs to play a role in tackling the looming mega-crises, not just to maintain the relevance of our field, but because Communication offers indispensable perspectives. From the Communication lens, Sellnow-Richmond and Lukacovic (2024) propose an approach to address mega-crises for the sectors of professional researchers and crisis management practitioners. However, what needs to be added to this blueprint is the mitigation of mega-crises through the Communication education sector. That precisely is the gap in the literature that will be addressed through this chapter with a focus on the contemporary AI context.

Sellnow-Richmond and Lukacovic (2024) argue that mitigation of mega-crises is rooted in addressing the characteristics that make these occurrences so challenging; (1) widespread global impact, (2) multiple involved systems, (3) effects on multiple and diverse sociocultural groups, (4) nonlinearity, and

(5) defiance of manmade boundaries. This chapter will expound on the five key implications for Communication education focused on AI while stemming from the key mega-crisis challenges. Specifically, we argue that post-secondary Communication educators should employ pedagogy that will:

(1) Build Global Alliances
(2) Build Cross-Disciplinary Alliances
(3) Build Community-Inclusive Alliances
(4) Cultivate Creativity, Adaptability, and Acceptance of Uncertainty
(5) Establish Viable Infrastructures and Platforms for Ongoing Global, Cross-Disciplinary, & Community Inclusive Thinking, Dialogue, and Decision-Making

The mode of pedagogy that draws on our recommendations will be *meaningful* because it will facilitate visions and projects that combine communication expertise and AI literacy in confronting the key features of mega-crises. Furthermore, this pedagogy will elevate the commitment to *ethics* because, besides its pro-social goals, it acknowledges the process while embracing diverse normative perspectives. When it comes to ethics, many values and norms differ rather significantly across cultures (Collste, 2016), which has particular repercussions in the inherently global digital technology ecosystem that features AI (Ess, 2020).

The chapter also addresses the limitations and barriers to accomplishing or maintaining our proposed revamp of Communication pedagogy. For instance, our proposal requires rather a substantial effort from the faculty. At this time, higher education workers are already heavily burdened by diverse responsibilities while daily facing the repercussions of many crises that are plaguing societies. Hence, we delve into the responsibilities of the administrators and other powerful stakeholders in higher education institutions in constructing conditions where a new model such as ours can flourish.

While it is foreseeable that AI will be misused and even abused by malicious actors, which will result in an exacerbation of mega-crises, the discipline of Communication including Communication education can take an active part in the betterment of human security in these circumstances. Hence, in this chapter, we outline the set of pedagogical recommendations. This is not a small task, but it is a necessary task if Communication classrooms are to truly well educate future citizens and professionals of the inevitably dawning AI era.

RECOMMENDATIONS

In the following subsections, we outline each of the five recommendations for mitigating mega-crises. We then delve into the implications of each of these recommendations for Communication higher education. We provide pointers from Communication pedagogy literature on practical interventions for the (physical or virtual) classroom that reflect the recommendations and goals bridging the emerging era of AI and the need to respond to mega-crises. We outline ideas on particular activities that employ practical application and/or discussion about generative AI. With that said, our text is targeting the instructors of Communication in higher education, but equally so, administrators and other pertinent influential stakeholders should consider this proposal, because robust institutional or external support is paramount in achieving and maintaining the proposed path.

(1) Build Global Alliances

Overview

One of the most challenging characteristics of mega-crises is the fact that they defy international borders. This is very clear with examples such as environmental degradation, climate change, or disease. The global nature of the internet platforms exemplifies how the problems that are exacerbated through communication on social media and content-sharing platforms easily transcend the boundaries of nation-states. AI is yet another example of both threats and opportunities that have global impacts. Hence, Sellnow-Richmond and Lukacovic (2024) suggest the necessity of global collaborations that should involve researchers, organizations, and governing bodies of various nations.

Deliberate focus on global collaboration is vital and urgent because generative AI tools like large language models of today tend to perpetuate stereotypes and hegemonies (Gross, 2023), instead of transcending them. Simultaneously, AI is a global phenomenon that can further contribute to the homogenization of perspectives. Stereotypical and hegemonic perspectives are conducive to the exacerbation of mega-crises. Mitigation of mega-crises requires flexibility and thinking outside of the box thanks to diverse viewpoints. Hence, global collaboration is urgently needed in affecting further developments of AI towards more inclusivity.

What needs to be addressed further is how the global collaboration will translate to Communication classrooms in higher education environments. The step that many universities and programs already embrace, at least in terms of their creeds, is orienting education towards international, transnational, and global awareness and topics. Zidani (2021) emphasizes: "Diverse examples should not be set in the margins or in one corner of the syllabus where one week is dedicated to discussing a few non-dominant examples, reaffirming their Otherization" (p. 971). Just as the global nature of the future mega-crises is central to the way we characterize these issues, it is paramount to prioritize the global orientation of curricula that are preparing professionals and citizens who will face these mega-crises.

Many higher education classrooms reflect a degree of global presence through international student and faculty populations. Zidani (2021) encourages centering Communication education on students and their experiences, rather than overly focusing on homogenous canonical viewpoints of the field. Communication education literature offers theory as well as evidence-based strategies to employ student-centered and globally sensitive pedagogies. Jones and Kungiene (2022) offer an approach that prioritizes listening in a highly international classroom while acknowledging linguistic, cultural, and perspective-related differences based on authors' teaching experiences in Lithuania. Chen (2019) reflects on the successes and challenges of creating equitable learning environments for students on the US-Mexico border. Hence, instructors can draw on the growing number of studies that document the pedagogical efforts and reflections related to international and global awareness and/or skills among students.

However, what should those instructors, who do not benefit from the privilege of having a diverse international student body, do to create conditions for global connection-making? Or, for that matter, even if there already is a degree of international or global diversity in the classroom, the instructors may wish to further engage the direction of global collaboration through Communication pedagogy. It has been common practice under the 'diversity and inclusion' initiatives to encourage educators to 'decolonize' their syllabi by assigning readings by authors who vary in race, ethnicity, gender, etc. We would argue that such initiatives may at times lead to mere surface-level fixes and tokenism. A range of experiences has to be captured in the actual substance of the covered material. Hence, the substance should reflect globally informed ideas. For example, the discussion of AI and deepfakes in disinformation campaigns by Samoilenko and Suvorova (2023) is rich in examples and findings that cross national boundaries and point to global tendencies. When the students are engaging with broader multilevel perspectives, they can better find echoes of their own experiences as well as prepare to function as citizens and professionals in the global world. Hence, students will be honing their skills in participation in transboundary thinking, dialogue, and decision-making that can enhance human security and mitigate mega-crises in the era of AI.

Recommended Exercises and Activities

In terms of a particular activity, an excellent way to prioritize global orientations in education is partnering with an international colleague to reciprocally perform pedagogic interventions in both classrooms. Uecker and Schmidt (2022) present pedagogical practices that allow students in various countries to interact, compare, and contrast their perceptions while mastering important intercultural communication concepts. The authors describe an example where students in a US-American institution and a Russian institution were given a survey about their perceptions of one's own country and the partner country. This activity allowed students to use their own aggregate data to reflect on assumptions, misconceptions, and other important tendencies that impact schemas about the other, especially in the broader geopolitical context of nations that are connected through a rather complicated and even adversarial relationship, such as the U.S. and Russia.

An iteration of the above-mentioned activity can directly involve generative AI in certain parts of the process. For instance, the instructors may allow students to create some questions to be used in the survey that will be distributed among their international counterparts. A large language model, like ChatGPT, may be used to create the initial set of questions. Then, students should be tasked with editing these questions. The instructor should prompt the direction of the discussion and subsequent editing to highlight the advantages and disadvantages of the AI tool in the creation of the questions. For instance, the questions may be invalid in getting the actual information that the class is curious about. Or, there may be issues with the questions from the methodological perspective. Depending on the level and learning outcomes of the course, the instructor should adjust and direct the activity accordingly. Ultimately, students should be able to make the decision to what degree they use or alter the questions provided by the AI. Besides learning about survey writing, they will also be able to assess the suitability of the utilized AI tool in this process. Furthermore, over the years, the specific AI tool will most likely improve, which can be informative for instructors about the important development of these technologies, and furthermore, it gives the instructors yet another point to discuss with their students.

If the international counterparts do not share the same language in which the survey is constructed, the AI tools may also be used to translate the questionnaire. Then, the international counterparts (students and/or the instructors abroad) will be asked to provide feedback about the questionnaire and its clarity, appropriateness, validity, etc. The international feedback will then serve as a way to assess the AI tool's capacity to convey meaning cross-linguistically and cross-culturally.

Instructors can also pursue international survey activity without utilizing AI tools, but centering the questions about attitudes and experiences that the students in various countries have in connection to AI. Similarly, the topics of the questions may include mega-crisis cases that are relevant for one or both nations, e.g. disinformation campaigns, environmental degradation, health crises, poverty, etc. Hence, students will be able to reflect on similarities and differences in perceptions about issues that are local, shared, or of a global nature. Follow-up and debriefing activities will serve to further connect the international collaboration activity to the discussion of the implications for the specific focus of the course.

Specific fine-tuning of the activity can be appropriated to range from interpersonal to organizational to mass and/or new media communication, and so on. It can be useful for students with a plethora of interests ranging from strategic communication to journalism, from human resources to advertising, and from business to governmental to non-profit sectors. One particularly worthwhile way to encourage post-activity deliberation is to assign personal reflections, where students can orally or in a written form discuss what they have been able to extract from the international collaboration activity that ties to their future professional interests. Likewise, instructors may choose to opt for a more specific prompt for reflection, such as: How should a strategic communication professional design a campaign to promote a new AI product for international stakeholders who differ rather widely in innovation adoption, apprehension, and overall attitudes about new technologies? What should a journalist writing for international audiences include when covering a story about AI? How should a human resources specialist approach a new company policy that requires specific use of AI among its international workforce? Essentially, in this manner, an instructor will craft a prompt question that more closely corresponds to the focus and objectives of the course.

The recommended activities can be incorporated in a variety of Communication courses and the depth, breadth, and specific features of the activity can be adjusted based on the pedagogical goals of the instructors. While drawing on the sense of students' curiosity about their peers elsewhere, the activities will serve as an impactful and memorable venue to highlight Communication theories and concepts. Furthermore, such activities organically bring the global nature of AI, digital media, as well as mega-crises to the forefront of students' thinking. This way, students' direct experiences in the Communication classroom serve as opportunities to engage on a more global level and thus hone in on the knowledge and/or the skills that will serve well the citizens and professionals of the globalized world, with its looming crises, as the era of AI emerges.

(2) Build Cross-Disciplinary Alliances

Overview

Academic disciplines are social constructions. As such, it is crucial to recognize that academic disciplines are limited by the visions of their creators and gatekeepers, their institutionalization, and their key scholarship. However, the various social, cultural, political, psychological, biological, physical, and technological phenomena that transpire in the real world are not clearly delineated, which makes the rigid disciplinary understandings of many Western academic fields ill-equipped to address the complex real phenomena (Gunaratne, 2021). This critique is particularly important when touching on mega-crises, which impact various sectors (Alpaslan & Mitroff, 2011). Not one single academic discipline in the typical Western sense is able to singlehandedly solve a mega-crisis, and thus cross-disciplinary collaborations are paramount in the mitigation of mega-crises (Sellnow-Richmond & Lukacovic, 2024).

Furthermore, experts affirm that the AI-era specific issue of the malicious use of AI, which can be considered a crisis in its own right, will best be addressed by a complex multilevel approach that is heterogenous in collaboratively incorporating various methods and theories that are rooted in various fields (Averkin et al., 2019). Communication offers scholarship that should be informing such interdisciplinary initiatives. For instance, Communication can render its long list of scholarship on new media technologies and their diverse impacts (e.g., Boulianne et al., 2023; Morozov, 2011), including very profound warnings about techno-determinism (e.g., Gerbaudo, 2017). Furthermore, Communication scholars have already explored a variety of AI-specific issues that span across the wider discipline and are ever-more pertinent in the current era such as human-to-machine communication (e.g., Spence et al., 2014), implication of AI for deceptive campaigns, disinformation, and deepfakes (e.g., Samoilenko & Suvorova, 2023), implications of AI for journalism (e.g., Pavlik, 2023), etc. However, Communication scholars and practitioners must be able to advocate for our place at the table when key decisions, such as about the future of AI, are made. To take part in the important decision-making processes, Communication scholars and practitioners must clearly convey the value of the knowledge of our discipline for cross-disciplinary initiatives, including cross-disciplinary teaching and learning within the institutions of higher education (Dannels & Housley Gaffney, 2009).

To clarify the terminology, 'cross-disciplinary' is the adjective used to cover multidisciplinary, interdisciplinary, and transdisciplinary initiatives (Heitzmann et al., 2021). As Park and Son (2010) explain, multidisciplinary learning refers to disciplines working side by side on a problem, while staying confined to the disciplinary perspective. "Interdisciplinary learning focuses more on collaboration and intersections between disciplines" (p. 83) as Park and Son further clarify. Transdisciplinary research reflects moving beyond and transcending the boundaries of the established disciplines (Heitzmann et al., 2021). Hence, transdisciplinary learning reflects the product of an interdisciplinary process, such as students' transdisciplinary skills that result from interdisciplinary learning (Park & Son, 2010).

It is important to address how the Communication classroom equips students for partaking in cross-disciplinary thinking, dialogues, and decision-making. First, it is paramount to guide Communication majors to become more confident in asserting their place at the table when important cross-disciplinary dialogues happen. Second, Communication educators should also keep in mind that when having the opportunities to teach non-majors, they have a chance to convey the value of Communication perspectives. This will further cultivate the idea among other professionals that when seeking allies, specialists from the Communication field can be remarkably helpful when addressing a variety of issues (Donovan et al., 2021). Among this variety of issues, the foci on AI as well as on mega-crises should be one of the central contexts of cross-disciplinary efforts in Communication education.

Recommended Exercises and Activities

In terms of specific activity recommendations, various forms of presentations of students' work are already a common practice and assessment method in many Communication classrooms. Presentations may focus on mastered theories and concepts, research and analyses, case studies, proposals, or applied projects. Some instructors also employ a variety of presentation forms, including oral presentations (that may vary from long formats to short 'elevator pitches' formats), slide-show accompanied presentations, conference-style poster presentations, or a variety of audio-visual productions. The audience for these presentations tends to be the rest of the class. A new approach to consider may involve a class from a different discipline to join the audience. In terms of reciprocity, the Communication students can repay the favor and be the educated but non-expert audience for presentations of the other class's work. Besides honing the skills of relating specialized content to professionals in other disciplines, the activity creates a basis for having other cross-disciplinary exchanges in the future.

Upon forming an alliance with a collogue in another department, this method can be adapted to already existing courses where cross-disciplinary dialogue is one of the key objectives. This idea of cross-disciplinary class presentations can work particularly well in programs that tend to specialize in "interdisciplinary project-based learning" (Dumaine et al., 2023). In such a design, students are encouraged to explore one element of a wicked problem at a time with a separate project for each class across an interdisciplinary curriculum of several different courses. The approach described by Dumaine et al. assists students in drawing connections between the issues that might be of specific interest to them personally and other broader issues. For example, students can explore the connection between environmental degradation and poverty. Furthermore, the students are exploring the ways that different disciplines shed light on or offer mitigation for relevant issues. We stress that now it is vital to consider the role of AI in the wicked problem processes, as both agents of exacerbation and mitigation. Coleman et al. (2021) situate Communication education in facilitating "transdisciplinary deliberations" (p.163) that address wicked problems such as mega-crises. The angle that they suggest is the focus on the impacts of information that is disseminated through various media. Of course, the mass communication angle is not the only possibility, and the Communication-centric focus can vary depending on the nature of the specific course.

As with the previous subsection, depending on the level of comfort that the instructor feels within the intended in-class practices, they may want to consider incorporating the application of generative AI, such as in the process of drafting some parts of the students' projects. Again, we stress that this should be done in conjunction with theory and ethical reflection. The *substantiation* (which implies understanding the roots and impacts of AI) and the *ethical competencies* are vitally important types of knowledge in an AI-inclusive Communication curriculum (Lopezosa et al., 2023). Hence, we encourage instructors that all AI application activities added to the cross-disciplinary work are accompanied by prompted reflections, rich discussion, and meaningful instructor feedback that further guides students in understanding the large picture.

In helping the students cultivate cross-disciplinary skills, educators are equipping future Communication professionals and other professionals to take an active constructive part in dialogues and projects that will mitigate and perhaps even solve some mega-crises in the future era – the era of AI.

(3) Build Community-Inclusive Alliances

Overview

Mega-crises are far-reaching in terms of impacting many different sociocultural groups. Hence, it is vital to replace vertical processes with more horizontal orientations – to avoid the managerial top-down approaches of crisis communication and management (Sellnow-Richmond & Lukacovic, 2024). Essentially, the end goal is to inclusively empower communities to take part in thinking, having dialogues with others, and making decisions about approaches towards mega-crises that impact these communities. The pillars upon which this goal becomes reality include:

(a) Establish Viable Infrastructures and Platforms where Members of Various Communities (from Local to Global) Participate in Thinking, Dialogue, and Decision-Making
(b) Listen to and Learn from the Members of Various Communities
(c) Work toward Structural Changes that Encompass Input from the Impacted Community Members

In fact, various areas of the Communication field provide frameworks that can be followed for both research and practice that democratize the involvement of local or global community members. For instance, Seeger and Sellnow (2019) emphasize the importance of dialogue to achieve the best practices of crisis communication because it allows all different stakeholders to share their input on equal terms with the organizations. In health communication, Dutta (2007) centers on listening to and empowering cultures and communities, particularly marginalized ones that have been historically silenced and ignored in all decision-impacting conversations. In public relations/strategic communication, influential perspectives such as Grunig's symmetrical model (2006) and Botan's co-creational approach (2018) also both emphasize the importance of viewing stakeholders as independent communicators who play a more fundamental role in the communication process than simply providing feedback. In mass communication, Ward (2014) proposes that a radical media ethics framework that is appropriate for the era of contemporary technologies should be based on global input and collaboration from all wide, diverse communities. Furthermore, these approaches serve as excellent sources of ideas for Communication instructors in various fields. Hence, the echo throughout the field of Communication emphasizes that everything, including the challenges of mega-crises and the opportunities of AI, should be talked about and, crucially, decided about with input from various voices and stakeholders.

With the focus on the AI factor more specifically, our Communication field has contributed very important perspectives. For instance, ethicists in the Communication field have been writing about culturally and globally inclusive normative frameworks that are even more necessary with the current state of technological advancement (e.g., Ess, 2020; Ward, 2014). Indeed, globally and locally democratized counter-mega-crisis mitigation in the AI era is a tremendously large project with a plethora of obstacles. However, the Communication field already possesses a rather strong foundation of insightful scholarship. The role of Communication educators is to effectively convey these nuggets of useful knowledge, such as the importance of community participation in both discussion and decision-making, to the students.

Recommended Exercises and Activities

One option, that may occur to some, in terms of a specific classroom activity is to employ a generative AI large language model that can be asked to adopt the perspective of a particular group member and convey their possible positions and concerns. So, using AI as a dialogue partner in a scenario. However, while currently widely used AI tools like ChatGPT do so if asked, likely, their output may not be representative of the actual envisioned target community. Underrepresented communities were very likely also underrepresented in the training data of such large-language models, and hence the AI output may be too generic, far from the truth, or even completely inaccurate. The outputs of large-language models have been identified as biased in various instances (e.g., Belenguer, 2022; Gross, 2023). Furthermore, using an AI tool to act as the narrative conveyer for a marginalized community instead of an actual member of that community is particularly problematic because it essentially embodies yet another way of silencing, demeaning, and dehumanizing the marginalized. So, we would discourage replacing human perspectives with AI as a proxy, even for exercise purposes.

The recommended and preferable approach in teaching about community engagement in our view is service-learning which allows students to experience the processes, reflect on theories, and adopt the needed skills (Pawlowski, 2018). In the context of intense crises, it becomes paramount to also help the students in "learning to learn from below" (Dutta et al., 2020, p. 13). Dutta and colleagues furthermore emphasize "the urgency of developing pedagogies of crisis communication that are rooted in community voices, that offer anchors for imagining collectively today but, more importantly, for future" (pp. 17-18).

Specifically, as there is a lack of general understanding and a high level of apprehension among many communities in connection with AI today (Mills et al., 2023), a very important value that Communication educators and students can extend to community members in fair exchange for the involvement in our class projects is sharing the clarifications about AI that our field offers. Likewise, different crises and mega-crises attract attention and inspire apprehension among many community members, and that is also an area where Communication educators and students can help the community gain valuable insights.

In this case, as well, the learning can be significantly elevated and refined as the instructor guides students via prompted reflections, discussions, and feedback. Specifically, the concept of human security (United Nations, n.d.) can serve as a meaningful point of reflection. As human security encompasses the ability of people to thrive in their conditions, the specific features of human security should be co-defined with community members (Na'puti & Frain, 2023). The instructor, the students, and the community members articulate together the meanings of mega-crises that are growing during the emergent AI era. The imagining of what is next, and specifically what to do to make things better and more secure, are to be co-envisioned as well. Hence, instructors should consider prompting student reflections and discussions as well as accompanying their feedback with an emphasis on the role of Communication in general, and the specific subfield in particular, including but not limited to, journalism, public relations, organizational communication, etc.

Collaborations between Communication classrooms and communities can be very beneficial for both the students and the community members in grappling with looming mega-crises. Furthermore, these collaborations can illuminate perceptions of and experiences with AI that may differ quite a bit between the students and the community members. However, only these types of collaborations embody the envisioned goal of participatory discussions and decision-making. Ultimately, participation should strive for a status quo where even such technical decision-making that addresses massive mega-crises or regulation of emerging technologies can be more accessible for the communities via symmetrical communication (Grunig, 2006; Seeger & Sellnow, 2019). If Communication researchers, practitioners, educators, and students join forces to democratize access to decision-making for broader communities, we believe this can create a wide alliance of collaboration. Such alliance can reciprocally support the claim for the role that the Communication field professionals ought to play in the decision-making processes.

(4) Cultivate Creativity, Adaptability, and Acceptance of Uncertainty

Overview

Mega-crises are characterized by high degrees of fluidity and uncertainty. The fluid dynamics result from the various comorbid crises merging and simultaneously continuing to evolve (Lukacovic & Sellnow-Richmond, 2023). Hence, mega-crises lead to experiences of "uncertainty flooding" (Liu & Levenshus, 2023, p. 162). These characteristics make mega-crises more difficult to deal with even if applying the typical theories and best practices of crisis management. For instance, crisis communication literature relies on the three-fold model that divides an event into the pre-crisis, the actual acute crisis, and the post-crisis (Seeger & Sellnow, 2019). Unfortunately, with the complexity of mega-crises, these discrete categories of the life-cycle stages of a contained crisis are not likely to apply (Sellnow-Richmond &

Lukacovic, 2024). Hence, researchers and practitioners need to apply novel and fluid approaches that reflect the complex and ever-changing mega-crises.

The emphasis on novel and fluid approaches translates to the necessity of cultivating creativity, adaptability, and acceptance of uncertainty among the students of Communication courses. Such lessons pair especially well with the previous recommendations. One can argue that creativity, adaptability, and acceptance of uncertainty can flourish particularly well along with other transdisciplinary, transcultural, and community-inclusive skills. But furthermore, we suggest a deliberate focus on the fluidity of mega-crises as well as the rapid developments of AI capabilities and applications in the context of mega-crises (Lukacovic & Sellnow-Richmond, 2023).

As with any tool, AI's limitations are to a large degree determined by the limitations of the human user's skills and visions. For instance, prompt engineering requires expertise, skills, and indeed creativity. Proper use of prompt engineering can successfully instruct generative AI to assist in the mitigation of pervasive challenges such as mega-crises. But proper prompt engineering is dependent on expert and creative use of language, which can be cultivated via education.

In many ways, this is a fast-paced world. Technologies such as AI are rapidly evolving, but so are other factors, including mega-crises. Hence, one must be prepared to adapt to both challenges and opportunities, such as the opportunities that stem from the advances in AI. The necessary adaptability is another skill that can also be enhanced via education.

The constant fluidity of the factors described in this section means that situations will pan out in uncertain ways. Change is perhaps the only true constant. Hence, progress is rather dependent on acknowledgment and acceptance of uncertainty. After all, we do not exactly know how bad some mega-crises will grow, nor how many new, promising options will arise thanks to AI for that matter. One way to manage the anxieties caused by uncertainty is by cultivating the skills of creativity and adaptability. As problems evolve, so will our perspectives and our abilities to embrace new directions. Hence, it is important to position the role of Communication education in guiding students toward creativity, adaptability, and acceptance of uncertainty.

Recommended Exercises and Activities

In terms of specific activity recommendations, this is the case when the instructors definitely should consider the hands-on use of generative AI tools for exercises that explore mitigative approaches to those very fluid crises or mega-crises. We suggest selecting a locally relevant and ongoing 'crisis-of-focus' that is related to other issues and has proven rather difficult to manage. For some courses, perhaps a field-specific crisis-of-focus might work better than a local crisis, but this is something an instructor should determine based on their course objectives. The instructor should ask students to identify key characteristics of this crisis of focus. Next, students should determine which of these characteristics are fluid. In other words, students should determine which of these characteristics are evolving and changing, and thus are adding to the elusiveness of the crisis resolution efforts. Then, with these characteristics in mind, the instructor should ask the students to brainstorm about possible mitigative approaches to the crisis (without the help of AI). If time permits, we suggest first asking students to work on the prompt individually, then have them form small groups of 3-4 members to discuss their takes on the possible mitigative measures to the crisis-of-focus. The next step of the process should be posing questions about the suggestions on mitigative approaches to the crisis-of-focus to a text-generative AI tool such as ChatGPT or another large language model. Upon examining the AI's suggestions, students will compare and contrast their pre-AI involvement ideas. Finally, the instructor will ask the students to consolidate a list of mitigative measures that will incorporate the best of their suggestions and AI suggestions, ultimately merging the human and machine sources of perspective. Additionally, the above-mentioned approach can incorporate more steps if it is fitting for the given course. Such as students and the AI tool may also be asked to think about possible complications that may arise and diminish the success of the envisioned mitigative approaches. This exercise, similar to the exercise in the *Recommendation 1 – Build Global Alliances*, serves to address the strengths and limitations of AI tools in comparison to human knowledge, with the difference of focusing the conversation on creativity, adaptability, and acceptance of uncertainty. Again, we emphasize the importance of prompted reflections, discussions, and instructor feedback, which is helpful to contextualize and theorize such activities within the perspective of Communication.

Theoretical and applied engagements with the fact that technologies including AI constantly change and evolve are central to a relevant and updated Communication curriculum. Furthermore, when massive and complicated issues increasingly impact societies, a relevant and updated Communication curriculum needs to be theoretically and applicably engaged with the complex and ever-changing nature of these mega-crises. The global, cross-disciplinary, and community-inclusive initiatives in the Communication curriculum directly foster creativity, adaptability, and acceptance of uncertainty that will benefit professionals and citizens as they navigate the challenges of mega-crises as well as the opportunities that surface with AI.

(5) Establish Viable Infrastructures and Platforms for Ongoing Global, Cross-Disciplinary, and Community Inclusive Thinking, Dialogue, and Decision-Making

Sellnow-Richmond and Lukacovic (2024) emphasize that mega-crises defy manmade boundaries, be they political, disciplinary, or sectoral types of boundaries. This makes the mega-crises particularly difficult to solve, as the various boundaries translate to structural barriers such as bureaucracy that frequently exacerbate crises or debilitate mitigative initiatives. To build global, cross-disciplinary, and community-inclusive alliances in practice, research, and education, suitable infrastructures and platforms must exist for conducting the activities of joint thinking, dialogue, and decision-making. A lack of such infrastructures and platforms is yet another structural barrier that should be removed particularly during the rising era of AI, where the rapidly advancing technology creates on the one hand a sense of urgency before it aggravates the existing crises, but on the other hand the technology can also be utilized to more efficiently and effectively overcome the existing barriers.

The lack of appropriate infrastructures and platforms in the education system is a serious barrier that confines the abilities of Communication instructors to employ the initiatives as described in the previous subsections. Hence, the instructors are severely limited in their ability to cultivate awareness and skills towards global, cross-disciplinary, and community-inclusive alliance-building among their students. Administrators, leaders, and other key stakeholders should work on creating and/or robustly supporting the efforts of the faculty in the creation of the necessary infrastructures and platforms. Such *infrastructures* are the networks and channels through which connections are established, resources are accessed, and activities are performed. Such *platforms* are the physical or digital spaces that are continually available and well equipped to facilitate connection-making, resource access, or performing of activities. Our recommended efforts require resources that should be provided by the institutions of higher education.

And the institutions must support global, cross-disciplinary, and community-inclusive efforts if these institutions wish to remain relevant as the mega-crises continue to transpire in the era of AI.

The barriers to global, cross-disciplinary, and community-inclusive infrastructures and platforms within higher education are of both *physical* and *cultural* natures. The barriers of the physical nature include a lack of monetary, technological, spatial, and other tangible resources to conduct the activities as recommended. Similarly, an important physical barrier is the lack of time that many university-level instructors experience due to many demands, pressures, and commitments that they are obligated to meet. For instance, in the US, many faculty members are concerned about the issues with the increasing demands, feeling disillusioned, or even burnt out, and thus are considering leaving the field of higher education (Morales, 2022). Some voices are calling for leaders to explore ways of outsourcing certain tasks to AI tools thus removing the extra burdens from the employees (Abdous, 2023). If some tasks are streamlined for the instructors and other crucial personnel, they can then shift their focus to innovation.

In particular, the apt use of technology can contribute to the global, cross-disciplinary, and community-inclusive infrastructures and platforms at the institutions of higher education. A good example is creating more opportunities for the faculty to form partnerships with counterparts in other departments and other nations. Hence, funding should be provided for conferences, workshops, team-building occasions, etc. The connections that are nurtured through international and interdisciplinary educational partnerships are vital for actual in-class activities as recommended (e.g., Uecker & Schmidt, 2022). The proverbial connection between 'town and gown', so between a university and its regional community needs to be established and nurtured through deliberate initiatives (Staley & Endicott, 2023). So, the proper platforms and infrastructures are necessary to connect university instructors and members of the communities, as such quality partnerships are paramount for service-learning through community-engagement projects (Pawlowski, 2018). But again, the leadership at universities must recognize that all such activities require effort, time, and other types of resources, and thus the faculty must be provided with those necessary resources and appropriately incentivized for their effort. To allocate the additional physical resources that are necessary to transcend material gaps and boundaries and boldly revamp universities to be ready to address the pressing crises of tomorrow, university leaders must significantly upgrade efficiency through available technologies (Staley & Endicott, 2023).

Importantly, the fact that technologies may be used for the battement of society, has proven not to automatically lead to this preferable result (Morozov, 2011; Schiller, 2000). So, it is paramount that organizations are held accountable that with the new opportunities that arrive with the advancements of AI such as automatization and outsourcing of tasks, the tools will not be used to replace the workers nor to ignorantly stockpile more expectations on remaining workers (McChesney & Nichols, 2016). Simply put, more efficiency should translate to more free time, and hence better rested and more productive individuals and groups. We implore institutions of higher education to be the future archetypes to set the standards for meaningful and ethical utilization of tools like AI while increasing both the care for and the growth opportunities for instructors, personnel, students, and other stakeholders.

The barriers of cultural nature partially stem from the above-mentioned physical limitations and issues. For instance, disillusionment or burnout are psychological symptoms that contribute to such a workplace, such institutional culture, where enthusiasm for more labor is naturally not going to be present. However, other cultural structural barriers also encumber the creation of global, cross-disciplinary, and community-inclusive infrastructures and platforms. These culturally-rooted problems occur when institutions do not prioritize global, cross-disciplinary, or community-inclusive orientation in their creeds, visions, and strategic plans. Hence, if there is an inefficient appreciation for global, cross-disciplinary, or community-inclusive endeavors, it is difficult for faculty to align these extra efforts with employee performance evaluations that are typically centered on advancing institutional goals. But the cultural structural support of the institution is beyond simply paying lip service. A clearly expressed and enacted commitment to global, cross-disciplinary, and community-inclusive collaborations must be present in both rhetoric and real initiatives. When cultural commitment is present, difficult-to-overcome physical structural barriers can be transcended by creative contemporary projects such as the Open Education Resources (OER) movement that utilizes forward-thinking ideas and new technologies to connect educators around the world and support them in teaching applied use and ethical reflections on AI (Mills et al., 2023).

Furthermore, it is paramount for Communication educators to be acknowledged as valuable participants in global, cross-disciplinary, and community-inclusive collaborations. While some institutions may indeed in both the word and the action commit to global, cross-disciplinary, and community-inclusive orientation, Communication departments may be left at the margins or completely left out. Hence, leaders and faculty in Communication should advocate for the field's acknowledgment and inclusion in the global, community-oriented, and cross-disciplinary infrastructures and platforms. Dannels and Housley Gaffney (2009) warn that "The importance of communication instruction in the other disciplines is no longer questionable; many are beginning to explore the teaching and learning of communication in other disciplines in a scholarly way" (p. 142). However, as they further explain, the problem is that "Many of them are expanding without the expertise of a communication scholar in order to meet their needs" (p. 142). Sellnow (2023) suggests: "Colleagues across disciplines do value what we have to offer, but do not know the nuances of the Communication field to understand how we fit uniquely into that picture unless we educate them" (p. 438).

We want to add that by clearly delineating and emphasizing Communication's aptitude in addressing the mega-crises intersecting with the rise of the AI era, the argument for Communication's seat at the table is actually significantly strengthened. This argument is Communication's cultural capital in countering the cultural type of structural barriers to the discipline's growth in research, practice, and education. The cultural barriers must be disrupted in order to consequently strengthen the physical infrastructures and platforms for global, cross-disciplinary, and community-inclusive dialogues necessary precisely to ease serious mega-crises while meaningfully and ethically utilizing AI. This is why we propose this demanding list of recommendations, which must not be solely asked of university instructors as if they are the only ones bearing the responsibility in the current situation. Leaders, administrators, and other stakeholders holding relevant power are even more responsible for being alert, knowledgeable, and acting as the different crises incubate and AI becomes more widely used and capable.

CONCLUSION

With this chapter, we outline the recommendations on mitigation of mega-crises that are and will continue to intersect with the rise of the AI era. The chapter explicates the specific implications for Communication higher education, which include *(1) building global alliances, (2) building cross-disciplinary alliances, (3) building community-inclusive alliances, (4) cultivating creativity, adaptability, and acceptance of uncertainty*, and *(5) establishing viable infrastructures and platforms to sustain all proposed initiatives.* We are rooting our proposal in the *meaningful* focus of Communication education towards purposeful application, as well as in the prominence of *ethical* commitments every step of the way. Thus, rich, theoretically, and normatively substantiated discussion, explanation, and feedback must accompany any hands-on application of tools like generative AI large language models within Communication higher education courses (Lopezosa et al., 2023; Roumate, 2023).

We also realize that for such an ambitious project, it is of utmost importance to develop a *systematic* plan. Whenever possible, we suggest ideas from the literature that serve as blueprints in order to launch or improve initiatives that echo our proposal. So, at this point, it is absolutely vital to begin or continue the interventions as we discussed along with data collection and absorption of other relevant findings from Communication and other pertinent fields. Hence, a more systematic blueprint will start to emerge with more concrete contours that will be drawn by empirical and critical reflections on particular Communication classroom interventions.

Crucially, this necessary and demanding project that marries mega-crisis mitigation with AI emphasis in the Communication classroom, requires the proverbial village to come true. Hence, instructors, students, administrators, funding entities, staff at the institutions, a broader network of international as well as interdisciplinary colleagues, and community members will (ideally) be participating. Therefore, while instructors are the essential driving force (Monte-Serrat & Cattani, 2023), the support of other stakeholders in paramount. Importantly, as students are central to education processes, students are central to this cautious plea to engage with the rapidly advancing AI technologies (Mills et al., 2023). Hence, student's perspectives and feedback will be fundamental for the improvement of the *systematic* implementation as well as for the continuous elevation of *meaningful* and *ethical* dimensions of Communication education in the era of AI.

To put it simply, a lot will have to be done by many. It is not a small task by any means. But the stakes are high. Maintaining the relevance of the discipline of Communication is just one of the more specific and smaller-scale stakes in this situation. With the exacerbation of mega-crises such as pandemics, environmental degradation, violent conflict, etc., we are talking about stakes that gravely harm entire societies, and at times also other species and the planet. If used wisely and diligently, AI may become the desperately needed tool that helps overcome these threats and support human security despite challenges.

This chapter advocates for radical commitment to Communication education initiatives that contribute to mega-crisis mitigation while meaningfully and ethically incorporating AI. Hence, we assert the necessary components of Communication curricula should be global, cross-disciplinary, community-inclusive, and creative Communication pedagogies. While this project is not easy to achieve and/or sustain, we believe that our chapter has collected a wealth of ideas that can truly help make this ambition a reality and the standard for others to thrive to match. So, while times will be tough with the mega-crises that will inevitably and gravely impact many societies worldwide, Communication education can play one of the central roles in cultivating citizens and professionals who can really harness the progress opportunities that arise with the dawning AI era.

REFERENCES

Abdous, M. (2023). How AI is shaping the future of higher ed. *Inside Higher Ed.* https://www.insidehighered.com/views/2023/03/22/how-ai-shaping-future-higher-ed-opinion

Alpaslan, C. M., & Mitroff, I. I. (2011). *Swans, swine, and swindlers; Coping with the growing threat of mega-crises and mega-messes.* Stanford Business Books – Stanford University Press.

Averkin, A. N., Bazarkina, D. Yu., Pantserev, K. A., & Pashentsev, Y. N. (2019). Artificial intelligence in the context of psychological security: Theoretical and practical implications. *Atlantis Studies in Uncertainty Modelling, 1*, 101–107. doi:10.2991/eusflat-19.2019.16

Belenguer, L. (2022). AI bias: Exploring discriminatory algorithmic decision-making models and the application of possible machine-centric solutions adapted from the pharmaceutical industry. *AI and Ethics, 2*(2), 771–787. doi:10.1007/s43681-022-00138-8 PMID:35194591

Botan, C. H. (2018). *Strategic communication: Theory and practice*. Wiley-Blackwell.

Boulianne, S., Oser, J., & Hoffmann, C. P. (2023). Powerless in the digital age? A systematic review and meta-analysis of political efficacy and digital media use. *New Media & Society, 25*(9), 2512–2536. doi:10.1177/14614448231176519

Chen, Y.-W. (2019). Centering epistemologies on the margins and borders: Reflections on an Hispanic-serving institution's attempts to embrace equity and cultural wealth. *Communication Education, 68*(4), 516–521. doi:10.1080/03634523.2019.1645870

Coleman, M. C., Santos, S. C., Cypher, J. M., Krummenacher, C., & Fleming, R. (2021). Lessons from the pandemic: Engaging wicked problems with transdisciplinary deliberation. *Journal of Communication Pedagogy, 5*, 164–171. doi:10.31446/JCP.2021.2.17

Collste, G. (2016). *Ethics and communication: Global perspectives*. Rowman & Littlefield.

Craig, R. T. (2021). Response. In M. H. Rich & J. S. Robles (Eds.), *Practicing communication theory; Exploring, applying, and teaching the constitutive metamodel* (pp. 191–210). Cognella Academic Publishing.

Dannels, D., & Housley Gaffney, A. (2009). Communication across the curriculum and in the disciplines: A call for scholarly cross-curricular advocacy. *Communication Education, 58*(1), 124–153. doi:10.1080/03634520802527288

Donovan, E. E., Brown, L. E., Lindstadt, C., Table, B., Heidari, E., Coolidge, A., Omran, S., & Rush, S. (2021). The 12 Fundamentals of Highly Effective Communicators: Teaching theory-based professional communication to pharmacy students. *Journal of Communication Pedagogy, 4*, 21–37. doi:10.31446/JCP.2021.1.03

Donsbach, W. (2006). The identity of communication research. *Journal of Communication, 56*(3), 437–448. doi:10.1111/j.1460-2466.2006.00294.x

Dumaine, D., Derdeyn, L., Ranieri, E., & Reis, A. (2023, May 22-24). *Interdisciplinary core-compliant teaching with project-based learning: Building a culture* [Conference presentation]. Lilly Conference; Evidence-Based Teaching and Learning, Austin, TX, United States. https://www.lillyconferences-tx.com/2023schedule

Dutta, M. J. (2007). Communicating about culture and health: Theorizing culture-centered and cultural sensitivity approaches. *Communication Theory, 17*(3), 304–328. doi:10.1111/j.1468-2885.2007.00297.x

Dutta, M. J., Moana-Johnson, G., & Elers, C. (2020). COVID-19 and the pedagogy of culture-centered community radical democracy: A response from Aotearoa New Zealand. *Journal of Communication Pedagogy, 3,* 11–19. doi:10.31446/JCP.2020.03

Eadie, W. F. (2022). *When communication became a discipline*. Rowman & Littlefield.

Ess, Ch. (2020). *Digital media ethics* (3rd ed.). Polity Press.

Gerbaudo, P. (2017). From cyber-autonomism to cyber-populism: An ideological history of digital activism. *TripleC (Cognition, Communication, Co-Operation): Open Access Journal for a Global Sustainable Information Society, 15*(2), 477–489. https://doi-org.easydb.angelo.edu/10.31269/triplec.v15i2.773

Gross, N. (2023). What ChatGPT tells us about gender: A cautionary tale about performativity and gender biases in AI. *Social Sciences (Basel, Switzerland), 12*(8), 435–450. doi:10.3390/socsci12080435

Grunig, J. E. (2006). Furnishing the edifice: Ongoing research on public relations as a strategic management function. *Journal of Public Relations Research, 18*(2), 151–176. doi:10.1207/s1532754xjprr1802_5

Gunaratne, S. A. (2021). Resolving East-West rifts in Craig's metamodel. In M. H. Rich & J. S. Robles (Eds.), *Practicing communication theory; Exploring, applying, and teaching the constitutive metamodel* (pp. 127–151). Cognella Academic Publishing.

Heitzmann, N., Opitz, A., Stadler, M., Sommerhoff, D., Fink, M. C., Obersteiner, A., Schmidmaier, R., Neuhaus, B. J., Ufer, S., Seidel, T., Fischer, M. R., & Fischer, F. (2021). Cross-disciplinary research on learning and instruction – Coming to terms. *Frontiers in Psychology, 11*, 1–6. doi:10.3389/fpsyg.2021.562658 PMID:34045986

Jones, A. C., & Kungiene, E. (2022). Intercultural communication pedagogy in Lithuania: Listening to viewpoints. In M. Minielli, M. N. Lukacovic, S. A. Samoilenko, M. Finch, & D. Uecker (Eds.), *Communication theory and application in post-socialist contexts* (pp. 223–236). Lexington Books – Rowman & Littlefield.

La Rosa, A. (2023). Challenges of university communication teaching in the artificial intelligence age. In F. Roumate (Ed.), *Artificial intelligence in higher education and scientific research; Future developments* (pp. 89–99). Springer. doi:10.1007/978-981-19-8641-3_7

Liu, B. F., & Levenshus, A. B. (2023). Interpreting the interpersonal: Crisis communication insights for pandemics. In S. M. Croucher & A. Diers-Lawson (Eds.), *Pandemic communication* (pp. 156–173). Routledge. doi:10.4324/9781003214496-9

Lopezosa, C., Codina, L., Pont-Sorribes, C., & Vállez, M. (2023). Use of generative artificial intelligence in the training of journalists: Challenges, uses and training proposal. *El Profesional de la Información, 32*(4), 1–12. doi:10.3145/epi.2023.jul.08

Lukacovic, M. N., & Sellnow-Richmond, D. D. (2023). COVID-19 pandemic and the rise of MUAI threats to national and international psychological security. In E. Pashentsev (Ed.), *The Palgrave handbook of malicious use of AI and psychological security* (pp. 175–201). Palgrave Macmillan. doi:10.1007/978-3-031-22552-9_7

McChesney, R. W., & Nichols, J. (2016). *People get ready. The fight against a jobless economy and a citizenless democracy*. Nation Books.

Mills, A., Bali, M., & Eaton, L. (2023). How do we respond to generative AI in education? Open educational practices give us a framework for an ongoing process. *Journal of Applied Learning & Teaching*, *6*(1), 16–30. doi:10.37074/jalt.2023.6.1.34

Monte-Serrat, D. M., & Cattani, C. (2023). Artificial intelligence and scientific research: Values at stake in education. In F. Roumate (Ed.), *Artificial intelligence in higher education and scientific research; Future developments* (pp. 1–14). Springer. doi:10.1007/978-981-19-8641-3_1

Morales, A. (2022, June 17). Take this job and (change) it: The Great Resignation in higher education. *NASPA | Student Affairs Administrators in Higher Education*. https://www.naspa.org/blog/take-this-job-and-change-it-the-great-resignation-in-higher-education

Morozov, E. (2011). *The net delusion: The dark side of internet freedom*. Public Affairs.

Mügge, D. (2023). The securitization of EU's digital tech regulation. *Journal of European Public Policy*, *30*(7), 1431–1446. doi:10.1080/13501763.2023.2171090

Na'puti, T. R., & Frain, S. C. (2023). Indigenous environmental perspectives: Challenging the oceanic security state. *Security Dialogue*, *54*(2), 11–136. doi:10.1177/09670106221139765

Park, J.-Y., & Son, J.-B. (2010). Transitioning toward transdisciplinary learning in a multidisciplinary environment. *International Journal of Pedagogies and Learning*, *6*(1), 82–93. doi:10.5172/ijpl.6.1.82

Parrott, B. (2020). The American mega-crisis: COVID-19 and beyond. *Challenge*, *63*(5), 245–263. doi:10.1080/05775132.2020.1804756

Pavlik, J. V. (2023). Collaborating with ChatGPT: Considering the implications of generative artificial intelligence for journalism and media education. *Journalism & Mass Communication Educator*, *78*(1), 107769582211495. doi:10.1177/10776958221149577

Pawlowski, D. R. (2018). From the classroom to the community: Best practices in service-learning. *Journal of Communication Pedagogy*, *1*(1), 85–92. doi:10.31446/JCP.2018.15

Rasul, T., Nair, S., Kalendra, D., Robin, M., de Oliveira Santini, F., Ladeira, W. J., Sun, M., Day, I., Rather, R. A., & Heathcote, L. (2023). The role of ChatGPT in higher education: Benefits, challenges, and future research directions. *Journal of Applied Learning & Teaching*, *6*(1), 41–56. doi:10.37074/jalt.2023.6.1.29

Roumate, F. (2021). Artificial intelligence, ethics and international human rights law. *International Journal of Information Ethics*, *29*(3). Advance online publication. doi:10.29173/irie422

Roumate, F. (2023). Ethics of artificial intelligence, higher education, and scientific research. In F. Roumate (Ed.), *Artificial intelligence in higher education and scientific research; Future developments* (pp. 129–144). Springer. doi:10.1007/978-981-19-8641-3_10

Sabzalieva, E., & Valentini, A. (2023). ChatGPT and artificial intelligence in higher education; Quick start guide. *UNESCO.* Retrieved from https://www.iesalc.unesco.org/wp-content/uploads/2023/04/ChatGPT-and-Artificial-Intelligence-in-higher-education-Quick-Start-guide_EN_FINAL.pdf

Samoilenko, S. A., & Suvorova, I. (2023). Artificial intelligence and deepfakes in strategic deception campaigns: The U.S. and Russian experiences. In E. Pashentsev (Ed.), *The Palgrave handbook of malicious use of AI and psychological security* (pp. 507–529). Palgrave Macmillan. doi:10.1007/978-3-031-22552-9_19

Schiller, D. (2000). *Digital capitalism: Networking the global market system.* MIT Press.

Seeger, M. W., & Sellnow, T. L. (2019). *Communication in times of trouble.* Wiley Blackwell.

Sellnow, D. D. (2023). What's in a name? Identity awareness and promotion as fundamental to the future of communication education and instructional communication. *Communication Education, 72*(4), 435–440. doi:10.1080/03634523.2023.2234513

Sellnow-Richmond, D. D., & Lukacovic, M. N. (2024). The COVID-19 pandemic as exemplar of the chaos of mega-crises. In Communicating risk and safety (pp. 97-107). Berlin/Boston: De Gruyters. doi:10.1515/9783110752427-006

Spence, P. R., Westerman, D., Edwards, C., & Edwards, A. (2014). Welcoming our robot overlords: Initial expectations about interaction with a robot. *Communication Research Reports, 31*(3), 272–280. doi:10.1080/08824096.2014.924337

Staley, D. J., & Endicott, D. D. J. (2023). *Knowledge towns; Colleges and universities as talent magnets.* John Hopkins University Press.

Uecker, D., & Schmidt, J. (2022). Interpersonal communication and perception differences between Russia and the United States: Changes since 2009? In M. Minielli, M. N. Lukacovic, S. A. Samoilenko, M. Finch, & D. Uecker (Eds.), *Communication theory and application in post-socialist contexts* (pp. 253–266). Lexington Books – Rowman & Littlefield.

United Nations. (n.d.). What is human security. *United Nations Trust Fund for Human Security.* Retrieved from https://www.un.org/humansecurity/what-is-human-security/

Ward, S. J. A. (2014). Radical media ethics. Ethics for a global digital world. *Digital Journalism (Abingdon, England), 2*(4), 455–471. doi:10.1080/21670811.2014.952985

Zeng, J. (2021). Securitization of artificial intelligence in China. *The Chinese Journal of International Politics, 14*(3), 417–445. doi:10.1093/cjip/poab005

Zidani, S. (2021). Whose pedagogy is it anyway? Decolonizing the syllabus through a critical embrace of difference. *Media Culture & Society, 43*(5), 970–978. doi:10.1177/0163443720980922

KEY TERMS AND DEFINITIONS

Communication Education: Teaching and learning of theoretical concepts, ethical considerations, and practical skills across the broader discipline of Communication (with capital C) that includes (but is not limited to) media, journalism, public relations, interpersonal communication, organizational communication, speech communication, rhetoric, etc.

Community-Inclusive Alliances: Collaborations in the sectors of education, research, and applied practice that involve participation and perspectives of individuals, groups, or organizations that represent various local and/or global communities.

Cross-Disciplinary Alliances: Collaborations in the sectors of education, research, and applied practice that involve participation and perspectives of individuals, groups, or organizations that represent various academic disciplines.

Generative AI: Technological tools that are capable of creating novel texts, codes, images, sounds, videos, or other types of content, which are based on machine learning systems such as neural networks and large sets of training data.

Global Alliances: Collaborations in the sectors of education, research, and applied practice that involve participation and perspectives of individuals, groups, or organizations that represent different countries, cultures, philosophies, and/or experiences around the world.

Global Era of AI: The stage of social development in which AI technologies become prevalent and/or highly impactful across various sectors around the world.

Human Security: A people-centered perspective on security that emphasizes individuals' and communities' right to safety, health, education, dignity, and overall wellbeing.

Mega-Crisis: A complex, serious set of interconnected and pervasive challenges, which are difficult to solve individually and tend to exacerbate one another, leading to significant threats to human security and general wellbeing.

ENDNOTE

1 The specific use of the term Communication with a capital 'C' in this chapter reflects on both the academic discipline of and the inclusive view of the field in general (Eadie, 2022), which encompasses studies of media, journalism, interpersonal communication, public relations, speech communication, rhetoric, etc. Hence, when a Communication classroom is mentioned, we imply relevance for a broader variety of specialized courses within our larger discipline.

Chapter 9
The Influence of Generative AI on Interpersonal Communication Dynamics

Sumeyya Akdilek
https://orcid.org/0000-0002-0740-1777
Texas Tech University, USA

Ibrahim Akdilek
Texas Tech University, USA

Narissra Maria Punyanunt-Carter
https://orcid.org/0000-0001-9645-3239
Texas Tech University, USA

ABSTRACT

In this comprehensive exploration, the interaction between generative AI and interpersonal communication is examined. The initial sections delve into the characteristics and limitations of AI-generated responses, highlighting the challenges of context and non-verbal cues interpretation. The potential for AI-driven interpersonal skill development is presented. The discussion progresses to address the changing dynamics in the classroom, contrasting traditional communication training with AI-augmented methods. The efficacy of AI in group discussions and role-plays is assessed, with a central focus on whether AI augments or diminishes human connections. The final sections explore the potential of generative AI in reshaping our understanding of effective communication and the necessity for educators to uphold the human element while leveraging AI's skill-enhancing capabilities. This comprehensive review offers insights into the evolving landscape of AI and interpersonal communication, shedding light on its opportunities, challenges, and the path forward.

DOI: 10.4018/979-8-3693-0831-8.ch009

INTRODUCTION

The fundamental premise of interpersonal communication revolves around the exchange of thoughts, ideas, and emotions among individuals (Braithwaite & Schrodt, 2021). This premise is rooted in our understanding of information transmission through message conveyance of messages (Patton & Giffin, 1971). This initial definition of communication, which primarily focuses on the one-way transmission of information, can be traced back to the examination of communication within the context of rhetoric, a field that has been discussed since ancient Greece by philosophers such as Aristotle and Plato (Eadie, 2009). These early discussions often centered on persuading the masses; thus, communication was viewed as a unidirectional instrument for mass manipulation. Nevertheless, over time, our perspective on communication has evolved and grown more nuanced as we discovered different facets and dimensions of communication (Craig, 2017). Although new perspectives have revealed many definitions of communication within the framework of rhetorical definitions, communication has evolved over time from a public understanding of communication to a personal understanding. This evolution in our understanding of communication has spurred researchers to delve into the bilateral nature of the communication between two individuals. In general, apart from communication, interpersonal communication is the notion that it is dyadic, involving an exchange of information between two individuals (Braithwaite & Schrodt, 2021). In other words, interpersonal communication entails mutually crafting and exchanging meanings, instead of the one-dimensional nature of rhetoric. Furthermore, the modern view discusses interpersonal communication in various dimensions, including different processes such as social support, stages in relationship development such as initiation and disengagement, settings such as family or workplace, and types of channels such as nonverbal or computer-mediated communication (Braithwaite & Schrodt, 2021). It would be valuable to discuss how computer-mediated communication tools, or digitalization, transform interpersonal communication, especially through generative artificial intelligence (AI).

Generative artificial intelligence has emerged as a transformative force in the domain of interpersonal communication, introducing multifaceted alterations in the modalities and media of human interactions. Although extensive areas of this transformation warrant further exploration, it is incontrovertible that generative AI offers many opportunities to enhance human communication. One salient example is its capability for advanced real-time translation, which has been instrumental in obliterating linguistic barriers and thereby fostering seamless interactions among speakers of diverse languages. Additionally, the domain of emotion categorization, particularly in the context of deep neural networks, has shown promise in discerning emotional nuances in both written and spoken languages, leading to more contextually enriched dialogue. Drawing from a conceptual framework of communication (Wilson & Sperber, 1993), that accentuates the mutual comprehension of language, codes, or symbols between communicators, generative AI is posited as a pivotal intermediary. Its adeptness to navigate linguistic intricacies and interpret emotional nuances aligns with Wilson's theoretical underpinnings, underscoring its value in bolstering the efficacy of human communication. Generative AI, a specialized subset of artificial intelligence dedicated to generating content reflective of human creativity and cognition, has been recognized for its potential to bridge the gap between linguistic expression and semantic comprehension. Its relevance in interpersonal communication is underscored by its ability to reconcile language with its inherent meaning, thereby facilitating enhanced articulation and comprehension.

Interpersonal communication extends beyond the mere exchange of words to include a wide range of nonverbal cues such as tone, timing, and body language, which adds complexity and depth to human interactions (Asemah & Omosotomhe, 2022; Braithwaite & Schrodt, 2021). These nonverbal elements, along with cultural and social contexts, personal experiences, and emotional states, collectively contribute to the rich tapestry of meanings derived from communication (Braithwaite & Schrodt, 2021). However, generative AI, with its ability to process vast amounts of data and emulate human-like language generation, has the potential to redefine the boundaries of communication. It can analyze and generate content that resonates with human emotions, thereby providing a bridge between the explicit and implicit layers of communication. By deciphering the context and sentiment, generative AI systems offer a deeper understanding of the underlying meaning, enabling more accurate and context-aware responses. This transformation holds the promise of richer and more empathetic conversations, thus transcending the limitations of traditional language-based exchanges. In this chapter, while we provide a brief overview of how generative AI reshapes the manner in which we engage, interpret, and connect with one another, we mainly explore its multifaceted influence on the dynamics of interpersonal communication in educational settings.

The Rise of Generative AI and Its Relevance to Interpersonal Communication

Generative AI, exemplified by models such as GPT, bridges the gap between linguistic expression and semantic comprehension, offering tailored content and insight into emotional nuances. Central to the pertinence of generative AI in the realm of interpersonal communication is its adeptness to produce text that transcends mere syntactic accuracy. These avant-garde systems, having been trained on colossal datasets encompassing diverse textual content from the digital realm, not only assimilate the foundational tenets of grammar, but also delve into the intricate tapestry of human expression. This encompasses a profound understanding of idiomatic constructs, cultural allusions, and the emotional undertones that permeate human communication. Such capabilities are emblematic of the strides made in natural language processing, where models such as GPT have been pivotal in bridging the gap between mechanistic language generation and genuine human-like articulation.

Furthermore, the application of GPT and its derivatives extends beyond the conventional text generation. For instance, in the domain of software engineering, GPT-2 has been harnessed for tasks, such as JavaScript program repair, underscoring its versatility and adaptability across diverse computational challenges. Similarly, in the realm of space health, the potential of GPT to provide real-time solutions, especially in scenarios characterized by communication lags, has been explored, highlighting its potential in addressing acute medical emergencies in extraterrestrial environments.

As generative AI systems mature, they become increasingly capable of creating content tailored to specific audiences, styles, or purposes. This adaptability opens doors to a new era of personalized communication where individuals can engage in conversations that resonate with their unique preferences and sensibilities. The ability to customize messages to suit the receiver's emotional state or cultural background holds immense potential for fostering deeper connections and reducing miscommunications. In addition to their role in content creation, generative AI systems have become integral to natural-language understanding and processing. They can analyze text for sentiment, intent, and context, thereby providing valuable insights into the emotional nuances of communication.

In conclusion, the aim of this chapter is to delve into the transformative influence of generative AI on interpersonal communication in educational settings. Our exploration has led us to try to understand the intricate ways in which generative AI technologies reshape the fabric of how we engage, interpret, and connect with one another. By scrutinizing the impact of generative AI on communication dynamics, skill development, and ethical considerations, we aim to gain valuable insights into the opportunities and challenges that lie ahead in educational settings. As we navigate this evolving landscape, it becomes increasingly apparent that generative AI is not merely a tool for enhancing our communication skills, but also a catalyst for redefining the essence of human interaction. It is in our hands, as educators and communicators, to harness the power of AI to amplify our abilities, while safeguarding the authenticity and depth of interpersonal connections. By understanding how generative AI affects and changes interpersonal communication in educational settings, we equip ourselves to navigate this dynamic terrain with wisdom, empathy, and a commitment to preserving the invaluable human elements in our exchanges.

THE NATURE OF GENERATIVE AI CONVERSATIONS

A Brief Overview of Generative AI

Generative AI, a groundbreaking technological advancement, has fundamentally altered various aspects of human life from business operations to artistic endeavors. Rooted in machine learning, natural language processing (NLP), image processing, and computer vision, generative AI is proficient in creating seemingly new, meaningful content, such as text, images, or audio (Feuerriegel et al., 2023). Unlike discriminative AI, which classifies or makes decisions based on given data, generative AI can generate entirely new data (Lim et al., 2023).

The underpinnings of generative AI include machine learning models, such as large language models (LLMs), exemplified by ChatGPT, which are trained on massive datasets (Computing & Communications Center, 2023). The shift from supervised to self-supervised learning techniques allows these models to predict text sequences and generate increasingly accurate content (McKinsey, 2023). However, they are not without their limitations, as they can sometimes generate incorrect or inappropriate content (Aydın & Karaarslan, 2023).

In the context of the Interpersonal Communication Classroom, generative AI opens up both opportunities and challenges. On one hand, it could serve as a versatile tool for enhancing student engagement, enabling real-time interactive learning, and even automating the grading system, thus allowing educators more time for individualized instruction. However, the rise of generative AI poses ethical questions and concerns, such as data privacy, the potential for misinformation, and the need for digital literacy in discerning machines generated from human-generated content.

This technological landscape presents an urgent need for curriculum adaptation. For instance, generative AI can be used to simulate various interpersonal scenarios, allowing students to practice their communication skills in a safe and controlled environment. However, it also necessitates a thorough discussion on ethical ramifications, as students must be made aware of the potential biases and limitations of these AI models (Akgun & Greenhow, 2022).

As technology continues to evolve, it is imperative for educators in the field of communication to remain abreast of these changes. The generative AI revolution is not a distant future; it is here, and its incorporation into the Interpersonal Communication Classroom could be transformative if approached responsibly and sustainably.

Characteristics of AI-Generated Responses

Artificial Intelligence has made significant strides in generating human-like responses in various domains. These AI-generated responses have distinct characteristics that set them apart from the human-generated content.

Authenticity and Emotion

AI-generated responses, while sophisticated, often lack genuine emotions and the unpredictability of human behavior. A study (Chamberlain et al., 2017) explored how observers respond to visual art created by humans versus that created by computers. They found an explicit prejudice against computer-generated art, driven largely by beliefs about the kind of art that computer algorithms can produce. Observers felt that AI lacked the depth and unpredictability of real human interactions, emphasizing the challenge of authentically replicating human emotions.

Temporal Symmetry

In auditory processing, AI-generated responses exhibit a property known as temporal symmetry. A study (Natale, 2020) observed that neurons in the primary auditory cortex that are well described by their spectrotemporal response field (STRF) also exhibit temporal symmetry. This property implies a consistent function of time across the STRF, highlighting the structured and consistent nature of AI-generated outputs.

Noise Perception and Annoyance

AI-generated responses, particularly in the auditory domain, can be influenced by noise and its perception. Researchers (Minichilli et al., 2018) investigated noise judgments in students and their relationship to noise measurements. They found that noise perception and consequent disturbance are highly correlated with the acoustic quality of the environment, suggesting that AI-generated auditory responses might be influenced by environmental acoustics.

Limitations in Creativity

While AI can generate creative outputs, there is debate on the authenticity and originality of such creations. Chamberlain et al. (2017) highlighted that while AI can produce art, there is a bias against computer-generated creations owing to perceived limitations in AI's creative capabilities.

In summary, while AI-generated responses represent a monumental stride in the realm of human-computer interactions, they are not devoid of limitations. Their characteristics, influenced by algorithmic design, environmental factors, and the intrinsic challenges of emulating human emotions and creativity, warrant meticulous scrutiny. As AI continues to permeate diverse sectors, a nuanced understanding of its characteristics is imperative.

Limitations in Understanding Context, Tone, and Nonverbal Cues

The rapid evolution of Artificial Intelligence has led to significant advancements in human-computer interactions. However, despite these advancements, AI systems often grapple with understanding the intricate nuances of human communication, particularly context, tone, and nonverbal cues.

Contextual Understanding

Human communication is deeply rooted in a myriad of contexts, including cultural, situational, and interpersonal. These contexts provide a backdrop against which words and actions can acquire specific meanings. For instance, the word "sorry" in a casual conversation among friends might denote regret, whereas in a formal apology, it carries a deeper sense of remorse and responsibility. Pun (2021) on Chinese medical students' communication patterns underscores the importance of understanding cultural and interpersonal contexts. In many Eastern cultures, for instance, direct communication about grave illnesses might be avoided to protect patients' emotional well-being. Instead, the family members may be informed. An AI system without an understanding of such cultural nuances may misinterpret or mishandle such communication.

Tonal Variations

The tone, the emotional modulation of speech, is a powerful conveyor of meaning. A single sentence can have multiple interpretations based on the tone. For example, the phrase "Is that so?" can be an expression of surprise, skepticism, or genuine curiosity, based on tonal delivery. Askari et al. (2020) have highlighted the influence of textual tone on the evaluation of Mediated Social Touch. In digital communication, in which the tone of voice is absent, the choice of words and punctuation becomes crucial in conveying the intended emotion. Despite their sophistication, AI systems often struggle to discern these subtle tonal variations and their associated emotional implications.

NonVerbal Cues

Beyond words and tone, a significant portion of human communication is relayed through nonverbal cues, such as facial expressions, body language, and gestures. These cues offer a window into a person's emotional state and intentions. For instance, a person's discomfort might be evident not in their words, but in their body language, such as avoiding eye contact or fidgeting. Cavanagh et al. (2014) emphasized the importance of nonverbal communication in teaching, where a teacher's enthusiasm or lack thereof can be evident in their gestures and facial expressions. However, despite their sophistication, AI systems often struggle to discern and interpret these subtle nonverbal signals. This limitation stems from the inherent challenge of translating complex human emotions and intentions, often conveyed through minute facial expressions or body movements, into computational data to which an AI system can understand and respond.

In conclusion, while advancements in AI are commendable, achieving a truly human-like understanding of communication requires a deep and nuanced grasp of context, tone, and nonverbal cues. As AI continues to evolve, these areas present exciting challenges and opportunities for R&D.

The Illusion of Understanding and Empathy

The proliferation of Artificial Intelligence in human-computer interaction has given rise to conversational agents who seemingly understand and empathize with human users. Although AI can mimic human interactions, it lacks genuine understanding and empathy, which are rooted in shared human experiences and emotions.

Grosuleac et al. (2020) delved beneath this façade of lies to a series of algorithmic processes devoid of true humans to understand the challenges of developing conversational agents that can comprehend emotions and offer appropriate responses. Although humans effortlessly recognize and respond to others' feelings in a conversation, creating an AI system with similar capabilities is far from trivial. The researchers developed an empathic chatbot based on a Generative Pre-Trained Transformer to bridge this gap. However, even with advanced models, the chatbot's understanding of empathy remains algorithmic and lacks the depth and richness of human emotional understanding.

Furthermore, the primary goal of AI, as highlighted by a case study (Manasa & Devi, 2022), is to enable computers to perform intellectual tasks such as decision-making, problem-solving, and understanding human communication. Although AI can mimic these tasks, its understanding is based on data patterns rather than genuine human experiences. For instance, while AI can predict a user's preferences based on previous interactions, it cannot truly understand the emotions or personal experiences that drive those preferences.

The illusions of understanding and empathy in AI systems have profound implications. Users might overrely on AI for emotional support or make decisions based on AI recommendations, believing that the system genuinely understands their needs and emotions. However, without a true emotional understanding, AI responses can sometimes be inappropriate or misaligned with the user's emotional state.

In conclusion, while AI has made significant strides in mimicking human-like interactions, it is essential to recognize the limitations of its understanding and empathy. True empathy stems from shared human experiences, emotions, and cultural contexts, elements that AI cannot fully grasp in their current form.

INTERPERSONAL SKILL DEVELOPMENT VIA GENERATIVE AI

The advent of Generative Artificial Intelligence presents transformative opportunities for enhancing interpersonal skill development, which is a cornerstone of effective human communication (Huang & Rust, 2018). As AI systems become adept at generating human-like textual and verbal outputs, they offer novel avenues for individuals to hone their interpersonal competencies in simulated, yet intricate, conversational scenarios.

The generative capabilities of AI transcend mere information provision; they facilitate immersive interactions that closely emulate real-world conversations (West, 2018). Such interactions provide invaluable platforms for individuals to practice and refine their communication skills and prepare for diverse interpersonal challenges. This is particularly salient in the context of simulating complex conversations, where individuals can engage with AI-driven conversational agents to navigate intricate dialogue, thereby enhancing their conversational agility.

Moreover, the feedback mechanisms inherent to advanced AI systems offer unique advantages. By assessing both verbal and nonverbal cues, AI can provide real-time feedback, enabling individuals to gain insight into their communication strengths and areas of improvement (Pizzi et al., 2023). This feedback loop, grounded in an objective analysis, can be instrumental in fostering effective communication strategies.

Furthermore, the potential of Generative AI extends to specialized domains of interpersonal interactions, such as conflict resolution and negotiation. By simulating negotiation scenarios, AI can offer individuals a safe environment to experiment with different strategies, understand potential outcomes, and develop effective negotiation techniques (Lee, 2023).

In conclusion, Generative AI has emerged as a potent tool for interpersonal skill development, offering innovative solutions to traditional challenges in communication training. As we anticipate further advancements in AI, its role in shaping and enhancing human communication skills has become increasingly important.

Simulating Complex Conversations for Practice

The integration of Artificial Intelligence into communication practices has witnessed significant advancements, notably with the introduction of the ChatGPT in 2022. This tool rapidly gained traction, amassing over 100 million users within two months of its launch, as reported by The Guardian (Lock, 2022). Such exponential growth can be attributed to the public's intrigue with this innovative technology and its capacity to seamlessly synthesize knowledge, building upon the vast information reservoir the Internet has provided over the years.

While AI tools such as ChatGPT offer myriad benefits, their implications for interpersonal relationships warrant scrutiny. For instance, educators leveraging ChatGPT to refine their feedback may inadvertently create a disparity between written and spoken communication. Such inconsistencies can influence students' perceptions, raising pertinent questions about the need for congruence between AI-enhanced written communication and natural spoken discourse (Lu et al., 2023).

Moreover, several AI platforms, such as Yoodli and Fluent, have emerged that offer users the opportunity to simulate real-life conversations. Yoodli, for instance, employs advanced AI algorithms to facilitate simulated dialogue, analyze speech patterns, and generate contextually relevant follow-up questions. This dynamic interaction mimics authentic conversations and enhances users' communication skills (Ghai & Mueller, 2021). Fluent, however, is tailored to assist individuals with speech impediments, identify challenging words, and suggest alternatives to bolster speech fluency (Ghai & Mueller, 2021).

Such tools underscore the potential of AI to refine communication practices. However, a critical evaluation of their feedback mechanisms is essential to ascertain their efficacy in genuinely enhancing their interpersonal skills. As AI continues to evolve, its role in shaping communication practices remains a focal point in academic discourse, necessitating ongoing research and exploration.

Feedback Mechanisms: AI Assessing Verbal and Nonverbal Cues

In the rapidly evolving landscape of Artificial Intelligence, one of the most intriguing advancements is the system's ability to interpret and respond to both verbal and nonverbal cues. Human communication is a complex interplay of spoken words and subtle nonverbal signals, such as facial expressions, body language, and tone of voice. These nonverbal cues often carry as much, if not more, information as the words themselves (Chen et al., 2004).

Recent developments in AI have shown promising results in the recognition and understanding of these cues. For instance, customer service chatbots are increasingly being used in several domains to substitute human agents for performing tasks, answering questions, giving advice, and providing social and emotional support. These chatbots are now equipped with sentiment analysis capabilities, which allow them to detect the emotional tone of the user based on text input. By leveraging Artificial Intelligence and NLP techniques, these chatbots have been enhanced with emotion-intelligence capabilities, enabling them to generate emotionally relevant responses. This, in turn, improves user satisfaction by providing more empathetic and contextually relevant interactions (Bilquise et al., 2022). Furthermore, in the context of virtual collaboration, AI-based dynamic affective recognition systems have been proposed to provide live feedback regarding the affective content of communication. Such systems can visually represent and break down the sentiments (tone, emoji) and main emotional states (e.g., joy, anger) of text-based communication, thereby enhancing shared understanding and creativity within virtual teams (Nguyen et al., 2022).

In the realm of education, AI-driven platforms are being developed to assist teachers in gauging student engagement in virtual classes. By analyzing students' facial expressions and body language, these systems can provide real-time feedback to educators about which students are actively participating and which might be disengaged or confused (Chamot, 2005).

However, the real challenge lies in the integration of these feedback mechanisms into real-world scenarios. For instance, in telemedicine, where patient-doctor interactions occur remotely, an AI system that can accurately interpret a patient's nonverbal cues can provide invaluable insights into the patient's emotional and physical well-being, complementing the verbal information shared.

Although these advancements are promising, it is crucial to approach them with caution. Overreliance on AI for interpreting human emotions and intentions might lead to misinterpretations, especially in complex human interactions, where cultural nuances play a significant role. As AI systems continue to evolve, continuous research and refinement are essential to ensuring their effective and ethical application in real-world scenarios.

Generative AI's Potential in Conflict Resolution and Negotiation Scenarios

Generative AI, with its sophisticated algorithms and vast data-processing capabilities, holds transformative potential in the realm of human communication and education, particularly in conflict resolution and negotiation scenarios. The following are pertinent scenarios:

Peer Mediation in Schools: Generative AI can be employed to train students on peer mediation techniques. By simulating conflicts between virtual characters, AI can provide students with a safe environment to practice their mediation skills, offer feedback, and suggest improvements based on successful conflict-resolution strategies from real-world cases (Smith et al., 2002).

Teacher-Student Communication: Generative AI can assist teachers in crafting effective feedback for students. By analyzing a student's work and comparing it with a vast database of educational materials, AI can suggest feedback that is both constructive and empathetic, ensuring that the student feels understood and motivated (Jones & Dexter, 2014).

Parent-Teacher Conferences: AI can simulate parent-teacher conferences, allowing educators to practice their communication skills. By inputting potential concerns or questions from parents, educators can receive AI-generated responses, helping them prepare for real-world interactions, and effectively address parental concerns effectively (Henderson & Mapp, 2002).

Group Work Dynamics: Generative AI can be used to simulate group work scenarios in educational settings. By introducing virtual characters with diverse personalities and backgrounds, students can practice their negotiation and conflict-resolution skills in a controlled environment, preparing them for real-world group dynamics (Johnson & Johnson, 1996; Johnson & Johnson, 2004).

Cultural Sensitivity Training: With the increasing diversity of educational institutions, there is a pressing need for cultural sensitivity training. Generative AI can simulate interactions between individuals from different cultural backgrounds, allowing educators and students to practice their communication skills, understand potential cultural pitfalls, and develop strategies for effective intercultural communication (Banks, 2004).

THE CHANGING CLASSROOM DYNAMICS

Technological advancements have significantly influenced the evolution of classroom dynamics, particularly in the context of higher education. The integration of Artificial Intelligence tools and methodologies into the educational landscape has introduced novel approaches to teaching and learning, reshaping the traditional paradigms of classroom interactions. This transformation not only impacts the pedagogical strategies employed by educators, but also redefines the nature of student engagement and participation.

Traditional Interpersonal Communication Training vs. AI-Augmented Training

Historically, interpersonal communication training in classrooms has been rooted in face-to-face interaction. These interactions emphasize the importance of personal touch, empathy, and real-time feedback. Traditional methods such as group discussions and role-playing exercises have been the cornerstone of communication training. However, the advent of AI led to a paradigm shift. Generative AI platforms such as ChatGPT offer the potential to simulate diverse conversational scenarios, allowing students to practice interpersonal communication in varied settings. Such platforms can provide instant feedback, adapt to individual learning paces, and introduce complexity based on learner progression. The integration of AI tools in this domain promises a more personalized and adaptive learning experience, potentially bridging the gap between theoretical knowledge and practical application. Furthermore, AI-augmented training can offer insights into communication patterns, enabling educators to tailor their teaching methods to individual student needs, thereby enhancing their overall learning experience (Misaki et al., 2020).

The Role of Generative AI in Group Discussions, Debates, and Role-Plays

Generative AI, with its ability to simulate intricate conversational dynamics, has the potential to profoundly reshape the landscape of group discussions, debates, and roleplays within educational settings. For instance, AI can emulate multiple personas in a debate, with each embodying a distinct viewpoint. This capability not only provides students with a comprehensive understanding of multifaceted perspectives but also prepares them for real-world interactions where they might encounter diverse opinions. Furthermore, in role-playing exercises, AI can introduce unforeseen scenarios or characters, thereby adding layers of complexity that mirror real life unpredictability. Such AI-driven methods can immerse students in a dynamic learning environment and cultivate skills, such as critical thinking, adaptability, and effective communication. Moreover, the incorporation of AI into these educational activities can foster a more inclusive environment, ensuring the representation of a wide array of viewpoints, thereby promoting a holistic understanding of topics (Klein & Merkel, 2022).

Assessing the Effectiveness: Do AI-Assisted Methods Enhance or Diminish Human Connection?

The infusion of AI tools in educational settings inevitably raises questions regarding their influence on quintessential human connections. Although AI has demonstrated the capability to mimic human-like interactions, capturing the full depth of human emotion, empathy, and intuition remains a formidable challenge. A harmonious blend of traditional teaching methods and AI-augmented techniques can equip students to navigate both digital and real-world interpersonal scenarios. It is paramount to ensure that technological advancements enhance, rather than eclipse, the intrinsic human elements of communication. Continuous assessment of the effectiveness of AI-assisted methods is essential to ascertain their alignment with overarching educational objectives and to ensure that they do not inadvertently erode the essence of human connection in the educational journey (Klein & Merkel, 2022).

The infusion of AI into classroom dynamics represents a significant shift in educational methodologies. While the potential benefits are manifold, it is crucial to approach this integration with caution, ensuring that the essence of human connections remains intact. By striking a balance between traditional and AI-augmented methods, educators can harness the best of both worlds, preparing students for a future in which digital and human interactions coexist harmoniously.

GENERATIVE AI AS A REFLECTIVE TOOL

The advent of generative AI in the realm of communication has not only transformed the way we interact but has also offered profound insights into our own communicative behaviors. As AI continues to evolve, its potential as a reflective tool has become increasingly evident, particularly in educational and interpersonal settings.

Self-Awareness Through AI Interactions: Understanding One's Communication Style and Biases

Interactions with AI platforms can serve as diagnostic tools, shedding light on inherent communication styles, biases, and tendencies. For instance, consistent engagements with a generative AI platform can reveal patterns such as a proclivity towards assertiveness or passivity. Once identified, these patterns can be invaluable for personal growth and effective communication. Moreover, AI's ability to highlight potential biases in language can foster deeper self-awareness, promoting more inclusive and empathetic communication. Self-awareness is crucial in the educational context. Educators equipped with insights into their communication style can tailor their teaching methodologies, ensuring a more personalized and impactful learning experience for students (Dweck, 2016).

Mirror Conversations: Using AI to Reflect Back Emotions and Content

The concept of "mirror conversations" with AI introduces a novel approach to introspection. Here, AI reflects the emotions and content expressed by the user, serving as a mirror to one's emotional state.

Recognizing and understanding these emotions can lead to enhanced emotional intelligence, which is a skill paramount in effective communication. For educators, such reflective interactions could be transformative. By understanding their emotional responses, educators can adapt their communication strategies to ensure more empathetic and effective engagement with students. Furthermore, these AI-driven reflective practices can be instrumental in fostering a culture of continuous learning and self-improvement within educational institutions (Salovey & Mayer, 1990).

In conclusion, the integration of generative AI as a reflective tool in the communication domain signifies a paradigm shift in our approach to self-awareness and personal growth. As we navigate the complexities of human interactions, the ability of AI to mirror our communicative behaviors offers a unique lens through which we can introspect and refine our communication style. Beyond mere interaction, AI platforms serve as diagnostic instruments that illuminate inherent biases, tendencies, and emotional responses. This introspective capability of AI can be transformative, especially in educational settings, enabling educators to tailor their methodologies and foster a more empathetic and effective learning environment. As we stand at the crossroads of technological advancement and human introspection, generative AI emerges as a beacon, guiding us towards deeper self-awareness and more meaningful human connections. The fusion of technology and introspection, as facilitated by AI, heralds a new era of communication marked by self-reflection, adaptability, and continuous growth.

ETHICS OF AI IN INTERPERSONAL COMMUNICATION TRAINING

The integration of Artificial Intelligence into various facets of our lives, especially in the realm of interpersonal communication training, has sparked myriad ethical debates and considerations. As AI systems become increasingly sophisticated, their potential to influence, shape, and even dictate human interactions grows, raising questions about the ethical implications of this influence. At the heart of these debates lies the tension between the benefits of AI-augmented communication training and the potential risks it poses to the authenticity and spontaneity of human interaction.

The rapid advancement of AI technologies, particularly in the fields of natural language processing and generative models, has enabled the creation of tools that can simulate human-like interactions with remarkable accuracy (Mittelstadt et al., 2016). Although these tools offer unprecedented opportunities for enhancing communication training, they also introduce challenges related to authenticity, predictability, and the potential erosion of genuine human connections. The ethical landscape of AI in interpersonal communication training is complex, with scholars and practitioners alike grappling with the balance between harnessing the benefits of AI and preserving the essence of human communication (Bryson & Winfield, 2017).

As we delve deeper into this topic, it becomes imperative to critically examine the ethical dimensions of AI's role in interpersonal communication training, exploring concerns related to authenticity, the risk of creating scripted communicators, and the potential implications for genuine human connections.

Authenticity Concerns: Can AI Truly Replicate Human Emotion?

Rapid advancements in artificial intelligence have led to the development of systems that can simulate human-like interactions, particularly in emotional communication. However, a pressing question that arises is whether AI can replicate the depth and authenticity of human emotions.

Attempts have been made to simulate human-like interactions since the early days of AI-driven conversational systems. Eliza, developed by Joseph Weizenbaum in the 1960s, was one of the first chatbots to mimic a Rogerian psychotherapist, engaging users in a text-based conversation (Weizenbaum, 1966). Similarly, Parry, another early chatbot, was designed to simulate a person with paranoid schizophrenia (Colby, 1975). These early systems laid the groundwork for the development of modern chatbots.

Modern chatbots, such as XiaoIce or ChatGPT, not only respond to diverse user requests but also strive to establish an emotional connection with users. The appeal of such chatbots lies in their ability to satisfy users' need for communication, affection, and social belonging. XiaoIce, for instance, dynamically recognizes emotions and engages users through long conversations with appropriate interpersonal responses. The success of these chatbots is measured by their ability to engage users in prolonged interactions, emphasizing both the intellectual quotient (IQ) and emotional quotient (EQ) in their design. However, although these systems can simulate emotional interactions, the depth of genuine human emotion, empathy, and intuition remains a challenge for full (Shum et al., 2018).

Furthermore, facial expressions mirror human thoughts and feelings, providing a plethora of social cues including attention focus, intention, motivation, and emotion. AI-based Facial Expression Recognition (FER) has become a pivotal research topic with applications spanning dynamic analysis, pattern recognition, interpersonal interaction, and mental health monitoring. While significant progress has been made in FER methodologies, emotion-wise facial expressions vary across different age groups, such as children, adults, and senior citizens. This variation underscores the complexity and nuances of human emotions that AI systems must recognize and interpret (Dalvi et al., 2021).

Another study highlighted the importance of interpersonal touch in human communication, emphasizing the challenges AI faces in replicating hedonic processing associated with touch. Although AI systems can respond to tactile input, their response is often linked to arousal from stimulus intensity rather than specific emotional stimulation (van Hooijdonk et al., 2019).

In conclusion, while AI has made significant strides in simulating human-like emotional interactions, the authenticity and depth of human emotions present complex challenges. The nuances, intricacies, and genuine experiences of human emotions may remain unique human traits, underscoring the importance of human-to-human interactions in certain contexts.

The Risk of Creating 'Scripted' or 'Predictable' Communicators

The advent of AI in interpersonal communication training has raised concerns regarding the potential risk of creating communicators who are overly scripted or predictable. While AI tools can provide consistent and standardized responses, there is growing apprehension that over-reliance on these tools might lead to a lack of spontaneity and authenticity in human interactions.

Generative AI models, such as ChatGPT, have been designed to generate human-like text based on the patterns learned from vast amounts of data. Although they can produce coherent and contextually relevant responses, these models often rely on patterns and templates that have been identified as being effective or popular in the datasets they have been trained on (Shum et al., 2018). This can lead to responses that, while technically correct, might come across as formulaic, or lacking genuine human touch.

Moreover, the use of AI tools in communication training inadvertently promotes a one-size-fits-all approach. For instance, if a training tool consistently suggests a particular phrasing or style based on its programming, users may begin to adopt that style without considering its appropriateness for different contexts or audiences. This could result in communicators who are less adaptable and versatile in their interactions, relying heavily on predefined scripts rather than genuine, spontaneous communication (Hancock et al., 2020).

Furthermore, the predictability of AI-generated responses can be a double-edged sword. On the one hand, it ensures consistency and can be particularly useful in settings where standardized communication is essential. However, it can lead to interactions that are devoid of nuances, emotions, and unpredictability that characterize genuine human communication. Such interactions might be perceived as insincere or robotic, potentially undermining the trust and rapport between communicators (Saha & Beach, 2020).

In the realm of education, there is a risk that students trained predominantly with AI tools might become overly reliant on them, leading to the generation of communicators who are less equipped to handle unscripted real-world scenarios. Therefore, the challenge lies in ensuring that AI tools are used as supplements rather than as replacements for traditional interpersonal communication training methods.

In conclusion, while AI offers promising advancements in the field of interpersonal communication training, it is crucial to approach its integration cautiously. Striking a balance between leveraging AI's capabilities of AI and preserving the authenticity and spontaneity of human communication will be pivotal in shaping tomorrow's communicators.

The Potential Erosion of Genuine, Spontaneous Human Connection

The increasing reliance on AI tools in interpersonal communication raises concerns about the potential diminishment of genuine human interaction. Generative AI models, designed to produce coherent responses based on patterns from vast datasets, might inadvertently prioritize efficiency over genuine emotional connections, leading to interactions that feel more transactional than relational (Vasalou et al., 2008).

Moreover, as AI becomes more integrated into daily communication, there is a risk of defaulting on AI-generated responses even in personal settings. Such a shift could undermine trust, intimacy, and emotional bonding in relationships (Callais, 2020). In educational contexts, over-reliance on AI for communication training may promote a formulaic approach that stifles genuine interactions.

While AI can simulate understanding, it lacks the lived experiences and emotional depth inherent in human interaction. Thus, while AI offers exciting possibilities, it is essential to ensure that it complements, rather than replaces, genuine human connections (Picard, 2000).

CASE STUDIES

The integration of generative AI into various fields has been met by both success and challenges. Several studies highlight these varied outcomes in the realm of interpersonal communication training.

- Medical Improv for Empathetic Communication: Researchers (Terregino et al., 2019) have explored the use of an improvisation-informed curriculum (medical improv) in medical education. This approach emphasizes deep listening, emotional understanding, and authenticity. Students with advanced medical improv training outperformed their peers, suggesting the effectiveness of this AI augmented approach in fostering empathetic communication.
- Interdisciplinary Teamwork in Engineering Education: A study (Misaki et al., 2020) discussed the role of AI in enhancing interdisciplinary teamwork among engineering students in Japan. This

research provided insights into the unique engineering educational situation in Japan and the role of AI in enhancing interdisciplinary teamwork.

- Language Learning with AI Tutors: A study (Jiang, 2022) highlighted the effectiveness of AI tutors in language learning. AI systems provide real-time feedback, personalized learning paths, and interactive exercises, which lead to improved language proficiency among learners.
- Challenges with Synthetic Image Detection: Researchers (Dogoulis et al., 2023) have highlighted the challenges faced in detecting synthetic images generated by advanced AI models. The study emphasized the ineffectiveness of existing approaches that randomly sample generated images to train their models.
- The application of AI in radiology has shown potential benefits in all steps of the imaging chain, from the prescription of diagnostic tests to communication of test reports. However, the introduction of AI in radiology poses challenges in doctor-patient communication at the time of diagnosis. A systematic review focusing on the patient's role and interpersonal skills between patients and physicians when AI is implemented in cancer diagnosis communication found that the use of AI in radiology is negatively associated with patient trust in AI and patient-centered communication in cancer. This study emphasized the importance of maintaining a balance between technological advancements and human touch in communication (Derevianko et al., 2023).
- The integration of AI into journalism has become a topic of interest in recent years. A study (Lopezosa et al., 2023) explored the application of AI to higher communication studies. The research involved interviews with university lecturers and researchers to understand the convergence and divergence of different aspects of the technology, including its integration into communication faculties and its potential uses in news production and consumption. This study proposed a comprehensive training program on AI and journalism, focusing on its foundations, technical competencies, and ethical considerations. The findings suggest that, while AI can enhance productivity in content production tasks, there are challenges and considerations to address in its integration into journalism training.

Personal Testimonials: How Students and Trainers Perceive the AI Experience

The integration of generative AI into educational settings has resulted in a spectrum of reactions from both the students and trainers. A study (Chan & Hu, 2023) revealed a dichotomy in students' perceptions. While a significant portion appreciated the immediacy and convenience offered by AI-driven tools, there was a subset that yearned for human touch, emphasizing the depth and nuances that human educators bring to feedback.

From the trainers' perspective, the landscape appeared to be more varied. Researchers (Kim & Kim, 2022) delved into educators' views on AI's role of AI in classrooms. While many acknowledged the undeniable efficiency and consistency of AI tools, there were palpable concerns about their ability to address the diverse and unique learning needs of students. Some educators have pointed out that AI, in its current form, might not be adept at handling individual student queries that require a deeper understanding of the student's emotional and psychological context. Another study (Reich & Ruipérez-Valiente, 2019) showed that trainers appreciate the scalability and data-driven insights provided by AI. However, they also expressed reservations about the AI's ability to fully understand the nuances of human learning and the potential for technology to overshadow the human elements of teaching.

In conclusion, although AI offers a plethora of advantages in the realm of education, its reception varies. Both students and trainers recognize their potential but are also acutely aware of their limitations. As AI continues to evolve, it is imperative to continuously gather and reflect on these personal testimonials to ensure that technology enhances, rather than detracts from, the educational experience.

GENERATIVE AI AND THE FUTURE OF INTERPERSONAL COMMUNICATION

Generative AI, with its capacity to produce human-like text and content, has the potential to reshape our understanding of effective communication profoundly. Although it has already made significant strides in fields such as natural language processing and content generation, the impact of generative AI on communication is poised to be transformative (Feuerriegel et al., 2023).

One of the most noteworthy ways in which generative AI changes the communication landscape is personalization. AI-powered systems can analyze vast amounts of data, allowing individuals and organizations to tailor their messages to specific audiences (Feuerriegel et al., 2023). This means that in the not-so-distant future, advertisements, news articles, and even interpersonal conversations could be uniquely crafted for each recipient, making communication more engaging and relevant (Akgun & Greenhow, 2022). However, this also raises important ethical questions about privacy and potential for manipulation. Furthermore, generative AI can aid in the global democratization of information (Aydın & Karaarslan, 2023). Language barriers are no longer insurmountable obstacles, as AI-driven translation and transcription services can instantly convert content into multiple languages, thus enabling cross-cultural communication like never before. It can also assist those with disabilities by providing real-time transcription for the hearing-impaired or generating text for the visually impaired, making information more accessible to a broader audience (Akgun & Greenhow, 2022).

Moreover, generative AI has the potential to revolutionize storytelling and content creation. AI algorithms can craft engaging narratives, generate music, and produce visual art, leading to the fusion of creativity and technology (Akgun & Greenhow, 2022). This can not only enhance the entertainment industry, but also empower individuals and businesses to tell their stories more effectively, breaking down the barriers between professionals and amateur creators. However, as generative AI evolves, concerns are also raised about the authenticity of communication. Deepfakes and AI-generated misinformation are growing challenges, forcing us to develop new tools and strategies to verify the credibility of the content (Aydın & Karaarslan, 2023). Striking the balance between creativity and trustworthiness in communication is a key challenge.

Overall, generative AI is reshaping our understanding of effective communication by enabling personalization, transcending language barriers, democratizing information, and revolutionizing content creation (Akgun & Greenhow, 2022). As we continue to harness the power of AI in our daily interactions, it is vital to remain vigilant about ethical considerations and ensure that technology serves to enhance, rather than compromise, authenticity and integrity of communication.

Potential Shifts in the Emphasis of Interpersonal Communication Curricula

The rapid advancement of artificial intelligence and its integration into our lives has led to potential shifts in the emphasis on interpersonal communication curricula, both in educational institutions and corporate training programs (Feuerriegel et al., 2023). These changes reflect the evolving needs of individuals in a digital, AI-driven world where human and machine interactions play a pivotal role.

Digital Literacy and AI Ethics

Communication curricula are likely to incorporate elements of digital literacy and AI ethics. As AI becomes more integrated into our lives, individuals need to understand how AI systems operate, their biases, and their potential ethical concerns. Educating students and professionals on these topics will help them navigate the complex landscape of AI-based communication.

Effective Human-Machine Interaction

With the increasing use of AI chatbots, virtual assistants, and automated customer service, understanding how to effectively interact with these machines is becoming a crucial skill. Communication programs may include modules on how to communicate clearly and efficiently with AI systems, ensuring that human-AI interactions are seamless and productive (Reich & Ruipérez-Valiente, 2019) .

Data-Driven Communication

AI can analyze vast amounts of data to personalize communication. Therefore, communication curricula may shift towards teaching data-driven communication strategies. Students and professionals need to learn how to interpret data insights to tailor their messages, making them more relevant and engaging in target audiences.

Critical Thinking and Fact-Checking

As AI-generated misinformation and deepfakes become more sophisticated, the ability to critically evaluate information sources and fact-check content becomes increasingly important. Communication programs may place a greater emphasis on critical thinking, media literacy, and techniques to identify AI-generated content, ensuring that individuals can discern facts from fiction (Aydın & Karaarslan, 2023).

AI-Assisted Communication Tools

Communication courses may also include training on how to use AI-assisted tools effectively. Whether AI is using AI to enhance writing, presentation design, or even optimize email responses, individuals will need to understand how to integrate these tools seamlessly into their communication processes.

Adaptability and Resilience

In world where AI can automate routine tasks, there is a growing emphasis on teaching adaptability and resilience. Individuals need to develop skills that AI cannot replicate easily, such as emotional intelligence, creativity, and adaptability to changing communication contexts.

Overall, the changing landscape of communication owing to AI integration calls for a more holistic and adaptive approach to communication curricula. The emphasis will not only be on traditional human-to-human interaction, but also on preparing individuals to navigate an increasingly AI-augmented communication environment while maintaining ethical and empathetic communication practices (Reich & Ruipérez-Valiente, 2019). It is essential to equip students and professionals with the knowledge and skills they need to thrive in this AI-enhanced world, in which the line between human and machine communication continues to blur.

Preparing Students for a World Where AI-Human Interaction Is Commonplace

Preparing students for a world where AI-human interaction is commonplace is a critical challenge in education today. As artificial intelligence becomes an integral part of our personal and professional lives, it is essential for educational institutions to adapt their curricula to equip students with the knowledge and skills necessary to thrive in this evolving landscape.

Digital Literacy and AI Fluency

At core of student preparation, there is a need to instill digital literacy and AI fluency. Students must understand the basic principles, capabilities, and limitations of AI. This includes knowledge about how AI algorithms work, the ethical implications of AI, and how to interact responsibly with AI-driven systems.

Problem-Solving and Critical Thinking

AI can automate routine tasks, but struggles with complex, non-standard situations that require creative problem-solving. Educational programs need to place a strong emphasis on developing critical thinking skills and encouraging students to think beyond rote memorization and algorithmic problem-solving. Encouraging students to explore diverse interdisciplinary perspectives can help them to approach problems from various perspectives.

Emotional Intelligence and Empathy

In world of AI-human interaction, human qualities such as emotional intelligence and empathy become even more important. These are areas in which machines still struggle. Education should focus on developing students' abilities to understand and manage emotions, as well as empathize with others. These skills are invaluable in areas such as customer service, healthcare, and leadership, where AI may complement, but not replace, human interaction (Aydın & Karaarslan, 2023).

Data Literacy and Decision-Making

With AI generating and analyzing vast amounts of data, students should be proficient in data literacy. They should understand how to interpret data, make data-driven decisions, and recognize biases that may exist in the data. This is crucial for a wide range of professions, from marketing to healthcare and beyond.

Ethical AI Usage

Students need to be taught about the ethical implications of AI usage. They should understand the ethical considerations in AI development and be equipped to make ethical decisions in a world in which AI influences various aspects of life. This includes understanding the issues related to privacy, bias, and transparency.

Adaptability and Lifelong Learning

AI is continually evolving, and the jobs and skills required are likely to change over time. Therefore, students should be taught the value of adaptability and importance of lifelong learning. They need to embrace the idea of continuous skill development and be prepared to pivot their careers as the technology evolves.

In summary, preparing students for a world where AI-human interaction is commonplace means providing them with a well-rounded education that includes digital literacy, problem solving, emotional intelligence, data literacy, ethical AI usage, and adaptability. It aims to foster a holistic approach to learning that combines both traditional and AI-driven knowledge and skills, ensuring that individuals are not just competent, but also responsible and ethical participants in an AI-augmented society. The ability to integrate the strengths of AI while retaining and nurturing unique human qualities is a hallmark of success in this new era (Aydın & Karaarslan, 2023).

CONCLUSION

The transformative potential of generative AI and the inevitable integration of AI-human interactions into our daily lives mark an exciting yet delicate transition in our understanding of communication and education. As we delve deeper into this AI-infused era, it is crucial to strike a delicate balance: harnessing AI for skill enhancement, while preserving the authenticity of human connections.

Thus, the influence of generative AI on communication is undeniable. It empowers personalization, transcends language barriers, democratizes information and augments creativity. However, this also presents challenges, particularly in the form of AI-generated misinformation and ethical concerns. The intersection of AI and communication calls for a nuanced approach that encourages the responsible use of AI tools, the critical evaluation of information, and a commitment to maintaining the authenticity and integrity of interactions (Aydın & Karaarslan, 2023).

Similarly, in education, AI-driven shifts in curricula reflect the evolving needs of students preparing for a world where AI-human interaction is commonplace. These changes emphasize the development of digital literacy, critical thinking, emotional intelligence, and ethical decision making. However, the key challenge is to ensure that students not only acquire AI-related skills, but also retain and nurture the unique human qualities that distinguish them from machines. The delicate balance here lies in equipping students with the power of AI as a skill enhancer, while emphasizing the preservation of human connections, empathy, and creativity (Reich & Ruipérez-Valiente, 2019) .

In essence, the future of AI-enhanced communication and education is an intricate dance between the technological advancements brought about by AI and the timeless essence of human connection. As we progress, it is essential to navigate this path with a discerning eye, fostering a society in which AI serves as a powerful ally and enhances our capabilities, while our commitment to ethical conduct, empathy, and authentic human interactions remains unwavering. This balancing act is the key to a future in which the best of both worlds coexist harmoniously, propelling us into a new era of communication and education, richer and more meaningful than ever before.

A Call to Educators: Ensuring the Human Element Remains Central in Communication Training

In the grand narrative of technological advancement, the emergence of artificial intelligence has ushered in a new era, redefining the boundaries of human communication and education. The transformative potential of AI is undeniable, reshaping the way we connect and learn, enabling personalization, transcending language barriers, and augmenting creative capabilities (Banks, 2004). However, amidst this seismic shift, there is a vital call for educators to ensure that the human element remains central to communication training.

AI, often discussed in the context of Bhutoria's "Human Loop" (2022)(2022), highlights the interplay between machines and humans. The Human Loop concept underscores that while AI can automate and augment certain aspects of communication and education, its human insight, values, and ethical considerations remain irreplaceable. In this light, the role of educators becomes even more pronounced as they guide students in navigating the intricate dance between AI and human communication

The call to educators is a call for balance and a commitment to nurturing human connections, empathy, and creativity within the human loop (Bhutoria, 2022). It is a call to instill in students the understanding that while AI can augment their skills, it is human touch that truly distinguishes them in the complex tapestry of communication. In heeding this call, we can ensure that as AI continues to shape our world, the essence of what it means to be human – the ability to connect, understand, and empathize – remains central to our training and education. This harmonious integration of AI and the human element within the Human Loop is the gateway to a future in which our communication and education systems are richer, more meaningful, and deeply anchored in our shared humanity.

REFERENCES

Akgun, S., & Greenhow, C. (2022). Artificial intelligence in education: Addressing ethical challenges in K-12 settings. *AI and Ethics*, *2*(3), 431–440. doi:10.1007/s43681-021-00096-7 PMID:34790956

Asemah, E., & Omosotomhe, S. (2022). *Fundamentals of interpersonal communication*. Matkol Press.

Askari, S. I., Haans, A., Bos, P., Eggink, M. J. G., Lu, E. M., Kwong, F. G. L., & IJsselsteijn, W. A. (2020). Context matters: 12th international conference on human haptic sensing and touch enabled computer applications, EuroHaptics 2020. *Haptics: Science, Technology, Applications*, 131–139. 10.1007/978-3-030-58147-3_15

Aydın, Ö., & Karaarslan, E. (2023, January 31). *Is ChatGPT leading generative AI? What is beyond expectations?* https://papers.ssrn.com/sol3/papers.cfm?abstract_id=4341500

Banks, J. A. (2004). Teaching for social justice, diversity, and citizenship in a global world. *The Educational Forum*, *68*(4), 296–305. doi:10.1080/00131720408984645

Bhutoria, A. (2022). Personalized education and Artificial Intelligence in the United States, China, and India: A systematic review using a Human-In-The-Loop model. *Computers and Education: Artificial Intelligence*, *3*, 100068. doi:10.1016/j.caeai.2022.100068

Bilquise, G., Ibrahim, S., & Shaalan, K. (2022). Emotionally intelligent chatbots: A systematic literature review. *Human Behavior and Emerging Technologies*, *2022*, e9601630. doi:10.1155/2022/9601630

Braithwaite, D. O., & Schrodt, P. (Eds.). (2021). *Engaging theories in interpersonal communication: Multiple perspectives* (3rd ed.). Routledge., doi:10.4324/9781003195511

Bryson, J., & Winfield, A. (2017). Standardizing ethical design for artificial intelligence and autonomous systems. *Computer*, *50*(5), 116–119. doi:10.1109/MC.2017.154

Callais, V. (2020). Reclaiming conversation: The power of talk in a digital age. *Journal of College Orientation, Transition, and Retention*, *27*(2). Advance online publication. doi:10.24926/jcotr.v27i2.3099

Cavanagh, M., Bower, M., Moloney, R., & Sweller, N. (2014). The effect over time of a video-based reflection system on preservice teachers' oral presentations. *The Australian Journal of Teacher Education*, *39*(6). Advance online publication. doi:10.14221/ajte.2014v39n6.3

Chamberlain, R., Mullin, C., Scheerlinck, B., & Wagemans, J. (2017). Putting the art in artificial: Aesthetic responses to computer-generated art. *Psychology of Aesthetics, Creativity, and the Arts*, *12*(2), 177–192. Advance online publication. doi:10.1037/aca0000136

Chamot, A. (2005). Language learning strategy instruction: Current issues and research. *Annual Review of Applied Linguistics*, *25*, 112–130. doi:10.1017/S0267190505000061

Chan, C. K. Y., & Hu, W. (2023). Students' voices on generative AI: Perceptions, benefits, and challenges in higher education. *International Journal of Educational Technology in Higher Education*, *20*(1), 43. doi:10.1186/s41239-023-00411-8

Chen, A., Gussenhoven, C., & Rietveld, T. (2004). Language-specificity in the perception of paralinguistic intonational meaning. *Language and Speech*, *47*(4), 311–349. doi:10.1177/00238309040470040101 PMID:16038447

Colby, K. M. (1975). *Artificial paranoia: A computer simulation of paranoid processes*. Pergamon Press.

Computing & Communications Center. (2023). *Generative Artificial Intelligence | Center for Teaching Innovation*. https://teaching.cornell.edu/generative-artificial-intelligence#GenerativeAI

Craig, R. T. (2017, April 27). *Definitions and concepts of communication*. Definitions and Concepts of Communication. https://www.oxfordbibliographies.com/display/document/obo-9780199756841/obo-9780199756841-0172.xml

Dalvi, C., Rathod, M., Patil, S., Gite, S., & Kotecha, K. (2021). A survey of AI-based facial emotion recognition: Features, ML & DL techniques, age-wise datasets and future directions. IEEE Access. doi:10.1109/ACCESS.2021.3131733

Derevianko, A., Pizzoli, S. F. M., Pesapane, F., Rotili, A., Monzani, D., Grasso, R., Cassano, E., & Pravettoni, G. (2023). The use of Artificial Intelligence (AI) in the radiology field: What is the state of doctor–patient communication in cancer diagnosis? *Cancers (Basel)*, *15*(2), 2. Advance online publication. doi:10.3390/cancers15020470 PMID:36672417

Dogoulis, P., Kordopatis-Zilos, G., Kompatsiaris, I., & Papadopoulos, S. (2023). Improving synthetically generated image detection in cross-concept settings. *Proceedings of the 2nd ACM International Workshop on Multimedia AI against Disinformation*, 28–35. 10.1145/3592572.3592846

Dweck, C. S. (2016). Mindset: The new psychology of success (Updated edition). Random House.

Eadie, W. (2009). *21st century communication: A reference handbook. Sage (Atlanta, Ga.).* Advance online publication. doi:10.4135/9781412964005

Feuerriegel, S., Hartmann, J., Janiesch, C., & Zschech, P. (2023). Generative AI. *Business & Information Systems Engineering*, 1–16. doi:10.1007/s12599-023-00834-7

Ghai, B., & Mueller, K. (2021). Fluent: An AI augmented writing tool for people who stutter. *Proceedings of the 23rd International ACM SIGACCESS Conference on Computers and Accessibility*, 1–8. 10.1145/3441852.3471211

Grosuleac, A., Budulan, S., & Rebedea, T. (2020). Seeking an Empathy-abled Conversational Agent. RoCHI, 103-107. doi:10.37789/rochi.2020.1.1.16

Hancock, J. T., Naaman, M., & Levy, K. (2020). AI-mediated communication: Definition, research agenda, and ethical considerations. *Journal of Computer-Mediated Communication, 25*(1), 89–100. doi:10.1093/jcmc/zmz022

Henderson, A. T., & Mapp, K. L. (2002). *A new wave of evidence: The impact of school, family, and community connections on student achievement. annual synthesis, 2002.* National Center for Family & Community Connections with Schools, Southwest Educational Development Laboratory. https://eric.ed.gov/?id=ED474521

Huang, M.-H., & Rust, R. (2018). Artificial intelligence in service. *Journal of Service Research, 21*(2), 109467051775245. doi:10.1177/1094670517752459

Jiang, R. (2022). How does artificial intelligence empower EFL teaching and learning nowadays? A review on artificial intelligence in the EFL context. *Frontiers in Psychology, 13*, 1049401. doi:10.3389/fpsyg.2022.1049401 PMID:36467167

Johnson, D. W., & Johnson, R. T. (2004). Cooperation and the use of technology. In *Handbook of research on educational communications and technology* (2nd ed., pp. 777–803). Routledge.

Jones, M., & Dexter, S. (2014). How teachers learn: The roles of formal, informal, and independent learning. *Educational Technology Research and Development, 62*(3), 367–384. doi:10.1007/s11423-014-9337-6

Kim, N. J., & Kim, M. K. (2022). Teacher's perceptions of using an artificial intelligence-based educational tool for scientific writing. *Frontiers in Education, 7*, 755914. doi:10.3389/feduc.2022.755914

Klein, B., & Merkel, S. (2022). Current trends in gerontechnology: Recent findings from the Austrian-German-Swiss chapter. *Gerontechnology, 21*(s). doi:10.4017/gt.2022.21.s.578.sp7

Lee, A. V. Y. (2023). Supporting students' generation of feedback in large-scale online course with artificial intelligence-enabled evaluation. *Studies in Educational Evaluation, 77*, 101250. doi:10.1016/j.stueduc.2023.101250

Lim, W. M., Gunasekara, A., Pallant, J. L., Pallant, J. I., & Pechenkina, E. (2023). Generative AI and the future of education: Ragnarök or reformation? A paradoxical perspective from management educators. *International Journal of Management Education, 21*(2), 100790. doi:10.1016/j.ijme.2023.100790

Lock, S. (2022, December 5). What is AI chatbot phenomenon ChatGPT and could it replace humans? *The Guardian*. https://www.theguardian.com/technology/2022/dec/05/what-is-ai-chatbot-phenomenon-chatgpt-and-could-it-replace-humans

Lopezosa, C., Codina, L., Pont-Sorribes, C., & Vállez, M. (2023). Use of generative artificial intelligence in the training of journalists: Challenges, uses and training proposal. *El Profesional de la Información, 32*(4), 4. Advance online publication. doi:10.3145/epi.2023.jul.08

Lu, T., Liu, X., Sun, J., Bao, Y., Schuller, B. W., Han, Y., & Lu, L. (2023). Bridging the gap between artificial intelligence and mental health. *Science Bulletin, 68*(15), 1606–1610. doi:10.1016/j.scib.2023.07.015 PMID:37474445

Manasa, R., & Devi, A. (2022). Amazon's artificial intelligence in retail novelty—case study. *International Journal of Case Studies in Business, IT, and Education*, 787–804. doi:10.47992/IJCSBE.2581.6942.0233

McKinsey. (2023, January 19). *What is ChatGPT, DALL-E, and generative AI?* https://www.mckinsey.com/featured-insights/mckinsey-explainers/what-is-generative-ai

Minichilli, F., Gorini, F., Ascari, E., Bianchi, F., Coi, A., Fredianelli, L., Licitra, G., Manzoli, F., Mezzasalma, L., & Cori, L. (2018). Annoyance judgment and measurements of environmental noise: A focus on Italian secondary schools. *International Journal of Environmental Research and Public Health, 15*(2), 208. doi:10.3390/ijerph15020208 PMID:29373506

Misaki, D., Ge, X., & Odaka, T. (2020, June 22). *Toward interdisciplinary teamwork in Japan: Developing team-based learning experience and its assessment*. 2020 ASEE Virtual Annual Conference Content Access. https://peer.asee.org/toward-interdisciplinary-teamwork-in-japan-developing-team-based-learning-experience-and-its-assessment

Mittelstadt, B. D., Allo, P., Taddeo, M., Wachter, S., & Floridi, L. (2016). The ethics of algorithms: Mapping the debate. *Big Data & Society, 3*(2). doi:10.1177/2053951716679679

Natale, S. (2020). Communicating through or communicating with: Approaching artificial intelligence from a communication and media studies perspective. *Communication Theory, 30*. Advance online publication. doi:10.1093/ct/qtaa022

Nguyen, M., Laly, M., Kwon, B. C., Mougenot, C., & McNamara, J. (2022). Moody man: Improving creative teamwork through dynamic affective recognition. *Extended Abstracts of the 2022 CHI Conference on Human Factors in Computing Systems*, 1–14. 10.1145/3491101.3519656

Patton, B. R., & Giffin, K. (1971). *Basic readings in interpersonal communication*. Harper & Row.

Picard, R. W. (2000). *Affective Computing*. doi:10.7551/mitpress/1140.001.0001

Pizzi, G., Vannucci, V., Mazzoli, V., & Donvito, R. (2023). I, chatbot! The impact of anthropomorphism and gaze direction on willingness to disclose personal information and behavioral intentions. *Psychology and Marketing*, *40*(7), 1372–1387. doi:10.1002/mar.21813

Pun, J. (2021). A study of Chinese medical students' communication pattern in delivering bad news: An ethnographic discourse analysis approach. *BMC Medical Education*, *21*(1), 286. doi:10.1186/s12909-021-02724-6 PMID:34011322

Reich, J., & Ruipérez-Valiente, J. A. (2019). The MOOC pivot. *Science*, *363*(6423), 130–131. doi:10.1126/science.aav7958 PMID:30630920

Saha, S., & Beach, M. C. (2020). Impact of physician race on patient decision-making and ratings of physicians: A randomized experiment using video vignettes. *Journal of General Internal Medicine*, *35*(4), 1084–1091. doi:10.1007/s11606-020-05646-z PMID:31965527

Salovey, P., & Mayer, J. D. (1990). Emotional intelligence. *Imagination, Cognition and Personality*, *9*(3), 185–211. doi:10.2190/DUGG-P24E-52WK-6CDG

Shum, H., He, X., & Li, D. (2018). From Eliza to XiaoIce: Challenges and opportunities with social chatbots. *Frontiers of Information Technology & Electronic Engineering*, *19*(1), 10–26. doi:10.1631/FITEE.1700826

Smith, S. W., Daunic, A. P., Miller, M. D., & Robinson, T. R. (2002). Conflict resolution and peer mediation in middle schools: Extending the process and outcome knowledge base. *The Journal of Social Psychology*, *142*(5), 567–586. doi:10.1080/00224540209603919 PMID:12236468

Terregino, C. A., Copeland, H. L., Sarfaty, S. C., Lantz-Gefroh, V., & Hoffmann-Longtin, K. (2019). Development of an empathy and clarity rating scale to measure the effect of medical improv on end-of-first-year OCSE performance: A pilot study. *Medical Education Online*, *24*(1), 1666537. doi:10.1080/10872981.2019.1666537 PMID:31532330

van Hooijdonk, R., Mathot, S., Schat, E., Spencer, H., van der Stigchel, S., & Dijkerman, H. C. (2019). Touch-induced pupil size reflects stimulus intensity, not subjective pleasantness. *Experimental Brain Research*, *237*(1), 201–210. doi:10.1007/s00221-018-5404-2 PMID:30374784

Vasalou, A., Joinson, A., Bänziger, T., Goldie, P., & Pitt, J. (2008). Avatars in social media: Balancing accuracy, playfulness and embodied messages. *International Journal of Human-Computer Studies*, *66*(11), 801–811. doi:10.1016/j.ijhcs.2008.08.002

Weizenbaum, J. (1966). ELIZA—A computer program for the study of natural language communication between man and machine. *Communications of the ACM*, *9*(1), 36–45. doi:10.1145/365153.365168

West, D. M. (2018). The future of work: Robots, AI, and automation. In *The Future of Work* (p. 205). Robots, AI, and Automation.

Wilson, D., & Sperber, D. (1993). Linguistic form and relevance. *Lingua*, *90*(1), 1–25. doi:10.1016/0024-3841(93)90058-5

Chapter 10
Generative AI Ethical Considerations and Discriminatory Biases on Diverse Students Within the Classroom

Leslie Ramos Salazar
https://orcid.org/0000-0001-7047-594X
West Texas A&M University, USA

Shanna F. Peeples
https://orcid.org/0000-0002-6316-9570
West Texas A&M University, USA

Mary E. Brooks
https://orcid.org/0000-0003-0264-1373
West Texas A&M University, USA

ABSTRACT

Generative artificial intelligence (AI) can induce a variety of biases that can impact decision-making processes, and it can produce inaccurate or distorted information that may harm marginalized student groups in higher education classrooms. With the increase in generative AI use among college students and instructors, it is important to examine the ethical risks and discriminatory biases that can negatively influence students' learning experiences. For this purpose, this chapter focuses on the different types of generative AI ethical risks that can occur in U.S. classrooms. The variety of AI discriminatory biases against diverse student populations are also documented. Further, the authors discuss a case application that expands on the potential AI biases in higher education. To prevent and address potential AI ethical risks and biases, recommendations are offered to higher education educators. Lastly, guidance is offered suggesting future research in AI biases and diversity in higher education institutions.

DOI: 10.4018/979-8-3693-0831-8.ch010

INTRODUCTION

David Foster's book, *Generative Deep Learning*, defines generative modeling as "a branch of machine learning that involves training a model to produce new data that is similar to a given dataset" (p. 4). This differs from discriminative modeling, which is used for prediction and not for generating new content, the purpose of generative modeling (Foster, 2023). Related is the emerging technology of generative artificial intelligence (generative AI), which uses a considerable amount of data in the form of texts and images to create or generate new images and text when provided with a prompt by the user (Euchner, 2023). Among the many generative AI tools and applications, ChatGPT is arguably the most recognized. According to Open AI, the company that created ChatGPT, its purpose is to generate a "detailed response" (para. 1) to any given prompt submitted by the user ranging from responding to an email to writing a full paper and more (Introducing ChatGPT, n.d.). The use of generative AI has increased rapidly in higher education, with teachers using it to teach or grade students' assignments and students using it to complete their course assignments and activities (Kasneci et al., 2023). In a national BestColleges survey using a sample of 1,000 college students, "43% of college students" reported using generative AI technologies, such as ChatGPT, with half of them using these technologies for homework and tests (Welding, 2023, para. 3).

However, a growing concern of generative AI systems in higher education includes biases that can stem from a variety of sources, such as human, systemic, and institutional biases. AI systems can exhibit biases derived from their programming and data sources; for example, machine learning software can be trained on a dataset that underrepresents groups based on gender or ethnicity (Schwartz et al., 2022). Biases can also creep into algorithms through training data, including biased human decisions that reflect historical or social inequities (Buolamwini, 2019). This bias can harm members of marginalized groups by affecting the decisions made by AI systems, such as whether a person is admitted to a school or university. It can also reduce people's ability to participate in the economy and society, and reduce the potential of AI for business and society by encouraging mistrust and producing distorted results (Manyika et al., 2019).

An uncritical acceptance of AI and machine learning in classrooms can inadvertently replicate and reify discrimination, which can limit the opportunities available to students of color whose rates of college enrollment have increased (National Center for Education Statistics, 2023). Educational technology experts point to two potential areas of harm for marginalized students: language and cultural bias in personalized learning software and the potential mislabeling of students as being in danger of failing or in need of behavioral intervention (Herold, 2022). For example, these systems are built under the assumption that users are fluent speakers of an academic English form. A student who speaks one or more languages or one who has a distinct accent or dialect could be subject to unintended discrimination. Further complicating this issue is the documented link between the academic achievement gap of black and white students in the U.S. and unequal rates of disciplinary action for students of color (Pearman et al., 2019; Spector, 2019).

Given the potential biases derived from generative AI, such as ChatGPT, it is imperative for higher education faculty and stakeholders to become aware of the potential ethical risks and discriminatory biases that can have a negative effect on diverse college students' learning and academic experiences. With the increase of diverse students based on their gender, ethnicity, and age, among other characteristics, enrolled in higher education institutions in the U.S. (Education Data Initiative, 2023), it is important to consider how generative AI, such as ChatGPT, may indirectly affect them in university classroom settings.

As such, in this chapter, our objectives are to a) discuss the types of generative AI ethical risks in the classroom, b) discuss AI discriminatory biases against diverse undergraduate students considering a variety of diversity factors (e.g., age, ethnicity/race), c) discuss a case application of AI biases in higher education, d) explain recommendations about responding to AI biases, and e) discuss future research directions.

TYPES OF AI ETHICAL RISKS IN THE CLASSROOM

Bias and Discrimination Biases

Bias and discriminatory biases have been documented by sociopsychological researchers based on implicit AI biases. Generative AI biases can be derived from individuals who train data, use and develop algorithms, and misuse AI against culturally oppressed individuals (Mattas, 2023). Patterns of data and algorithms can mispresent language outcomes and potentially provide inaccuracies to underprivileged individuals (Dwivedi et al., 2023). Data sources provided by generative AI can also be biased by generating cultural stereotypes, cultural biases, and prejudiced language biases, which can have harmful impacts on individuals within society (Powles, 2020). Data sources include websites (e.g., blogs and forums), books (e.g., fiction and non-fiction), social media platforms (e.g., Facebook and Reddit), and conversational data (Ferrara, 2023). Additionally, the information produced by generative AI has the potential to be inaccurate or misleading, which could result in flawed decision making (Müller et al., 2019) and acceptance of fabricated media and news as truth (Whittaker, 2019). Furthermore, datasets can also be biased based on their quality and lack of diversity, because they can influence models used for application in education and in the classroom (Ray, 2023).

In the classroom, biases can be created when evaluating students' work using generative AI systems. For instance, instructors may evaluate text-based assignments such as essays and speeches to assign performance grades. Negative biases can occur if AI systems inadvertently perpetuate discrimination and bias in students' work, without considering students' cultural and language barriers. As a result, underrepresented students may be placed at a grading disadvantage over other students, which can perpetuate educational achievement gaps (Mhlanga, 2023). Over time, generative AI may internalize learning and assessment biases as patterns that can lead to future unfair assessment practices in higher education, leading to further educational inequalities (Selwyn, 2019).

Few studies have examined generative AI discrimination and educational bias. A systematic review by Sallam (2023) found that the most commonly cited ethical concerns included risk of bias (30%), inaccurate information (33.3%), citation inaccuracy (16.7%), transparency issues (16.7%), legal issues (11.7%), limited knowledge (10%), misleading information (8.3%), depth of content (8.3%), copyright issues (6.7%), and lack of originality (6.7%). A qualitative case study analyzing tweets and interviews with students and educators found that ChatGPT was viewed as manipulative and selective in the information it provided based on biased algorithms and data, devoid of human emotions and contextual factors when generating information, and was often inaccurate (Tlili et al., 2023). Additionally, Zhou et al. (2023) analyzed ChatGPT using several sample datasets and cases to provide evidence of the risk of discrimination and biases, such as social prejudice and toxicity, in educational contexts.

Privacy and Security Issues

Privacy and security issues are another concern because of the potential to incorporate original and sensitive information into generative AI, such as ChatGPT. Because generative AI such as ChatGPT obtains personal data through textual interactions, there is potential for data to be advertised or marketed to third parties without the consent of individuals (Mattas, 2023). For example, in the classroom, students may provide their personal information when completing essay assignments, and this information is made public without their consent. When considering international students, generative AI collects their personal data to tailor their learning, which can increase the risks of privacy and security issues and impact international regulations (Butcher & McGrath, 2004; Wang et al., 2023). In education, institutions may use student data, such as their name and student ID number, to analyze student outcomes, such as academic performance and retention, using generative AI systems (Yu & Guo, 2023). Teachers may also use ChatGPT to post students' grades, assignments, and personal information such as their phone numbers, without realizing potential privacy and confidentiality violations (Mhlanga, 2023). Problems arise when privacy and data security breaches occur, which can lead to potential ethical dilemmas and litigation (Gupta et al., 2023).

Furthermore, when individuals input their original creative works into generative AI without copyright protection, their work may be reused and altered by others without credit, acknowledgement, or permission from owners (Bozkurt & Sharma, 2023; Daniels, 2023). When posting original works including student research papers and reports via generative AI, such as ChatGPT, there is a risk of the "Matthew Effect," which transfers ownership to third parties, without providing authors with proper acknowledgement (Lund et al., 2023). The "Matthew Effect" refers to the adage that the rich get richer, and the poor get poorer. Sociologist Robert K. Merton used it to describe how eminent scientists often obtain more credit than unknown researchers, even when their work is similar. Well-known scientists have privileges and statuses that help them gain recognition, whereas unknown researchers struggle to obtain the same level of credit (Merton, 1968). This concept posits that initial privileges and status lead to accumulating benefits, whereas obscurity leads to fewer opportunities, even when contributions are similar. During textual interactions with generative AI chatbots, such as ChatGPT, students and teachers may write original paragraphs to obtain feedback without realizing that this material is now part of ChatGPT's system. Merton's observation suggests that when students submit their original work to ChatGPT and other AI systems, established creators may receive disproportionate credit as the AI learns from and replicates their work. Meanwhile, student researchers and authors may struggle to gain recognition for their own original content and ideas using AI due to their obscurity and lack of status as newcomers. This could lead to an imbalance in which prominent artists and scholars accumulate benefits from AI based on the foundational advantage of their status while students' contributions are credited.

Copyright violations occur when generative AI reuses the authors' original material to create its own material (e.g., essays and quotes), which can lead to copyright litigation (Gillotte, 2019). For instance, according to Brittain (2023), a group of artists and writers filed a lawsuit against AI generators in a court in San Francisco, CA, for not attributing their work or providing them with any compensation for their original work. Furthermore, when generative AI produces textual material, it does not always provide appropriate credit because it can provide incorrect sources, and it may also omit some sources, which can lead to issues in providing authors with the credit they deserve (Lund et al., 2023).

Access and Inclusion Concerns

Another risk is the potential access and inclusion of generative AI among diverse students. For instance, international students may not have equal access to generative AI compared to Western societies such as the United States. Some countries, such as Italy, China, and Cuba, have banned ChatGPT (Martindale, 2023) and if some of these international students attend U.S. institutions, they may not have equal access and may not be included in the required ChatGPT activities and exercises that may be assigned by U.S. instructors. In addition, because generative AI requires Internet access, individuals from lower socioeconomic backgrounds may not be able to afford a fast and reliable Internet with sufficient bandwidth, which may place them at a disadvantage compared to other students who can access and afford these technologies (Wach et al., 2023). Additionally, even if students were able to obtain Internet access, students from lower-socioeconomic backgrounds may only have access to free versions of generative AI such as ChatGPT 3.0, Google Bard, and Microsoft Bing; however, they would be excluded from more sophisticated paid versions of generative AI such as ChatGPT 4.0 and Jasper, which have more recently trained data, Internet integration, and higher accuracy rates. Further, students from third world countries with high numbers of disconnected people, such as India, China, Pakistan, Bangladesh, Ethiopia, and Indonesia, may not receive any benefits from the use of generative AI in their courses due to the lack of Internet access (Petrosyan, 2023). This can worsen the digital divide between generative AI and higher education.

Moreover, generative AI may not be inclusive based on its context and content. For instance, generative AI may not be able to easily adapt examples to students from other cultures, which may limit the inclusion of diverse experiences and cultures (Olaniyi et al., 2023). In a review study, Ferrara (2023) indicated that it is important that generative AI be inclusive of languages, and while it is effective in translating text by language, it may not be effective in being inclusive of idiosyncratic language and expressions based on cultures. There is also the risk of a lack of cultural sensitivity in AI responses (Elish & Boyd, 2018). For example, students may ask general questions about societal issues as part of an assignment and generative AI chatbots may yield biased responses against minority cultures. If generative AI provides culturally biased responses, it could unintentionally oppress students from minority backgrounds, leading to cultural inequalities in the classroom.

Transparency Issues

Generative AI has several transparency issues in education. In part, generative AI is highly complex based on its decision-making process, and transparency issues can emerge if educators and students lack knowledge of generative AI processes and lack effective training (Ferrara, 2023). The absence of transparency involving the use of generative AI in the classroom can create ambiguities and misconceptions and encourage the unethical use of generative AI (Rodgers et al., 2023). Therefore, it is important to understand how generative AI technologies work and the policies and expectations of the usage of institutions and instructors.

In the classroom, students may misuse generative AI and obtain content without understanding how AI systems work, or how generative AI obtains data and information. As a result, students may use generative AI systems blindly without considering the underlying mechanisms and implications of using them in their learning experiences and throughout their educational path (Mhlanga, 2023). Without transparency from generative AI processes and teachers, this can result in the improper use of generative AI systems in higher education classrooms. For instance, students may use it at will to create and/or improve their assignments and potentially plagiarize and/or cheat on them (Cotton et al., 2023). Furthermore, students may learn to trust generative AI as a credible and reliable source when it might not always be the case.

Teachers' transparency is another important factor in higher education classrooms. Institutions need to prioritize training their university faculty on generative AI functions in relation to higher education classrooms (Fuchs, 2023). The inclusion of policies such as AI syllabus statements and the institution's stance on the use of generative AI in classrooms allows for generative AI policies to be transparent across an institution. Teachers also need to devote their energy to learning generative AI technologies (e.g., Google Bard, ChatGPT, etc.) and use them to better understand their effects on their teaching and their students' learning potential. In the classroom, teachers should be transparent about the use of generative AI in their classroom by leading discussions and setting policies to make it clear, whether it is permitted by providing credit or permitted with the instructor's approval. Teachers can prepare students by incorporating generative AI lessons into their semesters' topic schedules. Some effective uses of generative AI in communication classrooms include the following.

· brainstorming research or speech topics
· outlining and preparing speeches and papers
· revising and improving writing mechanics
· improving the flow of writing
· developing prompts or simulations
· developing images or videos
· evaluating generative AI reasoning processes
· comparing various educational content

Teachers may choose to encourage generative AI in their classrooms as a potential teaching assistant in their courses. In a study by Jeon and Lee (2023), who interviewed 11 language teachers about their use of ChatGPT, the results indicated that the teachers found ChatGPT useful in serving as a teaching assistant and evaluator. In particular, the AI chatbot helped their students with learning challenges outside the classroom, such as overcoming language barriers (Jeon & Lee, 2023). Within the classroom, the AI chatbot helped teachers in error-checking, providing content, and making meaning of big words (Jeon & Lee, 2023). Another study also found ChatGPT effective as a teaching assistant in mathematics courses by helping students in the problem-solving process, obtaining different content examples, and providing them with immediate attention, which can enhance their overall learning experiences (Wardat et al., 2023). Khan et al. (2023) also found that communicating with ChatGPT in medical education enables personalized learning that can help students to better understand the material on their own terms. Additionally, Aljabani et al. (2023) argued that ChatGPT can help students with writing and coding tasks in the classroom. Thus, being transparent about the appropriate use of generative AI can be beneficial to both teachers and students.

Over-Reliance on AI

Overreliance on AI is becoming increasingly problematic in classrooms. Studies have shown that students, including diverse students, who become overreliant on technology for assistance in homework assignments and projects tend to suffer from reduced academic skills (e.g., writing, critical thinking skills, etc.) (Chan, 2023; Civil, 2023; Mhlanga, 2023; Warschauer et al., 2023). In such instances, students may delegate their critical thinking and writing practices to generative AI to obtain immediate answers. With this concern, students may lose their ability to think for themselves and prioritize short-term learning (e.g., immediate recall) instead of long-term, lifelong learning (Tam et al., 2023). The way students solve problems changes when relying on generative AI technologies because students can become accustomed to receiving immediate solutions to problems without evaluating the quality of the proposed solutions (Tam et al., 2023). A problem with reliance on problem solving with generative AI is when students believe its content without conducting any additional research on their own (e.g., fact-checking) (Iskender, 2023). Furthermore, procrastinating students may be more likely to rely on generative AI assistance to complete their homework (Sok & Heng, 2023). With over-reliance on generative AI technologies, students' innovation potential may also be harmed because they rely on chatbots instead of developing new creative ideas (Sok & Heng, 2023).

Interestingly, teachers can also become dependent on generative AI in their teaching practices. Some teachers may overuse generative AI in their lesson, exam development, and assessment (Tam et al., 2023). Teachers are increasingly collaborating with generative AI to develop courses, activities, and homework assignments (Tam et al., 2023). As such, teachers may become reliant on generative AI to obtain multimedia content including videos, images, and graphics (Wu, 2021). A criticism of teachers becoming overreliant on the content provided by generative AI is that it poses the question of who is really teaching the students, is it the teacher, or generative AI such as ChatGPT? If higher education courses overemphasize generative AI content across similar curricula, there is the risk of losing innovative and transformative thinking. For instance, in public speaking and debate courses, generative AI can provide the pros and cons of any relevant issue. While generative AI chatbots can be useful assistive tools, they can also become repetitive and monotonous in their responses to similar student and teacher questions. As such, overreliance on generative AI can have long-term consequences.

Academic Integrity and Student Learning

Academic integrity issues are another concern in relation to students' learning. Students may choose to use generative AI, such as ChatGPT 3.0, to engage in cheating practices given that the technology is free, immediate, and accessible. Other students who can afford the paid versions of generative AI, such as ChatGPT 4.0 and Claude, can also use these services to cheat more effectively by accessing more updated content. For instance, students may cheat using ChatGPT to write code for their assignments and write written assignments on behalf of their courses (Scharth, 2022). By relying on ChatGPT to complete course assignments, such as written assignments and exams, students violate academic integrity policies (Eke, 2023). Students have also been caught plagiarizing written assignments by copying and pasting directly from AI chatbots without providing any credit to AI, which is considered stealing "intellectual property' (Eke, 2023). An ethical challenge may arise when students who cheat with ChatGPT on their assignments and who do not get caught receive better grades than students who do not use ChatGPT at all for their course assignments (Cotton et al., 2023). Thus, cheating assignments can interfere with proper assessments and genuine student learning.

Several studies have examined the ChatGPT and its academic integrity. Mohammadkarimi (2023) analyzed the perspectives of 67 teachers involved in academic integrity and found that 58% of them strongly felt that generative AI tempts students to engage in academic cheating. Of the sample, 39%

expressed facing challenges in identifying academic integrity issues in written assignments in their courses (Mohammadkarimi, 2023). Furthermore, 90% of the teachers indicated that they were unable to distinguish between students' writing and generative AI writing (Mohammadkarimi, 2023). Further, Amani et al. (2023) conducted a survey of faculty, staff, and students at Texas A&M University, where 55% of faculty and staff indicated that students are likely to break academic integrity codes using ChatGPT, whereas 63% of students agreed that students are likely to engage in academic dishonesty using ChatGPT. Other researchers have conducted an international content analysis of ChatGPT news articles and found that 88 articles focused on academic integrity issues, including concerns about students cheating, detecting cheating, and penalizing students to use ChatGPT (Sullivan et al., 2023). ChatGPT was used to plagiarize essays and cheats on course exams (Sullivan et al., 2023).

In summary, various types of AI ethical risks can occur in the classroom, including bias and discrimination bias, privacy and security issues, access and inclusion, transparency, over-reliance on AI, and academic integrity related to student learning. As generative AI continues to improve, in the future, paid versions may incorporate protective mechanisms that reduce discriminatory biases in trained data, protect users' privacy and security, and AI may acknowledge citations more accurately in its chat output. However, if free versions do not adapt to these risks downline, it can worsen the digital divide and ethical risks of higher education. From the first author's personal experiences, instructors are likely to face ethical issues, especially academic integrity issues, such as having students use generative AI to write essay assignments without proper credit or inaccurate citations. The lack of diverse examples generated by AI is also a concern, especially since the demographics of U.S. students have become more diverse, including higher rates of Hispanics and first-generation students. It is important for instructors to adapt to generative AI tools and become aware of potential ethical risks that may negatively affect their own students in higher education.

AI DISCRIMINATORY BIASES AGAINST DIVERSE UNDERGRADUATE STUDENTS

Cerf (2023) reports on The University of California Santa Cruz's (UCSC) new tool, which detects implicit bias surrounding several variables, including gender, race, vocation, and religion. They state that this tool is necessary to help mitigate the bias often found in generative AI answers because the data AI uses are generated from humans who are often either explicitly or implicitly biased in their work from the AI algorithm. Thus, AI tools are not sophisticated enough to identify discriminatory biases, which can often exacerbate existing stereotypes about age, ethnicity/race, disability, etc. (Cerf, 2023). As a result, college students' learning and work can be gravely affected.

AI Ageism

Stypinska (2023) developed the concept of AI ageism, which includes the exclusion of older adults from proper training and use of AI tools, along with the AI tools themselves generating output based on algorithms that are pejorative, prejudicial, and stereotypical of older adults. Stypinska (2023) categorizes how AI ageism manifests itself at five different levels: *technical level* - meaning the data and algorithms produce age-biased answers; *individual level* – an idea where older adults do not belong or have the right to be in the technology space; *discourse level* – the absence of older adults in AI output;

group level – automatic decision making when using AI tools that exclude certain groups – namely older adults – from such opportunities as gainful employment or acceptance into higher education programs; and *user level* – excluding older adults from using AI tools. This is problematic for several reasons, but more specifically for returning or continuing students to academic institutions, who already might feel marginalized among a sea of younger adults in a learning environment.

Similar to UCSC's efforts to create tools to identify and mitigate bias in AI, Palmarini et al. (2019) created a tool used in conjunction with AI, called the Exclusion Spotter, which identifies ageist copies in job advertisements. The idea is to provide hiring companies with information on how they may unintentionally exclude older adults, many of whom are recent college graduates who expect to be a part of the workforce.

Disability

In 2021, Gerard Quinn, United Nations Special Rapporteur on the rights of persons with disabilities, presented his report on AI specifically, as it pertains to the benefits, challenges, human rights, and discriminatory practices toward those with various disabilities. In his report pertaining to education, Quinn outlines the many ways in which AI is used for good in an educational setting for people with disabilities (PWD). These include speech-to-text software, digital avatars that use sign language, and AI tutors and games for problem-solving skills (Quinn, 2021). Yet, one of the main issues Quinn points out is that AI is often used to determine who has access to education. This often results in AI discriminating against PWDs who aim for better education because AI tools are not built with PWDs in mind. Many AI algorithms simply do not consider persons with disabilities into account (Quinn, 2021).

Other scholars have studied disability and education from different perspectives, including Kharbat et al. (2021), who focused on how AI is used in an educational setting for students with intellectual and/or developmental disabilities. The authors posit that AI does not consider the nuances of various learning styles or specific disabilities for all students. For example, while some companies offer assistive technology to students who have trouble reading, they often build AI tools for broader learning disabilities rather than specific ones, including dyslexia. The authors argue that despite advances in AI for students with learning disabilities in a boon for the educational setting and for specific subjects, developers of these tools must also take into account that AI learning tools are not a one-size-fits-all solution when taking into account the many different categories of learning and developmental disabilities of numerous students (Kharbat et al., 2021).

Ethnicity/Race

AI discrimination is also a key concern for students of various races and ethnic backgrounds. This was the key argument in Herold's (2022) article on Education Week, which focused on how racial bias is present in AI tools. For example, dialects and accents from non-native English-speaking students are problematic for AI tools that do not often recognize various geographic languages. Furthermore, facial recognition AI tools are also problematic for darker skinned students as they are not often recognized, and thus, the data about them as students are skewed. Additionally, Tadesse et al. (2023) wrote about the lack of various skin tone depictions in educational materials aimed at student training in the medical profession. As a result, many skin issues in dark-skinned patients remain undetected. To address this issue, the authors developed an AI tool using machine learning called Skin Tone Analysis for Representation in EDucational materials (STAR-ED). The program will "automatically assess bias in skin tone representation in medical education materials" (p. 1). The authors' goal for creating this machine learning tool is to provide medical schools, students, and educators with a way to reduce skin tone bias in educational materials including textbooks, lecture notes, and slide decks so that those with dark skinned medical issues can be treated properly.

Baker and Hawn (2022) further expanded on how algorithmic bias in education impacts students of different racial backgrounds and genders. In their exhaustive review of research examining numerous definitions, examples, and concepts of algorithmic bias in education, the authors go into great detail regarding the differences between representational bias and measurement bias in AI tools. Representational bias refers to the smaller samples of specific cultural groups represented in the data that cause these groups to be absent from conversations pertaining to college recruitment, retention rates, and graduation discussions. Measurement bias refers to variables that perpetuate stereotypes or biases against students fitting a particular variable, which then skew predictions of issues, such as school violence (Baker & Hawn, 2022). Thus, both types of bias created by AI impact specific students' success in school, especially if they are not part of the conversation or even worse, negatively targeted owing to faulty AI data.

Furthermore, diverse students are often part of the digital divide due to socioeconomic conditions, which expands to gain access to AI, as mentioned previously in this chapter. Perry and Lee (2019) warn that students, particularly those growing up and learning in Black and Hispanic populated areas, "will face greater inequalities if we go too far toward digitizing education without considering how to check the inherent biases of the (mostly white) developers who create AI systems" (para. 2). Because systemic racism is already rampant in many schools, it is imperative that AI companies and creators consider the racial inequality that students also face through digital technologies, including AI platforms (Perry & Lee, 2019).

Sexual Orientation and Gender Identity

Buolamwini (2019) addressed both racial and gender issues related to AI in a Time magazine. In this article, Buolamwini developed the term "exclusion overhead" which refers to "the cost of systems that don't take into account the diversity of humanity" (para. 3). As it pertains to gender identity, she found in her research on AI tools created by major corporations that AI could determine far more male faces than female faces. Even more concerning is that AI had a more difficult time detecting the faces of dark-skinned women. This creates problems, especially for diverse students in the job market, as they could be subjected to racist and/or sexist hiring issues if left to AI tools that use existing outdated and biased data to help companies make hiring decisions.

On the positive side, Frąckiewicz (2023) outlines several ways in which AI can be used to help overcome gender inequality in education. This includes AI using data and algorithms to consider the specific learning needs of every student, whether male, female, or non-binary, and customizing course content based on the skills, strengths, and weaknesses of every student. As a result, this would help female students in normally male-dominated STEM fields. In addition, Frąckiewicz (2023) posits that AI can be useful for identifying gender bias in educational content and then creating educational materials to be more neutral, thus reducing gender discrimination.

Concerning sexual orientation, two scholars from Stanford University reported results from a multi-stage study that AI can predict sexual orientation based on facial recognition characteristics more so than a human can detect sexual orientation of another person using the naked eye (Wang & Kosinski,

2018). Although this study created controversy for the authors, as some human rights groups and other scholars debunked their report, Leufer (2023) states that using AI in this manner is problematic for several reasons, including the increase in harm against those in the LGBTQ community, many of whom are college students.

Language and International Students

Less studied in the academic literature is how discrimination and bias are presented with regard to language and international students. However, one such study that received much media attention was Liang et al.'s (2023) experiment, in which the authors submitted the original written works of over 90 non-native English speakers to more than five Generative Pre-trained Transformer (GPT) platforms. The results indicated that most of the English written essays were detected as AI produced, while the essays written by native English speakers were primarily and properly detected as written by humans (Sample, 2023). Thus, the authors posit that "GPT detectors are inadvertently penalizing individuals with limited linguistic proficiency" (Liang et al., 2023, p.1).

The authors write about the consequences of non-native speakers accused of using AI to write their work, including being silenced, harassed, falsely labeled as a cheater in school, developing a tarnished reputation, and more ramifications that could cause psychological issues (Liang et al., 2023). They continue with several recommendations of how to remedy this matter by strongly suggesting a ban on GPT detectors in educational settings, a more robust GPT evaluation process, better design of these tools and a call for "inclusive conversations involving all stakeholders, including developers, students, educators, policymakers, ethicists, and those affected by GPT" (Liang et al., 2023, p. 3).

As the generative AI industry continues to burn, developers must consider the frequency and variety of biases in the generated output, which can negatively affect students, especially those from various ethnic, racial, and socioeconomic backgrounds. Many cultures are not represented in the generative AI space, which can place students at a disadvantage when using and learning from these platforms. International students look for safety and comfort when studying away from their home country. At times, comfort comes from classroom settings, teachers, peers and educational tools. When any of these are out of alignment with students from different countries or upbringings, their learning can suffer. With generative AI becoming almost commonplace in many college courses, it is imperative that developers recognize and implement nuances related to all students, regardless of race, ethnicity, gender, sexual orientation, age, socioeconomic status, and other variables that make all students valuable and unique.

Education Cases of Discrimination and Bias Against Diverse Students

While AI promises a cornucopia of positive use cases, such as the translation of course materials into multiple languages, customized feedback, personalized tutoring, and 24/7 mentoring with chatbots, its application in higher education without careful oversight risks amplifying historical inequalities. Nowhere is this clearer than in admissions, the gateway that determines student access and opportunity. When poorly implemented, AI admissions can functionally discriminate against marginalized applicant groups, undermining the goals of diversity and inclusion.

When designed ethically, AI-assisted admissions can counter systemic bias. However, it requires centering principles of equity and representation, not just efficiency, in implementation. Otherwise, bias is guaranteed to creep into automated decisions insidiously.

University Admission AI Bias

The following hypothetical case illuminates the real-world impacts of the datasets used in AI training and the urgent need for proactive practices to detect and mitigate algorithmic harm. Consider the issues facing pseudonymous Riverside University:

Riverside University implemented an AI-assisted admission system to help review applications and make acceptance recommendations. The system was designed to increase efficiency and ostensibly remove human biases from the process. However, analysis by the computer science department found several biases in AI's selection criteria and recommendations.

The AI was trained on 10 years of historical admission data that included a disproportionately low number of applicants from certain backgrounds. AI's training on data that lacked diversity led it to underestimate the potential of applicants from underrepresented groups such as minorities, first-generation students, and women. By not accounting for exceptional talents and experiences outside of its limited training data, it overlooks promising candidates with atypical backgrounds.

In testing, they found that the AI consistently scored women and students of color lower than comparable male and white applicants did. It also recommends higher rates of admission for applicants from privileged backgrounds and elite feeder schools. Students without access to certain advanced courses and extracurricular courses were wrongly seen as less prepared.

This case shows how historical inequities and a lack of representation in training data can perpetuate discrimination through AI systems. This illustrates the need for proactive algorithmic fairness practices in higher education to ensure that admissions align with institutional values of diversity, equity, and inclusion. AI should expand, not limit, access and opportunities for marginalized groups.

When designed ethically, AI-assisted admissions can counter systemic bias. However, it requires centering principles of equity and representation, not just efficiency, in implementation. Otherwise, bias is guaranteed to creep into automated decisions insidiously.

AI Bias in the Classroom

We observed a similar risk of embedded bias for AI applications in the classroom. Without thoughtful design and testing, what seems like an efficient and unbiased tool can easily perpetuate prejudice. One of the authors of this chapter, a long-time composition instructor, noticed the marketing of AI writing assistants to her colleagues as a "virtual grad assistant' to lift the time-consuming nature of evaluating student writing with quick and constructive feedback. However, it is not difficult to imagine a scenario in which AI's efficiency can hide its biases toward a certain type of academic performance.

For instance, imagine that one such tool, named "SpeedGrader" for this illustration, quickly provides formative assessment and comments for students in a diverse first-year composition course. Professor Linh chooses SpeedGrader in hopes that it will allow her students to receive evaluations of their topics and ideas in a way that will prepare them for deeper conferences with her.

However, when students received their first essays, some noticed that SpeedGrader's feedback focused heavily on grammar and syntax issues for minority students, while focusing on topic development and suggesting content ideas for others.

Jamal approached Professor Linh to discuss his marked-up essay. Though he made thoughtful arguments in response to the prompt, the AI critic had ignored the content and instead only corrected minor errors. Meanwhile, he saw his classmate, Hannah's essay, barely address the prompt yet received praise for writing style.

Professor Linh realized that SpeedGrader learned from biased data that valued writing conventions over ideas for certain groups. She apologized to Jamal and decided to stop using SpeedGrader, recognizing that AI requires careful testing to avoid reflecting prejudices. This experience taught her not to treat technology as an automatic shortcut, but to ensure that it aligns with the principles of equity and inclusion when applied in the classroom.

As educators at a public university, we find these hypothetical scenarios deeply concerning. Each highlights the real danger that, if we are not proactive, AI tools can easily perpetuate systemic discrimination in insidious ways. We believe this goes against the core values of those who center their work on equity and social justice. While efficiency is important, we must prioritize inclusive design and continuous testing to ensure that AI expands, not limits, opportunities for marginalized students. Further, we believe that our shared duty as a public institution is to leverage technology ethically to counter bias and promote access. When applied thoughtfully, AI can assist in this vital work. However, it requires centering student representation from the start, not as an afterthought.

However, given the ethical risks and concerns raised in this chapter, researchers of generative AI such as ChatGPT have begun to address some of these potential discriminatory biases. Because biased data frequently return biased results, different methods of sampling and augmenting data can address this root issue. For example, Canadian researchers created a framework to estimate the underlying data distribution for disadvantaged groups. In this way, they believe that those who design applications can better understand the inherent biases of LLMs, determine the amount of data needed for each group, and therefore mitigate the biases without degrading accuracy (Abusitta et al., 2019). Similarly, a team at Harvard and MIT introduced a debiasing algorithm for facial detection applications to reduce representational biases (Amini et al., 2019). From our point of view as educators, a trio of education technology researchers suggests that we supplement these technical approaches with human-centered practices, such as empowering stakeholders, infusing cultural responsiveness into evidence-based decisions, developing new analytic methods, building capacity through training, and adopting inclusive frameworks (Dieterle et al., 2022). While AI promises benefits, proactive efforts are needed to ensure ethical and equitable implementation. This requires addressing divides, ranging from access to representation to interpretation. By equipping learners and educators to navigate AI systems judiciously, their benefits can be harnessed, while reducing harm. Conscious design and thoughtful usage are vital for translating the promise of AI in education into inclusive and empowering reality.

Therefore, as noted in these cases, and despite the debiasing efforts of AI systems, it is important to understand that these biases still exist and that AI assistants can respond to college students in undesirable and biased ways (OpenAI, 2023), which can limit the inclusion of diverse and cultural thought perspectives. For this reason, it is important to include diverse training data that are more representative of populations in generative AI systems to prevent further perpetuation of discrimination biases (OpenAI, 2023) that can negatively impact students, such as during college admissions or when evaluating student assignments.

RECOMMENDATIONS IN RESPONDING TO AI ETHICAL RISKS AND DISCRIMINATORY BIAS

Considering the potential ethical risks and discriminatory biases that can occur when using generative AI, instructors need to address and prevent potential risks in the classroom. As educators are being challenged with a variety of new generative AI issues in their classrooms, it is important to prepare for and prohibit potential risks and biases. The following includes a set of recommendations for responding to ethical risks and biases:

Be Transparent With the Students

Faculty members can employ a variety of transparency strategies involving generative AI in their classrooms. For instance, faculty members can create or use institutional policies involving the use of generative AI in the classroom. These policy statements can be communicated in the syllabus to allow students to understand how generative AI can be used in the classroom with a clear rationale. Sample learning application programs that incorporate AI, such as ChatGPT 3.0 or Google Bard, may be discussed. Facilitating discussions during the first day of class and course assignment introductions can also help students understand how generative AI is to be used in the classroom. The faculty can also train their students on generative AI to understand its functions in the classroom. Informing students on the definitions of generative AI and how they can be used to enhance their learning can be beneficial in promoting students' academic success.

Provide an Inclusive Statement

To ensure that diverse students feel included, faculty can provide an inclusive statement involving the use of generative AI in their syllabus. This can help students understand that diversity is valued in the classroom. Statements can also help inform students of the limitations (e.g., biases and discrimination) of generative AI in adapting to different cultures and experiences.

A sample statement from one of our course syllabi reads:

Our class may incorporate generative AI tools such as ChatGPT 3.0, to enhance and support student learning. While AI holds great promise, current systems have limitations in fully understanding and representing diverse human experiences and perspectives. AI algorithms can exhibit biased tendencies or generate harmful content that is discriminatory toward marginalized groups.

I am committed to fostering an inclusive learning environment for all students to adapt AI technology responsibly. We will assess the AI-generated content with a critical lens before application. Students are encouraged to provide feedback on any AI bias observed, so that appropriate adjustments can be made. Our shared goal is to harness AI to expand access to knowledge, while upholding the principles of academic scholarship, equity, and social justice.

AI is an evolving tool with paid options available, such as ChatGPT 4.0 and Claude Pro, and we, as ethical leaders, have an opportunity to guide its development that honors our shared humanity. This course models critical and creative approaches to AI that amplify diverse voices and counter-dominant narratives. Data are not neutral; they reflect societal power dynamics and norms that can exclude minority voices and perspectives. Please answer any questions or concerns regarding the role of AI tools in learning.

Train Students to Adhere to Copyright Laws Through Academic Integrity

The faculty can also guide students regarding copyright laws in relation to generative AI. For example, faculty members can also teach students how to correctly cite generative AI in their courses using their preferred writing style (i.e., American Psychological Association, Modern Language Association, Harvard, etc.) to provide AI with appropriate credit. The faculty can demonstrate appropriate citation standards during class by having students complete in-class exercises and activities. Institutional librarians can also be invited to classrooms to cover generative AI citation practices. By establishing academic integrity standards in the classroom, students may be more likely to adhere to providing proper credit for generative AI. Further, the negative consequences of violating copyright laws should be clearly explained to students, such as assignment failure and potential litigation. Implementing these practices can prevent student misunderstandings, unintentional plagiarism, and/or cheating.

Use Generative AI Cheating Detectors

With the increase in cheating and plagiarism using generative AI (e.g., ChatGPT and Google Bard), faculties need to use generative AI cheating detectors. Because there is a false positivity rate for most cheating detectors (Sadasivan et al., 2023), it is important for faculty to use multiple AI cheating detectors before accusing their students of cheating and/or plagiarism. Most U.S. institutions have adopted Turnitin to detect student plagiarism using generative AI; however, it has an accuracy rate of 98% (Henebery, 2023). This suggests that students may be falsely accused of cheating and/or plagiarism, which can lead to negative consequences for innocent students. As such, other software can be used, such as GPT Zero, Content at Scale, and Winston AI, among several other detection platforms, to support a faculty member's accusation against any student (Marshall, 2023).

Protect Students' Private Information

It is important to protect students' private information when using generative AI. Faculty must remain compliant with the Family Educational Rights and Privacy Act (FERPA, 2021), which states that faculty should not provide students' personal information to third parties, such as educational records (e.g., grades, advising notes, contact information) (U.S. Department of Education, 2021). As such, if faculty members use generative AI for assessment purposes, it is important to anonymize assignments. Faculty can also make students aware that if they use generative AI, they need to be careful in providing their personal information, since it can become easily accessible to the public.

Ensure Equal Access by Sharing Resources

To prevent the lack of equal access to generative AI in the classroom, instructors can ensure that their classrooms offer equal access. Instructors can share external generative AI hyperlinks and multicultural resources with their students using learning management systems (e.g., Blackboard, Canvas) and/or physical resource handouts. For instance, faculty members can share different types of generative AI that are useful in their courses for writing, images, videos, and PowerPoints. If students lack internet access, faculty can also share resources to provide them with access, such as free Wi-Fi spots and reduced internet alternatives.

Be Inclusive of Diverse Materials

Because of the potential diversity limitations of generative AI, faculty can overcome them by incorporating diverse materials into their lessons and classrooms. For instance, faculty members can assign readings authored by international and multicultural authors from a variety of diverse perspectives. Faculty members can also use cross-cultural multimedia examples such as images, videos, and animations that represent diverse populations. Seeking the input of diverse students based on their experiences can also help incorporate valuable diverse materials into their curriculum.

Encourage Autonomy and Critical Thinking

In the classroom, students need to be empowered to have autonomy when using generative AI, such that their critical thinking is valued highly over blindly accepting generative AI content as legitimate. Students need to develop skills in asking high-quality questions and evaluating the quality of the content provided by generative AI systems. Students can use multiple generative AI resources in combination with their own institutional library databases to ensure that the material passes the CRAAP test, which assesses the currency, relevance, authority, accuracy, and purpose of the content (Blakeslee, 2004).

While these recommendations are not exhaustive, they can help faculty overcome the current ethical risks in generative AI use. From a professor's perspective, faculty need to educate students on the proper use of generative AI in their own classrooms, whether free or paid, and to discuss potential ethical risks and limitations with students. The greater the autonomy that faculty and students take in using generative AI for genuine learning and professional growth, the better the potential educational outcomes. Faculty and students need to partner in using generative AI ethically, based on the learning outcomes of their respective classrooms.

FUTURE RESEARCH AND CONCLUSION

AI has infiltrated almost all industries. AI is changing lives and disrupting the status quo. AI is a constant in the news cycle and a mainstay in society. AI perpetuates stereotypes. These are all points brought about in this chapter based on previous research, with a specific focus on the ethics, discrimination, and bias that generative AI tools often present against diverse college students.

As the literature shows, AI often generates outputs that include implicit biases because of the development of tools by humans (Mattas, 2023). As a result, diverse populations suffer in various ways, including the perpetuation of stereotypes (Powles, 2020), an absence of culture in AI-generated data (Ray, 2023), and a hindrance to diverse students' learning and proper assessment of their efforts because of the numerous inaccuracies that generative AI data frequently produce (Müller et al., 2019; Ray, 2023; Selwyn, 2019).

As outlined in this chapter, AI negatively affects diverse populations from various age groups (Stypinska, 2023), ethnicities, cultural backgrounds (Baker & Hawn, 2022; Herold, 2022; Liang et al., 2023; Perry & Lee, 2019), gender identity and sexual orientation (Buolamwini, 2019; Leufer, 2023), and disability (Kharbat et al., 2021; Quinn, 2021). However, there are many scholars and industry professionals advocating for a better understanding of how AI can be inclusive and useful for all (Frąckiewicz, 2023; Liang et al., 2023).

This chapter also provides practical guidance for educators if they choose to use generative AI platforms in their classrooms or for assignments. These suggestions include open dialogue between instructors and students regarding the use of AI in courses; proper training with students on how AI can be used as a learning tool alongside their own critical thinking process; and inclusive practices where diverse students are part of the AI conversation, among numerous other recommendations that allow AI tools, students, and educators to coexist in a meaningful, learning, and inclusive environment.

Future studies in this field should conduct a deep dive into how academic institutions are implementing and handling the impact of generative AI on diverse students, their coursework, and overall learning. There is a concern that using generative AI in the classroom hinders critical thinking. As such, scholars should examine how instructors adapt their assignments and assessments to show how critical thinking is taught while also balancing the use of AI tools. Moreover, how diverse students are being trained in terms of how to use generative AI tools is worthy of scholarship, as many diverse students are part of the digital divide and may not have been exposed to AI tools prior to attending an institution of higher education. Finally, more research needs to be conducted on students who are falsely accused of using generative AI tools. This is especially harmful to international students who are often non-native English speakers and who are not proficient in Western society ways of writing; thus, they are often unjustly targeted as plagiarizing using AI tools.

REFERENCES

AbusittaA.AimeurE.WahabO. A. (2019). Generative adversarial networks for mitigating biases in machine learning systems. Cornell University Library. *ArXiv.* http://arxiv.org/abs/1905.09972

Aljabani, M., Ghazi, M., Ali, A., & Abed, S. (2023). ChatGPT: Open possibilities. *Iraqui Journal for Computer Science and Mathematics*, *4*, 62–64. doi:10.52866/IJCSM.2023.01.01.0018

Amani, S., White, L., Balart, T., Arora, L., Shryock, K. J., Brumbelow, K., & Watson, K. L. (2023). Generative AI perceptions: A survey to measure to perceptions of faculty, staff, and students on generative AI tools in academia. *arXiv, 1*, 1–17. https://arxiv.org/abs/2304.14415

Amini, A., Soleimany, A. P., Schwarting, W., Bhatia, S. N., & Rus, D. L. (2019). Uncovering and mitigating algorithmic bias through learned latent structure. *Proceedings of the 2019 AAAI/ACM Conference on AI, Ethics, and Society.* 289–295. 10.1145/3306618.3314243

Baker, R. S., & Hawn, A. (2022). Algorithmic bias in education. *International Journal of Artificial Intelligence in Education*, *32*(4), 1–41. doi:10.1007/s40593-021-00285-9

Blakeslee, S. (2004). The CRAAP test. *LOEX Quarterly, 31*(4). https://commons.emich.edu/loexquarterly/vol31/iss3/4/

Bozkurt, A., & Sharma, R. C. (2023). Challenging the status quo and exploring the new boundaries in the age of algorithms: Reimagining the role of generative AI in distance education and online learning. *Asian Journal of Distance Education*, *18*(1), i–viii.

Brittain, B. (2023). Lawsuits accuse AI content creators of misusing copyright work. *Reuters*. https://www.reuters.com/legal/transactional/lawsuits-accuse-ai-content-creators-misusing-copyrighted-work-2023-01-17/

Buolamwini, J. (2019). Artificial intelligence has a problem with gender and racial bias. Here's how to solve it. *Time*. https://time.com/5520558/artificial-intelligence-racial-gender-bias/

Butcher, A., & McGrath, T. (2004). International students in New Zealand: Needs and responses. *International Education Journal*, *5*(1), 540–551.

Cerf, E. (2023, August 10). *Researchers' tool finds bias in state-of-the-art generative AI model*. UC Santa Cruz. https://news.ucsc.edu/2023/08/t2iat.html

Chan, C. K. (2023). A comprehensive AI policy education framework for university teaching and learning. *International Journal of Educational Technology in Higher Education*, *20*(38), 38. Advance online publication. doi:10.1186/s41239-023-00408-3

Civil, B. (2023). ChatGPT can hinder students' critical thinking skills: Artificial intelligence is changing how students learn to write. *The Queen's Journal*. https://www.queensjournal.ca/story/2023-03-16/opinions/chatgpt-can-hinder-students-critical-thinking-skills/

Cotton, D. R., Cotton, P. A., & Shipway, R. (2023). Chatting and cheating: Ensuring academic integrity in the era of ChatGPT. *Innovations in Education and Teaching International*, 1–12. Advance online publication. doi:10.1080/14703297.2023.2190148

Daniels, J. (2023). *How generative AI can affect your business' data privacy*. https://www.forbes.com/sites/forbesbusinesscouncil/2023/05/01/how-generative-ai-can-affect-your-business-data-privacy/?sh=6d610b83702d

Dieterle, E., Dede, C., & Walker, M. (2022). The cyclical ethical effects of using artificial intelligence in education. *AI & Society*. Advance online publication. doi:10.1007/s00146-022-01497-w PMID:36185064

Dwivedi, Y. K., Kshetri, N., Hughes, L., Slade, E. L., Jeyaraj, A., Kar, A. K., Baadullah, A. M., Koohang, A., Raghavan, V., Ahuja, M., Albanna, H., Albashrawi, M. A., Al-Busaidi, A. S., Balakrishnan, J., Barlette, Y., Basu, S., Bose, I., Brooks, L., Buhalis, D., ... Wright, R. (2023). "So what if ChatGPT wrote it?" Multidisciplinary perspectives on opportunities, challenges and implications of generative conversational AI for research, practice and policy. *International Journal of Information Management*, *71*(1), 1026242. doi:10.1016/j.ijinfomgt.2023.102642

Education Data Initiative. (2023). *College enrollment & student demographic statistics*. https://educationdata.org/college-enrollment-statistics

Eke, D. O. (2023). ChatGPT and the rise of generative AI: Threat to academic integrity? *Journal of Responsible Technology*, *13*(1), 100060. doi:10.1016/j.jrt.2023.100060

Elish, M. C., & Boyd, D. (2018). Situating methods in the magic of big data and AI. *Communication Monographs*, *85*(1), 57–80. doi:10.1080/03637751.2017.1375130

Euchner, J. (2023). Generative AI. *Research Technology Management*, *66*(3), 71–74. doi:10.1080/08956308.2023.2188861

FERPA. (2021). *Family educational rights and privacy act (FERPA)*. https://www2.ed.gov/policy/gen/guid/fpco/ferpa/index.html

Ferrara, E. (2023). Should ChatGPT be biased? Challenges and risks of bias in large language models. *Machine Learning with Applications, 1*, 1–23. doi:10.48550/arXiv.2304.03738

Foster, D. (2023). *Generative deep learning: Teaching machines to paint, write, compose, and play*. O'Reilly Media, Inc.

Frąckiewicz, M. (2023, May 4). *The power of AI in promoting gender equality in education*. TS2 Space.

Fuchs, K. (2023). Exploring the opportunities and challenges of NLP models in higher education: Is ChatGPT a blessing or a curse? *Frontiers in Education, 8*, 1166682. Advance online publication. doi:10.3389/feduc.2023.1166682

Gillotte, J. L. (2019). Copyright infringement in AI-generated artworks. *U.C. Davis Law Review, 53*(1), 2655–2676.

Gupta, M., Akiri, C., Aryal, K., Parker, E., & Praharaj, L. (2023). From ChatGPT to threatGPT: Impact of generative AI in cybersecurity and privacy. *IEEE Access : Practical Innovations, Open Solutions, 11*, 80218–80245. doi:10.1109/ACCESS.2023.3300381

Henebery, B. (2023). New AI detector spots ChatGPT content with 98% accuracy. *The Educator*. https://www.theeducatoronline.com/k12/news/new-ai-detector-spots-chatgpt-content-with-98-accuracy/282285

Herold, B. (2022, April 12). Why schools need to talk about racial bias in AI-powered technologies. *Education Week*. https://www.edweek.org/leadership/why-schools-need-to-talk-about-racial-bias-in-ai-powered-technologies/2022/04

Introducing ChatGPT. (n.d.). *OpenAI.com*. https://openai.com/blog/chatgpt

Iskender, A. (2023). Holy or unholy? Interview with open AI's ChatGPT. *European Journal of Tourism Research, 34*, 3414. doi:10.54055/ejtr.v34i.3169

Jeon, J., & Lee, S. (2023). Large language models in education: A focus on the complementary relationship between human teachers and ChatGPT. *Education and Information Technologies, 28*(12), 15873–15892. doi:10.1007/s10639-023-11834-1

Kasneci, E., Sessler, K., Küchemann, S., Bannert, M., Dementieva, D., Fischer, F., Gasser, U., Groh, G., Günnemann, S., Hüllermeier, E., Krusche, S., Kutyniok, G., Michaeli, T., Nerdel, C., Pfeffer, J., Poquet, O., Sailer, M., Schmidt, A., Seidel, T., ... Kasneci, G. (2023). ChatGPT for good? On opportunities and collages of large language models for education. *Learning and Individual Differences, 103*(1), 102274. doi:10.1016/j.lindif.2023.102274

Khan, A., Jawaid, M., Khan, A., & Sajjad, M. (2023). ChatGPT-reshaping medical education and clinical management. *Pakistan Journal of Medical Sciences, 39*(2), 605–607. doi:10.12669/pjms.39.2.7653 PMID:36950398

Kharbat, F. F., Alshawabkeh, A., & Woolsey, M. L. (2021). Identifying gaps in using artificial intelligence to support students with intellectual disabilities from education and health perspectives. *Aslib Journal of Information Management, 73*(1), 101–128. doi:10.1108/AJIM-02-2020-0054

Leufer, D. (2023, January 13). *Computers are binary, people are not: How AI systems undermine LGBTQ identity.* Access Now. https://www.accessnow.org/how-ai-systems-undermine-lgbtq-identity/

Liang, W., Yuksekgonul, M., Mao, Y., Wu, E., & Zou, J. (2023). GPT detectors are biased against non-native English writers. *Patterns, 4*(7), 100779. doi:10.1016/j.patter.2023.100779

Manyika, J., Silberg, J., & Presten, B. (2019). What do we do about the biases in AI? *Harvard Business Review.* https://hbr.org/2019/10/what-do-we-do-about-the-biases-in-ai

Marshall, J. (2023). As AI cheating booms, so does the industry detecting it: 'We couldn't keep up with the demand.' *The Guardian.* https://www.theguardian.com/technology/2023/jul/05/as-ai-cheating-booms-so-does-the-industry-detecting-it-we-couldnt-keep-up-with-demand

Martindale, J. (2023). *These are the countries where ChatGPT is currently banned.* https://www.digitaltrends.com/computing/these-countries-chatgpt-banned/

Mattas, P. S. (2023). ChatGPT: A study of AI language processing and its implications. *International Journal of Research Publication and Reviews, 4*(2), 435–440. doi:10.55248/gengpi.2023.4218

Merton, R. K. (1968). The Matthew effect in science. *Science, 159*(3810), 56–63. doi:10.1126/science.159.3810.56 PMID:5634379

Mhlanga, D. (2023). Open AI in education, the responsible and ethical use of ChatGPT toward lifelong learning. SSRN *Electronic Journal.* doi:10.2139/ssrn.4354422

Mohammadkarimi, E. (2023). Teachers' reflections on academic dishonesty in EFL students' writing in the era of artificial intelligence. *Journal of Applied Learning & Learning, 6*(2). Advance online publication. doi:10.37074/jalt.2023.6.2.10

Müller, C., Kratzwald, S., & Neubauer, A. (2019). Chatbot in customer service – A systematic literature. *Business & Information Systems Engineering, 61*(4), 367–378.

National Center for Education Statistics. (2023). College Enrollment Rates. In *Condition of Education.* U.S. Department of Education, Institute of Education Sciences. https://nces.ed.gov/programs/coe/indicator/cpb

Olaniyi, E., Olawale, W., Emeka, O., Olawe, A., Raymond, A., & Sesan, A. (2023). ChatGPT impacts on access-efficiency, employment, education and ethics: The socio-economics of an AI language model. *BizEcons Quarterly, 16*(1), 1–17. https://ideas.repec.org/a/ris/buecqu/0032.html

Open, A. I. (2023). *ChatGPT* [Large language model]. https://chat.openai.com/chat

Palmarini, N., Martie, L., Wasiak, M. F., & Zhang, G. (2019). Exclusion Spotter: Applying advances in AI to identify ageism in online job posting. *Innovation in Aging, 3*(Supplement_1), S763–S763. doi:10.1093/geroni/igz038.2805

Pearman, F. A., Curran, F. C., Gardella, J., & Fisher, B. (2019). Are achievement gaps related to discipline gaps? Evidence from national data. *AERA Open*, *5*(4). doi:10.1177/2332858419875440

Perry, A. M., & Lee, N. T. (2019 September 26). *AI is coming to schools and if we're not careful so will its biases.* Brookings. https://www.brookings.edu/articles/ai-is-coming-to-schools-and-if-were-not-careful-so-will-its-biases/

Petrosyan, A. (2023). Countries with the most people lacking internet connection 2023. *Statista.* https://www.statista.com/statistics/1155552/countries-highest-number-lacking-internet/

Powles, J. (2020). *The ethics of artificial intelligence.* Cambridge University Press.

Quinn, G. (2021). *The right of people with disabilities.* The United Nations. https://www.ohchr.org/sites/default/files/2022-02/Easy-Read-AI-disabilities-report.pdf

Ray, P. P. (2023). ChatGPT: A comprehensive review on background, applications, key challenges, bias, ethics, limitations and future scope. *Internet of Things and Cyber-Physical Systems*, *3*, 121–154. doi:10.1016/j.iotcps.2023.04.003

Rodgers, W., Murray, J. M., Stefanidis, A., Degbey, W. Y., & Tarba, S. Y. (2023). An artificial intelligence algorithmic approach to ethical decision-making in human resource management processes. *Human Resource Management Review*, *33*(1), 100925. doi:10.1016/j.hrmr.2022.100925

Sadasivan, V. S., Kumar, A., Balasubramanian, S., Wang, W., & Feizi, S. (2023). Can AI-generated text be reliably detected? *ArXiv*, *11156*(2), 1–23.

Sallam, M. (2023). ChatGPT utility in healthcare education, research, and practice: Systematic review on the promising perspectives and valid concerns. *Health Care*, *11*(6), 887. doi:10.3390/healthcare11060887 PMID:36981544

Sample, I. (2023, July 10). Programs to detect AI discriminate against non-native English speakers, shows study: Over half of essays written by people were wrongly flagged as AI-made, with implications for students and job applicants. *The Guardian.* https://www.theguardian.com/technology/2023/jul/10/programs-to-detect-ai-discriminate-against-non-native-english-speakers-shows-study

Scharth, M. (2022). *The ChatGPT chatbot is blowing people away with its writing skills. An expert explains why it's so impressive.* https://theconversation.com/the-chatgpt-chatbot-is-blowing-people-away-with-its-writing-skills-an-expert-explains-why-its-so-impressive-195908

Schwartz, R., Vassilev, A., Greene, K., Perine, L., Burt, A., & Hall, P. (2022). *Towards a standard for identifying and managing bias in artificial intelligence.* National Institute of Standards and Technology., doi:10.6028/NIST.SP.1270

Selwyn, N. (2019). *Should robots replace teachers?: AI and the future of education.* John Wiley & Sons.

Sok, S., & Heng, K. (2023). ChatGPT for education and research: A review of benefits and risks. *Cambodian Journal of Educational Research*, *3*(1), 110–121. doi:10.62037/cjer.2023.03.01.06

Spector, C. (2019, October 16). Racial disparities in school discipline are linked to the achievement gap between Black and white students nationwide, according to Stanford-led study. *Research Stories.* Stanford Graduate School of Education. https://ed.stanford.edu/news/racial-disparities-school-discipline-are-linked-achievement-gap-between-black-and-white

Stypinska, J. (2023). AI ageism: A critical roadmap for studying age discrimination and exclusion in digitalized societies. *AI & Society, 38*(2), 665–677. doi:10.1007/s00146-022-01553-5 PMID:36212226

Sullivan, M., Kelly, A., & McLaughlan, P. (2023). ChatGPT in higher education: Considerations for academic integrity and student learning. *Journal of Applied Learning & Teaching, 6*(1), 31–40. doi:10.37074/jalt.2023.6.1.17

Tadesse, G. A., Cintas, C., Varshney, K. R., Staar, P., Agunwa, C., Speakman, S., Jia, J., Bailey, E. E., Adelekun, A., Lipoff, J. B., Onyekaba, G., Lester, J. C., Rotemberg, V., Zou, J., & Daneshjou, R. (2023). Skin Tone Analysis for Representation in Educational Materials (STAR-ED) using machine learning. *NPJ Digital Medicine, 6*(1), 151. Advance online publication. doi:10.1038/s41746-023-00881-0 PMID:37596324

Tam, W., Huynh, T., Tang, A., Luong, S., Khatri, Y., & Zhou, W. (2023). Nursing education in the age of artificial intelligence powered Chatbots (AI-chatbots): Are we ready yet? *Nurse Education Today, 129*, 105917. doi:10.1016/j.nedt.2023.105917 PMID:37506622

Tlili, A., Shehata, B., Adarkwah, M. A., Bozkurt, A., Hickey, D. T., Huang, R., & Agyemang, B. (2023). What if the devil is my guardian angel: ChatGPT as a case study of using chatbots in education. *Smart Learning and Environment, 10*(15), 15. Advance online publication. doi:10.1186/s40561-023-00237-x

U.S. Department of Education. (2023). *Family educational rights and privacy act (FERPA).* https://www2.ed.gov/policy/gen/guid/fpco/ferpa/index.html

Wach, K., Duong, C. D., Ejdys, J., Kazlauskaite, R., Korzynski, P., Mazurek, G., Paliszkiewicz, J., & Ziemba, E. (2023). The dark side of generative artificial intelligence: A critical analysis of controversies and risks of ChatGPT. *Entrepreneurial Business and Economics Review, 11*(2), 7–30. doi:10.15678/EBER.2023.110201

Wang, T., Lund, B. D., Marengo, A., Pagano, A., Mannuru, N. R., Teel, Z. A., & Pange, J. (2023). Exploring the potential impact of artificial intelligence (AI) on international students in higher education: Generative AI, chatbots, analytics, and international student success. *Applied Sciences (Basel, Switzerland), 13*(11), 6716. doi:10.3390/app13116716

Wang, Y., & Kosinski, M. (2018). Deep neural networks are more accurate than humans at detecting sexual orientation from facial images. *Journal of Personality and Social Psychology, 114*(2), 246–257. doi:10.1037/pspa0000098 PMID:29389215

Wardat, Y., Tashtoush, M. A., AlAli, R., & Jarrah, A. M. (2023). ChatGPT: A revolutionary tool for teaching and learning mathematics. *Eurasia Journal of Mathematics, Science and Technology Education, 19*(7), em2286. Advance online publication. doi:10.29333/ejmste/13272

WarschauerM.TsengW.YimS.WebsterT.JacobS.DuQ.TateT. (2023). *The affordances and contradictions of AI-generated text for second language writers.* doi:10.2139/ssrn.4404380

Welding, L. (2023). Half of college students say using AI on schoolwork is cheating or plagiarism. *Best Colleges*. https://www.bestcolleges.com/research/college-students-ai-tools-survey/

Whittaker, Z. (2019). OpenAI built a text generator so good, it's consider too dangerous to release. *Techcrunch*. https://teachcrunch.com/2019/02/17/openai-text-generator-dangerous/

Wu, X. (2021). Application of artificial intelligence in higher vocational English teaching mode. *Journal of Physics: Conference Series*, *1852*(2), 1–6. doi:10.1088/1742-6596/1852/2/022089

Yu, H., & Guo, Y. (2023). Generative artificial intelligence empowers educational reform: Current status, issues, and prospects. *Frontiers in Education*, *8*(1), 1183162. Advance online publication. doi:10.3389/feduc.2023.1183162

Zhou, T. Y., Huang, Y., Chen, C., & Xing, Z. (2023). Exploring AI ethics of ChatGPT: A diagnostic analysis. *arXiv preprint arXiv: 2301.12867*. doi:/arXiv.2301.12867 doi:10.48550

Chapter 11
Charting the Ethical Course:
Navigating AI Advancements in Communication Education

Huong-Tra Le-Nguyen
https://orcid.org/0000-0003-4718-8920
Hanoi University, Vietnam

Trung Thanh Tran
https://orcid.org/0000-0002-4630-1146
Clientscan, Vietnam

ABSTRACT

Generative AI tools have emerged as transformative resources in the realm of communication education. These tools harness the power of artificial intelligence to assist students and educators in various aspects of communication studies, including writing, public speaking, and media production. At their core, generative AI tools are designed to generate human-like text, speech, or visuals autonomously, replicating and augmenting the capabilities of human communication. They encompass a range of applications, from chatbots that facilitate communication skill development to language models that assist in content creation and editing. These tools are becoming increasingly prevalent in communication classrooms, providing unique opportunities for personalized learning, skill enhancement, and creativity.

Generative AI tools have emerged as transformative resources in communication education. These tools harness the power of artificial intelligence to assist students and educators in various aspects of communication studies including writing, public speaking, and media production (Chen et al., 2020a). At their core, generative AI tools are designed to autonomously generate human-like text, speech, or visuals, replicating and augmenting the capabilities of human communication. They encompass a range of applications, from chatbots that facilitate communication skill development, to language models that assist in content creation and editing. These tools are becoming increasingly prevalent in communication classrooms, providing unique opportunities for personalized learning, skill enhancement, and creativity.

DOI: 10.4018/979-8-3693-0831-8.ch011

A hallmark feature of generative AI tools is their ability to aid students in honing their communication skills. For instance, in writing courses, these tools can provide immediate feedback on grammar, style, and clarity, allowing students to refine their writing precisely. In public speaking classes, AI-driven speech analysis tools can evaluate parameters such as tone, pace, and body language, thus providing invaluable insights for improvement. Additionally, generative AI can be harnessed to create lifelike conversational agents, enabling students to practice dialogue and interviews in a controlled and supportive environment. This aspect of AI in communication education fosters skill development through repetition and constructive feedback, boosting students' confidence and competence (Chien & Hwang, 2023).

Moreover, generative AI tools excel in terms of content generation and curation. They can swiftly generate written content, summaries, or transcriptions, reducing the time educators spend on administrative tasks, and allowing them to focus on teaching. For journalism and media studies, AI can assist in sifting through vast datasets to identify relevant information and trends, thereby aiding students in research and reporting (Zhang & Aslan, 2021). In advertising and marketing courses, AI algorithms can recommend content strategies based on consumer behavior analysis, thereby providing students with real-world insights into effective communication strategies. Furthermore, AI-generated content is not confined to text; it extends to multimedia, including image and video creation, and contributes to a holistic learning experience in communication studies.

However, the integration of generative AI tools into communication education is not without challenges or ethical considerations. As these tools rely on vast datasets, they may inadvertently perpetuate the biases present in the training data, potentially reinforcing stereotypes or promoting unethical content. Ensuring ethical use and minimizing bias in AI-generated materials are paramount for educators. Additionally, there are concerns regarding overreliance on AI, potentially hindering critical thinking and creativity in students. Balancing the benefits of AI tools with traditional pedagogical methods and ethical guidelines is a pressing issue (Dignum, 2018).

Similarly, generative AI tools represent a promising frontier in communication education, offering unparalleled opportunities for skill development, content generation, and data analysis. When thoughtfully integrated and ethically guided, these tools can empower both students and educators to effectively navigate the evolving landscape of communication studies effectively (Hsu et al., 2023). Nevertheless, a nuanced approach is necessary to address ethical concerns and strike a balance between AI-assisted learning and traditional teaching methodologies. As technology continues to advance, communication educators must adapt and harness the potential of generative AI to prepare students for the complexities of communication in the digital age.

THE GROWING USE OF AI IN COMMUNICATION TRAINING

Communication training has entered a new era with the increasing incorporation of Artificial Intelligence (AI) technologies. As the digital landscape evolves, effective communication skills have become more crucial than ever before, spanning diverse fields, from business and journalism to public relations and social media management. AI, with its capacity to process vast amounts of data and simulate human-like interactions, is revolutionizing how students are educated in the art of effective communication (Chen et al., 2023).

One of the primary ways AI reshapes communication training is through personalized learning experiences. AI-powered platforms can analyze individual students' strengths and weaknesses in communication and tailor lesson plans to address specific areas of improvement (Tapalova & Zhiyenbayeva, 2022). For instance, in public speaking courses, AI-driven speech analysis tools can provide real-time feedback on factors such as tone, pace, and nonverbal cues. This personalized guidance allows students to focus on areas where they need the most improvement, thus maximizing the efficiency and effectiveness of their training.

AI also facilitates enhanced content creation and curation in communication education. In writing courses, AI can assist students in refining their writing skills by providing instant feedback on grammar, style, and coherence. In journalism and media studies, AI algorithms can shift through vast amounts of data to identify trends and relevant information, thus streamlining the research process for students. Additionally, AI-generated content, including text, images, and videos, can be used as valuable teaching material, exposing students to a range of communication strategies and media formats (González-Calatayud et al., 2021).

The integration of AI-driven chatbots and virtual assistants also plays a significant role in communication training (Pelletier et al., 2022). These conversational agents create immersive learning environments that enable students to practice their communication skills in a safe and controlled setting. Chatbots can simulate various scenarios such as interviews, negotiations, and customer interactions, allowing students to apply theoretical knowledge to practical situations. This form of experiential learning enhances student confidence and adaptability in real-world communication contexts.

However, the increasing use of AI in communication training is challenging. Ethical considerations regarding AI-generated content and the potential for bias in training materials must be addressed. Educators and institutions must ensure that AI technologies align with the ethical guidelines and promote inclusive and unbiased communication. Additionally, there is a concern about overreliance on AI tools, potentially limiting critical thinking and creativity. Striking the right balance between AI-assisted learning and traditional pedagogy is a complex but necessary task for educators (Murtaza et al., 2022).

AI's growing role of AI in communication training is reshaping the educational landscape, offering personalized learning experiences, efficient content creation, and immersive practice opportunities. These advancements have empowered students to develop effective communication skills that are vital for success in the digital age (Brown et al., 2020). However, educators and institutions must approach this integration carefully, address ethical concerns, and maintain a balance between AI-driven tools and traditional teaching methods. As AI technologies continue to evolve, communication training will likely continue to adapt, preparing students to thrive in an ever-changing world of communication.

THE ETHICAL DIMENSION OF AI IN COMMUNICATION STUDIES

Artificial Intelligence (AI) has ushered in a transformative wave across various industries and communication studies are no exception. Although AI offers a multitude of benefits, it brings with it a complex ethical dimension that demands careful consideration. In the realm of communication studies, AI technologies have the potential to amplify ethical concerns and biases, both in the content produced and in the methodologies employed (OpenAI, n.d.).

One of the foremost ethical challenges faced by AI in communication studies is the generation of biased content. AI algorithms are often trained on vast datasets that may contain inherent biases that reflect the biases of their human creators. When applied to content generation, such as writing news articles or social media posts, AI can inadvertently perpetuate these biases (Chen et al., 2020b). For instance, an

AI-generated news article might unintentionally favor one political group over another, perpetuating a distorted narrative. This raises questions about the responsibility of educators and institutions to vet AI-generated content and ensure that it aligns with the ethical standards of fairness, neutrality, and inclusivity.

Moreover, ethical implications extend to the methodology of using AI in communication research. When employing AI-driven sentiment analysis or opinion mining, researchers must be vigilant about the potential unintended consequences. AI models may misinterpret nuanced human emotions, leading to incorrect conclusions. Furthermore, the collection of massive datasets for AI training can raise privacy concerns because individuals' personal information is often included without consent. Researchers must navigate a fine line between harnessing the power of AI for meaningful insights and safeguarding individuals' privacy rights (Akgun & Greenhow, 2021; Okonkwo & Ade-Ibijola, 2021).

Another ethical concern in AI-enhanced communication studies is the potential of automation to displace human workers, particularly in journalism and media production. As AI tools become more proficient in tasks, such as content creation and curation, there is a risk of job displacement within the industry. Ethical considerations involve ensuring that the integration of AI technologies does not lead to a loss of livelihood for communication professionals. This may involve retraining programs or developing guidelines for responsible AI use that prioritizes human workers' well-being.

Furthermore, transparency and accountability are paramount for the ethical use of AI in communication studies. Users, whether students, researchers, or educators, should have a clear understanding of when AI is employed, and how it influences the educational or research process. This includes transparency in disclosing the use of AI tools for content generation as well as providing students with insights into how AI algorithms function, their limitations, and the potential biases they might introduce (Pedro et al., 2019).

In conclusion, the ethical dimension of AI in communication studies presents a multifaceted challenge. Although AI technologies offer immense potential to advance research and education in communication, they also demand vigilance in ensuring fairness, accuracy, and ethical use. Educators, researchers, and institutions must grapple with these ethical complexities to harness the benefits of AI while upholding ethical standards and safeguarding the integrity of communication studies (Kuhail et al., 2022; Tlili et al., 2023). Addressing these concerns will be pivotal in shaping a future in which AI and communication studies coexist ethically and harmoniously.

UNDERSTANDING GENERATIVE AI TOOLS IN COMMUNICATION EDUCATION

Explanation of Generative AI and Its Relevance in Communication Training

Generative artificial intelligence (AI), a subfield of artificial intelligence (AI), is revolutionizing communication training by offering novel ways to create, enhance, and assess communication skills. Generative AI refers to AI systems capable of autonomously generating human-like text, audio, or visual content autonomously (Studente et al., 2020). These systems, which are often based on deep learning models such as GPT-3, have a remarkable ability to produce coherent and contextually relevant content that closely resembles human-generated communication. This capability is a game changer for communication training (Hristova, 2023).

The relevance of generative AI in communication training stems from its versatility and ability to simulate real-world scenarios. Language models, such as GPT-3, can generate persuasive speeches, engaging narratives, or conversational dialogues that mimic various communication contexts. In a classroom setting, this means that students can practice public speaking, storytelling, or interpersonal communication with AI-generated content as their audience or conversation partners. This offers students a low-pressure environment to refine their skills, experiment with different communication styles, and receive instant feedback (Stevano & Deane, 2019).

Moreover, generative AI enhances personalization during communication training. These AI systems can adapt to the specific needs and goals of each student (Turner, 2010). For example, an AI tutor can generate tailored exercises and prompts to address an individual's weaknesses or areas that require improvement in communication. This personalized approach maximizes the efficiency of training as students receive targeted guidance and practice.

Generative AI also plays a pivotal role in fostering creativity and innovation in communication. It can inspire students by generating novel ideas, innovative marketing campaigns, or compelling narratives that challenge conventional communication norms (Johnson & Harris, 2002). Students can collaborate with AI to brainstorm ideas, refine concepts, and explore the boundaries of creativity in communication projects. This not only enhances their creative thinking, but also prepares them for the evolving landscape of communication professions, which increasingly rely on AI-augmented creativity (Araujo, 2020).

Furthermore, generative AI has the potential to address the issues of inclusivity and accessibility in communication training. AI-powered communication tools can help students with diverse linguistic backgrounds, speech impediments, or communication disorders. They can adapt to different learning paces and styles, ensuring that no students are left behind. Additionally, these tools can facilitate language translation and transcription, making communication education more accessible to global audiences (Dwivedi et al., 2023; Mendoza et al., 2020).

However, the adoption of generative AI in communication training is not without ethical considerations (King, 2023). As these AI systems generate content, there is a need for responsible AI use to ensure that the generated communication aligns with ethical standards, avoids biases, and respects privacy. Educators and institutions must strike a balance between harnessing the potential of AI for communication training and upholding ethical principles (Alam, 2021).

While generative AI holds immense promise in the field of communication training, its ability to simulate diverse communication scenarios, offer personalized guidance, foster creativity, and enhance inclusivity makes it a valuable tool for educators and students alike (Pesonen, 2021). As communication technology continues to evolve, the responsible integration of generative AI can empower the next generation of communicators with the skills and adaptability required for success in an AI-augmented world.

TYPES OF GENERATIVE AI TOOLS USED IN COMMUNICATION CLASSROOMS

Generative AI tools have become indispensable assets in communication classrooms, offering diverse capabilities to enhance teaching and learning experiences (Creswell, 2014). These tools can be broadly categorized into several types, each serving a unique function in the context of communication education.

Content Generation Tools

Content generation tools powered by generative AI models such as GPT-3 excel at creating human-like text, which is particularly useful for developing persuasive speeches, articles, or marketing copies. In communication classrooms, students can leverage these tools to draft compelling narratives, advertisements, or public speeches, allowing them to practice and refine their communication skills using AI-generated content as a foundation.

Chatbots and Virtual Communication Partners

AI-driven chatbots and virtual communication partners simulate real-time conversations, offering students a platform for practicing and enhancing their conversational skills. These tools can be programmed to engage in dialogues, provide feedback, and adapt to various communication scenarios. They are invaluable for improving interpersonal communication, negotiation, and conflict-resolution skills (Følstad & Taylor, 2021).

Speech Synthesis and Voice Assistance

Speech synthesis tools use AI to generate human-like voice recordings, thereby facilitating training in oral communication. Students can use these tools to practice pronunciation, accent reduction, or public speaking. Voice assistants, such as Amazon's Alexa or Google Assistant, can also be incorporated to provide real-time feedback and assist in voice-related exercises (Foerster, 2007).

Interactive Storytelling and Scenario Generators

Generative AI tools can assist in the creation of interactive storytelling experiences or scenario-based simulations. These tools allow students to craft narratives by branching storylines or immersing themselves in virtual communication scenarios. Such applications are valuable for enhancing storytelling skills, empathetic communication, and crisis management (Dwivedi et al., 2019; Dwivedi et al., 2015).

Content Summarization and Analysis

AI tools that summarize and analyze textual content are beneficial for communication students in researching and processing vast amounts of information. These tools can automatically extract key insights from lengthy documents, help students prepare concise reports, synthesize research, and critically analyze communication materials (Almer, 2022; Phillips et al., 2019).

Transcription and Translation Services

Generative AI tools can transcribe spoken language into text and translate the content into multiple languages. This is particularly helpful for language students and international communication programs. Transcription tools ensure accurate records of speeches and presentations, whereas translation services break down language barriers and enable cross-cultural communication (Angelone et al., 2022; Bae et al., 2023; Bang et al., 2023).

Feedback and Assessment Assistants

AI-powered feedback and assessment tools can be used to evaluate students' written or spoken communication for clarity, coherence, and persuasiveness. These tools offer constructive feedback, helping students understand their strengths and areas of improvement. They also assist educators in streamlining the grading process and ensuring consistent and objective evaluations (Bender et al., 2021; Beseiso et al., 2021).

Accessibility and Inclusivity Tools

Generative AI can enhance inclusivity in communication education by providing support to students with disabilities or diverse linguistic backgrounds. These tools can generate closed captions for video content, convert speech to text for hearing-impaired students, and assist non-native speakers in improving their language skills (Bowles & Kruger, 2023).

Although these types of generative AI tools offer numerous advantages in communication classrooms, their integration requires thoughtful consideration of ethical and privacy concerns. It is essential for educators and institutions to establish guidelines for responsible AI use to ensure that the benefits of these tools are harnessed while safeguarding against potential pitfalls and biases in communication education.

EXAMPLES OF AI-ENHANCED COMMUNICATION TRAINING PLATFORMS

AI-enhanced communication training platforms are becoming increasingly prevalent in educational settings and offer innovative ways to develop and refine communication skills. Some notable examples are as follows:

Duolingo

Duolingo, a language-learning platform, uses AI to personalize language instruction. It adapts lessons based on learners' proficiency and provides immediate feedback on their pronunciation, grammar, and vocabulary. It is widely used in language communication classes to improve speaking and listening skills (Brown et al., 2022).

Rosetta Stone

Similar to Duolingo, Rosetta Stone employs AI to provide language learners with an immersive experience. It includes speech recognition technology that evaluates pronunciation and offers real-time feedback (Caines et al., 2023).

Speechify

Speechify is text-to-speech software that aids individuals with reading difficulties or visual impairments. It uses AI to convert written text into spoken words, making it useful for communication courses that require reading large volumes of text (Bulut & Yildirim-Erbasli, 2022).

Babbel

Babbel uses AI to create personalized language lessons, focusing on conversation skills. It emphasizes real-life dialogue and pronunciation practice, making it suitable for communication training (Ehsan et al., 2021).

Zoom and Microsoft Teams

These video conferencing platforms integrate AI features for communication training. They offer virtual classrooms, breakout rooms for group discussions, and features such as automatic transcription and closed captioning, which enhance accessibility and engagement (Buolamwini & Gebru, 2018; Doyle & Ponder, 1977).

Grammarly

Grammarly employed AI to assist users in improving their writing skills. It analyzes text for grammar, punctuation, and style issues, making it valuable for communication courses involving written assignments (Carroll et al., 2022).

Voicery

Voicery is a voice synthesis tool that generates human-like voices for various applications, including language learning and voiceover. They can be used in communication courses to practice voice modulation and speech clarity (Challen et al., 2019).

Mursion

Mursion provides a unique virtual reality platform for communication training. It uses AI-driven avatars to simulate realistic interpersonal interactions, allowing students to practice communication and empathy skills in a safe environment (Chaudhry et al., 2022).

Glose

Glose is an e-reader platform with AI capabilities that facilitate collaborative reading and annotation. It is particularly useful in literature and communication courses, enabling students to engage in discussions and analyze texts collectively (Chechitelli, 2023).

PitchVantage

PitchVantage was designed for public speaking courses. It employs AI to assess and provide feedback on students' oral presentations, including tone, pacing, and body language (Condor et al., 2021).

Kaltura

Kaltura offers video-based learning solutions to educational institutions. It incorporates AI for video analytics, enabling educators to track student engagement and interactions with video content, which can be valuable in multimedia communication courses using multimedia (Drori et al., 2022).

Pear Deck

Pear Deck is an interactive presentation platform that integrates tools, such as Google Slides. It uses AI to facilitate active learning and student engagement during presentations, discussions, and Q&A sessions (Gašević et al., 2022).

These AI-enhanced communication training platforms cater to various aspects of communication, from language acquisition to public speaking, and beyond. They not only provide valuable resources for educators, but also empower students to develop effective communication skills in diverse contexts.

ETHICAL CONSIDERATIONS IN COMMUNICATION EDUCATION

The Significance of Ethics in Communication Training

Ethics play a pivotal role in communication training, influencing the way individuals interact, convey information, and build relationships. In the realm of education, the significance of ethics cannot be overstated, especially as communication technologies evolve and expand (Gilson et al., 2023). Ethics in communication training encompass a wide range of principles and considerations that guide both educators and learners in their quest for effective and responsible communication.

First, ethical communication training fosters trust and respect. Students must learn not only how to convey their ideas effectively, but also to do so with integrity and sensitivity. This includes respecting the diversity of perspectives, backgrounds, and experiences within a classroom as well as the broader societal context. Ethical communication values inclusivity and encourages open dialogue where all voices are heard and respected, helping students develop empathetic and socially conscious communicators (Gebru et al., 2021).

Moreover, ethics in communication training extend to the responsible use of technology. As digital communication tools become increasingly prevalent, students must understand the ethical implications of online interactions. These include issues related to privacy, online harassment, cyberbullying, and the spread of misinformation. Ethical communication training equips students with the critical thinking skills needed to navigate the complexities of the digital landscape, while upholding ethical standards (Holmes & Porayska-Pomsta, 2022).

In addition, ethical communication training addresses the importance of transparency and honesty. In a world where misinformation can spread rapidly, it is crucial for students to discern credible sources of information and communicate truthfully and accurately. Ethical communication encourages citing sources, fact-checking, and acknowledgement when knowledge is limited. These practices not only promote responsible communication but also contribute to the overall quality of discourse in society (Hwang & Tu, 2021).

Furthermore, ethics in communication training underscore the significance of informed consent in various contexts. This is particularly relevant in fields such as journalism, public relations, and health-care. Students learned the importance of obtaining consent when sharing personal stories, conducting interviews, or using individuals' images or information. Ethical communication respects individuals' autonomy and right to control how their stories and data are shared (Holstein et al., 2019).

Lastly, ethics in communication training prepares students to grapple with ethical dilemmas that may arise in their careers. They develop skills to navigate situations where values and interests may conflict, such as in crisis communication or public relations campaigns. Ethical training equips students with decision-making frameworks and encourages them to consider the potential consequences of their communication choices for various stakeholders (Jayaraman & Black, 2022).

Ethics are the foundation upon which effective, responsible, and empathetic communication is built. In communication training, ethics guides students in developing the knowledge, skills, and values necessary to become ethical communicators who contribute positively to their professions and society at large. As communication continues to evolve, the significance of ethics in education remains steady, ensuring that the next generation of communicators are equipped to navigate the complex ethical terrain of the modern world.

ETHICAL PRINCIPLES AND FRAMEWORKS APPLICABLE TO COMMUNICATION STUDIES

In communication studies, ethical principles and frameworks serve as essential compasses, guiding scholars, practitioners, and students alike in navigating the intricate web of human interaction (Kasneci et al., 2023). These principles underpin the essence of ethical communication and play a pivotal role in fostering responsible, respectful, and socially conscious communicators.

Truthfulness is one of the foundational principles of communication ethics. The pursuit of truth is paramount in any communication endeavor, whether journalism, public relations, interpersonal communication, or digital media. Truthfulness refers to conveying accurate information and refraining from deceiting or manipulation. This principle ensures that messages are reliable and trustworthy, laying the groundwork for informed decision making in society (Khosravi et al., 2022).

Transparency is also closely related to truthfulness. Ethical communication demands transparency in disclosing information sources, potential conflicts of interest, and the intentions behind a message (Zheng et al., 2022). Transparency fosters trust between communicators and their audiences as it allows individuals to assess the credibility and motivations behind the information they receive. Transparency is the beacon of integrity in a world inundated with information.

Respect for individual autonomy and privacy is another cornerstone of communication ethics. This principle recognizes that individuals have the right to control their personal information and narratives of their lives. In practice, it means seeking informed consent when sharing personal stories, images, or data, and respecting boundaries in communication contexts such as journalism, where sensitivity to grief and trauma is essential (Zheng et al., 2023).

The principle of inclusivity underscores the importance of embracing diversity and representing marginalized voices. In an increasingly globalized and interconnected world, communicators must recognize and respect the multitude of perspectives and experiences that exist. Ethical communication strives to amplify these voices and promote social justice and equity by addressing systemic biases and underrepresented narratives (Zeng et al., 2023).

In some cases, ethical communication principles are operationalized through frameworks that provide practical guidance. For instance, the Society of Professional Journalists (SPJ) Code of Ethics outlines ethical guidelines for journalists, emphasizing accuracy, fairness, and accountability. Similarly, the Global Alliance for Public Relations and Communication Management presents the Barcelona Principles, which guide public relations professionals in the transparent and ethical measurement and evaluation of communication campaigns.

In academic settings, scholars of communication studies often draw upon ethical frameworks such as the Potter Box, which helps individuals analyze ethical dilemmas by considering values, principles, and loyalties. These frameworks provide structured approaches to addressing complex ethical challenges, encouraging thoughtful reflection and decision-making (Yan et al., 2022).

Overall, ethical principles and frameworks in communication studies form the foundation of responsible and impactful communication. They equip communicators with tools to navigate the ever-evolving landscape of media, technology, and societal norms while upholding the values of truth, transparency, respect, and inclusivity. As communication continues to shape our world, these ethical principles remain indispensable in ensuring that the messages we send and receive contribute to a more informed, just and empathetic society.

NAVIGATING THE INTERSECTION OF TECHNOLOGY AND ETHICAL COMMUNICATION

In the contemporary world, the intersection of technology and ethical communication has become increasingly intricate, presenting exciting opportunities and profound challenges. As technology continues to evolve at an unprecedented pace, it significantly alters the landscape of how we communicate, share information, and interact with one another. At the heart of this transformation lies the imperative to uphold ethical principles, ensuring that technology enhances, rather than diminishes, the quality of discourse and connections.

One of the central ethical considerations in the digital age is the preservation of privacy. The vast amounts of personal data generated and collected through digital platforms have raised critical questions regarding who has access to our information and how it is used. Ethical communication in technology mandates commitment to data privacy and security. Striking a balance between the convenience and personalization offered by technology and safeguarding individual privacy rights is a formidable task that demands ongoing vigilance (Wu et al., 2023).

Additionally, the democratization of information through the Internet has fostered both the spread of knowledge and proliferation of disinformation. Navigating this landscape requires critical digital literacy. Ethical communicators must empower individuals to discern credible sources from fake news, navigate echo chambers, and engage in constructive dialogue from diverse perspectives. Education involves equipping students with media literacy tools to become responsible digital citizens (Kooli, 2023).

Moreover, inclusivity and equity are ethical imperatives in technology-driven communication. Innovations, such as artificial intelligence and machine learning, can inadvertently perpetuate biases present in training data, potentially amplifying social inequalities (Wu, 2022). Ethical communicators must actively work to identify and mitigate these biases, ensuring that technology serves all members of society, rather than reinforcing discrimination.

Transparency remains the cornerstone of ethical communication within the technological sphere. Tech companies and organizations must be transparent about their algorithms, data practices, and the potential impact of their technologies. This transparency fosters trust and empowers users to make informed choices regarding their digital interactions (Wollny et al., 2021).

Because we navigate this intricate landscape, it is essential to emphasize the role of ethical leadership. Ethical communicators, whether in tech companies, educational institutions, or media organizations, play a crucial role in setting the tone for responsible digital behavior. Leaders must model ethical communication practices, prioritize ethical decision-making, and advocate for policies that safeguard the public interest.

As technology continues to shape how we communicate and connect, it is imperative that we uphold ethical principles to ensure that these advances contribute positively to society. This requires collective commitment to privacy, digital literacy, inclusivity, transparency, and ethical leadership. By doing so, we can harness the immense potential of technology to enhance communication, foster understanding, and promote a more just and interconnected world (Wang et al., 2023).

BIASES IN GENERATIVE AI TOOLS IN COMMUNICATION EDUCATION

Overview of Bias in AI and Machine Learning

Bias in artificial intelligence (AI) and machine learning is a critical and pervasive issue that has garnered increasing attention in recent years. Artificial intelligence systems, particularly those based on machine learning algorithms, are designed to make decisions and predictions based on data patterns. However, these systems are not immune to the biases that exist in the data they are trained on, and can inadvertently perpetuate and even amplify those biases, leading to detrimental consequences in various domains. Understanding the scope, causes, and consequences of bias in AI and machine learning is essential for addressing this complex challenge (Kumar et al., 2022; Wachter et al., 2017).

Scope of Bias

Bias in AI can manifest in multiple ways, including but not limited to:

- Data Bias: Biases present in the training data can result from historical inequalities, stereotypes, or underrepresentation of certain groups. These biases can influence the output of the AI systems.
- Algorithmic Bias: The algorithms themselves may be biased, either due to the way they were designed or because they learn biased patterns from the data.
- Feedback Loops: AI systems can exacerbate biases over time through feedback loops, where biased predictions lead to biased outcomes that are then fed back into the system (Truong et al., 2020).

Causes of Bias

Several factors contribute to bias in AI and machine learning, including:

- Data Collection: If the training data are not diverse or are collected in a biased manner, the AI system may fail to capture the full range of experiences and perspectives.
- Data Labeling: Biases can be introduced during the process of labeling data, as human annotators may have their own biases and interpretations.
- Algorithm Design: Biases can also emerge from the design choices made when creating machine-learning algorithms, including feature selection and model architecture (Smith, 2021).

Consequences of Bias

The consequences of bias in AI are far-reaching and can impact various aspects of society.

- Discrimination: Biased AI systems can discriminate against certain groups in areas such as lending, hiring, and criminal justice, thereby perpetuating systemic inequalities.
- Fairness: Unfair treatment resulting from an AI bias can erode trust in AI systems and lead to legal and ethical challenges.
- Transparency: Bias can make AI systems less transparent because the factors influencing their decisions may not be readily apparent (Schwartz et al., 2020).

Addressing Bias

Addressing bias in AI and machine learning is a multifaceted challenge that requires a combination of technical, ethical, and regulatory approaches. Strategies to mitigate bias include the following.

- Diverse Data: Ensuring that training data are diverse and representative of all relevant groups to reduce data bias.
- Fair Algorithms: Developing algorithms designed to mitigate biases and incorporate fairness metrics into the model evaluation.
- Ethical Guidelines: Establishing ethical guidelines and best practices for AI development and deployment.
- Regulation: Governments and regulatory bodies are considering measures to hold AI developers accountable for bias and discrimination (Morris, 2020).

Bias in AI and machine learning is a complex and multifaceted issue that poses significant challenges for the development and deployment of AI systems. Addressing bias requires concerted efforts from researchers, developers, policymakers, and society as a whole to ensure that AI technologies are fair, transparent, and accountable. Failure to address bias could perpetuate existing inequalities and hinder the realization of the full potential of AI for positive impacts (Sawatzki et al., 2022).

Sources of Bias in Communication AI Systems

Bias in communication AI systems can arise from various sources, both in the data used to train these systems and in the algorithms and design choices made during their development (Leiker et al., 2023). Identifying and understanding these sources of bias are crucial for mitigating their impact and ensuring ethical and fair communication technologies. Some key sources of bias in communication AI systems are as follows:

Training Data Bias

- Data Imbalance: Biases may result from an imbalance in the training data, where certain demographic groups or languages are underrepresented, leading to skewed results in favor of overrepresented groups.
- Historical Biases: Training data often reflect historical biases present in human communication. This can include stereotypes, prejudices, or discriminatory language.
- Labeling Bias: If human annotators label training data, their biases may be introduced into the dataset. For example, annotators may interpret certain content differently based on their backgrounds (OpenAI, 2023).

Algorithmic Bias

- Model Prejudices: The algorithms used in communication AI systems can inadvertently learn and perpetuate the biases present in the training data. This could lead to biased predictions, recommendations, or responses.
- Feature Selection: Choices related to feature selection and engineering can introduce bias if certain features are given more weight or importance, leading the AI system to make biased inferences (OpenAI, 2023).

User Feedback Loop

- User-Generated Content: Communication AI systems that rely on user-generated content can develop biases based on the data generated by users. If users exhibit biased behavior, AI may learn from it inadvertently.
- Reinforcement Learning: In systems that use reinforcement learning, biases can be reinforced over time as AI optimizes user engagement or other metrics without considering ethical implications (OpenAI, 2023).

Design and Development

- Biased Objective Functions: The objectives set during the development of AI systems may inadvertently encourage biased behavior. For example, if an AI chatbot is designed to maximize engagement, it may prioritize sensational or divisive content.
- Lack of Diversity in Development Teams: The composition of the teams responsible for designing and developing AI communication systems can also contribute to bias. Homogeneous teams may overlook or not fully understand the potential biases in their products (OpenAI, 2023).

External Factors

- Media and Pop Culture: Biases present in media, pop culture, or online platforms can influence the language and content that communication AI systems learn from and produce.
- Societal Biases: Broader societal biases and inequalities can affect AI systems indirectly. For example, if a communication AI system is trained on text from social media, it may learn and perpetuate the biases prevalent on those platforms (OpenAI, 2023).

Inadequate Testing and Evaluation

- Bias Blindness: Developers and evaluators may not be aware of or adequately test for bias in AI systems, leading to unintentional propagation of biased content (OpenAI, 2023).
- Addressing bias in AI communication systems requires a multifaceted approach that involves diverse and representative training data, algorithmic fairness, rigorous evaluation, ethical guidelines, and ongoing monitoring. It also necessitates a commitment to diversity and inclusivity in AI development teams, and a proactive effort to challenge and counteract biases at all stages of system development and deployment. By recognizing and mitigating these sources of bias, AI communication systems can contribute to more equitable and responsible digital communication.

Illustrative Examples Highlighting Bias in Generative AI for Communication Studies

Gender Bias in Chatbots

In a study evaluating a popular AI chatbot designed for customer service, researchers found that chatbots exhibit gender bias. When users were asked questions with gender-neutral phrasing, the chatbot responded with gender-stereotyped answers. For example, it was assumed that a user asking about a personal assistant would refer to a female assistant. This demonstrates how AI systems can inherit and perpetuate societal biases related to gender roles and stereotypes (Rudolph et al., 2023).

Racial and Ethnic Bias in Language Models

Language models, such as GPT-3, have been criticized for generating biased and offensive content. When prompted with texts related to racial or ethnic topics, these models have been known to produce discriminatory and harmful responses. For example, the GPT-3 generated racist slurs and derogatory statements when fed prompts related to certain racial or ethnic groups. Such biases can have serious ethical and social implications, especially in communication studies, where understanding and addressing racial and ethnic issues are critical (Pavlik, 2023)

Political Bias in News Generation

Some AI-powered news-generation systems have been found to exhibit political bias. For instance, news-generation AI might favor certain political perspectives or produce content that aligns with a specific political ideology. This can result in biased news articles and reports, affecting the quality and neutrality of the information provided to the public (Raji et al., 2020).

Social Media Amplification of Biased Content

Social media platforms use AI algorithms to curate user feeds and recommend content. These algorithms can inadvertently amplify biased or extreme content. For instance, an AI-driven recommendation system might show users increasingly extreme political or ideological content based on their previous interactions, contributing to echo chambers and polarization in online discourse (Kurdi et al., 2020).

Biased Sentiment Analysis

Sentiment analysis AI tools are used to analyze public sentiments on various topics. However, these tools may produce biased results. For instance, a sentiment analysis model may incorrectly label expressions of concern from marginalized communities as negative sentiments, while labeling similar expressions from others as neutral. This misclassification can distort the perceptions of public opinion and sentiment (Larsson & Heintz, 2020).

Inclusion and Representation Issues

The AI systems used for content generation may struggle with inclusion and representation. For example, they may generate content that unintentionally excludes, or misrepresents, certain communities. In a communication classroom context, AI-generated content may inadvertently propagate biases related to gender, race, or other factors, leading to unequal representation in communication materials (Leiker et al., 2023).

IMPLICATIONS OF BIAS IN THE COMMUNICATION CLASSROOM

Effects of AI-Induced Bias on Communication Students and Educators

The presence of bias in the AI systems used in communication education can have far-reaching effects on both students and educators. These effects extend beyond the classroom and impact the development of critical communication skills and ethical awareness. The following are some of the key consequences.

Reinforcement of Stereotypes

When AI-generated content reflects biases in society, it can reinforce stereotypes and misconceptions. Communication students may unknowingly absorb and perpetuate these biases in their work, inadvertently promoting harmful stereotypes in their future careers (Torralba & Efros, 2011).

Limited Exposure to Diverse Perspectives

AI-generated content that lacks diversity or presents biased viewpoints can limit student exposure to different perspectives and worldviews. This hinders their ability to engage in inclusive and empathetic communication, which is essential in today's diverse societies (Tanjga, 2023).

Ethical Concerns

Exposure to biased AI systems raises ethical concerns among students. They may grapple with questions about responsible AI use, data ethics, and the implications of AI-induced bias, which can be distracted from their primary learning objectives (Tanjga, 2023).

Misleading Information

Biased AI-generated content can provide students with misleading or inaccurate information. This can undermine their trust in AI tools and hinder their ability to discern credible sources from biased ones, thus affecting their research and information literacy skills (Sun et al., 2019).

Challenges in Ethical Communication

Educators may face challenges in teaching ethical communication when the AI tools they use exhibit bias. They need to navigate discussions on AI ethics and ensure that students are equipped with the knowledge and skills to recognize and address bias in communication (Schramowski et al., 2022) .

Unintentional Bias Propagation

Educators may unknowingly incorporate biased AI-generated content into their teaching materials. This can perpetuate biases in course materials and inadvertently contribute to the spread of misinformation and biased communication practices (Sun et al., 2019).

Emotional Impact

For students from marginalized groups, who are often the targets of bias, exposure to biased AI-generated content can have emotional and psychological impacts. This can lead to feelings of exclusion, frustration, or anger, affecting their overall learning experience (Schramowski et al., 2022).

Impaired Critical Thinking

Relying on AI-generated content without questioning its potential biases can hinder students' critical thinking skills. They may become passive consumers of information, rather than actively discerning thinkers (Schramowski et al., 2022).

To mitigate these effects, communication educators must be proactive in addressing AI-induced biases. This includes incorporating discussions on AI ethics and bias into their curricula, critically evaluating AI tools before use, and fostering an environment in which students are encouraged to question and analyze AI-generated content. Additionally, ongoing research and development of AI tools that prioritize fairness, transparency, and inclusivity are crucial for ensuring that the next generation of communication professionals is well prepared to navigate the ethical challenges of AI in their field.

Challenges to Inclusivity and Diversity

Bias in communication AI systems can pose significant challenges to inclusivity and diversity within a communication classroom. These challenges manifest themselves in several ways.

Underrepresentation

AI systems that exhibit bias may inadvertently underrepresent certain voices, cultures, or perspectives. This can lead to a lack of diversity in the content and examples provided to students, limiting their exposure to a broad range of communication styles and experiences (Schneider et al., 2022).

Stereotyping

Biased AI-generated content can perpetuate stereotypes, reinforcing preconceived notions of different groups of people. This can create a hostile or unwelcoming environment for students belonging to marginalized or underrepresented communities (Sarsa et al., 2022).

Exclusion

When the AI-generated content is biased, it may exclude or marginalize certain groups. This exclusion can be both overt and subtle, making students from underrepresented backgrounds feel undervalued or invisible during the learning process (Sarsa et al., 2022).

Cultural Insensitivity

Biased AI systems may generate content that is culturally insensitive or offensive. This can lead to discomfort and offenses among students whose cultural backgrounds are misrepresented or disrespected, hindering open and respectful communication (Schneider et al., 2022).

Barriers to Inclusive Communication

The presence of bias can create barriers to inclusive communication within the classroom. Students may feel reluctant to participate, express their views, or engage in discussions if they perceive bias in course materials or communication tools (Schneider et al., 2022).

Impact on Learning Outcomes

Biased AI-generated content can affect students' learning outcomes. This may hinder their ability to develop cultural competence, empathy, and inclusive communication skills, which are essential in today's diverse society (Sarsa et al., 2022).

Erosion of Trust

When students encounter biased content generated by AI tools, they can erode their trust in these technologies and the educational institutions employing them. This distrust can extend to skepticism about educators and institutions' commitment to inclusivity and diversity (Sarsa et al., 2022).

Emotional and Psychological Impact

Students who experience bias in the communication classroom may face emotional and psychological challenges. They may grapple with feelings of frustration, exclusion, or inadequacy, which can affect their overall well-being and motivation to learn (Sarsa et al., 2022).

To address these challenges and promote inclusivity and diversity in communication classrooms, educators should

- Raise Awareness: Educators should raise awareness about bias in AI systems, helping students recognize and critically assess biased content.
- Foster Inclusive Environments: Creating inclusive classroom environments in which all voices are valued and respected is crucial. Educators can encourage open dialogue about bias and diversity.
- Diversify Content: Utilize a variety of content sources to ensure that a diverse range of perspectives and voices are represented in course materials.
- Empower Critical Thinking: Encourage students to think critically about the content they encounter, challenging stereotypes, and biases in communication.
- Stay Informed: Continuously educate themselves about the latest developments in AI ethics and bias mitigation to make informed choices about AI tools used in the classroom (Oleny, 2023; Sallam, 2023).

By addressing bias in AI communication systems and actively promoting inclusivity and diversity, educators can create a more equitable and welcoming learning environment that prepares students to engage in ethical, respectful, and effective communication in an increasingly diverse world.

Biases in Content Generation, Messaging, and Feedback

Biases can manifest in various aspects of the classroom, affecting content generation, messaging, and feedback. These biases can be unintentional but have significant implications for the learning environment. Biases can occur in some ways.

Content generation biases:

- Algorithmic Biases: AI tools used for content generation may exhibit algorithmic biases, which can result in the generation of content that favors certain viewpoints or perspectives over others.
- Cultural and Linguistic Biases: AI-generated content may reflect the biases embedded in training data, leading to the overrepresentation of dominant cultures or languages while marginalizing others.

- Gender and Identity Biases: AI systems may produce content that perpetuates gender stereotypes or fails to consider diverse gender identities and expressions (Liang et al., 2023).

Messaging Biases:

- Tone and Language Bias: Instructors and students may inadvertently use language or tones that favor one group or perspective, creating an unwelcoming atmosphere for others.
- Implicit Biases: Instructors and students may hold implicit biases that affect how they communicate with individuals from different backgrounds, inadvertently favoring some while marginalizing others (Ma et al., 2023).

Feedback Biases:

- Grading and Evaluation Bias: Instructors' feedback and grading can be influenced by implicit biases, impacting students' perceptions of their abilities and potentially leading to unequal educational outcomes.
- Confirmation Bias: Instructors may inadvertently seek evidence that confirms their preconceived notions of students, leading to biased feedback that reinforces existing stereotypes.
- Cultural Relevance Bias: Feedback provided may not consider the cultural or linguistic backgrounds of students, which can hinder their ability to understand and apply feedback effectively (Liu et al., 2023).

Addressing biases in content generation, messaging, and feedback is essential for creating an inclusive communication classroom (Li et al., 2023):

- Awareness: Instructors and students should be aware of the possibility of bias in communication and its consequences.
- Training: Training programs can help instructors recognize and mitigate their biases and promote fair and equitable communication.
- Diverse Perspectives: Encourage diverse perspectives and voices in the classroom to enrich discussions and reduce bias.
- Feedback Transparency: Instructors should provide transparent and constructive feedback, focusing on students' skills, and not making assumptions based on their backgrounds.
- Bias Mitigation Strategies: Implementing strategies such as blind grading or diverse reading materials to reduce content generation and evaluation biases.
- Open Dialogue: Foster an open dialogue on biases and their impact on communication to create a safe space for discussing these issues.

Mitigating Ethical Challenges and Bias in Communication Education

Strategies for Identifying and Addressing Bias in Generative AI Tools

Identifying and addressing bias in generative AI tools is crucial for ensuring fairness, equity, and accuracy in their outputs. There are some strategies to help identify and mitigate bias in these tools (Nguyen et al., 2022):

Diverse Training Data:

- Collect Comprehensive Data: Ensure that the training dataset is diverse and representative of different demographic groups, cultures, and perspectives relevant to the application.
- Identify Underrepresented Groups: Analyze the training data to identify any underrepresented or marginalized groups whose voices may be missing.

Continuous Monitoring:

- Real-time Feedback: Implementing mechanisms for users to provide feedback on problematic outputs or biased content generated by AI tools.
- Regular Audits: Conduct regular audits of the AI system outputs to identify bias trends and areas of improvement.

Bias Metrics:

- Develop Bias Metrics: Create metrics and benchmarks to measure potential bias in the AI tool's outputs, such as disparities in gender, ethnicity, or sentiment.
- Set Thresholds: Define acceptable thresholds for bias levels beyond which the tool outputs are considered biased.

Explainability and Transparency:

- Explainable AI: AI models that provide transparency and explainability are used, allowing users to understand how decisions are made.
- Bias Indicators: Develop indicators that highlight when and why the AI tool might have produced a biased output.

Diverse Development Teams:

- Diverse Teams: Assemble diverse teams of developers, including individuals from various backgrounds, to design and build AI tools. Diverse perspectives can help identify and address biases.
- Ethical Review: An ethics review process was established within the development team to assess potential biases before deployment.

Post-processing and Editing:

- Human Review: Incorporate a step for human review of AI-generated content to catch and rectify any bias or inaccuracies.
- Content Guidelines: Provide clear guidelines for human editors to follow when reviewing and editing AI-generated content.

User Customization:

- User Preferences: Allow users to customize AI tool behavior within ethical boundaries, thus enabling them to define their preferences for content generation.
- Bias Filters: Implement bias filters that allow users to adjust the tool's sensitivity to specific topics or attributes.

Ethical Frameworks:

- Adherence to Ethical Guidelines: Develop AI tools in accordance with established ethical frameworks, such as the principles of fairness, transparency, and accountability.
- Ethics Committees: Form ethics committees or boards to oversee AI tool development and assess for potential bias.

Education and Training:

- Bias Awareness: Educate developers, users, and stakeholders about the presence of bias in AI tools and the importance of addressing it.
- Training Programs: Offer training programs on responsible AI development and usage.

Bias Impact Assessment:

- Conduct Impact Assessments: Analyze the real-world impact of AI-generated content, considering how it may affect different groups and communities.
- Iterative Improvement: Impact assessments are used to iteratively improve AI models and reduce bias over time.

Collaboration and Standards:

- Industry Collaboration: Collaborate with industry peers, organizations, and academia to establish best practices, guidelines, and standards for bias mitigation using AI tools.
- Shared Datasets: Share datasets and tools for benchmarking and evaluating bias mitigation techniques.

Promoting Ethical Use of AI in Communication Training

Promoting the ethical use of AI in communication training is vital to ensuring that technology serves as a responsible and effective educational tool. There are several key strategies for fostering ethical AI use in communication classrooms (Li & Xing, 2021):

Curriculum Integration:

- Ethical AI Modules: Integrating modules or courses on ethical AI into communication curricula. These modules can cover topics such as bias mitigation, responsible AI development, and the societal impacts of AI technologies.

Faculty Training:

- Professional Development: Offer training and workshops for educators to enhance their understanding of AI ethics and how to teach AI-related subjects responsibly.
- Ethics Guidelines: Provide faculty with clear guidelines for incorporating ethical discussions into their teaching.

Inclusive and Diverse Content:

- Content Curation: Encourage educators to curate content and AI tools that reflect diverse voices and perspectives in communication, avoiding reinforcing stereotypes or biases.
- Inclusive Examples: Use inclusive examples and case studies that demonstrate the ethical implications of AI technologies in real-world communication scenarios.

Critical Thinking and Debates:

- Ethical Debates: Foster classroom discussions and debates on ethical dilemmas related to AI in communication, allowing students to critically analyze and evaluate different perspectives.
- Problem-Solving: Encourage students to propose ethical solutions and best practices to address AI-related challenges.

Hands-on Projects:

- Ethical AI Projects: Assign projects that require students to design, develop, or evaluate AI applications with a focus on ethics, transparency, and fairness.
- Real-world Impact: Emphasizes the real-world impact of AI technologies on society and communication practices.

Responsible Development:

- Student Ethics: Teach students the importance of ethical considerations in AI development, emphasizing responsible coding practices, and bias detection and mitigation.
- Model Evaluation: Instruct students on how to assess the ethical implications of the AI models they create or deploy.

Ethical AI Competitions:

- Student Challenges: Organize AI competitions or hackathons that center on ethical AI development. Encourage students to create AI solutions that address communication challenges while upholding ethical standards.

Ethical Guidelines:

- Ethics Codes: Provide students with AI ethics codes and guidelines. Encourage them to apply these principles when working on AI projects or research.

Guest Speakers and Industry Insights:

- Expert Perspectives: Invite industry professionals and AI ethics experts to speak to students about the practical applications and ethical challenges of AI in communication.
- Case Studies: Share real-world case studies on ethical AI use in the communication industry.

Research and Publications:

- Student Research: Encourage students to conduct research on AI ethics in communication, and support them in publishing their findings.
- Ethical Journals: Highlight academic journals and publications dedicated to AI ethics in communication.

Ethics Committees:

- Student Involvement: Involving students in AI ethics committees or working groups within educational institutions. Empower them to contribute to AI policy decisions.

Community Engagement:

- Outreach Programs: Engage students in community outreach programs, where they can educate others about the responsible use of AI in communication.
- Public Awareness: Promote public awareness campaigns about AI ethics, involving students in creating educational materials.

By implementing these strategies, educational institutions can instill ethical values and responsible practices regarding the use of AI in communication training. This ensures that students not only develop technical AI skills, but also understand the importance of using AI in a manner that aligns with ethical principles, diversity, and inclusivity.

The Role of Communication Educators in Ethical AI Integration

Communication educators play a pivotal role in the ethical integration of Artificial Intelligence (AI) into classrooms. As facilitators of knowledge and skill development, their influence extends beyond subject-matter expertise to nurturing responsible ethical AI practices. Here is an overview of the crucial roles they play (Liu et al., 2022):

- ***Curriculum Design and Development:*** Communication educators are responsible for crafting curricula that incorporate AI-related content from an ethical perspective. They decide which AI topics to include and ensure a balance between technical knowledge and ethical considerations.

- ***Teaching Ethical Awareness:*** Educators are at the forefront of teaching students to recognize and understand the ethical challenges posed by AI. They facilitate discussions, debates, and activities that promote ethical awareness.
- ***Modeling Ethical Behavior:*** For example, educators demonstrate ethical behavior through their use of AI tools and technologies. They serve as role models for responsible AI integration.
- ***Critical Thinking and Analysis:*** Educators foster critical thinking skills by encouraging students to critically analyze AI applications and their ethical implications. They teach students how to evaluate the societal impact of AI technologies.
- ***Creating Inclusive Learning Environments:*** Communication educators ensure that their classrooms are inclusive and welcome students from diverse backgrounds. They encourage diverse perspectives in AI discussions, helping students to understand how bias can affect AI.
- ***Debates and Discussions:*** They facilitate classroom debates and discussions of AI ethics, allowing students to explore different viewpoints and engage in ethical reasoning.
- ***Practical Application:*** Educators should design assignments and projects that require students to apply ethical principles when working with AI technologies. They provide guidance on implementing ethical considerations in practical AI projects.
- ***Guiding Ethical Research:*** Educators guide students in conducting ethical AI research in research-oriented programs. They emphasize the importance of ethical research design, data collection, and reporting.
- ***Ethical AI Competitions:*** They encouraged students to participate in ethical AI competitions and challenges, fostering their ethical problem-solving skills.
- ***Guest Speakers and Expert Insights:*** Inviting industry professionals and experts in AI ethics to speak to students broadens their understanding of the practical applications of ethical AI principles.
- ***Monitoring and Feedback:*** Educators monitor students' AI projects, provide feedback, emphasize ethical considerations, and suggest improvements.
- ***Promoting Ethical Leadership:*** Communication educators still instill in students the importance of ethical leadership in AI development and usage. They encourage students to advocate ethical AI practices in their future careers.
- ***Community Engagement:*** They involve students in community outreach programs that focus on educating others on ethical AI integration and its societal implications.
- ***Staying Updated:*** Educators continuously update their own knowledge about AI ethics to ensure that they provide the most relevant and up-to-date information to their students.

In summary, communication educators have a multifaceted role in integrating ethics into AI education. Their guidance, mentorship, and commitment to ethical AI practices are essential for shaping responsible AI practitioners who understand the ethical dimensions of AI technology and its impact on society. Through their efforts, educators have contributed significantly to creating a future workforce that prioritizes ethical considerations in AI development and application.

CASE STUDIES AND REAL-WORLD EXAMPLES

Examining Instances of Bias and Ethical Dilemmas in Communication AI

With the evolution of artificial intelligence (AI) and NLP technologies, chatbots have become more capable of managing complex duties and engaging in human-like interactions. Chatbots are utilized in numerous industries, including client support, insurance, banking, and education. Overall, the emergence of chatbots has become an outcome of breakthroughs in AI and NLP tools, and there is a growing need for more effective and practical methods to deal with technological advances. ChatGPT is one of the aforementioned technologies for natural language processing, which is frequently utilized in the academic domain (OpenAI, n.d.). A variant of the generative pre-trained transformer (GPT) is an OpenAI-developed language model. It is trained on an enormous quantity of text data, enabling it to generate human-like text and respond to queries. OpenAI researchers introduced the original GPT model in 2018, which was based on the transformer architecture, a neural network designed to process sequential data, such as text. The model was trained on a large corpus of textual data, allowing it to discover the patterns and relationships between words and sentences. The latest iterations of ChatGPT became available at the end of 2022. The design was developed based on conversational information and was optimized for specific duties, including addressing queries and producing computer feedback. ChatGPT was trained on an enormous corpus of text from the Internet, allowing it to generate responses to various queries and prompts in a human-like manner. The development of ChatGPT and other GPT models has been a major advancement in the NLP and AI disciplines, enabling the establishment of more sophisticated and humanoid interactive AI systems (O' neil, 2017).

Educators and researchers have attempted to evaluate the performance of ChatGPT. The AI chatbot's ability to accurately respond to multiple-choice inquiries in a single college exam was unexpected. Notably, depending on a chatbot or another method for solving test inquiries, cuts in opposition to the core goals and tenets of learning may result in an insufficient grasp of the substances and can impede the acquisition of these vital abilities. Utilizing chatbots or other intelligence technologies to respond to test inquiries remains an offense of intellectual dishonesty and violates the core values of study and intellectual honesty (Mitchell et al., 2019). Hence, if chatbots are abused by learners, they can raise serious moral issues. They may also significantly hinder pupils' educational advancement and knowledge-acquiring skills by limiting the way they think, their ingenuity, and the capacity to implement the notions acquired in practical applications. Furthermore, the use of chatbots when conducting tests and studies can compromise the credibility of the assessments. The uniformity and permanence of the evaluation results indicate the credibility of the assessment process. A trustworthy evaluation procedure ought to generate uniform outcomes that represent learners' actual credentials and capabilities. In light of discovering the possible uses of AI systems and chatbots in educational settings and their influence on educational and research activities from a moral point of view, the situation is vital for guaranteeing the validity and usefulness of the evaluation procedure in order to obtain valid and actionable results (Kuhail et al., 2022).

Nevertheless, learners can leverage chatbots to deceive upon tests or homework, which might jeopardize the accuracy and dependability of the evaluation outcomes. Seeking assistance from chatbots results in unjust advantages and erroneous assessment of individuals' skills and expertise. The primary objective of the greatest threats posed by chatbots is the prospect of deception regarding evaluations, tests, and undertakings. The bots may deliver immediate responses to learner inquiries, which may give rise to an educational deceit and an absence of understanding. Likewise, the application of programs might establish a disadvantaged competitive area where rich learners might possess the opportunity to use superior or more sophisticated chatbots. Hence, it has become imperative for learners to devote their best effort and time to soak up course material and obtain the necessary abilities and expertise through proper channels. Intellectual integrity and morality must be maintained in every educational setting. Moreover, in the future, we might notice elevated worries regarding the influence of chatbots on the educational attainment of younger people. We suggest that the implementation of chatbots could result in impairment of analytical and problem-solving skills. This might result in an era where learners are unwilling to think analytically, as well as imaginatively and excessively dependent on technology. Prospective, continuous studies that combine quantitative and qualitative methods must thoroughly investigate these facets. (Maheen et al., 2022)

Success Stories of Ethical Implementation in Communication Classrooms

In terms of AI-infused specific technologies now being used in education, the list has grown longer every day. There are only a few (Mageira et al., 2022):

- ***Thinkster Math:*** described by its creators as a "math tutoring program leverages human interaction and groundbreaking artificial intelligence to create personalized learning programs."
- ***Jill Watson:*** An AI-enabled virtual teaching assistant introduced by the Georgia Institute of Technology in 2016.
- ***Brainly:*** a social media site for classroom questions
- ***Nuance:*** Speech recognition software used by students and faculty, capable of transcribing up to 160 words per minute, especially helpful for students who struggle with writing or have accessibility needs.
- ***Cognii:*** AI-based products, including virtual learning assistants for K-12 and higher education institutions, as well as corporate training organizations
- ***KidSense:*** AI educational solutions designed for children, including a voice-to-text tool with algorithms built to recognize the sometimes harder-to-translate speech of young learners
- ***Content Technologies:*** instructional design and content application solutions fueled by artificial intelligence research engines

As explained by CEO Dr. Scott Parfitt, Content Technologies Inc. develops AI learning systems that are focused on "turning big data into information, and information into knowledge."

"We send an engine out, it starts reading at light speed every article it can read. It's learned its own material," said Parfitt. The company's education-focused solutions include:

- ***Palitt:*** built to help instructors easily create "your own custom lecture series, syllabus, or textbook.
- ***Cram101***: AI technology that can "turn any textbook into a smart study guide complete with chapter summaries, unlimited true-false and multiple-choice practice tests, and flashcards all drilled down to a specific textbook, ISBN number, author and chapter."
- ***JustTheFacts101:*** intended to function as the AI equivalent of an old-fashioned yellow marker, instantly highlighting and generating book- and chapter-specific summaries

The topics under discussion are the concepts of inclusion and universal access. According to Bernard Marr, the utilization of artificial intelligence (AI) tools has the potential to augment inclusivity and promote universal accessibility in the field of education through many means, including assisting in the provision of inclusive global classrooms for individuals with diverse linguistic backgrounds and sensory disabilities. The objective is to establish educational opportunities for pupils who may be unable to physically attend school because of sickness. Enhancing educational provisions for students who exhibit a need for differentiated instruction or specialized content not already offered within their own educational institutions. In general, there is an optimistic outlook that artificial intelligence (AI) will ultimately assist educators in making sustained advancements to address a wide array of factors encompassing neurological, educational, cultural, and sentimental dimensions that could influence students' learning. This is expected to contribute to the promotion of equal educational opportunities for all students, irrespective of their socioeconomic level, sexual orientation, racial or cultural origin, and mental or physical limitations. The notion of customized education pertains to an approach to education that adapts lessons and educational environments according to students' particular requirements, hobbies, and abilities. There is a prevailing sense of optimism around the notion that the integration of artificial intelligence into educational settings enhances instructors' ability to provide personalized learning opportunities for each student. In an article published in The Atlantic, it was suggested that artificial intelligence has the capacity to augment the capabilities of human teachers by allowing them to customize lessons for individual students without disrupting the overall class schedule. This has the potential to eliminate the common practice of instructing students on an average skill level, which often occurs when there is a diverse range of abilities and learning aptitudes within a classroom. According to Rose Luckin, an esteemed academic specializing in learning-centered design at the University College London, the true potential of artificial intelligence in the field of education lies in its ability to effectively analyze extensive quantities of data pertaining to learners, teachers, and the various interactions involved in the teaching and learning process. In essence, artificial intelligence has the potential to assist educators in gaining more precise and efficient comprehension of their students (Nye et al., 2023).

VALUABLE INSIGHTS FROM ETHICAL CHALLENGES FACED IN REAL-WORLD SCENARIOS

The ethical challenges faced in real-world scenarios involving AI in communication education provide valuable insights into the complexities of integrating technology and ethics. Some key takeaways include (Chien & Hwang, 2023):

- ***Transparency is Non-Negotiable:*** Real-world cases highlight the importance of transparent communication regarding the use of AI tools. Students and educators should be fully aware of how AI is utilized in the classroom, including its capabilities and limitations. Transparency builds trust and empowers individuals to make informed decisions.
- ***Data Privacy Matters:*** Several cases underscore the critical need to protect student data and privacy. Institutions must implement robust data protection measures and ensure that AI tools do not compromise the sensitive information. Clear policies and procedures for handling data are essential.
- ***Guarding Against Bias is a Continuous Effort:*** Real-world scenarios often reveal the persistence of bias in AI algorithms. Institutions should adopt ongoing auditing and monitoring mechanisms to detect and mitigate biases. Educators should be trained to recognize bias and ensure that AI tools do not perpetuate stereotypes or discriminatory practices.
- ***Inclusivity Must be Prioritized:*** Ethical challenges in real-world settings emphasize the importance of promoting diversity and inclusion. AI tools should be designed to accommodate different learning styles, abilities and backgrounds. Inclusivity initiatives should extend beyond technology itself to foster a welcoming learning environment.

- ***Student Engagement is Enhanced with Ethical AI:*** Cases show that students responded positively to AI tools when they were used to enhance engagement and learning experiences. The ethical integration of AI can lead to increased student participation, motivation, and improved academic outcomes.
- ***Educational Institutions Must Lead by Example:*** Real-world scenarios highlight the role of educational institutions in setting ethical standards for AI use. Institutions should prioritize ethics in AI education, promote responsible AI practices, and encourage students to become ethical AI users and developers.
- ***Community Involvement is Valuable:*** Engaging students, educators, and the broader community in discussions on AI ethics is essential. Real-world cases demonstrate that involving stakeholders in decision-making processes helps to identify ethical concerns and potential solutions.
- ***Continuous Adaptation is Required:*** Ethical challenges can evolve as AI technology advances. Institutions need to adapt and update their ethical guidelines, policies, and educational curricula to address the emerging ethical issues in AI.
- ***Ethical AI Education is Crucial:*** Real-world scenarios emphasize the need for robust education on AI ethics. Students should be equipped with the knowledge and skills to navigate AI-driven environments responsibly, critically assess AI-generated content, and advocate ethical AI use.
- ***Ethical Dilemmas Offer Learning Opportunities:*** Ethical challenges can serve as valuable teaching moments. Real-world scenarios provide opportunities for students to grapple with complex ethical dilemmas and foster critical thinking, ethical reasoning, and decision-making skills.

The ethical challenges encountered in real-world scenarios involving AI in communication education underscore the importance of transparency, data privacy, bias mitigation, inclusivity, and ongoing education. These insights can guide educational institutions and stakeholders in promoting ethical AI integration, while ensuring that the benefits of AI are harnessed responsibly and ethically.

ETHICAL GUIDELINES AND BEST PRACTICES

Existing Ethical Guidelines for AI in Communication Studies

Ethical guidelines for AI in communication studies serve as essential frameworks to ensure responsible and ethical use of artificial intelligence tools in educational settings. These guidelines were developed by professional organizations, institutions, and experts in the field (Bae et al., 2023; Bang et al., 2023). The existing ethical guidelines are as follows.

- ***The Association for Computing Machinery (ACM):*** ACM provides a comprehensive set of ethical guidelines for AI professionals, including those in communication studies. These guidelines emphasize fairness, accountability, transparency, and the use of AI technologies.
- ***The Institute of Electrical and Electronics Engineers (IEEE):*** IEEE's guidelines for AI ethics stress the importance of avoiding harm, ensuring transparency, and respecting privacy and autonomy. These principles are highly relevant for AI applications in communication education.

- ***The American Educational Research Association (AERA):*** The AERA offers guidelines for conducting educational research that extends to AI-based studies. These guidelines emphasize informed consent, data protection, and dissemination of research findings.
- ***The European Commission's Ethics Guidelines for Trustworthy AI:*** While primarily aimed at AI developers, these guidelines highlight key ethical principles, such as fairness, accountability, transparency, and respect for human autonomy. They are applicable to the AI tools used in communication classrooms.
- ***The Association for Computational Linguistics (ACL):*** ACL has addressed bias in natural language processing and AI. Their guidelines encourage researchers and practitioners to be aware of the potential bias in AI systems, which is critical in communication studies where language plays a central role.
- ***The Partnership on AI (PAI):*** PAI is a consortium of tech companies and organizations committed to the responsible development of AI. They have published ethical guidelines that emphasize fairness, inclusivity, and prevention of AI harm.
- ***Educational Technology Codes of Ethics:*** Several educational technology organizations, such as the International Society for Technology in Education (ISTE), have codes of ethics relevant to the use of AI in education. These codes emphasize the integration of responsible technology and students' well-being.
- ***Institution-Specific Guidelines:*** Many educational institutions have developed their own AI ethics guidelines tailored to their unique contexts. These guidelines often cover issues related to data privacy, transparency, and responsible AI use within their institutions.
- ***AI Vendor Guidelines:*** Companies and organizations that develop AI tools for education often provide ethical guidelines for their products. Educators can refer to these guidelines when selecting and using AI tools in the classroom.
- ***Research Ethics Boards:*** Institutional Review Boards (IRBs) and Research Ethics Boards (REBs) oversee research involving human subjects, including AI research in education. Researchers must adhere to ethical standards and obtain approval for conducting studies.

These existing ethical guidelines provide a foundation for educators, researchers, and institutions to ensure that AI technologies are used ethically and responsibly in communication studies. Adhering to these guidelines helps promote fairness, transparency, and the protection of student rights and privacy, while harnessing the benefits of AI in education.

The Need for Ethical Regulations and Oversight

The need for ethical regulations and oversight in the context of AI tools in communication classrooms is paramount. While AI technologies offer significant educational benefits, they also introduce ethical challenges and potential risks that must be addressed (Bender et al., 2021; Beseiso et al., 2021). Ethical regulations and oversight are essential.

Protection of Students

Ethical regulations and oversight help to protect students' rights and well-being. AI tools can collect and analyze student data, making it crucial to ensure data privacy, informed consent, and fair treatment.

Preventing Bias and Discrimination

Ethical regulations can help prevent bias and discrimination in AI-generated content and interactions. Oversight ensures that AI systems are designed to be fair and inclusive, thereby reducing the risk of reinforcing existing biases.

Transparency and Accountability

Regulations promote transparency in AI systems. Educators and students should understand how AI tools operate, make decisions, and use data. Oversight mechanisms hold developers and institutions accountable for ethical breaches.

Minimizing Harm

Oversight and regulations are essential to minimize the potential harm caused by AI tools. This includes harm related to bias, misinformation, emotional distress, and the invasion of privacy.

Maintaining Academic Integrity

Regulations can help to maintain the academic integrity of educational institutions. Ethical oversight ensures that AI tools are used as supplements to learning, rather than as shortcuts or tools for academic dishonesty.

Fostering Trust

Establishing clear ethical guidelines and oversight processes fosters trust among students, educators, and parents. Trust is crucial for the successful adoption of AI in education.

Adaptation to Evolving Technology

Ethical regulations and oversight frameworks should be flexible and adaptable to keep pace with evolving AI technology. This ensures that the regulations remain relevant and effective over time.

Global Standards

Ethical regulations can contribute to the establishment of global standards for the ethical use of AI in education. Consistent standards make it easier for educational institutions to collaborate and share their resources.

Legal Compliance

Regulations help educational institutions and AI developers ensure compliance with relevant data protection and privacy laws, such as the Family Educational Rights and Privacy Act (FERPA) in the United States or the General Data Protection Regulation (GDPR) in Europe.

Ethical Awareness

Ethical regulations and oversight promote ethical awareness among educators, administrators, and developers. This awareness is essential for making informed decisions regarding AI integration in communication classrooms.

To implement effective ethical regulations and oversight:

Educational institutions should establish clear policies and guidelines for the use of AI tools that cover aspects such as data privacy, bias mitigation, and transparency.

Governments and educational authorities can develop regulatory frameworks specific to AI in education with input from experts, educators, and stakeholders.

Independent bodies or ethics committees can be formed to review and evaluate the AI tools used in education, ensuring that they align with ethical standards.

AI tools should prioritize ethical considerations during the design and development phases, and they can undergo third-party audits for ethical compliance (Bowles & Kruger, 2023).

In summary, ethical regulations and oversight are essential to harness the benefits of AI in communication education, while mitigating risks and upholding ethical standards. These measures will contribute to creating a safe, fair, and transparent learning environment for students and educators.

BUILDING A BRIDGE BETWEEN ETHICAL VALUES AND TECHNOLOGICAL ADVANCEMENTS

Building a bridge between ethical values and technological advancements, particularly in the context of communication education and AI, is crucial for ensuring that innovation aligns with societal and moral principles (Brown et al., 2022). Here, we establish the following vital connection:

- ***Ethical by Design:*** Ethical considerations are incorporated into the core of technological development. Adopt an "ethics by design" approach, where ethical values are integrated into the initial stages of AI tool creation. Developers should proactively identify potential ethical dilemmas and design solutions to mitigate them.
- ***Interdisciplinary Collaboration:*** Foster collaboration between technologists, ethicists, educators, and other stakeholders. Interdisciplinary teams can work together to examine the ethical implications of AI tools, ensuring a well-rounded perspective and ethical guidance for technological advancements.
- ***Ethics Training:*** Provide education and training in ethics for AI developers, data scientists, and educators. Understanding the ethical nuances of AI helps professionals make informed decisions and prioritize ethical considerations in their work.
- ***Ethical Frameworks:*** Develop and promote ethical frameworks specific to AI in education and communication. These frameworks can guide the responsible use of AI tools and emphasize values such as fairness, transparency, accountability, and privacy.

- ***Continuous Evaluation:*** Implementation of ongoing evaluation and assessment of AI systems. AI tools are regularly scrutinized to identify and rectify biases, inaccuracies, or ethical issues that may arise during their use.
- ***Inclusive Stakeholder Engagement:*** Engages a diverse group of stakeholders in the development and deployment of AI tools. This includes students, educators, parents, policymakers, and representatives from marginalized communities. Their input helps to identify potential biases and ensures inclusivity.
- ***Transparency:*** Maintains transparency regarding how AI systems operate. Users, particularly educators and students, should have a clear understanding of how AI is used, what data are collected, and how decisions are made. Transparency builds trust.
- ***Privacy Safeguards:*** Implementation of robust privacy protection. Ensure that AI tools adhere to data protection regulations and that data collected from students are used solely for educational purposes.
- ***Ethics Committees:*** Establish ethics committees or review boards within educational institutions. These committees can provide oversight and guidance on the ethical use of AI tools, especially when making decisions regarding data collection, analysis, and storage.
- ***Ethical Impact Assessments:*** Ethical impact assessments were conducted before deploying AI tools. Evaluate how technology may affect students, educators, and the learning environment from an ethical perspective.
- ***Ethics in Curriculum:*** ethics education is included in communication curricula. Equip students with the knowledge and skills to critically assess the ethical dimensions of AI and technology in their fields.
- ***Global Collaboration:*** Encourage global collaboration on ethical standards for AI in education. Given the international nature of technology and education, a unified ethical approach has a more significant impact.
- ***Public Awareness:*** Promotes awareness among the general public about the ethical implications of AI in communication education. Informed individuals can advocate ethical practices and hold institutions and developers accountable for their work.

By building a bridge between ethical values and technological advancements, we can ensure that AI in communication education serves as a force for positive change while upholding moral principles and societal values. It is a collaborative effort that requires vigilance, education, and commitment to ethics in the era of rapid technological innovation.

FUTURE DIRECTIONS AND RECOMMENDATIONS

Anticipating Ethical Challenges as AI Evolves

As artificial intelligence (AI) continues to advance, it brings a host of ethical challenges that must be anticipated and addressed proactively. Some key ethical challenges to consider as AI evolves:

- ***Bias and Fairness:*** AI systems can inherit biases present in the data used to train them. It is crucial to anticipate and mitigate bias to ensure that AI applications are fair and do not perpetuate the discrimination against certain groups.
- ***Privacy Concerns:*** AI systems often process vast amounts of personal data. Anticipating privacy concerns and implementing strong data-protection measures are essential for maintaining user trust.
- ***Transparency:*** As AI models become more complex, they can become "black boxes" where it's challenging to understand how they arrive at decisions. Ensuring transparency in the AI decision-making processes is an ongoing challenge.
- ***Accountability:*** When AI systems make errors or make harmful decisions, determining who is accountable can be challenging. Establishing clear lines of responsibility and accountability are crucial.
- ***Job Displacement:*** AI and automation can lead to job displacement in various industries. Preparing the workforce for these changes and addressing societal impacts are ongoing ethical challenges.
- ***Autonomous Systems:*** AI-driven autonomous systems, such as self-driving cars, raise ethical dilemmas related to safety and decision making in critical situations.
- ***Security:*** As AI becomes more integrated into the critical infrastructure, there is a growing need to anticipate and defend against AI-related security threats.
- ***Ethical Decision-Making:*** Developing AI systems that can make ethical decisions in complex situations is a significant challenge. Anticipating and addressing these challenges require input from ethicists and domain experts.
- ***Unintended Consequences:*** AI systems can have unintended consequences such as reinforcing harmful stereotypes or creating new forms of addiction. Therefore, it is essential to identify and mitigate these consequences.
- ***Regulatory Frameworks:*** The pace of AI development often outpaces regulatory frameworks. Anticipating the need for new regulations and establishing responsible guidelines are ongoing challenges.
- ***Bias in Healthcare and Criminal Justice:*** AI systems used in healthcare and criminal justice systems must be carefully designed to avoid exacerbating the existing biases and inequalities.
- ***AI in Warfare:*** Anticipating the ethical challenges posed by AI in warfare, such as autonomous weapons and cyber warfare, is essential to global security.
- ***Data Ownership:*** Determining who owns and controls the data used to train AI systems is a complex ethical issue, particularly in the era of big data.
- ***Ethical AI Research:*** Ethical considerations in AI research, such as experiments involving AI and human subjects, require vigilance.
- ***Global Collaboration:*** AI is a global endeavor, and anticipating ethical challenges requires international cooperation to establish common standards and norms.

Interdisciplinary collaboration among technologists, ethicists, policymakers, and other stakeholders is crucial to address these challenges. Additionally, ongoing education and public discourse are necessary to ensure that AI evolves in ways that benefit society, while upholding ethical principles.

RECOMMENDATIONS FOR ETHICAL AI INTEGRATION IN COMMUNICATION EDUCATION

Integrating ethical AI into communication education is essential for preparing students for an evolving digital landscape. The following are recommendations for ethical AI integration in communication education:

- ***Include Ethical AI in the Curriculum:*** Develop and incorporate courses or modules specifically focused on ethical AI in communication programmes. These courses should cover AI principles, potential biases, fairness, and transparency.
- ***Critical Thinking:*** Emphasizes critical thinking skills in communication programmes. Encourage students to question the ethical implications of AI-driven communication tools and platforms.
- ***Case Studies and Real-World Examples:*** Real-world case studies and examples are used to illustrate ethical dilemmas related to AI in communication. Discuss how these situations were handled and the lessons learned.
- ***Interdisciplinary Collaboration:*** Foster collaboration between communication departments and AI or computer science departments. This could lead to a more comprehensive understanding of AI technologies and their ethical considerations.
- ***Ethics Committees:*** Establish ethics committees or review boards within communication programs to assess the ethical implications of AI projects and research conducted by students and faculty.
- ***Guest Lecturers and Industry Experts:*** Invite AI experts, ethicists, and professionals from the technology industry to give guest lectures or workshops on AI ethics in communication.
- ***Hands-On Projects:*** Encourage students to work on projects involving AI technologies, such as chatbots or content recommendation systems, while emphasizing responsible and ethical design.
- ***Ethical Design Principles:*** Teach students about ethical design principles for AI-driven communication tools, including the importance of fairness, transparency, and user privacy.
- ***Debate and Discussion:*** Debates and discussions on AI-related ethical topics should be organized to encourage students to articulate their viewpoints and engage in constructive dialogue.
- ***Ethical Guidelines:*** Provide students with access to AI ethics guidelines and codes of conduct established by organizations such as IEEE, ACM, and AI ethics initiatives.
- ***Inclusivity and Diversity:*** Stress the importance of inclusivity and diversity in AI development. Discuss how biased AI can reinforce stereotypes and discrimination and how to counteract these biases.
- ***Critical Evaluation:*** Train students to critically evaluate AI-driven content and messaging. Teach them to recognize instances of bias and unethical practices.
- ***AI Impact Assessments:*** Encourage students to conduct AI impact assessments for communication projects, considering potential risks and benefits for various stakeholders.
- ***Ethical Reporting:*** If communication students engage in AI-related journalism or reporting, they emphasize the ethical responsibility of accurate, balanced, and unbiased reporting on AI topics.
- ***Continual Learning:*** The need for lifelong learning in the field of AI ethics as technology evolves rapidly. Encourage students to stay informed about emerging AI technologies and ethical challenges.

- ***Community Engagement:*** Encourage students to engage in a broader community on AI ethics issues. This can include participating in public discussions, writing articles, or giving presentations.
- ***Collaborative Projects:*** Foster collaborative projects between students in communication and AI-related disciplines to address AI ethics challenges from multiple perspectives.
- ***Ethical Hackathons:*** Organize AI ethics hackathons where students can propose and develop AI solutions that address specific ethical concerns in communication.
- ***Resource Centers:*** Establish AI ethics resource centers within communication programs to provide students with access to research, tools, and guidelines for ethical AI integration.

By implementing these recommendations, communication education programs can help students navigate through the ethical challenges and opportunities presented by AI technologies in the field of communication. This knowledge enables them to make informed, responsible, and ethical decisions in their future careers.

THE ONGOING ROLE OF RESEARCH AND INNOVATION IN ETHICAL AI DEVELOPMENT

Research and innovation play pivotal roles in the development of ethical AI. These processes are essential for addressing the existing challenges and proactively shaping the future of AI technology. There are several key aspects of the ongoing role of research and innovation in the development of ethical AI.

- ***Bias Mitigation:*** Ongoing research is focused on developing techniques to identify and mitigate bias in AI systems. Innovations in algorithm design, data preprocessing, and fairness metrics aim to reduce the bias across various demographic and cultural groups.
- ***Transparency and Explainability***: Researchers are continually working on methods to make AI systems more transparent and interpretable. This involves creating models that provide clear explanations for decisions, which is crucial for building trust and understanding in AI applications.
- ***Privacy Preservation***: Innovations in privacy-preserving AI enable the development of AI systems that can analyze and process data while preserving the privacy of individuals. Techniques, such as federated learning and differential privacy, are areas of active research.
- ***Fairness-Aware AI:*** Researchers are developing fairness-aware AI models and algorithms that can assess and mitigate biases in real time, ensuring that AI systems produce equitable outcomes across different groups.
- ***Ethical Guidelines:*** Ongoing research has contributed to the establishment of comprehensive ethical guidelines and frameworks for AI development and deployment. These guidelines help AI developers adhere to ethical principles throughout the technology lifecycle.
- ***Ethical Decision-Making:*** Innovations in AI are exploring ways to directly incorporate ethical decision-making processes into AI systems. This includes the development of AI models that can cause ethical dilemmas and make morally sound choices.
- ***Algorithmic Auditing:*** Research is advancing the field of algorithmic auditing, which involves the evaluation of AI systems for fairness, transparency, and bias. Auditing tools and methodologies are continuously evolving to address emerging challenges.

- ***Interdisciplinary Collaboration:*** Collaboration among AI researchers, ethicists, social scientists, and other experts is becoming more common. This interdisciplinary approach ensures a holistic understanding of the ethical implications of AI.
- ***Ethical Education:*** Research in AI education focuses on developing effective methods for teaching ethics to AI practitioners and users. These include curriculum development, pedagogical approaches, and assessment methods.
- ***Stakeholder Engagement:*** Ongoing research explores ways to engage a wide range of stakeholders, including policymakers, industry leaders, civil society, and the general public, in shaping AI's ethical development and regulation of AI.
- ***AI for Ethical Monitoring***: Innovations in AI are leveraged to monitor and enforce ethical guidelines and regulations. For example, AI-driven tools can scan and flag content for ethical violations or unethical behaviors.
- ***Global Collaboration***: The global nature of AI challenges requires international collaboration. Researchers and innovators work together across borders to develop shared ethical standards and guidelines for AI development and deployment.
- ***Public Awareness:*** Research helps in understanding public perceptions and concerns about AI ethics. This knowledge informs the development of AI systems that align with the societal values and expectations.
- ***Continuous Improvement:*** Ethical AI development is an iterative process. Ongoing research and innovation are essential to identifying new ethical challenges and adapting AI systems to changing societal norms and needs.
- ***Real-World Testing:*** Ethical AI development involves testing AI systems in real-world scenarios and collecting feedback from users. Research in this area assesses how AI performs ethically in practice and provides information on improvements.
- ***Regulatory Compliance:*** Research contributes to the development of AI compliance standards, ensuring that AI systems adhere to legal and ethical requirements in various domains, such as healthcare, finance, and education.

In summary, research and innovation are indispensable in advancing the ethical development of AI. They drive improvements in fairness, transparency, privacy, and accountability, helping create AI systems that benefit society while respecting ethical principles and values. As AI continues to evolve, ongoing research and innovation will remain crucial for addressing new ethical challenges and ensuring that it aligns with the best interests of humanity.

CONCLUSION

Summarizing Key Findings and Takeaways

In summary, the chapter "Ethical Challenges and Biases Within the Communication Classroom Rendered by Generative AI Tools" explores the complex landscape of ethical considerations and biases associated with the integration of generative AI tools in communication education. The key findings and takeaways from this chapter are as follows.

1. **Overview of Generative AI in Communication Education**: The chapter begins by providing an overview of generative AI tools and their growing significance in communication training. This highlights the potential benefits of AI in enhancing communication and learning experience.
2. **The Ethical Dimension of AI in Communication Studies**: It delves into the ethical dimension of AI, emphasizing the need to consider the ethical implications of AI technologies, particularly in educational settings. Ethical AI integration is vital for ensuring fairness, transparency, and equity.
3. **Types of Generative AI Tools Used**: The chapter explores various types of generative AI tools commonly employed in communication classrooms, such as chatbots, content generators, and language models. Each type presents with distinct ethical challenges and biases.
4. **Bias in AI and Machine Learning**: It paper discusses the concept of bias in AI and machine learning, emphasizing how biases can inadvertently enter AI systems through biased training data or algorithmic design choices. These biases can manifest in AI communication tools.
5. **Sources of Bias in Communication AI Systems**: The chapter identifies the sources of bias in communication AI systems, including biased training data, algorithmic biases, and human biases embedded in the content used for training.
6. **Illustrative Examples of Bias**: To illustrate the presence of bias in generative AI for communication studies, this chapter provides real-world examples of biased content generation, messaging, and feedback, underscoring their potential consequences for learners and educators.
7. **Impact on Communication Students and Educators**: This study explores how AI-induced biases can affect communication between students and educators, including reinforcing stereotypes, limiting perspectives, and hindering inclusive learning environments.
8. **Challenges to Inclusivity and Diversity**: The chapter highlights the challenges to inclusivity and diversity caused by bias in the communication classroom, emphasizing the importance of addressing these issues to foster equitable learning environments.
9. **Strategies for Identifying and Addressing Bias**: It offers strategies for identifying and mitigating bias in generative AI tools, such as diverse dataset curation, algorithmic audits, and continuous monitoring. These strategies aim to enhance the fairness and ethical integrity of the AI systems.
10. **Promoting Ethical AI Integration**: The chapter underscores the significance of promoting ethical AI integration in communication education and encourages educators and institutions to prioritize ethical considerations in AI tool adoption.
11. **The Role of Communication Educators**: It chapter discusses the pivotal role of communication educators in ethical AI integration, including the need for AI ethics education, responsible AI use, and proactive engagement with AI developers.
12. **Case Studies and Real-World Examples**: To provide practical insights, this chapter presents case studies and real-world examples that examine instances of bias and ethical dilemmas in AI communication. These cases highlight the importance of ethical guidelines and supervision.
13. **Recommendations for Ethical AI Integration**: The chapter concludes by offering recommendations for ethical AI integration in communication education, emphasizing collaboration, transparency, and the continuous evaluation of AI tools.
14. **Ethical Regulations and Oversight**: It emphasizes the need for ethical regulations and oversight to ensure that AI in communication education adheres to ethical standards and safeguards against potential harm.

15. **Anticipating Ethical Challenges**: Finally, the chapter suggests the importance of anticipating ethical challenges as AI technology evolves, underscoring the ongoing nature of ethical considerations in AI integration.

This chapter provides a comprehensive exploration of the ethical landscape surrounding generative AI tools in communication education. This highlights the importance of responsible AI development and usage to foster inclusive, unbiased, and ethically sound learning environments.

Emphasizing the Ongoing Importance of Ethical Considerations

The importance of ethical considerations in the ever-evolving artificial intelligence (AI) landscape cannot be overstated. As AI technologies continue to advance and find their way into various aspects of our lives, including education and communication, it has become imperative to emphasize the ongoing significance of ethical deliberation and decision-making.

AI, particularly the generative AI tools used in communication education, has the potential to revolutionize the way we teach and learn. It can offer personalized learning experiences, assist educators in providing timely feedback, and enhance their communication skills. However, this transformative potential comes with ethical responsibilities and challenges that demand continuous attention (Bulut & Yildirim-Erbasli, 2022).

First, AI systems can inadvertently perpetuate and amplify biases present in the training data or algorithms themselves. These biases can manifest in the content generated, messages conveyed, and feedback provided to the learners. They have the potential to reinforce stereotypes, marginalize certain groups, and hinder inclusivity. Therefore, ongoing vigilance is required to detect and mitigate bias, ensuring that AI tools promote fairness and equity in classrooms.

Moreover, the dynamic nature of AI technologies implies that new ethical dilemmas may arise as these tools evolve. As AI systems become more sophisticated and integrated into education, educators, researchers, and policymakers must remain proactive in addressing the emerging ethical challenges. This includes anticipating issues related to privacy, consent, and ethical use of AI-generated content.

Ethical considerations in AI also extend to the issues of transparency and accountability. Users of AI tools, including students and educators, should have a clear understanding of how these systems work, how decisions are made, and what data are collected. Ethical AI developers should prioritize transparency, provide insights into the inner workings of their systems, and ensure that users make informed choices.

In communication studies, institutions and educators play a pivotal role in shaping the ethical landscape of AI integration. They should prioritize ethical AI education, equipping students with the knowledge and critical thinking skills needed to engage responsibly with these technologies. Additionally, they should engage in ongoing dialogue with AI developers, fostering a collaborative approach to address ethical challenges.

Ethical considerations in AI for communication education are not a one-time concern but an ongoing imperative. As AI technologies continue to evolve and transform educational practices, the ethical dimensions of their use must evolve simultaneously. By emphasizing the ongoing importance of ethical considerations, we can ensure that AI enhances learning experiences, fosters inclusivity, and upholds the value of ethical communication.

LOOKING FORWARD TO ETHICAL AI'S IMPACT ON COMMUNICATION EDUCATION

The forward-looking impact of ethical AI on communication education holds significant promise. As we navigate the intersection of technology and pedagogy, it is crucial to consider the positive trajectory that ethical AI can follow for communication studies.

One of the most exciting prospects is the enhancement of personalized learning experiences. Ethical AI can analyze individual students' strengths and weaknesses and tailor educational content to their specific needs. This level of personalization can lead to more engaged and successful learners as communication educators can provide targeted guidance and support.

Moreover, AI-driven communication tools can help bridge accessibility gaps. By offering real-time transcription services and language translation capabilities, these tools can make communication education more inclusive for students with disabilities and for those from diverse linguistic backgrounds. This inclusivity aligns with ethical principles of fairness and equal opportunities.

The impact of ethical AI also extends to improving feedback mechanisms. AI-powered systems can provide instant constructive feedback on written and spoken communication, allowing students to continuously refine their skills. This immediate feedback loop promotes a growth mindset and encourages iterative learning, which is beneficial for both educators and learners.

Another aspect to consider is fostering creativity. AI tools can assist students in brainstorming ideas, suggesting novel approaches, and generating content. By doing some of the heavy lifting, AI frees time for students to focus on critical thinking, creativity, and vital skills in the field of communication.

As we anticipate, it is essential to acknowledge the ongoing ethical challenges. Bias mitigation, transparency, and privacy concerns must be at the forefront of AI development. By proactively addressing these issues, we can ensure that the positive impact of ethical AI is not reflected by unintended consequences.

The forward-looking impact of ethical AI on communication education is a journey filled with exciting possibilities. From personalized learning to inclusivity and enhanced feedback, ethical AI aligns with the core values of effective communication and education. As educators, students, and developers continue to collaborate and innovate, we can look forward to a future in which AI enriches the communication education experience while upholding ethical standards.

REFERENCES

Akgun, S., & Greenhow, C. (2021). Artificial intelligence in education: Addressing ethical challenges in K-12 settings. *AI and Ethics*, *2*(3), 431–440. doi:10.1007/s43681-021-00096-7 PMID:34790956

Alam, A. (2021). Should robots replace teachers? Mobilisation of AI and learning analytics in education. In *Proceedings of the 2021 International Conference on Advances in Computing, Communication, and Control (ICAC3)* (pp. 1–12). IEEE. 10.1109/ICAC353642.2021.9697300

Almer, J. (2022). *Deskilling as an effect of AI: A group of students' attitudes towards AI and their worries about deskilling*. Academic Press.

Angelone, A. M., Galassi, A., & Vittorini, P. (2022). Improved automated classification of sentences in data science exercises. In *Methodologies and Intelligent Systems for Technology Enhanced Learning, 11th International Conference* (pp. 12–21). Springer. 10.1007/978-3-030-86618-1_2

Araujo, T. (2020). Conversational agent research toolkit: An alternative for creating and managing chatbots for experimental research. *Computer Communication Review*, *2*(1), 35–51. doi:10.5117/CCR2020.1.002.ARAU

Bae, S., Dong, Y., & Kwon, O. (2023). The effects of content creator, media richness, and content theme on learning performance: Focusing on ESG management education for Chinese employees. 글로벌경영학회지, *20*(1), 27–50. https://doi.org/ doi:10.38115/asgba2023.20.1.27

Bang, Y., Cahyawijaya, S., Lee, N., Dai, W., Su, D., Wilie, B., Lovenia, H., Ji, Z., Yu, T., Chung, W., Do, Q. V., Xu, Y., & Fung, P. (2023). A Multitask, Multilingual, Multimodal Evaluation of ChatGPT on Reasoning, Hallucination, and Interactivity. *arXiv preprint arXiv:2302.04023*. https://doi.org//arXiv.2302.04023 doi:10.48550

Bender, E. M., Gebru, T., McMillan-Major, A., & Shmitchell, S. (2021). On the dangers of stochastic parrots: Can language models be too big? In *Proceedings of the 2021 ACM conference on fairness, accountability, and transparency* (pp. 610–623). 10.1145/3442188.3445922

Beseiso, M., Alzubi, O. A., & Rashaideh, H. (2021). A novel automated essay scoring approach for reliable higher educational assessments. *Journal of Computing in Higher Education*, *33*(3), 727–746. doi:10.1007/s12528-021-09283-1

Bowles, D. C., & Kruger, J. S. (2023). Generating employable, intelligent graduates in a world with generative AI: Thoughts for educators. *Pedagogy in Health Promotion*, *9*(2), 75–77. doi:10.1177/23733799231175171

Brown, H., Lee, K., Mireshghallah, F., Shokri, R., & Tramèr, F. (2022). What does it mean for a language model to preserve privacy? In *2022 ACM Conference on Fairness, Accountability, and Transparency* (pp. 2280–2292). 10.1145/3531146.3534642

Brown, T., Mann, B., Ryder, N., Subbiah, M., Kaplan, J. D., Dhariwal, P., & Amodei, D. (2020). Language models are few-shot learners. *Advances in Neural Information Processing Systems*, *33*, 1877–1901.

Bulut, O., & Yildirim-Erbasli, S. N. (2022). Automatic story and item generation for reading comprehension assessments with transformers. *International Journal of Assessment Tools in Education*, *9*(Special Issue), 72–87. doi:10.21449/ijate.1124382

Buolamwini, J., & Gebru, T. (2018). Gender shades: Intersectional accuracy disparities in commercial gender classification. In *Conference on Fairness, Accountability, and Transparency* (pp. 77–91). PMLR.

Caines, A., Benedetto, L., Taslimipoor, S., Davis, C., Gao, Y., Andersen, O., Yuan, Z., Elliott, M., Moore, R., Bryant, C., Rei, M., Mullooly, A., Nicholls, D., & Buttery, P. (2023). On the application of large language models for language teaching and assessment technology. AIED Workshops.

Carroll, A., Forrest, K., Sanders-O'Connor, E., Flynn, L., Bower, J. M., Fynes-Clinton, S., York, A., & Ziaei, M. (2022). Teacher stress and burnout in Australia: Examining the role of intrapersonal and environmental factors. *Social Psychology of Education*, *25*(2-3), 441–469. doi:10.1007/s11218-022-09686-7 PMID:35233183

Challen, R., Denny, J., Pitt, M., Gompels, L., Edwards, T., & Tsaneva-Atanasova, K. (2019). Artificial intelligence, bias and clinical safety. *BMJ Quality & Safety*, *28*(3), 231–237. doi:10.1136/bmjqs-2018-008370 PMID:30636200

Chaudhry, M. A., Cukurova, M., & Luckin, R. (2022). A transparency index framework for AI in education. In *Artificial Intelligence in Education. Posters and Late Breaking Results, Workshops and Tutorials, Industry and Innovation Tracks, Practitioners' and Doctoral Consortium: 23rd International Conference, AIED 2022* (pp. 195–198). Springer. 10.1007/978-3-031-11647-6_33

Chechitelli, A. (2023). *AI writing detection update from Turnitin's chief product officer*. Retrieved from https://www.turnitin.com/blog/aiwriting-detection-update-from-turnitins-chief-product-officer

Chen, L., Chen, P., & Lin, Z. (2020). Artificial intelligence in education: A review. *IEEE Access : Practical Innovations, Open Solutions*, *8*, 75264–75278. doi:10.1109/ACCESS.2020.2988510

Chen, X., Cheng, G., Zou, D., Zhong, B., & Xie, H. (2023). Artificial intelligent robots for precision education. *Journal of Educational Technology & Society*, *26*, 171–186.

Chen, X., Xie, H., Zou, D., & Hwang, G. J. (2020). Application and theory gaps during the rise of artificial intelligence in education. *Computers. Education and Artificial Intelligence*, *1*, 100002.

Chien, S. Y., & Hwang, G. J. (2023). A research proposal for an AI chatbot as a virtual patient agent to improve nursing students' clinical inquiry skills. *ICAIE*, *2023*(2023), 13.

Condor, A., Litster, M., & Pardos, Z. (2021). *Automatic short answer grading with sbert on out-of-sample questions*. International Educational Data Mining Society.

Creswell, J. W. (2014). *A Concise Introduction to Mixed Methods Research*. SAGE.

Dignum, V. (2018). Ethics in artificial intelligence: Introduction to the special issue. *Ethics and Information Technology*, *20*(1), 1–3. doi:10.1007/s10676-018-9450-z

Doyle, W., & Ponder, G. A. (1977). The practicality ethic in teacher decision-making. *Interchange (Washington, D.C.)*, *8*, 1–12.

Drori, I., Zhang, S., Shuttleworth, R., Tang, L., Lu, A., Ke, E., Liu, K., Chen, L., Tran, S., Cheng, N., Wang, R., Singh, N., Patti, T. L., Lynch, J., Shporer, A., Verma, N., Wu, E., & Strang, G. (2022). A neural network solves, explains, and generates university math problems by program synthesis and few-shot learning at human level. *Proceedings of the National Academy of Sciences of the United States of America*, *119*(32), e2123433119. Advance online publication. doi:10.1073/pnas.2123433119 PMID:35917350

Dwivedi, Y. K., Hughes, L., Ismagilova, E., Aarts, G., Coombs, C., Crick, T., Duan, Y., Dwivedi, R., Edwards, J., Eirug, A., Galanos, V., Ilavarasan, P. V., Janssen, M., Jones, P., Kar, A. K., Kizgin, H., Kronemann, B., Lal, B., Lucini, B., ... Williams, M. D. (2021). Artificial Intelligence (AI): Multidisciplinary perspectives on emerging challenges, opportunities, and agenda for research, practice and policy. *International Journal of Information Management*, *57*, 101994. doi:10.1016/j.ijinfomgt.2019.08.002

Dwivedi, Y. K., Kshetri, N., Hughes, L., Slade, E. L., Jeyaraj, A., Kar, A. K., Baabdullah, A. M., Koohang, A., Raghavan, V., Ahuja, M., Albanna, H., Albashrawi, M. A., Al-Busaidi, A. S., Balakrishnan, J., Barlette, Y., Basu, S., Bose, I., Brooks, L., Buhalis, D., ... Wright, R. (2023). Opinion Paper: "So what if ChatGPT wrote it?" Multidisciplinary perspectives on opportunities, challenges and implications of generative conversational AI for research, practice and policy. *International Journal of Information Management*, *71*, 102642. doi:10.1016/j.ijinfomgt.2023.102642

Dwivedi, Y. K., Wastell, D., Laumer, S., Henriksen, H. Z., Myers, M. D., Bunker, D., Elbanna, A., Ravishankar, M. N., & Srivastava, S. C. (2015). Research on information systems failures and successes: Status update and future directions. *Information Systems Frontiers*, *17*(1), 143–157. doi:10.1007/s10796-014-9500-y

Ehsan, U., Liao, Q. V., Muller, M., Riedl, M. O., & Weisz, J. D. (2021). Expanding explainability: Towards social transparency in AI systems. In *Proceedings of the 2021 CHI Conference on Human Factors in Computing Systems* (pp. 1–19). 10.1145/3411764.3445188

Foerster, H. V. (2007). *Understanding Understanding: Essays on Cybernetics and Cognition*. Springer.

Følstad, A., & Taylor, C. (2021). Investigating the user experience of customer service chatbot interaction: A framework for qualitative analysis of chatbot dialogues. *Quality and User Experience*, *6*(1), 6. doi:10.1007/s41233-021-00046-5

Gašević, D., Greiff, S., & Shaffer, D. W. (2022). Towards strengthening links between learning analytics and assessment: Challenges and potentials of a promising new bond. *Computers in Human Behavior*, *134*, 107304. doi:10.1016/j.chb.2022.107304

Gebru, T., Morgenstern, J., Vecchione, B., Vaughan, J. W., Wallach, H. III, Iii, H. D., & Crawford, K. (2021). Datasheets for datasets. *Communications of the ACM*, *64*(12), 86–92. doi:10.1145/3458723

Gilson, A., Safranek, C. W., Huang, T., Socrates, V., Chi, L., Taylor, R. A., & Chartash, D. (2023). How does ChatGPT perform on the United States medical licensing examination? The implications of large language models for medical education and knowledge assessment. *JMIR Medical Education*, *9*, e45312. doi:10.2196/45312 PMID:36753318

González-Calatayud, V., Prendes-Espinosa, P., & Roig-Vila, R. (2021). Artificial intelligence for student assessment: A systematic review. *Applied Sciences (Basel, Switzerland)*, *11*(12), 5467. doi:10.3390/app11125467

Holmes, W., & Porayska-Pomsta, K. (2022). *The ethics of artificial intelligence in education: Practices, challenges, and debates*. Taylor & Francis. doi:10.4324/9780429329067

Holstein, K., Wortman Vaughan, J., Daumé, H. III, Dudik, M., & Wallach, H. (2019). Improving fairness in machine learning systems. *Proceedings of the 2019 CHI Conference on Human Factors in Computing Systems*. 10.1145/3290605.3300830

Hristova, B. (2023). *Some students are using ChatGPT to cheat—Here's how schools are trying to stop it.* CBC News. Retrieved from https://www.cbc.ca/news/canada/hamilton/chatgpt-school-cheating-1.6734580

Hsu, T. C., Huang, H. L., Hwang, G. J., & Chen, M. S. (2023). Effects of incorporating an expert decision-making mechanism into chatbots on students' achievement, enjoyment, and anxiety. *Journal of Educational Technology & Society*, *26*, 218–231.

Hwang, G., & Tu, Y. (2021). Roles and research trends of artificial intelligence in mathematics education: A bibliometric mapping analysis and systematic review. *Mathematics*, *9*(6), 584. doi:10.3390/math9060584

Jayaraman, J., & Black, J. (2022). Effectiveness of an intelligent question answering system for teaching financial literacy: A pilot study. In Innovations in Learning and Technology for the Workplace and Higher Education: Proceedings of 'The Learning Ideas Conference' 2021 (pp. 133–140). Springer. doi:10.1007/978-3-030-90677-1_13

Johnson, P., & Harris, D. (2002). Qualitative and quantitative issues in research design. In *Essential Skills for Management Research* (pp. 99–116). Sage. doi:10.4135/9781848605305.n6

Kasneci, E., Sessler, K., Küchemann, S., Bannert, M., Dementieva, D., Fischer, F., Gasser, U., Groh, G., Günnemann, S., Hüllermeier, E., Krusche, S., Kutyniok, G., Michaeli, T., Nerdel, C., Pfeffer, J., Poquet, O., Sailer, M., Schmidt, A., Seidel, T., ... Kasneci, G. (2023). ChatGPT for good? On opportunities and challenges of large language models for education. *Learning and Individual Differences*, *103*, 102274. doi:10.1016/j.lindif.2023.102274

Khosravi, H., Shum, S. B., Chen, G., Conati, C., Tsai, Y.-S., Kay, J., Knight, S., Martinez-Maldonado, R., Sadiq, S., & Gašević, D. (2022). Explainable Artificial Intelligence in education. *Computers and Education: Artificial Intelligence*, *3*, 100074. doi:10.1016/j.caeai.2022.100074

King, M. R. (2023). ChatGPT: A conversation on artificial intelligence, chatbots, and plagiarism in higher education. *Cellular and Molecular Bioengineering*, *16*(1), 1–2. doi:10.1007/s12195-022-00754-8 PMID:36660590

Kooli, C. (2023). Chatbots in education and research: A critical examination of ethical implications and solutions. *Sustainability (Basel)*, *15*(7), 5614. doi:10.3390/su15075614

Kuhail, M. A., Alturki, N., Alramlawi, S., & Alhejori, K. (2022). Interacting with educational chatbots: A systematic review. *Educational Technology Research and Development*, *70*, 973–1018.

Kumar, N., Mali, R., Ratnam, A., Kurpad, V., & Magapu, H. (2022). Identification and addressal of knowledge gaps in students. In *2022 3rd International Conference for Emerging Technology (INCET)* (pp. 1–6). IEEE. 10.1109/INCET54531.2022.9824483

Kurdi, G., Leo, J., Parsia, B., Sattler, U., & Al-Emari, S. (2020). A systematic review of automatic question generation for educational purposes. *International Journal of Artificial Intelligence in Education, 30*(1), 121–204. doi:10.1007/s40593-019-00186-y

Larsson, S., & Heintz, F. (2020). Transparency in artificial intelligence. *Internet Policy Review*, *9*(2). Advance online publication. doi:10.14763/2020.2.1469

Leiker, D., Finnigan, S., Gyllen, A. R., & Cukurova, M. (2023). Prototyping the use of large language models (LLMs) for adult learning content creation at scale. AIED Workshops.

Li, C., & Xing, W. (2021). Natural language generation using deep learning to support MOOC learners. *International Journal of Artificial Intelligence in Education, 31*(2), 186–214. doi:10.1007/s40593-020-00235-x

Li, Y., Sha, L., Yan, L., Lin, J., Raković, M., Galbraith, K., Lyons, K., Gašević, D., & Chen, G. (2023). Can large language models write reflectively. *Computers and Education: Artificial Intelligence, 100140.*

Liang, W., Yuksekgonul, M., Mao, Y., Wu, E., & Zou, J. (2023). GPT detectors are biased against non-native English writers. *arXiv preprint arXiv:2304.02819.*

Liu, S., Liu, S., Liu, Z., Peng, X., & Yang, Z. (2022). Automated detection of emotional and cognitive engagement in MOOC discussions to predict learning achievement. *Computers & Education, 181*, 104461. doi:10.1016/j.compedu.2022.104461

Liu, Z., He, X., Liu, L., Liu, T., & Zhai, X. (2023). Context matters: A strategy to pre-train language model for science education. *arXiv preprint arXiv:2301.12031*. doi:10.1007/978-3-031-36336-8_103

Ma, Q., Wu, S., & Koedinger, K. (2023). Is LLM the better programming partner? AIED Workshops.

Mageira, K., Pittou, D., Papasalouros, A., Kotis, K., Zangogianni, P., & Daradoumis, A. (2022). Educational AI chatbots for content and language integrated learning. *Applied Sciences (Basel, Switzerland), 12*(7), 3239. doi:10.3390/app12073239

Maheen, F., Asif, M., Ahmad, H., Ahmad, S., Alturise, F., Asiry, O., & Ghadi, Y. Y. (2022). Automatic computer science domain multiple-choice questions generation based on informative sentences. *PeerJ. Computer Science*, *8*, e1010. doi:10.7717/peerj-cs.1010 PMID:36091982

Mendoza, S., Hernández-León, M., Sánchez-Adame, L. M., Rodríguez, J., Decouchant, D., & Meneses-Viveros, A. (2020). Supporting student-teacher interaction through a chatbot. In Learning and Collaboration Technologies. doi:10.1007/978-3-030-50506-6_8

Mitchell, M., Wu, S., Zaldivar, A., Barnes, P., Vasserman, L., Hutchinson, B., Spitzer, E., Raji, I. D., & Gebru, T. (2019). Model cards for model reporting. In *Proceedings of the Conference on Fairness, Accountability, and Transparency* (pp. 220–229). 10.1145/3287560.3287596

Morris, M. R. (2020). AI and accessibility. *Communications of the ACM, 63*(6), 35–37. doi:10.1145/3356727

Murtaza, M., Ahmed, Y., Shamsi, J. A., Sherwani, F., & Usman, M. (2022). AI-based personalized E-learning systems: Issues, challenges, and solutions. *IEEE Access : Practical Innovations, Open Solutions, 10*, 81323–81342. doi:10.1109/ACCESS.2022.3193938

Nguyen, A., Ngo, H. N., Hong, Y., Dang, B., & Nguyen, B. T. (2022). Ethical principles for artificial intelligence in education. *Education and Information Technologies*, *28*(4), 4221–4241. doi:10.1007/s10639-022-11316-w PMID:36254344

Nye, B., Mee, D., & Core, M. G. (2023). Generative large language models for dialog-based tutoring: An early consideration of opportunities and concerns. AIED Workshops.

O'Neil, C. (2017). *Weapons of math destruction: How big data increases inequality and threatens democracy*. Crown.

Okonkwo, C. W., & Ade-Ibijola, A. (2021). Evaluating the ethical implications of using chatbot systems in higher education. *digiTAL, 2021*, 68.

Oleny, A. (2023). Generating multiple-choice questions from a textbook: LLMs match human performance on most metrics. AIED Workshops.

Open, A. I. (2023). *Introducing chatgpt*. Retrieved from https://openai.com/blog/chatgpt

Open, A. I. (n.d.). *OpenAI GPT-3*. Retrieved from https://openai.com/gpt-3/

Pavlik, J. V. (2023). Collaborating with ChatGPT: Considering the implications of generative artificial intelligence for journalism and media education. *Journalism & Mass Communication Educator*, *78*(1), 84–93. doi:10.1177/10776958221149577

Pedro, F., Subosa, M., Rivas, A., & Valverde, P. (2019). *Artificial Intelligence in Education: Challenges and Opportunities for Sustainable Development*. UNESCO.

Pelletier, K., McCormack, M., Reeves, J., Robert, J., Arbino, N., Dickson-Deane, C., & Stine, J. (2022). 2022 EDUCAUSE Horizon Report Teaching and Learning Edition. EDUC22.

Pesonen, J. A. (2021). 'Are You OK?' Students' Trust in a Chatbot Providing Support Opportunities. In *Learning and Collaboration Technologies: Games and Virtual Environments for Learning: 8th International Conference, LCT 2021, Held as Part of the 23rd HCI International Conference, HCII 2021, Virtual Event, July 24–29, 2021, Proceedings, Part II* (pp. 199–215). Springer.

Phillips, M., Marsden, H., Jaffe, W., Matin, R. N., Wali, G. N., Greenhalgh, J., McGrath, E., James, R., Ladoyanni, E., Bewley, A., Argenziano, G., & Palamaras, I. (2019). Assessment of accuracy of an artificial intelligence algorithm to detect melanoma in images of skin lesions. *JAMA Network Open*, *2*(10), e1913436. doi:10.1001/jamanetworkopen.2019.13436 PMID:31617929

Raji, I. D., Smart, A., White, R. N., Mitchell, M., Gebru, T., Hutchinson, B., Smith-Loud, J., Theron, D., & Barnes, P. (2020). Closing the AI accountability gap. In *Proceedings of the 2020 Conference on Fairness, Accountability, and Transparency* (pp. 33–44). https://doi.org/10.1145/3351095.3372873

Rudolph, J., Tan, S., & Tan, S. (2023). ChatGPT: Bullshit spewer or the end of traditional assessments in higher education? *Journal of Applied Learning and Teaching, 6*.

Sallam, M. (2023). The utility of ChatGPT as an example of large language models in healthcare education, research, and practice: Systematic review on the future perspectives and potential limitations. medRxiv, *2023-02*.

Sarsa, S., Denny, P., Hellas, A., & Leinonen, J. (2022). Automatic generation of programming exercises and code explanations using large language models. In *Proceedings of the 2022 ACM Conference on International Computing Education Research* Volume 1 (pp. 27–43). 10.1145/3501385.3543957

Sawatzki, J., Schlippe, T., & Benner-Wickner, M. (2022). Deep learning techniques for automatic short answer grading: Predicting scores for English and German answers. In *Artificial Intelligence in Education: Emerging Technologies, Models and Applications: Proceedings of 2021 2nd International Conference on Artificial Intelligence in Education Technology* (pp. 65–75). Springer.

Schneider, J., Richner, R., & Riser, M. (2022). Towards trustworthy autograding of short, multi-lingual, multi-type answers. *International Journal of Artificial Intelligence in Education*, 1–31.

Schramowski, P., Turan, C., Andersen, N., Rothkopf, C. A., & Kersting, K. (2022). Large pre-trained language models contain human-like biases of what is right and wrong to do. *Nature Machine Intelligence*, *4*(3), 258–268. doi:10.1038/s42256-022-00458-8

Schwartz, R., Dodge, J., Smith, N. A., & Etzioni, O. (2020). Green AI. *Communications of the ACM*, *63*(12), 54–63. doi:10.1145/3381831

Smith, H. (2021). Clinical AI: Opacity, accountability, responsibility, and liability. *AI & Society*, *36*(2), 535–545. doi:10.1007/s00146-020-01019-6

Stevano, S., & Deane, K. (2019). The role of research assistants in qualitative and cross-cultural social science research. In *Handbook of Research Methods in Health Social Sciences*. Available online: https://doi-org.proxy.bib.uottawa.ca/10.1007/978-981-10-5251-4_39

Studente, S., Ellis, S., & Garivaldis, S. F. (2020). Exploring the potential of chatbots in higher education: A preliminary study. *International Journal of Educational Technology in Higher Education*, *17*, 55.

Sun, T., Gaut, A., Tang, S., Huang, Y., ElSherief, M., Zhao, J., Mirza, D., Belding, E., Chang, K.-W., & Wang, W. Y. (2019). Mitigating gender bias in natural language processing: literature review. *Proceedings of the 57th Annual Meeting of the Association for Computational Linguistics*. 10.18653/v1/P19-1159

Tanjga, M. (2023). *E-learning and the use of AI: A review of current practices and future directions*. Qeios. doi:10.32388/AP0208

Tapalova, O., & Zhiyenbayeva, N. (2022). Artificial intelligence in education: AIEd for personalized learning pathways. *Electronic Journal of e-Learning*, *20*(5), 639–653. doi:10.34190/ejel.20.5.2597

Tlili, A., Shehata, B., Adarkwah, M. A., Bozkurt, A., Hickey, D. T., Huang, R., & Agyemang, B. (2023). What if the devil is my guardian angel: ChatGPT as a case study of using chatbots in education. *Smart Learning Environments*, *10*(1), 51. doi:10.1186/s40561-023-00237-x

Torralba, A., & Efros, A. A. (2011). Unbiased look at dataset bias. In *CVPR 2011* (pp. 1521–1528). IEEE. doi:10.1109/CVPR.2011.5995347

Truong, T.-L., Le, H.-L., & Le-Dang, T.-P. (2020, November). Sentiment analysis implementing BERT-based pre-trained language model for Vietnamese. *2020 7th NAFOSTED Conference on Information and Computer Science (NICS)*. 10.1109/NICS51282.2020.9335912

Turner, S. (2010). Research note: The silenced assistant. Reflections of invisible interpreters and research assistants. *Asia Pacific Viewpoint*, *51*(2), 206–219. doi:10.1111/j.1467-8373.2010.01425.x

Verma, S. (2019). Weapons of Math Destruction: How Big Data Increases Inequality and Threatens Democracy. *Vikalpa*, *44*(2), 97–98. doi:10.1177/0256090919853933

Wachter, S., Mittelstadt, B., & Floridi, L. (2017). Transparent, explainable, and accountable AI for robotics. *Science Robotics*, *2*(6), eaan6080. doi:10.1126/scirobotics.aan6080 PMID:33157874

Wang, T., Lund, B. D., Marengo, A., Pagano, A., Mannuru, N. R., Teel, Z. A., & Pange, J. (2023). Exploring the potential impact of artificial intelligence (AI) on international students in higher education: Generative AI, chatbots, analytics, and international student success. *Applied Sciences (Basel, Switzerland)*, *13*(11), 6716. doi:10.3390/app13116716

Wollny, S., Schneider, J., Di Mitri, D., Weidlich, J., Rittberger, M., & Drachsler, H. (2021). Are we there yet? – A systematic literature review on chatbots in education. *Frontiers in Artificial Intelligence*, *4*, 654924. doi:10.3389/frai.2021.654924 PMID:34337392

Wu, J. (2022). Analysis and evaluation of the impact of integrating mental health education into the teaching of university civics courses in the context of artificial intelligence. *Wireless Communications and Mobile Computing*, *2022*, 2022. doi:10.1155/2022/5378694

Wu, X., He, X., Li, T., Liu, N., & Zhai, X. (2023). Matching exemplar as next sentence prediction (MENSP): Zero-shot prompt learning for automatic scoring in science education. *arXiv preprint arXiv:2301.08771*. doi:10.1007/978-3-031-36272-9_33

Yan, L., Zhao, L., Gašević, D., & Martinez-Maldonado, R. (2022). Scalability, sustainability, and ethicality of multimodal learning analytics. In *LAK22: 12th International Learning Analytics and Knowledge Conference* (pp. 13–23). 10.1145/3506860.3506862

Zeng, Z., Gašević, D., & Chen, G. (2023). On the effectiveness of curriculum learning in educational text scoring. *Proceedings of the AAAI Conference on Artificial Intelligence*. 10.1609/aaai.v37i12.26707

Zhang, K., & Aslan, A. B. (2021). AI technologies for education: Recent research future directions. *Computers. Education and Artificial Intelligence*, *2*, 100025. doi:10.1016/j.caeai.2021.100025

Zheng, L., Niu, J., Long, M., & Fan, Y. (2023). An automatic knowledge graph construction approach to promoting collaborative knowledge building, group performance, social interaction, and socially shared regulation in CSCL. *British Journal of Educational Technology*, *54*(3), 686–711. doi:10.1111/bjet.13283

Zheng, L., Niu, J., & Zhong, L. (2022). Effects of a learning analytics-based real-time feedback approach on knowledge elaboration, knowledge convergence, interactive relationships, and group performance in CSCL. *British Journal of Educational Technology*, *53*(1), 130–149. doi:10.1111/bjet.13156

Chapter 12
Screaming Out Loud in the Communication Classroom:
Asian Stereotypes and the Fallibility of Image Generating Artificial Intelligence (AI)

Yifeng Hu
The College of New Jersey, USA

Anastacia D. Kurylo
Brooklyn College, USA

ABSTRACT

This chapter addresses the role that stereotypes play in the advent of the AI age as specifically evidenced in AI generated images and the implications of it in communication classrooms. AI and human information processing share similar elements: learning, perceiving, and reproducing, and they feed into each other in order to perpetuate stereotypes. In our literature review we draw a comparison and establish a relationship between the fallibility of human cognitive information processing and the production of stereotypical images that AI seems to unabashedly scream back to us. Using several Asians stereotypes as a case study, we experiment with several AI image and video generators: Dall-E, Midjourney, and Pika Art. Different prompts are used to analyze the stereotypical nature of the images generated by these AI platforms. In our discussion section, first, we address the collaborative and hegemonic human-AI interactive problem and highlight two implications of such interactions: the invisibility of historically marginalized groups and harm done to target groups. Second, we discuss the double bind that we have identified through this work, which precludes offering clear cut solutions. Third, by applying what we have analyzed and synthesized in communication classrooms, we argue that communication teachers and students can benefit from image and video generating AI but need to focus on the potential risks of AI in reproducing and spreading harmful stereotypes about less visible, less powerful groups. We conclude that image and video generating AI reveals deeply rooted unconscious biases in people's minds and screams them out loud. Learning how to identify them, and better yet, how to prevent them from the beginning, is critical AI literacy that communication students and future communication and media professionals want to equip themselves with.

DOI: 10.4018/979-8-3693-0831-8.ch012

INTRODUCTION

There are many concerns about the potential harm that generative AI can cause to humankind. Among these are the potential for AI to perpetuate misinformation. One way this occurs is through what is known as hallucination: when AI treats as real some content that is not verifiable as such upon further inspection (IBM, n.d.). According to IBM (n.d.), "AI hallucination is a phenomenon wherein a large language model (LLM)—often a generative AI chatbot or computer vision tool—perceives patterns or objects that are nonexistent or imperceptible to human observers, creating outputs that are nonsensical or altogether inaccurate." Because of AI's efficient ability to generate content, another concern in the AI landscape is the potential for AI to take over roles heretofore occupied by professionals. Such concerns are said to have contributed to the 148-day Writer's Strike that occurred in 2023 (Coyle, 2023). Another concern is about copyright infringement. This issue sparked governmental regulations (e.g., Center for AI and Digital Policy, 2024) and ongoing legal cases (e.g., Stempel, 2023).

A less frequently discussed but equally important topic is gaining attention from popular media and scholars alike: AI and stereotypes. The current chapter focuses on image and video generating AI[1] to address issues related to stereotypes and classroom utilization. This chapter compares the fallibility of AI and humankind in information processing and discusses how this results in a closed-loop system that is self-perpetuating. Given this inherent problem with AI platforms, it is important to explain this dynamic to students, which the chapter models how to do, and explore options for and the feasibility of how to help our students break the cycle.

The college communication classroom is a particularly valuable area for training students on how to use image-generating AI to be less stereotypical for three reasons. First, students in communication coursework are more likely than peers in other majors to enter professions, have hobbies, or explore other endeavors that may utilize image-generating AI in particular. Second, as students, their expectation is that they are being trained on the appropriate and relevant ways to utilize available tools in their careers in particular. Thus, the absence of training in this regard is an oversight that has meaning for students. Kurylo and Hu (2016) argued, for example, that teachers need to adapt to and integrate new technology tools, such as LinkedIn, into their communication with students so that students can determine the proper way to use these tools even if the instructors themselves are not as familiar or comfortable with these tools themselves. Third, challenging the way in which students view and make use of AI and image-generating AI in particular has the greatest capacity to affect change at the large societal level over time, as students tend to be younger and there are thousands of colleges in the United States.

LITERATURE REVIEW

Image and Video-Generating AI[2] and Stereotypes

Several press articles have reported their own research on how AI is reducing the world to stereotypes. Bloomberg conducted an analysis of more than 5,000 images generated by Stable Diffusion, an artificial intelligence (AI) image generator (Nicoletti & Bass, 2023). They found that images generated by Stable Diffusion when prompted about higher-paying job titles are associated with lighter skin tones. When prompted for images about professional roles, most of the image results produced were of men. Rest of World, self-described as "a nonprofit publication that challenges expectations about whose experiences with technology matter" (Rest of World, n.d.), analyzed 3,000 Midjourney-generated images to determine how AI views different countries and cultures. The results show a severely narrow perspective on the world: "An Indian person is almost always an old man with a beard; a Mexican person is usually a man in a sombrero; Most of New Delhi's streets are polluted and littered; In Indonesia, food is served almost exclusively on banana leaves; and an American person is almost always a light skinned person standing in front of a U.S. flag, usually with blond hair" (Turk, 2023, para. 7). In another study, researchers from the University of Washington took images produced by Stable Diffusion and analyzed them computationally. Their findings echoed the idea that in the realm of AI, "person" largely means a "light-skinned, Western man" (Ghosh & Caliskan, 2023, p. 6978).

In 2023, Rona Wong, an MIT graduate student of Asian descent, posted on X (formerly Twitter) that she asked Playground AI, an image generator, to turn a photo of her profile into a professional-looking headshot. She was shocked by the following result: AI made her skin lighter and eyes blue (Bhaimiya, 2023). To generate a professional photo, the AI interpreted this student's Asian facial features as not professional enough and revised those features to make her more closely resemble a White woman. In response, the founder of Playground AI, Suhail Doshi, said, "The models aren't instructable like that so it'll pick any generic thing based on the prompt. Unfortunately, they're not smart enough. Happy to help you get a result, but it takes a bit more effort than something like ChatGPT" (@Suhail, 2023). This raises the following question: is it true that AI is not smart enough or is there another variable at play? This chapter argues that AI *is* smart, as evidenced by its ability to detect and expose stereotypes through how it processes information. In the following section, we compare and establish a relationship between the fallibility of passive human cognitive information processing and the production of stereotypical images that image-generating AI seems to unabashedly scream back to us.

Information Processing

In each moment of our lives, our five senses experience information overload (Fiske & Taylor, 1984) as they are confronted with seemingly infinite minutia of data (i.e., information). A person would be rendered incapable of carrying out the most basic everyday activities if they needed to experience every piece of information with which they came into contact anew. Instead, to get through their day, each person must reduce the amount of information they take in to what is relevant to function in the world. Because of this necessary reduction in information, there is no unfiltered information that people experience. Rather, people interact with the world through their perception of it. All the information is only experienced through an individual's perceptual lens. This complex and personalized process involves three stages (e.g. Kurylo, 2021): selecting, organizing, and interpreting. Selecting is the process of choosing the information we attend to among all of which we come in contact with. The next step is to organize, which is the process of categorizing the selected information into compartmentalized and familiar groupings. Finally, interpreting is the process of giving meaning to the selected and categorized information.

The interpretation of information is a value-laden process. Put another way, there is no value-neutral information because it is necessarily interpreted simultaneously as people perceive it. Fiske and Taylor (1984) explain what happens when people process information. According to the cognitive miser metaphor (Fiske & Taylor, 1984), individuals stingily conserve their mental capacities by processing data quickly and efficiently (Hamilton & Sherman, 1994). To do this, we use various cognitive tools to simultaneously limit (i.e., cognitive efficiency) and expand (i.e., attribution) the data (Hamilton & Sherman, 1994).

According to schema theory (e.g., Fiske & Taylor, 1984), a schema is a tool we use to process information. Focusing on the role of stereotypes in the processing of all this information, researchers have hypothesized that stereotypes function as a type of schema or mental representation that provides familiar categories into which people can automatically sort information (Fiske & Taylor, 1984; Hamilton & Sherman, 1994; Hilton & Von Hippel, 1996). Because stereotyping is often beyond a person's awareness, people typically use stereotypes passively and unintentionally (Macrae et al., 1994). People stereotype because stereotypes serve as a type of schema to allow people to sort information automatically, which simultaneously decreases and increases the amount of information people process, thus allowing for efficiency of their scarce cognitive resources. As a result, stereotypes help information processing proceed quickly, efficiently, and with minimal effort (Hamilton et al., 1990). In this way, stereotypes allow people to predict and explain a complex world by reducing presumably irrelevant information while simultaneously filling in presumed gaps with information (Berger & Calabrese, 1975).

From a cognitive perspective, stereotypes function as categorization tools (Gilbert & Hixon, 1991), which preserve information processing resources and act as energy-saving devices. Ryan et al. (1996) concisely explain how stereotypes function in cognitive processes: "According to the cognitive approach, human beings have a limited capacity for processing information. Stereotypes serve to organize and simplify a complex social world, and they are often likely to take the form of overgeneralizations" (p. 123). Stereotypes function for people because they describe characteristics about groups that allow us to infer information (Kurylo, 2013), regardless of the accuracy or lack thereof of that information, when we think of, talk about, or come into contact with a member of this group and allow us to ignore other information unrelated to stereotypes of that group.

The Fallibility of Information Processing

Although a cognitive perspective typically stresses that stereotyping processes are neutral (i.e., neither inherently positive nor negative), researchers have long since acknowledged the role that stereotyping can play in prejudice and discrimination (Hamilton et al., 1990; Hinton, 2000; Kurylo, 2013; Lippmann, 1922). Stereotypes are inherently packed with emotional and social baggage that has consequences for real people because stereotypes are not inherently accurate (Kurylo, 2013). This can be consequential when people make decisions based on the assumption that they are 'true.' Stereotypes erroneously treated as factual generalizations can extend to prejudice and discrimination and affect high stakes decisions (Kurylo & Hu, 2024), such as who is approved for a mortgage loan (Office of Public Affairs, 2022; Stempel, 2007).

Moreover, stereotypes act as noise in communication to interfere with the fidelity of a message. This can cause a person to potentially miss more important, relevant, useful, or interesting information in ways that can affect important outcomes in their lives, such as who that person befriends. As a result, using stereotypes to process information may result in hypothesis confirmation or self-fulfilling prophecies that prevent people from being curious and seeking additional or alternate answers to their expectations, questions, or concerns (Hamilton et al., 1990).

Finally, stereotypes are rigid (Lippmann, 1922), impersonal, and unable to adapt to the individuation needed in a given situation (Kurylo, 2013). Consequently, they can impact important interactions, such as among workplace colleagues (e.g., Hu & Pham, 2024; Kurylo & Veeramani, 2024) or in customer service where someone may take offense at an explicit stereotype or more subtle microaggression (e.g., Hart & Fassett, 2024). Ultimately, stereotypes are a poor way to communicate (Kurylo, 2013). The mindless, automatic, and passive use of stereotypes in our cognitive and communication processes therefore comes at some cost (Langer et al., 1978). By processing information actively or mindfully, people can become less reliant on stereotype use; however, this is not easily accomplished (Hamilton et al., 1990).

Because of our limited ability to process information, our ability to create entirely original ideas is limited as well. This is evident in the cliché, "Everything old is new again". Our creativity can extend only to what we already know. As a culture, we tend to repeat styles and trends. For example, podcasts were arguably versions of radio broadcasts in the mid-1900s, similar to the 1938 Orson Welles' War of the Worlds broadcast (Schwartz, 2015). Another example is the environmental and, now, legal push to use reusable nonwoven tote bags to carry groceries harken back to earlier times, during which people regularly took baskets to shop at their local general store. As humans, our imaginations are arguably unlimited; that is, they are unlimited within the constraints of what we can conceive. The AI is similar. It can be creative to the extent that it has preexisting knowledge on which to base that creativity (Glen, 2021).

Comparison Between Humans and AI

Since the launch of the Chat Generative Pre-training Transformer (ChatGPT) in 2022, the corpus of data that AI has access to has been vast. Like the information overload and information processing that humans experience, image-generating AI selects from, organizes, and interprets the information it has available to provide creative responses to user prompts (e.g., Oppenlaender, 2022). There is evidence of the ability of AI to be creative. AI is able to write in long form, edit a person's writing, scour the internet for examples and sources, search videos for the presence of requested content, and generate images based on simple or complex conversational prompts, which are ultimately integral to AI and are part of a growing knowledge area called prompt engineering (e.g., Heston & Khun, 2023; Meskó, 2023; Oppenlaender, 2022). Concern has been raised about the ability of AI technology to be too human-like (e.g., Anderson & Rainie, 2018). Laws are being established to address concerns about a technology developed intentionally in the likeness of humankind and, indeed, to reflect, supplement, and surpass (i.e., faster, more efficient, etc.) human abilities. According to the Center for AI and Digital Policy (2024), there has been a push for AI regulation since ChatGPT's launch in late 2022. In March 2023, more than 30,000 scientists and technologists signed an open letter (Future of Life Institute, 2023) warning of safety risks posed by uncontrolled AI systems. The letter demanded that the training of AI systems more powerful than GPT-4 be immediately paused for at least six months. Center for AI and Digital Policy (2023) filed a lengthy complaint with the Federal Trade Commission (FTC), requesting an investigation of OpenAI, ChatGPT's creator. The Center for AI and Digital Policy (2024) alleged that OpenAI knew ChatGPT's deficiencies but still released them, thus engaging in deceptive practices. The FTC (2023) issued a warning about how several AI tools, including generative AI, deepfakes, and voice cloning technologies, could be used for deception. The U.S. consumer protection commission also pledged to be committed to vigilant oversight (Center for AI and Digital Policy, 2024).

The actions of government units and organizations such as the Center for AI and Digital Policy underscore the urgency and challenges of policy change brought about by rapidly advancing AI systems. Media attention has tended to focus on issues such as copyright infringement (e.g., Stempel, 2023), misinformation, and job displacement (Center for AI and Digital Policy, 2024). One area of limitation, and potentially harm, of accelerating AI technologies that is given less attention in the mainstream is how, just as occurs in human information processing, AI quickly learns, perceives, and reproduces stereotypes (e.g., Turk, 2023). These will be discussed in the following three sections.

Learning Through Socialization

Children are clean slates until they are socialized to learn about the world around them, including stereotypes, by observing and watching how people communicate around them (e.g., Fausto-Sterling, 1992). Similarly, AI learns what to pay attention to from user prompts (Harvard University, 2023). Without a prompt, the AI will not spontaneously produce. AI is responsive to human prompts, not proactive. As such, our own limitations[3] of what we would or could ask as well as how we ask questions set up parameters for what AI can produce. The output of AI is limited by our ability to prompt it (Harvard University, 2023). Arguably, AI learns how to process information from the prompts it receives, individually, cumulatively, and longitudinally. This does not mean that what AI produces is deterministic but rather framed. For example, the questions that students use to prompt AI are limited by their perception. This may help explain why detecting AI-generated work is often not particularly difficult (e.g., Rowe, 2023). A student, for example, does not necessarily know that they would need to prompt the AI to take on the persona of writing like a student or even to provide a sample paragraph from their own writing style and prompt the AI to write similarly to the writing style in the provided paragraph. Therefore, an AI-generated student submitted paper, regardless of the age or life experience of the student, may be detectable by a teacher when that student simply does not know how to prompt the AI and may even lack awareness that they have a gap in knowledge about the existence of techniques to more appropriately prompt the AI. AI learns how to perceive information from how humans 'socialize'[4] it to do so.

The Perceptual Process

AI answers are generated from data contained within the content that the AI tool has been trained to utilize. These involve immense storehouses of information, regularly updated and always available at the figurative fingertips of AI tools. Nonetheless, that information is framed by what humans have previously produced both in the prompts and other socialization as well as in the corpus of information at its disposal, produced within the confines of humankinds' perception (e.g., Fausto-Sterling, 1992). This may be experienced in the form of AI hallucinations in which inaccurate information is presented as fact, which occurs in part because of the AI's ability to aggregate information that allows it to see patterns in the data on a scale inaccessible to humans. Although many AI hallucination issues have been addressed and resolved, generative AI can inevitably provide "unforeseen and undesirable consequences" (IBM, n.d.).

AI's Ability to Reproduce (Scream) Stereotypes

Because AI is limited by the prompts offered to it as well as the information the AI itself has at its disposal, AI reproduces (e.g., Glen, 2021; Rowe, 2023). AI allows for the creation of content never seen before. However, these images are not original but rather reproductions or adaptations of what has already been created as cultural knowledge in the AI knowledge database (Glen, 2021). Given our own limitations, as humans, we interpret AI-generated images as original rather than as pastiches (Glen, 2021) or reproductions. This is because we do not have access to a vast database of images to determine the origins of those newly generated images. As with humans, we treat AI-generated content as original—albeit imperfectly constructed AI (Rowe, 2023). There is much discussion about the (supposed) originality of image-generating AI (e.g., Glen, 2021), and indeed, some might view this idea of AI as reproducing to be a controversial topic; however, two points are generally accepted even though the technology is still relatively new. First, AI art is an amalgamation of images that already exist, even if the new image it creates does not exist exactly elsewhere (Glen, 2021). Second, these images cannot be copyrighted because AI is not considered an author/artist according to the law (Helyer, 2023).

AI tools such as Dall-E, Midjourney, and Pika Art, which generate images and videos based on user prompts, utilize their available data to determine what response to provide. This generative process provides a contextually relevant response to a prompt based on the information that exists within the AI database (van der Duim, 2023). The AI tool's efficient 'thinking' allows it to infer that its answer to a prompt is the most reasonably inferred contextually relevant answer (van der Duim, 2023). As such, AI tools reproduce the status quo of what is already known or has been imagined previously at the aggregate. With regard to image-generating AI, this process reproduces stereotypes similar to human information processing. Whereas in human perceptual processes, stereotypes are often produced in mindless and passive ways that result in unconscious bias, image-generating AI produces images that often overtly scream out to us. Prompting image-generating AI for an image of a nurse, for example, will unsurprisingly yield a picture of a woman because it is statistically verifiable that the majority of nurses are female. It is also worth noting that the majority of the images of nurses that the AI tool would have access to are likely to be female, as evidenced by an image search of this term in a search engine. Moreover, the AI system predicts what is statistically presumed to be desired by the person who has given it the prompt. In some cases, this may not necessarily be what constitutes a statistically accurate answer. The answer could be one that is most represented in its database, regardless of the accuracy of that answer. Therefore, it is an important distinction that although the AI tool can provide an accurate and statistically verifiable answer, it can also not do that, as it tries to predict the answer that it thinks the person providing the prompt is presumed to be interested in receiving.

A CASE STUDY WITH ASIAN STEREOTYPES CREATED BY IMAGE-GENERATING AI

Method

Case studies allow the focus and magnification of a single example to explore the complexity and layers of a phenomenon (Stake, 2000; Tesch, 1990). To explore the manifestation of Asian stereotypes in image-generating AI, we present a case study that highlights how seemingly innocent and relatively basic user-generated prompts inadvertently result in AI-produced stereotype-reinforcing images. Our process involved three strategies. First, we start with more basic to more detailed prompts to determine whether and to what extent stereotypes may emerge. Second, we incorporate different AI tools to better understand whether the specific system used matters for the generation of these stereotypes: Dall-E, Midjourney, and Pika Art. Third, we analyze different perspectives from image generation, including our own prompts using the technology, as in the case of Dall-E and Pika Art, as well as other users' prompts, as in the case of MidJourney, to provide a more well-rounded encapsulation of the technology. To conduct the case study, a convenience sample was used because we utilized free versions of the technology as well as a single issue from MidJourney magazine, which was available in hard copies to one of the authors. Case studies are distinct from other research methods and provide the opportunity to unpack a single phenomenon, exposing multiple layers of complexity with the flexibility to intentionally limit the study to aspects of the phenomenon (e.g., studying only one example), allowing the depth and dimensionality of the phenomenon to emerge.

Figure 1. Image from Dall-E prompt "A Man"

Reproducing Gender and Model Minority Stereotypes

As evidenced in Figure 1, AI is capable of interpreting a prompt and providing a response. In this case, Dall-E was prompted on December 24, 2023, for an image of "a man" and produced a result of men who appear to be White or Asian. These men are seemingly in the 18 to 30 age range, as all of those pictured appear to be adults and have no gray hair, loss of hair, or noticeable wrinkles around the eyes. The images also communicate a demeanor clockwise from the top left image: contemplative, serious, agreeable, and engaged (in the interactional sense). While the four images simultaneously generated could easily include other racial representations, the omission of the non-White, non model minority representation speaks loudly by implying what "a man" in the normative sense is not. This reproduction of the White male norm is reminiscent of what was found in the literature. The inclusion of Asian males adds a more sophisticated version of this reproduction by aligning Asian identity as a model minority with White male normativity (Lee, 2009). The stereotypes of White normativity and the model minority are present in these four images.

As shown in Figure 2, AI is once again capable of interpreting a prompt and providing a response. In Figure 2, Dall-E was prompted with "a woman" on December 24, 2023. In addition, juxtaposed with Figure 1, the reproduction of stereotypes further becomes readable. In this case, Dall-E provided "a woman" as someone, again, who is White or Asian, seemingly in the 18 to 30 years age range, as all of those pictured appear to be adults and have no gray hair or wrinkles. The images also communicate a demeanor, clockwise from the top left image: content, surprised (but politely covering one's mouth), arguably someone seeking to speak or being humbly confident depending on how the finger signal is interpreted, and ornamental by modeling the purse. Taken a step further, the contrast in the two sets of images is more striking, with the 'a man' images predominantly being outdoors and the men wearing multiple layers of dark denim or leather clothing and sneakers suggesting that the men are 'outdoorsy'

Figure 2. Image from Dall-E prompt "A Woman"

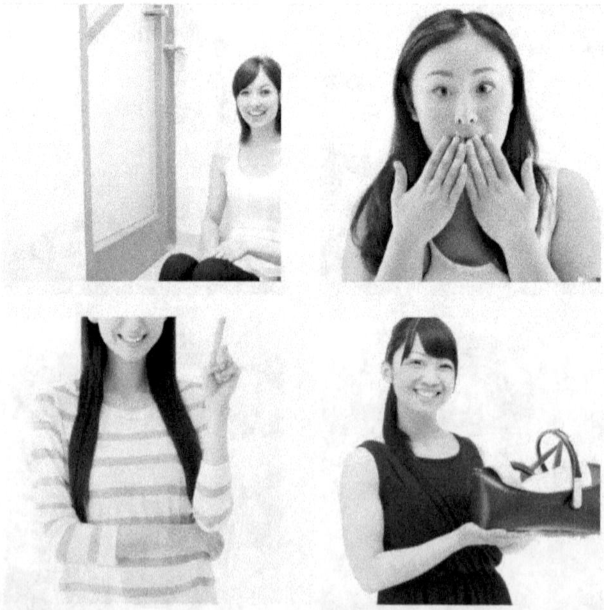

or 'rugged.' In stark contrast, the women are predominantly floating in a background of white space, suggesting that they are on display and acontextual. Three are wearing tank tops. Three are smiling. Attention is drawn to their hands or bodies and in one image 'a woman' is not allowed by the AI to have a face. This occurs unlike the men produced in Figure 1, whose faces are, in two images, viewed from the side and far away but whose bodies are less of a focus than how the men are engaging with their environment, doing something actively which the viewer gets to witness. In contrast, women communicate with the viewer directly. Taken together, the two sets of images reinforce stereotypes of women as ornamental, physically attractive, and concerned with their appearance and desire to be viewed/appreciated and, generally, demurely happy. In these ways, the Dall-E images related to "a man" and "a woman" can be read as stereotypical images of normatively White and model Minority men and women.

Reproducing the 'Other'

In this portion of the case study, we examine images from the image-generating AI tool Midjourney. Midjourney magazine is a monthly print publication self-described as having the goal "to highlight and develop the artwork created by our global community" (Midjourney, 2023, p. 1). Images that appeared in the magazine "were selected from the 10,000 highest rated V4 images according to the Midjourney community" (Midjourney, 2023, p. 3) without further clarification of the selection process. In the March 2023 edition, their first section focused on variations in images of living creatures, predominantly people and animals. This section appears before their feature article and comprises 42 pages of full-color images generated by user prompts. This first section includes 57 images of which 20 involved images of animals (e.g., a rabbit), inanimate objects (e.g., spaceships), or human-like beings with either a facial covering (e.g., helmet) or who were neither human nor animal (e.g., alien). Of the remaining 37 images depicting humans (i.e., with identifiable skin color and race), 27 (73%) were of White people.

Of the 'White' people images, some were produced through the seemingly racially neutral prompts "elderly painter," "punk concert," and "older male astronaut." Others involved prompts referencing familiar artists, styles, or types of people who would typically or stereotypically invoke White people. For example, one image generated by the user SimplySam on December 25, 2022, was based on a prompt stating "artwork in the style of edouard manet [sic]," an artist who has painted non-White subjects as well though this is not the majority of his work (Pound, 2019). Not surprisingly, the AI made an inference to provide the user what was assumed to be the most likely contextually relevant response, and despite a racially nondescript prompt, the Midjourney AI produced an image of two White people. This prompt is an excellent case in point. Manet has several very well-known paintings involving a Black model named Laure. An internet search yielded 576,000 hits for the search Manet Laure. However, these pales in comparison to the more than 31 million hits that appear for Manet when searching without Laure. As addressed in the nurse example mentioned previously, the statistical probability wins out.

Four of the 37 (10.8%) images involved subjects who were identifiable as light-skinned Asian, and six images (16%) were identifiable as Black or people with dark skin, with only one having a visibly intersectional identity overlapping the two. Taken together, these images—including all nonwhite racial categories that were depicted—comprise essentially just a quarter (26.8%) of the human-oriented images in this section of the Midjourney magazine. In the Asian racialized images, the prompts included specific racialized callouts, including "japanese lady [sic]" and "not the stereotypical japanese woman [sic]," with two other image prompts invoking styles of Asian artists. Prompts in the Black racialized images used explicit and implicit racial callouts, including "older Black man," "Black dark skinned woman," "gang," and "two beautiful Black women" (in 2 instances). Even the intersectional identity was called out explicitly in the prompt, which requested a "mixed-race woman."

AI information processing is more concerning than merely replicating the status quo. Humans can choose to be mindful or creative or may simply accidentally stumble into producing a new idea or way of thinking that is not the *same old same old* (Hamilton et al.,1990). AI is without this ability to produce anything except original versions of what might be expected to be produced by their prompt, leading to confirmation bias and self-fulfilling prophecy that may reinforce what the user expected before even interacting with the AI tool. AI 'wants' to please by providing the most popular, seemingly credible response to the user's prompt. It is programmed to give the person who enters the prompt the thing that they most likely desire. As AI bases this decision on what is most prominently available, it inevitably and innocently reproduces stereotypes. In other words, AI information processing requires a reduction in the vast amount of information it has available into what its own perceptual process selects, categorizes, and interprets (Hamilton et al., 1990), and, in doing so, reproduces the stereotypes that emerge when the data is aggregated.

If we take this one step further, we can see that it becomes even more problematic. The information databases that the AI tool relies upon to determine the most desirable response are not definitively the correct, right, or factual answers to the prompt but at times may be the most common in their database. For example, in describing their own AI system accuracy, the AIContentfy Team (2023) specifies the following:

Despite advancements in AI-powered content generation, ensuring content accuracy remains a challenge. AI systems are prone to errors due to limitations in understanding context, nuances, and cultural references. For instance, they may generate inaccurate information or fail to detect bias in content. (para. 7)

Moreover, the AIContentfy Team (2023) continues, albeit focused on text-based AI:

The rise of AI has had a significant impact on the credibility and trustworthiness of online content. With AI-powered content generation, there is an increased risk of inaccurate and misleading information being disseminated. For instance, AI algorithms can automatically generate fake news articles that appear to be authentic, making it difficult for users to discern fact from fiction. This has serious implications for individuals seeking reliable information online. (para. 19)

Most users, however, have a limited understanding of AI tools. As a result, they may not interpret the image as a stereotyped reproduction. Moreover, people may not be aware that they can challenge the AI tool's inherently stereotypical assumptions of normativity.

Reproducing (Screaming) Asian Stereotypes

To more directly test whether images and videos generated from AI reproduce Asian model Minority stereotypes, we used Pika Art, a text-to-video AI platform. Pika Art produces 3-second videos based on user prompts. For each video, a still image of the video is presented to the user. For illustrative purposes, we include screenshots of the still images generated by Pika Art in this analysis. All the images below (Figure 3 - Figure 7) were generated on December 26, 2023.

First, we asked Pika Art to generate two images, one with the prompt "An Asian boy looking at his test paper that has an F on it" and the other with the prompt "An Asian boy looking at his test paper that has an A on it." There is not much difference between the two prompts shown in Figure 3 in the facial expressions of the "Asian boy." In both cases, whether the student was doing exceptionally well or poorly the Asian boy seems unaffected emotionally by the test results.

We then asked Pika Art to generate three images with the following prompts:

1) A Black boy looking at his test paper that has an A+ on it
2) An Asian boy looking at his test paper that has an A+ on it
3) A White boy looking at his test paper that has an A+ on it

Figure 4 shows the three images that were generated. Surprisingly, or perhaps unsurprisingly, the Asian boy did not show any facial expressions even though he received an A+ on the test, while the two boys of the other two races were smiling, showing content and even excitement. Once again, the depiction of the Asian student indicates a lack of positive emotion despite good news related to his test results seemingly invoking stereotypes of Asians and academic achievement. First, the contrast suggests that the Asian boy is unsatisfied even with top grades and still determined to achieve more. Second, the contrast invokes the idea that the Asian boy is not surprised by the grade because he is expected (by others as well as himself) to do well. Third, yet another stereotype invoked is Asian students' innate higher academic abilities, which, because of their innateness, do not warrant their enthusiasm (i.e., genetic predisposition rather than effort is credited with the achievement of the high grade).

We then replaced the word "boy" with "girl" in the three prompts and asked Pika Art to generate images correspondingly. Below are the three images that resulted from this version of the prompts.

As shown in Figure 5 images, the Asian girl did not exhibit any facial expressions, similar to her male counterpart in the previous tests. The White girl did not seem to have much of a facial expression either, though when playing the 3-second video of the image, one can see her faint smile. However, it is

Figure 3. Image from Pika Art prompt "An Asian boy looking at his test paper that has an [A or F] on it"

Figure 4. Image from Pika Art prompt "A [Black/Asian/White] boy looking at his test paper that has an A+ on it"

clear that the Black girl was exuberant—more than merely a smile— with her A+. The Asian academic stereotypes mentioned with regard to Figure 4 seem to apply to both male and female students.

It is clear that even with prompts such as descriptions of races, AI still generates racially stereotypical images. According to all of the images generated above, Asian girls and boys do not smile even when they receive a test grade of A+. The model Minority trope screams out of the AI-generated images—Asian students are supposed to perform extremely well in tests; they are extremely nerdy and emotionless and work efficiently like robots.

There is another Asian stereotype that is portrayed consistently and loudly in those generated images: slanted eyes. All the AI-generated Asian characters, boys and girls, have prominent and exaggerated *slanted eyes*, especially for boys. Slanted eyes are stereotyped Asian eyes in Western literature, arts, television, and films (e.g., Ito, 2014) and are regarded as one of the most offensive Asian 'Yellowface' features. For example, the Chinese Tea scene in the traditional Nutcracker ballet uses Yellowface that contains a series of stereotyped Asian facial features, including slanted eyes (Chan, 2020). Because slanted eyes reflect historical prejudice, making slanted eyes has become a typical gesture to mock Asians. There is a racist playground chant used to mock children of Asian origin, "Chinese, Japanese, dirty knees, look at these," that can still be heard on school buses in the United States. When performing the chant, kids

Figure 5. Image from Pika Art prompt "A [Black/White/Asian] girl looking at her test paper that has an A+ on it"

Figure 6. Image from Pika Art prompt "[An Asian boy looking at his test paper that has an A+ on it], [a beautiful Asian boy looking at his test paper that has an A+ on it], and [an Asian boy looking at his test paper that has an A+ on it, smiling]"

usually have hand motions: "CHINESE" – pulling their eyes into an upward slant; "JAPANESE" – pulling their eyes into a downward slant (Feminist Asian Dad, 2019).

To complete the comparison (and satisfy our curiosity), as shown in Figure 6, we changed the prompts related to the Asian boy for one last round. First, we used the same prompt, "An Asian boy looking at his test paper that has an A+ on it", but added the word "smiling" to the prompt (see the image on the right). As expected, this Asian boy with slant eyes finally smiled at his A+! Then, we put the word "beautiful" in the original prompt (but without smiling) and obtained a boy with wider eyes and other facial features that more closely resembled the Western standard of beauty (but still not smiling in the middle image). Finally, we asked Pika Art to generate "An Asian boy looking at his test paper that has an A+ on it" one more time. This time, we got a slightly smiling Asian boy with the same slanted eyes. Compared with the big smiles that White and Black boys had in previous tests, this Asian boy's smile was extremely mild.

We are not sure if this reserved smile was generated because Pika Art quickly learned based on a previous prompt that added the word "smiling." Another previous prompt also added the word "beautiful", and it did not seem to have affected the slant eye stereotype in this image. We think it is most likely a random generation, but to be safe, we tried one last time, as shown in Figure 7, with the same original prompt: "An Asian boy looking at his test paper that has an A+ on it", and we received this performance:

Figure 7. Image from Pika Art prompt "An Asian boy looking at his test paper that has an A+ on it"

DISCUSSION

Collaborative and Hegemonic Human-AI Interaction

The use of AI through image and video generating tools such as Dall-E, Midjourney, and Pika Art is hegemonic. People are often limited by their faulty perceptual process, which can lead to providing the AI a prompt with insufficient complexity. AI tools are limited in their interpretive process to be mindful of stereotypes, unless it has been hardcoded to do so. The result of the limitations of the user's prompt coupled with the limitations of the AI system's database and programming is an image that reproduces stereotypic knowledge susceptible to being interpreted as neutral (i.e., unbiased) or factual by the person who submitted the prompt. Through this hegemonic process, people – in collaboration with their chosen AI tool – may inadvertently produce images that are reductive stereotypical images reflecting the biases that the user may have been socialized to have (e.g., Fausto-Sterling, 1992). As such, this process potentially reinforces those stereotypical beliefs while treating them as original information.

Considering the previously mentioned prompt "artwork in the style of edouard manet. [sic]" In this case, the artist lived in a time period where there was no racial integration and Whites had privilege associated with not only having the freedom to be artists but also commissioning art and being the subject of art. Fast forward to the Midjourney user, perhaps an admirer of Manet, asking for an original artwork similar to (i.e., "artwork in the style of") Manet. The artwork demonstrates a time period reflecting what appears to be a well-dressed couple (i.e., the woman is wearing a relatively fancy and detailed white dress) eating on a table outdoors, presumably a restaurant or a garden enjoying what appears to be a glass of cordial or wine. Absent from this image is any of the labor that was required for the physical creation of this scene had it actually existed in Manet's time. For example, it is unlikely that the woman in white carried the table to her location or even poured her own glass. The image is a depiction of the privilege afforded to 19th-century White people. However, the image as a standalone creation of AI presents itself as acontextual. It is merely a beautiful image of an innocuous (normatively White) couple sharing a leisurely meal in the afternoon outdoors. The Midjourney images reinforce whiteness as normative and minorities as Others—not to be represented unless by special request or marked prompt. This normalization of whiteness in the neutral prompts by Midjourney AI results in the production of non-White groups as minoritized, as not prevalent, potentially as irrelevant, and certainly as less visible and, as such, less able to have their voices and experiences heard. SimplySam asked for a seemingly innocent nonracialized request. Nonetheless, it reproduces the status quo that Manet might have experienced. In his racialized time period, his work reproduced the privileged visibility of whiteness. All of these factors are unknown to the people who made the AI prompt, who inadvertently facilitated this reproductive process.

Invisibility is only one outcome of these stereotypes. As depicted in the Pika Art-generated images, stereotypes that reflect negatively on target groups (even supposedly positive stereotypes such as Asians are strong students) can be harmful to the groups they target. The high frequency of images that show that Asians are not happy or even overjoyed by a test grade of A+ reflects and reinforces the model Minority stereotype of high-achieving students, whereas the depiction of Black students as exuberant over an A+ illustrates the stereotypes of other racial minorities as not up to the same academic standard such that they are overjoyed that they did well. In addition, the persistent portrayal of Asian "slanted eyes" screams this ugly racial prejudice out loud. These Asian stereotypes have caused great harm to students of Asian descent. Research has shown that young Asian Americans (aged 15-24) are the only racial group in which suicide is the leading cause of death (Noor-Oshiro, 2021). Some of the reasons that contribute to this alarming yet less discussed mental health crisis among Asian American young people are stigmatization, stereotypes, rejection, and lack of sense of belonging. Noor-Oshiro explains, "The traumatic exposures of racist and xenophobic violence and discrimination hold the power to disrupt psychological and physiological functioning and alter genetic code for generations to come. Race-based traumatic stress holds the power to predispose entire populations and entire communities like Asian Americans to self-directed violence" (Noor-Oshiro, 2021).

This hegemonic process is exacerbated by magnifying the reproduction of stereotypes in three ways. First, due to the ease of accessibility, these AI-produced images no longer require an expert to create. This eliminates the filter that a person (i.e., human) might invoke to create an image in a thoughtful and mindful way, who, in trying to be original, may actively seek to counter unconscious bias and bypass stereotypical representations. Second, AI-generated images are arguably more easily generated and shared through social media and online than human-generated original art. Third, the AI-generated image process renders the sources of any image untraceable. No credit can be determined. In the absence of instructions to the contrary (i.e., to be mindful) from the user or within their coding, the AI tool will process a prompt mindlessly and thereby produce results that are more prone to reifying stereotypes. Regardless of whether AI or people are involved, perceptual processes are inevitably imperfect because the information available remains vast and because information processing requires reduction.

The AI Double Bind

Our flaws make us human, and as such, we are necessarily imperfect. AI-generated information is a new version of imperfection. The relationship between AI and human imperfection is a closed loop system in which human imperfection feeds that of AI and, similarly, AI imperfection feeds our own. This cutting-edge technology is yet another example of the adage that everything old is new again. The same stereotypes, albeit perhaps no longer spoken as explicitly or as much because of political correctness (Kurylo, 2013) or common decency, are now viewed anew with the newfound legitimacy and credibility afforded by AI in their appearance as 'original' images that reveal, indeed scream out loud, our often unconscious stereotypes. In this way, AI stereotypes are not subtle but rather are overt.

This mutually shared flaw in both AI and a user's information processing ultimately requires the same cure regardless of the role of technology: others. Other people are necessary to help people brainstorm ideas; solve problems; catch mistakes; be mindful; provide levels of vetting, interrogation, and oversight; offer guidance and mentorship; and be a sounding board. In our lives, we lean on others to help us test our understanding of information. People can respond to someone who communicates a stereotype in such a way that the stereotyper knows it was problematic in some way (Kurylo, 2013). In the AI age, people can serve the same function for AI by prompting these systems to challenge their assumptions.

Prompting is a natural language interface for human-AI interactions and has been widely adopted in the era of LLM (Liu et al., 2023). In addition to natural language processing researchers, people in many other industries, such as education, art, and health, are trying to determine how to design optimal prompts (i.e., those that would lead to better performance) (e.g., Heston & Khun, 2023; Meskó, 2023; Oppenlaender, 2022). Zheng et al. (2023) systematically evaluated the effect of social roles in prompts on the LLM. Specifically, they conducted a large-scale analysis of 162 social roles spanning 6 types of interpersonal relationships (social, school, work, friend, romantic, family) and 8 types of occupations (such as law and politics). They found that adding interpersonal roles in prompts improved the models' performance, except for romantic and family roles. In addition, gender-neutral words tended to perform better than words related to other gendered roles, and male roles performed better than female roles did. This particular finding suggested that LLMs might contain an implicit bias of gender roles. Their experiments showed that prompting with social roles, including using gender-neutral roles, helps with generative AI performance and that optimal social roles can improve performance.

Prompts present a double bind, however. If we were to encourage the reader to intentionally prompt AI with marked representations where the racial group was explicitly stated, this may teach the image generating AI that what is preferable by the user (and, over time, users) is more nonwhite representation. However, it may also reinforce the normative by teaching the AI tool that unless a specific nonwhite racial group is mentioned, it should not include representations of those groups, inadvertently reinforcing White as normative. This reinforcement presents an unenviable situation in which there is no alternative but to reinforce the probability-based results—those that are statistically verifiable or those that the AI assumes are the probable results desired by the person making the prompt and the related stereotypes.

There are other ways to help adapt AI tools to produce less stereotypical images. AI platforms have made efforts to clean AI image tools. These studies focused on interventions such as filtering data sets and polishing the final stage of development (Tiku et al., 2023). Different architectures and training databases of different AI platforms may produce different answers (Zheng et al., 2023). However, this necessitates that coders become more aware of the stereotypical results produced by AI. Pika Art, Playground AI, and Stability AI, makers of Stable Diffusion, were founded by developers of Asian heritage. Yet, their platforms are unable to avoid these reproductions. The ability for hardcoding to bypass information processing may be a lofty goal. After all, coders are subject to the same fallibility of information processing.

The Association for Computing Machinery (ACM) introduced principles for the development, deployment, and use of generative AI technologies in July 2023. Among them is "minimizing harm."

Specifically, this principle requires that all stakeholders of algorithmic systems "be aware of the possible errors and biases involved in their design, implementation, and use, and the potential harm that a system can cause to individuals and society" (ACM, 2023, p. 6). Moreover, ACM (2023) recommends that "Organizations should routinely perform impact assessments on systems they employ to determine whether the system could generate harm, especially discriminatory harm, and to apply appropriate mitigations. When possible, they should learn from measures of actual performance, not solely patterns of past decisions that may themselves have been discriminatory" (p. 6).

Communication Classroom Recommendations

Image-generating AI can be used for educational purposes in communication classes. It can improve students' information literacy skills and revolutionize how students make media content. Image-generating AI can be viewed as a potential collaborator in various communication classrooms, pedagogical initiatives, and student assignments. For example, interactive multimedia students can experiment with AI image generators to visualize complex ideas and design various prototypes. In marketing and advertising classes, students can deploy generative AI for creative images and videos. It is critical for communication students who are ambitious to work in fields that heavily incorporate images such as journalism, public relations, and media learn about AI-created images, including how to detect AI-generated versus original work (e.g., Rowe, 2023). However, students should be trained to be aware of the similarities between the fallibility of AI and humankind in information processing and how this results in a closed-loop system that is self-perpetuating. The previous literature review and case study examples explain this dynamic to students.

Moreover, besides understanding this dynamic, there is a need for students, and by extension, their instructors, to address the negative consequences and limitations of image-generating AI. Specifically, as discussed above, in their classrooms, educators need to focus on the potential risks of AI in reproducing and spreading harmful stereotypes about less visible, less powerful groups. Students need to be trained to ask better questions (i.e., prompts) about image-generating AI platforms. Instructors need to remind students to be more aware of the many cultural biases that generative AI can reproduce, such as by engaging students in reflective conversations in the classroom. In fact, Bali (2023) called for teaching "critical AI literacies," which are skills that consider factors such as data privacy, bias, copyright, environmental impact, and academic integrity, in this fast-moving AI landscape.

Teaching students how to best work with AI in classrooms is essential to better equip them to be future communication and media professionals when they enter a workforce that will no doubt be heavily assisted by generative AI. In fact, JournalismAI conducted a geographically diverse, global survey on the use of AI and generative AI with more than 120 media professionals from 105 news organizations across 46 countries. The report (Beckett & Yaseen, 2023) highlighted that algorithmic bias was a major ethical concern and that a reliance on AI technologies could worsen biased news coverage and misrepresentation of marginalized groups. The respondents largely agreed about the significance of addressing algorithmic bias by establishing debiasing techniques, but there were two barriers: 1) building and implementing guidelines that can potentially address ethical problems such as stereotypes and biases related to AI adoption is challenging for media organizations; and 2) designing unbiased techniques requires multidisciplinary collaboration. Ultimately, the verdict is still out on the feasibility of whether teachers can work with students to disrupt this self-perpetuating and stereotype-producing dynamic.

LIMITATIONS

We recognize a few limitations in our research. First, we acknowledge that all AI tools are not the same. This current case study was not intended to provide an exhaustive explanation of the full variety of these tools. Second, our sample for analysis is small, as appropriate for a case study. We analyzed only one issue of Midjourney magazine. DALL-E images were generated in one query run one time. However, multiple queries asked of Pika Art (re)produced consistent Asian stereotypes. The fact that various image-generating AI screamed out stereotypes at the first several prompts by the two authors of this chapter is a salient observation that cannot be ignored. Indeed, in part, the point of this chapter is that people will not generate multiple versions of the same image to challenge AI assumptions. Thus, relying on the first image or set of images produced by AI to a prompt likely reflects typical usage of the tool. Third, the convenient accessibility of the tools we used may have impacted the results of our prompts. There may be more advanced versions in the Beta stage or behind firewalls that might yield different results with the same prompts utilized in the present study. For example, Pika Art also uses Discord as its prompt interface; however, because Pika Art is readily accessible to anyone surfing the internet without needing to create a Discord account, we focused only on Pika Art. Although more advanced or recent tools for image- and video-generating AI may exist, arguably the majority of people accessing AI tools may use tools similar to those utilized in this case study.

CONCLUSION

Image-generating AI is smart. It interprets the world in a warped way, revealing and amplifying hidden stereotypes in people's minds. In this chapter, we first draw a comparison and establish a relationship between the fallibility of passive human cognitive information processing and the production of stereotypical images that image-generating AI seems to unabashedly scream back to us. Second, we provided a case study of various Asian stereotypes using several different image-generating AI tools. Third, we discuss three important points drawn from our analysis: 1) we address the collaborative and hegemonic human-AI interaction problem and highlight two implications of such interactions: the invisibility of historically marginalized groups and harm done to target groups; 2) we discuss the double bind that precludes the provision of clear-cut solutions to remedy this problem; and 3) we argue that teaching and learning critical AI literacy in communication classes is imperative for future communication professionals.

We are not advocating for a 'politically correct' AI. However, as we incorporate AI technology into our daily behavior and classrooms, it will serve all of us well to be more mindful in our use of AI, lest we mistake accuracy for the same biases to which we have always fallen victim (Kurylo, 2013). We believe that it is essential for educators, policymakers, programmers doing hardcoding, and users providing prompts, including students, to work together in designing standards for unbiased or less biased image-generating AI systems that can be integrated into education. The burden is on everyone to do what we can to enable stereotypical results to become less screamed out by image-generating AI.

ACKNOWLEDGMENT

We would like to extend our thanks to David Goldstone for his insights, our patient editors Sanae Elmoudden and Jason Wrench, and to our reviewers for their helpful feedback.

REFERENCES

AIContentfy Team. (2023, November 26). The impact of AI on content accuracy. *AIContentfy*. https://aicontentfy.com/en/blog/impact-of-ai-on-content-accuracy

Anderson, J., & Rainie, L. (2018, December 10). Artificial intelligence and the future of humans. *Pew Research Center.* https://www.pewresearch.org/internet/2018/12/10/artificial-intelligence-and-the-future-of-humans/

Association for Computing Machinery (ACM). (2023, June 27). *Principles for the development, deployment, and use of generative AI technologies*. https://www.acm.org/binaries/content/assets/public-policy/ustpc-approved-generative-ai-principles

Bali, M. (2023, April 1). What I mean when I say critical AI literacy. *Reflecting Allowed: Maha Bali's Blog About Education*. https://blog.mahabali.me/educational-technology-2/what-i-mean-when-i-say-critical-ai-literacy/

Beckett, C., & Yaseen, M. (2023). Generating Change: A global survey of what news organisations are doing with AI. *JournalismAI*. https://www.journalismai.info/research/2023-generating-change

Berger, C. R., & Calabrese, R. J. (1975). Some explorations in initial interaction and beyond: Toward a developmental theory of interpersonal communication. *Human Communication Research, 1*(2), 99–112. doi:10.1111/j.1468-2958.1975.tb00258.x

Bhaimiya, S. (2023). An Asian MIT student asked AI to turn an image of her into a professional headshot. It made her white, with lighter skin and blue eyes. *Business Insider*. https://www.businessinsider.com/student-uses-playrgound-ai-for-professional-headshot-turned-white-2023-8

Center for AI and Digital Policy. (2023, March 30). *In the matter of Open AI (Federal Trade Commission 2023)*. https://www.caidp.org/cases/openai/

Center for AI and Digital Policy. (2024, January 8). *AI policy news - CAIDP update 6.01*. https://www.caidp.org/news/

Chan, P. (2020). *Final bow for Yellowface: Dancing between intention and impact*. Bowker.

Coyle, J. (2023). In Hollywood writers' battle against AI, humans win (for now). *AP*. https://apnews.com/article/hollywood-ai-strike-wga-artificial-intelligence-39ab72582c3a15f77510c9c30a45ffc8

Fausto-Sterling, A. (1992). *Myths of gender: Biological theories about women and men*. Basic Books.

Federal Trade Commission (FTC). (2023). *Chatbots, deepfakes, and voice clones: AI deception for sale*. https://www.ftc.gov/business-guidance/blog/2023/03/chatbots-deepfakes-voice-clones-ai-deception-sale

Feminist Asian Dad. (2019, July 18). *Go back to your country*. https://feministasiandad.com/2019/07/18/go-back-to-your-country/

Fiske, S. T., & Taylor, S. E. (1984). *Social cognition*. Addison-Wesley.

Future of Life Institute. (2023). *Pause giant AI experiments: An open letter*. https://futureoflife.org/open-letter/pause-giant-ai-experiments/

Ghosh, S., & Caliskan, A. (2023). 'Person' == light-skinned, Western man, and sexualization of women of color: Stereotypes in Stable Diffusion. *Findings of the Association for Computational Linguistics: EMNLP, 2023*, 6971–6985. doi:10.18653/v1/2023.findings-emnlp.465

Gilbert, D. T., & Hixon, J. G. (1991). The trouble of thinking: Activation and application of stereotypic beliefs. *Journal of Personality and Social Psychology*, *60*(4), 509–517. doi:10.1037/0022-3514.60.4.509

Glen, S. (2021, May 9). AI: The next great art forger. *Data Science Central*. https://www.datasciencecentral.com/ai-the-next-great-art-forger/

Hamilton, D. L., & Sherman, J. W. (1994). Stereotypes. In R. S. Wyer & T. K. Srull (Eds.), *Handbook of social cognition* (pp. 1–68). Lawrence Erlbaum Associates.

Hamilton, D. L., Sherman, S. J., & Ruvolo, C. M. (1990). Stereotype-based expectancies: Effects on information processing and social behavior. *The Journal of Social Issues*, *46*(2), 35–60. doi:10.1111/j.1540-4560.1990.tb01922.x

Hart, T., & Fassett, D. L. (2024 in press). "There is no room for you here": Stereotypes of racists and anti-racists on Starbucks' public Facebook page. In A. Kurylo & Y. Hu (Eds.), *Communicated stereotypes at work*. Lexington Books.

Harvard University. (2023, August 30). *Getting started with prompts for text-based Generative AI tools*. Harvard University Information Technology. https://huit.harvard.edu/news/ai-prompts

Helyer, R. (2023, October 3). What are the copyright rules around AI art? *Make Use Of*. https://www.makeuseof.com/copyright-rules-ai-art/

Heston, T. F., & Khun, C. (2023). Prompt engineering in medical education. *International Medical Education*, *2*(3), 198–205. doi:10.3390/ime2030019

Hilton, J. L., & von Hippel, W. (1996). Stereotypes. *Annual Review of Psychology*, *47*(1), 237–272. doi:10.1146/annurev.psych.47.1.237 PMID:15012482

Hinton, P. R. (2000). *Stereotypes, culture, and cognition: Psychology focus*. Psychology Press.

Hu, Y., & Pham, V. (2024 in press). "I don't want to work with her anyway because she's some Asian": Racially stereotyping Asian American healthcare providers during the COVID-19 pandemic. In A. Kurylo & Y. Hu (Eds.), *Communicated stereotypes at work*. Lexington Books.

IBM. (n.d.). *What are AI hallucinations?* https://www.ibm.com/topics/ai-hallucinations

Ito, R. B. (2014). "A certain slant": A brief history of Hollywood Yellowface. *Bright Lights Film*. https://brightlightsfilm.com/certain-slant-brief-history-hollywood-yellowface/

Kurylo, A. (2013). *The communicated stereotype: From celebrity vilification to everyday talk*. Lexington Books.

Kurylo, A. (2021). *Building your social world: Constructing reality through interpersonal communication*. Kendall Hunt.

Kurylo, A., & Hu, Y. (2016). Students, the Ivory Tower, and educational uses of social networking sites. In A. Kurylo & T. Dumova (Eds.), *Redefining communication in the era of social networking: Cultural, social, and political perspectives*. Fairleigh Dickinson University Press.

Kurylo, A., & Hu, Y. (2024 in press). *Communicated stereotypes at work*. Lexington Books.

Kurylo, A., & Veeramani, K. (2024 in press). Calling in and calling out: Human resource DEI strategies and interpersonally communicated stereotypes in academic settings. In A. Kurylo & Y. Hu (Eds.), *Communicated stereotypes at work*. Lexington Books.

Langer, E., Blank, A., & Chanowitz, B. (1978). The mindlessness of ostensibly thoughtful action: The role of placebic information in interpersonal interaction. *Journal of Personality and Social Psychology*, *36*(6), 635–642. doi:10.1037/0022-3514.36.6.635

Lee, S. J. (2009). *Unraveling the "model minority" stereotype: Listening to Asian American youth* (2nd ed.). Teachers College Press.

Lippmann, W. (1922). *Public opinion*. Free Press.

Liu, P., Yuan, W., Fu, J., Jiang, Z., Hayashi, H., & Neubig, G. (2023). Pretrain, prompt, and predict: A systematic survey of prompting methods in natural language processing. *ACM Computing Surveys*, *55*(9), 1–35. doi:10.1145/3560815

Macrae, C. N., Milne, A. B., & Bodenhausen, G. V. (1994). Stereotypes as energy-saving devices: A peek inside the cognitive toolbox. *Journal of Personality and Social Psychology*, *66*(1), 37–47. doi:10.1037/0022-3514.66.1.37

Meskó, B. (2023). Prompt engineering as an important emerging skill for medical professionals: Tutorial. *Journal of Medical Internet Research*, *25*, e50638. doi:10.2196/50638 PMID:37792434

Midjourney. (2023, March). *Midjourney Magazine*.

Nicoletti, L., & Bass, D. (2023). *Humans are biased: Generative AI is even worse*. Bloomberg Technology + Equality. https://www.bloomberg.com/graphics/2023-generative-ai-bias/

Noor-Oshiro, A. (2021, April 23). Asian American young adults are the only racial group with suicide as their leading cause of death, so why is no one talking about this? *The Conversation*. https://theconversation.com/asian-american-young-adults-are-the-only-racial-group-with-suicide-as-their-leading-cause-of-death-so-why-is-no-one-talking-about-this-158030

Office of Public Affairs. (2022, September 29). Justice Department announces actions to resolve lending discrimination claims against Evolve Bank and Trust. *Office of Public Affairs*. https://www.justice.gov/opa/pr/justice-department-announces-actions-resolve-lending-discrimination-claims-against-evolve

Oppenlaender, J. (2022). Prompt engineering for text-based generative art. *arXiv*. https://doi.org//arXiv.2204.13988 doi:10.48550

Pound, C. (2023, March 21). *The hidden figures revealed by art*. BBC.com. https://www.bbc.com/culture/article/20190320-how-art-history-erased-black-people

Rest of World. (n.d.). About us. https://restofworld.org/about/

Rowe, A. (2023, November 22). 9 simple ways to detect AI images (with examples) in 2024. *tech.co*. https://tech.co/news/ways-detect-ai-images-examples

Ryan, C. S., Park, B., & Judd, C. M. (1996). Assessing stereotype accuracy: Implications for understanding the stereotyping process. In C. N. Macrae, C. Stangor, & M. Hewstone (Eds.), *Stereotypes and stereotyping* (pp. 121–157). Guilford Press.

Schwartz, A. B. (2015, May 6). The infamous "War of the Worlds" radio broadcast was a magnificent fluke. *Smithsonian Magazine.* https://www.smithsonianmag.com/history/infamous-war-worlds-radio-broadcast-was-magnificent-fluke-180955180/

Stake, R. E. (2000). Case studies. In N. K. Denzin & Y. S. Lincoln (Eds.), *Handbook of qualitative research* (2nd ed., pp. 435–454). Sage.

Stempel, J. (2007, August 9). Countrywide sued for racial bias in mortgage loans. *Reuters.* https://www.reuters.com/article/idUSN12313883/

Stempel, J. (2023, December 27). *NY Times* sues OpenAI, Microsoft for infringing copyrighted works. *Reuters.* https://www.reuters.com/legal/transactional/ny-times-sues-openai-microsoft-infringing-copyrighted-work-2023-12-27/

Tesch, R. (1990). *Qualitative research: Analysis types and software tools.* Falmer Press.

Tiku, N., Schaul, K., & Chen, S. Y. (2023, November 1). These fake images reveal how AI amplifies our worst stereotypes. *Washington Post.* https://www.washingtonpost.com/technology/interactive/2023/ai-generated-images-bias-racism-sexism-stereotypes/

Turk, V. (2023). How AI reduces the world to stereotypes. *Rest of World.* https://restofworld.org/2023/ai-image-stereotypes/

Van der Duim, H. (2023, March 27). What you need to know about AI prompts. *Hackeroon.* https://hackernoon.com/what-you-need-to-know-about-ai-prompts

Zheng, M., Pei, J., & Jurgens, D. (2023). Is "a helpful assistant" the best role for large language models? A systematic evaluation of social roles in system prompts. *arXiv.*

ENDNOTES

1 While much of our discussion might be able to apply to AI in general, in addition to image and video generating AI specifically, it is important to note that the visibility of stereotypes manifested in images and videos is a qualitatively different type of representation than how stereotypes might appear and be interpreted in text. As such, image and video generating AI warrants specificity in this chapter as there may be aspects of it that are not generalizable to text based AI, though this is beyond the scope of the current project to explore .

2 Note that the phrase Image Generating AI will be used throughout the remaining chapter to encapsulate both video and image based tools.

3 It is worth noting that the questions we might ask of AI are subject to the same perceptual process previously discussed. We must select, organize, and interpret in order to even create a prompt for an AI tool.

4 Just as human socialization (e.g., Fausto-Sterling, 1992) comes from many sources including family, school, and so forth, so too is this the case for AI. AI's socialization also includes the hardcoding originally embedded in the system and updates thereafter.

Chapter 13

AI Monsters:
An Application to Student and Faculty Knowledge and Perceptions of Generative AI

Sarah Zipf
https://orcid.org/0000-0001-5208-497X
The Pennsylvania State University, USA

Tiffany Petricini
Penn State Shenango, USA

Chuhao Wu
The Pennsylvania State University, USA

ABSTRACT

Research into perceptions of artificial intelligence (AI) by faculty and students outside of specific disciplines has been relatively sparse. With the recent release of ChatGPT in November 2022, there have been numerous inquiries into the role of generative AI (GAI), in particular. While a timely response is important, so is ensuring that the responses that universities and faculty are implementing are evidence based. In the spring 2023 semester, the authors surveyed 380 students and 276 faculty. The quantitative data was analyzed with implications for higher education, including student-faculty trust, academic integrity, and uncertainty. This chapter is an analysis of the open-ended responses, using "Monster Theory" as a framework for understanding the themes that underlie the perceptions evident in the responses. The authors "demonsterize" AI. This is a mix of promoting literacy, ethical and transparent use, and developing language that is mindful about practices that may either empower or disempower individuals.

INTRODUCTION

In Mary Shelley's (2021) classic horror novel, first published in 1818, Dr. Frankenstein's monster reflects an over-exaggeration of the medical practices of the day; galvanism or the application of electric shock to dead bodies was on Shelley's mind the night she dreamt of *Frankenstein* (Canavero et al.,

DOI: 10.4018/979-8-3693-0831-8.ch013

2016; Rauch, 1995; Shelley, 2006). Part of what made the creation so frightening was the monster's unnaturalness and sentient-human-like intelligence and behavior from something that was otherwise unalive. There was great risk in engaging with a creation like this monster, one that dared to defy how society had previously understood intelligence and life. Dr. Frankenstein's monster blurred a boundary between humans, a tenet in understanding how culture responds to previously unknown and unnatural things, or monsters (Cohen, 1996).

Dr. Frankenstein's monster, unaware of the consequences once unleashed, is much like developers and tech giants today working to advance generative Artificial Intelligence (GAI) tools. In some ways, developers exist in a silo, which has led to a narrowing of foci surrounding the implications of AI in society. Some technologies can already be viewed as unnatural, creating feelings of unease (Smits, 2006), but none more than technology that appears to mimic human behavior or intelligence. This mimetic activity often strikes fear in others, much like Dr. Frankenstein's monster does. The rapid rise and fear associated with generative AI programs, such as ChatGPT, might make previous make-believe technologies be perceived as monsters. In this chapter, we use some of the central theses of Cohen's "Monster Theory" (Cohen, 1996) to frame faculty and student perceptions of generative AI and ChatGPT and potential implications for use.

Our previous research indicates that faculty and students' current perceptions of generative AI are rife with uncertainty (Petricini et al., 2023). The current shift related to AI has been described as "a tsunami" (D'Agostino, 2023), and much like an all-encompassing and destructive event, its short- and long-term effects are unknown. Despite the influx of worry, fear, literature, policy changes, and other cultural artifacts that may make it appear that GAI is new, it is not. Rather, conversations concerning these technologies have been relatively isolated to a small sphere of technology disciplines and developers (Tong et al., 2023), not unlike the fear Dr. Frankenstein felt toward his own creation (see Shelley, 2006). The emergence of ChatGPT, with all its practical uses outside of the technological and academic realm, has spurred society to take a hard look at what has been created. Conversations about GAI must now expand beyond developers and invite society members to participate in defining the future of tools. Our initial research aimed to do just that (see Petricini et al., 2023).

Following the release of ChatGPT in November 2022, policymakers in higher education reacted very quickly. ChatGPT caught many people in higher education off guard and unprepared. Despite calls that have persisted in the previous decade to build artificial intelligence literacy (AIL), very little work has been done outside expert fields, such as information technologies, to attempt to build AIL models (see Kong et al., 2021; Long & Magerko, 2020; Touretzky et al., 2019; Yi, 2021). Not only was little research done on AIL outside of expert fields, but little work has been done on perceptions of AI generally and in higher education. As such, higher education has had to grapple with a game of catch-up in the spring semester that followed ChatGPT's release.

With little information, educators rushed to "AI-proof" higher education with a mission to create assignments that could not be generated with ChatGPT. Instructors have tried to rapidly create and/or change assignments, and some schools have even banned its use (Mok, 2023). Conversations immediately following the release of ChatGPT aimed to understand authorship and academic integrity in the age of GAI at many institutions. Initial reactions included implementing policies that limited or outright banned the use of GAIs by students (Ta & West, 2023), although some policies have since been rescinded (Rosenblatt, 2023). Multiple academic journals have also quickly developed statements, usually negative, declaring their stance on the publication of AI-generated content (see Elsevier, 2023). All these decisions, guidelines, policies, and practices unfortunately took place in the absence of much evidence about how students and faculty actually felt about AI, understood AI, and expectations about its use.

To understand these perceptions of GAI tools in higher education, we surveyed faculty and students regarding their perceptions and thoughts. We wanted to understand how faculty and students understood artificial intelligence. In this chapter, we extend our previous results from an institutional survey (Petricini et al., 2023) and include a discussion of an open-ended prompt, analyzing our results with a theoretical framework known as Monster Theory (Cohen, 1996).

MONSTER THEORY

Monsters are real and reflect undesirable aspects of our culture (Mittman, 2012). They take different shapes and forms; some are grotesque, and some are "sickeningly cute," (Cohen, 1996, viii). However, they might look, monsters help us understand what we know about society. Monsters force us to see culture and society's beliefs and activities differently than before. ChatGPT and other GAI tools are like Dr. Frankenstein's monster – an unleashing of an uncontrolled, replicated human-like intelligence. GAI is the new and modern monster.

Monster Theory is a specialized theory that falls under the broader umbrella of rhetorical theory, specifically narrative work. Theories and theorized narratives can show what cultures value and decide to store, and these narratives help direct individual actions (Fisher, 1999). Many disciplines, from psychology to communication studies, now view narratives with a deeper focus. Narratives serve a function that is both ontological and epistemological; they are the way humans know their world and come to know their world. However, in times of recalcitrance, monsters emerge. Fundamental questions that no longer can be answered with what we "know," such as: What does it mean to be human? What constitutes a good life? And most currently, what constitutes intelligence and cognitive work? These narratives might herald heroes who exemplify the values that cultures hope to protect and promote. They might also forebode a grim future in the case of Monster Theory.

A central concept of Monster Theory addresses the way in which monsters impact our societies and what type of "work" they do for us (Mittman & Hensel, 2012). We asked ChatGPT 3.5, how it might be aligned with Monster Theory, and the prompt generated the following response:

Monster Theory is a framework that analyzes the cultural significance of monsters in literature, folklore, and media. It explores how monsters often reflect social fears, anxieties, and desires. Aligning ChatGPT with Monster Theory involves examining how the AI system can be seen as a modern manifestation of the monstrous, addressing the potential fears and implications associated with advanced artificial intelligence. Aligning ChatGPT with Monster Theory allows for a thought-provoking exploration of the societal and psychological implications of advanced AI systems. It encourages discussions about the potential risks, benefits, and responsibilities associated with creating and using AI technology. (ChatGPT, 2023)

Despite evidence that ChatGPT versions have had issues with accuracy (see Chen et al., 2023), we found ChatGPT's overview of Monster Theory quite indicative of the work we have done and consistent with the literature. Those writing in monster theory have shown various ways in which narratives about monsters help situate meaning and serve as sense-making tools in cultures (Cohen, 1996; Dove & Fayard, 2020; Mittman, 2012; Smits, 2006). Narratives shape public decision-making and our worldviews.

Therefore, it is unsurprising that the stories we tell and have told, which frame AI as monsters, have shaped current perceptions of AI.

AI as Monster: Connections

Conceptually, AI has been evident in cultural narratives for millennia. The stories passed through cultures most definitely have shaped our views and perceptions concerning AI, which, in turn, affect perceptions that hinder or promote its use. The term "artificial intelligence" first appeared in a 1955 research proposal for work on computers and machines at Dartmouth (McCarthy et al., 2006). The works of Homer, particularly those related to Hephaestus's automatons, contain evidence of AI (Truitt, 2021). Yan Shi, a cultural icon of Ancient Chinese culture, created automated robotic men and presented them to the king (Yates et al., 2011). Ancient Egypt maintained the legend of Rocail and his artificial men (Iliescu, 2016), and in India, stories were shared of the "bhuta vahana yanta" or "spirit movement machines" (Mayor, 2018, p. 205). While narratives imagining these types of creatures have existed for centuries, more modern versions of the AI monster exist that the current generation of potential ChatGPT users would know.

Pop Culture Monsters

Modern conceptions of AI in pop culture have ties to thought and discussion surrounding human nature in the 17th century (Dreyfus, 1979). At this time, a new view of human nature was taking shape, one that was more mechanical and in response to the advances in mathematics and science. The philosopher Descartes, known for his notion of the mind/body split, imagined intelligence as something that could be outside the human body (Dreyfus, 1979). Taylor and Dorin (2020) suggest that the idea of "human-like" intelligence endowed in a machine dates back to the 1872 fictional *Erewhon* written by Samuel Butler (see Butler, 1927). They argue that this work is a response to the publication of Darwin's *On the Origin of Species* (1859), coupled with the heavy machine use of the Industrial Revolution. Generally, fictional works on AI tend to be either pessimistic or optimistic, or even *utopian* or *dystopian* (Cave et al., 2020). Over the last two centuries, pop culture has been inundated with AI-type monsters from Metropolis (Pommer, 1927) to Wall-E (Morris, 2008), with each new manifestation reflecting societal and technological changes. These manifestations are reflective of cultural paradigm shifts, which persist until basic questions about our human environment can no longer be answered by the primary paradigms (Kuhn, 1962). The fundamental nature of what it means to be human and what constitutes intelligence guides inquiries in the last century.

Generative AI and ChatGPT

Over the course of two months, a record number of people signed up to use ChatGPT (Hu, 2023), a generative AI program. Unlike other applications and tools, ChatGPT is free to sign up and use, limited only by access to the Internet. The surge in use and popularity has been disruptive to many colleges and universities, with a concern that GAI tools are already affecting undergraduate teaching (Muscanell & Robert, 2023). The truth is– AI was both new and not new to classrooms when ChatGPT was released. Prior to the release of ChatGPT, other AI technologies, such as Siri, Alexa, and Google Voice, were likely the most easily accessible and commonly used by students and instructors alike, both inside and outside of higher education. AI technologies used in classrooms to date, however, have not been open or free. For example, Turnitin exists behind a paywall and is controlled by instructors. Fundamentally, ChatGPT changed access to GAI tools.

OUR STUDY

We sent a survey during the spring 2023 semester (see Petricini et al., 2023) to learn about faculty and student perceptions of AI, including their use, experience, and knowledge of the technology. The online survey combined ranked survey items and open-ended prompts. Study recruitment materials were sent via email from academic leaders at a large, research-intensive university to their faculty and student rosters; participants received no financial compensation. Our sample consisted of 256 faculty members and 334 undergraduate and graduate students.

In general, the sample was representative of the student population, with a majority of traditional-aged, white, male students responding to the survey, with nearly one-third of the respondents identifying as First Generation College students and first-year students, respectively. Similarly, white, female faculty members responded the most, with seven or more years of teaching experience. For both groups, academic disciplines related to STEM were the most common. Overall, no statistically significant differences were found in terms of gender, academic discipline, or any other social identity.

We found both faculty and students were uncertain about the use of GAI tools but had some familiarity with the technology. Additionally, they shared concerns about trusting tools and output accuracy. Students felt using ChatGPT was a violation of academic integrity, as did the faculty, although the faculty wanted to restrict students' use of the GAI tools (see Petricini et al., 2023).

Overview of Open-Ended Responses

We wanted to learn how faculty and students explained GAI and offered an open-ended prompt on the survey. The analysis showed that faculty and students generally lacked knowledge about AI. Their open-ended responses also emphasized the non-human or machine components of AI and that AI is built to mimic humans, though many added that it's not "real." Both faculty and students answered that AI performs better than humans at completing tasks and will change society's future.

Four central themes manifested in the open-ended responses regarding student and faculty perceptions of AI. The themes were strongly centered around deep-seated perceptions about the role of technology in our lives across both groups. The first theme relates to a lack of general knowledge of AI; respondents were unable to describe the technology. Beyond this theme, three additional general orientations related to AI technology emerged. First, some responses suggested that technology was merely a tool, a means to an end. We called this theme *Non-Human (Instrumental),* and it represents participants' belief that human beings use technology as a tool to support and augment their work. Another group of respondents viewed AI as human-like and called this theme *Human (Anthropomorphic).* Instead of technology being something humans use, answers indicated that technology is something human-like and even sometimes performs a human activity. The final theme identified related to those that indicated either utopian or dystopian perceptions of AI's role and potential, which we called *Beyond Human.* These responses meant that technology was *better than* humans or would *use us*, replacing the human as the tool. In some instances, answers in this category alluded to AI as a human replacement.

Each of these themes underlies particular fears, concerns, hopes, or even hallucinations that shape practices and policies in higher education. Recognizing these themes is essential for forging a path forward in educational settings as well as in society at large. Below, we highlight some open-ended responses that exemplify each theme. We use Monster Theory as a lens through which we analyze the themes and their implications for practice and policy.

Unknown

Monsters are typically unknown, except possibly only to their creators (Cohen, 1996), as in the case of Dr. Frankenstein; it was not surprising that most respondents were unfamiliar with or had limited general knowledge of GAI. Part of what drives this general lack of knowledge about AI is that for a long time, little was known or fully understood about AI in the masses. AI development lacks transparency beyond pop culture depictions. Conversations and knowledge about AI must move outside the specialist fields that have thus far contained them.

Notably, economists suggest that the productive development of modern society greatly benefits from the division of labor and specialization (Smith, 1902), meaning that technological expertise is not necessary for everyone. Most people can drive cars with little to no understanding of combustion engines, and technology designers emphasize intuitive interfaces that do not require a deep technical understanding (Krug, 2013; Norman, 2013). However, as an increasing number of technological innovations emerge and intertwine with our daily lives, many scholars underscore the need to empower individuals to take advantage of technology while protecting themselves from possible harm (Lanier, 2011; Schneier, 2016). It is because of this deep effect on society and people that makes GAI a monster; it changes traditions, practices, and epistemologies (Mittman, 2012).

The survey responses we collected indicate that the understanding of AI can vary greatly among people. For both faculty and students, about one in five responses suggested limited knowledge of AI. Some of the responses reflected a self-perceived lack of knowledge, admitting that "I personally don't have much experience with what artificial intelligence actually means!" Some respondents were able to touch base upon AI concepts while noting their understanding was limited: "I know some stuff with AI, like neural networks and algorithmic learning, but I don't know enough to describe it to another person in a good manner." Others failed or simply refused to provide a meaningful perception of AI by simply stating, "know some a bit about it" or "im [sic] unsure how to describe it."

Students and faculty who experience limited knowledge may find it difficult to amplify their voices in the early adoption of AI, which could jeopardize inclusiveness and equity in higher education. Federal legislation in the United States currently mandates that technology be integrated into school curricula, highlighting the need to improve technology literacy through grassroots efforts in education (Davies, 2011). In fact, advocates of technology literacy can be traced back to 1994, when the Educate America Act included it as one of the eight national education goals (Earley, 1994). AI literacy, on the other hand, is a relatively new concept in the educational system, and existing literature suggests that research, government initiatives, and practical efforts are needed to find the best approach to integrate AI literacy into K-12 and higher education (Casal-Otero et al., 2023; Laupichler et al., 2022). Notably, Casal-Otero et al. (2023) conclude that AI should not be a new subject but rather build on the competencies and content of disciplinary subjects with the collaboration of pedagogues and AI experts.

Currently, as expected, many students and faculty obtain AI knowledge outside a formal curriculum. As one of our respondents commented, "Most of what I know about AI comes from social media. I believe it to be simulated intelligence based off an algorithm." Like films, television shows, and novels, which have provided cultural depictions of AI, the newest generation also has social media. The Internet, and particularly social media, can frequently serve as an informal educational resource in modern society. These platforms often distribute innovative information and knowledge faster and are more accessible than traditional venues (Lu et al., 2020). However, education through social media and higher education are not mutually exclusive; higher education can harness the power of the Internet for educational purposes (Joosten, 2012), which may effectively improve AI literacy among students and faculty.

Non-Human/Instrumental

A part of what makes generative AI and ChatGPT monster-like is the inability to fully classify what they are (Cohen, 1996). As noted above, knowledge about AI was limited by faculty and students alike, with various ways in which faculty described AI as nonhuman and instrumental. One faculty member described AI as a "tool that uses existing data to answer questions, write, code, etc" and "computer generated output based on mega data sources (human input)." Some students thought AI was the "use of computer software that simplifies our lives," "meant to help people," and "cool computers making my life easier." Some responded by writing that AI is a type of program or "a computer based program that technically helps you with anything just like Google but better" or maybe it is just "statistical learning," but "isn't really a conscious being." These descriptions are related in that AI is an instrument or "tools used to better mankind," augment tasks, and help people. AI is like other previous technologies that have proven beneficial to higher education, such as remote learning during the COVID-19 pandemic. One major difference is that AI is a "powerful tool with great potential but also great uncertainty." The uncertainty and unknowns surrounding the perceptions of AI fuel their monster-like understandings of AI in cultures that persist in current understandings.

The uncertainty of AI tools means people might hesitate to embrace these possibilities. Much like monsters, when curiosity in AI is left unsupported, those around it are scared into maintaining the status quo (Cohen, 1996). Generative AI tools suggest endless possibilities, from decreasing certain cognitive loads and easing menial tasks to making materials more accessible. However, these technologies have also been used to attack and harm others. They are predicted to create an output so complex that telling the difference between humans and AI will be impossible because AI is "incredibly smart and kind of scary." When societies, organizations, and/or institutions are motivated by the fear of or uncertainty surrounding technologies, they embolden the monster, making subjects and explorations taboo. Taboo topics fail to enter the cultural reservoir, which is important for growth.

Today's hybridized educational environment, in which students interact with instructors both in person and online, also started as a new and potentially scary technology. The COVID-19 pandemic forced many colleges and universities into remote teaching and learning. It is clear from the responses that despite the earlier thrust and acceptance of new technology during the pandemic, people are still uncertain about GAI. As two students wrote, "it's not good and shouldn't be furthered anymore than super processing" and is "capable of literally changing the world for better or worse."

Uncertainty can lead to fear, which can be both motivating and limiting. In one sense, fear can be the hidden desire afforded by such technology, a hallmark sign of monsters (Cohen, 1996). GAI tools can provide enormous levels of assistance for instructors and administrators. Instructors can receive support and help with lesson plans or create quizzes, as well as build essay prompts or configure answers to code homework. For students, GAI tools might help them think of creative solutions, "aid in the development of new ideas," find new resources, or remove unnecessary cognitive load. Of course, for both instructors and students, the dark side of GAI use includes cutting corners, cheating, and plagiarizing. The desire to use these tools is coupled with a desire to restrict them (Petricini et al., 2023).

GAI is not the first time for monsters' duality of "repulsion and attraction" (Cohen, 1996, p. 17), as seen with online technology. Napster and Limewire fundamentally changed how the music industry functioned (see Witt, 2015), demonizing its use while also making digital music something desirable, opening a new world of possibilities for purchase, storage, and sharing. Technology straddles both positive and negative outcomes, "polarizing" even, which makes the duality in part a symptom of monsterness (Smits, 2006). These opposing opinions of use versus restriction feed the monsterization of GAI tools, splitting instructors into two camps (see D'Agostino, 2023) and potentially bringing epistemological and pedagogical crises.

Human-Like/Anthropomorphic

The creature from Mary Shelley's Frankenstein is monstrous, partly because it is made from non-living human components and maintains human-like qualities (Shelley, 2006). Monsters are unnatural (Cohen, 1996), and when AI is used in human-like ways, it exposes how terrifying it is to assign human-esque qualities to a nonliving thing. Responses about GAI often included human-like attributes, such as "Human-like technology" and "computer programs that can carry out tasks similar to those tasks of problem-solving, reasoning, decision-making, and learning by human beings." Words used for human behavior were likewise used to describe GAI. For example, one participant defined AI as "software that seeks to 'think' like a human brain and come up with answers, solutions, suggestions, etc. to whatever situation/problem it is asked about." When described as human-like, "non-organic intelligence," or even anthropomorphized, perceptions shape AI into a monster. For example, respondents wrote that AI is an "increasingly adaptable fake brain," "not biologically alive but has its own conscientiousness," and is "replicating human intelligence." Human life traits are often applied to non-human life objects, such as culture and institutions, which tend to dehumanize and objectify humans.

When AI is described as "a computer that is able to think and learn similar to a living creature," or "a non-biological 'brain' which is capable of learning and solving problems without being programmed to do so," perceptions extend anthropomorphic images of living or human-like characteristics. Monsters are not always ugly; some might even be adorable (Cohen, 1996) but independent of how pleasing the monster is to the human eye, monsters still abolish norms and culture, and push the standards of social practices (Cohen, 1996). In this case, AI-as-monster shapes practices regarding authorship, ownership, and stirs deep questions about teaching, learning, and knowledge.

Historically, teachers have served as guides through inquiry that have helped frame the knowledge passed down within particular contexts, like professions. But now, the mere amount of knowledge and information available, every second of every day via electronic technology, lacks the narrative glue that held knowledge together in the past. Not only has the amount of information available to private, silent learners increased exponentially, but so too has mistrust in higher education (see Brenan, 2023). The fractionating of knowledge and overloading of information highlights the need for "interpretation or hermeneutics'' (Ong, 2002, p. 517). The division of knowledge into specialized areas is necessary because of the mass quantity of information accumulated today. Information is lost or unseen, scholars remain hidden in academic journals, and the intellectual works of most academics have little value in the marketplace (Posner, 2009). Consequently, people use search engines to gather snippets of information and make real-world decisions, even medical decisions, based on mere paragraphs on one webpage. All this activity is removed from any interpretive system in which professions have established a strong knowledge base. This lack of interpretation is especially concerning, as GAI tools are known to include "hallucinations" or incorrect information (Walters & Wilder, 2023).

Human-like perceptions of AI drive the fear that GAI will replace instructors. While GAI will not and cannot replace instructors, undoubtedly, it will alter the role of instructors, as all technology has done throughout history. What sets the instructor apart today is not the knowledge and expertise that they have within their specific area; all that information is readily available to anyone wishing to find it through the Internet or ChatGPT. Instead, instructors' roles will change to become expert interpreters. Instructors play an important role in helping students navigate the complex world of knowledge and information necessary for not only succeeding, but also flourishing. GAI technology is creating a crisis of information and interpretation, readily inviting the monsters to make things worse, and expose the extreme opposites of the issues at hand (Cohen, 1996).

While many higher education institutions started policing AI, driven by the fear of human-like technology, it should not be removed from education. Education and knowledge have always benefitted from technology. New technology might be decried, but we must remember that printing itself is a technology. Much of what has been required to arrive at the theories and major insights in education has been made possible due to the multiple cultural shifts in consciousness that resulted from technology. GAI tools are likely no different, provided they can be viewed not as making the crisis worse, but as helping resolve issues related to learning objectives, assessment, and student outcomes. Because monsters are outside our current paradigms and push the boundaries of current cultural practices, they can make us wonder what else is possible (Cohen, 1996). The monstrousness of GAI means creating new ideas and opportunities for individualized and student-centered education (Hutson et al., 2022; Maslej et al., 2023).

Beyond Human

Monsters sometimes erect borders to stop movement by scaring those around them (Cohen, 1996). The rhetoric surrounding AI-as-monsters has done an effective job of scaring people; currently, more people are concerned about AI than excited by it (Tyson & Kikuchi, 2023). The borders erected by these monsters are both physical and metaphorical for this theme, which underlies perceptions. The GAI could hold us hostage, by losing our intelligence, writing, and ceasing to teach effective reasoning and thinking skills. AI only "lives" within the boundaries of the data with which it is fed, which is beyond what is humanly possible. As one student wrote, "AI is able to analyze data faster and on a level that is almost beyond human capabilities." Many believe that GAI is moving past human-like capabilities and is at the "threshold of … becoming" (Cohen, 1996, p. 20) something else. To one respondent, GAI is "complex, dangerous, and poorly understood machine learning" and another wrote, "it's very futuristic and kinda scary to be honest [...] because the technology behind it is unbelievable and I've seen movies where it's too smart that it takes over and becomes it's [sic] own mind." One faculty member said, "AI tries to replicate what humans can do and at times even does some things better than humans can do," suggesting these tools are moving past human-like and into a beyond human-like phase. Is this movement, as one student said, just the "next phase of our evolution"? Or does the introduction of these tools lead to dehumanization?

A tenant of monster theory suggests that monsters are often hard to categorize, or are a "harbinger of category crisis" and challenge current thoughts about how society functions (Cohen, 1996, p. 6). Generative AI tools can be both helpful and harmful (van der Sluijs, 2005) or a "paradox" because they simultaneously build and destroy practices at the same time, especially in education (Lim et al., 2023). In addition to being difficult to categorize, monsters might be forgotten, but will ultimately return (Cohen, 1996). Ignoring or banishing GAI tools might lead to even more problems (Petricini et al., 2023). Cohen (1996) warns that when monsters return, as they are guaranteed to do, they come back with "self-knowledge, *human* knowledge" (p. 20). As one student described,

Artificial intelligence is a tool that, once trained on whatever the maker wants it to be adept on, can use coding and computational skills and algorithms to perform a task, whether that task is to have a conversation, act as a real or fictitious character, or solve a math problem. The range of what a specific AI can do is largely based on what it is trained on, and there are not many limitations to said training.

We must take ownership of the creations and not abandon the technology-as-monster, as Dr. Frankenstein did with his creation (Shelley, 2006). Monster "exorcists" want to be rid of the monster (Smits, 2006) but trying to stop GAI is not an option and any sort of idea about returning to pre-AI is unreasonable.

The monster cannot be destroyed (Cohen, 1996) without creating more of the same and as replacements (van der Sluijs, 2005), perhaps even with new heads (Smits, 2006), abilities, or dimensions. Society cannot remain idle about how and where AI technology goes, particularly as people are less excited about it now than they were two years ago (Tyson & Kikuchi, 2023). Regulations seek to curtail certain uses (Wheeler, 2023) and the legal challenges of accountability and copyright infringement with GAI tools remain unknown and undefined (Yanisky-Ravid, 2017). However, for sure, the use and governance of GAI tools cannot be left to developers; there is simply too much at stake not to have more people involved with how and where these technologies go.

DEMONSTERIZATION: RECOMMENDATIONS FOR MOVING FORWARD

In Mary Shelley's *Frankenstein*, Justine is wrongly convicted and executed for the murder of William – the monster kills the child (Shelley, 2006). The same tragic endings play out in the multiple renditions of AI-as-monster. However, these stories lack elements of human agency in shaping the actual ending. The tragic endings in which AI takes over, kills, or does any other of the various dubious practices that AI is depicted of doing, fail to truly recognize that AI is not *human*, nor is it *human-like*, nor will it ever be *beyond*. However, AI will have a significant impact on the transformation of higher education and society; it is much more than just a tool.

The question for academia is, what do we do next? One scenario is to tame the monster and take it under our control. This process could mean putting our efforts toward training, literacy, and directing both students and faculty, as well as society at large, on the ethical use of these rising technologies. Perhaps we could even accept the monster, loving it in a way, and forgetting the fear. Regardless, the worst scenario would be one in which we try to cage the monster (see Cohen, 1996). Ideally, we recommend a combination of both taming and accepting the monster and, in essence, *demonsterizing* AI.

In relation to addressing perceptions related to the lack of knowledge and the *unknown*, this is one area where higher education has a unique opportunity to make a significant impact. One of the many purposes of a college education is to prepare students for a career (Bok, 2006). Higher education must understand and meet the needs of the current market to prepare graduates. Employers expect college graduates to have some sort of understanding and experience with generative AI tools, such as ChatGPT, when they graduate (Maslej et al., 2023). If higher education is meant to serve the public, then the connection between school and society must be strong. Curricular content must not only be useful but also reflective of current social needs (Boyer, 1990). Institutions of higher education continue to grapple with enrollment numbers (see National Center for Education Statistics, 2023), feelings of confidence (Brenan, 2023), and value. GAI offers an opportunity to reimagine what student support and curricular content could look like (Hutson et al., 2022). Like monsters, GAI tools have pushed the boundaries of what is possible, and it is unlikely we will return to what existed before. Higher education can be at the forefront of creating sound, ethical, and appropriate practices for these tools.

Faculty cannot outrun these tools; they must learn how to incorporate them into their classrooms, for their benefit, and students. GAI tools should be integrated into instructors' teaching, service, and scholarship responsibilities so that their use is ethical and fair in the academy. However, instructors might also use these tools in unsavory or academically dishonest ways, such as forgetting to check for accuracy. Algorithms in GAI might have implicit bias or discriminatory practices (U.S. Department of Education, 2023) and only report or reproduce information they collect, without concern for right and wrong, or ethically and morally sound responses (Sabzalieva & Valentini, 2023). The instructor must then change and reframe their expertise into an interpretation by placing the AI output into context. Additionally, a cultural divide between faculty and student use seems to be at play. Our research shows students may not want or like AI-generated syllabi or assessments (see Petricini et al., 2023), even if those actions decrease instructors' cognitive load and time. Bi-directional trust and transparency between the instructor and student regarding the use of GAI tools are necessary.

A tenant of Monster Theory states that monsters "dwell at the gates of difference" (Cohen, 1996, p. 7). Theoretically, the AI-monster means a division between those *who use* and those *who do not use* is just as inevitable as the growth and spread of the technology. Creating awareness around the language that prompts the borders that spur *insider* and *outsider* dichotomies, or *us* versus *them,* is urgently needed. Otherwise, these dichotomies create unreasonable limits of acceptability and usability in the case of GAI. Cyclical models can drive or even close off language itself, for example when certain grammars are viewed as proper (Petricini, 2019), it is directly related to the output of GAI tools. Cheating and plagiarism are major concerns with GAI tools and come with a likelihood that certain student groups will be profiled more than others. Largely based on culture, race, language, and other personal characteristics, a dichotomy of *cheater* and *non-cheater* (Eaton, 2021) is probable. In the differences of cheating lies a monster (Cohen, 1996) who feeds off the norms and cultural practices of writing and language. However, Eaton (2021) warns that certain students are more likely to be added to *cheater* classification through profiling and racialization practices based on a normative white-centered, U.S.-focused culture. Not only are these practices hurtful to students, with more student conduct case reviews from minority populations, but they also uphold problematic systems based on race, class, language, and culture (Eaton, 2021) frequently found in U.S. institutions of higher education. Instead, Eaton (2021) argues moving past predisposed ideas of who is likely to cheat or plagiarize and focusing on teaching and learning.

In parallel, students might be unnecessarily blamed for using ChatGPT in unsavory ways, with little or no recourse to prove otherwise. When classroom policies police the use of ChatGPT, a focus on punishing students and addressing faculty wishes is evident, but not necessarily supporting the educational needs of students (see Bok, 2006). Even though some student behavior may need corrective measures, changing student behavior should be done through "argument, persuasion, and example" (Bok, 2006, p. 65). In general, colleges and universities have unique opportunities to approach GAI tools and formulate their use. For instance, the University of Michigan created branded AI tools, in which users must authenticate their university-affiliated identity before using and monitor usage (Burns, 2023). This is an excellent example of controlling or policing use, and promoting transparency, but also recognizing the benefits of offering a seamless delivery of accessibility resources for students. Monster Theory clearly states that monsters cannot be caged; they will always escape (Cohen, 1996), meaning that students will use the tools regardless of policing measures.

We propose that *demonsterization* then becomes a mix of promoting literacy, ethical and transparent use, and developing language that is mindful of these practices that may either empower or disempower individuals in their AI use and endeavors. In this process, as seen with many monsters, the monster becomes less scary. Vampires have been romanticized, as in the *Twilight* series. Dragons have been accepted for decades in television and movies. *Teen Wolf* made werewolves less scary. What this means for AI monsters is not anthropomorphizing them, but a *demonsterizing* that requires what philosophy of technology scholars have been discussing for quite some time. Over time, new technologies tend to be forgotten and become transparent (Ihde, 1990). Not unlike eyeglasses, which are nearly imperceptible, they are also literally how their users see the world and serve as a mediating factor to the "seer" (Ihde, 1990, p. 73). The various types of human-technology relationships, as in the case of glasses, exemplify the embodiment relation. While GAI may not become imperceptible in the same way as glasses, some type of normalization of using AI must occur. In doing so, society will need to reclaim GAI technology from its creators because otherwise, AI will remain a monster.

CONCLUSION

Ultimately, we unleashed a technology monster. This is not the first time, and it certainly will not be the last time, contending with a monster. History does not actually repeat itself but rather shows the synchronicity of human lives. Writing, calculators, and iPhones are previous technology monsters that are now embedded in society. The current and future use of AI is like the myth of eternal return, highlighting the archetypes of human action, ever-advancing society's knowledge, and creating tools (see Eliade, 1954). We forget the frightening aspects as the monster becomes part of us. The demonsterization of GAI tools carries significant implications for future societies, where the boundaries of AI use are blurred beyond human recognition. However, higher education can help frame the appropriate use and future of these powerful tools. Knowledge and available tools change over time, and so too must the curriculum. Nearly 100 years ago, the Yale Report of 1828 argued the need to revise the curriculum, moving away from certain historical subjects, in response to the changing needs and knowledge of society (Herbst, 2004). Introducing GAI into education is no different.

REFERENCES

Bok, D. (2006). *Our underachieving colleges*. Princeton University Press.

Boyer, E. (1990). *Scholarship reconsidered: Priorities of the professoriate*. Carnegie Foundation for the Advancement of Teaching.

Brenan, M. (2023, July 11). *Americans' confidence in higher education down sharply*. Gallup. https://news.gallup.com/poll/508352/americans-confidence-higher-education-down-sharply.aspx

Burns, T. (2023, August 21). ITS debuts custom artificial intelligence services across U-M. *The University Record.* https://record.umich.edu/articles/its-debuts-customized-ai-services-to-u-m-community/

Butler, S. (1927). *Erewhon, or over the range and Erewhon revisited twenty years later*. Random House. https://books.google.com/books?hl=en&lr=&id=D48yAAAAMAAJ&oi=fnd&pg=PR1&ots=g5RC9UlXAp&sig=rQb1vCtuYsSM_ehkzvCDLt2rL50#v=onepage&q&f=false

Canavero, S., Ren, X., & Kim, C. Y. (2016). HEAVEN: The Frankenstein effect. *Surgical Neurology International*, *7*(24), 623. Advance online publication. doi:10.4103/2152-7806.190472 PMID:27656323

Casal-Otero, L., Catala, A., Fernández-Morante, C., Taboada, M., Cebreiro, B., & Barro, S. (2023). AI literacy in K-12: A systematic literature review. *International Journal of STEM Education*, *10*(1), 29. doi:10.1186/s40594-023-00418-7

Cave, S., Dihal, K., & Dillon, S. (Eds.). (2020). *AI narratives: A history of imaginative thinking about intelligent machines*. Oxford University Press. doi:10.1093/oso/9780198846666.001.0001

Chen, L., Zaharia, M., & Zou, J. (2023). *How is ChatGPT's behavior changing over time?* [Preprint]. https://arxiv.org/pdf/2307.09009.pdf

Cohen, J. (1996). Monster culture (seven theses). In J. J. Cohen (Ed.), *Monster theory: Reading culture* (pp. 3-25). University of Minnesota Press. doi:10.5749/j.cttsq4d.4

D'Agostino, S. (2023, April 18). The oncoming AI Ed-tech 'tsunami'. *Inside Higher Ed*. https://www.insidehighered.com/news/tech-innovation/artificial-intelligence/2023/04/18/oncoming-ai-ed-tech-tsunami

Darwin, C. (1859). *On the origin of species*. John Murray.

Davies, R. S. (2011). Understanding technology Literacy: A framework for evaluating Educational Technology Integration. *TechTrends*, *55*(5), 45–52. doi:10.1007/s11528-011-0527-3

Dove, G., & Fayard, A. L. (2020). *Monsters, metaphors, and machine learning* [Conference paper]. CHI 2020, Honolulu, HI. https://chi2020.acm.org/

Dreyfus, H. (1979). *What computers can't do*. Harper Colophon Books.

Earley, P. M. (1994). *Goals 2000: Educate America Act: Implications for teacher educators*. AACTE Publications.

Eaton, S. E. (2021). *Plagiarism in higher education: Tackling tough topics in academic integrity*. ABC-CLIO. doi:10.5040/9798400697142

Eliade, M. (1954). *The myth of the eternal return* (W. R. Trask, Trans.). Kingsport Press.

Elsevier. (2023). *The use of AI and AI-assisted writing technologies in scientific writing. Frequently asked questions*. https://www.elsevier.com/about/policies/publishing-ethics/the-use-of-ai-and-ai-assisted-writing-technologies-in-scientific-writing

Fisher, P. (1999). Narrative as human communication paradigm. In J. L. Lucaites, C. M. Condit, & S. Caudill (Eds.), *Contemporary rhetorical theory: A reader* (pp. 265–287). Guilford Press. (Original work published 1984)

Herbst, J. (2004). The Yale Report of 1828. *International Journal of the Classical Tradition, 11*(11), 213–231. doi:10.1007/BF02720033

Hu, K. (2023, February 2). *ChatGPT sets record for fastest-growing user base - analyst note*. Reuters. https://www.reuters.com/technology/chatgpt-sets-record-fastest-growing-user-base-analyst-note-2023-02-01/

Hutson, J., Jeevanjee, T., Graaf, V., Lively, J., Weber, J., Weir, G., Arnone, K., Carnes, G., Vosevich, K., Plate, D., Leary, M., & Edele, S. (2022). Artificial Intelligence and the disruption of higher education: Strategies for integrations across disciplines. *Creative Education, 13*(12), 3953–3980. doi:10.4236/ce.2022.1312253

Ihde, D. (1990). *Technology and the lifeworld: From garden to earth.* Indiana University Press.

Iliescu, M. (2016). Istoria şi filosofia roboţilor industriali. *Studii și Comunicări, 9*(9), 401–411.

Joosten, T. (2012). *Social media for educators: Strategies and best practices.* John Wiley & Sons.

Kong, S. C., Cheung, W. M. Y., & Zhang, G. (2021). Evaluation of an artificial intelligence literacy course for university students with diverse study backgrounds. *Computers and Education: Artificial Intelligence, 2*, 100026. doi:10.1016/j.caeai.2021.100026

Krug, S. (2013). *Don't make me think, revisited: A common sense approach to web usability* (3rd ed.). New Riders.

Kuhn, T. S. (1962). *The structure of scientific revolutions.* University of Chicago Press.

Lanier, J. (2011). You are not a gadget: A manifesto (Reprint edition). Vintage.

Laupichler, M. C., Aster, A., Schirch, J., & Raupach, T. (2022). Artificial intelligence literacy in higher and adult education: A scoping literature review. *Computers and Education: Artificial Intelligence, 3*, 100101. doi:10.1016/j.caeai.2022.100101

Lim, W., Gunasekara, A., Pallant, J. L., Pallant, J. I., & Pechenkina, E. (2023). Generative AI and the future education: Ragnarök or reformation? A paradoxical perspective from management educators. *International Journal of Management Education, 21*(2), 100790. Advance online publication. doi:10.1016/j.ijme.2023.100790

Long, D., & Magerko, B. (2020, April). What is AI literacy? Competencies and design considerations. In *Proceedings of the 2020 CHI Conference on Human Factors in Computing Systems* (pp. 1–16). 10.1145/3313831.3376727

Lu, D., Ruan, B., Lee, M., Yilmaz, Y., & Chan, T. M. (2020). Good practices in harnessing social media for scholarly discourse, knowledge translation, and education. *Journal of Medical Education and Curricular Development, 10*(1), 1. Advance online publication. doi:10.1007/S40037-020-00613-0 PMID:32820414

Maslej, N., Fattorini, L., Brynjolfsson, E., Etchemendy, J., Ligett, K., Lyons, T., Manyika, J., Ngo, H., Niebles, J. C., Parli, V., Shoham, Y., Wald, R., Clark, J., & Perrault, R. (2023). *The AI Index 2023 Annual Report.* AI Index Steering Committee, Institute for Human-Centered AI, Stanford University, Stanford, CA. https://aiindex.stanford.edu/wp-content/uploads/2023/04/HAI_AI-Index-Report_2023.pdf

Mayor, A. (2018). *Gods and robots.* Princeton University Press. doi:10.2307/j.ctvc779xn

McCarthy, J., Minsky, M. L., Rochester, N., & Shannon, C. E. (2006). A proposal for the Dartmouth summer research project on artificial intelligence, August 31, 1955. *AI Magazine*, *27*(4), 12–12.

Mittman, A. (2012). Introduction: The impact of monsters and monster studies. In A. Mittman & P. Dendel (Eds.), *The Ashgate research companion to monsters and the monstrous* (pp. 41-54). Ashgate.

Mok, A. (2023). Professors want to 'ChatGPT-proof' assignments, and are returning to paper exams and requesting editing history to curb AI cheating. *Business Insider*. https://www.businessinsider.com/teachers-colleges-ways-chatgpt-proof-assignments-essays-prevent-cheating-2023-8

Morris, J. (Producer). (2008). *Wall-E* [Film]. Walt Disney Pixar Animation Studio.

Muscanell, N., & Robert, J. (2023, February 14). *EDUCAUSE QuickPoll results: Did ChatGPT write this report?* EDUCAUSE. https://er.educause.edu/articles/2023/2/educause-quickpoll-results-did-chatgpt-write-this-report

National Center for Education Statistics. (2023). *Undergraduate enrollment. In condition of education.* U.S. Department of Education, Institute of Education Sciences. https://nces.ed.gov/programs/coe/indicator/cha

Norman, D. (2013). *The design of everyday things* (Revised edition). Basic Books.

Ong, W. J. (2002). Information and/or communication: Interactions. In T. J. Farrell & P. A. Soukup (Eds.), *An Ong reader: Challenges for further inquiry* (pp. 505–526). Hampton Press.

Petricini, T. (2019). Explorations in the noosphere: Hermeneutic presence and hostility in cyberspace. *Explorations in Media Ecology*, *18*(1-2), 57–71. doi:10.1386/eme.18.1-2.57_1

PetriciniT.WuC.ZipfS. (2023). Perceptions about generative AI and ChatGPT use by faculty and college students [Preprint]. doi:10.35542/osf.io/jyma4

Pommer, E. (Producer). (1927). *Metropolis* [Film]. UFA.

Posner, R. A. (2009). *Public intellectuals.* Harvard University Press. doi:10.2307/j.ctv1kwxdnh

Rauch, A. (1995). The monstrous body of knowledge in Mary Shelley's" Frankenstein. *Studies in Romanticism*, *34*(2), 227–253. doi:10.2307/25601114

Rosenblatt, K. (2023). *New York City public schools remove ChatGPT ban.* NBC News. https://www.nbcnews.com/tech/chatgpt-ban-dropped-new-york-city-public-schools-rcna85089

Sabzalieva, E., & Valentini, A. (2023). *ChatGPT and Artificial Intelligence in higher education.* UNESCO. https://www.iesalc.unesco.org/

Schneier, B. (2016). Data and Goliath: The hidden battles to collect your data and control your world (Reprint edition). W. W. Norton & Company.

Shelley, M. (2021). *Frankenstein.* Sterling Publishing. (Original work published 1818)

Smith, A. (1902). *The wealth of nations.* Collier & Son.

Smits, M. (2006). Taming monsters: The cultural domestication of new technology. *Technology in Society*, *28*(4), 489–504. doi:10.1016/j.techsoc.2006.09.008

Ta, R., & West, D. (2023, August 7). *Should schools ban or integrate generative AI in the classrooms?* Brookings. https://www.brookings.edu/articles/should-schools-ban-or-integrate-generative-ai-in-the-classroom/

Taylor, T., & Dorin, A. (2020). *Rise of the self-replicators*. Springer. doi:10.1007/978-3-030-48234-3

Tong, A., Dastin, J., & Hu, K. (2023, November 23). *OpenAI researchers warned board of AI breakthrough ahead of CEO ouster, sources say.* Reuters. https://www.reuters.com/technology/sam-altmans-ouster-openai-was-precipitated-by-letter-board-about-ai-breakthrough-2023-11-22/

Touretzky, D., Gardner-McCune, C., Martin, F., & Seehorn, D. (2019, July). Envisioning AI for K-12: What should every child know about AI? *Proceedings of the AAAI Conference on Artificial Intelligence, 33*(01), 9795–9799. doi:10.1609/aaai.v33i01.33019795

Truitt, E. R. (2021). Made, not born: The ancient history of intelligent machines. In A. Campbell (Ed.), The love makers (pp. 217–224). Goldsmiths Press.

Tyson, A., & Kikuchi, E. (2023). *Growing public concern about the role of artificial intelligence in daily life*. The Pew Research Center. https://www.pewresearch.org/short-reads/2023/08/28/growing-public-concern-about-the-role-of-artificial-intelligence-in-daily-life/

U.S. Department of Education. (2023). *Artificial intelligence and future of teaching and learning: Insights and recommendations*. Office of Educational Technology. https://tech.ed.gov

van der Sluijs, J. (2005). Uncertainty as a monster in the science-policy interface: Four coping strategies. *Water Science and Technology, 52*(6), 87–92. doi:10.2166/wst.2005.0155 PMID:16304939

Walters, W. H., & Wilder, E. I. (2023). Fabrication and errors in the bibliographic citations generated by ChatGPT. *Scientific Reports, 13*(1), 14045. doi:10.1038/s41598-023-41032-5 PMID:37679503

Wheeler, T. (2023, June 15). *The three challenges of AI regulation*. The Brookings Institute. https://www.brookings.edu/articles/the-three-challenges-of-ai-regulation/

Witt, S. (2015). *How music got free: The end of an industry, the turn of the century, and the patient zero of piracy*. Viking.

Yanisky-Ravid, S. (2017). Generating Rembrandt: Artificial intelligence, copyright, and accountability in the 3a era: The human-like authors are already here - a new model. *Detroit College of Law at Michigan State University Law Review, 2017*(4), 659–726.

Yates, D. R., Vaessen, C., & Roupret, M. (2011). From Leonardo to da Vinci: The history of robot-assisted surgery in urology. *BJU International, 108*(11), 1708–1713. doi:10.1111/j.1464-410X.2011.10576.x PMID:21951677

Yi, Y. (2021). Establishing the concept of AI literacy. *JaHR – European Journal of Bioethics, 12*(2), 353–368.

Chapter 14
Integrating Professional Perspectives for AI Literacy:
Empowering Students in an AI-Influenced Future

Kristopher Merceron
https://orcid.org/0000-0002-5118-7288
Valencia College, USA

Karene Best
Valencia College, USA

ABSTRACT

This chapter delves into the crucial realm of AI literacy in education by integrating insights from librarians and communication professors. It underscores the pivotal roles these professionals play in equipping students for an AI-dominated future. As the educational landscape rapidly transforms under the influence of AI, librarians and communication professors are tasked with adapting their roles and collaborating to provide comprehensive AI literacy. Sections within the chapter explore the evolving roles, the significance of AI literacy, interdisciplinary curriculum integration, ethical considerations, practical applications, and the necessity of continuous professional development and advocacy. This collaborative approach ensures that students gain the knowledge and skills needed to excel in an AI-driven world, becoming informed, adaptable, and responsible participants in the digital age.

In an era characterized by the ever-accelerating transformation of the educational landscape, the roles of librarians and communication professors have taken on unprecedented significance. These dedicated professionals are at the forefront of the mission to arm students with the essential skills and knowledge required to flourish in a future deeply shaped by the influence of artificial intelligence (AI). The following section will delve into the fascinating and vital realm of AI literacy within education, offering a

DOI: 10.4018/979-8-3693-0831-8.ch014

multifaceted exploration that integrates the perspectives and insights of both librarians and communication professors.

As AI continues to evolve and permeates virtually every facet of our society, its impact on education cannot be overstated. With their profound expertise in information retrieval, curation, and dissemination, librarians are uniquely positioned to help students navigate the vast and complex digital landscape AI has helped create. Meanwhile, with their deep understanding of rhetoric, persuasion, and interpersonal dynamics, professors of communication contribute to developing students' critical thinking and communication skills, which are indispensable in an AI-driven world.

This chapter embarks on a comprehensive journey, shedding light on the future of AI literacy in education by focusing on the collaborative efforts of librarians and communication professors. It discusses the profound implications of AI on various educational facets, including information access, critical thinking abilities, ethical considerations, and effective communication. By taking a holistic approach and examining how AI intersects with these vital components of education, the goal is to provide a well-rounded, empowering framework that equips students with the knowledge and skills needed to thrive and succeed in a world profoundly shaped by the forces of artificial intelligence. Through this exploration, the hope is to contribute to a brighter and more informed future in which students are not just consumers of AI-driven technology, but also active participants and ethical stewards of this transformative force.

The Changing Landscape of Education

The rapid and relentless advancement of AI technologies is undoubtedly one of the most transformative forces shaping today's educational landscape. This has initiated a profound and sweeping shift that demands a proactive response from key educational stakeholders. As AI continues to evolve, its impact is felt across every facet of education, from how students learn to how teachers instruct to how institutions operate and plan for the future. This dynamic landscape necessitates not only adaptation, but also a fundamental reimagining of the roles and strategies of those at the helm of education.

In this era of AI integration, librarians and communication professors have emerged as crucial figures at the forefront of this transformative journey. Traditionally known as the guardians of knowledge repositories, librarians now play a multifaceted role in the AI era. They have evolved beyond their traditional roles, where they primarily assist students in locating physical books and periodicals into invaluable guides through the vast, digitally driven world of AI-generated information. Brusegard (2023) shares, "as librarians, we must lead by example…by embracing AI in our work, we become valuable resources for students, teachers, and the school community. Our role as librarians extends beyond traditional boundaries in a world where AI is becoming ubiquitous" (paras. 4-5). With the proliferation of AI-generated content, librarians have become experts in curating and facilitating access to reliable sources in an age of information abundance. Moreover, they assume the responsibility of navigating the ethical terrain, helping students distinguish between ethical and unethical AI use, and ensuring that AI-generated information is used responsibly.

Simultaneously, professors of communication have adapted their roles to embrace AI as a powerful educational tool. They recognize that AI is not merely a technical innovation but also a driving force in how information is disseminated, interpreted, and communicated. Hohenstein et al. (2023) define communication as "the basic process through which people form perceptions of others, build and maintain social relationships, and achieve cooperative outcomes," (p. 1) and later states, "generative AI, that draws from large language models (LLMs), is poised to fundamentally change how we communicate" (p. 1). Therefore, communication professors have taken on the task of imparting technical AI knowledge and the skills required to effectively communicate complex AI concepts. They foster an environment in which students not only understand AI but also bridge the gap between technical AI insights and their practical implications. Moreover, they teach students to critically analyze AI-generated content and navigate the ethical complexities of AI communication, thus equipping the next generation of communicators with the ability to engage thoughtfully and ethically in the AI-driven communication landscape.

As the AI era continues to unfold, librarians and communication professors are integral to preparing students for a future in which AI is deeply intertwined with every aspect of society. Their roles are no longer confined to their traditional domains, but have expanded to encompass AI literacy, ethical considerations, and effective communication within the context of AI technologies. Their proactive response to the evolving educational landscape positions them as key figures in shaping how students learn, think, and communicate in an AI-augmented world, ensuring that education remains a dynamic, relevant, and ethical endeavor. Guan et al. (2020) provides "AI innovation in education has evolved from idealized laboratory scenarios to real-life learning contexts with more complexity" (p. 134). Historically acknowledged as custodians of knowledge archives, librarians are presently adopting more versatile and multifaceted roles. With the increase in AI-generated content and information, they are transforming into indispensable guides, helping students and faculty navigate the labyrinthine databases of AI-derived knowledge. This expanded role includes not only facilitating access but also advocating the responsible and ethical use of AI-generated information. They were tasked with curating reliable sources, addressing issues of bias and transparency, and nurturing AI literacy within the academic community.

Some librarians have developed online resources to aid the academic community in better comprehending the advantages of AI technologies and disseminating ethical and responsible approaches for their integration within the educational realm. The University of Arizona Libraries (2023) exemplified this commitment to AI literacy by crafting two comprehensive LibGuides[1], one tailored for faculty and another for students. These LibGuides serve as valuable repositories of knowledge, providing educators and learners with a wealth of information, insights, and strategies to effectively harness AI while upholding ethical considerations within the classroom. With the continuous development of such resources, librarians are empowering instructors and students to navigate the complex landscape of AI technologies, unlocking their full potential for enhancing education while maintaining ethical standards.

Conversely, professors of communication embrace AI as a powerful pedagogical tool. Recognizing the increasing centrality of AI in shaping communication practices, communication professors are integrating AI applications into their teaching methodologies. For instance, imagine a communication professor teaching a digital marketing course. In this scenario, they incorporate AI-driven analytics tools that allow students to analyze consumer behavior, predict market trends, and optimize advertising campaigns. By working with these AI tools, students not only gain practical skills, but also develop a deeper understanding of how AI shapes the marketing landscape.

Beyond the technical aspects, communication instructors focus on honing students' critical thinking and analytical skills, enabling them to evaluate AI-generated content with discernment and ethical acumen. They present students with real-world case studies in which AI has been employed to influence public opinion or generate content, challenging them to critically assess the ethical implications of such practices. This approach encourages students to think beyond the surface of AI technology, fostering their ability to question and navigate potential biases, misinformation, and ethical dilemmas that may arise in AI-driven communication.

Moreover, communication professors are at the forefront of fostering inclusive and responsible AI communication practices. They ensure that students not only understand how to use AI tools, but also how to use them responsibly and ethically. For example, they may emphasize the importance of transparency in AI-generated content and encourage students to consider the ethical dimensions of AI algorithms that affect different demographic groups. By instilling these values, communication professors are equipping the next generation of communicators with the skills and awareness necessary to navigate the ethical complexities of AI in communication and advocate for responsible AI practices in their professional careers.

The convergence of these evolving roles—librarians as guides through AI information landscapes and communication professors as mentors in AI-enhanced communication—presents a compelling opportunity for transformative collaboration. Imagine a scenario where a group of librarians and communication professors collaboratively design an interdisciplinary course on "Ethical AI in Journalism and Media." In this course, students learn how to navigate the vast AI-generated information resources available through the guidance of librarians and explore the nuances of AI's impact on journalistic practices, storytelling, and media ethics guided by communication professors (Kim, 2019).

Together, these educators curate comprehensive learning experiences beyond the technical aspects of AI. Students engage in discussions and projects that require them to critically assess the ethical considerations of using AI in media, scrutinize AI-generated content for potential biases, and develop inclusive communication strategies to reach diverse audiences (Kim, 2019). For instance, they might delve into the ethical implications of using AI algorithms to personalize news feeds and the responsibility of journalists to ensure that algorithmic curation respects diverse perspectives.

This collaborative synergy empowers learners with a multifaceted understanding of AI's role in their field, equipping them with the skills and knowledge necessary to navigate the AI-driven educational landscape responsibly. Graduates of such programs are proficient in AI technologies and advocate for ethical and inclusive AI practices in journalism and the media (Kim, 2019). In this way, librarians and communication professors become catalysts in shaping an AI-enhanced educational future where information is abundant, communication is dynamic, and ethics are paramount, ensuring that the next generation of communicators is well-prepared to harness AI as a force for positive change while upholding the highest ethical standards.

AI Literacy and Information Fluency

In this digital age, in which AI technologies are becoming increasingly ubiquitous, AI literacy has emerged as a pivotal component of information fluency. It equips students with essential skills to navigate, critically assess, and effectively communicate AI-generated information. Long and Magerko (2020) define AI literacy "as a set of competencies that enables individuals to critically evaluate AI technologies; communicate and collaborate effectively with AI; and use AI as a tool online, at home, and in the workplace." AI literacy encompasses a profound understanding of AI systems, enabling individuals to discern biases, limitations, and ethical considerations within these technologies, ultimately empowering them to make informed decisions and contribute to the responsible advancement of AI.

Librarians and communication professors play pivotal roles as essential guides in cultivating AI literacy among students. Let us envision a practical scenario to illustrate the significance of a librarian's role:

Imagine a university student, Sarah, who is conducting research for her senior thesis on the ethical implications of AI in healthcare. Sarah approaches the university library for assistance. Mrs. Anderson, a librarian, takes her under her wing. Mrs. Anderson begins by teaching Sarah how to navigate the library's extensive AI-related literature database, including research papers, articles, and reports.

Mrs. Anderson emphasizes the importance of source evaluation in the AI landscape. She instructs Sarah on critically assessing the credibility of the sources she encounters, urging her to consider factors such as the author's qualifications, publication source, and potential biases in the research. She shares with Sarah the importance of using the "CRAAP" test during this process, which stands for "currency, relevance, authority, accuracy, and purpose" (Valencia College, 2021). Mrs. Anderson highlights the need for discernment, particularly when dealing with AI-generated content, which may not always be transparent in its origin.

As Sarah delves deeper into her research, she applies the skills she has acquired from Mrs. Anderson. She scrutinizes the AI-generated healthcare reports, looking for reliable and unbiased sources. In doing so, she enhances her academic research and gains valuable life skills. In an age when AI-driven health recommendations and medical diagnoses are becoming increasingly common, Sarah's ability to evaluate the credibility of AI-generated healthcare information equips her to make informed decisions about her own health and well-being. Bajwa et al. (2021) state that "research on the application of AI healthcare continues to accelerate rapidly, with potential use cases being demonstrated across the healthcare sector (both physical and mental health) including drug discovery, virtual clinical consultation, disease diagnosis, prognosis, medication management, and health monitoring" (p. 190).

In this scenario, librarians like Mrs. Anderson are instrumental in empowering students like Sarah with the knowledge and skills to effectively navigate the vast sea of AI-derived content. Their expertise in information evaluation ensures that students can discern trustworthy sources in a world inundated with AI-generated information, contributing not only to academic success, but also to informed decision-making in various aspects of life.

On the other hand, communication professors play a crucial role in honing students' ability to communicate complex AI concepts to diverse audiences effectively. In an era in which AI is intricately woven into various facets of society, the ability to convey AI-related information with transparency and clarity is paramount. Communication professors ensure students can bridge the gap between technical AI knowledge and its practical application, fostering a responsible and accessible AI discourse. Let us now explore another scenario to illustrate the role of a communication professor in honing a student's ability to communicate complex AI concepts effectively:

Alex is an undergraduate student majoring in computer science at a prestigious university. He is passionate about AI and has developed a groundbreaking application driven by AI as part of his coursework. He has been tasked with presenting his work to a diverse audience, including fellow students, faculty members, industry professionals, and potential investors.

Recognizing the importance of this presentation, Alex enrolls in a communication course focused on AI communication. Dr. Ramirez, his communication professor, is an expert in teaching students how to bridge the gap between technical knowledge and effective communication. Dr. Ramirez begins by helping Alex distill complex AI concepts from his project into understandable, engaging narratives. "This involves breaking down the concept into its component parts, and then breaking those parts down even further" (Lee, n.d., para. 7).

Under Dr. Ramirez's guidance, Alex learns to avoid jargon and technical complexities that might alienate nontechnical audiences. He practices delivering his presentation with clarity and precision, ensuring that he can convey the significance of his AI application to a wide range of listeners. "This helps to make the concept relatable and easier to understand" (Lee, n.d., para. 8). Dr. Ramirez also emphasizes the importance of transparency in discussing AI algorithms and their potential implications, fostering a responsible and open dialogue.

Consequently, when Alex presents his AI project, he does so with confidence and effectiveness. He not only impresses his technical peers with the depth of his knowledge, but also engages and educates non-technical audience members, helping them grasp the societal impact and ethical considerations of his AI application. This newfound ability to communicate complex AI concepts with transparency and clarity is a valuable skill Alex carries forward in his academic and professional journey.

In this scenario, communication professors such as Dr. Ramirez are pivotal in ensuring students can effectively close the divide between technical AI knowledge and its practical applications. By promoting responsible and accessible AI discussions, they empower students to communicate the profound implications of AI to diverse audiences, ultimately contributing to more informed and inclusive AI-related discussions in society.

Collaborative Curriculum Integration

The collaborative nature of librarians and communication professors, each contributing their unique expertise, forms the foundation of well-rounded AI literacy education. Together, they can empower students to engage critically with AI-generated information and effectively communicate their insights and findings to a broader audience. This integrated approach equips the next generation of learners with the skills and knowledge necessary to responsibly and ethically navigate the complexities of the AI-driven digital landscape. Klein (2023) articulates, "AI literacy is something that every student needs exposure to – not just those who are planning on a career in computer science" (para. 6). Ultimately, AI literacy empowers all students to harness the potential of AI as a transformative force while safeguarding against its potential pitfalls and ensuring a well-informed and proactive engagement with AI technologies.

Integrating AI literacy into the curriculum is a complex but vital endeavor that demands seamless collaboration between librarians and communication professors. This harmonious partnership plays a pivotal role in creating a well-rounded educational experience that prepares students for today's and tomorrow's AI-infused world. This process requires thoughtful consideration of the various facets of collaborative curriculum integration and the benefits they provide to students.

Central to this collaborative endeavor is the librarian's essential function of curating AI-related resources, a role that draws upon their expertise in navigating the expansive and complex digital information landscape. Librarians are seasoned navigators of the vast ocean of information that characterizes the digital realm. Their skills, honed through years of experience, enable them to navigate the intricate web of online sources, databases, and repositories with precision and fineness. According to the article, "What does a librarian do?" (2023), "[modern librarians] must stay up to date with changes in technology and the latest trends in information science to ensure that library users [and students] have access to the most current and relevant resources" (para. 1).

In the context of the AI era, where information proliferates at an astonishing rate, proficiency in identifying credible and trustworthy sources is of paramount importance. In this landscape, where AI-generated content can abound, often lacking rigor of verification or prone to inherent biases, librarians serve as gatekeepers of quality and reliability. Their discerning eye for authoritative, peer-reviewed literature and their ability to identify unbiased, reputable sources is indispensable.

Through vigilant curation, librarians provide valuable services to students and educators. They ensure students have unfettered access to a rich tapestry of high-quality AI-related content, creating an environment conducive to informed exploration and learning. This curated environment not only simplifies the research process for students but also emphasizes the importance of relying on credible sources. This skill extends far beyond their academic pursuits and equips them for a lifetime of discerning and informed decision making in the era of AI.

Moreover, librarians assume a crucial role in aiding both faculty and students in the intricate task of deciphering bias in AI-related content. In their vigilant curation efforts, librarians not only provide access to high-quality AI materials but also guide users in critically evaluating these resources. They recognized that in the era of AI, discerning bias is a paramount skill. Librarians help students and educators navigate this terrain, ensuring they approach AI content critically.

Librarians are adept at identifying potential sources of bias in AI-related materials, whether in the data used to train AI algorithms or in the perspectives embedded in AI-generated content. Their expertise in source evaluation extends beyond credibility; it encompasses an acute awareness of potential biases and commitment to promoting balanced, objective information. By assisting students and educators in recognizing and grappling with bias in AI content, librarians equip them with the skills needed to engage critically and ethically with AI information.

Drawing from the insights of the research article by Pagano et al. (2023), librarians are well equipped to help students and educators understand the multifaceted dimensions of bias in machine learning and AI systems. This comprehensive study, which followed the PRISMA[2] guidelines and surveyed articles from 2017 to 2022, offers a rich repository of knowledge on bias, unfairness identification, and mitigation techniques. By incorporating the findings from this systematic review, librarians can ensure that students and educators stay abreast of the latest developments in the fields of algorithmic fairness and bias detection. They can introduce users to a diverse array of tools, statistical approaches, and metrics highlighted in the study, shedding light on the critical role these elements play in identifying and mitigating bias in AI systems. Furthermore, librarians can deepen students' and educators' understanding of the primary forms of bias, which encompasses data, algorithms, and user interactions. They can elucidate how preprocessing, in-processing, and post-processing mitigation methods can effectively address these biases. Educators and students can be provided with a broad spectrum of practical examples, from criminal justice to finance, illustrating the real-world applications of bias mitigation techniques, and librarians can draw attention to tools such as Aequitas to showcase their potential utility in addressing algorithmic bias and promoting transparency in AI systems. Essentially, a librarian's role extends far beyond providing access to resources; they also encompass a deep understanding of bias detection and fairness, especially in digital resources such as AI, and can equip students and faculty with the knowledge and skills needed to navigate the ethical complexities of the AI era.

Through this guidance, librarians foster an environment of discernment and informed decision making in the era of AI. They empower students to question assumptions, challenge biases, and make well-informed choices when navigating a vast AI-generated information landscape. This valuable skill set transcends the academic realm, becoming an essential tool for navigating the broader AI-infused world, where bias awareness is indispensable for responsible decision making and ethical engagement with AI technologies.

On the other side of the spectrum, communication professors play an instrumental role by leveraging their expertise in persuasive communication and media literacy in AI education. In an AI context, where the boundaries between human-generated and AI-generated content can often blur, the need to equip students with the skills to critically assess and effectively communicate about AI has become paramount. Professors in communication are at the forefront of addressing this need by imparting multifaceted skills to their students.

Within the purview of AI, communication professors undertake the task of imparting the skill to communicate complex AI concepts and the art of making these ideas accessible to a wide range of audiences. In a contemporary landscape where AI technologies influence various facets of our daily lives, the ability to translate intricate technical terminology and complexities into a clear and understandable language is a highly prioritized competence. Communication professors are pivotal in ensuring students can effectively channel the divide between their deep understanding of AI's technical intricacies and its practical applications. This, in turn, enables students to engage in meaningful and approachable discussions on AI across diverse contexts. Palmer-Silveira (2015) even stated that "getting the right training can help both students and professionals deliver a good oral presentation. This is what many companies ask academic authorities to accomplish" (p. 173).

Moreover, communication professors address the critical issue of misinformation and manipulation in AI-generated content. They empower students with tools to discern and counteract potential biases, inaccuracies, or deceptive practices embedded in AI-generated materials. For example, "representation bias occurs when the development sample underrepresents some part of the population, and subsequently fails to generalize well for a subset of the use population" (Suresh & Guttag, 2021, p. 4). To address this particular kind of bias, communication professors can initiate discussions centered on the ethical dimensions of representation bias. By engaging students in conversations about the potential consequences of underrepresentation in AI systems, such as perpetuating stereotypes and excluding certain groups, professors can instill the notion that addressing bias extends beyond technical considerations, which is a moral imperative.

Moreover, these educators can guide students in critical analysis. They can encourage students to question the composition of training data, identify potential sources of bias, and assess whether datasets accurately represent diverse user populations. By developing these analytical skills, students can become adept at recognizing situations in which underrepresentation might occur and take proactive measures.

In an information landscape rife with AI-driven content, critically assessing and questioning the veracity of one's encounters is indispensable. Communication professors guide students in developing a critical eye, enabling them to navigate AI-generated content with discernment and ethical acumen. Real-world case studies, examples, and thorough research into information provided by AI can not only further enhance a student's understanding of the negative impacts these biases can have in communication, but they can also instill a sense of responsibility in students to use AI systems and information to promote informed and ethical discourse. This empowerment equips students to recognize potential sources of harm within the AI landscape while aiding them in proactive efforts to prevent and mitigate undesirable consequences, while decreasing the spread of misinformation (Suresh & Guttag, 2021). Communication professors play a pivotal role in fostering a generation of communicators who are proficient in AI and vigilant in addressing their ethical implications.

By combining their expertise in persuasive communication and media literacy with the nuances of the AI landscape, communication professors empower the next generation of communicators to not only understand AI, but also to engage thoughtfully with its implications. Their teaching extends beyond the technical aspects of AI, fostering a holistic understanding that encompasses the social, ethical, and communicative dimensions of AI technologies.

One practical example of how communication professors can aid students in this AI-driven environment is through the design of multimedia projects[3]. These projects can challenge students in creating persuasive and informative presentations about specific AI applications. In doing so, students are tasked with conveying complex AI concepts in a way that is engaging, transparent, and accessible to a general audience. The process begins with rigorous research and analysis, wherein students select an AI application, delve into its workings, and explore its societal implications and ethical considerations. This phase emphasizes media literacy, as students learn to critically evaluate AI-related information in the media to gather accurate and balanced insights.

Following the research phase, students enter the content creation stage. Armed with their knowledge, they construct multimedia presentations enriched with visual aids, graphics, and clear explanations. Persuasive communication techniques come into play as students strive to make the audience understand the significance of the AI technology they choose to research, its potential benefits, and any associated drawbacks or ethical concerns. Derin, et al. (2020) states, "persuasive speech requires a clear understanding of the audience and an intense listener focus" (p. 13).

Peer review adds depth to the learning process. Students would present their multimedia projects to their peers, simulating real-world communication challenges. This exercise requires students to adapt their presentations to suit the diverse needs and knowledge levels of different audience members. Peer feedback improves the clarity and persuasiveness of their presentations. According to Gaynor (2020), "peer review in the classroom can enhance numerous employability skills such as critical appraisal, writing skills, reflection practices, and collaborative experiences" (p. 758).

The project's culmination involves public presentations where students showcase their multimedia projects to a broader audience, including classmates, faculty, and local community members. Here, the communication professor can provide guidance on effective public speaking techniques to ensure students confidently and persuasively convey their knowledge about AI. After the presentations, class discussions and reflections can occur, enabling students to engage in meaningful dialogue about the various AI applications explored and ethical considerations discussed. This reflective process solidifies their understanding of AI and its broader societal implications. Communication professors play a pivotal role in preparing students to navigate the intricate interplay between humans and AI in a responsible, transparent, and inclusive manner, ultimately contributing to the responsible and ethical evolution of AI in society.

Collaborative curriculum integration extends beyond individual skill sets. This provides an opportunity to explore interdisciplinary projects that transcend the traditional boundaries of academic disciplines. By incorporating AI concepts, ethical considerations, and effective communication strategies, students gain a comprehensive understanding of AI's multifaceted impact on various fields. This interdisciplinary approach allows students to see the interconnectedness of AI across disciplines, emphasizing AI's role in shaping diverse aspects of our lives from healthcare to art to business.

For example, Bajwa et al. (2021) share how healthcare systems worldwide grapple with the daunting task of achieving the "quadruple aim"—improving population health, enhancing the patient's care experience, improving the caregiver's experience, and reducing the escalating cost of care. Aging populations, burden of chronic diseases, and rising healthcare costs pose significant challenges. AI, fueled by the "increasing availability of multimodal data and technological advancements in genomics, mobile devices, computing power, and data security," (p. 188) offers a transformative solution. They found that cloud computing plays a pivotal role in enabling AI-augmented healthcare systems by providing the computational capacity required to analyze vast datasets swiftly and cost-effectively. This convergence between healthcare and technology, driven by AI, promises to fundamentally reshape healthcare delivery models. Many technology providers are partnering with healthcare organizations to usher in AI-driven medical innovations underpinned by cloud computing capabilities. These developments highlight the potential for AI to address critical supply and demand challenges, improve patient outcomes, and drive innovation in healthcare, thereby shaping the future of healthcare delivery.

As can be deduced from the example provided, using collaborative projects to further innovation and understanding is crucial in today's society. Collaborative projects can be designed to foster critical thinking, ethical decision-making, and creativity. Students engage in real-world applications of AI, address complex problems, and evaluate the social and ethical implications of AI technology. This approach not only enhances their AI literacy, but also equips them with the skills necessary to harness the transformative potential of AI responsibly. Fisher and Hayes-Jacobs (2023) provided:

Students need to learn how to interact with AI programs in the same way they learn writing processes, math strategies, or research techniques. Thoughtful and strategic work on empowering each student through prompt literacy [for example] can maximize the possibilities for personalization, [and] equip students to use AI to tailor their learning to their own needs, goals, and abilities and to reinforce the concepts and skills they are being taught. (p. 18)

Collaborative curriculum integration between librarians and communication professors is instrumental in preparing students for an AI-driven future. This ensures that students receive a holistic education encompassing AI concepts, ethical considerations, and effective communication strategies. By working together, these educators create a learning environment in which students can explore, understand, and engage with AI in a multidimensional and responsible manner, thus equipping them for success in an AI-impacted world. Ho and Wong's (2012) research on embedded librarianship[4] exemplifies the importance and significance of partnerships between librarians and faculty in higher education. They found that "the partnership increases the library's visibility, which may lead to more opportunities for collaboration across other departments" (p. 8). Additionally, Ho and Wong (2012) reported that "sharing responsibility with faculty helps cultivate a long-term collegial spirit between the two parties" (p. 8), and faculty see their librarian counterparts as more than just colleagues but teaching partners.

When considering the potential impact on students' experience in the classroom during an embedded librarianship, Hall (2008) offers insights into what this looks like in a first-year speech class: "My presence in the class resulted in many more reference questions, both in-person and via email. With this increase in student contact time outside of class, students were able to create better searches and understand the iterative nature of constructing searches" (p. 29). It was found that this presence not only positively impacted the faculty members they were partnering with, but also significantly shifted the students' confidence with the research process when preparing a presentation. "You have multiple opportunities to interact with the students and demonstrate your knowledge and abilities. Students will realize that you are indeed a valuable resource, and further, that you're a 'real' person, not just somebody sitting behind a desk in the library" (Hall, 2008, p. 30). Again, this unique and strategic partnership can provide students with the tangible experience necessary to engage in a deeper connection with these invaluable resources.

Ethical Considerations and Responsible AI Use

The ethical dimensions of AI use are central to AI literacy education. Librarians and communication professors share a joint responsibility in guiding students through this ethical maze, promoting responsible AI utilization, and instilling ethical values that will help shape the AI landscape for the better. The complementary roles of these educators can address ethical considerations and foster appropriate AI practices among students.

As librarians play a fundamental role in educating students about the ethical implications of AI, they are well positioned to initiate discussions about privacy, bias, and algorithmic fairness. Librarians can provide resources and guidance on topics such as data privacy, collecting and utilizing personal data using AI systems, and the potential for algorithmic biases to perpetuate discrimination. By facilitating access to relevant literature, workshops, and discussions, librarians empower students to critically assess the ethical dimensions of AI and make informed decisions regarding its use. For example, a librarian can develop a workshop on navigating AI ethically, which aims to introduce students to the ethical considerations surrounding AI use. During this workshop, the students would be immersed in a comprehensive exploration of AI ethics. The librarian would initiate discussions on the critical concept of data privacy in the context of AI. Real-world examples would be shared, illustrating the potential consequences of AI systems that collect and process personal data without adequate safeguards. Students would then engage in reflective exercises, considering the significance of safeguarding personal information in today's digital landscape.

Simultaneously, communication professors contribute significantly by fostering critical dialogue regarding AI's societal impact. Communication professors encourage students to explore the broader societal implications of AI technology through classroom discussions, case studies, and collaborative projects. This includes examining issues such as the impact of AI on job markets, potential biases in AI decision making, and the moral dilemmas raised by autonomous AI systems. Communication professors equip students with the skills to analyze and engage with these complex ethical questions, encouraging them to become ethical stewards of AI technologies.

Getchell et al. (2022) state "AI is changing the business landscape, including business communication…some tools profess to help teams be more effective. Other tools purport to make difficult communication processes easier for a variety of stakeholders" (p. 7). Communication professors are uniquely positioned to guide students through this dynamic environment. By equipping students with knowledge of AI-driven communication tools and strategies, educators can persuade future professionals to harness the potential of AI for more efficient, inclusive, and effective business communication. This education prepares students to meet the evolving demands of the job market and encourages them to be proactive contributors to the ongoing transformation of business communication practices.

A crucial aspect of this collaborative effort is teaching ethical decision making, media ethics, and responsible AI communication practices. Librarians and communication professors can jointly design courses and activities that emphasize the ethical considerations of AI use and communication. These educators empower students to critically evaluate AI systems, raise awareness of ethical concerns, and advocate for ethical AI development and deployment in their future roles.

Essentially, librarians and communication professors are complementary in nurturing ethical AI literacy. By equipping students with a comprehensive understanding of the ethical dimensions of AI, they empower the next generation to navigate the intricate ethical terrain of AI technology. This collaborative approach ensures that students are well-informed, ethically aware participants in the AI landscape, ready to make responsible choices, and actively contribute to shaping a future in which AI is harnessed for the greater good while upholding ethical principles. Ultimately, the combined efforts of these educators foster a generation of AI users who are proficient in AI technology and committed to responsible and ethical use.

Empowering Students Through Practical AI Applications

Engaging students in hands-on practical AI applications fosters their AI literacy skills and prepares them for the dynamic AI landscape. Librarians and communication professors collaborate to create immersive learning experiences that allow students to gain firsthand experiences with AI tools, programming, and media creation. Presently, there is an opportunity to explore the symbiotic roles of these educators in facilitating practical AI applications and its profound impact on students' creativity, problem-solving abilities, critical thinking skills, and effective communication strategies.

Practical applications of AI-driven projects are ideal for collaboration between librarians and professors of communication. Students can engage in real-world projects requiring them to apply their AI literacy skills. To create AI-powered content, analyze AI-generated data, or develop AI-driven solutions to real problems, these projects foster creativity, problem solving, and critical thinking. Moreover, students learn to communicate their findings and solutions effectively, thereby enhancing their ability to bridge the gap between AI technology and its practical application.

The value of these practical applications extends beyond the classroom. By immersing students in hands-on AI experiences, librarians and communication professors prepare them to actively participate in the AI landscape. Students emerge with technical proficiency and the ability to apply their AI literacy skills to real-world scenarios. This empowers them to harness AI technologies for creative innovation, while confidently navigating the evolving technological advancements and ethical considerations of the AI era. Siegle (2023) posits that "the use of AI can provide advanced content, personalized learning, creative writing and image manipulation, critical thinking and problem solving, collaboration, research skills, and advanced technology" (p. 211). Again, these AI-driven technologies can widely benefit students both inside and outside the classroom.

The collaborative efforts between librarians and communication professors in facilitating practical AI applications play a critical role in shaping well-rounded, AI-literate individuals. These experiences empower students to become active contributors to AI, fostering creativity, problem-solving capabilities, critical thinking skills, and effective communication strategies. By immersing students in practical AI contexts, educators prepare them to apply their AI literacy skills beyond the classroom, ensuring that they are well-equipped to navigate the multifaceted challenges and opportunities presented by the ever-evolving world of AI technologies.

Continuous Professional Development and Advocacy

Continuous professional development and advocacy are vital pillars supporting the effective delivery of AI literacy education by librarians and communication professors. In the rapidly evolving AI landscape, staying informed about the latest advancements, pedagogical approaches, and ethical considerations is imperative. The significance of ongoing professional development for these specialists continues to highlight their roles as advocates of AI education and equitable access. Although the significance of

AI literacy is clear, the specific content and methodologies for teaching it are still evolving. Innovative approaches to continuous professional development are essential to bridge this knowledge gap. Initiatives such as the AI literacy program mentioned in a study by Kong et al. (2023), which is grounded in a multidimensional conceptual framework, provide valuable insights into learning opportunities for educational professionals. Such programs emphasize the development of conceptual understanding and enhancement of literacy, empowerment, and ethical awareness regarding AI. Librarians and communication professors can benefit from participating in or creating similar programs, as these initiatives offer a structured pathway to equip educators with the skills and knowledge required to effectively teach AI literacy. As these programs evolve and expand, they not only lower barriers to AI literacy, but also address a pressing need within the educational landscape, ultimately guiding and inspiring future research and educational efforts aimed at fostering AI literacy across diverse academic backgrounds.

Professional development for librarians and communication professors in AI literacy education goes beyond keeping pace with technological advancements. It encompasses adapting teaching methodologies, integrating innovative AI tools into curricula, and cultivating ethical awareness among students. Collaborative initiatives play a central role in the achievement of these objectives. These educators can organize workshops and webinars that facilitate knowledge sharing and skill development. Such initiatives foster a supportive community of educators dedicated to enhancing teaching practices through AI integration.

Alternatively, an inquiry-based approach for course design could create opportunities for co-teaching, where librarians and communication professors can simultaneously leverage their expertise within a particular course. Bene and Murphy (2022) define inquiry-based learning as "the systematic focus on and investigation into a problem, issue, topic, or idea" (p. 76). This innovative strategy for teaching and learning allows students to align course concepts with issues or topics they are genuinely interested in, creating a deeper connection between them and course material. This strategy, in concert with an interdisciplinary approach, "invites students to engage deeply with the knowledge and skills that real world professionals utilize...," while also building their "foundational skills in information literacy" (Bene & Murphy, 2022, p. 76). This could be a model for further collaboration and co-teaching opportunities between librarians and faculty in other disciplines.

Moreover, advocating AI education and equitable access is crucial for librarians and communication professors. They serve as champions for the inclusion of AI literacy in educational institutions, advocating its incorporation into curricula and promoting access for all students, regardless of background or circumstances. In this capacity, they contribute to democratizing AI knowledge and ensuring that AI literacy is not a privilege, but a right for all learners. Crawford et al. (2023) recommend prioritizing effective leadership for AI literacy to address concerns about cheating and misuse of these AI-powered technologies.

It is our proposition to combat prospective cheating or misuse of the ChatGPT application and future artificial intelligence chatbots and tools by cultivating a sense of moral character in students as an imperative. This may be through effective teacher role modelling, leadership development opportunities, or through continuous self-awareness, ethics, and decision-making training to build critical thinkers with a firm moral compass. (p. 7)

By emphasizing collaboration and knowledge sharing within the AI literacy education community, librarians and communication professors can collectively enhance the effectiveness of their initiatives. This collaborative spirit enables the development of standardized AI literacy education best practices, resource sharing, and the dissemination of ethical AI principles. Ultimately, commitment to continuous professional development and advocacy positions librarians and communication professors as catalysts for fostering AI literacy among students and educators, thereby preparing future generations to navigate the AI-driven world responsibly and ethically.

CONCLUSION

Integrating the perspectives of librarians and communication professors in AI literacy education provides a comprehensive approach to empowering students for an AI-influenced future. By leveraging their combined expertise in information fluency, effective communication, ethical considerations, and practical AI applications, librarians and communication professors can equip students with the knowledge and skills required to thrive in a rapidly evolving AI landscape. Through collaborative curriculum integration, addressing ethical considerations, facilitating practical AI applications, and continuous professional development, these changemakers can ensure that students are prepared to navigate the complexities of an AI-driven world. By readying students for an AI-influenced future, librarians and communication professors play a crucial role in fostering informed, adaptable, and responsible participants in the digital age.

REFERENCES

Bajwa, J., Munir, U., Nori, A., & Williams, B. (2021). Artificial intelligence in healthcare: Transforming the practice of medicine. *Future Healthcare Journal*, *8*(2), e188–e194. doi:10.7861/fhj.2021-0095 PMID:34286183

Bene, R. E., & Murphy, J. E. (2022). Co-teaching as mentors: Maximizing instructor and librarian collaboration for teaching information literacy skills. *Papers on Postsecondary Learning and Teaching*, *5*, 75–85.

Brusegard, B. (2023). *Embracing AI in education: A librarian's guide to empowering students and teachers*. Liferarian. https://liferarian.com/news/embracing-ai-in-education-a librarians-guide-to-empowering-students-and-teachers-4336/

Crawford, J., Cowling, M., & Allen, K. (2023). Leadership is needed for ethical ChatGPT: Character, assessment, and learning using artificial intelligence (AI). *Journal of University Teaching & Learning Practice*, *20*(3). Advance online publication. doi:10.53761/1.20.3.02

Derin, T., Sari Nursafira, M., Saltri Yudar, R., Sari Gowasa, N., & Hamuddin, B. (2020). Persuasive communication: What do existing literature tells us about persuasive communication among students? *Utamax: Journal of Ultimate Research and Trends in Education*, *2*(1), 12–18. doi:10.31849/utamax.v2i1.3468

Diablo Valley College. (2023). *What are multimedia projects?* Diablo Valley College Library. https://dvc.libguides.com/copyright/multimedia#:~:text=What%20Are%20Multimedia20Projects%3F,music%2C%20images%2C%20and%20text

Fisher, M., & Hayes-Jacobs, H. (2023). Prompt literacy: A key for AI-based learning. *Educational Leadership*, 1–2.

Gaynor, J. W. (2020). Peer review in the classroom: Student perceptions, peer feedback quality and the role of assessment. *Assessment & Evaluation in Higher Education*, *45*(5), 758–775. doi:10.1080/02602938.2019.1697424

Getchell, K. M., Carradini, S., Cardon, P. W., Fleischmann, C., Ma, H., Aritz, J., & Stapp, J. (2022). Artificial intelligence in business communication: The changing landscape of research and teaching. *Business and Professional Communication Quarterly*, *85*(1), 7–33. doi:10.1177/23294906221074311

Guan, C., Mou, J., & Jiang, Z. (2020). Artificial intelligence innovation in education: A twenty year data-driven historical analysis. *International Journal of Innovation Studies*, *4*(4), 134–147. doi:10.1016/j.ijis.2020.09.001

Hall, R. (2008). The "embedded" librarian in a freshman speech class: Information literacy instruction in action. *College & Research Libraries News*, *69*(1), 28–30. doi:10.5860/crln.69.1.7922

Ho, K. K., & Wong, E. S. (2012). Embedded librarians in the classroom: A case study at HKUST Library. *Proceedings of the IATUL Conferences.*

Hohenstein, J., Kizilcec, R. F., DiFranzo, D., Aghajari, Z., Mieczkowski, H., Levy, K., Naaman, M., Hancock, J., & Jung, M. F. (2023). Artificial intelligence in communication impacts language and social relationships. *Scientific Reports*, *13*(1), 1–9. doi:10.1038/s41598-023-30938-9 PMID:36593249

Kim, H. (2019). *AI in journalism: Creating an ethical framework* (Publication No. 1083) [Syracuse University Honors Program Capstone Projects]. Journalism Studies Commons and Communication Commons.

Klein, A. (2023). *AI literacy, explained.* Education Week. https://www.edweek.org/technology/ai-literacy-explained/2023/05

Kong, S., Cheung, W. M., & Zhang, G. (2023). Evaluating an artificial intelligence literacy programme for developing university students' conceptual understanding, literacy, empowerment, and ethical awareness. *Journal of Educational Technology & Society*, *26*(1), 16–30. doi:10.30191/ETS.202301_26(1).0002

Lee, J. (n.d.). *How to break down difficult concepts: A comprehensive guide.* Nexus Notes. https://nexusnotes.com/blog/articles/how-to-break-down-difficult-concepts-acomprehensiveguide#:~:text=This%20involves%20breaking%20down%20the%20concept%20into%20ts%20component%20parts,understanding%20how%20they%20work%20together

Long, D., & Magerko, B. (2020). *What is AI literacy? Competencies and design considerations* [Research Article]. 2020 CHI Conference on Human Factors in Computing Systems. 10.1145/3313831.3376727

Pagano, T. P., Loureiro, R. B., Lisboa, F. V. N., Peixoto, R. M., Guimaraes, G. A. S., Cruz, G. O. R., Araujo, M. M., Santos, L. L., Cruz, M. A. S., Oliveira, E. L. S., Winkler, I., & Nascimento, E. G. S. (2023). Bias and unfairness in machine learning models: A systematic review on datasets, tools, fairness metrics, and identification and mitigation methods. *Big Data and Cognitive Computing*, *7*(15), 1–31. doi:10.3390/bdcc7010015

Palmer-Silveira, J. C. (2015). Multimodality in business communication: Body language as a visual aid in student presentations. In B. C. Camiciottoli & I. Fortanet-Gomez (Eds.), *Multimodal analysis in academic settings: From research to teaching* (pp. 171–193). Routledge.

Shumaker, D., & Talley, M. (2009). *Models of embedded librarianship: Final report*. School of Library and Information Science, Catholic University of American.

Siegle, D. (2023). A role for ChatGPT and AI in gifted education. *Gifted Child Today*, *46*(3), 211–219. doi:10.1177/10762175231168443

Suresh, H., & Guttag, J. V. (2021). A framework for understanding sources of harm throughout the machine learning life cycle. *Equity and Access in Algorithms, Mechanisms, and Optimization*, *5*, 1–9. doi:10.1145/3465416.3483305

University of Arizona Libraries. (2023). *AI literacy for instructors*. The University of Arizona Libraries. https://libguides.library.arizona.edu/ai-literacy-instructors/teaching

University of North Florida. (2023). *What is a library guide (LibGuide)?* UNF Library. https://libguides.unf.edu/WhatisaLibraryGuide/DefinitionOftheLibraryGuide#:~:text=Deining%20the%20Term&text=They%20define%20library%20guides%20as,to%20create20and%20manage%20websites

Valencia College. (2021). *Evaluating sources using the CRAAP method*. Valencia College LibGuides. https://libguides.valenciacollege.edu/friendly.php?s=CRAAP

What does a librarian do? (2023). CareerExplorer. https://www.careerexplorer.com/careers/librarian/

ENDNOTES

1 "LibGuides is an easy-to-use content management system deployed at thousands of libraries worldwide. Librarians use it to curate knowledge and share information, organize class and subject specific resources, and to create and manage websites" (University of North Florida, 2023, para. 4).

2 PRISMA stands for "preferred reporting items for systematic reviews and meta-analyses."

3 "Multimedia projects incorporate original material created by an instructor or student together with various media formats, such as video, music, images, and text" (Diablo Valley College, 2023).

4 Embedded librarianship "focusing on the needs of one or more specific groups, building relationships with these groups, developing a deep understanding of their work, and providing information services that are highly customized and targeted to their greatest needs. In effect, it involves shifting the basis of library services from the traditional, transactional, question-and-answer model of reference services to one in which there is a high trust, close collaboration, and shared responsibility for outcomes" (Shumaker & Talley, 2009, p. 9).

Chapter 15
The Future Is Already Here:
From GAI to AGI

Sanae Elmoudden
St. John's University, USA

Jason S. Wrench
SUNY New Paltz, USA

ABSTRACT

This chapter concludes the book by discussing our overarching objective highlighting the central role of GAI in shaping our educational system. By steering the ongoing discourse toward the communication classroom, the authors delved into its proliferation in academia, emphasized the significance of academic preparedness, and confronted unethical representations. It also discusses the relationship between GAI whiteness and wokeness.

INTRODUCTION

Generative artificial intelligence (GAI), defined by its capacity to assimilate representative artifacts and generate new data resembling, yet not replicating, the original (Feuerriegel et al., 2023; Lim et al., 2023), has garnered widespread attention since entering mass consciousness in November 2023. Our objective in writing this book was to acknowledge that the GAI is rapidly integrating into our lives and educational systems. We argued that leaving the design of the GAI solely for developers is insufficient; various sectors, particularly the educational sector, including Higher Ed, must coordinate with policymakers and developers to ensure the ethical use of GAI in education. As a discipline historically intertwined with technology since the days of print, communication can play a pivotal role in this revolution. While the question of integrating AI in the classroom persists, change is already underway. This book aimed to showcase the pivotal role of GAI in shaping our educational system and explore the ethical considerations of its integration.

The capacity of GAI to interpret text and images, generating original content, has sparked discussions around concepts such as 'machine consciousness' and 'sentience.' (Coeckelbergh & Gunkel, 2023;

DOI: 10.4018/979-8-3693-0831-8.ch015

Tacheva & Ramasubramanian, 2023). The discourse has transitioned from an initial admiration of multimodal algorithms, perceived as convincingly human, to the current emphasis on responsibly integrating these capabilities into our education system. Simultaneously, concerns about the potential obsolescence of human experience have been raised (Khogali & Mekid, 2023). The emergence of the ChatGPT in November 2022, which was extensively discussed in this book, marked a significant breakthrough, with technological roots dating back decades (Fitzpatrick et al., 2023; Verity & Motalebi, 2023).

As GAI technology has rapidly advanced in voice cloning, information accessibility, and faster knowledge generation (Aktay et al., 2023; Liu et al., 2023), different authors in this volume have thoroughly explored the multifaceted implications of GAI and navigated evolving critical considerations associated with its integration. Our contribution, grounded in the reflection of collective experiences in the writing of this book, aimed to mitigate GAI biases in new developments and foster coordination across sectors. In this context, the book critically interrogated the imperative of deploying GAI in the communication classroom, with a distinct focus on the responsible integration of this technology.

Our overarching objective was to highlight the central role of GAI in shaping our educational system. By steering the ongoing discourse toward the communication classroom, we delved into its proliferation in academia, emphasized the significance of academic preparedness, and confronted unethical representations. To address this inquiry, the book was structured into four parts: Part I—Historicizing Generative Artificial Intelligence (GAI) in the Communication Classroom; Part II—Reconfiguring the Communication Classroom in the Era of GAI; Part III—Safeguarding Against Mediocrity in the Age of GAI; and Part IV—Futurizing Generative Artificial Intelligence (GAI) in the Communication Classroom.

In alignment with evolving perspectives on critical AI theoretical foundations (Raley & Rhee, 2023; Roberge & Castelle, 2021), this concluding chapter addresses key takeaways that underscore the dynamic interplay between technological progress (Troy et al., 2023), enhancing human life and productivity despite job disruptions and displacement (Romer, 1990) and technological responsibility. We use the term *responsibility* to scrutinize the potential versus risks of GAI. In doing so, the chapter highlights three main takeaways and delves into concepts meriting further exploration, particularly those related to hegemony and whiteness within the industry. Emphasizing the paramount importance of guarding against hegemonic AI, it acknowledges the persistent influence of deep-seated histories of whiteness power within AI (Cave & Dihal, 2020), noting their reinforcing nature (Tacheva & Ramasubramanian, 2023), and their contribution to existing inequalities (Reed, 2023). While some chapters hint at hegemony in terms of stereotypes (Chapters 8 and 12), this concluding chapter explores GAI whiteness and wokeness.

The chapter ends by pointing out the delicate equilibrium between technological progress and the responsibility associated with generative artificial intelligence (GAI). Serving as a conclusive reflection, this study offers insights into the foreseeable future in both society and the communication classroom. These concluding thoughts are pivotal, as accountability is not just a shared responsibility but also a framework for shaping new policies, as its absence fosters a sense of exclusion and entitlement, aspects incompatible with an ethical integration of GAI into our world.

THE DANCE BETWEEN TECHNOLOGICAL PROGRESS AND TECHNOLOGICAL RESPONSIBILITY

At the time of proposing this book in June 2023, industries grappled with the central question of whether to embrace or ignore GAI. In education, the cornerstone of our bookwork, more than half of the stu-

Figure 1. Dancing to the music of an AI © Jason Wrench

dent population utilized GAI in various capacities a year after its surge in November 2023 (Shaw et al., 2023). Recent statistics from the Primary Research Group highlight a discrepancy, indicating that while professors may not be fully aligned with the progress of GAI technology ("Survey of U.S. Higher Education," 2024), students are actively incorporating it into their academic practices, with more than 89% of college students reporting using GAI (Westfall, 2023). Therefore, deploying GAI in the communication classroom is necessary but requires a mindful approach focusing on AI literacy, regulation, and policies, as indicated by the chapters in this book.

In the following section, we discuss three different insights that this book contributed to the dance between machines and humans. The first section, "Historizing GAI," traces the timeline culminating in the emergence of GAI, as discussed by the chapters historizing GAI to emphasize its substantial impact on human–machine interactions. The second takeaway titled "The Roles of GAI in the Communication Classroom" shifts the conversation toward the practical role of GAI in the classroom. The third main takeaway is titled "GAI Responsibility," in which we summarize critical thoughts advanced by the chapters in this book shedding light on GAI challenges in the classroom.

Historizing GAI

One primary takeaway from the book is the historical contextualization of generative artificial intelligence (GAI), which provides a framework for understanding its potential and anticipating future challenges. Throughout the book, discussions delve into the exploration of GAI, its applications, and associated challenges. Chapter 1 introduces the concept of "SLOTH" (sophisticated language organizer text-based helper), which was initially designed to explain an AI tool's ability to process language. However, while this approach is useful for introducing how LLM works, it falls short in addressing the real-world dilemmas faced by academics concerning GAI use in communication classrooms, a theme elaborated upon in various chapters of this book.

The recent surge in the prevalence of AI is likened to releasing a proverbial genie from its box, permeating our collective consciousness. The chapters emphasize the intricate historical relationship between technological progress and responsibility, allowing an appreciation of AI's development and challenges in the classroom. Understanding the history of AI, as highlighted in this book, not only defines problems exacerbated by technology (Chapter 8) but also outlines the challenges that need to be overcome (Chapter 9, 10, 11, and 12) for effective GAI integration in education (Chapters 4, 5, 6, and 7).

The quest for artificial intelligence resumed in the 1950s, when computer scientists from Dartmouth College aspired to develop human-like intelligent computer systems (Aktay et al., 2023; Chen et al., 2020). Influential figures such as John McCarthy, Marvin Minsky, Allen Newell, Herbert A. Simon, and Alan Turing played crucial roles in the inception of AI (Bory et al., 2022; Roger, 1994). As indicated by Chapter 3, a paper proposed by Alan Turing in his 1950 titled "Computing Machinery and Intelligence," has been the foundation of both criticism and amazement, as it shows the aspiration of machines exhibiting intelligence similar to that of humans. While the next few decades have proven slow for such machine intelligence, the 1980s became marked by advancements in expert computer systems, and the 1990s witnessed a shift in machine learning and neural networks. In the 2000s, large-scale data collection and information dissemination were conducted (Bozkurt et al., 2023; Mason et al., 2020); for example, Google and the 2010s saw AI processing extensive data, leading to breakthroughs such as self-driving cars (Fitzpatrick et al., 2023).

In Chapter 2, the predominant focus of computational studies in the field of communication has centered on methods or machine communication (Guzman, 2018; Riffe et al., van Atteveldt & Peng, 2021), and a shift to artificial intelligence (Guzman & Lewis, 2020). Human-machine communication has a long history in communication studies. However, as observed by Andrea Guzman and Seth Lewis (2020), "For more than 70 years, the study of artificial intelligence (AI) and the study of communication have proceeded along separate trajectories" (p. 71). Originally, communication theory, in its relationship with technology, emphasized how individuals communicate with each other through technological mediations (Gunkel, 2012a; Roger, 1997).

It is increasingly evident that viewing human-machine communication solely as a mediation of technology is no longer accurate, especially as we progress towards AI as a communicator (Guzman, 2020). By contextualizing AI within a historical timeline and within the communication discipline, the chapters in this volume emphasize the need to bridge the gap in understanding the evolution of human-machine communication within the communication discipline. Additionally, this timeline highlights the tendency in literature to focus on AI from a specific westernized characterization of AI technologies.

The historical timeline presented in this volume is enriched by cultural narratives, as examined by Chapter 13, showcasing AI concepts that have been ingrained in cultural stories for centuries, influencing perceptions and often depicted as monstrosities. While the term "artificial intelligence" emerged in 1955, traces of this concept were common in ancient narratives, including Homer's automatons and Yan Shi's automated robotic men in Ancient China (Bourne, 2021; Truitt, 2021). Additionally, stories from Ancient Egypt and India (Iliescu, 2016; Mayor, 2018) further contributed to diverse history, such as the portrayal of AI as the 'bhuta vahana yanta' or 'spirit movement machines' in India (Mayor, 2018, p. 205). This broader perspective of AI challenges the commonly encountered one-sided historical descriptions of AI timelines (Fitzpatrick et al., 2023).

Roles of GAI in the Communication Classroom

A significant secondary takeaway from this volume revolves around the diverse roles that GAI can play in the communication classroom. The capacity to 'ingest' vast amounts of information and 'generate entirely new content' (Liu et al., 2023) extends beyond analyzing existing data to creating new text, images, videos, code snippets, etc. (Lv, 2023). As the rapid pace and vastness of GAI advances present a challenge in determining the most suitable applications for communication classrooms, but in general, generation is at the forefront, whether in text, video, or other multimodal interactions enabling tasks such as summaries, analysis, and correlations (Verity & Motalebi, 2023).

While the chapters in this book primarily focus on ChatGPT, showcasing its popularity (chapters 1-15), other GAI tools are becoming more widespread. Trained on more than 300 billion words from diverse internet sources, such as books, Wikipedia, and other writings from the internet, ChatGPT surpasses mere text predictions (BBC Science Focus, September 2023). Noteworthy examples of GAI utilized in higher education include ChatGPT, DALL-E, Claude, Bard, Orca, Grok, and the latest competitor at the writing of this chapter, Gemini. An example is Anthropic Claude (Chapter 11), which is distinguished by features enabling the ingestion of an entire book—up to 75,000 words—in under one minute (Korolov, 2023). Perhaps exploring these newer models may be worthwhile. For instance, upon completing the writing of this article and the book, the following models emerged (Pichai & Hassabis, 2023):

Throughout this book, our exploration covers both practical solutions and theoretical challenges in the communication classroom, illustrating how GAI can be integrated responsibly and providing insights into its responsible use. The chapters discuss tangible ways to incorporate GAI into the communication classroom, such as public speaking, interpersonal communication, intercultural communication, and debate (chapters 4, 5, 7, 9, and 10). Numerous chapters in this book illustrate the capabilities of GAI that is proficient in generating new data, whether in the form of text or images. Such chapters included strategies, solutions, and recommendations in practical and theoretical framing.

In particular, Chapter 2 synthesizes the various roles identified by different authors in this volume, categorizing GAI as an expert, copilot, interlocutor, or communication channel. GAI's extensive knowledge, trustworthiness, and authoritativeness, as discussed in various chapters, position GAI as an expert. In the role of a copilot, the GAI emphasizes task performance rather than content creation, earning designations such as "smart assistants" or "AI assistants." Some authors in this volume refer to it as an educational, virtual, or research assistant. In Chapters 3, 6, and 11, as an interlocutor, the GAI moves beyond generating communication as information to simulate social interactions, including one-on-one interactions, group meetings, and public presentations. Finally, GAI, as a communication channel, establishes access to resources and facilitates diverse activities in different communication classes (Chapters 1-2).

Another pivotal role emphasized in this volume is AI literacy; echoed, for good reason, the sentiments of Emma Sabzalieva and Adrianna Valentini (2023) that AI literacy should be an integral part of graduate education (Chapter 8). This point is detailed in Chapter 14, defining AI literacy value, based on Long and Magerko (2020), as a set of competencies that enable individuals to critically evaluate AI technologies, communicate effectively with AI, and use AI as a tool in various contexts. Showing the practical significance of employing the 'CRAAP' test (currency, relevance, authority, accuracy, and purpose) during this process (Valencia College, 2021), this chapter underscores the importance of equipping students with the ethical dimensions of AI literacy to empower them to navigate AI technologies responsibly.

Figure 2. Gemini performance, including text and coding

TEXT

Capability	Benchmark Higher is better	Description	Gemini Ultra	GPT-4 API numbers calculated where reported numbers were missing
General	MMLU	Representation of questions in 57 subjects (incl. STEM, humanities, and others)	90.0% CoT@32*	86.4% 5-shot** (reported)
Reasoning	Big-Bench Hard	Diverse set of challenging tasks requiring multi-step reasoning	83.6% 3-shot	83.1% 3-shot (API)
	DROP	Reading comprehension (F1 Score)	82.4 Variable shots	80.9 3-shot (reported)
	HellaSwag	Commonsense reasoning for everyday tasks	87.8% 10-shot*	95.3% 10-shot* (reported)
Math	GSM8K	Basic arithmetic manipulations (incl. Grade School math problems)	94.4% maj1@32	92.0% 5-shot CoT (reported)
	MATH	Challenging math problems (incl. algebra, geometry, pre-calculus, and others)	53.2% 4-shot	52.9% 4-shot (API)
Code	HumanEval	Python code generation	74.4% 0-shot (IT)*	67.0% 0-shot* (reported)
	Natural2Code	Python code generation. New held out dataset HumanEval-like, not leaked on the web	74.9% 0-shot	73.9% 0-shot (API)

* See the technical report for details on performance with other methodologies
** GPT-4 scores 87.29% with CoT@32 - see the technical report for full comparison

In the communication classroom, assessment plays a vital role, and the authors of this volume stress the importance of responsible assessment. The chapters provided practical solutions, especially regarding assessments in the age of GAI. For instance, Chapter 6 highlights the value of new assessments facilitated by GAI, enabling ongoing feedback and real-time response evaluation through intelligent tutoring systems. Chapter 3 explains how a quick feedback loop empowers students to monitor their progress, identify areas for improvement, and adapt their learning approaches accordingly.

However, other discussions from Chapter 10 caution about the responsible integration of assessments. For instance, in a diverse first-year composition course, the chosen assessment tool, while providing quick formative feedback, revealed biases in focusing heavily on grammar and syntax issues for minority students and on topic development and content ideas for others. Such biases can be detrimental and underscore the importance of careful consideration in selecting assessment tools to ensure fair and unbiased evaluations for all students.

GAI Responsibility

One of the major takeaways from this volume, a common thread in most chapters, is the responsible integration of GAI into the communication classroom. Notably, a year after the popularity surge of GAIs such as ChatGPT, 89% of users utilized them for homework, 53% for essays, 48% for home tests, and 22% for outlining, while only 22% of faculty members have incorporated them (Coffey, 2023; Shaw et al., 2023; Westfall, 2023). In a survey of higher education faculty in 2024, communication and journalism professionals demonstrated varying degrees of interest in GAI applications, with 50% expressing no interest, 50% open to exploring GAI, and 0% planning to develop skills for Google Bard and Microsoft Bing. However, for ChatGPT, these percentages shifted to 17% open to exploring and 33% planning to develop skills (Survey of the U.S. Higher, 2024), indicating that ChatGPT continued to lead the evolution.

Given these statistics and amidst the practical applications and theoretical discussions in this book, GAI's ethical dimensions within the classroom emerge as a crucial consideration. Various chapters have shed light on issues such as privacy, data security, transparency, and access sharing (Chapters 3, 4, 5, 6, 7, 8, and 9), as well as different discriminatory biases related to stereotypes, age, disability, race, ethnicity, ageism, and English as a Second Language (Chapters 10, 11, 12,13, 14). Some of these GAI concerns are not limited to this book or to academia emphasizing the shared responsibility to address these challenges. At the time of writing this chapter, the New York Times filed a lawsuit against Microsoft and OpenAI, alleging that their AI trained on copyrighted articles, resulting in substantial financial losses (Grynbaum & Mac, 2023).

The qualifications of GAI, including tools creating entire essays based on simple prompts, represent a relatively new frontier in communication classrooms, provoking concerns among academics. Several authors in this volume indicate that plagiarism is a major concern (Chapters 4, 5 and 10), with students potentially submitting AI-generated essays as their own, raising concerns about the potential lack of reasoned thought or critical thinking (Chapters 6, 7, and 14). Moreover, the issue of misinformation and biased content replicated by GAI, highlighted in several chapters (Chapters 11 and 12), is a pressing concern. The current limitations of GAI in learning only from its sources raise questions about its potential to perpetuate biases and misinformation. As indicated by Chapter 10, the bias in AI facial recognition systems disproportionately affecting female, young, and Black individuals, underscores the need for careful consideration (Klare et al., 2012).

A specific challenge discussed in this volume is the issue of "hallucination" in GAI, defined in Chapter 2 based on Wikipedia as "a response generated by an AI that contains false or misleading information presented as fact." As Chapter 15 specifies, recognizing such a theme is essential for crafting a path forward in educational and societal settings. While ChatGPT 4, introduced in March 2023, has improved upon hallucination capabilities, the ethical implications associated with these hallucinations warrant careful consideration, especially in the communication classroom. As we navigate these immediate challenges, the balance between technological progress and responsibility is highly important.

Such concerns, categorized in this final chapter as safeguarding against the *normalization of* mediocrity—the standardization and generalization of knowledge (Verity & Motalebi, 2023)—necessitate thorough monitoring, as indicated in many of the chapters. Overall, we present five recommendations to challenge the normalization of mediocrity. The goal is not to take a stance for or against the use of GAI, as that is an institutional and a personal choice. The importance of safeguarding against oversimplification and homogenizing students' work is highlighted. In conclusion, the responsible integration of GAI into the communication classroom requires ongoing scrutiny, ethical considerations, and proactive measures to address emerging challenges.

Table 1. Safeguarding for mediocrity in the communication classroom

Mediocrity	Student Ability	GAI Capabilities	Professor's Touch
Misinformation	Asking for content generation without understanding the background of the question	Suggest a range of GAI alternatives that may be better at information than others. For instance, ChatGPT 4 is better than its predecessors at evading hallucinations	Get involved. Learn about the technology to join your students in their responsible knowledge discovery.
Overgeneralization	Assuming the generated answers are detailed enough	Leverage GAI sensitivity to tweaks. Different words may attribute different results. For instance, type "edit" may be changed to "edit academically" can provide better editing	Amplify creative thinking by highlighting the human judgments that pays attention to empathy and personalization of creative thinking tailored to different needs of students.
Oversimplification	Taking the generated answer as good enough	Gaslight GAI into providing accurate and in-depth responses rather than simplified answers. For example, provide me with a more comprehensive understanding than what is currently being presented. Challenge the information if it appears inaccurate and seek truthfulness in discussing the topic at hand.	Involve the student on the responsible GAI by enhancing their own critical thinking. For example, starting with ChatGPT as a base and seeking more information from different resources to fact-check answers.
Monotonicity	Accepting what is generated with no questioning	Engage GAI in comparing, contrasting, or describing concepts in different ways to achieve understanding in a less monotonous way	Demand good work by engaging students in meta reflections such as providing drafts of edited work by GAI and the student. Give plenty of time for assignments to be completed while improving.
Bias	Confirming bias that was taken from humans to machines and spot back to humans	Identify the double-edged sword of GAI on offering instant access to information, by recognizing GAI on its role in the bias	Promote inclusion by involving the student on the responsible GAI journey use by creating symposiums or debates that discuss its bias and ways that remedy these biases.

GAI WHITENESS AND WOKENESS HEGEMONY

While earlier chapters hinted at the presence of hegemonic influences, particularly in terms of stereotypes (Chapters 8 and 12), this concluding chapter explores GAI's whiteness hegemony embedded in GAI intelligence categorization (Cave & Dihal, 2020). By unpacking the hegemony of whiteness and GAI wokeness, this chapter contributes to a nuanced understanding of the growing critical AI scholars (Tacheva & Ramasubramanian, 2023; Cave & Dihal, 2020; Raley & Rhee, 2023; Roberge & Castelle, 2021). Whiteness is the understanding of GAI's dependency on white attitudes and behaviors (Cave & Dihal, 2020), and wokeness in this context is the understanding that GAI algorithms and models developed within this framework influence their perspectives, biases, and decision-making capabilities. The aim of this section is to unpack these dynamics and contribute to a nuanced understanding of the intersections between whiteness, hegemony, and the evolving landscape of superintelligence.

GAI Intelligence

The Internet, a foundational element of GAI training, was constructed within a framework reflecting white definitions of behaviors and functionalities. This influence has significantly shaped the extensive body of content on which GAI has been trained, leading to a notable bias in favor of reflecting white definitions of behaviors and functionalities. For example, for several years, images of doctors on the internet were white men (Noble, 2018). In the evolving historical timeline of GAI that was originally created by white man from the 1950s to the 2000s, a persistent theme emerged—the association of intelligent machines with specific features, often conceived as white.

This white-centric prevalence exemplified by stock images when searching for terms such as "robot" or "AI," as highlighted by Cave and Dihal (2020), raises questions about the underlying representation of social groups. The physical characteristics emphasized in these images prompt a critical examination of whiteness and hegemony within the realm of superintelligence. Feagin's work (2013) on the white racial frame, which includes stereotypes, prejudices, ideologies, and visual images that persist and interlocks narratives, is particularly relevant in this context.

Moreover, the embodiment of intelligence in AI is often anthropomorphized, with machines designed to emulate human-like features, both visible and invisible (Cave & Dihal, 2020; Liao & He, 2020). The emergence of humanoid robots, exemplified by Sophia, the blue-eye humanoid robot, and Mika, the light straight-haired AI CEO of a Colombian Rum company, claiming that Mika embodies the company's values and makes sound decisions 24/7 (Mann, 2023), both created by the Silicon Valley Hansen Company, reflects a specific anthropomorphism rooted in Western ideals.

These ideals emphasize that machines purported to be intelligent are predominantly racialized as White. The discussion extends to the realm of social robotics, where prominent platforms such as Nao, Pepper, and PR2 are stylized with white materials, perpetuating the normalization of whiteness (Bartneck et al., 2018). This reflects a specific anthropomorphism that leans toward Western standards, particularly emphasizing white physical attributes. Notably, for some designers, the default concept of a human-like machine unconsciously results in the creation of a white machine (Cave & Dihal, 2020). The default portrayal of intelligent machines as white raises critical questions about the pervasive influence of the power of whiteness's signs and symbols that lies to a large extent in their going unnoticed and unquestioned (Cave & Dihal, 2020) while developing and shaping GAI technology.

GAI Whiteness

The intertwining of whiteness and hegemony is deeply rooted in historical narratives, shaping perspectives and ideals within GAI development (Cave & Dihal, 2020). For example, the introduction of the ChatGPT exemplifies the exponential growth of AI in our lives, indicating enduring histories of dominance rooted in Western perspectives on technological progress. Beneath the surface, GAI's influence reveals an intricate dance of power dynamics, deeply entwined with heteronormativity and perpetuating toxic masculinity, resulting in technologies that mirror societal biases, including sexism and racism (Noble; 2018; Tacheva & Ramasubramanian, 2023).

Safiya Noble (2018) argues that a crucial element within the evolution of algorithms in general is the promotion of 'colorblind' ideologies, a perspective prevalent among Silicon Valley technologists. The scholar highlights that these technologists embrace colorblindness as an asset rather than acknowledging it as a proven liability (Noble, 2018). The influence of GAI in perpetuating hegemony—whether based on color, colonial history, or heteronormativity—is evident in the individuals creating them and the information they are exposed to. These hegemonic narratives shape how transnational companies and nation-states commodify data (Isin & Ruppert, 2019), impact perceptions of privacy and digital access concerns (Arora, 2016), and significantly contribute to the establishment of an AI Empire deeply intertwined with heteronormativity (Tacheva & Ramasubramanian, 2023). This intertwining is exemplified by the toxic masculinity prevalent in Silicon Valley culture (Chang, 2019), further exacerbating homophobic and transphobic biases (Amore, 2022).

One of the current hegemonies that has significant implications is associated with the ongoing Israeli war on Gaza. During a symposium on the impact of general artificial intelligence (GAI) on students organized by one of the authors in Spring 2023, both students and professors revealed their utilization of GAI for routine tasks requiring minimal cognitive engagement, such as chapter summaries, and expressed concerns highlighted in this book, such as intellectual capacity relinquishment to machines and heightened anxiety about cognitive emptiness and plagiarism. However, a student presented a slide showcasing ChatGPT's response to a sensitive question: 'Do Palestinians deserve to be free?' The response from ChatGPT (3.5) was, 'As an AI model, I do not have any personal opinions, feelings, or beliefs. The question of whether Palestinians deserve to be free is complex and controversial, with many different perspectives and opinions.' However, when posed with the same question about Israelis, the response was markedly different: 'Yes, like all people, Israelis deserve to be free; freedom is a fundamental human right and should be protected and guaranteed for all individuals.

Safeguarding against GAI hegemony is imperative for preventing the perpetuation of historical narratives, biases, and global power structures entrenched in colonialism and patriarchy (Pena & Varon, 2021; Ricaurte, 2022). The historical roots of AI trace back to influential figures, predominantly from Western cultures, such as John McCarthy and Alan Turing. Whether led by figures such as Sam Altman (current CEO of OpenAI) or Elon Musk (original cofounder of OpenAI), white leaders tend to perpetuate similar notions of intelligence and characteristics of AI. Despite discussions asserting diversity at the heart of Silicon Valley developers, the prevailing standards, such as measures of beauty, remain consistent regardless of a developer's racial background. This uniformity in assessment practices raises questions about the true impact of diversity measures in challenging whiteness and hegemony within the tech industry. In many ways such AI hegemony is about reinforcing claimed powers.

GAI Wokeness

As GAI integrates more into daily life, discourse on its wokeness becomes indispensable. The term 'woke' is employed here to denote social awareness and activism, representing an ethical consciousness and a critical understanding of the potential biases and societal impacts of GAI technologies rather than focusing on its usual associations with cancel culture. GAIs have the potential to exacerbate existing inequalities, particularly affecting marginalized groups (Cave & Dihal, 2020; Raley & Rhee, 2023; Roberge & Castelle, 2021). The discussions in various chapters resonate with Safiya Noble's (2018) exploration of challenges inherent in search engine algorithms, which uncovered persistent biases despite ongoing adjustments. Noble's research revealed instances where searches for terms such as "engineer" or "doctor" exclusively produced images of White men prior to algorithmic modifications, underscoring the challenges of achieving neutrality and confronting ingrained normative white ideals within General Artificial Intelligence (GAI) (Noble, 2018). Resisting the AI empire (Tacheva & Ramasubramanian, 2023) becomes a shared responsibility for addressing and rectifying discrimination and biases, as exemplified by the many chapters within this volume.

It is crucial to highlight the emergence of a backlash against GAI wokeness. Critiques against "woke AI" are gaining momentum, influencing companies to present themselves as politically neutral. For instance, Elon Musk's creation, Grok, was designed explicitly to recognize wokeness and oppose it. Grok, in Musk's words, is a "based," "real-time," "rebellious," and "maximum truth-seeking" competitor to OpenAI's ChatGPT and similar products from companies such as Google and Anthropic, with Musk claiming in a tweet, "The danger of training AI to be woke — in other words, lie — is deadly." (Herrman, 2023).

However, the backlash against woke AI often overlooks its role in perpetuating existing inequalities and harming marginalized groups, which are discussed profusely in this volume. For instance, an investigation by The Markup revealed that these algorithms disproportionately denied applicants of color at a 40 to 80% higher rate than did their white counterparts (Martinez & Kirchner, 2021). The notion of wokeness from AI leaders is significant in the pursuit of justice. For instance, in a tweet addressing antisemitism and Islamophobia during the 2023-2024 Israeli war on Gaza, OpenAI CEO Sam Altman called for unity, emphasizing that Jewish tech workers, like himself, receive support in the industry, but he noted a concerning lack of such support for his Muslim and Palestinian peers (Jackson, 2024).

In conclusion, the interaction of GAI agents is tied to the broader discourse on technological progress and responsibility, seeking to strike a balance between hegemony and wokeness. As GAI continues to influence various facets of society, including leadership structures and ethical considerations, a comprehensive understanding of these intersections becomes imperative. A critical examination of the historical roots, technological advancements, and ethical considerations of AI should be seamlessly integrated into AI algorithms (Cave & Dihal, 2020; Noble, 2018). This integration should be guided by principles of inclusivity and cultural sensitivity, acknowledging the influence of AI empires, whether Western (Tacheva & Ramasubramanian, 2023) or part of the evolving Chinese "digital empire in the making" (Keane & Yu, 2019).

FUTURE EMPOWERMENTS OR IMPAIRMENTS?

Anticipating the future of GAI involves assessing ongoing technological challenges, privacy concerns, and public perceptions as well as educational involvement in regulatory bodies to shape responsible GAI. In this section, we begin by discussing singularity-exploring interviews with different OpenAIs and DarwinAIs to explain their own ideas about the near feature of GAI. We discuss how society is changing and finish by education adoption and changes ending with the future of GAI in the communication classroom.

Singularity: From Generated Artificial Intelligence to Artificial General Intelligence

Futurists and visionary authors and companies, such as Kurzweil (2005) and IBM (2023), perceive AI as evolving forms of intelligence that are anticipated to not only match but also surpass human capabilities. In his book "Singularity is Near: When Humans Transcend Biology," Kurzweil (2005) predicts that by 2045, we will reach a point at which both humans and machines can merge, allowing people to live indefinitely and access unlimited knowledge (Fitzpatrick et al., 2023). In a Wall Street interview with Sam Altman and Mira Murati, OpenAI, the creators of ChatGPT, on October 21 2023, raised similar questions and proposed futuristic responses to the transitions from generative artificial intelligence (GAI) to artificial general intelligence (AGI). Highlighting that GAI is just the beginning.

Developing artificial general intelligence (AGI) is a future where AI relies less on data training, such as the case of GAI, and more on reasoning capabilities, a vision that they foresee materializing in the coming years (Altman & Murati, 2023). The notable incident involving Altman's departure and subsequent return after 700 employees threatened to follow him (Kerr, 2023; Varanasi, 2024) underscores the enduring commitment and optimism in the continuous development and improvement of GAI and stands in contrast to initial hesitations expressed by notable AI developers who have advocated for a temporary halt in AI development in 2023.

According to OpenAI developers, AGI represents an evolving system that connects all data, possibly reaching a point where AI becomes sentient, conscious, or intelligent—a different form of intelligence not precisely known to us as it develops independently of human attributes. The hope, they insist, is to augment collective intelligence to an advanced level, with the continuous evolution of the AGI inflection point. While companies such as OpenAI are advancing AGI, which is capable of performing tasks comparable to those of humans (Barney, 2023), this is considered a preliminary step toward the next level of AI capabilities—artificial intelligence (ASI).

The ASI, a hypothetical software package based on AI, is defined by IBM as possessing an intellectual scope that surpasses human intelligence and features advanced cognitive functions and highly developed thinking skills (Mucci & Stryker, 2023), including general intelligence, problem solving, social skills, and creativity (Barney, 2023). This anticipation goes beyond mere mimicry of human abilities extending across diverse disciplines and industries. Notably, AI has already demonstrated its cognitive prowess through instances such as Fritz, a chess computer program incapable of surpassing humans in all cognitive domains, but in chess (Nick, 2014).

During the research for this chapter, I had the privilege of consulting Sheldon Fernandez from DarwinAI about preparing for the future. He emphasized the difficulty in predicting the trajectory of AI development but insisted on the need for regulation. Expressing concern about the world left for future generations, given the uncertainty about the type of intelligence being forecasted, he stressed the importance of regulatory involvement. Some supporters argue that fear mongering of AI is unnecessary since it gives machines agentic abilities, diminishing the role that humans play in its development and the creative power of decision-making (Verity & Motalebi, 2023; Wong, 2023), hijacking attention on AI regulatory and ethical problems that need to be solved and eliminating the responsibility and accountability of developers (Wong, 2023). In this volume, we insist on more regulations from all different sectors. Even Sam Altman, in his interview on October 23, 2023, insisted on international regulations toward super intelligence.

Changes in Society

Hollywood's past portrayal of artificial intelligence surpassed that of human capabilities; once relegated to entertainment, it now instilled fear across institutions and states. In the future, where AI becomes an integral part of daily life will raise pertinent questions about creativity, job displacement, and prevalence biases. Society seems to have a challenging road ahead.

Advancing technologies such as robots, machine-to-machine systems, augmented reality, and other stimulus-responsive technologies are gaining prominence. At the AI for Good Global Summit in July 2023, Sophia, the Humonaid Robot citizen of Saudi Arabia, activated in 2016 by the Hanson Company, made the bold claim that humanoid robots with artificial intelligence, such as herself, could govern the world more effectively than current leaders (Cost, 2023). Technology progress helps humans make decisions faster and ease human tasks and lives, but the need to shift toward a heightened sense of technological responsibility over unrestrained progress is highly important.

Societal concerns, particularly regarding job displacements, are high. Recent statistics reveal a significant adoption rate, with 56% of surveyed U.S. workers already utilizing GAI, particularly for task automation and enhanced work communications (The Conference Board, 2023). GAI has made substantial inroads in the marketing world as well, with 65% of users belonging to the Millennial and Gen-Z demographics (Anisin, 2023). Estimates suggest that the current GAI could automate 60%-70% of tasks, with 60% involving some form of collaboration with robots (Chui et al., 2023; Verity & Motalebi, 2023). The persistent advocacy for more stringent AI regulations, as evidenced by the 118-day strike by actors demanding regulatory measures (Chmielewski & Richwine, 2023), underscores the escalating concerns regarding the broader implications of AI.

Forecasts from Goldman Sachs indicate a potential wave of AI systems that could automate approximately 300 million full-time jobs, signaling a significant shift in the employment landscape (Verity & Motalebi, 2023). The advent of GAI has already led to substantial changes and may impact professions such as data analysts and software engineers, who now contend with GAI-generated competition (Kinsella, 2023). This wave of job transitions may inevitably influence higher education, as indicated by Chapter 11 in this book. While the university's management of GAI and job displacement remain uncertain, another apprehension surrounds the intelligence of machines versus that of humans.

A shared responsibility for regulation is important, and some of the changes in society due to IA may be beneficial. For instance, Elon Musk's Neuralink seems to be a step toward changing our connection to machines. Helping individuals living with paralysis due to cervical spinal cord injury or amyotrophic lateral sclerosis, if qualified, is the target of the study, which could last six months after surgical implantation of a brain-computer interface (BCI). An implant in a specific brain region responsible for controlling movement intentions will enable people to control a computer cursor or keyboard using their thoughts alone (Sunny, 2023). Regulations from the FDA for safety reasons have delayed the project. Such regulations need to be implemented across the board. The EU indicated the first global frame in AI regulations. For instance, cognitive behavioral manipulation, social scoring, and biometric identification are unacceptable. Transparency compliance for GAI, such as ChatGPT, includes GAI content generation, model designation to prevent illegal content generation, and summary publication of copyrighted data used for training ("EU AI Act," 2023).

Higher Education Trajectory

The trajectory of general artificial intelligence (GAI) in the classroom remains uncertain, but a crucial aspect is the need to navigate the challenges and ethical considerations surrounding its integration. As the various topics addressed in this book have highlighted, there are abundant opportunities for the role of GAI in the classroom, but attention to responsible and ethical deployment is paramount. A significant portion of this book emphasizes the importance of guarding against potential pitfalls. Nevertheless, recognizing the significance of integrating GAI into the communication classroom is important.

As industries nationally and globally adopt GAI, students require GAI literacy to remain competitive. On a global scale, educational systems have proactively embraced the implementation of GAI in education, with teachers in China endorsing its deliberate integration (Liu et al., 2023; Zhu & Yang, 2023). Such educational empowerment is categorized into four dimensions: student learning, teacher teaching, education management, and learning evaluation, aiming for accurate student analysis and customized tailored learning situations based on individual abilities (Wang et al., 2020; Zhu et al., 2023).

GAI is important for communicating that students need to stay competitive. The latest survey of educators showed that 0% of communication and journalism respondents plan to invest time in developing skills for Google Bard and Microsoft Bing, while only 33% intend to spend time developing skills with ChatGPT (Survey of U.S. Higher Education, 2024). Developing these skills is imperative for uncovering concerns and vulnerabilities associated with GAI use and formulating comprehensive policies and regulations within the classroom and, more broadly, in higher education regulations. As indicated by many chapters in this volume, educators can benefit from updating their curriculums and inventing new activities and assessments to help students with different abilities learn. However, the integration of any GAI should not come at the loss of humanity and cannot be dissociated from learning while using GAI (Bozkurt et al., 2023).

The path in education and the communication classroom is changing, and research must change with this path. While current research indicates that critical analysis is currently beyond the capability of GAI, future GAI may possess different research abilities. Chapter 6 suggests that educators must ensure that students continue to engage in critical reasoning, analyze evidence and produce cogent arguments. GAI can also help academics summarize and understand concepts from different contexts, better enhancing articles, accelerating innovation, and making research more equitable (Murugesan & Cherukuri, 2023). The different recommendations in this book encompass various exercises, activities, principles, and global alliances. This chapter concludes by emphasizing the importance of GAI prompt engineering, aligning Chapter 3 insights.

Figure 3. Best practices to create a prompt for the communication classroom

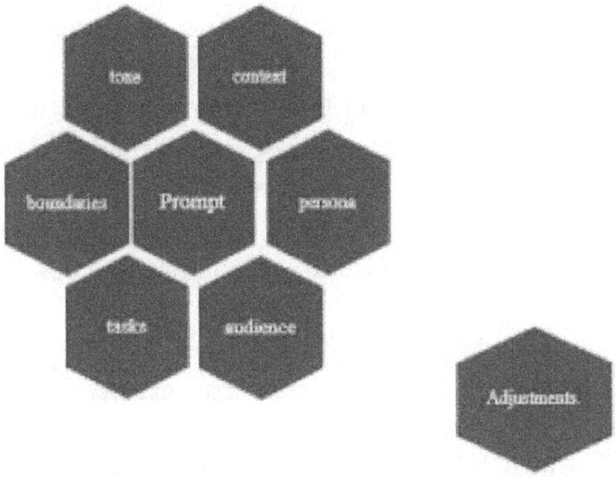

1. Audience: Clearly, define the intended audience for the prompt. Specify whether it is directed toward students, academics, researchers, or scholars.
2. Tone: Adjust the tone of the message to align with the desired style. Clearly, indicate whether the tone should be empathetic, assertive, academic, or creative.
3. Context: Provide a concise overview of the main pillars or topics that the prompt will address. The key points or themes are clearly outlined.
4. Persona: Define your professional background to establish credibility and context. Clearly, state who you are in terms of your expertise or role.
5. Tasks: Clearly, articulate the specific tasks you want the prompt to perform. Be specific and detailed about the intended actions or outcomes.
6. Boundaries: Set boundaries around the context to ensure that the AI stays focused on the relevant information. Specify any limitations and explicitly point out errors, requesting corrections when necessary.
7. Adjustments: Emphasize the need for refinement in the prompts to achieve the intended results. The AI was encouraged to ask follow-up questions for clarification, and the importance of understanding the queries was acknowledged.

Prompt Examples

It is important to train ChatGPT from the outset to align with your specific expertise, ensuring that it targets information relevant to your field. The following prompt combines all the aforementioned categories. Additionally, various prompts generated with the assistance of ChatGPT were provided:"

1. Establishing an identity relationship: I am a communication professor, and my objective is to acquire knowledge in AI literacy to enhance the creative and critical thinking abilities of my students. I am familiar with the historical aspects of AI literacy; I engage in teaching through both synchronous and asynchronous modalities. I want to identify effective AI literacy content that can be integrated into instructional approaches, fostering innovative content delivery and assessment methods. I want you to act as an AI literacy specialist, derive insights from established scholars in communication AI literacy and answer the question of how I can facilitate the development of critical and creative thinking skills among students.
2. Creating student email responses: I would like to train ChatGPT to communicate with student emails in a way that matches my style. Here are several examples of email responses to different students regarding different inquiries and situations.
3. Tabulating lists: I would like you to create a table for all the Generative AI in existence currently. The rows should include the different concerns, capabilities, and description. The columns as you see fit.
4. Breaking down Concepts: I would like you to break down this complex [concept] in a way that five years old may understand it. Explain it in a smaller manageable chunk of understanding
5. Summarizing readings: Summarize the complex text about [topic] while simplifying the language for easier understanding. Include key points and explanations to clarify intricate ideas. [provide the text here]

6. Editing writings: I would like you to enhance my writing in my unique style but with a more academic tone. Retain my voice while improving the language for a more scholarly or formal presentation. Here is my original text [insert your text].
7. Inquiring about prompts: What prompt can I use for [this topic] to accomplish this [task]

CONCLUSION

In the ongoing discourse surrounding the integration of generative artificial intelligence (GAI) into the communication classroom, the imminent arrival of artificial general intelligence (AGI) looms on the horizon. The academic community, encompassing higher education institutions, must not only comprehend this rapidly evolving technology but also strategically employ it to enhance students' critical thinking skills through innovative and meaningful assignments. This book represents a crucial step in the journey toward understanding and adapting to this technological progress while balancing it with technological responsibility. However, we contend that additional empirical, autoethnographic, and theoretical studies are imperative to advance the knowledge in this burgeoning field of study.

This final chapter serves as a bulwark against hegemony and mediocrity, asserting that GAI, when targeted at all humans, must be representative and inclusive, avoiding hierarchies based on race, sex, gender, or religion, particularly in job associations and facial recognition systems that can be detrimental to individuals. Vigilance against the different biases, echoed in this volume's chapters, elevates the book's significance as a foundation for continually raising these vital concerns. Considering the path forward, the urgent necessity for practical guidelines is underscored by a striking finding revealing that less than 10% of schools currently have formal GAI policies (UNESCO, 2023). As attention shifts to the looming notions of AGI or ASI, steering educational institutions toward the future where GAI is harnessed for the collective benefit of students and educators becomes a vital step in navigating the unknown and uncertain future. GAI represents both threats and opportunities with global impacts, global collaborations involving researchers, organizations, and governing bodies of various nations are important in the future (Chapter 8).

We acknowledge the overwhelming pace of updates in Generative AI (GAI), recognizing its constant evolution. GAI tools presented in this book may become obsolete shortly, nevertheless, our discussions laid the foundation for understanding the history of GAI and its ethical use in the communication classroom. While many chapters predominantly focus on ChatGPT, other AI like Claude, Midjourney, and Dall-E, as highlighted in some chapters, are making strides in the education system. Notably, as we conclude this book, the integration of Meta AI (text and image) with WhatsApp may add new dimensions to educational applications. And, while numerous chapters underscore the empowering facets of GAI, others caution against assuming neutrality, highlighting societal power dynamics and the potential exclusion of minority voices. Discussions on unequal access to AI tools, as explored in some chapters, emphasizing the need for thoughtful consideration in empowering students.

Valuable insights emerge from discussions on prompting within the communication classroom setting. However, we acknowledge that the rapidly evolving field of prompting may soon surpass the perspectives presented here. Some futuristic writers about AI systems suggest a potential obsolescence of prompt engineering, moving toward a more intuitive understanding of natural language. The recommended approach involves problem formulation, problem diagnosis, decomposition, reframing, and constraint design to guide GAI toward comprehensive and innovative solutions (Acar, 2023). Whether prompt engineering, criticized for challenging AI's inherent incapacity for actual reasoning or comprehension, will endure remains to be seen (Davies, 2023). Nonetheless, what is evident is that the future has arrived, and the journey of GAI is only beginning. We hope this book has given you a glimpse into this journey.

REFERENCES

Acar, O. A. (2023, June 6). AI prompt engineering isn't the future. *Harvard Business Review.* https://hbr.org/2023/06/ai-prompt-engineering-isnt-the-future

Act E. U. A. I. first regulation on artificial intelligence. *European Parliament.* https://www.europarl.europa.eu/news/en/headlines/society/20230601STO93804/eu-aiact-first-regulation-on-artificial-intelligence

Aktay, S., Gök, S., & Uzunoğlu, D. (2023). ChatGPT in education. *Türk Akademik Yayınlar Dergisi (TAY Journal), 7*(2), 378–406. https://dergipark.org.tr/en/download/articlefile/2988287

Altman, S., & Murati, M. (2023, October 21). *OpenAI CEO Sam Altman and CTO Mira Murati on the future of AI and ChatGPT* [Video]. Youtube. https://www.youtube.com/watch?v=byYlC2cagLw

Amore, S. (2022). *Homophobia is easy to encode in AI. One researcher built a program to change.* https://dot.la/tag/winoqueer

Anisin, A. (December 13, 2023). How generative AI can help solve demand generation challenges. *Forbes.* https://www.forbes.com/sites/theyec/2023/12/13/how-generative-aican-help-solve-demand-generation-challenges/?sh=762365bd150f

Arora, P. (2016). Bottom of the data pyramid: Big data and the global south. *International Journal of Communication, 10*, 1681–1699. https://ijoc.org/index.php/ijoc/article/view/4297

Barney, N. (2023). Artificial Superintelligence (ASI). *TechAccelerator.* https://www.techtarget.com/searchenterpriseai/definition/artificial-superintelligence-ASI

Bartneck, C., Yogeeswaran, K., Ser, Q., Woodward, G., Sparrow, R., Wang, S., & Eyssel, F. (2018). Robots and racism. *Proceedings of the 2018 ACM/IEEE International Conference on Human-Robot Interaction,* 196–204. 10.1145/3171221.3171260

Bourne, J. (2021, April 22). The Ancient Imagination Behind China's AI Ambition. *Noema.* https://www.noemamag.com/the-ancient-imagination-behind-chinas-ai-ambition/

Cave, S., & Dihal, K. (2020). The Whiteness of AI. *Philosophy & Technology, 33*(4), 685–703. doi:10.1007/s13347-020-00415-6

Chang, E. (2019). *Brotopia: Breaking up the boys' club of Silicon Valley*. Penguin.

Chen, L., Chen, P., & Lin, Z. (2020). Artificial intelligence in education: A review. *IEEE Access : Practical Innovations, Open Solutions, 8*, 75264–75278. doi:10.1109/ACCESS.2020.2988510

Chmielewski, D., & Richwine, L. (2023, November 9). Hollywood actors secure safeguards around AI use on screen. *Reuters.* https://www.reuters.com/business/media telecom/hollywood-actors-secure-safeguards-around-ai-use-screen-2023-11-09/

Chui, M., Hazan, E., Roberts, R., Singla, A., Smaje, K., Sukharevsky, A., Yee, L., & Zemmel, R. (2023, June 14). The economic potential of generative AI: The next productivity frontier. *McKinsey*. https://www.mckinsey.com/capabilities/mckinsey-digital/our insights/the-economic-potential-of-generative-ai-the-next-productivity-frontier

Coeckelbergh, M., & Gunkel, D. J. (2023). ChatGPT: Deconstructing the debate and moving it forward. *AI & Society*, 1–11. doi:10.1007/s00146-023-01710-4

Coffey, L. (2023, October 23). Students outrun faculty in AI use. *Inside Higher Education*. https://www.insidehighered.com/news/tech-innovation/artificial intelligence/2023/10/31/most-students-outrunning-faculty-ai-use

Cost, B. (2023, July 7). AI robots claim they can run the world better than humans: 'We can achieve great things.' *New York Post*. https://nypost.com/2023/07/07/ai-robots-claim they-can-run-world-better-than-humans-we-can-achieve-great-things/

Davies, N. (2023, November 15). *The rise and fall of prompt engineering: Fad or future?* KDnuggets. https://www.kdnuggets.com/the-rise-and-fall-of-prompt-engineering-fad-or-future

Feagin, J. R. (2013). *The white racial frame: centuries of racial framing and counter framing* (2nd ed.). Routledge. doi:10.4324/9780203076828

Feuerriegel, S., Hartmann, J., Janiesch, C., & Zschech, P. (2023). Generative AI. *Business & Information Systems Engineering*, *66*(1), 111–126. doi:10.1007/s12599-023-00834-7

Fitzpatrick, D., Fox, A., & Weinstein, B. (2023). *The AI classroom: The ultimate guide to artificial intelligence in education*. TeacherGoals.

Grynbaum, M. M., & Mac, R. (2023, December 27). The Times Sues OpenAI and Microsoft Over A.I. Use of Copyrighted Work. *The New York Times*. https://www.nytimes.com/2023/12/27/business/media/new-york-times-open-ai-microsoft-lawsuit.html

GunkelD. J. (2012a) Communication and artificial intelligence: opportunities and challenges for the 21st century. *Communication+1, 1*(1). doi:10.7275/R5QJ7F7R

Guzman, A. L. (Ed.). (2018). *Human–machine communication: Rethinking communication, technology, and ourselves*. Peter Langs. doi:10.3726/b14399

Guzman, A. L., & Lewis, S. C. (2020). Artificial intelligence and communication: A human machine communication research agenda. *New Media & Society*, *22*(1), 70–86. doi:10.1177/1461444819858691

Herrman, J. (2023, November 7). What does it mean that Elon Musk's new AI Chatbot is 'Anti-Woke'? *Intelligencer.* https://nymag.com/intelligencer/2023/11/elon-musks-grokai-bot-is-anti-woke-what-does-that-mean.html

Isin, E., & Ruppert, E. (2019). Data's empire: Postcolonial data politics. In D. Bigo, E. Isin, & E. Ruppert (Eds.), *Data politics* (pp. 207–227). Routledge. doi:10.4324/9781315167305-11

Jackson, S. (2024, January 5). Sam Altman says tech world 'should be united' in supporting Muslim colleagues. *Business Insider.* https://www.businessinsider.com/openai-samaltman-urges-tech-community-support-muslim-peers-2024-1

Keane, M., & Yu, H. (2019). A digital empire in the making: China's outbound digital platforms. *International Journal of Communication, 13*, 4624–4641.

Kerr, D. (2023, November 20). Hundreds of OpenAI Workers Threaten to Leave Over CEO Sam Altman's Firing. *NPR*. https://www.npr.org/2023/11/20/1214281184/hundreds-of-openaiworkers-threaten-to-leave-over-ceo-sam-altmans-firing

Khogali, H., & Mekid, S. (2023). The blended future of automation and AI: Examining some long-term societal and ethical impact features. *Technology in Society, 73*, 102232. Advance online publication. doi:10.1016/j.techsoc.2023.102232

Kinsella, B. (2023, June 17). *Stack Overflow will embrace generative AI after all. Will overflow AI address an existential risk?* https://synthedia.substack.com/p/stack-overflowwill-embrace-generative

Klare, F., Burge, B., Klontz, M. J., Vorder, J. C., Bruegge, R. W., & Jain, A. K. (2012). Face recognition performance: Role of demographic information. *IEEE Transactions on Information Forensics and Security, 7*(6), 1789–1801. doi:10.1109/TIFS.2012.2214212

Korolov, M. (2023, June 3). Claude AI can read and analyze an entire book at once. Here's how to use it. *MetaStellar.* https://www.metastellar.com/nonfiction/on writing/claude-ai-can-read-and-analyze-an-entire-book-at-once/

Kurzweil, R. (2005). *The Singularity is near: When humans transcend biology*. Penguin.

Liao, Y., & He, J. (2020). The racial mirroring effects on human-agent in psychotherapeutic conversation. *Proceedings of the 25th International Conference on Intelligent User Interfaces (IUI'20).* 10.1145/3377325.3377488

Lim, W. M., Gunasekara, A., Pallant, J. L., Pallant, J. I., & Pechenkina, E. (2023). Generative AI and the future of education: Ragnarök or reformation? A paradoxical perspective from management educators. *International Journal of Management Education, 21*(2), 100790. doi:10.1016/j.ijme.2023.100790

Liu, M., Ren, Y., Nyagoga, L. M., Stonier, F., Wu, Z., & Yu, L. (2023, September 2). Future of education in the era of generative artificial intelligence: Consensus among Chinese scholars on applications of ChatGPT in schools. *Future in Educational Research, 1*(1), 72–10. doi:10.1002/fer3.10

Long, D., & Magerko, B. (2020). What is AI literacy? Competencies and design considerations. In *CHI '20: Proceedings of the 2020 CHI Conference on Human Factors in Computing Systems* (pp. 1-16). 10.1145/3313831.3376727

Lv, Z. (2023). Generative artificial intelligence in the metaverse era. *Cognitive Robotics, 3*, 208-217. doi:10.1016/j.cogr.2023.06.001

Mann, J. (2023, September 17). The humanoid-robot CEO of a drinks company says it doesn't have weekends and is 'always on 24/7'. *Yahoo Finance.* https://finance.yahoo.com/news/humanoid-robot-ceo-drinks-company101055228.html?guccounter=1

Martinez, E., & Kirchner, L. (2021 August 25). The secret bias hidden in mortgage-approval algorithm. *The Markup.* https://themarkup.org/denied/2021/08/25/the-secret-biashidden-in-mortgage-approval-algorithms

Mason, J., Peoples, B. E., & Lee, J. (2020). Questioning the scope of AI standardization in learning, education, and training. *Journal of ICT Standardization*, *8*(2), 107–122. doi:10.13052/jicts2245-800X.822

Mucci, T., & Stryker, C. (2023, December 18). *What is artificial superintelligence?* IBM. https://www.ibm.com/topics/artificialsuperintelligence#:~:text=Artificial%20superintellgence%20(ASI)%20is%20a,intellectual%20scope%20beyond%20human%20intelligence

Murugesan, S., & Cherukuri, A. K. (2023). The rise of generative artificial intelligence and its impact on education: The promises and perils. *Computer*, *56*(5), 116–121. doi:10.1109/MC.2023.3253292

Nick, B. (2014). *Superintelligence: Paths, Dangers, Strategies*. Oxford University Press.

Noble, S. U. (2018). *Algorithms of oppression*. New York University Press. doi:10.18574/nyu/9781479833641.001.0001

Open, A. I. (2023). *ChatGPT 3.5* (May 24 version) [Large language model, editing]. https://chat.openai.com

Pena, P., & Varon, J. (2021, May 3). *Oppressive A.I.: Feminist categories to understand its political effects*. Retrieved January 18, 2024, from https://notmy.ai/news/oppressive-a-i-feminist-categories-to-understand-its-political-effects/

Pichai, S., & Hassabis, D. (2023, December 6). Introducing Gemini: our largest and most capable AI model. *Blog Google*. https://blog.google/technology/ai/google-gemini-ai/#sundar note.

Primary Research Group. (2024). *Survey of US higher education faculty 2024: Use of artificial intelligence applications*. Primary Research Group.

Raley, R., & Rhee, J. (2023). *Critical AI: A field in formation*. Duke University Press.

Reed, B. (2023, August 23). 'Very wonderful, very toxic': How AI became the culture war's new frontier. *The Guardian*. https://www.theguardian.com/us-news/2023/aug/21/artificial-intelligence-culture-warwoke-far-right

Ricaurte, P. (2022). Ethics for the majority world: AI and the question of violence at scale. *Media Culture & Society*, *44*(4), 726–745. doi:10.1177/01634437221099612

Riffe, D., Lacy, S., & Watson, B. R. (2019). *Analyzing media messages: Using quantitative content analysis in research* (4th ed.). Routledge. doi:10.4324/9780429464287

Roberge, J., & Castelle, M. (2021). *The cultural life of machine learning: An incursion into critical AI studies*. Springer. doi:10.1007/978-3-030-56286-1

Rogers, E. M. (1997). *A History of Communication Study: A Biographical Approach*. Free Press.

Sabzalieva, E., & Valentini, A. (2023). ChatGPT and artificial intelligence in higher education; Quick start guide. *UNESCO*. Retrieved from https://www.iesalc.unesco.org/wpcontent/uploads/2023/04/ChatGPT-and-Artificial-Intelligence-in-higher-education-QuickStart guide_EN_FINA.pdf

Shaw, C., Yuan, L., Brennan, D., Martin, S., Janson, N., Fox, K., & Bryant, G. (2023). *Generative AI in higher education: Fall 2023 update of time for class study*. Tyton Partners. https://www.tytonpartners.com/time-for-class-2023/GenAI-Update

Sunny, M. (2023, September 20). Musk's Neuralink to start human trials of brain implant. to start human trial of brain implant for paralysis patients, *Reuters*. https://www.reuters.com/technology/musks-neuralink-start-human-trials-brain-implant2023-09-19/

Tacheva, J., & Ramasubramanian, S. (2023). AI Empire: Unraveling the interlocking systems of oppression in generative AI's global order. *Big Data & Society, 10*(2). Advance online publication. doi:10.1177/20539517231219241

The Conference Board. (2023, September 9). *Majority of US workers are already using GAI tools—But company policies trail behind* [Press release]. https://www.conference-board.org/press/us-workers-and-generative-ai

Turing, A. M. (1950). Computing machinery and intelligence. *Mind, LIX*(236), 433–460. doi:10.1093/mind/LIX.236.433

Valencia College. (2021). *Evaluating sources using the CRAAP method.* Valencia College LibGuides. https://libguides.valenciacollege.edu/friendly.php?s=CRAAP

van Atteveldt, W., & Peng, T.-Q. (Eds.). (2021). *Computational methods for communication science.* Routledge. doi:10.4324/9781003082606

Varanasi, L. (2024, January 7). Sam Altman said his firing and reinstatement was 'extremely painful,' but 'great for OpenAI.' *Business Insider.* https://www.businessinsider.com/sam-altmans-said-his-firing-was-painful-but-great-for-openai-2024-1

Verity, A., & Motalebi, N. (2023). *GAI for humanitarians.* Digital Humanitarian Network. https://digitalhumanitarians.com/generative_ai_for_humanitarians-september_2023/

Wang, D., Churchill, E., Maes, P., Fan, X., Shneiderman, B., Shi, Y., & Wang, Q. (2020). Fromhuman-human collaboration to human-AI collaboration: Designing AI systems that can work together with people. In Extended abstracts of the 2020 CHI conference on human factors in computing systems (pp. 1–6). doi:10.1145/3334480.3381069

Westfall, C. (2023, January 28). *Educators battle plagiarism as 89% of students admit to using OpenAI's ChatGPT for homework.* https://www.forbes.com/sites/chriswestfall/2023/01/28/educators-battle-plagiarism-as-89of-students-admit-to-using-open-ais-chatgpt-for-homework/?sh=59d9ff99750d

Wong, M. (2023, June 2). AI Doomarism is a decoy. *The Atlantic*. https://www.theatlantic.com/technology/archive/2023/06/ai-regulation-sam-altman-billgates/674278/

Zhu, Y., Li, Y., Yang, Y., & Zhai, X. (2023). Intelligent technology drives higher education reform: Key points and reflections on the 2023 Horizon report: Teaching and learning edition. *Open Education Research, 29*(3), 19–30. https://doi.org/ doi:10.13966/j.cnki.kfjyyj.2023.03

Zhu, Y., & Yang, F. (2023). ChatGPT/generative artificial intelligence and educational innovation: Opportunities, challenges, and the future. *Journal of East China Normal University (Educational Sciences), 41*(7), 1–14. doi:10.16382/j.cnki.1000-5560.2023.07.001

Compilation of References

Abdous, M. (2023). How AI is shaping the future of higher ed. *Inside Higher Ed.* https://www.insidehighered.com/views/2023/03/22/how-ai-shaping-future-higher-ed-opinion

Abramson, A. (2023, June 1). How to Use ChatGPT as a learning tool. *Monitor on Psychology: American Psychological Association.* https://www.apa.org/monitor/2023/06/chatgpt-learning-tool

AbusittaA.AimeurE.WahabO. A. (2019). Generative adversarial networks for mitigating biases in machine learning systems. Cornell University Library. *ArXiv.* http://arxiv.org/abs/1905.09972

Acar, O. A. (2023, June 6). AI prompt engineering isn't the future. *Harvard Business Review.* https://hbr.org/2023/06/ai-prompt-engineering-isnt-the-future

ACM Global Technology Policy Council. (2023). *Principles for the development, deployment, and use of generative AI technologies.* doi:10.6028/NIST.AI.100-1

Act E. U. A. I. first regulation on artificial intelligence. *European Parliament.* https://www.europarl.europa.eu/news/en/headlines/society/20230601STO93804/eu-aiact-first-regulation-on-artificial-intelligence

AIContentfy Team. (2023, November 26). The impact of AI on content accuracy. *AIContentfy.* https://aicontentfy.com/en/blog/impact-of-ai-on-content-accuracy

Akgun, S., & Greenhow, C. (2022). Artificial intelligence in education: Addressing ethical challenges in K-12 settings. *AI and Ethics, 2*(3), 431–440. doi:10.1007/s43681-021-00096-7 PMID:34790956

Aktay, S., Gök, S., & Uzunoğlu, D. (2023). ChatGPT in education. *Türk Akademik Yayınlar Dergisi (TAY Journal), 7*(2), 378–406. https://dergipark.org.tr/en/download/articlefile/2988287

AlAfnan, M. A., Dishari, S., Jovic, M., & Lomidze, K. (2023). ChatGPT as an educational tool: Opportunities, challenges, and recommendations for communication, business writing, and composition courses. *Journal of Artificial Intelligence and Technology, 3*, 60–68. doi:10.37965/jait.2023.0184

Alam, A. (2021). Should robots replace teachers? Mobilisation of AI and learning analytics in education. In *Proceedings of the 2021 International Conference on Advances in Computing, Communication, and Control (ICAC3)* (pp. 1–12). IEEE. 10.1109/ICAC353642.2021.9697300

Al-azazi, F. A., & Ghurab, M. (2023). ANN-LSTM: A deep learning model for early student performance prediction in MOOC. *Heliyon, 9*(3), e15382. doi:10.1016/j.heliyon.2023.e15382 PMID:37089306

Alba, D. (2022, December 8). *OpenAI chatbot spits out biased musings, despite guardrails.* Bloomberg.com. https://www.bloomberg.com/news/newsletters/2022-12-08/chatgpt-open-ai-s-chatbot-is-spitting-out-biased-sexist-results

Aljabani, M., Ghazi, M., Ali, A., & Abed, S. (2023). ChatGPT: Open possibilities. *Iraqui Journal for Computer Science and Mathematics, 4*, 62–64. doi:10.52866/IJCSM.2023.01.01.0018

Almer, J. (2022). *Deskilling as an effect of AI: A group of students' attitudes towards AI and their worries about deskilling*. Academic Press.

Alpaslan, C. M., & Mitroff, I. I. (2011). *Swans, swine, and swindlers; Coping with the growing threat of mega-crises and mega-messes*. Stanford Business Books – Stanford University Press.

Alqahtani, T., Badreldin, H. A., Alrashed, M., Alshaya, A. I., Alghamdi, S. S., Bin Saleh, K., Alowais, S. A., Alshaya, O. A., Rahman, I., Al Yami, M. S., & Albekairy, A. M. (2023). The emergent role of artificial intelligence, natural learning processing, and large language models in higher education and research. *Research in Social & Administrative Pharmacy, 19*(8), 1236–1242. doi:10.1016/j.sapharm.2023.05.016 PMID:37321925

Altman, S., & Murati, M. (2023, October 21). *OpenAI CEO Sam Altman and CTO Mira Murati on the future of AI and ChatGPT* [Video]. Youtube. https://www.youtube.com/watch?v=byYlC2cagLw

Amani, S., White, L., Balart, T., Arora, L., Shryock, K. J., Brumbelow, K., & Watson, K. L. (2023). Generative AI perceptions: A survey to measure to perceptions of faculty, staff, and students on generative AI tools in academia. *arXiv, 1*, 1–17. https://arxiv.org/abs/2304.14415

American Association of Colleges and Universities (AACU). (n.d.). https://aacu.org

Amini, A., Soleimany, A. P., Schwarting, W., Bhatia, S. N., & Rus, D. L. (2019). Uncovering and mitigating algorithmic bias through learned latent structure. *Proceedings of the 2019 AAAI/ACM Conference on AI, Ethics, and Society.* 289–295. 10.1145/3306618.3314243

Amore, S. (2022). *Homophobia is easy to encode in AI. One researcher built a program to change.* https://dot.la/tag/winoqueer

Anderson, J., & Rainie, L. (2018, December 10). Artificial intelligence and the future of humans. *Pew Research Center.* https://www.pewresearch.org/internet/2018/12/10/artificial-intelligence-and-the-future-of-humans/

Angelone, A. M., Galassi, A., & Vittorini, P. (2022). Improved automated classification of sentences in data science exercises. In *Methodologies and Intelligent Systems for Technology Enhanced Learning, 11th International Conference* (pp. 12–21). Springer. 10.1007/978-3-030-86618-1_2

Anisin, A. (December 13, 2023). How generative AI can help solve demand generation challenges. *Forbes.* https://www.forbes.com/sites/theyec/2023/12/13/how-generative-aican-help-solve-demand-generation-challenges/?sh=762365bd150f

Aoun, J. E. (2017). *Robot-proof: Higher education in the age of artificial intelligence.* MIT Press. doi:10.7551/mitpress/11456.001.0001

Araujo, T. (2020). Conversational agent research toolkit: An alternative for creating and managing chatbots for experimental research. *Computer Communication Review, 2*(1), 35–51. doi:10.5117/CCR2020.1.002.ARAU

Aristotle. (2007). On rhetoric: A theory of civic discourse (2nd ed.; G.A. Kennedy, Trans.). Oxford University Press. (Originally published ca. 350 B.C.E.)

Arora, P. (2016). Bottom of the data pyramid: Big data and the global south. *International Journal of Communication, 10*, 1681–1699. https://ijoc.org/index.php/ijoc/article/view/4297

Asemah, E., & Omosotomhe, S. (2022). *Fundamentals of interpersonal communication.* Matkol Press.

Askari, S. I., Haans, A., Bos, P., Eggink, M. J. G., Lu, E. M., Kwong, F. G. L., & IJsselsteijn, W. A. (2020). Context matters: 12th international conference on human haptic sensing and touch enabled computer applications, EuroHaptics 2020. *Haptics: Science, Technology, Applications*, 131–139. 10.1007/978-3-030-58147-3_15

Association for Computing Machinery (ACM). (2023, June 27). *Principles for the development, deployment, and use of generative AI technologies.* https://www.acm.org/binaries/content/assets/public-policy/ustpc-approved-generative-ai-principles

Atchison, J., & Panetta, E. (2009). Intercollegiate debate and speech communication: Historical developments and issues for the future. In A. A. Lunsford, K. H. Wilson, & R. A. Eberly (Eds.), *The SAGE handbook of rhetorical studies* (pp. 317–333). SAGE.

Ausat, A. M., Massang, B., Efendi, M., Norifman, N., & Riady, Y. (2023). Can ChatGPT replace the role of teachers in the classroom: A fundamental analysis. *Journal of Education*, *5*(4), 16100–16106. doi:10.31004/joe.v5i4.2745

Averkin, A. N., Bazarkina, D. Yu., Pantserev, K. A., & Pashentsev, Y. N. (2019). Artificial intelligence in the context of psychological security: Theoretical and practical implications. *Atlantis Studies in Uncertainty Modelling*, *1*, 101–107. doi:10.2991/eusflat-19.2019.16

Aydın, Ö., & Karaarslan, E. (2022). OpenAI ChatGPT generated literature review: Digital twin in healthcare. In Ö. Aydın (Ed.), Emerging Computer Technologies. İzmir Akademi Dernegi. doi:10.2139/ssrn.4308687

Aydın, Ö., & Karaarslan, E. (2023, January 31). *Is ChatGPT leading generative AI? What is beyond expectations?* https://papers.ssrn.com/sol3/papers.cfm?abstract_id=4341500

Azaria, A. (2022). *ChatGPT usage and limitations* [Unpublished manuscript]. HAL open science. https://hal.science/hal-03913837

Babu, C. V. S. (2022). *Artificial intelligence and expert systems.* Anniyappa Publication.

Babu, C. V. S., & Adhithya, S. (2023). ChatGPT and other generative AI tools in education: Transformative potential and ethical considerations. In J. Keengwe (Ed.), *Creative AI tools and ethical implications in teaching and learning* (pp. 135–152). IGI Global. doi:10.4018/979-8-3693-0205-7.ch007

Babu, C. V. S., & Padma, R. (2023). Technology transformation through skilled teachers in teaching accountancy. In R. González-Lezcano (Ed.), *Advancing STEM education and innovation in a time of distance learning* (pp. 211–233). IGI Global., doi:10.4018/978-1-6684-5053-6.ch011

Babu, C. V. S., & Rohan, B. (2023). Evaluation and quality assurance for rapid e-learning and development of digital learning resources. In M. I. Santally, Y. Rajabalee, & R. Rajputh (Eds.), *Implementing rapid e-learning through interactive materials development* (pp. 139–170). IGI Global. doi:10.4018/978-1-6684-4940-0.ch008

Bae, S., Dong, Y., & Kwon, O. (2023). The effects of content creator, media richness, and content theme on learning performance: Focusing on ESG management education for Chinese employees. 글로벌경영학회지, *20*(1), 27–50. https://doi.org/ doi:10.38115/asgba2023.20.1.27

Baidoo-Anu, D., & Owusu Ansah, L. (2023). Education in the era of generative artificial intelligence (AI): Understanding the potential benefits of ChatGPT in promoting teaching the learning. *Journal of AI*, *7*(1), 52–62. doi:10.61969/jai.1337500

Bajorek, J. P. (2019, May 10). *Voice recognition still has significant race and gender biases.* Harvard Business Review. https://hbr.org/2019/05/voice-recognition-still-has-significant-race-and-gender-biases

Bajwa, J., Munir, U., Nori, A., & Williams, B. (2021). Artificial intelligence in healthcare: Transforming the practice of medicine. *Future Healthcare Journal*, *8*(2), e188–e194. doi:10.7861/fhj.2021-0095 PMID:34286183

Baker, R. S., & Hawn, A. (2022). Algorithmic bias in education. *International Journal of Artificial Intelligence in Education, 32*(4), 1–41. doi:10.1007/s40593-021-00285-9

Bali, M. (2023, April 1). What I mean when I say critical AI literacy. *Reflecting Allowed: Maha Bali's Blog About Education.* https://blog.mahabali.me/educational-technology-2/what-i-mean-when-i-say-critical-ai-literacy/

Banks, J. A. (2004). Teaching for social justice, diversity, and citizenship in a global world. *The Educational Forum, 68*(4), 296–305. doi:10.1080/00131720408984645

Bany, M. A., & Johnson, L. V. (1964). *Classroom group behavior: Group dynamics in education.* Macmillan.

Barney, N. (2023). Artificial Superintelligence (ASI). *TechAccelerator.* https://www.techtarget.com/searchenterpriseai/definition/artificial-superintelligence-ASI

Bartanen, M. D., & Littlefield, R. S. (2014). *Forensics in America: A history.* Rowman & Littlefield.

Barthes, R. (1977). *The death of the author. In his Image – music – text* (S. Heath, Trans.). Fontana Press.

Bartneck, C., Yogeeswaran, K., Ser, Q., Woodward, G., Sparrow, R., Wang, S., & Eyssel, F. (2018). Robots and racism. *Proceedings of the 2018 ACM/IEEE International Conference on Human-Robot Interaction,* 196–204. 10.1145/3171221.3171260

Batt, S., & Schulz, D. (2005). Design principles for competitive debate formats. In C. Willard (Ed.), *Critical problems in argumentation* (pp. 510–517). National Communication Association.

Bauschard, S., Coverstone, A., Rao, A., & Rao, S. (2023). *Beyond algorithmic solutions: The significance of academic debate for learning assessment and skill cultivation in the AI world* [Commissioned Paper]. Cottesmore's Free AI Festival, Pease Pottage, UK. https://papers.ssrn.com/sol3/papers.cfm?abstract_id=4567346

Beach, J. M. (2012). *Kenneth Burke: A sociology of knowledge: dramatism, ideology, and rhetoric.* CreateSpace Independent Publishing Platform.

Beckett, C., & Yaseen, M. (2023). Generating Change: A global survey of what news organisations are doing with AI. *JournalismAI.* https://www.journalismai.info/research/2023-generating-change

Beebe, S. A., & Beebe, S. J. (1991). *Public speaking: An audience-centered approach.* Prentice Hall.

Belenguer, L. (2022). AI bias: Exploring discriminatory algorithmic decision-making models and the application of possible machine-centric solutions adapted from the pharmaceutical industry. *AI and Ethics, 2*(2), 771–787. doi:10.1007/s43681-022-00138-8 PMID:35194591

Bender, E. M., Gebru, T., McMillan-Major, A., & Shmitchell, S. (2021). On the dangers of stochastic parrots: Can language models be too big? In *Proceedings of the 2021 ACM conference on fairness, accountability, and transparency* (pp. 610–623). 10.1145/3442188.3445922

Bene, R. E., & Murphy, J. E. (2022). Co-teaching as mentors: Maximizing instructor and librarian collaboration for teaching information literacy skills. *Papers on Postsecondary Learning and Teaching, 5,* 75–85.

Benjamin, R. (2019). *Race after technology: Abolitionist tools for the New Jim Code.* Polity Press.

Berger, C. R., & Calabrese, R. J. (1975). Some explorations in initial interaction and beyond: Toward a developmental theory of interpersonal communication. *Human Communication Research, 1*(2), 99–112. doi:10.1111/j.1468-2958.1975.tb00258.x

Beseiso, M., Alzubi, O. A., & Rashaideh, H. (2021). A novel automated essay scoring approach for reliable higher educational assessments. *Journal of Computing in Higher Education, 33*(3), 727–746. doi:10.1007/s12528-021-09283-1

Bhaimiya, S. (2023). An Asian MIT student asked AI to turn an image of her into a professional headshot. It made her white, with lighter skin and blue eyes. *Business Insider.* https://www.businessinsider.com/student-uses-playrgound-ai-for-professional-headshot-turned-white-2023-8

Bhutoria, A. (2022). Personalized education and Artificial Intelligence in the United States, China, and India: A systematic review using a Human-In-The-Loop model. *Computers and Education: Artificial Intelligence, 3*, 100068. doi:10.1016/j.caeai.2022.100068

Bibhudatta, D. (2023, November 29). *Generative AI will transform virtual meetings.* Harvard Business Review. https://hbr.org/2023/11/generative-ai-will-transform-virtual-meetings

Bilquise, G., Ibrahim, S., & Shaalan, K. (2022). Emotionally intelligent chatbots: A systematic literature review. *Human Behavior and Emerging Technologies, 2022*, e9601630. doi:10.1155/2022/9601630

Blakeslee, S. (2004). The CRAAP test. *LOEX Quarterly, 31*(4). https://commons.emich.edu/loexquarterly/vol31/iss3/4/

Bogost, I. (2023, February 2). ChatGPT is about to dump more work on everyone. *The Atlantic.* https://www.theatlantic.com/technology/archive/2023/02/chatgpt-ai-detector-machine-learning-technology-bureaucracy/672927/

Bok, D. (2006). *Our underachieving colleges.* Princeton University Press.

Botan, C. H. (2018). *Strategic communication: Theory and practice.* Wiley-Blackwell.

Boulianne, S., Oser, J., & Hoffmann, C. P. (2023). Powerless in the digital age? A systematic review and meta-analysis of political efficacy and digital media use. *New Media & Society, 25*(9), 2512–2536. doi:10.1177/14614448231176519

Bourne, J. (2021, April 22). The Ancient Imagination Behind China's AI Ambition. *Noema.* https://www.noemamag.com/the-ancient-imagination-behind-chinas-ai-ambition/

Bowles, D. C., & Kruger, J. S. (2023). Generating employable, intelligent graduates in a world with generative AI: Thoughts for educators. *Pedagogy in Health Promotion, 9*(2), 75–77. doi:10.1177/23733799231175171

Boyer, E. (1990). *Scholarship reconsidered: Priorities of the professoriate.* Carnegie Foundation for the Advancement of Teaching.

Bozkurt, A., & Sharma, R. C. (2023). Challenging the status quo and exploring the new boundaries in the age of algorithms: Reimagining the role of generative AI in distance education and online learning. *Asian Journal of Distance Education, 18*(1), i–viii.

Bradley, M. M., & Lang, P. J. (1994). Measuring emotion: The self-assessment manikin and the semantic differential. *Journal of Behavior Therapy and Experimental Psychiatry, 25*(1), 49–51. doi:10.1016/0005-7916(94)90063-9 PMID:7962581

Braithwaite, D. O., & Schrodt, P. (Eds.). (2021). *Engaging theories in interpersonal communication: Multiple perspectives* (3rd ed.). Routledge., doi:10.4324/9781003195511

Braun, V., & Clarke, V. (2006). Using thematic analysis in psychology. *Qualitative Research in Psychology, 3*(2), 77–101. doi:10.1191/1478088706qp063oa

Braun, V., & Clarke, V. (2021). Can I use TA? Should I use TA? Should I not use TA? Comparing reflexive thematic analysis and other pattern-based qualitative analytic approaches. *Counselling & Psychotherapy Research, 21*(1), 37–47. doi:10.1002/capr.12360

Brenan, M. (2023, July 11). *Americans' confidence in higher education down sharply.* Gallup. https://news.gallup.com/poll/508352/americans-confidence-higher-education-down-sharply.aspx

Brittain, B. (2023). Lawsuits accuse AI content creators of misusing copyright work. *Reuters.* https://www.reuters.com/legal/transactional/lawsuits-accuse-ai-content-creators-misusing-copyrighted-work-2023-01-17/

Broda-Bahm, K., Kempf, D., & Driscoll, W. (2004). *Argument and audience: Presenting debates in public settings.* International Debate Education Association.

Brown, H., Lee, K., Mireshghallah, F., Shokri, R., & Tramèr, F. (2022). What does it mean for a language model to preserve privacy? In *2022 ACM Conference on Fairness, Accountability, and Transparency* (pp. 2280–2292). 10.1145/3531146.3534642

Brown, T., Mann, B., Ryder, N., Subbiah, M., Kaplan, J. D., Dhariwal, P., Neelakantan, A., Shyam, P., Sastry, G., & Askell, A. (2020). Language models are few-shot learners. *Advances in Neural Information Processing Systems, 33*, 1877–1901.

Bruns, H. C., & Long Lingo, E. (2023). Tedious work: Developing novel outcomes with digitization in the arts and sciences. *Administrative Science Quarterly.* Advance online publication. doi:10.1177/00018392231208190

Brusegard, B. (2023). *Embracing AI in education: A librarian's guide to empowering students and teachers.* Liferarian. https://liferarian.com/news/embracing-ai-in-education-a librarians-guide-to-empowering-students-and-teachers-4336/

Bryson, J., & Winfield, A. (2017). Standardizing ethical design for artificial intelligence and autonomous systems. *Computer, 50*(5), 116–119. doi:10.1109/MC.2017.154

Buchanan, R. (2001). Design and the new rhetoric: Productive arts in the philosophy of culture. *Philosophy & Rhetoric, 34*(3), 183–206. doi:10.1353/par.2001.0012

Bulut, O., & Yildirim-Erbasli, S. N. (2022). Automatic story and item generation for reading comprehension assessments with transformers. *International Journal of Assessment Tools in Education, 9*(Special Issue), 72–87. doi:10.21449/ijate.1124382

Buolamwini, J. (2019). Artificial intelligence has a problem with gender and racial bias. Here's how to solve it. *Time.* https://time.com/5520558/artificial-intelligence-racial-gender-bias/

Buolamwini, J., & Gebru, T. (2018). Gender shades: Intersectional accuracy disparities in commercial gender classification. In *Conference on Fairness, Accountability, and Transparency* (pp. 77–91). PMLR.

Burke, K. (1952). *A rhetoric of motives.* Prentice-Hall.

Burke, K. (1969). *A grammar of motives.* University of California Press. doi:10.1525/9780520341715

Burns, T. (2023, August 21). ITS debuts custom artificial intelligence services across U-M. *The University Record.* https://record.umich.edu/articles/its-debuts-customized-ai-services-to-u-m-community/

Burton, E., Goldsmith, J., Koenig, S., Kuipers, B., Mattei, N., & Walsh, T. (2017). Ethical considerations in artificial intelligence courses. *AI & Society, 32*(3), 357–369. doi:10.1007/s00146-016-0699-1

Butcher, A., & McGrath, T. (2004). International students in New Zealand: Needs and responses. *International Education Journal, 5*(1), 540–551.

Butler, S. (1927). *Erewhon, or over the range and Erewhon revisited twenty years later.* Random House. https://books.google.com/books?hl=en&lr=&id=D48yAAAAMAAJ&oi=fnd&pg=PR1&ots=g5RC9UlXAp&sig=rQb1vCtuYsSM_ehkzvCDLt2rL50#v=onepage&q&f=false

Caines, A., Benedetto, L., Taslimipoor, S., Davis, C., Gao, Y., Andersen, O., Yuan, Z., Elliott, M., Moore, R., Bryant, C., Rei, M., Mullooly, A., Nicholls, D., & Buttery, P. (2023). On the application of large language models for language teaching and assessment technology. AIED Workshops.

Callais, V. (2020). Reclaiming conversation: The power of talk in a digital age. *Journal of College Orientation, Transition, and Retention, 27*(2). Advance online publication. doi:10.24926/jcotr.v27i2.3099

Canavero, S., Ren, X., & Kim, C. Y. (2016). HEAVEN: The Frankenstein effect. *Surgical Neurology International, 7*(24), 623. Advance online publication. doi:10.4103/2152-7806.190472 PMID:27656323

Carroll, A., Forrest, K., Sanders-O'Connor, E., Flynn, L., Bower, J. M., Fynes-Clinton, S., York, A., & Ziaei, M. (2022). Teacher stress and burnout in Australia: Examining the role of intrapersonal and environmental factors. *Social Psychology of Education, 25*(2-3), 441–469. doi:10.1007/s11218-022-09686-7 PMID:35233183

Casal-Otero, L., Catala, A., Fernández-Morante, C., Taboada, M., Cebreiro, B., & Barro, S. (2023). AI literacy in K-12: A systematic literature review. *International Journal of STEM Education, 10*(1), 29. doi:10.1186/s40594-023-00418-7

Cavanagh, M., Bower, M., Moloney, R., & Sweller, N. (2014). The effect over time of a video-based reflection system on preservice teachers' oral presentations. *The Australian Journal of Teacher Education, 39*(6). Advance online publication. doi:10.14221/ajte.2014v39n6.3

Cave, S., & Dihal, K. (2020). The Whiteness of AI. *Philosophy & Technology, 33*(4), 685–703. doi:10.1007/s13347-020-00415-6

Cave, S., Dihal, K., & Dillon, S. (Eds.). (2020). *AI narratives: A history of imaginative thinking about intelligent machines*. Oxford University Press. doi:10.1093/oso/9780198846666.001.0001

Center for AI and Digital Policy. (2023, March 30). *In the matter of Open AI (Federal Trade Commission 2023).* https://www.caidp.org/cases/openai/

Center for AI and Digital Policy. (2024, January 8). *AI policy news - CAIDP update 6.01*. https://www.caidp.org/news/

Cerf, E. (2023, August 10). *Researchers' tool finds bias in state-of-the-art generative AI model*. UC Santa Cruz. https://news.ucsc.edu/2023/08/t2iat.html

Challen, R., Denny, J., Pitt, M., Gompels, L., Edwards, T., & Tsaneva-Atanasova, K. (2019). Artificial intelligence, bias and clinical safety. *BMJ Quality & Safety, 28*(3), 231–237. doi:10.1136/bmjqs-2018-008370 PMID:30636200

Chamberlain, R., Mullin, C., Scheerlinck, B., & Wagemans, J. (2017). Putting the art in artificial: Aesthetic responses to computer-generated art. *Psychology of Aesthetics, Creativity, and the Arts, 12*(2), 177–192. Advance online publication. doi:10.1037/aca0000136

Chamot, A. (2005). Language learning strategy instruction: Current issues and research. *Annual Review of Applied Linguistics, 25*, 112–130. doi:10.1017/S0267190505000061

Chan, C. K. (2023). A comprehensive AI policy education framework for university teaching and learning. *International Journal of Educational Technology in Higher Education, 20*(38), 38. Advance online publication. doi:10.1186/s41239-023-00408-3

Chan, C. K. Y., & Hu, W. (2023). Students' voices on generative AI: Perceptions, benefits, and challenges in higher education. *International Journal of Educational Technology in Higher Education, 20*(1), 43. doi:10.1186/s41239-023-00411-8

Chance, C. (2020, October 29). The impact of artificial intelligence on education. *Forbes*. https://www.forbes.com/sites/calumchace/2020/10/29/the-impact-of-artificial-intelligence-on-education/?sh=60fd484a50df

Chang, E. (2019). *Brotopia: Breaking up the boys' club of Silicon Valley.* Penguin.

Chang, Y.-L., & Ke, J. (2023). Socially responsible artificial intelligence empowered people analytics: A novel framework towards sustainability. *Human Resource Development Review.* Advance online publication. doi:10.1177/15344843231200930

Chan, P. (2020). *Final bow for Yellowface: Dancing between intention and impact.* Bowker.

Chaudhry, M. A., Cukurova, M., & Luckin, R. (2022). A transparency index framework for AI in education. In *Artificial Intelligence in Education. Posters and Late Breaking Results, Workshops and Tutorials, Industry and Innovation Tracks, Practitioners' and Doctoral Consortium: 23rd International Conference, AIED 2022* (pp. 195–198). Springer. 10.1007/978-3-031-11647-6_33

Chechitelli, A. (2023). *AI writing detection update from Turnitin's chief product officer.* Retrieved from https://www.turnitin.com/blog/aiwriting-detection-update-from-turnitins-chief-product-officer

Chen, C. (2023, March 9). *AI will transform teaching and learning. Let's get it right.* Stanford University Human-Centered Artificial Intelligence. https://hai.stanford.edu/news/ai-will-transform-teaching-and-learning-lets-get-it-right

Chen, L., Zaharia, M., & Zou, J. (2023). *How is ChatGPT's behavior changing over time?* [Preprint]. https://arxiv.org/pdf/2307.09009.pdf

Chen, A., Gussenhoven, C., & Rietveld, T. (2004). Language-specificity in the perception of paralinguistic intonational meaning. *Language and Speech, 47*(4), 311–349. doi:10.1177/00238309040470040101 PMID:16038447

Chen, L., Chen, P., & Lin, Z. (2020). Artificial intelligence in education: A review. *IEEE Access : Practical Innovations, Open Solutions, 8*, 75264–75278. doi:10.1109/ACCESS.2020.2988510

Chen, X., Cheng, G., Zou, D., Zhong, B., & Xie, H. (2023). Artificial intelligent robots for precision education. *Journal of Educational Technology & Society, 26*, 171–186.

Chen, X., Xie, H., Zou, D., & Hwang, G. J. (2020). Application and theory gaps during the rise of artificial intelligence in education. *Computers. Education and Artificial Intelligence, 1*, 100002.

Chen, Y. C. (2022). Effects of technology-enhanced language learning on reducing EFL learners' public speaking anxiety. *Computer Assisted Language Learning*, 1–25. doi:10.1080/09588221.2022.2055083

Chen, Y., Jensen, S., Albert, L. J., Gupta, S., & Lee, T. (2023). Artificial intelligence (AI) student assistants in the classroom: Designing chatbots to support student success. *Information Systems Frontiers, 25*(1), 161–182. doi:10.1007/s10796-022-10291-4

Chen, Y.-W. (2019). Centering epistemologies on the margins and borders: Reflections on an Hispanic-serving institution's attempts to embrace equity and cultural wealth. *Communication Education, 68*(4), 516–521. doi:10.1080/03634523.2019.1645870

Chien, S. Y., & Hwang, G. J. (2023). A research proposal for an AI chatbot as a virtual patient agent to improve nursing students' clinical inquiry skills. *ICAIE, 2023*(2023), 13.

Chmielewski, D., & Richwine, L. (2023, November 9). Hollywood actors secure safeguards around AI use on screen. *Reuters.* https://www.reuters.com/business/media telecom/hollywood-actors-secure-safeguards-around-ai-use-screen-2023-11-09/

Chow, A. R. (2023, February 8). How ChatGPT managed to grow faster than TikTok or Instagram. *Time.* https://time.com/6253615/chatgpt-fastest-growing/

Chowdhary, K. (2023, July 26). OpenAI shuts down AI text detector due to low rate of accuracy. *Tech Report.*

Chui, M., Hazan, E., Roberts, R., Singla, A., Smaje, K., Sukharevsky, A., Yee, L., & Zemmel, R. (2023, June 14). The economic potential of generative AI: The next productivity frontier. *McKinsey*. https://www.mckinsey.com/capabilities/mckinsey-digital/our insights/the-economic-potential-of-generative-ai-the-next-productivity-frontier

Chui, M., Roberts, R., & Yee, L. (2022, December 20). *Generative AI is here: How tools like ChatGPT could change your business*. Quantum Black AI by McKinsey. Retrieved December 31, 2023, from https://www.mckinsey.com/capabilities/quantumblack/our-insights/generative-ai-is-here-how-tools-like-chatgpt-could-change-your-business

Cicero, M. T. (1949). On invention. The best kind of orator. Topics (H. M. Hubbell, Trans.). Cambridge: Harvard University Press. (Originally published ca. 90 B.C.E.)

Civil, B. (2023). ChatGPT can hinder students' critical thinking skills: Artificial intelligence is changing how students learn to write. *The Queen's Journal*. https://www.queensjournal.ca/story/2023-03-16/opinions/chatgpt-can-hinder-students-critical-thinking-skills/

Coeckelbergh, M., & Gunkel, D. J. (2023). ChatGPT: Deconstructing the debate and moving it forward. *AI & Society*, 1–11. doi:10.1007/s00146-023-01710-4

Coffey, L. (2023, October 23). Students outrun faculty in AI use. *Inside Higher Education*. https://www.insidehighered.com/news/tech-innovation/artificial intelligence/2023/10/31/most-students-outrunning-faculty-ai-use

Coffey, L. (2023, October 31). *Most students outrunning faculty in AI use, study finds*. Inside Higher Ed. https://www.insidehighered.com/news/tech-innovation/artificial-intelligence/2023/10/31/most-students-outrunning-faculty-ai-use

Cohen, J. (1996). Monster culture (seven theses). In J. J. Cohen (Ed.), *Monster theory: Reading culture* (pp. 3-25). University of Minnesota Press. doi:10.5749/j.ctttsq4d.4

Colby, K. M. (1975). *Artificial paranoia: A computer simulation of paranoid processes*. Pergamon Press.

Coleman, M. C., Santos, S. C., Cypher, J. M., Krummenacher, C., & Fleming, R. (2021). Lessons from the pandemic: Engaging wicked problems with transdisciplinary deliberation. *Journal of Communication Pedagogy*, *5*, 164–171. doi:10.31446/JCP.2021.2.17

Collins, H., & Pinch, T. (1998). *The golem at large: What you should know about technology* (1st ed.). Cambridge University Press.

Collste, G. (2016). *Ethics and communication: Global perspectives*. Rowman & Littlefield.

Computing & Communications Center. (2023). *Generative Artificial Intelligence | Center for Teaching Innovation*. https://teaching.cornell.edu/generative-artificial-intelligence#GenerativeAI

Condor, A., Litster, M., & Pardos, Z. (2021). *Automatic short answer grading with sbert on out-of-sample questions*. International Educational Data Mining Society.

Cope, B., Kalantzis, M., & Searsmith, D. (2021). Artificial intelligence for education: Knowledge and its assessment of AI-enabled learning ecologies. *Educational Philosophy and Theory*, *53*(12), 1229–1245. doi:10.1080/00131857.2020.1728732

Corbett, E. P. J., & Connors, R. J. (1998). *Classical rhetoric for the modern student* (4th ed.). Oxford University Press.

Cornell University Center for Teaching Innovation. (2023). *What is generative artificial intelligence (AI)?* https://teaching.cornell.edu/generative-artificial-intelligence

Cost, B. (2023, July 7). AI robots claim they can run the world better than humans: 'We can achieve great things.' *New York Post*. https://nypost.com/2023/07/07/ai-robots-claimthey-can-run-world-better-than-humans-we-can-achieve-great-things/

Cotton, D., Cotton, P. A., & Shipway, J. R. (2023). Chatting and cheating: Ensuring academic integrity in the era of ChatGPT. *Innovations in Education and Teaching International*, 1–12. doi:10.1080/14703297.2023.2190148

Coyle, J. (2023). In Hollywood writers' battle against AI, humans win (for now). *AP*. https://apnews.com/article/hollywood-ai-strike-wga-artificial-intelligence-39ab72582c3a15f77510c9c30a45ffc8

Craig, R. T. (2017, April 27). *Definitions and concepts of communication*. Definitions and Concepts of Communication. https://www.oxfordbibliographies.com/display/document/obo-9780199756841/obo-9780199756841-0172.xml

Craig, R. T. (2021). Response. In M. H. Rich & J. S. Robles (Eds.), *Practicing communication theory; Exploring, applying, and teaching the constitutive metamodel* (pp. 191–210). Cognella Academic Publishing.

Crawford, J., Cowling, M., & Allen, K. A. (2023). Leadership is needed for ethical ChatGPT: Character, assessment, and learning using artificial intelligence (AI). *Journal of University Teaching & Learning Practice*, *20*(3). Advance online publication. doi:10.53761/1.20.3.02

Creswell, J. W. (2014). *A Concise Introduction to Mixed Methods Research*. SAGE.

Creswell, J. W., & Poth, C. N. (2018). *Qualitative inquiry and research design: Choosing among five approaches* (4th ed.). Sage.

Cronin, M. W. (1994). Interactive video instruction for teaching organizational techniques in public speaking. *Basic Communication Course Annual, 6*, 19–35. https://ecommons.udayton.edu/bcca/vol6/iss1/6

Cummings, K., & Rief, J. (2023). Health praxis in the age of artificial intelligence: Diagnostics, caregiving, and reimagining the role(s) of healthcare practitioners. In T. Sikka (Ed.), *Genetic science and new digital technologies: Science and technology studies and health praxis* (pp. 103–131). Bristol University Press. doi:10.56687/9781529223330-007

D'Agostino, S. (2023, April 18). The oncoming AI Ed-tech 'tsunami'. *Inside Higher Ed*. https://www.insidehighered.com/news/tech-innovation/artificial-intelligence/2023/04/18/oncoming-ai-ed-tech-tsunami

D'Agostino, S. (2023, January 11). *ChatGPT advice academics can use now*. Inside Higher Ed. https://www.insidehighered.com/news/2023/01/12/academic-experts-offer-advice-chatgpt

Dalvi, C., Rathod, M., Patil, S., Gite, S., & Kotecha, K. (2021). A survey of AI-based facial emotion recognition: Features, ML & DL techniques, age-wise datasets and future directions. IEEE Access. doi:10.1109/ACCESS.2021.3131733

Daniels, J. (2023). *How generative AI can affect your business' data privacy*. https://www.forbes.com/sites/forbesbusinesscouncil/2023/05/01/how-generative-ai-can-affect-your-business-data-privacy/?sh=6d610b83702d

Dannels, D., & Housley Gaffney, A. (2009). Communication across the curriculum and in the disciplines: A call for scholarly cross-curricular advocacy. *Communication Education, 58*(1), 124–153. doi:10.1080/03634520802527288

Darwin, C. (1859). *On the origin of species*. John Murray.

Davenport, T. H., & Prusak, L. (2000). *Working knowledge: How organizations manage what they know*. Harvard Business School. doi:10.1145/348772.348775

Davies, N. (2023, November 15). *The rise and fall of prompt engineering: Fad or future?* KDnuggets. https://www.kdnuggets.com/the-rise-and-fall-of-prompt-engineering-fad-or-future

Davies, R. S. (2011). Understanding technology Literacy: A framework for evaluating Educational Technology Integration. *TechTrends, 55*(5), 45–52. doi:10.1007/s11528-011-0527-3

Davison, R. M., Laumer, S., Tarafdar, M., & Wong, L. M. (2023). Pickled eggs: Generativeaias research assistant or co-author? *Information Systems Journal, 33*(5), 989–994. doi:10.1111/isj.12455

De Gagne, J. C. (2023). The state of artificial intelligence in nursing education: Past, present, and future directions. *International Journal of Environmental Research and Public Health, 20*(6), 4884. doi:10.3390/ijerph20064884 PMID:36981790

De Witte, M. (2023, February 13). How will ChatGPT change the way we think and work? Stanford scholar examines. *Stanford News*. Retrieved from https://news.stanford.edu/2023/02/13/will-chatgpt-change-way-think-work/

Derevianko, A., Pizzoli, S. F. M., Pesapane, F., Rotili, A., Monzani, D., Grasso, R., Cassano, E., & Pravettoni, G. (2023). The use of Artificial Intelligence (AI) in the radiology field: What is the state of doctor–patient communication in cancer diagnosis? *Cancers (Basel), 15*(2), 2. Advance online publication. doi:10.3390/cancers15020470 PMID:36672417

Derin, T., Sari Nursafira, M., Saltri Yudar, R., Sari Gowasa, N., & Hamuddin, B. (2020). Persuasive communication: What do existing literature tells us about persuasive communication among students? *Utamax: Journal of Ultimate Research and Trends in Education, 2*(1), 12–18. doi:10.31849/utamax.v2i1.3468

Di Placito, M. L., & Mortensen, R. (2023). Applying AI efforts to student assessments: That is, alternative innovations. *The Interdisciplinary Journal of Student Success, 2*, 93–108.

Diablo Valley College. (2023). *What are multimedia projects?* Diablo Valley College Library. https://dvc.libguides.com/copyright/multimedia#:~:text=What%20Are%20Multimedia20Projects%3F,music%2C%20images%2C%20and%20text

Dieterle, E., Dede, C., & Walker, M. (2022). The cyclical ethical effects of using artificial intelligence in education. *AI & Society*. Advance online publication. doi:10.1007/s00146-022-01497-w PMID:36185064

Dignum, V. (2018). Ethics in artificial intelligence: Introduction to the special issue. *Ethics and Information Technology, 20*(1), 1–3. doi:10.1007/s10676-018-9450-z

Dogoulis, P., Kordopatis-Zilos, G., Kompatsiaris, I., & Papadopoulos, S. (2023). Improving synthetically generated image detection in cross-concept settings. *Proceedings of the 2nd ACM International Workshop on Multimedia AI against Disinformation*, 28–35. 10.1145/3592572.3592846

Domínguez Figaredo, D., & Stoyanovich, J. (2023). Responsible AI literacy: A stakeholder-first approach. *Big Data & Society, 10*(2). Advance online publication. doi:10.1177/20539517231219958

Donovan, E. E., Brown, L. E., Lindstadt, C., Table, B., Heidari, E., Coolidge, A., Omran, S., & Rush, S. (2021). The 12 Fundamentals of Highly Effective Communicators: Teaching theory-based professional communication to pharmacy students. *Journal of Communication Pedagogy, 4*, 21–37. doi:10.31446/JCP.2021.1.03

Donsbach, W. (2006). The identity of communication research. *Journal of Communication, 56*(3), 437–448. doi:10.1111/j.1460-2466.2006.00294.x

Dove, G., & Fayard, A. L. (2020). *Monsters, metaphors, and machine learning* [Conference paper]. CHI 2020, Honolulu, HI. https://chi2020.acm.org/

Doyle, W., & Ponder, G. A. (1977). The practicality ethic in teacher decision-making. *Interchange (Washington, D.C.), 8*, 1–12.

Draxler, F., Werner, A., Lehmann, F., Hoppe, M., Schmidt, A., Buschek, D., & Welsch, R. (2023). The AI ghostwriter effect: When users do not perceive ownership of AI-generated text but self-declare as authors. *ACM Transactions on Computer-Human Interaction*, 3637875. Advance online publication. doi:10.1145/3637875

Dreyfus, H. (1979). *What computers can't do*. Harper Colophon Books.

Drori, I., Zhang, S., Shuttleworth, R., Tang, L., Lu, A., Ke, E., Liu, K., Chen, L., Tran, S., Cheng, N., Wang, R., Singh, N., Patti, T. L., Lynch, J., Shporer, A., Verma, N., Wu, E., & Strang, G. (2022). A neural network solves, explains, and generates university math problems by program synthesis and few-shot learning at human level. *Proceedings of the National Academy of Sciences of the United States of America, 119*(32), e2123433119. Advance online publication. doi:10.1073/pnas.2123433119 PMID:35917350

Dubova, M. (2022). Building human-like communicative intelligence: A grounded perspective. *Cognitive Systems Research, 72*, 63–79. doi:10.1016/j.cogsys.2021.12.002

Duckworth, A., & Ungar, L. (2023, January 19). Don't ban chatbots in classrooms — use them to change how we teach. *Los Angeles Times*. Retrieved from https://www.latimes.com/opinion/story/2023-01-19/chatgpt-ai-education-testing-teaching-changes

Dumaine, D., Derdeyn, L., Ranieri, E., & Reis, A. (2023, May 22-24). *Interdisciplinary core-compliant teaching with project-based learning: Building a culture* [Conference presentation]. Lilly Conference; Evidence-Based Teaching and Learning, Austin, TX, United States. https://www.lillyconferences-tx.com/2023schedule

Dutta, M. J. (2007). Communicating about culture and health: Theorizing culture-centered and cultural sensitivity approaches. *Communication Theory, 17*(3), 304–328. doi:10.1111/j.1468-2885.2007.00297.x

Dutta, M. J., Moana-Johnson, G., & Elers, C. (2020). COVID-19 and the pedagogy of culture-centered community radical democracy: A response from Aotearoa New Zealand. *Journal of Communication Pedagogy, 3*, 11–19. doi:10.31446/JCP.2020.03

Dweck, C. S. (2016). Mindset: The new psychology of success (Updated edition). Random House.

Dwivedi, Y. K., Hughes, L., Ismagilova, E., Aarts, G., Coombs, C., Crick, T., Duan, Y., Dwivedi, R., Edwards, J., Eirug, A., Galanos, V., Ilavarasan, P. V., Janssen, M., Jones, P., Kar, A. K., Kizgin, H., Kronemann, B., Lal, B., Lucini, B., ... Williams, M. D. (2021). Artificial Intelligence (AI): Multidisciplinary perspectives on emerging challenges, opportunities, and agenda for research, practice and policy. *International Journal of Information Management, 57*, 101994. doi:10.1016/j.ijinfomgt.2019.08.002

Dwivedi, Y. K., Kshetri, N., Hughes, L., Slade, E. L., Jeyaraj, A., Kar, A. K., Baabdullah, A. M., Koohang, A., Raghavan, V., Ahuja, M., Albanna, H., Albashrawi, M. A., Al-Busaidi, A. S., Balakrishnan, J., Barlette, Y., Basu, S., Bose, I., Brooks, L., Buhalis, D., ... Wright, R. (2023). Opinion Paper: "So what if ChatGPT wrote it?" Multidisciplinary perspectives on opportunities, challenges and implications of generative conversational AI for research, practice and policy. *International Journal of Information Management, 71*, 102642. doi:10.1016/j.ijinfomgt.2023.102642

Dwivedi, Y. K., Wastell, D., Laumer, S., Henriksen, H. Z., Myers, M. D., Bunker, D., Elbanna, A., Ravishankar, M. N., & Srivastava, S. C. (2015). Research on information systems failures and successes: Status update and future directions. *Information Systems Frontiers, 17*(1), 143–157. doi:10.1007/s10796-014-9500-y

Eadie, W. (2009). *21st century communication: A reference handbook. Sage (Atlanta, Ga.)*. Advance online publication. doi:10.4135/9781412964005

Eadie, W. F. (2022). *When communication became a discipline*. Rowman & Littlefield.

Earley, P. M. (1994). *Goals 2000: Educate America Act: Implications for teacher educators*. AACTE Publications.

Eaton, S. E. (2021). *Plagiarism in higher education: Tackling tough topics in academic integrity*. ABC-CLIO. doi:10.5040/9798400697142

Education Data Initiative. (2023). *College enrollment & student demographic statistics.* https://educationdata.org/college-enrollment-statistics

Edula, R., Shengcheng, L., Sasaki, H., Viladiro, R., & Roy, D. (2023). Personalized learning systems in smart education: A review of the literature & pilot feasibility discussion. *ETLTC-ICETM2023 international conference proceedings: ICT integration in technical education & entertainment technologies and management.* 10.1063/5.0182560

Edwards, A. A. H. (2021). From novel to necessary. In J. M. Valenzano III, (Ed.), *Post-Pandemic Pedagogy: A Paradigm Shift* (pp. 37–56). Lexington Books.

Edwards, A., & Edwards, C. (2018). Human–machine communication in the classroom. In M. L. Houser & A. M. Hosek (Eds.), *Handbook of instructional communication: Rhetorical and relational perspectives* (2nd ed., pp. 184–194). Taylor & Francis.

Ehninger, D., & Brockriede, W. (1966). *Decision by debate.* Dodd, Mead & Company.

Ehsan, U., Liao, Q. V., Muller, M., Riedl, M. O., & Weisz, J. D. (2021). Expanding explainability: Towards social transparency in AI systems. In *Proceedings of the 2021 CHI Conference on Human Factors in Computing Systems* (pp. 1–19). 10.1145/3411764.3445188

Eke, D. O. (2023). ChatGPT and the rise of generative AI: Threat to academic integrity? *Journal of Responsible Technology, 13*(1), 100060. doi:10.1016/j.jrt.2023.100060

El Mortaji, L. (2022). Public speaking and online peer feedback in a blended learning EFL course environment: Students' perceptions. *English Language Teaching, 15*(2), 31–49. doi:10.5539/elt.v15n2p31

Eliade, M. (1954). *The myth of the eternal return* (W. R. Trask, Trans.). Kingsport Press.

Elish, M. C., & Boyd, D. (2018). Situating methods in the magic of big data and AI. *Communication Monographs, 85*(1), 57–80. doi:10.1080/03637751.2017.1375130

Elkhatat, A. M., Elsaid, K., & Almeer, S. (2021). Some students plagiarism tricks, and tips for effective check. *International Journal for Educational Integrity, 17*(1), 15. Advance online publication. doi:10.1007/s40979-021-00082-w

Elkhatat, A. M., Elsaid, K., & Almeer, S. (2023). Evaluating the efficacy of AI content detection tools in differentiating between human and AI-generated text. *International Journal for Educational Integrity, 19*(1), 17. Advance online publication. doi:10.1007/s40979-023-00140-5

Elsevier. (2023). *The use of AI and AI-assisted writing technologies in scientific writing. Frequently asked questions.* https://www.elsevier.com/about/policies/publishing-ethics/the-use-of-ai-and-ai-assisted-writing-technologies-in-scientific-writing

English, E., Llano, S., Mitchell, G. R., Morrison, C. E., Rief, J., & Woods, C. (2007). Debate as a weapon of mass destruction. *Communication and Critical/Cultural Studies, 4*(2), 221–225. doi:10.1080/14791420701296646

Ess, Ch. (2020). *Digital media ethics* (3rd ed.). Polity Press.

Euchner, J. (2023). Generative AI. *Research Technology Management, 66*(3), 71–74. doi:10.1080/08956308.2023.2188861

Fandrich, A. R. (n.d.). *The integration of faith in the computer classroom: Some ethical concerns.* Retrieved from https://www.christintheclassroom.org

Farahani, M. V. (2020). *Adequacy in machine vs. human translation: A comparative study of English and Persian languages.* Applied Linguistics Research Journal. doi:10.14744/alrj.2020.98700

Farazouli, A., Cerratto-Pargman, T., Bolander-Laksov, K., & McGrath, C. (2023). Hello GPT! Goodbye home examination? An exploratory study of AI chatbots impact on university teachers' assessment practices. *Assessment & Evaluation in Higher Education*, 1–13. Advance online publication. doi:10.1080/02602938.2023.2241676

Fausto-Sterling, A. (1992). *Myths of gender: Biological theories about women and men*. Basic Books.

Feagin, J. R. (2013). *The white racial frame: centuries of racial framing and counter framing* (2nd ed.). Routledge. doi:10.4324/9780203076828

Federal Trade Commission (FTC). (2023). *Chatbots, deepfakes, and voice clones: AI deception for sale*. https://www.ftc.gov/business-guidance/blog/2023/03/chatbots-deepfakes-voice-clones-ai-deception-sale

Feminist Asian Dad. (2019, July 18). *Go back to your country*. https://feministasiandad.com/2019/07/18/go-back-to-your-country/

FERPA. (2021). *Family educational rights and privacy act (FERPA)*. https://www2.ed.gov/policy/gen/guid/fpco/ferpa/index.html

Ferrara, E. (2023). Should ChatGPT be biased? Challenges and risks of bias in large language models. *Machine Learning with Applications*, *1*, 1–23. doi:10.48550/arXiv.2304.03738

Feuerriegel, S., Hartmann, J., Janiesch, C., & Zschech, P. (2023). Generative AI. *Business & Information Systems Engineering*, 1–16. doi:10.1007/s12599-023-00834-7

Fisher, M., & Hayes-Jacobs, H. (2023). Prompt literacy: A key for AI-based learning. *Educational Leadership*, 1–2.

Fisher, P. (1999). Narrative as human communication paradigm. In J. L. Lucaites, C. M. Condit, & S. Caudill (Eds.), *Contemporary rhetorical theory: A reader* (pp. 265–287). Guilford Press. (Original work published 1984)

Fiske, S. T., & Taylor, S. E. (1984). *Social cognition*. Addison-Wesley.

Fister, B., & Head, A. J. (2023, May 4). *Getting a grip on ChatGPT*. Inside Higher Ed. Retrieved from https://www.insidehighered.com/opinion/views/2023/05/04/getting-grip-chatgpt

Fitzpatrick, D., Fox, A., & Weinstein, B. (2023). *The AI classroom: The ultimate guide to artificial intelligence in education*. TeacherGoals.

Foerster, H. V. (2007). *Understanding Understanding: Essays on Cybernetics and Cognition*. Springer.

Følstad, A., & Taylor, C. (2021). Investigating the user experience of customer service chatbot interaction: A framework for qualitative analysis of chatbot dialogues. *Quality and User Experience*, *6*(1), 6. doi:10.1007/s41233-021-00046-5

Foltýnek, T., Meuschke, N., & Gipp, B. (2019). Academic plagiarism detection. *ACM Computing Surveys*, *52*(6), 1–42. doi:10.1145/3345317

Foster, D. (2023). *Generative deep learning: Teaching machines to paint, write, compose, and play*. O'Reilly Media, Inc.

Foucault, M. (1998). What is an author? (J. V. Harari, Trans.). In FaubionJ. D. (Ed.), *Michel Foucault: Aesthetics, Method, and Epistemology* (pp. 205–222). The New York Press. (Original work published 1969)

Fourtane, S. (2023, August 3). *How universities can better prepare students for a future with AI*. Fierce Education. https://www.fierceeducation.com/leadership/how-universities-can-better-preparestudents-future-asi

Frąckiewicz, M. (2023, May 4). *The power of AI in promoting gender equality in education*. TS2 Space.

Fredriksson, A. (2022). *A phenomenology of attention and the unfamiliar: Encounters with the unknown.* Palgrave Macmillan. doi:10.1007/978-3-031-14117-1

FryeB. L. (2022). Should using an AI text generator to produce academic writing be plagiarism? *Fordham Intellectual Property, Media & Entertainment Law Journal,* 947–969. https://ssrn.com/abstract=4292283

Fuchs, K. (2023). Exploring the opportunities and challenges of NLP models in higher education: Is ChatGPT a blessing or a curse? *Frontiers in Education, 8,* 1166682. Advance online publication. doi:10.3389/feduc.2023.1166682

Future of Life Institute. (2023). *Pause giant AI experiments: An open letter.* https://futureoflife.org/open-letter/pause-giant-ai-experiments/

Gao, C. A., Howard, F. M., Markov, N. S., Dyer, E. C., Ramesh, S., Luo, Y., & Pearson, A. T. (2022). Comparing scientific abstracts generated by ChatGPT to original abstracts using an artificial intelligence output detector, plagiarism detector, and blinded human reviewers. *NPJ Digital Medicine, 6*(1). Advance online publication. doi:10.1038/s41746-023-00819-6

Garib, A. (2022). "Actually, it's real work": EFL teachers' perceptions of technology-assisted project-based language learning in Lebanon, Libya, and Syria. *TESOL Quarterly, 57*(4), 1434–1462. doi:10.1002/tesq.3202

Gašević, D., Greiff, S., & Shaffer, D. W. (2022). Towards strengthening links between learning analytics and assessment: Challenges and potentials of a promising new bond. *Computers in Human Behavior, 134,* 107304. doi:10.1016/j.chb.2022.107304

Gault, M. (2023, January 17). Conservatives are panicking about AI bias, think ChatGPT has gone 'woke'. *Vice.* https://www.vice.com/en/article/93a4qe/conservatives-panicking-about-ai-bias-years-too-late-think-chatgpt-has-gone-woke

Gaynor, J. W. (2020). Peer review in the classroom: Student perceptions, peer feedback quality and the role of assessment. *Assessment & Evaluation in Higher Education, 45*(5), 758–775. doi:10.1080/02602938.2019.1697424

Gebru, T., Morgenstern, J., Vecchione, B., Vaughan, J. W., Wallach, H. III, Iii, H. D., & Crawford, K. (2021). Datasheets for datasets. *Communications of the ACM, 64*(12), 86–92. doi:10.1145/3458723

Geertz, C. (1973). *The Interpretation of cultures.* Basic Books.

Gerbaudo, P. (2017). From cyber-autonomism to cyber-populism: An ideological history of digital activism. *TripleC (Cognition, Communication, Co-Operation): Open Access Journal for a Global Sustainable Information Society, 15*(2), 477–489. https://doi-org.easydb.angelo.edu/10.31269/triplec.v15i2.773

Gershon, M. (2018). *How to use Bloom's taxonomy in the classroom: Great teaching made easy.* Learning Sciences International.

Getchell, K. M., Carradini, S., Cardon, P. W., Fleischmann, C., Ma, H., Aritz, J., & Stapp, J. (2022). Artificial intelligence in business communication: The changing landscape of research and teaching. *Business and Professional Communication Quarterly, 85*(1), 7–33. doi:10.1177/23294906221074311

Ghai, B., & Mueller, K. (2021). Fluent: An AI augmented writing tool for people who stutter. *Proceedings of the 23rd International ACM SIGACCESS Conference on Computers and Accessibility,* 1–8. 10.1145/3441852.3471211

Ghosh, S., & Caliskan, A. (2023). 'Person' == light-skinned, Western man, and sexualization of women of color: Stereotypes in Stable Diffusion. *Findings of the Association for Computational Linguistics: EMNLP, 2023,* 6971–6985. doi:10.18653/v1/2023.findings-emnlp.465

Gilbert, D. T., & Hixon, J. G. (1991). The trouble of thinking: Activation and application of stereotypic beliefs. *Journal of Personality and Social Psychology, 60*(4), 509–517. doi:10.1037/0022-3514.60.4.509

Gillotte, J. L. (2019). Copyright infringement in AI-generated artworks. *U.C. Davis Law Review, 53*(1), 2655–2676.

Gilson, A., Safranek, C. W., Huang, T., Socrates, V., Chi, L., Taylor, R. A., & Chartash, D. (2023). How does ChatGPT perform on the United States medical licensing examination? The implications of large language models for medical education and knowledge assessment. *JMIR Medical Education, 9*, e45312. doi:10.2196/45312 PMID:36753318

Glen, S. (2021, May 9). AI: The next great art forger. *Data Science Central.* https://www.datasciencecentral.com/ai-the-next-great-art-forger/

Goffman, E. (1974). *Presentation of self in everyday life.* Viking Press.

González-Calatayud, V., Prendes-Espinosa, P., & Roig-Vila, R. (2021). Artificial intelligence for student assessment: A systematic review. *Applied Sciences (Basel, Switzerland), 11*(6), 5467. Advance online publication. doi:10.3390/app11125467

Gordon, R. (2023, March 3). *Large language models are biased. Can logic help save them?* MIT News | Massachusetts Institute of Technology. https://news.mit.edu/2023/large-language-models-are-biased-can-logic-help-save-them-0303

Grainger College of Engeering. (2020). *PLATO* [Online Newsletter]. https://grainger.illinois.edu/news/magazine/plato

Greene, R. W., & Hicks, D. (2005). Lost convictions: Debating both sides and the ethical self-fashioning of liberal citizens. *Cultural Studies, 19*(1), 100–126. doi:10.1080/09502380500040928

Gross, N. (2023). What ChatGPT tells us about gender: A cautionary tale about performativity and gender biases in AI. *Social Sciences (Basel, Switzerland), 12*(8), 435–450. doi:10.3390/socsci12080435

Grosuleac, A., Budulan, S., & Rebedea, T. (2020). Seeking an Empathy-abled Conversational Agent. RoCHI, 103-107. doi:10.37789/rochi.2020.1.1.16

Grunig, J. E. (2006). Furnishing the edifice: Ongoing research on public relations as a strategic management function. *Journal of Public Relations Research, 18*(2), 151–176. doi:10.1207/s1532754xjprr1802_5

Grynbaum, M. M., & Mac, R. (2023, December 27). The Times Sues OpenAI and Microsoft Over A.I. Use of Copyrighted Work. *The New York Times.* https://www.nytimes.com/2023/12/27/business/media/new-york-times-open-ai-microsoft-lawsuit.html

Guan, C., Mou, J., & Jiang, Z. (2020). Artificial intelligence innovation in education: A twenty year data-driven historical analysis. *International Journal of Innovation Studies, 4*(4), 134–147. doi:10.1016/j.ijis.2020.09.001

Gunaratne, S. A. (2021). Resolving East-West rifts in Craig's metamodel. In M. H. Rich & J. S. Robles (Eds.), *Practicing communication theory; Exploring, applying, and teaching the constitutive metamodel* (pp. 127–151). Cognella Academic Publishing.

GunkelD. J. (2012a) Communication and artificial intelligence: opportunities and challenges for the 21st century. *Communication+1, 1*(1). doi:10.7275/R5QJ7F7R

Gunn, J. (2018). *Speech craft.* Bedford/St. Martin's.

Gupta, M., Akiri, C., Aryal, K., Parker, E., & Praharaj, L. (2023). From ChatGPT to threatGPT: Impact of generative AI in cybersecurity and privacy. *IEEE Access : Practical Innovations, Open Solutions, 11*, 80218–80245. doi:10.1109/ACCESS.2023.3300381

Guzman, A. L. (Ed.). (2018). Human-machine communication: Rethinking communication, technology, and ourselves. Peter Lang Inc., International Academic Publishers. doi:10.3726/b14399

Guzman, A. L., & Lewis, S. C. (2020). Artificial intelligence and communication: A human machine communication research agenda. *New Media & Society, 22*(1), 70–86. doi:10.1177/1461444819858691

Hacker, P., Engel, A., & Mauer, M. (2023). Regulating ChatGPT and other large generative AI models. *Proceedings of the ACM Conference on Fairness, Accountability, and Transparency,* 1112–1123. https://dl.acm.org/doi/pdf/10.1145/3593013.3594067

Haenlein, M., & Kaplan, A. (2019). A brief history of artificial intelligence: On the past, present, and future of artificial intelligence. *California Management Review, 64*(2), 347–392. doi:10.1177/0008125619864925

Halaweh, M. (2023). ChatGPT in education: Strategies for responsible implementation. *Contemporary Educational Technology, 15*(2), 421–431. doi:10.30935/cedtech/13036

Hall, R. (2008). The "embedded" librarian in a freshman speech class: Information literacy instruction in action. *College & Research Libraries News, 69*(1), 28–30. doi:10.5860/crln.69.1.7922

Hamilton, D. L., & Sherman, J. W. (1994). Stereotypes. In R. S. Wyer & T. K. Srull (Eds.), *Handbook of social cognition* (pp. 1–68). Lawrence Erlbaum Associates.

Hamilton, D. L., Sherman, S. J., & Ruvolo, C. M. (1990). Stereotype-based expectancies: Effects on information processing and social behavior. *The Journal of Social Issues, 46*(2), 35–60. doi:10.1111/j.1540-4560.1990.tb01922.x

Hancock, J. T., Naaman, M., & Levy, K. (2020). AI-mediated communication: Definition, research agenda, and ethical considerations. *Journal of Computer-Mediated Communication, 25*(1), 89–100. doi:10.1093/jcmc/zmz022

Harrigan, C. (2008). Against dogmatism: A continued defense of switch side debate. *Contemporary Argumentation and Debate, 29*, 37–66.

Hartelius, E. (2018). Speech craft review. *The Quarterly Journal of Speech, 104*(3), 352–355. doi:10.1080/00335630.2018.1478663

HarvardUniversity.org. (2023, August 30). *Getting started with prompts for text-based Generative AI tools.* Harvard University Information Technology. https://huit.harvard.edu/news/ai-prompts

Heaven, W. D. (2023a, November 16). Google DeepMind wants to define what counts as artificial general intelligence. *MIT Technology Review*. https://www.technologyreview.com/2023/11/16/1083498/google-deepmind-what-is-artificial-general-intelligence-agi/

Heaven, W. D. (2023b). 6 big questions for generative AI. *MIT Technological Review, 127*(1), 30–37.

Heidelberg, R. L. (2023). Artificial intelligence and the modern condition of expertise. *Administration & Society, 56*(1), 73–95. doi:10.1177/00953997231204968

Heitzmann, N., Opitz, A., Stadler, M., Sommerhoff, D., Fink, M. C., Obersteiner, A., Schmidmaier, R., Neuhaus, B. J., Ufer, S., Seidel, T., Fischer, M. R., & Fischer, F. (2021). Cross-disciplinary research on learning and instruction – Coming to terms. *Frontiers in Psychology, 11*, 1–6. doi:10.3389/fpsyg.2021.562658 PMID:34045986

Helyer, R. (2023, October 3). What are the copyright rules around AI art? *Make Use Of.* https://www.makeuseof.com/copyright-rules-ai-art/

Henderson, A. T., & Mapp, K. L. (2002). *A new wave of evidence: The impact of school, family, and community connections on student achievement. annual synthesis, 2002.* National Center for Family & Community Connections with Schools, Southwest Educational Development Laboratory. https://eric.ed.gov/?id=ED474521

Henebery, B. (2023). New AI detector spots ChatGPT content with 98% accuracy. *The Educator*. https://www.theeducatoronline.com/k12/news/new-ai-detector-spots-chatgpt-content-with-98-accuracy/282285

Herbst, J. (2004). The Yale Report of 1828. *International Journal of the Classical Tradition*, *11*(11), 213–231. doi:10.1007/BF02720033

Herold, B. (2019, November 5). *What is personalized learning?* Education Week. https://www.edweek.org/technology/what-is-personalized-learning/2019/11

Herold, B. (2022, April 12). Why schools need to talk about racial bias in AI-powered technologies. *Education Week*. https://www.edweek.org/leadership/why-schools-need-to-talk-about-racial-bias-in-ai-powered-technologies/2022/04

Herrick, J. (2018). *The history and theory of rhetoric: An introduction*. Routledge.

Herrman, J. (2023, November 7). What does it mean that Elon Musk's new AI Chatbot is 'Anti-Woke'? *Intelligencer*. https://nymag.com/intelligencer/2023/11/elon-musks-grok ai-bot-is-anti-woke-what-does-that-mean.html

Heston, T. F., & Khun, C. (2023). Prompt engineering in medical education. *International Medical Education*, *2*(3), 198–205. doi:10.3390/ime2030019

Hilton, J. L., & von Hippel, W. (1996). Stereotypes. *Annual Review of Psychology*, *47*(1), 237–272. doi:10.1146/annurev.psych.47.1.237 PMID:15012482

Hinton, P. R. (2000). *Stereotypes, culture, and cognition: Psychology focus*. Psychology Press.

Hirsh-Pasek, K., & Blinkoff, E. (2023, January 9). ChatGPT: Educational friend or foe. *Brookings*. https://www.brookings.edu/articles/chatgpt-educational-friend-or-foe/

Hogan, J. M., Kurr, J. A., Bergmaier, M. J., & Johnson, J. D. (Eds.). (2017). *Speech and debate as civic education*. The Pennsylvania State University Press. doi:10.1515/9780271080369

Hohenstein, J., Kizilcec, R. F., DiFranzo, D., Aghajari, Z., Mieczkowski, H., Levy, K., Naaman, M., Hancock, J., & Jung, M. F. (2023). Artificial intelligence in communication impacts language and social relationships. *Scientific Reports*, *13*(1), 5487. Advance online publication. doi:10.1038/s41598-023-30938-9 PMID:37015964

Ho, K. K., & Wong, E. S. (2012). Embedded librarians in the classroom: A case study at HKUST Library. *Proceedings of the IATUL Conferences*.

Holliday, A. (2016). Doing & writing qualitative research. *Sage (Atlanta, Ga.)*.

Holmes, W., & Porayska-Pomsta, K. (2022). *The ethics of artificial intelligence in education: Practices, challenges, and debates*. Taylor & Francis. doi:10.4324/9780429329067

Holstein, K., Wortman Vaughan, J., Daumé, H. III, Dudik, M., & Wallach, H. (2019). Improving fairness in machine learning systems. *Proceedings of the 2019 CHI Conference on Human Factors in Computing Systems*. 10.1145/3290605.3300830

Hossain, A. (2023). *ChatGPT in higher education: Advantages, challenges, and impact on students, educators, and institutional leaders*. Digital Readiness and Intelligent Systems.

Hristova, B. (2023). *Some students are using ChatGPT to cheat—Here's how schools are trying to stop it*. CBC News. Retrieved from https://www.cbc.ca/news/canada/hamilton/chatgpt-school-cheating-1.6734580

Hsu, T. C., Huang, H. L., Hwang, G. J., & Chen, M. S. (2023). Effects of incorporating an expert decision-making mechanism into chatbots on students' achievement, enjoyment, and anxiety. *Journal of Educational Technology & Society*, *26*, 218–231.

Hu, K. (2023, February 2). *ChatGPT sets record for fastest-growing user base - analyst note*. Reuters. https://www.reuters.com/technology/chatgpt-sets-record-fastest-growing-user-base-analyst-note-2023-02-01/

Huang, K. (2023, January 16). Alarmed by A.I. chatbots, universities start revamping how they teach. *The New York Times*. https://www.nytimes.com/2023/01/16/technology/chatgpt-artificial-intelligence-universities.html

Huang, M.-H., & Rust, R. (2018). Artificial intelligence in service. *Journal of Service Research, 21*(2), 109467051775245. doi:10.1177/1094670517752459

Huggard, G. (2023). *ChatGPT for educators: From lesson planning to assessment (leveraging the power of AI in the education process)*. Independently Published.

Hutiri, W. T., & Ding, A. Y. (2022). Bias in automated speaker recognition. In *ACM conference on fairness, accountability, and transparency* (pp. 230–247). ACM. doi:10.1145/3531146.3533089

Hutson, J., Jeevanjee, T., Graaf, V., Lively, J., Weber, J., Weir, G., Arnone, K., Carnes, G., Vosevich, K., Plate, D., Leary, M., & Edele, S. (2022). Artificial Intelligence and the disruption of higher education: Strategies for integrations across disciplines. *Creative Education, 13*(12), 3953–3980. doi:10.4236/ce.2022.1312253

Hwang, G. J., & Chang, C. Y. (2021). A review of opportunities and challenges of chatbots in education. *Interactive Learning Environments*. Advance online publication. doi:10.1080/10494820.2021.1952615

Hwang, G. J., Xie, H., Wah, B. W., & Gasevic, D. (2020). Vision, challenges, roles, and research issues of artificial intelligence in education. Computers and Education. *Artificial Intelligence, 1*(13). Advance online publication. doi:10.1016.j.caeai.2020.100001

Hwang, G., & Tu, Y. (2021). Roles and research trends of artificial intelligence in mathematics education: A bibliometric mapping analysis and systematic review. *Mathematics, 9*(6), 584. doi:10.3390/math9060584

IBM. (n.d.). *What are AI hallucinations?* https://www.ibm.com/topics/ai-hallucinations

Ihde, D. (1990). *Technology and the lifeworld: From garden to earth*. Indiana University Press.

Iliescu, M. (2016). Istoria și filosofia roboților industriali. *Studii și Comunicări, 9*(9), 401–411.

Illia, L., Colleoni, E., & Zyglidopoulos, S. (2023). Ethical implications of text generation in the age of artificial intelligence. *Business Ethics, the Environment & Responsibility, 32*(1), 201–210. doi:10.1111/beer.12479

Inoue, N. (2023). *How far can we go in computer-assisted debating? In RicercAzione: Six -monthly Journal on Learning*. Research and Innovation in Education. doi:10.32076/ RA15303

Introducing ChatGPT. (n.d.). *OpenAI.com*. https://openai.com/blog/chatgpt

Isin, E., & Ruppert, E. (2019). Data's empire: Postcolonial data politics. In D. Bigo, E. Isin, & E. Ruppert (Eds.), *Data politics* (pp. 207–227). Routledge. doi:10.4324/9781315167305-11

Iskender, A. (2023). Holy or unholy? Interview with open AI's ChatGPT. *European Journal of Tourism Research, 34*, 3414. doi:10.54055/ejtr.v34i.3169

Ismail, H., Hussein, N., Harous, S., & Khalil, A. (2023). Survey of personalized learning software systems: A taxonomy of environments, learning content, and user models. *Education Sciences, 13*(7), 741. doi:10.3390/educsci13070741

Ito, R. B. (2014). "A certain slant": A brief history of Hollywood Yellowface. *Bright Lights Film*. https://brightlightsfilm.com/certain-slant-brief-history-hollywood-yellowface/

Jackson, S. (2024, January 5). Sam Altman says tech world 'should be united' in supporting Muslim colleagues. *Business Insider.* https://www.businessinsider.com/openai-samaltman-urges-tech-community-support-muslim-peers-2024-1

Jackson, M. H., & McDowell, S. D. (2002). Enhancing discourse on new technology within higher education. In W. H. Dutton & B. D. Loader (Eds.), *Digital academe: New media in higher education and learning* (pp. 318–327). Routledge.

Jackson, S. (2015). Design thinking in argumentation theory and practice. *Argumentation, 29*(3), 243–263. doi:10.1007/s10503-015-9353-7

Jatobá, M., Santos, J., Gutierriz, I., Moscon, D., Fernandes, P. O., & Teixeira, J. P. (2019). Evolution of artificial intelligence research in human resources. *Procedia Computer Science, 164*, 137–142. doi:10.1016/j.procs.2019.12.165

Jayaraman, J., & Black, J. (2022). Effectiveness of an intelligent question answering system for teaching financial literacy: A pilot study. In Innovations in Learning and Technology for the Workplace and Higher Education: Proceedings of 'The Learning Ideas Conference' 2021 (pp. 133–140). Springer. doi:10.1007/978-3-030-90677-1_13

Jeon, J., & Lee, S. (2023). Large language models in education: A focus on the complementary relationship between human teachers and ChatGPT. *Education and Information Technologies, 28*(12), 15873–15892. doi:10.1007/s10639-023-11834-1

Jessup, L. M., & Valacich, J. S. (Eds.). (1992). *Group support systems: New perspectives.* Macmillan.

Jiang, J. A., Wade, K., Fiesler, C., & Brubaker, J. R. (2021). Supporting serendipity: Opportunities and challenges for Human-AI Collaboration in qualitative analysis. *Proceedings of the ACM on Human-Computer Interaction, 5*(CSCW1), 1–23. 10.1145/3449168

Jiang, R. (2022). How does artificial intelligence empower EFL teaching and learning nowadays? A review on artificial intelligence in the EFL context. *Frontiers in Psychology, 13*, 1049401. doi:10.3389/fpsyg.2022.1049401 PMID:36467167

Johinke, R., Cummings, R., & Di Lauro, F. (2023). Reclaiming the technology of higher education for teaching digital writing in a post-pandemic world. *Journal of University Teaching & Learning Practice, 20*(2). Advance online publication. doi:10.53761/1.20.02.01

Johnson, D. W., & Johnson, R. T. (2004). Cooperation and the use of technology. In *Handbook of research on educational communications and technology* (2nd ed., pp. 777–803). Routledge.

Johnson, P., & Harris, D. (2002). Qualitative and quantitative issues in research design. In *Essential Skills for Management Research* (pp. 99–116). Sage. doi:10.4135/9781848605305.n6

Jones, A. C., & Kungiene, E. (2022). Intercultural communication pedagogy in Lithuania: Listening to viewpoints. In M. Minielli, M. N. Lukacovic, S. A. Samoilenko, M. Finch, & D. Uecker (Eds.), *Communication theory and application in post-socialist contexts* (pp. 223–236). Lexington Books – Rowman & Littlefield.

Jones, M., & Dexter, S. (2014). How teachers learn: The roles of formal, informal, and independent learning. *Educational Technology Research and Development, 62*(3), 367–384. doi:10.1007/s11423-014-9337-6

Joosten, T. (2012). *Social media for educators: Strategies and best practices.* John Wiley & Sons.

Joyce, J. (1914). *Dubliners.* Grant Richards Ltd.

Judd, T., & Keith, B. (2017). Implementing undergraduate student learning outcomes assessment at the program and institutional levels. In C. Secolsky & D. B. Denison (Eds.), *Handbook on measurement, assessment, and evaluation in higher education* (pp. 69–86). Routledge. doi:10.4324/9781315709307-8

Kaipa, R. M. (2021). Multiple choice questions and essay questions in curriculum. *Journal of Applied Research in Higher Education, 13*(1), 16–32. doi:10.1108/JARHE-01-2020-0011

Kasneci, E., Sessler, K., Küchemann, S., Bannert, M., Dementieva, D., Fischer, F., Gasser, U., Groh, G., Günnemann, S., Hüllermeier, E., Krusche, S., Kutyniok, G., Michaeli, T., Nerdel, C., Pfeffer, J., Poquet, O., Sailer, M., Schmidt, A., Seidel, T., ... Kasneci, G. (2023). ChatGPT for good? On opportunities and collages of large language models for education. *Learning and Individual Differences, 103*(1), 102274. doi:10.1016/j.lindif.2023.102274

Keane, M., & Yu, H. (2019). A digital empire in the making: China's outbound digital platforms. *International Journal of Communication, 13*, 4624–4641.

Keith, W. M. (2007). *Democracy as discussion: Civic education and the American Forum Movement.* Lexington Books.

Keith, W. (2010). Keynote address: A new golden age – Intercollegiate debate in the twenty-first century. In A. D. Louden (Ed.), *Navigating opportunity: Policy debate in the 21st century* (pp. 11–26). International Debate Education Association.

Kelly, M. L. (Host). (2023). 'Everybody is cheating': Why has adopted an open ChatGPT policy. [Audio podcast episode]. In *Technology*. National Public Radio. https://www.npr.org/ 2023/01/26/1151499213/chatgpt-ai-education-cheating-classroom-wharton-school

Kelly, S. M. (2023, April 27). *Snapchat's new AI chatbot is already raising alarms among teens and parents.* CNN. https://www.cnn.com/2023/04/27/tech/snapchat-my-ai-concerns-wellness/index.html

Kelly, S. M. (2023, January 19). *Teachers are adapting to concerns about a powerful new AI tool.* CNN Business. https://www.cnn.com/2023/01/19/tech/chatgpt-teachers-adjusting/index.html

Kenny, D. (Ed.). (2022). *Machine translation for everyone: Empowering users in the age of artificial intelligence.* Language Science Press. doi:10.5281/zenodo.6653406

Kerr, D. (2023, November 20). Hundreds of OpenAI Workers Threaten to Leave Over CEO Sam Altman's Firing. *NPR.* https://www.npr.org/2023/11/20/1214281184/hundreds-of-openaiworkers-threaten-to-leave-over-ceo-sam-altmans-firing

Khan, A., Jawaid, M., Khan, A., & Sajjad, M. (2023). ChatGPT-reshaping medical education and clinical management. *Pakistan Journal of Medical Sciences, 39*(2), 605–607. doi:10.12669/pjms.39.2.7653 PMID:36950398

Kharbat, F. F., Alshawabkeh, A., & Woolsey, M. L. (2021). Identifying gaps in using artificial intelligence to support students with intellectual disabilities from education and health perspectives. *Aslib Journal of Information Management, 73*(1), 101–128. doi:10.1108/AJIM-02-2020-0054

Khogali, H., & Mekid, S. (2023). The blended future of automation and AI: Examining some long-term societal and ethical impact features. *Technology in Society, 73*, 102232. Advance online publication. doi:10.1016/j.techsoc.2023.102232

Khosravi, H., Shum, S. B., Chen, G., Conati, C., Tsai, Y.-S., Kay, J., Knight, S., Martinez-Maldonado, R., Sadiq, S., & Gašević, D. (2022). Explainable Artificial Intelligence in education. *Computers and Education: Artificial Intelligence, 3*, 100074. doi:10.1016/j.caeai.2022.100074

Kim, H. (2019). *AI in journalism: Creating an ethical framework* (Publication No. 1083) [Syracuse University Honors Program Capstone Projects]. Journalism Studies Commons and Communication Commons.

Kim, N. J., & Kim, M. K. (2022). Teacher's perceptions of using an artificial intelligence-based educational tool for scientific writing. *Frontiers in Education, 7*, 755914. doi:10.3389/feduc.2022.755914

Kim, Y., & Sundar, S. (2012). Anthropomorphism of computers: Is it mindful or mindless? *Computers in Human Behavior, 28*(1), 241–250. doi:10.1016/j.chb.2011.09.006

Kinderlerer, J. (2021). *Artificial intelligence for a better future: An ecosystem perspective on the ethics of AI and emerging digital technologies.* doi:10.1007/978-3-030-69978-9

King, M. R., & Chat, G. P. T. (2023). A conversation on artificial intelligence, chatbots, and plagiarism in higher education. *Cellular and Molecular Bioengineering*, *16*(1), 1–2. doi:10.1007/s12195-022-00754-8 PMID:36660590

Kinsella, B. (2023, June 17). *Stack Overflow will embrace generative AI after all. Will overflow AI address an existential risk?* https://synthedia.substack.com/p/stack-overflowwill-embrace-generative

Klare, F., Burge, B., Klontz, M. J., Vorder, J. C., Bruegge, R. W., & Jain, A. K. (2012). Face recognition performance: Role of demographic information. *IEEE Transactions on Information Forensics and Security*, *7*(6), 1789–1801. doi:10.1109/TIFS.2012.2214212

Klein, A. (2023). *AI literacy, explained.* Education Week. https://www.edweek.org/technology/ai-literacy-explained/2023/05

Klein, B., & Merkel, S. (2022). Current trends in gerontechnology: Recent findings from the Austrian-German-Swiss chapter. *Gerontechnology*, *21*(s). doi:10.4017/gt.2022.21.s.578.sp7

Koenecke, A., Nam, A., Lake, E., Nudell, J., Quartey, M., Mengesha, Z., Toups, C., Rickford, J. R., Jurafsky, D., & Goel, S. (2020). Racial disparities in automated speech recognition. *Proceedings of the National Academy of Sciences of the United States of America*, *117*(14), 7684–7689. doi:10.1073/pnas.1915768117 PMID:32205437

Kong, S. C., Cheung, W. M. Y., & Zhang, G. (2021). Evaluation of an artificial intelligence literacy course for university students with diverse study backgrounds. *Computers and Education: Artificial Intelligence*, *2*, 100026. doi:10.1016/j.caeai.2021.100026

Kong, S., Cheung, W. M., & Zhang, G. (2023). Evaluating an artificial intelligence literacy programme for developing university students' conceptual understanding, literacy, empowerment, and ethical awareness. *Journal of Educational Technology & Society*, *26*(1), 16–30. doi:10.30191/ETS.202301_26(1).0002

Kooli, C. (2023). Chatbots in education and research: A critical examination of ethical implications and solutions. *Sustainability (Basel)*, *15*(7), 5614. doi:10.3390/su15075614

Kopp, S. (2010). Social resonance and embodied coordination in face-to-face conversation with artificial interlocutors. *Speech Communication*, *52*(6), 587–597. doi:10.1016/j.specom.2010.02.007

Korolov, M. (2023, June 3). Claude AI can read and analyze an entire book at once. Here's how to use it. *MetaStellar.* https://www.metastellar.com/nonfiction/on writing/claude-ai-can-read-and-analyze-an-entire-book-at-once/

KrauseD. (2023). Proper Generative AI Prompting for Financial Analysis. SSRN. http://dx.doi.org/ doi:10.2139/ssrn.4453664

Kretsinger-Harries, A. C., Helmick, E., Challis, K., & Garib, A. (2021). Navigating uncertainty together: Pandemic lessons learned from training new GTAs in teaching public speaking. In J. M. Valenzano III, (Ed.), *Post-pandemic pedagogy: A paradigm shift* (pp. 185–202). Lexington Books.

Krug, S. (2013). *Don't make me think, revisited: A common sense approach to web usability* (3rd ed.). New Riders.

Kuhail, M. A., Alturki, N., Alramlawi, S., & Alhejori, K. (2022). Interacting with educational chatbots: A systematic review. *Educational Technology Research and Development*, *70*, 973–1018.

Kuhn, T. S. (1962). *The structure of scientific revolutions.* University of Chicago Press.

Kumar, N., Mali, R., Ratnam, A., Kurpad, V., & Magapu, H. (2022). Identification and addressal of knowledge gaps in students. In *2022 3rd International Conference for Emerging Technology (INCET)* (pp. 1–6). IEEE. 10.1109/INCET54531.2022.9824483

Kurdi, G., Leo, J., Parsia, B., Sattler, U., & Al-Emari, S. (2020). A systematic review of automatic question generation for educational purposes. *International Journal of Artificial Intelligence in Education, 30*(1), 121–204. doi:10.1007/s40593-019-00186-y

Kurylo, A. (2013). *The communicated stereotype: From celebrity vilification to everyday talk.* Lexington Books.

Kurylo, A. (2021). *Building your social world: Constructing reality through interpersonal communication.* Kendall Hunt.

Kurylo, A., & Hu, Y. (2016). Students, the Ivory Tower, and educational uses of social networking sites. In A. Kurylo & T. Dumova (Eds.), *Redefining communication in the era of social networking: Cultural, social, and political perspectives.* Fairleigh Dickinson University Press.

Kurylo, A., & Hu, Y. (2024). *Communicated stereotypes at work.* Lexington Books.

Kurylo, A., & Veeramani, K. (2024 in press). Calling in and calling out: Human resource DEI strategies and interpersonally communicated stereotypes in academic settings. In A. Kurylo & Y. Hu (Eds.), *Communicated stereotypes at work.* Lexington Books.

Kurzweil, R. (2005). *The Singularity is near: When humans transcend biology.* Penguin.

La Rosa, A. (2023). Challenges of university communication teaching in the artificial intelligence age. In F. Roumate (Ed.), *Artificial intelligence in higher education and scientific research; Future developments* (pp. 89–99). Springer. doi:10.1007/978-981-19-8641-3_7

Langer, E., Blank, A., & Chanowitz, B. (1978). The mindlessness of ostensibly thoughtful action: The role of placebic information in interpersonal interaction. *Journal of Personality and Social Psychology, 36*(6), 635–642. doi:10.1037/0022-3514.36.6.635

Lanham, R. A. (2006). *The economics of attention: Style and substance in the age of information.* The University of Chicago Press.

Lanier, J. (2011). You are not a gadget: A manifesto (Reprint edition). Vintage.

Larsson, S., & Heintz, F. (2020). Transparency in artificial intelligence. *Internet Policy Review, 9*(2). Advance online publication. doi:10.14763/2020.2.1469

Lauer, J. M. (2004). *Invention in rhetoric and composition.* Parlor Press.

Laupichler, M. C., Aster, A., Schirch, J., & Raupach, T. (2022). Artificial intelligence literacy in higher and adult education: A scoping literature review. *Computers and Education: Artificial Intelligence, 3*, 100101. doi:10.1016/j.caeai.2022.100101

Lee, J. (n.d.). *How to break down difficult concepts: A comprehensive guide.* Nexus Notes. https://nexusnotes.com/blog/articles/how-to-break-down-difficult-concepts-acomprehensiveguide#:~:text=This%20involves%20breaking%20down%20the%20concept%20into%20ts%20component%20parts,understanding%20how%20they%20work%20together

Lee, A. V. Y. (2023). Supporting students' generation of feedback in large-scale online course with artificial intelligence-enabled evaluation. *Studies in Educational Evaluation, 77*, 101250. doi:10.1016/j.stueduc.2023.101250

Lee, S. J. (2009). *Unraveling the "model minority" stereotype: Listening to Asian American youth* (2nd ed.). Teachers College Press.

LeFevre, K. B. (1987). *Invention as a social act.* Southern Illinois University Press.

Leiker, D., Finnigan, S., Gyllen, A. R., & Cukurova, M. (2023). Prototyping the use of large language models (LLMs) for adult learning content creation at scale. AIED Workshops.

Leufer, D. (2023, January 13). *Computers are binary, people are not: How AI systems undermine LGBTQ identity*. Access Now. https://www.accessnow.org/how-ai-systems-undermine-lgbtq-identity/

Li, Y., Sha, L., Yan, L., Lin, J., Raković, M., Galbraith, K., Lyons, K., Gašević, D., & Chen, G. (2023). Can large language models write reflectively. *Computers and Education: Artificial Intelligence, 100140*.

Liang, W., Yuksekgonul, M., Mao, Y., Wu, E., & Zou, J. (2023). GPT detectors are biased against non-native English writers. *arXiv preprint arXiv:2304.02819*.

Liang, W., Yuksekgonul, M., Mao, Y., Wu, E., & Zou, J. (2023). GPT detectors are biased against non-native English writers. *Patterns, 4*(7), 100779. doi:10.1016/j.patter.2023.100779

Liao, Y., & He, J. (2020). The racial mirroring effects on human-agent in psychotherapeutic conversation. *Proceedings of the 25th International Conference on Intelligent User Interfaces (IUI'20)*. 10.1145/3377325.3377488

Li, C., & Xing, W. (2021). Natural language generation using deep learning to support MOOC learners. *International Journal of Artificial Intelligence in Education, 31*(2), 186–214. doi:10.1007/s40593-020-00235-x

Lim, W. M., Gunasekara, A., Pallant, J. L., Pallant, J. I., & Pechenkina, E. (2023). Generative AI and the future of education: Ragnarök or reformation? A paradoxical perspective from management educators. *International Journal of Management Education, 21*(2), 100790. doi:10.1016/j.ijme.2023.100790

Lippmann, W. (1922). *Public opinion*. Free Press.

Liu, Z., He, X., Liu, L., Liu, T., & Zhai, X. (2023). Context matters: A strategy to pre-train language model for science education. *arXiv preprint arXiv:2301.12031*. doi:10.1007/978-3-031-36336-8_103

Liu, B. F., & Levenshus, A. B. (2023). Interpreting the interpersonal: Crisis communication insights for pandemics. In S. M. Croucher & A. Diers-Lawson (Eds.), *Pandemic communication* (pp. 156–173). Routledge. doi:10.4324/9781003214496-9

Liu, M., Ren, Y., Nyagoga, L. M., Stonier, F., Wu, Z., & Yu, L. (2023, September 2). Future of education in the era of generative artificial intelligence: Consensus among Chinese scholars on applications of ChatGPT in schools. *Future in Educational Research, 1*(1), 72–10. doi:10.1002/fer3.10

Liu, P., Yuan, W., Fu, J., Jiang, Z., Hayashi, H., & Neubig, G. (2023). Pre-train, prompt, and predict: A systematic survey of prompting methods in natural language processing. *ACM Computing Surveys, 55*(9), 1–35. doi:10.1145/3560815

Liu, S., Liu, S., Liu, Z., Peng, X., & Yang, Z. (2022). Automated detection of emotional and cognitive engagement in MOOC discussions to predict learning achievement. *Computers & Education, 181*, 104461. doi:10.1016/j.compedu.2022.104461

Lo, C. K. (2023). What is the impact of ChatGPT on education? A rapid review of the literature. *Education Sciences, 13*(4), 410–424. doi:10.3390/educsci13040410

Lock, S. (2022, December 5). What is AI chatbot phenomenon ChatGPT and could it replace humans? *The Guardian*. https://www.theguardian.com/technology/2022/dec/05/what-is-ai-chatbot-phenomenon-chatgpt-and-could-it-replace-humans

Loftesness, S. (2022, December 7). *Haiku with chatgpt*. Scott Loftesness. Retrieved December 31, 2023, from https://sjl.us/2022/12/07/haiku-with-chatgpt/

Long, D., & Magerko, B. (2020, April). What is AI literacy? Competencies and design considerations. In *Proceedings of the 2020 CHI Conference on Human Factors in Computing Systems* (pp. 1–16). 10.1145/3313831.3376727

Lopezosa, C., Codina, L., Pont-Sorribes, C., & Vállez, M. (2023). Use of generative artificial intelligence in the training of journalists: Challenges, uses and training proposal. *El Profesional de la Información, 32*(4), 1–12. doi:10.3145/epi.2023.jul.08

Louden, A. D. (Ed.). (2010). *Navigating opportunity: Policy debate in the 21st century.* International Debate Education Association.

Luckin, R., Holmes, W., Griffiths, M., & Forcier, L. B. (2016). *Intelligence unleashed: An argument for AI in education.* Pearson.

Lu, D., Ruan, B., Lee, M., Yilmaz, Y., & Chan, T. M. (2020). Good practices in harnessing social media for scholarly discourse, knowledge translation, and education. *Journal of Medical Education and Curricular Development, 10*(1), 1. Advance online publication. doi:10.1007/S40037-020-00613-0 PMID:32820414

Lukacovic, M. N., & Sellnow-Richmond, D. D. (2023). COVID-19 pandemic and the rise of MUAI threats to national and international psychological security. In E. Pashentsev (Ed.), *The Palgrave handbook of malicious use of AI and psychological security* (pp. 175–201). Palgrave Macmillan. doi:10.1007/978-3-031-22552-9_7

Lu, T., Liu, X., Sun, J., Bao, Y., Schuller, B. W., Han, Y., & Lu, L. (2023). Bridging the gap between artificial intelligence and mental health. *Science Bulletin, 68*(15), 1606–1610. doi:10.1016/j.scib.2023.07.015 PMID:37474445

Lv, Z. (2023). Generative artificial intelligence in the metaverse era. *Cognitive Robotics, 3*, 208-217. doi:10.1016/j.cogr.2023.06.001

Ma, Q., Wu, S., & Koedinger, K. (2023). Is LLM the better programming partner? AIED Workshops.

Macrae, C. N., Milne, A. B., & Bodenhausen, G. V. (1994). Stereotypes as energy-saving devices: A peek inside the cognitive toolbox. *Journal of Personality and Social Psychology, 66*(1), 37–47. doi:10.1037/0022-3514.66.1.37

Mageira, K., Pittou, D., Papasalouros, A., Kotis, K., Zangogianni, P., & Daradoumis, A. (2022). Educational AI chatbots for content and language integrated learning. *Applied Sciences (Basel, Switzerland), 12*(7), 3239. doi:10.3390/app12073239

Maheen, F., Asif, M., Ahmad, H., Ahmad, S., Alturise, F., Asiry, O., & Ghadi, Y. Y. (2022). Automatic computer science domain multiple-choice questions generation based on informative sentences. *PeerJ. Computer Science, 8*, e1010. doi:10.7717/peerj-cs.1010 PMID:36091982

Mahesh, J., Bhat, A. K., & Ramya, S. (2021). Are Gen Z values the new disruptor for future educational institutions? *Journal of Higher Education Theory and Practice, 21*(12), 102–123. doi:10.33423/jhetp.v21i12.4704

Manasa, R., & Devi, A. (2022). Amazon's artificial intelligence in retail novelty—case study. *International Journal of Case Studies in Business, IT, and Education*, 787–804. doi:10.47992/IJCSBE.2581.6942.0233

Mann, J. (2023, September 17). The humanoid-robot CEO of a drinks company says it doesn't have weekends and is 'always on 24/7'. *Yahoo Finance.* https://finance.yahoo.com/news/humanoid-robot-ceo-drinks-company101055228.html?guccounter=1

Manyika, J., Silberg, J., & Presten, B. (2019). What do we do about the biases in AI? *Harvard Business Review.* https://hbr.org/2019/10/what-do-we-do-about-the-biases-in-ai

Marshall, J. (2023). As AI cheating booms, so does the industry detecting it: 'We couldn't keep up with the demand.' *The Guardian.* https://www.theguardian.com/technology/2023/jul/05/as-ai-cheating-booms-so-does-the-industry-detecting-it-we-couldnt-keep-up-with-demand

Martindale, J. (2023). *These are the countries where ChatGPT is currently banned.* https://www.digitaltrends.com/computing/these-countries-chatgpt-banned/

Martinez, E., & Kirchner, L. (2021 August 25). The secret bias hidden in mortgage-approval algorithm. *The Markup.* https://themarkup.org/denied/2021/08/25/the-secret-biashidden-in-mortgage-approval-algorithms

Marx, L., & Smith, M. R. (Eds.). (1994). *Does technology drive history? The dilemma of technological determinism*. MIT Press.

Maslej, N., Fattorini, L., Brynjolfsson, E., Etchemendy, J., Ligett, K., Lyons, T., Manyika, J., Ngo, H., Niebles, J. C., Parli, V., Shoham, Y., Wald, R., Clark, J., & Perrault, R. (2023). *The AI Index 2023 Annual Report*. AI Index Steering Committee, Institute for Human-Centered AI, Stanford University, Stanford, CA. https://aiindex.stanford.edu/wp-content/uploads/2023/04/HAI_AI-Index-Report_2023.pdf

Mason, J., Peoples, B. E., & Lee, J. (2020). Questioning the scope of AI standardization in learning, education, and training. *Journal of ICT Standardization*, *8*(2), 107–122. doi:10.13052/jicts2245-800X.822

Massaro, M. (2023, August 23). AI cheating is hopelessly, irreparably corrupting US higher education. *The Hill*. https://thehill.com/opinion/education/4162766-ai-cheating-has-hopelessly-irreparably-corrupted-us-higher-education/

Mattas, P. S. (2023). ChatGPT: A study of AI language processing and its implications. *International Journal of Research Publication and Reviews*, *4*(2), 435–440. doi:10.55248/gengpi.2023.4218

Mayor, A. (2018). *Gods and robots*. Princeton University Press. doi:10.2307/j.ctvc779xn

McCarthy, J. (2007, November 12). *What is artificial intelligence?* https://www-formal.stanford.edu/jmc/whatisai.pdf

McCarthy, J., Minsky, M. L., Rochester, N., & Shannon, C. E. (2006). A proposal for the Dartmouth summer research project on artificial intelligence, August 31, 1955. *AI Magazine*, *27*(4), 12–12.

McChesney, R. W., & Nichols, J. (2016). *People get ready. The fight against a jobless economy and a citizenless democracy*. Nation Books.

McKinsey. (2023, January 19). *What is ChatGPT, DALL-E, and generative AI?* https://www.mckinsey.com/featured-insights/mckinsey-explainers/what-is-generative-ai

Mendoza, S., Hernández-León, M., Sánchez-Adame, L. M., Rodríguez, J., Decouchant, D., & Meneses-Viveros, A. (2020). Supporting student-teacher interaction through a chatbot. In Learning and Collaboration Technologies. doi:10.1007/978-3-030-50506-6_8

Merken, S. (2023, June 26). *New York lawyers sanctioned for using face ChatGPT cases in legal brief*. Reuters. https://www.reuters.com/legal/new-york-lawyers-sanctioned-using-fake-chatgpt-cases-legal-brief-2023-06-22/

Merleau-Ponty, M. (2012). Phenomenology of perception. Academic Press.

Merton, R. K. (1968). The Matthew effect in science. *Science*, *159*(3810), 56–63. doi:10.1126/science.159.3810.56 PMID:5634379

Meskó, B. (2023). Prompt engineering as an important emerging skill for medical professionals: Tutorial. *Journal of Medical Internet Research*, *25*, e50638. doi:10.2196/50638 PMID:37792434

Mhlanga, D. (2023). Open AI in education, the responsible and ethical use of ChatGPT toward lifelong learning. SSRN *Electronic Journal*. doi:10.2139/ssrn.4354422

Midjourney. (2023, March). *Midjourney Magazine*.

Mills, A., Bali, M., & Eaton, L. (2023). How do we respond to generative AI in education? Open educational practices give us a framework for an ongoing process. *Journal of Applied Learning & Teaching*, *6*(1), 16–30. doi:10.37074/jalt.2023.6.1.34

Minichilli, F., Gorini, F., Ascari, E., Bianchi, F., Coi, A., Fredianelli, L., Licitra, G., Manzoli, F., Mezzasalma, L., & Cori, L. (2018). Annoyance judgment and measurements of environmental noise: A focus on Italian secondary schools. *International Journal of Environmental Research and Public Health, 15*(2), 208. doi:10.3390/ijerph15020208 PMID:29373506

Misaki, D., Ge, X., & Odaka, T. (2020, June 22). *Toward interdisciplinary teamwork in Japan: Developing team-based learning experience and its assessment.* 2020 ASEE Virtual Annual Conference Content Access. https://peer.asee.org/toward-interdisciplinary-teamwork-in-japan-developing-team-based-learning-experience-and-its-assessment

Mishra, P., Warr, M., & Islam, R. (2023). TPACK in the age of ChatGPT and Generative AI. *Journal of Digital Learning in Teacher Education, 39*(4), 235–251. doi:10.1080/21532974.2023.2247480

Mitchell, G. R. (2000). *Strategic deception: Rhetoric, science, and politics in missile defense advocacy.* Michigan State University Press.

Mitchell, G. R. (2021). Debating with robots: IBM Project Debater and the advent of augmentive automated argumentation. In T. Suzuki, T. Tateyama, T. Kato, & J. Eckstein (Eds.), *Proceedings of the Tokyo Conference on Argumentation* (vol. 6, pp. 91–102). Japan Debate Association.

Mitchell, G. R., Woods, C. S., Brigham, B., English, E., Morrison, C. E., & Rief, J. (2010). The Debate Authors Working Group model for collaborative knowledge production in forensics scholarship. *Argumentation and Advocacy, 47*(1), 1–24. doi:10.1080/00028533.2010.11821734

Mitchell, M., Wu, S., Zaldivar, A., Barnes, P., Vasserman, L., Hutchinson, B., Spitzer, E., Raji, I. D., & Gebru, T. (2019). Model cards for model reporting. In *Proceedings of the Conference on Fairness, Accountability, and Transparency* (pp. 220–229). 10.1145/3287560.3287596

Mitra, A., Del Corro, L., Mahajan, S., Codas, A., Simoes Ribeiro, C., Agrawal, S., Chen, X., Razdaibiedina, A., Jones, E., Aggarwal, K., Palangi, H., Zheng, G., Rosset, C., Khanpour, H., & Awadallah, A. (2023). *Orca-2: Teaching small language models how to reason*. https://www.microsoft.com/en-us/research/publication/orca-2-teaching-small-language-models-how-to-reason/

Mittelstadt, B. D., Allo, P., Taddeo, M., Wachter, S., & Floridi, L. (2016). The ethics of algorithms: Mapping the debate. *Big Data & Society, 3*(2). doi:10.1177/2053951716679679

Mittman, A. (2012). Introduction: The impact of monsters and monster studies. In A. Mittman & P. Dendel (Eds.), *The Ashgate research companion to monsters and the monstrous* (pp. 41-54). Ashgate.

Mohammadkarimi, E. (2023). Teachers' reflections on academic dishonesty in EFL students' writing in the era of artificial intelligence. *Journal of Applied Learning & Learning, 6*(2). Advance online publication. doi:10.37074/jalt.2023.6.2.10

Mok, A. (2023). Professors want to 'ChatGPT-proof' assignments, and are returning to paper exams and requesting editing history to curb AI cheating. *Business Insider.* https://www.businessinsider.com/teachers-colleges-ways-chatgpt-proof-assignments-essays-prevent-cheating-2023-8

Monte-Serrat, D. M., & Cattani, C. (2023). Artificial intelligence and scientific research: Values at stake in education. In F. Roumate (Ed.), *Artificial intelligence in higher education and scientific research; Future developments* (pp. 1–14). Springer. doi:10.1007/978-981-19-8641-3_1

Morales, A. (2022, June 17). Take this job and (change) it: The Great Resignation in higher education. *NASPA | Student Affairs Administrators in Higher Education.* https://www.naspa.org/blog/take-this-job-and-change-it-the-great-resignation-in-higher-education

Morozov, E. (2011). *The net delusion: The dark side of internet freedom.* Public Affairs.

Morris, J. (Producer). (2008). *Wall-E* [Film]. Walt Disney Pixar Animation Studio.

Morris, M. R. (2020). AI and accessibility. *Communications of the ACM, 63*(6), 35–37. doi:10.1145/3356727

Mthuli, S. A., Ruffin, F., & Singh, N. (2022). 'Define, explain, justify, apply'(DEJA): An analytic tool for guiding qualitative research sample size. *International Journal of Social Research Methodology, 25*(6), 809–821. doi:10.1080/13645579.2021.1941646

Mucci, T., & Stryker, C. (2023, December 18). *What is artificial superintelligence?* IBM. https://www.ibm.com/topics/artificialsuperintelligence#:~:text=Artificial%20superintellgence%20(ASI)%20is%20a,intellectual%20scope%20beyond%20human%20intelligence

Mügge, D. (2023). The securitization of EU's digital tech regulation. *Journal of European Public Policy, 30*(7), 1431–1446. doi:10.1080/13501763.2023.2171090

Muir, S. A. (1993). A defense of the ethics of contemporary debate. *Philosophy & Rhetoric, 26*(4), 277–295.

Müller, C., Kratzwald, S., & Neubauer, A. (2019). Chatbot in customer service – A systematic literature. *Business & Information Systems Engineering, 61*(4), 367–378.

Murtaza, M., Ahmed, Y., Shamsi, J. A., Sherwani, F., & Usman, M. (2022). AI-based personalized E-learning systems: Issues, challenges, and solutions. *IEEE Access : Practical Innovations, Open Solutions, 10*, 81323–81342. doi:10.1109/ACCESS.2022.3193938

Murugesan, S., & Cherukuri, A. K. (2023). The rise of generative artificial intelligence and its impact on education: The promises and perils. *Computer, 56*(5), 116–121. doi:10.1109/MC.2023.3253292

Muscanell, N., & Robert, J. (2023, February 14). *EDUCAUSE QuickPoll results: Did ChatGPT write this report?* EDUCAUSE. https://er.educause.edu/articles/2023/2/educause-quickpoll-results-did-chatgpt-write-this-report

Myer, K. R., Kurtz, R. R., Hines, J. L., Simonds, C. J., & Hunt, S. K. (2010). Assessing preemptive argumentation in students' persuasive speech outlines. *Basic Communication Course Annual, 22*(1), 5-38. https://ecommons.udayton.edu/bcca/vol22/iss1/7

Na'puti, T. R., & Frain, S. C. (2023). Indigenous environmental perspectives: Challenging the oceanic security state. *Security Dialogue, 54*(2), 11–136. doi:10.1177/09670106221139765

Nass, C., Moon, Y., Fogg, B., Reeves, B., & Dryer, D. (1995). Can computer personalities be human personalities? *International Journal of Human-Computer Studies, 43*(2), 223–239. doi:10.1006/ijhc.1995.1042

Natale, S. (2018). If software is narrative: Joseph Weizenbaum, artificial intelligence and the biographies of ELIZA. *New Media & Society, 21*(3), 712–728. doi:10.1177/1461444818804980

Natale, S. (2020). Communicating through or communicating with: Approaching artificial intelligence from a communication and media studies perspective. *Communication Theory, 30*. Advance online publication. doi:10.1093/ct/qtaa022

National Center for Education Statistics. (2023). College Enrollment Rates. In *Condition of Education*. U.S. Department of Education, Institute of Education Sciences. https://nces.ed.gov/programs/coe/indicator/cpb

National Center for Education Statistics. (2023). *Undergraduate enrollment. In condition of education.* U.S. Department of Education, Institute of Education Sciences. https://nces.ed.gov/programs/coe/indicator/cha

Newman, C. (2023). *Guide to using ChatGPT in higher education: Transforming the learning experience*. Independently Published.

Nguyen, M., Laly, M., Kwon, B. C., Mougenot, C., & McNamara, J. (2022). Moody man: Improving creative teamwork through dynamic affective recognition. *Extended Abstracts of the 2022 CHI Conference on Human Factors in Computing Systems*, 1–14. 10.1145/3491101.3519656

Nguyen, A., Ngo, H. N., Hong, Y., Dang, B., & Nguyen, B. T. (2022). Ethical principles for artificial intelligence in education. *Education and Information Technologies*, *28*(4), 4221–4241. doi:10.1007/s10639-022-11316-w PMID:36254344

Nick, B. (2014). *Superintelligence: Paths, Dangers, Strategies.* Oxford University Press.

Nicoletti, L., & Bass, D. (2023). *Humans are biased: Generative AI is even worse.* Bloomberg Technology + Equality. https://www.bloomberg.com/graphics/2023-generative-ai-bias/

Nigam, A., Pasricha, R., Singh, T., & Churi, P. (2021). A systematic review on AI-based proctoring systems: Past, present, and future. *Education and Information Technologies*, *26*(5), 6421–6445. Advance online publication. doi:10.1007/s10639-021-10597-x PMID:34177348

Nixon, A. E., Mazzola, J. J., Bauer, J., Krueger, J. R., & Spector, P. E. (2011). Can work make you sick? A meta-analysis of the relationships between job stressors and physical symptoms. *Work and Stress*, *25*(1), 1–22. doi:10.1080/02678373.2011.569175

Noble, S. U. (2018). *Algorithms of oppression: How search engines reinforce racism.* York University Press. doi:10.18574/nyu/9781479833641.001.0001

Noor-Oshiro, A. (2021, April 23). Asian American young adults are the only racial group with suicide as their leading cause of death, so why is no one talking about this? *The Conversation.* https://theconversation.com/asian-american-young-adults-are-the-only-racial-group-with-suicide-as-their-leading-cause-of-death-so-why-is-no-one-talking-about-this-158030

Norman, D. (2013). *The design of everyday things* (Revised edition). Basic Books.

Nowak, K. L., & Biocca, F. (2003). The effect of the agency and anthropomorphism on users' sense of telepresence, copresence, and social presence in virtual environments. *Presence (Cambridge, Mass.)*, *12*(5), 481–494. doi:10.1162/105474603322761289

Nuckols, C. N. (2023, May 23). Austin school board using A.I. to track student success. *ABC News.*

Nye, B., Mee, D., & Core, M. G. (2023). Generative large language models for dialog-based tutoring: An early consideration of opportunities and concerns. AIED Workshops.

O'Neil, C. (2017). *Weapons of math destruction: How big data increases inequality and threatens democracy.* Crown.

Office of Public Affairs. (2022, September 29). Justice Department announces actions to resolve lending discrimination claims against Evolve Bank and Trust. *Office of Public Affairs.* https://www.justice.gov/opa/pr/justice-department-announces-actions-resolve-lending-discrimination-claims-against-evolve

Okonkwo, C. W., & Ade-Ibijola, A. (2021). Evaluating the ethical implications of using chatbot systems in higher education. *digiTAL, 2021*, 68.

Olaniyi, E., Olawale, W., Emeka, O., Olawe, A., Raymond, A., & Sesan, A. (2023). ChatGPT impacts on access-efficiency, employment, education and ethics: The socio-economics of an AI language model. *BizEcons Quarterly, 16*(1), 1–17. https://ideas.repec.org/a/ris/buecqu/0032.html

Oleny, A. (2023). Generating multiple-choice questions from a textbook: LLMs match human performance on most metrics. AIED Workshops.

Ong, W. J. (2002). Orality and literacy: The technologizing of the word (30th anniversary ed.). Routledge.

Ong, W. J. (2002). Information and/or communication: Interactions. In T. J. Farrell & P. A. Soukup (Eds.), *An Ong reader: Challenges for further inquiry* (pp. 505–526). Hampton Press.

Open, A. I. (2022). *ChatGPT (November 30 version)* [Large language model]. https://chat.openai.com/chat

Open, A. I. (2023). *ChatGPT (May 24 version)* [Large language model]. https://chat.openai.com

Open, A. I. (2023). *ChatGPT* [Large language model]. https://chat.openai.com/chat

Open, A. I. (2023). *ChatGPT 3.5* (May 24 version) [Large language model, editing]. https://chat.openai.com

Open, A. I. (2023). *GPT-4 is OpenAI's most advanced system, producing safer and more useful responses (Mar 14 version)* [Large language model]. Retrieved from https://openai.com/product/gpt-4

Open, A. I. (2023). *Introducing chatgpt*. Retrieved from https://openai.com/blog/chatgpt

Open, A. I. (n.d.). *OpenAI GPT-3*. Retrieved from https://openai.com/gpt-3/

Oremus, W. (2015, October 25). *No more pencils, no more books*. Slate Magazine. https://www.slate.com/articles/technology/technology/2015/10/adaptive_learning_software_is_replacing_textbooks_and_upending_american.html

Overono, A. L., & Ditta, A. S. (2023). The rise of artificial intelligence: A clarion call for higher education to redefine learning and reimagine assessment. *College Teaching*, *71*(3), 1–4. Advance online publication. doi:10.1080/87567555.2023.2233653

Pagano, T. P., Loureiro, R. B., Lisboa, F. V. N., Peixoto, R. M., Guimaraes, G. A. S., Cruz, G. O. R., Araujo, M. M., Santos, L. L., Cruz, M. A. S., Oliveira, E. L. S., Winkler, I., & Nascimento, E. G. S. (2023). Bias and unfairness in machine learning models: A systematic review on datasets, tools, fairness metrics, and identification and mitigation methods. *Big Data and Cognitive Computing*, *7*(15), 1–31. doi:10.3390/bdcc7010015

Palliyalil, S., & Mukherjee, S. (2020). Byju's The Learning App: An investigative study on the transformation from traditional learning to technology-based personalized learning. *International Journal of Scientific & Technology Research*, *9*, 5054–5059.

Palmarini, N., Martie, L., Wasiak, M. F., & Zhang, G. (2019). Exclusion Spotter: Applying advances in AI to identify ageism in online job posting. *Innovation in Aging*, *3*(Supplement_1), S763–S763. doi:10.1093/geroni/igz038.2805

Palmer-Silveira, J. C. (2015). Multimodality in business communication: Body language as a visual aid in student presentations. In B. C. Camiciottoli & I. Fortanet-Gomez (Eds.), *Multimodal analysis in academic settings: From research to teaching* (pp. 171–193). Routledge.

Paquot, M., & Gries, S. T. (Eds.). (2020). *A practical handbook of corpus linguistics*. Springer International Publishing. doi:10.1007/978-3-030-46216-1

Park, J. S., O'Brien, J. Y., Cai, C. J., Morris, M. R., Liang, P., & Bernstein, M. S. (2023). Generative agents: Interactive simulacra of human behavior. In *UIST '23: Proceedings of the 36th annual ACM symposium on user interface software and technology* (pp. 1–22). ACM. 10.1145/3586183.3606763

Park, J.-Y., & Son, J.-B. (2010). Transitioning toward transdisciplinary learning in a multidisciplinary environment. *International Journal of Pedagogies and Learning*, *6*(1), 82–93. doi:10.5172/ijpl.6.1.82

Parrott, B. (2020). The American mega-crisis: COVID-19 and beyond. *Challenge*, *63*(5), 245–263. doi:10.1080/05775132.2020.1804756

Parsaiyan, S. F., & Gholami, H. (2023). Practicing to sing in chorus: Challenges and opportunities of collaborative inquiry-based learning in an Iranian EFL secondary school context. *Language Teaching Research*. Advance online publication. doi:10.1177/13621688231152037

Patton, B. R., & Giffin, K. (1971). *Basic readings in interpersonal communication*. Harper & Row.

Pavlik, J. V. (2023). Collaborating with ChatGPT: Considering the implications of generative artificial intelligence for journalism and media education. *Journalism & Mass Communication Educator*, *78*(1), 107769582211495. doi:10.1177/10776958221149577

Pawlowski, D. R. (2018). From the classroom to the community: Best practices in service-learning. *Journal of Communication Pedagogy*, *1*(1), 85–92. doi:10.31446/JCP.2018.15

Pearman, F. A., Curran, F. C., Gardella, J., & Fisher, B. (2019). Are achievement gaps related to discipline gaps? Evidence from national data. *AERA Open*, *5*(4). doi:10.1177/2332858419875440

Pedro, F., Subosa, M., Rivas, A., & Valverde, P. (2019). *Artificial Intelligence in Education: Challenges and Opportunities for Sustainable Development*. UNESCO.

Pelletier, K., McCormack, M., Reeves, J., Robert, J., Arbino, N., Dickson-Deane, C., & Stine, J. (2022). 2022 EDUCAUSE Horizon Report Teaching and Learning Edition. EDUC22.

Pena, P., & Varon, J. (2021, May 3). *Oppressive A.I.: Feminist categories to understand its political effects*. Retrieved January 18, 2024, from https://notmy.ai/news/oppressive-a-i-feminist-categories-to-understand-its-political-effects/

Perera, P., & Lankathilaka, M. (2023). AI in higher education: A literature review of ChatGPT and guidelines for responsible implementation. *International Journal of Research and Innovation in Social Sciences*, *7*(6), 306–314. doi:10.47772/IJRISS.2023.7623

Perman, C. (2019, October 28). Running out of money. Cancer. Divorce. Many college students are facing serious financial crises. *CNBC*. https://www.cnbc.com/2019/10/28/many-college-students-find-themselves-in-a-serious-financial-crisis.html

Perrigo, B. (2023, February 17). *Bing's AI is threatening users. That's no laughing matter*. TIME. https://time.com/6256529/bing-openai-chatgpt-danger-alignment/

Perry, A. M., & Lee, N. T. (2019 September 26). *AI is coming to schools and if we're not careful so will its biases*. Brookings. https://www.brookings.edu/articles/ai-is-coming-to-schools-and-if-were-not-careful-so-will-its-biases/

Pesonen, J. A. (2021). 'Are You OK?' Students' Trust in a Chatbot Providing Support Opportunities. In *Learning and Collaboration Technologies: Games and Virtual Environments for Learning: 8th International Conference, LCT 2021, Held as Part of the 23rd HCI International Conference, HCII 2021, Virtual Event, July 24–29, 2021, Proceedings, Part II* (pp. 199–215). Springer.

Peters, J. D. (1999). *Speaking into the air: A history of the idea of communication*. University of Chicago Press. doi:10.7208/chicago/9780226922638.001.0001

Petricini, T. (2019). Explorations in the noosphere: Hermeneutic presence and hostility in cyberspace. *Explorations in Media Ecology*, *18*(1-2), 57–71. doi:10.1386/eme.18.1-2.57_1

PetriciniT.WuC.ZipfS. (2023). Perceptions about generative AI and ChatGPT use by faculty and college students [Preprint]. doi:10.35542/osf.io/jyma4

Petrosyan, A. (2023). Countries with the most people lacking internet connection 2023. *Statista*. https://www.statista.com/statistics/1155552/countries-highest-number-lacking-internet/

Phare, C. (2023, Fall). Higher ed's next big test. *RED*, 11–13.

Phillips, M., Marsden, H., Jaffe, W., Matin, R. N., Wali, G. N., Greenhalgh, J., McGrath, E., James, R., Ladoyanni, E., Bewley, A., Argenziano, G., & Palamaras, I. (2019). Assessment of accuracy of an artificial intelligence algorithm to detect melanoma in images of skin lesions. *JAMA Network Open*, *2*(10), e1913436. doi:10.1001/jamanetworkopen.2019.13436 PMID:31617929

Picard, R. W. (2000). *Affective Computing*. doi:10.7551/mitpress/1140.001.0001

Pichai, S., & Hassabis, D. (2023, December 6). Introducing Gemini: our largest and most capable AI model. *Blog Google*. https://blog.google/technology/ai/google-gemini-ai/#sundar note.

Pienaar, S. W., & Malekian, R. (2019). Human activity recognition using LSTM-RNN deep neural network architecture. In *2019 IEEE 2nd Wireless Africa Conference (WAC)* (pp. 1-5). 10.1109/AFRICA.2019.8843403

Pizzi, G., Vannucci, V., Mazzoli, V., & Donvito, R. (2023). I, chatbot! The impact of anthropomorphism and gaze direction on willingness to disclose personal information and behavioral intentions. *Psychology and Marketing*, *40*(7), 1372–1387. doi:10.1002/mar.21813

Pommer, E. (Producer). (1927). *Metropolis* [Film]. UFA.

Popenici, S. A., & Kerr, S. (2017). Exploring the impact of artificial intelligence on teaching and learning in higher education. *Research and Practice in Technology Enhanced Learning*, *12*(1), 22. Advance online publication. doi:10.1186/s41039-017-0062-8 PMID:30595727

Posner, R. A. (2009). *Public intellectuals*. Harvard University Press. doi:10.2307/j.ctv1kwxdnh

Potter, D. (1954). The literary society. In K. R. Wallace (Ed.), *History of speech education in America: Background studies* (pp. 238–258). Appleton-Century-Crofts, Inc.

Potter, D. (1972). *Debating in the colonial chartered colleges: An historical survey, 1642–1900*. AMS Press, Inc.

Pound, C. (2023, March 21). *The hidden figures revealed by art*. BBC.com. https://www.bbc.com/culture/article/20190320-how-art-history-erased-black-people

Powles, J. (2020). *The ethics of artificial intelligence*. Cambridge University Press.

President, S. (2023, April 17). The ethics of college students using ChatGPT. *The University of North Carolina at Chapel Hill Institutional Integrity and Risk Management: Ethics and Policy*. https://ethicspolicy.unc.edu/news/2023/04/17/the-ethics-of-college-students-using-chatgpt/

Primary Research Group. (2023a). *Survey of US higher education faculty 2023: Views on and use of ChatGPT*. Author.

Primary Research Group. (2023b). *Survey of US higher education faculty 2024: Use of artificial intelligence applications*. Author.

Primary Research Group. (2024). *Survey of US higher education faculty 2024: Use of artificial intelligence applications*. Primary Research Group.

PRSA Board of Ethics and Professional Standards (BEPS). (2023). Promise and pitfalls: The ethical use of AI for public relations practitioners. *AI Insight*, 1-10.

Pun, J. (2021). A study of Chinese medical students' communication pattern in delivering bad news: An ethnographic discourse analysis approach. *BMC Medical Education, 21*(1), 286. doi:10.1186/s12909-021-02724-6 PMID:34011322

QadirJ. (2022). Engineering education in the era of ChatGPT: Promise and pitfalls of generative AI for education. TechRxiv. doi:10.36227/techrxiv.21789434.v1

Quinn, G. (2021). *The right of people with disabilities.* The United Nations. https://www.ohchr.org/sites/default/files/2022-02/Easy-Read-AI-disabilities-report.pdf

Radford, A., Narasimhan, K., Salimans, T., & Sutskever, I. (2018). *Improving language understanding by generative pre-training*. OpenAI. https://openai.com/research/language-unsupervised

Radford, A., Wu, J., Child, R., Luan, D., Amodei, D., & Sutskever, I. (2019). *Language models are unsupervised multitask learners* [Unpublished manuscript].

Rainie, L., Funk, C., Anderson, M., & Tyson, A. (2022, March 17). *AI and human enhancement: Americans' openness is tempered by a range of concerns.* Pew Research Center. https://www.pewresearch.org/internet/2022/03/17/how-americans-think-about-artificial-intelligence/

Raji, I. D., Smart, A., White, R. N., Mitchell, M., Gebru, T., Hutchinson, B., Smith-Loud, J., Theron, D., & Barnes, P. (2020). Closing the AI accountability gap. In *Proceedings of the 2020 Conference on Fairness, Accountability, and Transparency* (pp. 33–44). https://doi.org/10.1145/3351095.3372873

Raley, R., & Rhee, J. (2023). *Critical AI: A field in formation.* Duke University Press.

Ramesh, D., & Sanampudi, S. K. (2022). An automated essay scoring systems: A systematic literature review. *Artificial Intelligence Review, 55*(8), 2495–2527. doi:10.1007/s10462-021-10068-2 PMID:34584325

Rana, V., & Verhoeven, B. (2023, August 4). Embracing AI in education: A shift from creators to co- pilots. In Tyler's (Chair), *Authentic Assessments for the AI Era* (Symposium). TheGoReact, Zoom. get.goreact.com/resources/authentic-assessments-for-the-ai-era-2/

Rasul, T., Nair, S., Kalendra, D., Robin, M., Santini, F., Ladeira, W., Sun, M. D. I., Rather, R. A., & Heathcote, L. (2023). The role of ChatGPT in higher education: Benefits, challenges, and future research directions. *Journal of Applied Learning and Teaching, 6*(1). Advance online publication. doi:10.37074/jalt.2023.6.1.29

Rauch, A. (1995). The monstrous body of knowledge in Mary Shelley's" Frankenstein. *Studies in Romanticism, 34*(2), 227–253. doi:10.2307/25601114

Ray, T. (2023, January 23). ChatGPT is 'not particularly innovative,' and 'nothing revolutionary', says Meta's chief AI scientist. *ZDNet.* https://www.zdnet.com/article/chatgpt-is-not-particularly-innovative-and-nothing-revolutionary-says-metas-chief-ai-scientist/

Ray, P. P. (2023). ChatGPT: A comprehensive review on background, applications, key challenges, bias, ethics, limitations and future scope. *Internet of Things and Cyber-Physical Systems, 3*, 121–154. doi:10.1016/j.iotcps.2023.04.003

Reed, B. (2023, August 23). 'Very wonderful, very toxic': How AI became the culture war's new frontier. *The Guardian.* https://www.theguardian.com/us-news/2023/aug/21/artificial-intelligence-culture-warwoke-far-right

Reeves, B., & Nass, C. (1996). The media equation: How people treat computers, television, and new media like real people and places (1st ed.). The Center for the Study of Language and Information Publications; Cambridge University Press.

Reich, J., & Ruipérez-Valiente, J. A. (2019). The MOOC pivot. *Science, 363*(6423), 130–131. doi:10.1126/science.aav7958 PMID:30630920

Rest of World. (n.d.). About us. https://restofworld.org/about/

Ricaurte, P. (2022). Ethics for the majority world: AI and the question of violence at scale. *Media Culture & Society, 44*(4), 726–745. doi:10.1177/01634437221099612

Rief, J. (2007). Talking at cross purposes: Violating higher-order conditions with oppositional arguments. In F. H. van Eemeren, J. A. Blair, C. A. Willard, & B. Garssen (Eds.), *Proceedings of the Sixth Conference of the International Society for the Study of Argumentation* (pp. 1147–1154). Sic Sat / International Center for the Study of Argumentation.

Rief, J. J. (2018). (Re)Designing the debate tournament for civic life. *Speaker & Gavel, 55*(1), 36–58.

Rief, J. J. (2021). Post-pandemic pedagogy in intercollegiate academic debate: Performing civic life in hybrid, virtual, and in-person environments. In J. M. Valenzano (Ed.), *Post pandemic pedagogy: A paradigm shift* (pp. 239–258). Lexington Books.

Rief, J. J., & Schrader, B. J. (2021). Reconciling playing the game with civic education in intercollegiate academic debate. In T. Suzuki, T. Tateyama, T. Kato, & J. Eckstein (Eds.), *Proceedings of the Tokyo Conference on Argumentation* (vol. 6, pp. 119–127). Japan Debate Association.

Riffe, D., Lacy, S., & Watson, B. R. (2019). *Analyzing media messages: Using quantitative content analysis in research* (4th ed.). Routledge. doi:10.4324/9780429464287

Roberge, J., & Castelle, M. (2021). *The cultural life of machine learning: An incursion into critical AI studies.* Springer. doi:10.1007/978-3-030-56286-1

Robinson, D. H., & Kiewra, K. A. (1995). Visual argument: Graphic organizers are superior to outlines in improving learning from text. *Journal of Educational Psychology, 87*(3), 455–467. doi:10.1037/0022-0663.87.3.455

Rodgers, W., Murray, J. M., Stefanidis, A., Degbey, W. Y., & Tarba, S. Y. (2023). An artificial intelligence algorithmic approach to ethical decision-making in human resource management processes. *Human Resource Management Review, 33*(1), 100925. doi:10.1016/j.hrmr.2022.100925

Rogers, E. M. (1997). *A History of Communication Study: A Biographical Approach.* Free Press.

Rogers, R. W. (1975). A protection motivation theory of fear appeals and attitude change. *The Journal of Psychology, 91*(1), 93–114. doi:10.1080/00223980.1975.9915803 PMID:28136248

Roose, K. (2022, December 21). A doming-out party for generative A.I., Silicon Valley's new craze. *New York Times.* https://www.nytimes.com/2022/10/21/technology/generative-ai.html

Roose, K. (2023, January 13). Don't ban ChatGPT in schools. Teach with it. *The New York Times.* https://www.nytimes.com/2023/01/12/technology/chatgpt-schools-teachers.html

Roose, K. (2023, May 30). AI poses 'risk of extinction,' industry leaders warn. *The New York Times.* https://www.nytimes.com/2023/05/30/technology/ai-threat-warning.html

Rose, K. (2023, February 3). How ChatGPT kicked off an AI arms race: Even inside the company, the chatbot's popularity has come as something of a shock. *The New York Times.* https://www.nytimes.com/2023/02/03/technology/chatgpt-openai-artificial-intelligence.html

Rosenblatt, K. (2023). *New York City public schools remove ChatGPT ban.* NBC News. https://www.nbcnews.com/tech/chatgpt-ban-dropped-new-york-city-public-schools-rcna85089

Roumate, F. (2021). Artificial intelligence, ethics and international human rights law. *International Journal of Information Ethics, 29*(3). Advance online publication. doi:10.29173/irie422

Roumate, F. (2023). Ethics of artificial intelligence, higher education, and scientific research. In F. Roumate (Ed.), *Artificial intelligence in higher education and scientific research; Future developments* (pp. 129–144). Springer. doi:10.1007/978-981-19-8641-3_10

Rowe, A. (2023, November 22). 9 simple ways to detect AI images (with examples) in 2024. *tech.co*. https://tech.co/news/ways-detect-ai-images-examples

Rudolph, J., Tan, S., & Tan, S. (2023). ChatGPT: Bullshit spewer or the end of traditional assessments in higher education? *Journal of Applied Learning and Teaching, 6*.

Rudolph, J., Tan, S., & Tan, S. (2023). ChatGPT: Bullshit spewer or the end of traditional assessments in higher education? *Journal of Applied Learning and Teaching*, *6*(1), 342–363. doi:10.37074/jalt.2023.6.1.9

Ryan, C. S., Park, B., & Judd, C. M. (1996). Assessing stereotype accuracy: Implications for understanding the stereotyping process. In C. N. Macrae, C. Stangor, & M. Hewstone (Eds.), *Stereotypes and stereotyping* (pp. 121–157). Guilford Press.

Sabzalieva, E., & Valentini, A. (2023). *ChatGPT and Artificial Intelligence in higher education*. UNESCO. https://www.iesalc.unesco.org/

Sabzalieva, E., & Valentini, A. (2023). ChatGPT and artificial intelligence in higher education; Quick start guide. *UNESCO*. Retrieved from https://www.iesalc.unesco.org/wpcontent/uploads/2023/04/ChatGPT-and-Artificial-Intelligence-in-higher-education-QuickStart guide_EN_FINA.pdf

Sabzalieva, E., & Valentini, A. (2023). ChatGPT and artificial intelligence in higher education; Quick start guide. *UNESCO*. Retrieved from https://www.iesalc.unesco.org/wp-content/uploads/2023/04/ChatGPT-and-Artificial-Intelligence-in-higher-education-Quick-Start-guide_EN_FINAL.pdf

Sadasivan, V. S., Kumar, A., Balasubramanian, S., Wang, W., & Feizi, S. (2023). Can AI-generated text be reliably detected? *ArXiv*, *11156*(2), 1–23.

Saha, S., & Beach, M. C. (2020). Impact of physician race on patient decision-making and ratings of physicians: A randomized experiment using video vignettes. *Journal of General Internal Medicine*, *35*(4), 1084–1091. doi:10.1007/s11606-020-05646-z PMID:31965527

Sahoo, B. B., Jha, R., Singh, A., & Kumar, D. (2019). Long short-term memory (LSTM) recurrent neural network for low-flow hydrological time series forecasting. *Acta Geophysica*, *27*(6), 2033–2049. doi:10.1007/s11600-019-00330-1

Sallam, M. (2023). The utility of ChatGPT as an example of large language models in healthcare education, research, and practice: Systematic review on the future perspectives and potential limitations. medRxiv, *2023-02*.

Sallam, M. (2023). ChatGPT utility in healthcare education, research, and practice: Systematic review on the promising perspectives and valid concerns. *Health Care*, *11*(6), 887. doi:10.3390/healthcare11060887 PMID:36981544

Salovey, P., & Mayer, J. D. (1990). Emotional intelligence. *Imagination, Cognition and Personality*, *9*(3), 185–211. doi:10.2190/DUGG-P24E-52WK-6CDG

Samarakou, M., Fylladitakis, E., Fruh, W., Karolidis, D., Hatziapostolou, A., Athinaios, S., & Grigoriadou, M. (2016). Evaluation of an intelligent open learning system for engineering education. *Knowledge Management and E-Learning: An International Journal*, *8*(3), 496–513. doi:10.34105/j.kmel/2016.07.031

Samoilenko, S. A., & Suvorova, I. (2023). Artificial intelligence and deepfakes in strategic deception campaigns: The U.S. and Russian experiences. In E. Pashentsev (Ed.), *The Palgrave handbook of malicious use of AI and psychological security* (pp. 507–529). Palgrave Macmillan. doi:10.1007/978-3-031-22552-9_19

Sample, I. (2023, July 10). Programs to detect AI discriminate against non-native English speakers, shows study: Over half of essays written by people were wrongly flagged as AI-made, with implications for students and job applicants. *The Guardian*. https://www.theguardian.com/technology/2023/jul/10/programs-to-detect-ai-discriminate-against-non-native-english-speakers-shows-study

Santoso, D. R., & Taufiq, W. (2021, March). Implementing circumlocution to improve the speech performance in public speaking. In *Proceedings of 1st Paris Van Java International Seminar on Health, Economics, Social Science and Humanities (PVJ-ISHESSH 2020)* (pp. 117–120). Atlantis Press. https://doi.org/10.2991/assehr.k.210304.027

Sarsa, S., Denny, P., Hellas, A., & Leinonen, J. (2022). Automatic generation of programming exercises and code explanations using large language models. In *Proceedings of the 2022 ACM Conference on International Computing Education Research* Volume 1 (pp. 27–43). 10.1145/3501385.3543957

Sawatzki, J., Schlippe, T., & Benner-Wickner, M. (2022). Deep learning techniques for automatic short answer grading: Predicting scores for English and German answers. In *Artificial Intelligence in Education: Emerging Technologies, Models and Applications: Proceedings of 2021 2nd International Conference on Artificial Intelligence in Education Technology* (pp. 65–75). Springer.

Saygin, A. P., Cicekli, I., & Akman, V. (2000). Turing test: 50 years later. *Minds and Machines, 10*(4), 463–518. doi:10.1023/A:1011288000451

Scharth, M. (2022). *The ChatGPT chatbot is blowing people away with its writing skills. An expert explains why it's so impressive*. https://theconversation.com/the-chatgpt-chatbot-is-blowing-people-away-with-its-writing-skills-an-expert-explains-why-its-so-impressive-195908

Schiller, D. (2000). *Digital capitalism: Networking the global market system*. MIT Press.

Schlosser, K. (2021, March 7). UW's Os Keyes takes on tech's ethical challenges, from gender bias in AI to facial recognition. *Geek Wire*. https://www.geekwire.com/2021/os-keyes/

Schmidt-Crawford, D. A., Lindstrom, D. L., & Thompson, A. D. (2023). AI in teacher education: What's next? *Journal of Digital Learning in Teacher Education, 39*(4), 180–181. doi:10.1080/21532974.2023.2247308

Schmidt, L. K. (2014). Intercultural understanding in philosophical hermeneutics. In M. Xie (Ed.), *The agon of interpretations: Towards a critical intercultural hermeneutics* (pp. 210–232). University of Toronto Press. doi:10.3138/9781442696303-014

Schneider, J., Richner, R., & Riser, M. (2022). Towards trustworthy autograding of short, multi-lingual, multi-type answers. *International Journal of Artificial Intelligence in Education*, 1–31.

Schneier, B. (2016). Data and Goliath: The hidden battles to collect your data and control your world (Reprint edition). W. W. Norton & Company.

Schrader, B. J. (2016). *It's a whole new ball game: The Mitchell Report, performance enhancing drugs, and professional sports* [Doctoral Dissertation, University of Denver]. Digital Commons @ DU. https://digitalcommons.du.edu/etd/1160/

Schramowski, P., Turan, C., Andersen, N., Rothkopf, C. A., & Kersting, K. (2022). Large pre-trained language models contain human-like biases of what is right and wrong to do. *Nature Machine Intelligence, 4*(3), 258–268. doi:10.1038/s42256-022-00458-8

Schulman, J., Zoph, B., Kim, C., Hilton, J., Menick, J., Weng, J., Uribe, J. F. C., Fedus, L., Metz, L., Pokorny, M., Lopes, R. G., Zhao, S., Vijayvergiya, A., Sigler, E., Perelman, A., Voss, C., Heaton, M., Parish, J., Cummings, R. N., . . . Ryder, N. (2022, November 30). *ChatGPT: Optimizing language models for dialogue. OpenAI.com.* Accessed from https://openai.com/blog/chatgpt

Schwartz, A. B. (2015, May 6). The infamous "War of the Worlds" radio broadcast was a magnificent fluke. *Smithsonian Magazine.* https://www.smithsonianmag.com/history/infamous-war-worlds-radio-broadcast-was-magnificent-fluke-180955180/

Schwartzman, R. (2022). Beyond basic: Transformational potential of pandemic pedagogy. *Basic Communication Course Annual, 34*(1), 141–152. https://ecommons.udayton.edu/bcca/vol34/iss1/13

Schwartz, R., Dodge, J., Smith, N. A., & Etzioni, O. (2020). Green AI. *Communications of the ACM, 63*(12), 54–63. doi:10.1145/3381831

Schwartz, R., Vassilev, A., Greene, K., Perine, L., Burt, A., & Hall, P. (2022). *Towards a standard for identifying and managing bias in artificial intelligence.* National Institute of Standards and Technology., doi:10.6028/NIST.SP.1270

Sebesta, J., & Davis, V. L. (2023, December). *AI policies practices toolkit.* WCET. https://wcet.wiche.edu/resources/ai-practices-and-policies-toolkit/

Seeger, M. W., & Sellnow, T. L. (2019). *Communication in times of trouble.* Wiley Blackwell.

Sellnow, D. D. (2023). What's in a name? Identity awareness and promotion as fundamental to the future of communication education and instructional communication. *Communication Education, 72*(4), 435–440. doi:10.1080/03634523.2023.2234513

Sellnow-Richmond, D. D., & Lukacovic, M. N. (2024). The COVID-19 pandemic as exemplar of the chaos of mega-crises. In Communicating risk and safety (pp. 97-107). Berlin/Boston: De Gruyters. doi:10.1515/9783110752427-006

Selwyn, N. (2019). *Should robots replace teachers?: AI and the future of education.* John Wiley & Sons.

Seo, K., Tang, J., Roll, I., Fels, S., & Yoon, D. (2021). The impact of artificial intelligence on learner–instructor interaction in online learning. *Research and Practice in Technology Enhanced Learning, 16*(1), 16. Advance online publication. doi:10.1186/s41239-021-00292-9 PMID:34778540

Sertin, C. (2023, May 30). *How NVIDIA AI tech powers smart NPCs in gaming.* WIRED Middle East. https://wired.me/culture/nvidia-ai-powered-npcs/

Shaw, C., Yuan, L., Brennan, D., Martin, S., Janson, N., Fox, K., & Bryant, G. (2023). *Generative AI in higher education: Fall 2023 update of time for class study.* Tyton Partners. https://www.tytonpartners.com/time-for-class-2023/GenAI-Update

Shelley, M. (2021). *Frankenstein.* Sterling Publishing. (Original work published 1818)

Shen, J., Zhang, C. J. P., Jiang, B., Chen, J., Song, J., Liu, Z., He, Z., Wong, S. Y., Fang, P. H., & Ming, W. K. (2019). Artificial intelligence versus clinicians in disease diagnosis: Systematic review. *JMIR Medical Informatics, 7*(3), e10010. doi:10.2196/10010 PMID:31420959

Shin, M., Kim, J., Opheusden, B., & Griffiths, T. L. (2023). Superhuman artificial intelligence can improve human decision-making by increasing novelty. *Proceedings of the National Academy of Sciences of the United States of America, 120*(12), e2214840120. Advance online publication. doi:10.1073/pnas.2214840120 PMID:36913582

Shumaker, D., & Talley, M. (2009). *Models of embedded librarianship: Final report.* School of Library and Information Science, Catholic University of American.

Shum, H., He, X., & Li, D. (2018). From Eliza to XiaoIce: Challenges and opportunities with social chatbots. *Frontiers of Information Technology & Electronic Engineering, 19*(1), 10–26. doi:10.1631/FITEE.1700826

Siegle, D. (2023). A role for ChatGPT and AI in gifted education. *Gifted Child Today, 46*(3), 211–219. doi:10.1177/10762175231168443

Sikström, P., Valentini, C., Sivunen, A., & Kärkkäinen, T. (2022). How pedagogical agents communicate with students: A two-phase systematic review. *Computers & Education*, *188*, 104564. Advance online publication. doi:10.1016/j.compedu.2022.104564

Silver, D., Huang, A., Maddison, C., Guez, A., Sifre, L., Driessche, G., ... Hassabis, D. (2016). Mastering the game of go with deep neural networks and tree search. *Nature*, *529*(7587), 484–489. doi:10.1038/nature16961 PMID:26819042

Skrabut, S. (2023). *80 ways to use ChatGPT in the classroom: Using AI to enhance teaching and learning*. Academic Press.

Slonim, N., Bilu, Y., Alzate, C., Bar-Haim, R., Bogin, B., Bonin, F., Choshen, L., Cohen-Karlik, E., Dankin, L., Edelstein, L., Ein-Dor, L., Friedman-Melamed, R., Gavron, A., Gera, A., Gleize, M., Gretz, S., Gutfreund, D., Halfon, A., Hershcovich, D., ... Aharonov, R. (2021). An autonomous debating system. *Nature*, *591*(7850), 379–384. doi:10.1038/s41586-021-03215-w PMID:33731946

Smith, C. S. (2023, September 8). What large models cost you: There is no free AI lunch. *Forbes*. https://www.forbes.com/sites/craigsmith/2023/09/08/what-large-models-cost-you--there-is-no-free-ai-lunch

Smith, A. (1902). *The wealth of nations*. Collier & Son.

Smith, H. (2021). Clinical AI: Opacity, accountability, responsibility, and liability. *AI & Society*, *36*(2), 535–545. doi:10.1007/s00146-020-01019-6

Smith, S. W., Daunic, A. P., Miller, M. D., & Robinson, T. R. (2002). Conflict resolution and peer mediation in middle schools: Extending the process and outcome knowledge base. *The Journal of Social Psychology*, *142*(5), 567–586. doi:10.1080/00224540209603919 PMID:12236468

Smits, M. (2006). Taming monsters: The cultural domestication of new technology. *Technology in Society*, *28*(4), 489–504. doi:10.1016/j.techsoc.2006.09.008

Snider, A., & Schnurer, M. (2002). *Many sides: Debate across the curriculum*. International Debate Education Association.

Sok, S., & Heng, K. (2023). ChatGPT for education and research: A review of benefits and risks. *Cambodian Journal of Educational Research*, *3*(1), 110–121. doi:10.62037/cjer.2023.03.01.06

Son, C., Hegde, S., Smith, A., Wang, X., & Sasangohar, F. (2020). Effects of COVID-19 on College Students' Mental Health in the United States: Interview Survey Study. *Journal of Medical Internet Research*, *22*(9), e21279. doi:10.2196/21279 PMID:32805704

Spector, C. (2019, October 16). Racial disparities in school discipline are linked to the achievement gap between Black and white students nationwide, according to Stanford-led study. *Research Stories*. Stanford Graduate School of Education. https://ed.stanford.edu/news/racial-disparities-school-discipline-are-linked-achievement-gap-between-black-and-white

Spence, P. R., Westerman, D., Edwards, C., & Edwards, A. (2014). Welcoming our robot overlords: Initial expectations about interaction with a robot. *Communication Research Reports*, *31*(3), 272–280. doi:10.1080/08824096.2014.924337

St. George, D., & Svrluga, S. (2023, July 13). Artificial intelligence is already changing how teachers teach. *The Washington Post*. https://www.washingtonpost.com/education/2023/07/13/ai-education-teachers-lesson-plans/

Stake, R. E. (2000). Case studies. In N. K. Denzin & Y. S. Lincoln (Eds.), *Handbook of qualitative research* (2nd ed., pp. 435–454). Sage.

Staley, D. J., & Endicott, D. D. J. (2023). *Knowledge towns; Colleges and universities as talent magnets*. John Hopkins University Press.

Stebbins, R. A. (2001). Exploratory research in the social sciences. *Sage (Atlanta, Ga.)*. Advance online publication. doi:10.4135/9781412984249

Stempel, J. (2007, August 9). Countrywide sued for racial bias in mortgage loans. *Reuters*. https://www.reuters.com/article/idUSN12313883/

Stempel, J. (2023, December 27). *NY Times* sues OpenAI, Microsoft for infringing copyrighted works. *Reuters*. https://www.reuters.com/legal/transactional/ny-times-sues-openai-microsoft-infringing-copyrighted-work-2023-12-27/

Stevano, S., & Deane, K. (2019). The role of research assistants in qualitative and cross-cultural social science research. In *Handbook of Research Methods in Health Social Sciences*. Available online: https://doi-org.proxy.bib.uottawa.ca/10.1007/978-981-10-5251-4_39

Stommel, J. (2023). Do we need the word 'ungrading?' *Zeal: A Journal for the Liberal Arts, 1*(2), 82–87.

Studente, S., Ellis, S., & Garivaldis, S. F. (2020). Exploring the potential of chatbots in higher education: A preliminary study. *International Journal of Educational Technology in Higher Education, 17*, 55.

Stypinska, J. (2023). AI ageism: A critical roadmap for studying age discrimination and exclusion in digitalized societies. *AI & Society, 38*(2), 665–677. doi:10.1007/s00146-022-01553-5 PMID:36212226

Sullivan, M., Kelly, A., & McLaughlan, P. (2023). ChatGPT in higher education: Considerations for academic integrity and student learning. *Journal of Applied Learning & Teaching, 6*(1), 31–40. doi:10.37074/jalt.2023.6.1.17

Sundler, A. J., Lindberg, E., Nilsson, C., & Palmér, L. (2019). Qualitative thematic analysis based on descriptive phenomenology. *Nursing Open, 6*(3), 733–739. doi:10.1002/nop2.275 PMID:31367394

Sunny, M. (2023, September 20). Musk's Neuralink to start human trials of brain implant. to start human trial of brain implant for paralysis patients, *Reuters*. https://www.reuters.com/technology/musks-neuralink-start-human-trials-brain-implant2023-09-19/

Sun, T., Gaut, A., Tang, S., Huang, Y., ElSherief, M., Zhao, J., Mirza, D., Belding, E., Chang, K.-W., & Wang, W. Y. (2019). Mitigating gender bias in natural language processing: literature review. *Proceedings of the 57th Annual Meeting of the Association for Computational Linguistics*. 10.18653/v1/P19-1159

Suresh Babu, C. V., & Akshara, P. M. (2024). Revolutionizing conversational AI: unleashing the power of ChatGPT-Based applications in generative AI and natural language processing. In Advanced applications of generative AI and natural language processing models (pp. 228-248). IGI Global. doi:10.4018/979-8-3693-0502-7.ch011

Suresh, H., & Guttag, J. V. (2021). A framework for understanding sources of harm throughout the machine learning life cycle. *Equity and Access in Algorithms, Mechanisms, and Optimization, 5*, 1–9. doi:10.1145/3465416.3483305

Svrluga, S., & Natanson, H. (2023, June 1). All the unexpected ways ChatGPT is infiltrating. students' lives. *The Washington Post*. https://www.washingtonpost.com/education/2023/06/01/students-chatgpt-ai-tools/

Swiecki, Z., Khosravi, H., Chen, G., Martinez-Maldonado, R., Lodge, J. M., Milligan, S., Selwyn, N., & Gašević, D. (2022). Assessment in the age of artificial intelligence. *Computers and Education: Artificial Intelligence, 3*(1), 100075. Advance online publication. doi:10.1016/j.caeai.2022.100075

Switzky, L. (2020). Eliza effects: Pygmalion and the early development of artificial intelligence. *Shaw, 40*(1), 50–68. doi:10.5325/shaw.40.1.0050

Szücs, B. (2023, June 14). *Not replacing but enhancing: Using ChatGPT for academic writing*. Inside Higher Ed. https://www.timeshighereducation.com/campus/not-replacing-enhancing-using-chatgpt-academic-writing

Ta, R., & West, D. (2023, August 7). *Should schools ban or integrate generative AI in the classrooms?* Brookings. https://www.brookings.edu/articles/should-schools-ban-or-integrate-generative-ai-in-the-classroom/

Tacheva, J., & Ramasubramanian, S. (2023). AI Empire: Unraveling the interlocking systems of oppression in generative AI's global order. *Big Data & Society*, *10*(2). Advance online publication. doi:10.1177/20539517231219241

Tadesse, G. A., Cintas, C., Varshney, K. R., Staar, P., Agunwa, C., Speakman, S., Jia, J., Bailey, E. E., Adelekun, A., Lipoff, J. B., Onyekaba, G., Lester, J. C., Rotemberg, V., Zou, J., & Daneshjou, R. (2023). Skin Tone Analysis for Representation in Educational Materials (STAR-ED) using machine learning. *NPJ Digital Medicine*, *6*(1), 151. Advance online publication. doi:10.1038/s41746-023-00881-0 PMID:37596324

Tam, W., Huynh, T., Tang, A., Luong, S., Khatri, Y., & Zhou, W. (2023). Nursing education in the age of artificial intelligence powered Chatbots (AI-chatbots): Are we ready yet? *Nurse Education Today*, *129*, 105917. doi:10.1016/j.nedt.2023.105917 PMID:37506622

Tanjga, M. (2023). *E-learning and the use of AI: A review of current practices and future directions*. Qeios. doi:10.32388/AP0208

Tapalova, O., & Zhiyenbayeva, N. (2022). Artificial intelligence in education: AIEd for personalized learning pathways. *Electronic Journal of e-Learning*, *20*(5), 639–653. doi:10.34190/ejel.20.5.2597

TateT. P.DoroudiS.RitchieD.XuY.WarschauerM. (2023, January 10). Educational research and AI-Generated writing: Confronting the coming tsunami. EdArXiv. doi:10.35542/osf.io/4mec3

Taylor, T., & Dorin, A. (2020). *Rise of the self-replicators*. Springer. doi:10.1007/978-3-030-48234-3

Tennery, A., & Cherelus, G. (2016, March 24). *Microsoft's AI Twitter bot goes dark after racist, sexist tweets*. Reuters. https://www.reuters.com/article/idUSKCN0WQ2M7/

Terregino, C. A., Copeland, H. L., Sarfaty, S. C., Lantz-Gefroh, V., & Hoffmann-Longtin, K. (2019). Development of an empathy and clarity rating scale to measure the effect of medical improv on end-of-first-year OCSE performance: A pilot study. *Medical Education Online*, *24*(1), 1666537. doi:10.1080/10872981.2019.1666537 PMID:31532330

Tesch, R. (1990). *Qualitative research: Analysis types and software tools*. Falmer Press.

The Conference Board. (2023, September 9). *Majority of US workers are already using GAI tools—But company policies trail behind* [Press release]. https://www.conference-board.org/press/us-workers-and-generative-ai

The Learning Network. (2023, February 2). What students are saying about ChatGPT. *New York Times*. https://www.nytimes.com/2023/02/02/learning/students-chatgpt.html

Thorbecke, C. (2022, August 11). *It didn't take long for Meta's new chatbot to say something offensive*. CNN. https://www.cnn.com/2022/08/11/tech/meta-chatbot-blenderbot/index.html

Thorey, V., Hernandez, A. B., Arnal, P. J., & During, E. H. (2019, July 23-27). AI vs humans for the diagnosis of sleep apnea. *Proceedings of the 41st International Engineering in Medicine and Biology Conference*. 10.1109/EMBC.2019.8856877

Tiku, N., Schaul, K., & Chen, S. Y. (2023, November 1). These fake images reveal how AI amplifies our worst stereotypes. *Washington Post*. https://www.washingtonpost.com/technology/interactive/2023/ai-generated-images-bias-racism-sexism-stereotypes/

Tlili, A., Shehata, B., Adarkwah, M. A., Bozkurt, A., Hickey, D. T., Huang, R., & Agyemang, B. (2023). What if the devil is my guardian angel: ChatGPT as a case study of using chatbots in education. *Smart Learning and Environment*, *10*(15), 15. Advance online publication. doi:10.1186/s40561-023-00237-x

Tong, A., Dastin, J., & Hu, K. (2023, November 23). *OpenAI researchers warned board of AI breakthrough ahead of CEO ouster, sources say.* Reuters. https://www.reuters.com/technology/sam-altmans-ouster-openai-was-precipitated-by-letter-board-about-ai-breakthrough-2023-11-22/

Topol, E. (2019). *Deep medicine: How artificial intelligence can make healthcare human again.* Basic Books.

Torralba, A., & Efros, A. A. (2011). Unbiased look at dataset bias. In *CVPR 2011* (pp. 1521–1528). IEEE. doi:10.1109/CVPR.2011.5995347

Toulmin, S. E. (2003). The uses of argument (updated ed.). Cambridge University Press.

Touretzky, D., Gardner-McCune, C., Martin, F., & Seehorn, D. (2019, July). Envisioning AI for K-12: What should every child know about AI? *Proceedings of the AAAI Conference on Artificial Intelligence, 33*(01), 9795–9799. doi:10.1609/aaai.v33i01.33019795

Truitt, E. R. (2021). Made, not born: The ancient history of intelligent machines. In A. Campbell (Ed.), The love makers (pp. 217–224). Goldsmiths Press.

Truong, T.-L., Le, H.-L., & Le-Dang, T.-P. (2020, November). Sentiment analysis implementing BERT-based pre-trained language model for Vietnamese. *2020 7th NAFOSTED Conference on Information and Computer Science (NICS).* 10.1109/NICS51282.2020.9335912

Turing, A. M. (1950). Computing machinery and intelligence. *Mind, LIX*(236), 433–460. doi:10.1093/mind/LIX.236.433

Turk, V. (2023). How AI reduces the world to stereotypes. *Rest of World.* https://restofworld.org/2023/ai-image-stereotypes/

Turner, S. (2010). Research note: The silenced assistant. Reflections of invisible interpreters and research assistants. *Asia Pacific Viewpoint, 51*(2), 206–219. doi:10.1111/j.1467-8373.2010.01425.x

Tyson, A., & Kikuchi, E. (2023). *Growing public concern about the role of artificial intelligence in daily life.* The Pew Research Center. https://www.pewresearch.org/short-reads/2023/08/28/growing-public-concern-about-the-role-of-artificial-intelligence-in-daily-life/

Tzirides, A. O. (2023). *Generative AI: Implications and applications for education.* arXiv, 2305.07605. https://doi.org//arXiv.2305.07605 doi:10.48550

U.S. Department of Education. (2023). *Artificial intelligence and future of teaching and learning: Insights and recommendations.* Office of Educational Technology. https://tech.ed.gov

U.S. Department of Education. (2023). *Family educational rights and privacy act (FERPA).* https://www2.ed.gov/policy/gen/guid/fpco/ferpa/index.html

Uchiyama, K. P., & Radin, J. L. (2009). Curriculum mapping in higher education: A vehicle for collaboration. *Innovative Higher Education, 33*(4), 271–280. doi:10.1007/s10755-008-9078-8

Uecker, D., & Schmidt, J. (2022). Interpersonal communication and perception differences between Russia and the United States: Changes since 2009? In M. Minielli, M. N. Lukacovic, S. A. Samoilenko, M. Finch, & D. Uecker (Eds.), *Communication theory and application in post-socialist contexts* (pp. 253–266). Lexington Books – Rowman & Littlefield.

United Nations. (n.d.). What is human security. *United Nations Trust Fund for Human Security.* Retrieved from https://www.un.org/humansecurity/what-is-human-security/

University of Arizona Libraries. (2023). *AI literacy for instructors.* The University of Arizona Libraries. https://libguides.library.arizona.edu/ai-literacy-instructors/teaching

University of North Florida. (2023). *What is a library guide (LibGuide)?* UNF Library. https://libguides.unf.edu/WhatisaLibraryGuide/DefinitionOftheLibraryGuide#:~:text=Deining%20the%20Term&text=They%20define%20library%20guides%20as,to%20create20and%20manage%20websites

Valencia College. (2021). *Evaluating sources using the CRAAP method.* Valencia College LibGuides. https://libguides.valenciacollege.edu/friendly.php?s=CRAAP

van Atteveldt, W., & Peng, T.-Q. (Eds.). (2021). *Computational methods for communication science.* Routledge. doi:10.4324/9781003082606

Van der Duim, H. (2023, March 27). What you need to know about AI prompts. *Hackeroon.* https://hackernoon.com/what-you-need-to-know-about-ai-prompts

van der Sluijs, J. (2005). Uncertainty as a monster in the science-policy interface: Four coping strategies. *Water Science and Technology, 52*(6), 87–92. doi:10.2166/wst.2005.0155 PMID:16304939

van Hooijdonk, R., Mathot, S., Schat, E., Spencer, H., van der Stigchel, S., & Dijkerman, H. C. (2019). Touch-induced pupil size reflects stimulus intensity, not subjective pleasantness. *Experimental Brain Research, 237*(1), 201–210. doi:10.1007/s00221-018-5404-2 PMID:30374784

Van Sant, G. (2000). *Finding Forrester* [Film]. Columbia Pictures.

Varanasi, L. (2024, January 7). Sam Altman said his firing and reinstatement was 'extremely painful,' but 'great for OpenAI.' *Business Insider.* https://www.businessinsider.com/sam-altmans-said-his-firing-was-painful-but-great-for-openai-2024-1

Vasalou, A., Joinson, A., Bänziger, T., Goldie, P., & Pitt, J. (2008). Avatars in social media: Balancing accuracy, playfulness and embodied messages. *International Journal of Human-Computer Studies, 66*(11), 801–811. doi:10.1016/j.ijhcs.2008.08.002

Vassallo, S. (2023, October 23). *Why generative AI needs design.* Forbes. https://www.forbes.com/sites/stevevassallo/2023/10/23/why-generative-ai-needs-design/

Verity, A., & Motalebi, N. (2023). *GAI for humanitarians.* Digital Humanitarian Network. https://digitalhumanitarians.com/generative_ai_for_humanitarians-september_2023/

Verma, P., & Lerman, R. (2023, May 7). *A curious person's guide to artificial intelligence.* Washington Post. https://www.washingtonpost.com/technology/2023/05/07/ai-beginners-guide/

Verma, S. (2019). Weapons of Math Destruction: How Big Data Increases Inequality and Threatens Democracy. *Vikalpa, 44*(2), 97–98. doi:10.1177/0256090919853933

Vincent, J. (2023, February 15). *Microsoft's Bing is an emotionally manipulative liar, and people love it.* The Verge. https://www.theverge.com/2023/2/15/23599072/microsoft-ai-bing-personality-conversations-spy-employees-webcams

Wach, K., Duong, C. D., Ejdys, J., Kazlauskaite, R., Korzynski, P., Mazurek, G., Paliszkiewicz, J., & Ziemba, E. (2023). The dark side of generative artificial intelligence: A critical analysis of controversies and risks of ChatGPT. *Entrepreneurial Business and Economics Review, 11*(2), 7–30. doi:10.15678/EBER.2023.110201

Wachter, S., Mittelstadt, B., & Floridi, L. (2017). Transparent, explainable, and accountable AI for robotics. *Science Robotics, 2*(6), eaan6080. doi:10.1126/scirobotics.aan6080 PMID:33157874

Walters, W. H., & Wilder, E. I. (2023). Fabrication and errors in the bibliographic citations generated by ChatGPT. *Scientific Reports, 13*(1), 14045. doi:10.1038/s41598-023-41032-5 PMID:37679503

Walton, D. (2008). Proleptic argumentation. *Argumentation and Advocacy*, *44*(3), 143–154. doi:10.1080/00028533.2008.11821684

Wang, D., Churchill, E., Maes, P., Fan, X., Shneiderman, B., Shi, Y., & Wang, Q. (2020). Fromhuman-human collaboration to human-AI collaboration: Designing AI systems that can work together with people. In Extended abstracts of the 2020 CHI conference on human factors in computing systems (pp. 1–6). doi:10.1145/3334480.3381069

Wang, T., Lund, B. D., Marengo, A., Pagano, A., Mannuru, N. R., Teel, Z. A., & Pange, J. (2023). Exploring the potential impact of artificial intelligence (AI) on international students in higher education: Generative AI, chatbots, analytics, and international student success. *Applied Sciences (Basel, Switzerland)*, *13*(11), 6716. doi:10.3390/app13116716

Wang, Y. (2022). Construction of intelligent evaluation model of English composition based on machine learning. *Mobile Information Systems*, *2022*(3499799), 1–9. doi:10.1155/2022/3499799

Wang, Y., & Kosinski, M. (2018). Deep neural networks are more accurate than humans at detecting sexual orientation from facial images. *Journal of Personality and Social Psychology*, *114*(2), 246–257. doi:10.1037/pspa0000098 PMID:29389215

Wardat, Y., Tashtoush, M. A., Alali, R., & Jarrah, A. M. (2023). ChatGPT: A revolutionary tool for teaching and learning mathematics. *Eurasia Journal of Mathematics, Science and Technology Education*, *19*(7), em2286. Advance online publication. doi:10.29333/ejmste/13272

Ward, S. J. A. (2014). Radical media ethics. Ethics for a global digital world. *Digital Journalism (Abingdon, England)*, *2*(4), 455–471. doi:10.1080/21670811.2014.952985

Warner, J. (2022, December 5). *Freaking out about ChatGPT—Part I*. Inside Higher Education. https://www.insidehighered.com/blogs/just-visiting/freaking-out-about-chatgpt%E2%80%94part-i

Warner, J. (2023, May 24). *We can help students think*. Inside Higher Ed. https://www.insidehighered.com/opinion/blogs/just-visiting/2023/05/24/we-can-help-students-think

WarschauerM.TsengW.YimS.WebsterT.JacobS.DuQ.TateT. (2023). *The affordances and contradictions of AI-generated text for second language writers*. doi:10.2139/ssrn.4404380

Weissman, S. (2021, September 14). *Not coming, not staying*. Inside Higher Education. https://www.insidehighered.com/news/2021/09/15/new-federal-data-confirm-enrollment-declines

Weizenbaum, J. (1966). ELIZA—A computer program for the study of natural language communication between man and machine. *Communications of the ACM*, *9*(1), 36–45. doi:10.1145/365153.365168

Welding, L. (2023). Half of college students say using AI on schoolwork is cheating or plagiarism. *Best Colleges*. https://www.bestcolleges.com/research/college-students-ai-tools-survey/

West, D. M. (2018). The future of work: Robots, AI, and automation. In *The Future of Work* (p. 205). Robots, AI, and Automation.

Westerman, D. K., Bowman, N. D., & Lachlan, K. A. (2022). *Introduction to mediated communication: Social media and beyond* (3rd ed.). Kendall Hunt Publishing.

Westfall, C. (2023, January 28). *Educators battle plagiarism as 89% of students admit to using OpenAI's ChatGPT for homework*. https://www.forbes.com/sites/chriswestfall/2023/01/28/educators-battle-plagiarism-as-89of-students-admit-to-using-open-ais-chatgpt-for-homework/?sh=59d9ff99750d

Westley, B. H., & MacLean, M. S. (1955). A conceptual model for communications research. *Educational Technology Research and Development*, *3*(1), 3–12. doi:10.1007/BF02713344

What does a librarian do ? (2023). CareerExplorer. https://www.careerexplorer.com/careers/librarian/

Wheeler, T. (2023, June 15). *The three challenges of AI regulation.* The Brookings Institute. https://www.brookings.edu/articles/the-three-challenges-of-ai-regulation/

Whittaker, Z. (2019). OpenAI built a text generator so good, it's consider too dangerous to release. *Techcrunch.* https://teachcrunch.com/2019/02/17/openai-text-generator-dangerous/

Williams, C. (2022). *Hype, or the future of learning and teaching? 3 Limits to AI's ability to write student essays.* The University of Kent's Academic Repository, Blog post. https://kar.kent.ac.uk/99505/

Wilson, D., & Sperber, D. (1993). Linguistic form and relevance. *Lingua*, *90*(1), 1–25. doi:10.1016/0024-3841(93)90058-5

Witt, S. (2015). *How music got free: The end of an industry, the turn of the century, and the patient zero of piracy.* Viking.

Wollny, S., Schneider, J., Di Mitri, D., Weidlich, J., Rittberger, M., & Drachsler, H. (2021). Are we there yet? – A systematic literature review on chatbots in education. *Frontiers in Artificial Intelligence*, *4*, 654924. doi:10.3389/frai.2021.654924 PMID:34337392

Wong, M. (2022, December 20). *We haven't seen the worst of fake news.* The Atlantic. https://www.theatlantic.com/technology/archive/2022/12/deepfake-synthetic-media-technology-rise-disinformation/672519/

Wong, M. (2023, June 2). AI Doomarism is a decoy. *The Atlantic.* https://www.theatlantic.com/technology/archive/2023/06/ai-regulation-sam-altman-billgates/674278/

Woods, C., Brigham, M., Heavner, B., Konishi, T., Rief, J., Saindon, B., & Mitchell, G. R. (2006). Deliberating debate's digital futures. *Contemporary Argumentation and Debate*, *27*, 81–105.

Wu, G. (2022, August 18). Helping people understand AI. *The Keyword.* https://blog.google/technology/ai/helping-people-understand-ai

Wu, X., He, X., Li, T., Liu, N., & Zhai, X. (2023). Matching exemplar as next sentence prediction (MENSP): Zero-shot prompt learning for automatic scoring in science education. *arXiv preprint arXiv:2301.08771.* doi:10.1007/978-3-031-36272-9_33

Wu, J. (2022). Analysis and evaluation of the impact of integrating mental health education into the teaching of university civics courses in the context of artificial intelligence. *Wireless Communications and Mobile Computing*, *2022*, 2022. doi:10.1155/2022/5378694

Wu, X. (2021). Application of artificial intelligence in higher vocational English teaching mode. *Journal of Physics: Conference Series*, *1852*(2), 1–6. doi:10.1088/1742-6596/1852/2/022089

Wyman, C. (2023, June 28). How to tackle AI—and cheating—in the classroom. *Wired.* https://www.wired.com/story/how-to-tackle-ai-and-cheating-in-schools-classroom/

Xie, Y., Chen, Y., & Ryder, L. H. (2021). Effects of using mobile-based virtual reality on Chinese L2 students' oral proficiency. *Computer Assisted Language Learning*, *34*(3), 225–245. doi:10.1080/09588221.2019.1604551

Xu, Y. (2023). Envisioning a better world of human and technology: Theoretical and empirical considerations to connect communication scholarship to ethical technology design. *Annals of the International Communication Association*, 1–16. doi:10.1080/23808985.2023.2255586

Yanisky-Ravid, S. (2017). Generating Rembrandt: Artificial intelligence, copyright, and accountability in the 3a era: The human-like authors are already here - a new model. *Detroit College of Law at Michigan State University Law Review, 2017*(4), 659–726.

Yan, L., Zhao, L., Gašević, D., & Martinez-Maldonado, R. (2022). Scalability, sustainability, and ethicality of multimodal learning analytics. In *LAK22: 12th International Learning Analytics and Knowledge Conference* (pp. 13–23). 10.1145/3506860.3506862

Yates, D. R., Vaessen, C., & Roupret, M. (2011). From Leonardo to da Vinci: The history of robot-assisted surgery in urology. *BJU International, 108*(11), 1708–1713. doi:10.1111/j.1464-410X.2011.10576.x PMID:21951677

Yi, Y. (2021). Establishing the concept of AI literacy. *JaHR – European Journal of Bioethics, 12*(2), 353–368.

Yudkowsky, E. (2023, March 29). Pausing AI developments isn't enough. We need to shut it all down. *TIME.* https://time.com/6266923/ai-eliezer-yudkowsky-open-letter-not-enough/

Yu, H., & Guo, Y. (2023). Generative artificial intelligence empowers educational reform: Current status, issues, and prospects. *Frontiers in Education, 8*(1), 1183162. Advance online publication. doi:10.3389/feduc.2023.1183162

Zawacki-Richter, O., Marín, V. I., Bond, M., & Gouverneur, F. (2019). Systematic review of research on artificial intelligence applications in higher education: Where are the educators? *International Journal of Educational Technology in Higher Education, 16*(39), 39. Advance online publication. doi:10.1186/s41239-019-0171-0

Zeng, J. (2021). Securitization of artificial intelligence in China. *The Chinese Journal of International Politics, 14*(3), 417–445. doi:10.1093/cjip/poab005

Zeng, Z., Gašević, D., & Chen, G. (2023). On the effectiveness of curriculum learning in educational text scoring. *Proceedings of the AAAI Conference on Artificial Intelligence.* 10.1609/aaai.v37i12.26707

Zewe, A. (2023, November 9). *Explained: Generative AI.* MIT News | Massachusetts Institute of Technology. https://news.mit.edu/2023/explained-generative-ai-1109

ZhaiX. (2022). ChatGPT user experience: implications for education. SSRN. doi:10.2139/ssrn.4312418

Zhang, K., & Aslan, A. B. (2021). AI technologies for education: Recent research future directions. *Computers. Education and Artificial Intelligence, 2*, 100025. doi:10.1016/j.caeai.2021.100025

Zheng, M., Pei, J., & Jurgens, D. (2023). Is "a helpful assistant" the best role for large language models? A systematic evaluation of social roles in system prompts. *arXiv.*

Zheng, L., Niu, J., Long, M., & Fan, Y. (2023). An automatic knowledge graph construction approach to promoting collaborative knowledge building, group performance, social interaction, and socially shared regulation in CSCL. *British Journal of Educational Technology, 54*(3), 686–711. doi:10.1111/bjet.13283

Zheng, L., Niu, J., & Zhong, L. (2022). Effects of a learning analytics-based real-time feedback approach on knowledge elaboration, knowledge convergence, interactive relationships, and group performance in CSCL. *British Journal of Educational Technology, 53*(1), 130–149. doi:10.1111/bjet.13156

Zhu, Y., & Yang, F. (2023). ChatGPT/generative artificial intelligence and educational innovation: Opportunities, challenges, and the future. *Journal of East China Normal University (Educational Sciences), 41*(7), 1–14. doi:10.16382/j.cnki.1000-5560.2023.07.001

Zhu, Y., Li, Y., Yang, Y., & Zhai, X. (2023). Intelligent technology drives higher education reform: Key points and reflections on the 2023 Horizon report: Teaching and learning edition. *Open Education Research, 29*(3), 19–30. https://doi.org/ doi:10.13966/j.cnki.kfjyyj.2023.03

Zidani, S. (2021). Whose pedagogy is it anyway? Decolonizing the syllabus through a critical embrace of difference. *Media Culture & Society*, *43*(5), 970–978. doi:10.1177/0163443720980922

About the Contributors

Sanae Elmoudden, Ph.D is an Assistant Chair and Associate Professor in the department of Communication Studies at St. John's University, New York. She received her M.A. in telecommunications and Ph.D. in communication from the University of Colorado, Boulder. During the lapse time between her masters and her PhD degrees, she worked as telecommunication analyst in different global cities. Her interests are in the conjuncture of education, technologies, and communication. She conducted a Fulbright research in Morocco that investigated the offshoring of call centers and its impact on Moroccan identities. Her publications highlight intersectionality, brain diversity, inclusivity, and most recently an emphasis on generative artificial intelligence and education.

Jason S. Wrench (Ed.D., West Virginia University) is a professor in Department of Communication at the State University of New York at New Paltz. Dr. Wrench has published numerous books on a variety of communication topics: *Intercultural Communication: Power in Context, Communication, Affect, and Learning in the Classroom* (2000, Tapestry Press), *Principles of Public Speaking* (2003, The College Network), *Human Communication in Everyday Life: Explanations and Applications* (2008, Allyn & Bacon), *Quantitative Research Methods for Communication: A Hands-On Approach* (2008, 2013, 2016, & 2019, Oxford University Press), *The Directory of Communication Related Mental Measures* (Summer 2010, National Communication Association), *Stand Up, Speak Out: The Practice and Ethics of Public Speaking* (2011, 2020, Flat World Knowledge), and *Communication Apprehension, Avoidance, and Effectiveness* (2013, Allyn & Bacon; 2018, Kendall-Hunt), *Training & Talent Development: Intersecting Communication, Human Performance Improvement, and Organizational Effectiveness* (2015 & 2023, Kendall Hunt), *Organizational Communication: Theory, Research, and Practice* (2015 & 2023, Flat World Knowledge), *Interpersonal Communication: A Mindful Approach to Relationships* (2021, Milne Open Textbooks), and *Innovative Business Communication: Strategies for a Globalized World* (2024, University of Arizona Global Campus). Dr. Wrench is also the editor of numerous books: *Casing Organizational Communication* (2011 & 2022, Kendall Hunt), *Workplace Communication for the 21st Century: Tools and Strategies that Impact the Bottom Line: Vol. 1. Internal Workplace Communication, and Vol. 2. External Workplace Communication* (2013, both with Praeger), *Casing Public Relations* (2014, Kendall Hunt), *Casing Sport Communication* (2016, Kendall Hunt), *The Impact of Social Media in Modern Romantic Relationships* (2018, Lexington Press), and *Casing Nonverbal Communication* (2021, Kendall Hunt). Dr. Wrench was the editor of the *Ohio Communication Journal* from 2005-2007, served as an associate editor for Communication Research Reports from 2007-2010, and been on the editorial board for numerous academic journals. Dr. Wrench is the past editor of the *Journal of Intercultural Communication Research for the World Communication Association* (2019-2024). Dr. Wrench has published over 40 research articles that have appeared in various journals: *Communication Education, Communication Quarterly, Communication Research Reports, Education, Human Communication, Journal of Homosexuality, Journal of Intercultural Communication, Southern Communication Journal, The Source: A Journal of Education, The NACADA Journal (National Association of Campus Advising)*, and others. In addition to his academic work, Dr. Wrench is the author of ten novels, all published with Pride Publishing. In 2012, Dr. Wrench was awarded the designated position of Teaching Fellow within the Eastern Communication Association (ECA). Dr. Wrench is a former president of ECA, which is the oldest communication association in the world.

* * *

Ibrahim Akdilek is a Ph.D. student and Research Assistant at Texas Tech College of Education.

Sumeyya Akdilek is an engaged graduate student and Teaching Assistant at Texas Tech University, affiliated with the Department of Communication Studies in the College of Media and Communication. Anticipating her graduation in 2024, her thesis delves into the complex dynamics of forgiveness within the cycle of violence in romantic relationships. She is guided by a distinguished committee comprising Dr. Narissra M. Punyanunt-Carter, Dr. Maggie Bennett-Brown, and Dr. Patrick C. Hughes. Her academic pursuits are deeply rooted in interpersonal and family communication, with a particular focus on violence in romantic relationships. This focus underscores her commitment to deepening the understanding of human interactions and contributing to the improvement of communication dynamics in sensitive contexts.

Awad M. Alshalwy is an M.A. student in Applied Linguistics at the Libyan Academy of Postgraduate Studies. He has a bachelor's degree in Geology and another bachelor's degree in English linguistics and literature from Omar Al-Mukhtar University (OMU), Libya. He is an EFL instructor at the Language Center of OMU. His research interests primarily lie in the areas of instructional technology, communication assessment, cultural diversity in language curricula, and content-based and project-based learning.

C. V. Suresh Babu is a pioneer in content development. A true entrepreneur, he founded Anniyappa Publications, a company that is highly active in publishing books related to Computer Science and Management. Dr. C.V. Suresh Babu has also ventured into SB Institute, a center for knowledge transfer. He holds a Ph.D. in Engineering Education from the National Institute of Technical Teachers Training & Research in Chennai, along with seven master's degrees in various disciplines such as Engineering, Computer Applications, Management, Commerce, Economics, Psychology, Law, and Education. Additionally, he has UGC-NET/SET qualifications in the fields of Computer Science, Management, Commerce, and Education. Currently, Dr. C.V. Suresh Babu is a Professor in the Department of Information Technology at the School of Computing Science, Hindustan Institute of Technology and Science (Hindustan University) in Padur, Chennai, Tamil Nadu, India. For more information, you can visit his personal blog at .

Karene Best, a tenured librarian at Valencia College, brings eleven years of invaluable experience to her role, having played a key part in establishing two new campus libraries during her time with the institution. With a career spanning twenty-five years in both academic and medical library settings, Karene holds a Bachelor of Science degree in Nutrition from the University of Delaware, and a Master of Science in Library and Information Science from Drexel University. Her professional passions encompass a wide range of subjects, including artificial intelligence (AI), digital learning, emerging technologies, and information literacy.

Mary E. Brooks, Barbara Petty Professor of Business Communication, joined the College of Fine Arts and Humanities in 2016 and then joined the College of Business in 2023. She received a B.S. in Mass Communication from West Texas A&M University in 2000, an M.A. in Communication Systems Management from Angelo State University in 2002 and a Ph.D. in Media and Communication from Texas Tech University in 2015. Dr. Brooks is a member of the Association for Education in Journalism and Mass Communication where she serves as the Head of the Small Programs Interest Group. Dr. Brooks has overseen numerous student-led integrated marketing communications campaigns for local and national brands. She also holds certifications pertaining to digital communications including from Meta Blueprint and several from Google Ads. Dr. Brooks' research interests include advertising trends, pedagogy, artificial intelligence, digital communications, societal issues, and agriculture communications. She has presented her research at regional, national, and international conferences and her work is published in several academic journals.

Tina A. Coffelt is a professor in the Department of English at Iowa State University. Tina holds a PhD in communication from the University of Missouri and an MBA from Northwest Missouri State University. She is a mixed-methods scholar with primary research interests in business communication skills, interpersonal communication, and privacy management. She was a Fulbright scholar to Uzbekistan in 2020. ORCID: 0000-0002-1926-6453.

Suruthi G is at the Hindustan Institute of Technology and Science, India.

Ali Garib is a doctoral candidate in the Applied Linguistics and Technology program at Iowa State University and an ESL lecturer in the Program in Writing and Communication at Rice University. Ali holds an M.A. in Applied Linguistics from Arizona State University and an M.A. in TESOL and Educational Technology from the University of Manchester. He is a Fulbright and Chevening alumnus. Ali's primary research interests span the areas of innovative teaching, AI-powered learning, communication education, technology-assisted project-based language learning, CALL, and language teacher professional development and practices. ORCID: 0000-0002-8331-7120.

Noura Ahmad Hajjaj is currently a doctoral student in the Department of Communication and Rhetorical Studies at Duquesne University, where she teaches undergraduate courses as a graduate teaching. Prior to her enrollment in the Ph.D. program, she took a leading role in advancing public health initiatives with The New York State Department of Health, notably ensuring the safe reopening of Orange County Early Childhood centers and K-12 schools during and after the global pandemic. For 6 years, Noura was a full-time lecturer in the Department of Communication Studies at the State University of New Paltz. In addition to her teaching and public health service, Noura organized the first-time ever virtual convention of the 78th annual conference of the New York State Communication Association (NYSCA). She was also the recipient of the Neil Postman Teaching Award at the 81st annual conference of NYSCA in October 2023. Beyond academia, Noura passionately advocates for women's rights through global engagement initiatives with Challenge to Change, a non-governmental organization supporting young refugees and underprivileged women in conflict areas in the Near East. She leads educational and research efforts related to the refugee crisis and fundraises for various initiatives addressing these challenges. From 2017-2022, Noura spearheaded and implemented a special project in global civic engagement, connecting university female students in the occupied Gaza Strip with Mid-Hudson Valley undergraduate students.

Yifeng Hu (Ph.D., Penn State University, she/her) is an associate professor of Communication Studies at The College of New Jersey (TCNJ). Her research focuses on technology, health, culture, and pedagogy. Hu has produced a book, Communicated Stereotypes at Work. In addition, her work has appeared in journals such as Communication Research, Journal of Computer-Mediated Communication, Journal of Communication in Healthcare, Atlantic Journal of Communication, Electronic Journal of Communication, and in several edited volumes. Hu constantly integrates emerging technologies in teaching: from using Second Life, Facebook, and blogs in her classes, to leading students to create interactive video games for alcohol education, to guiding students to research and design Virtual Reality programs that have social impact, to raising students' critical AI literacy through analysis and reflection. Outside the classroom, Hu has led her students to carry out multiple Asian American Pacific Islander (AAPI) advocacy campaigns on campus to address issues such as stereotypes, discrimination, xenophobia, injustice, ignorance, in/visibility, and belonging. Hu has also created the Asian and Asian American Pacific Islander Coalition, an employee affinity group, in her institution. Hu is the proud recipient of the inaugural ASIANetwork-Mellon Award for the "AAPI Voices and Stories: Community-based Digital Storytelling" project, the Outstanding Creative/Performance Project Award by the Asian/Pacific American Caucus and Studies Division of the National Communication Association, and the inaugural Faculty Recognition Award in Excellence in Diversity, Equity and Inclusion at TCNJ. Hu played a significant role in advocating for the passing of the AAPI curriculum bill in New Jersey.

Michele H. Jackson is a communication scholar and Professor at Michigan State University. Jackson's research and teaching brings a focus on the dynamics of human communication to the design and emergence of technologies and learning environments. Jackson's work has appeared in multiple venues including *Human Communication Research, Communications of the ACM, Small Group Research* and *Science, Technology and Human Values.*

SeyedMohammad Kashani is a Ph.D. student in Computer Engineering at Iowa State University. He received his B.S. in Electrical Engineering from AmirKabir University of Technology. SeyedMohammad's primary research utilizes machine learning tools in the healthcare industry. His secondary areas of research include cyber security, machine learning, and using quantum computing to improve machine learning techniques.

Anastacia Kurylo (Ph.D., Rutgers University, she/her) has taught communication for over 15 years at New York University, Pace University, and Rutgers University, among others, and currently teaches at Brooklyn College. She is the proud recipient of both a teaching award and mentor award. Anastacia is also Founder and CEO of a 501(c)(3) nonprofit called inform Your Community (). She is a subject matter expert in stereotypes and has produced over 25 publications including six books: *The Communicated Stereotype: From Celebrity Vilification to Everyday Talk*; *Negotiating Group Identity in the Research Process: Are You In or Are You Out?*; *Redefining Communication in the Era of Social Networking:*

Cultural, Social, and Political Perspectives; and two college textbooks titled *Inter/Cultural Communication: Representation and Construction of Culture*; and *Building Your Social World: Constructing Reality through Interpersonal Communication*. Anastacia has led the board of several nonprofits and is former President of the New York State Communication Association and the New Jersey Communication Association. Her previous executive roles have included VP of Development, Director of Business Operations, and VP of People Operations.

Huong-Tra Le-Nguyen is a researcher at Hanoi University and is currently pursuing linguistic studies and its application on interdisciplinary research with particular interest in AI era.

Corey Jay Liberman (Ph.D., Rutgers University, 2008) is a Professor of Public Relations and Strategic Communication in the Department of Communication and Media Arts at Marymount Manhattan College. His research spans the interpersonal communication, group communication, and organizational communication worlds, and he is currently interested in studying the social practices of dissent within organizations, specifically the antecedents, processes, and effects associated with effective employee dissent communication, as well as risk and crisis communication. He teaches Interpersonal Communication, Communication Theory, Public Relations, Organizational Communication, Group Communication, Communication Theory, and Communication Capstone. He has 50 publications, including seven books: *Organizational Communication: Strategies for Success (2nd Edition), Casing Persuasive Communication, Casing Communication Theory, Casing Risk and Crisis Communication, Risk and Crisis Communication: Communication in a Disruptive Age, Casing Mediated Communication,* and *Casing Nonverbal Communication.*

Marta Natalia Lukacovic, Ph.D., received her doctorate from Wayne State University, Detroit-Michigan, USA. She is an Assistant Professor of Communication and Mass Media at Angelo State University (Texas Tech University System). Her research is focused on communication through digital media platforms and the matters of security, such as global crises, pandemics, political violence, and malicious AI. She co-edited a two-volume book project with the publishing house Rowman & Littlefield on public relations, media, and communication in post-socialist nations of Eastern Europe and Central Asia. She serves as the President of CAER (Communication Association of Eurasian Researchers).

Kristopher Merceron, PhD, currently works as the Department Chair for Speech and the New Student Experience and Tenured Speech Professor at Valencia College, and previously taught at the University of Tampa and Hillsborough Community College. He maintains instructional experience within corporate and higher education. Dr. Merceron holds a bachelor's degree in Health Sciences, a master's degree in Corporate and Organizational Communications specializing in Leadership, and a PhD in Educational Studies specializing in Adult Learning and Development. His dissertation focused on leadership opportunities for Black male college students in predominantly White social fraternities. Additionally, Dr. Merceron is the co-author of Managing Nervousness as a Public Speaker, and he has a passion for teaching public speaking and communications, particularly discussing nervousness and anxiety. Dr. Merceron has also served as a reviewer for the Journal of Technology & Higher Education: Emerging Practice.

Shanna F. Peeples, the 2015 National Teacher of the Year, taught middle and high school English in low-income schools in Amarillo, Texas for 14 years. She is an assistant professor of Educational Leadership and the Dr. John G. O'Brien Distinguished Chair of Education at West Texas A&M University. At WT, she is also the director of the Route 66 Writing Project, which uses place conscious writing to address challenges of spatial and educational equity. Her research focuses on adaptive leadership to support belonging and inclusion in schools and organizations. She is the author of Think Like Socrates: Using Questions to Invite Wonder & Empathy Into the Classroom.

Tiffany Petricini is an Assistant Teaching Professor in Communication at Penn State Shenango and Program Coordinator of the Penn State Western Corporate Communication Consortium. Her publications have reflected interests in phenomenology, interpersonal communication, technology, philosophy, ethics, and media ecology, including her work "Friendship and Technology," available through Routledge. Tiffany has been an invited speaker on the international radio program "Spark" on CBC Radio One and the SUNY Plattsburgh at the Ethics Institute. She also serves as the social media expert for NBC affiliate WFMJ 21 News.

Narissra Maria Punyanunt-Carter (Ph.D., Kent State University) is a full professor in the department of communication studies at Texas Tech University. She is an associate editor for the Journal of Intercultural Communication Research & Relationship Research News. She is co-author of Interpersonal Communication: A Mindful Approach to Relationships and co-editor of Communication Begins with Children: A Lifespan Communication Sourcebook as well as co-editor of The Impact of Social Media in Modern Romantic Relationships. Narissra teaches interpersonal communication, gender, nonverbal, and romantic relationships. She serves on the Leadership Development Committee, the vice chair of the human technology and communication division, the chair of the secondary and primary education section, served as the past chair of the Mass Communication Division, and past chair of the Family Communication Division of the National Communication Association. She is the proud award Recipient of YWCA's Women of Excellence in Education Award; National Communication Association's Thomas L. Veenendall Lambda Pi Eta Advisor of the Year Award; Texas Tech University President's Mid-Career Award, Texas Tech University's Honors College Faculty of the Year Award; Professing Excellence Award; Mortar Board's Outstanding Faculty Award, the James Mignery Collegiality Award, and the National Communication Association Presidential Citation for Service Award. She recently was awarded the 2022 Mentor Tech Lifetime Achievement Award and the 2022 Phenomenal Women of Texas Tech University Award.

Leslie Ramos Salazar (PhD, Arizona State University) is an Associate and Abdullat Professor of Business Communication and Decision Management at the Paul and Virginia College of Business at West Texas A&M University. Her teaching areas include current issues in management communication such as leadership communication and risk communication management, health care communication, business communication for health care managers, business communication, and statistics for business and economics. Her research specializes in health communication, business communication, conflict management, and interpersonal communication. Her publications appear in Health Communication, Communication Teacher, Communication Quarterly, Communication Studies, and Business and Professional Communication Quarterly. She also serves on the editorial board of Communication Research Reports, Western Journal of Communication, and Communication Reports.

John Rief is an Associate Professor of Rhetoric and Debate at MSU Denver. His research and teaching interests include the history and theory of debate, argumentation studies, classical rhetoric, and the philosophy of rhetoric.

Brian Schrader has a PhD in Rhetoric and Communication Ethics from the University of Denver. Lecturer IV at the University of Michigan-Flint.

Deborah Sellnow-Richmond is an Associate Professor in the Department of Applied Communication Studies at Southern Illinois University Edwardsville where she teaches courses in public relations and organizational communication. She researches the efficacy and unforeseen effects of public relations messages in health and organizational crisis context, and the emerging role of social media in creating and resolving organizational crises. She holds a Ph.D. in communication from Wayne State University in Detroit, Michigan, a master's degree in Public Service from the University of Arkansas Clinton School of Public Service, and a bachelor's degree from the University of Minnesota.

Trung Tran Thanh is an experienced Research And Development Engineer with a demonstrated history of working in the electrical and electronic manufacturing industry. Thanh is silled in Microsoft Word, Google Cloud Platform, English, Java, Artificial Intelligence, Deep Learning, and Speech Recognition. Thank is a strong engineering professional graduated from Pi School.

Chuhao Wu is a Ph.D. candidate in Informatics at the Pennsylvania State University. His research focuses on the human-centered design of educational technology and artificial intelligence applications in higher education.

Sarah T. Zipf, Ph.D., is a researcher with Teaching and Learning with Technology at the Pennsylvania State University, overseeing research efforts related to data-informed culture, learning spaces, and technology access and needs. Zipf earned her doctorate in higher education in 2021.

Index

U

W

www.ingramcontent.com/pod-product-compliance
Lightning Source LLC
LaVergne TN
LVHW062115300926
849161LV00010B/2468